About Island Press

Since 1984, the nonprofit Island Press has been stimulating, shaping, and communicating the ideas that are essential for solving environmental problems worldwide. With more than 800 titles in print and some 40 new releases each year, we are the nation's leading publisher on environmental issues. We identify innovative thinkers and emerging trends in the environmental field. We work with world-renowned experts and authors to develop cross-disciplinary solutions to environmental challenges.

Island Press designs and implements coordinated book publication campaigns in order to communicate our critical messages in print, in person, and online using the latest technologies, programs, and the media. Our goal: to reach targeted audiences—scientists, policymakers, environmental advocates, the media, and concerned citizens—who can and will take action to protect the plants and animals that enrich our world, the ecosystems we need to survive, the water we drink, and the air we breathe.

Island Press gratefully acknowledges the support of its work by the Agua Fund, Inc., Annenberg Foundation, The Christensen Fund, The Nathan Cummings Foundation, The Geraldine R. Dodge Foundation, Doris Duke Charitable Foundation, The Educational Foundation of America, Betsy and Jesse Fink Foundation, The William and Flora Hewlett Foundation, The Kendeda Fund, The Andrew W. Mellon Foundation, The Curtis and Edith Munson Foundation, Oak Foundation, The Overbrook Foundation, the David and Lucile Packard Foundation, The Summit Fund of Washington, Trust for Architectural Easements, Wallace Global Fund, The Winslow Foundation, and other generous donors.

The opinions expressed in this book are those of the author(s) and do not necessarily reflect the views of our donors.

Environmental Land Use Planning and Management

Environmental Land Use Planning and Management

SECOND EDITION

John Randolph

◑ **ISLAND**PRESS   Washington | Covelo | London

Island Press is a trademark of The Center for Resource Economics.

Library of Congress Cataloging-in-Publication Data

Randolph, John.
    Environmental land use planning and management / by John
Randolph. —2nd ed.
        p. cm.
    Includes bibliographical references and index.
    ISBN-13: 978-1-59726-730-4 (cloth : alk. paper)
    ISBN-10: 1-59726-730-9 (cloth : alk. paper)
    1. Land use—Environmental aspects. 2. Land use—
Planning. I. Title.
    HD108.3.R36   2011
    333.73—dc23   2011026558

British Cataloguing-in-Publication data available.

Printed on recycled, acid-free paper

Manufactured in the United States of America
10 9 8 7 6

To Sandy

Contents

Preface

The first edition of this book began with the following words, written in 2003:

> For thousands of years we humans have been learning how to manage our relationship with nature. Every generation creates a new set of circumstances as our population and economy grow, as our impacts on the natural environment increase, and as our knowledge of the consequences of our actions and means of controlling them advance. Every generation must adapt to those circumstances. Our evolving social and political system has enhanced our ability to make collective decisions about the use and management of the natural environment, as well as how to adapt to it…. Although we face a myriad of environmental and related economic and social challenges, the good news is that we continue to learn.

We *have*, in fact, continued to learn, and the reason for the second edition of this book is to chronicle what we have learned in the past decade. In our fast-changing world, it does not take a generation for "a new set of circumstances" to emerge, and we cannot wait a full generation to respond and adapt to them.

We are faced with new environmental challenges, led by climate change and its prospective impacts on water supplies, agriculture, ecosystems, and coastal cities due to sea level rise and increasing incidents of extreme weather events. We are under a climate change imperative that requires mitigating our impact by reducing emissions of greenhouse gases and adapting to the consequences of climate change that are likely to occur despite our mitigation efforts.

In addition to climate change, we are faced with population trends that have resulted in more than half the global population living in cities, with the prospect of 80% by 2050. This is actually good news for natural ecosystems, as urbanization tends to lead to a lower environmental impact per person and drives down fertility rates that should slow population growth to a stable 8–9 billion by mid-century.

The global challenge we face, as Stewart Brand puts it, is "to Green the hell out of our growing cities" (2009, 69), making them livable and sustainable, reducing their ecological footprint, and providing social and economic opportunities for their growing populations. The second challenge is to protect the newly emptied countryside, its agriculture, forest, and watershed resource lands and its biodiversity and ecological services.

The first edition chronicled emerging approaches to environmental land use planning and management. Providing a framework for teaching and learning interdisciplinary environmental planning, it emphasized land use, land analysis, methods, and policies for planning and managing urban development, as well as rural resource agriculture and forestlands in the United States. These emerging approaches included environmental and community design, environmental engineering and science, information systems, integrative approaches, collaborative processes, land conservation, smart urban growth management, and environmental regulatory and nonregulatory policies and their legal foundation.

The first edition traced the evolution of these approaches, with the assumption that our continuing learning process does (and must) get better to meet emerging challenges. This is no more evident than in the brief span of years that have passed since the first edition was published. Nearly all of these approaches have advanced, and this second edition presents this next generation of environmental planning. The community continues to be the laboratory, where new methods, technologies, designs, and policies are devised, tried, and judged. Therefore, this edition uses more case studies of these approaches "in action."

The new edition also has a slight shift in emphasis and includes emerging challenges and responses.

- **Sustainable communities.** Because of demographic and social trends, more emphasis is placed on urbanization and the growing movement toward sustainable and livable communities. Not only do we see citizens and cities creating this movement, but U.S. federal agencies are focusing on this theme. There are many dimensions to this movement, including energy and climate protection, stormwater management, green infrastructure, public health and active living, mobility, economic vibrancy, affordability, social interaction, community resilience, and environmental justice, among others. They are all interrelated and are all necessary for sustainable communities.
- **Climate change.** This has become the defining environmental issue of the century. Planning efforts focus on climate protection or mitigation through the reduction of greenhouse gas (GHG) emissions and carbon sequestration by advancing energy efficiency and low-carbon sources, reforestation, and soil management. Reducing GHG emissions also benefits energy security by lowering oil consumption, decreasing urban air pollution, and minimizing other fossil-fuel-related environmental impacts.
- **International efforts toward sustainability.** While the first edition emphasized policies and practices in the United States, the sustainability movement has accelerated around the world, and there is much to be learned from Europe, Australia, and Japan, as well as emerging approaches

in China, Brazil, and other developing nations. This edition highlights some of these efforts through case examples.

The second edition is also reorganized based on the teaching experience of many instructors, including myself. I have found that students need a big picture context on environmental planning to start, but they are more receptive to digging into the technical issues of environmental and land analysis that provide an analytical foundation before addressing design, planning, and policy issues. Therefore, the book is now organized into three parts:

Part I: A Framework for Environmental Land Use Planning and Management

This section, Chapters 1–4, contains the first four chapters from the first edition, revised to reflect emerging issues and approaches in environmental planning. Chapter 1 explores concepts of environmental management, Chapter 2 focuses on the interdisciplinary nature of environmental planning, and Chapter 3 discusses land use planning from the perspective of sustainable communities. Chapter 4 highlights the growing role of collaborative processes in engaging people in environmental planning decisions and implementation.

Part II: Environmental Planning: Technical Principles and Analysis

This section, Chapters 5–14, contains an updated and revised version of the material in the first edition's Chapters 11–18, focusing on the science, technical analysis, and engineering methods used in environmental planning. Many of these methods have improved since the first edition was published, especially geospatial tools and the development of digital and web-based techniques for soil evaluation, wetlands mapping, stormwater analysis, natural hazard mitigation, and forest and watershed assessment. Chapter 12 is a new chapter on land use and climate change addressing mitigation and adaptation planning, as well as related community energy planning and urban air quality protection.

Part III: Planning, Design, and Policy Tools for Environmental Land Management

This final section, Chapters 15–19, includes updated and revised versions of the first edition's Chapters 5–10 on design, financial, and policy approaches for sustainable communities, smart growth, and ecosystem and watershed management. The quest for sustainable cities has become a movement not only in the U.S. but around the world. The designers, engineers, planners, and policy makers continue to make advances in response to the growing market for green and livable buildings, neighborhoods, and communities.

Because of extensive new material and the desire to avoid expanding the text by using more resources, certain sections have been removed from the earlier edition. Many of these sections are still useful, and where appropriate, they are retained in PDF form on the book website (www.envirolanduse.org) and cited in the new second edition. In addition, because of the changing nature of this field, the book website is loaded with web-based resources linked to chapter references and case studies. The website will be periodically updated with new links and information as we continue to learn.

Acknowledgments

Much has changed in environmental planning since the first edition of this book came out in November 2003. In this second edition, I have tried to reflect the new emphases for planning sustainable and livable communities and mitigating and adapting to climate change, new methods for geospatial analysis, new science on urban ecology and climate change, innovations in design and policy, and growing social awareness of environmental problems and solutions. The movement toward sustainable communities has matured, and the community has been the laboratory for these new concepts, approaches, methods, and techniques. I gratefully acknowledge the practitioners whose innovative work is embodied in this text.

Among U.S. federal agencies, the Natural Resources Conservation Service, Environmental Protection Agency, Forest Service, Federal Emergency Management Agency, Fish and Wildlife Service, National Oceanic and Atmospheric Administration, and Geological Survey continue to develop and improve many of the techniques, methods, and information sources presented in this book. Certain state and regional agencies also stand out in advancing the practice of environmental land use planning. I have borrowed heavily from the work of state environmental agencies in California, Washington, Oregon, Massachusetts, Maryland, and New York, as well as regional agencies, including the Tahoe Regional Planning Agency, Twin Cities Metro Council, San Francisco Bay Conservation and Development Commission, and the Portland Metro Council.

I am especially grateful to the many local government agencies for their exemplary work that has helped define this field. Portland (Oregon) stands out, and this textbook reads almost like a Portland case study. I also lean heavily on the experience from Seattle and King County (Washington), Montgomery County (Maryland), Fairfax County (Virginia), Boulder (Colorado), Austin (Texas), my own Blacksburg (Virginia), and many others. Several environmental nonprofit groups also are key players in the field, especially land conservation, and I thank them for their work and their data that I use herein: The Nature Conservancy, the Trust for

A Framework for Environmental Land Use Planning and Management

Acknowledgments

Much has changed in environmental planning since the first edition of this book came out in November 2003. In this second edition, I have tried to reflect the new emphases for planning sustainable and livable communities and mitigating and adapting to climate change, new methods for geospatial analysis, new science on urban ecology and climate change, innovations in design and policy, and growing social awareness of environmental problems and solutions. The movement toward sustainable communities has matured, and the community has been the laboratory for these new concepts, approaches, methods, and techniques. I gratefully acknowledge the practitioners whose innovative work is embodied in this text.

Among U.S. federal agencies, the Natural Resources Conservation Service, Environmental Protection Agency, Forest Service, Federal Emergency Management Agency, Fish and Wildlife Service, National Oceanic and Atmospheric Administration, and Geological Survey continue to develop and improve many of the techniques, methods, and information sources presented in this book. Certain state and regional agencies also stand out in advancing the practice of environmental land use planning. I have borrowed heavily from the work of state environmental agencies in California, Washington, Oregon, Massachusetts, Maryland, and New York, as well as regional agencies, including the Tahoe Regional Planning Agency, Twin Cities Metro Council, San Francisco Bay Conservation and Development Commission, and the Portland Metro Council.

I am especially grateful to the many local government agencies for their exemplary work that has helped define this field. Portland (Oregon) stands out, and this textbook reads almost like a Portland case study. I also lean heavily on the experience from Seattle and King County (Washington), Montgomery County (Maryland), Fairfax County (Virginia), Boulder (Colorado), Austin (Texas), my own Blacksburg (Virginia), and many others. Several environmental nonprofit groups also are key players in the field, especially land conservation, and I thank them for their work and their data that I use herein: The Nature Conservancy, the Trust for

Public Land, the American Farmland Trust, and many regional and local organizations like the Piedmont Environmental Council (Virginia) and local volunteer groups.

Of course, many private and nonprofit planning firms have led the path to innovative environmental land use practices. Thanks especially to the Center for Watershed Protection for its good work on urban watersheds, wetlands, and forests—work that appears in many parts of this new edition. The Environmental Systems Research Institute (Esri), Google, and other firms have helped lead the geospatial revolution that has fundamentally changed how we look at and evaluate the land, its resources, and its use. The Congress for New Urbanism, Smart Growth America, the Smart Growth Network, and other associations have led the movement toward more livable communities. And private design firms, such as Calthorpe Associates; Duany, Plater-Zyberk & Company; Dover, Kohl & Partners; Mithūn; Wallace Roberts & Todd; and Jonathan Rose Companies, continue to demonstrate more sustainable land development practices.

This textbook includes extensive graphical material to help communicate trends and possibilities. I gratefully acknowledge the many sources of public domain artwork and the kind permission provided by holders of copyrighted material, including Esri, the Center for Watershed Protection, Elsevier, McGraw-Hill, John Wiley & Sons, W. H. Freeman, and the American Planning Association, among many others.

On a personal note, I wish to thank my many colleagues across the country who continue to develop new knowledge and approaches that I use throughout the book. They include Tom Schueler, Marina Alberti, Peter Calthorpe, Fritz Steiner, and a large group of promising young environmental planning faculty who will carry on this important work. I also want to thank Heather Boyer, Courtney Lix, Nick Columbo, Sharis Simonian, Betsy Dilernia, and others at Island Press who have once again helped so much on this, my fourth Island Press book.

Finally, special thanks to Sandy for her love and support, and especially her patience for putting up with me and the obsession required for a project like this.

1 ■ Environmental Management for Sustainability

Since the dawn of their time, humans have been dependent on, and part of, the natural forces of the Earth. As society advanced, people tried to separate themselves from the natural burdens and hazards of life common to all other living beings. Yet, like it or not, humans remain part of that natural environment, subject to natural disasters and dependent on natural systems for the necessities of life—clean air and water, energy, food, and health—and remain connected to their evolutionary heritage. And as human population grew and its technology developed, human activity increased to impact these critical natural systems, including biogeochemical cycles, large-scale ecosystems, and atmospheric processes.

Managing their relationship with the natural environment has been a continuous requirement and responsibility for people and society. How society has assumed that responsibility depends on technology, human ingenuity, and the values and norms of society, which vary across cultures and over time. Just as human beings and society have evolved, so too has their relationship with the environment and the way they manage that relationship. It is still evolving.

Evolve it must—and quickly. The need to achieve a sustainable relationship with the environment and natural systems has never been so apparent as it is in this second decade of the twenty-first century. More than ever before, human impacts on the environment are affecting not only nature, but also the natural services that support civilization, its economy, and its society. Climate change, energy constraints and the depletion of fossil fuels, fresh water scarcity and contamination, exacerbated natural disasters, the loss of biodiversity and agricultural land, and other impacts are posing major consequences for economic, environmental, and social systems, especially those of vulnerable populations. These impacts will become much worse as the human population grows to an estimated 9 billion by 2050. Sustainability has become not just an environmental necessity, but an economic and social imperative.

In May 2011, many Nobel laureates and renowned experts met at the Third Interdisciplinary Nobel Laureate Symposium on Global Sustainability in Stockholm,

neighborhoods. New designs for walkable communities aim to create opportunities for more active living.

Natural resources and managed natural systems are critical for human subsistence, livelihood, and quality of life. Nonrenewable resources, like fossil energy, minerals, and land, are subject to depletion. Sustainable management of water resources and productive "working landscapes," such as agriculture and forestry, is necessary for the sustained production of renewable resources, water, food, and fiber.

Human society's resource exploitation and pollution impact essential **natural services and ecosystems**. These services are important to human economic productivity, such as groundwater recharge, fisheries, climate regulation, and hydrologic and biogeochemical cycles. They also include the many productive benefits of wetlands (e.g., flood control, water quality enhancement), vegetation (e.g., erosion and slope stability), and natural areas (e.g., aesthetic and property value).

Resource use and pollution also affect **natural ecosystems**. Although our economy ultimately depends on functioning ecosystems and have significant macroeconomic value (Hawken et al. 1999), wildlife habitat, species biodiversity, and natural systems are undervalued in most economic valuations, including the marketplace. However, the environmental movement has heightened public value given to these "noneconomic" natural resources. This value stems from both an anthropocentric view based on human enjoyment of these resources, now and in the future, and a perspective that natural ecosystems and the life they support have value for their own sake.

Environmental management aims to control these interactions of people and the environment to achieve sustainability. Put very simply, management entails figuring out what to do and how to do it … and then doing it. "Figuring out what to do and how to do it" applies science, engineering, design, economic and financial analysis, and policy development—the collective task we call planning. "Doing it" involves implementing and administering plans, designs, and programs. Post-implementation evaluation of plan, design, and program outcome is both an administrative and a planning component, because it helps fine-tune implementation activities and informs new and revised actions using adaptive planning. Although a scientific and technical field, environmental management is also a political one driven by the process of social and institutional discourse. Environmental planning and management involve people interacting in a competition of ideas, data, and values, shaping the technical, institutional, legal, and policy means of managing human–environment interactions.

Participants and Roles in Sustainable Environmental Management

In the United States and most democratic countries, a great many participants or actors in government, the private market, and civil society are involved in environmental management. These interrelationships are illustrated in Figure 1.1.

Equity. I like to add two more, Engagement and Eternity, to draw attention to necessary political participation and a future orientation. Practitioners of sustainability must break from current narrow and short-term thinking and planning, and adopt a broad, long-term perspective.

Although sustainability has recently emerged as an environmental concept, it is important to always remember its economic, social justice, and democratic dimensions. Sustainability can never be achieved without addressing people's economic and social needs and embracing democratic processes that engage people in determining their own destiny. Sustainability thus captures a wide range of global and domestic concerns: climate change, energy systems, water resources, toxic pollution, natural hazards, food systems, population growth, public health, economic stability, and social and environmental justice.

Environmental management for sustainability emphasizes the human and natural environment. It is the means of controlling or guiding human-environment interactions to protect and enhance human health and welfare and environmental quality. We will discuss later that this task has evolved from a desire for living with nature to a responsibility for managing natural systems, because we both need them and impact them. These interactions can affect human welfare and the environment in the following ways:

1. The environment poses certain natural hazards to human society.
2. Society-generated pollution impacts human health through the environment.
3. Society exploits economically important natural resources at unsustainable rates.
4. Pollution and overuse undermine productive natural systems, services, and ecosystems.

Natural hazards include flooding, hurricanes, tornadoes, extreme heat, drought and other weather-related damages; geologic hazards, such as earthquakes, tsunamis, and landslides; wildfires; and natural pests and disease-transmitting organisms. These hazards may be caused by natural elements, but they can escalate to disasters by human actions that alter the natural system or locate vulnerable human settlements in harm's way. In 2010 and 2011, we witnessed some of the most damaging natural disasters on record across the globe and in the United States.

Human-generated pollution affects **human health**. Here the environment is a transfer medium. Contamination of air, drinking water, and food by toxic pollution can result in debilitating ailments, cancer, and genetic damage. Inadequate sanitation can foster the transmission of disease, and improper handling of dangerous materials can cause severe accidents. Both pollution and natural hazard impacts on human health and well-being usually affect the poor and disadvantaged disproportionally, since they are often relegated to live in more vulnerable locations. Human health is also influenced by environmental and community design; for example, the obesity epidemic in the U.S. is exacerbated by sedentary lifestyles fostered by an automobile culture and lack of pedestrian-oriented neighborhoods. New designs for walkable communities aim to create opportunities for more active living.

Natural resources and managed natural systems are critical for human subsistence, livelihood, and quality of life. Nonrenewable resources, like fossil energy, minerals, and land, are subject to depletion. Sustainable management of water resources and productive "working landscapes," such as agriculture and forestry, is necessary for the sustained production of renewable resources, water, food, and fiber.

Human society's resource exploitation and pollution impact essential **natural services and ecosystems**. These services are important to human economic productivity, such as groundwater recharge, fisheries, climate regulation, and hydrologic and biogeochemical cycles. They also include the many productive benefits of wetlands (e.g., flood control, water quality enhancement), vegetation (e.g., erosion and slope stability), and natural areas (e.g., aesthetic and property value).

Resource use and pollution also affect **natural ecosystems**. Although our economy ultimately depends on functioning ecosystems and have significant macroeconomic value (Hawken et al. 1999), wildlife habitat, species biodiversity, and natural systems are undervalued in most economic valuations, including the marketplace. However, the environmental movement has heightened public value given to these "noneconomic" natural resources. This value stems from both an anthropocentric view based on human enjoyment of these resources, now and in the future, and a perspective that natural ecosystems and the life they support have value for their own sake.

Environmental management aims to control these interactions of people and the environment to achieve sustainability. Put very simply, management entails figuring out what to do and how to do it … and then doing it. "Figuring out what to do and how to do it" applies science, engineering, design, economic and financial analysis, and policy development—the collective task we call planning. "Doing it" involves implementing and administering plans, designs, and programs. Post-implementation evaluation of plan, design, and program outcome is both an administrative and a planning component, because it helps fine-tune implementation activities and informs new and revised actions using adaptive planning. Although a scientific and technical field, environmental management is also a political one driven by the process of social and institutional discourse. Environmental planning and management involve people interacting in a competition of ideas, data, and values, shaping the technical, institutional, legal, and policy means of managing human–environment interactions.

Participants and Roles in Sustainable Environmental Management

In the United States and most democratic countries, a great many participants or actors in government, the private market, and civil society are involved in environmental management. These interrelationships are illustrated in Figure 1.1.

1 ■ Environmental Management for Sustainability

Since the dawn of their time, humans have been dependent on, and part of, the natural forces of the Earth. As society advanced, people tried to separate themselves from the natural burdens and hazards of life common to all other living beings. Yet, like it or not, humans remain part of that natural environment, subject to natural disasters and dependent on natural systems for the necessities of life—clean air and water, energy, food, and health—and remain connected to their evolutionary heritage. And as human population grew and its technology developed, human activity increased to impact these critical natural systems, including biogeochemical cycles, large-scale ecosystems, and atmospheric processes.

Managing their relationship with the natural environment has been a continuous requirement and responsibility for people and society. How society has assumed that responsibility depends on technology, human ingenuity, and the values and norms of society, which vary across cultures and over time. Just as human beings and society have evolved, so too has their relationship with the environment and the way they manage that relationship. It is still evolving.

Evolve it must—and quickly. The need to achieve a sustainable relationship with the environment and natural systems has never been so apparent as it is in this second decade of the twenty-first century. More than ever before, human impacts on the environment are affecting not only nature, but also the natural services that support civilization, its economy, and its society. Climate change, energy constraints and the depletion of fossil fuels, fresh water scarcity and contamination, exacerbated natural disasters, the loss of biodiversity and agricultural land, and other impacts are posing major consequences for economic, environmental, and social systems, especially those of vulnerable populations. These impacts will become much worse as the human population grows to an estimated 9 billion by 2050. Sustainability has become not just an environmental necessity, but an economic and social imperative.

In May 2011, many Nobel laureates and renowned experts met at the Third Interdisciplinary Nobel Laureate Symposium on Global Sustainability in Stockholm,

Sweden, to discuss scientific and political strategies for reconciling the conflicts of human civilization with its physical and ecological support systems. Like the 2007 Potsdam Memorandum and 2009 London Memorandum from the preceding symposiums, their resulting Stockholm Memorandum sums up the imperative we face:

> The Earth system is complex. There are many aspects that we do not yet understand. Nevertheless, we are the first generation with the insight of the new global risks facing humanity. We face the evidence that our progress as the dominant species has come at a very high price. Unsustainable patterns of production, consumption, and population growth are challenging the resilience of the planet to support human activity. We can no longer exclude the possibility that our collective actions will trigger tipping points, risking abrupt and irreversible consequences for human communities and ecological systems.
>
> We cannot continue on our current path. The time for procrastination is over. We cannot afford the luxury of denial. We must respond rationally, equipped with scientific evidence. Our predicament can only be redressed by reconnecting human development and global sustainability, moving away from the false dichotomy that places them in opposition. In an interconnected and constrained world, in which we have a symbiotic relationship with the planet, environmental sustainability is a precondition for poverty eradication, economic development, and social justice. (Stockholm Memorandum 2011, 3)

This book addresses this quest for what the Nobel laureate memoranda call the Great Transformation to sustainability. It focuses on the use of land by human society and its implications for environmental systems, and it emphasizes progress made in the United States. This chapter provides a context for the book by introducing some concepts of environmental management for sustainability, the range of human values and perspectives that influences it, and emerging approaches that are part of its current evolution.

What Is Environmental Management for Sustainability?

Let's first define some terms. Because "sustainability" has become such an overused term that to many it has lost meaning, it is important to provide an operable definition for our use in this book. Based on the Brundtland Commission (1987) and others, sustainable development is defined as the *paths of economic, social, environmental, and political progress that aim to meet the needs of today without compromising the ability of future generations to meet their needs.*

Sustainability is the quality of human life and of the environment that is not gained at the expense of the future (Gell-Mann 2010). It is usually characterized by the integration of the 3-E objective of Economy, Environment, and social

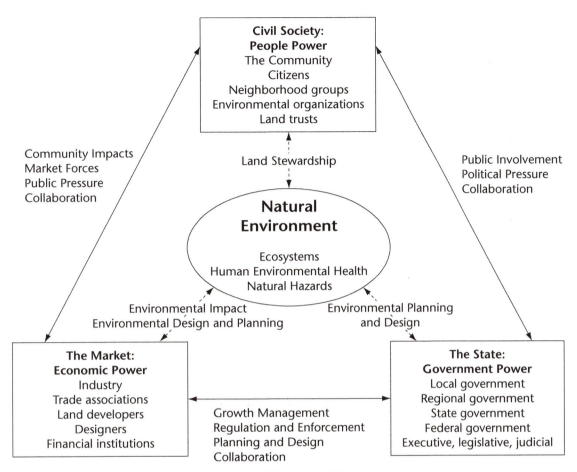

Figure 1.1 Participants and Relationships in Environmental Planning and Management.

The Market

In our strong market economy, **private** activities—**the market**—determine to a large extent the fate of the environment. Ultimately, the consuming public makes choices about products and designs that shape patterns of production and development. Growing consumer preference for sustainable products has spurred a recent market transformation for more sustainable goods, ranging from green buildings and ENERGY STAR appliances to hybrid cars and organic food. When retail giant Walmart launched an initiative in 2009 to green its stores, products, and delivery systems, the green consumer market movement went mainstream, because of Walmart's significant effect on the global market supply chain.

In addition to retailers, industrial firms, land developers, landowners, and farmers play critical roles as they initiate actions that impact the environment, respond to environmental regulations and programs, and develop innovative technologies and approaches for environmental control. Landowners and farmers have a special opportunity and responsibility for environmental stewardship of their lands and waters. Landowners, developers, and associated firms, including financial institutions, real estate agents, and designers, are sometimes referred to collectively, and with some contempt, as the "growth machine," because their profit-motivated land use practices and development projects often adversely impact the environment.

During the past decade, however, planners and designers in the land development industry have also been the source of innovative sustainable designs and practices to create livable communities and protect the environment. Examples include compact, mixed-use, pedestrian- and transit-oriented development; conservation subdivisions; low-impact development to reduce runoff pollution; green buildings and neighborhoods; and watershed and land stewardship. These innovative practices were born from creative design, but they have also been driven by consumer preference for more livable and sustainable neighborhoods.

The State

In other cases, the land developers have changed their practices in response to regulatory or public pressure from other participants (see Figure 1.1). **Government—the state**—plays an important role, using its "police power" to protect public health and welfare to regulate private activity that affects the environment. It also has a public interest in promoting effective development activity that is socially, environmentally, and economically beneficial. Environmental management by government has involved all three levels—federal, state, and local (in some cases, regional)—and all three branches—executive, legislative, and judicial. The legislature enacts laws establishing programs and policies, the courts interpret laws, and agencies in the executive branch (such as the U.S. Environmental Protection Agency or a local planning department) develop plans and administer programs.

In the management of land use in the United States, state and county and municipal local governments take the lead, although the federal government also administers some land use programs, such as wetlands permitting and endangered species habitat protection. State and local **growth management** aims to control land use and development. In the past decade, these efforts have promoted Smart Growth, or patterns of development and redevelopment in areas of existing infrastructure with the goals of revitalizing existing communities, arresting urban sprawl, and achieving densities that support transit and pedestrian mobility. Among regulatory tools used in growth management to control the location and impact of development are zoning, subdivision regulations, and more innovative performance standards and urban growth boundaries. Increasingly, state and local agencies have used nonregulatory measures, such as location of infrastructure, tax policies, land acquisition, education, environmental design guidelines, and other measures, to influence land use and development practices.

Civil Society

The third sector or category is the **public**, or **civil society**, which includes nongovernmental organizations (NGOs), environmental and citizen groups, land trusts, property owners, and others with an interest in the activities of the market or the state. Public groups can affect activities in a number of ways: by partici-

BOX 1.1—Blessed Unrest: The Million-Org Movement Toward Sustainability

On his lecture tours, environmentalist Paul Hawken often met with a lingering group of attendees who would tell their stories and share their business cards, which he would save. Through the years his collection grew to the point where he recognized the immense number and diversity of people and nongovernmental organizations working in the common quest for environmental and social justice—by looking after rivers, educating people to grow their own food, retrofitting houses with solar panels, fighting polluters, or teaching children about the environment.

After checking government records and databases, Hawken explained:

> I initially estimated a total of 30,000 environmental organizations around the globe. When I added social justice and indigenous people's rights organizations, the number exceeded 100,000. I then researched to see if there had ever been any equals to this movement in scale and scope, but I couldn't find anything, past or present. The more I probed, the more I unearthed, and the number continued to climb. . . . I soon realized that my initial estimate of 100,000 organization was off by at least a factor of ten, and I now believe there are over one—and maybe even two—million organizations working toward ecological and social justice. (2007, 2)

This collective, diverse, and intermingled movement he calls Blessed Unrest and argues that it has become a major force working toward sustainability. Yet, he also states that it is not a typical movement, because movements have leaders and ideologies, and people join them, identify themselves with the group, and become followers. But this Blessed Unrest movement is dispersed and fiercely independent, with no manifesto. Rather, it is organic and self-organizing, involving tens of millions of people dedicated to change. In his book, *Blessed Unrest: How the Largest Movement in the World Came into Being and Why No One Saw It Coming* (2007), Hawken chronicles the development of this movement and the hope it provides for a sustainable world.

pating in government planning and decision making, by pressuring or directly negotiating private development project proposals, and/or by actively preserving environmental resources through land trusts and conservation easements. In *Blessed Unrest* (2007), Paul Hawken estimates that more than 1 million NGOs are working worldwide to improve ecological and social justice (Box 1.1).

The civil society sector includes the hundreds of thousands of local nonprofit environmental and justice organizations working in small but effective ways to improve their communities. It also includes the large national and global environmental groups that engage in three important roles in environmental management: education, resource protection, and oversight. Some in the U.S., like the National Wildlife Federation and the Sierra Club, provide environmental information to the public; others, such as The Nature Conservancy (TNC) and hundreds of state and local land trusts, establish and protect trusts, nature preserves, and sanctuaries; still others, including the Natural Resources Defense Council (NRDC) and the Environmental Defense Fund, use the administrative review process and the judicial courts to clarify and interpret environmental laws and policies. In this latter role, these nongovernmental organizations have been important watchdogs of environmental management in the United States and around the world.

Environmental Management: A Reflection of Social Culture, Values, and Ethics

Ultimately, how the environment is managed is based on society's culture and values. However, a complex society does not have just one set of values. Different cultures and different people within cultures have differing values and ideologies about their relationship with the natural environment. These are influenced by religious belief, ethical and moral persuasion, educational and personal experience, awareness, personal security, livelihood, and many other factors. Culture is not static and uniform but varies over time and across society. It is important to understand culture and values for two reasons. First, a society's approach to managing the environment is usually a reflection of its values, culture, and norms. And second, we need to understand and integrate these values in planning and making decisions to engage people in environmental management.

Society's values are manifested in **ethics**, or making and defending choices based on those values. In a democratic society, these choices are shown in political persuasions and ideologies that prompt political debate to resolve differences. In the United States, we have seen an expanding adoption of sustainability values and environmental ethics, but in 2011 we also saw a growing political debate about the role of government and personal liberty in managing the environment and the economy.

Environmental ethics has its roots deep in human history. Native Americans had a strong environmental ethic and effective environmental management. The emergence of an environmental ethic in U.S. culture dates back to the nineteenth-century writings of Marsh, Emerson, Thoreau, and Muir, and mid-twentieth-century books by Leopold and Carson (discussed in more detail below). In a society based largely on utilitarianism and economic efficiency, these writings struck a chord as people realized that both personal and public decisions should be based not only on utility but also on duty, responsibility, and stewardship.

Beatley (1994) suggests that natural objects have three types of value:

- **Instrumental value**: what people can do with an object (e.g., converting a forest to timber).
- **Intrinsic value**: what people appreciate in an object (e.g., seeing and experiencing the forest).
- **Inherent worth**: value for its own sake, irrespective of the instrumental and intrinsic value humans hold for it (e.g., the forest as a living organism). (See also Stone 1974.)

Instrumental and intrinsic values are largely human-based or anthropocentric (what's in it for me?). Inherent worth is nonanthropocentric, implying a human sense of duty and responsibility for other living things and the environment.

Environmental ethics are rooted in nature's intrinsic and inherent values and remain important philosophical, spiritual, and romantic tenets of the modern environmental movement. These values are manifest in environmental management through, for example, the establishment of national and state parks and wildlife refuges, endangered species acts, land conservation programs, and private land stewardship.

But environmental values and ethics continue to evolve, from a focus on humans' relationship with nature to the collective needs of human and natural systems, to what we might call "sustainability ethics." Sustainability ethics include the protection of nature's values, as well as human economic and social justice. As a result, the environmental movement is evolving from a romantic preservation of nature to more pragmatic science-based and duty-based problem solving to achieve sustainable human–environment interactions. We now trace this evolution of environmentalism.

The Evolution of Environmentalism

Many historians and analysts have traced the development of the environmental movement and its reflection in policy and management. Stewart Brand loosely defines the environmental movement as "a body of science, technology and emotion engaged in directing public discourse, public policy, and private behavior toward ensuring health of natural systems" (2009, 208). Most agree that major steps in the evolution of environmentalism occurred in response to influential people, major events, and social movements that led to political action. And environmentalism was heavily influenced by civil society organizations established in response to the movement. The environmental movement is diverse and is best understood by looking at its submovements in a roughly chronological order.

Although environmental concerns over sanitation and hunting date back centuries, most historians trace the roots of U.S. environmentalism to the mid to late nineteenth century and the writings of Henry David Thoreau ("In Wildness Is the Preservation of the World," 1851, and *Walden*, 1854); George Perkins Marsh (*Man and Nature: The Earth as Modified by Human Action*, 1864); and John Muir (1890s). These largely philosophical works contributed to the **Preservation Movement**, which advocated protecting nature's wonders and wildlife for spiritual renewal and for their own sake. The movement led to the first national parks (Yellowstone in 1872 and Yosemite in 1890), Muir's founding of the Sierra Club (1892), the first wildlife refuge (1903), and the National Park Service (1916). Principal U.S. civil society preservation organizations include the Sierra Club (1892), the National Audubon Society (1905), the Wilderness Society (1935), the National Wildlife Federation (1936), and The Nature Conservancy (1951).

Around the same time, the parallel **Conservation Movement** fostered by Gifford Pinchot, first head of the Forest Service, and President Theodore Roosevelt advocated the wise use of resources and established concepts of reforestation and sustainable yields. The Preservation and Conservation movements conflicted over the damming of Hetch Hetchy Valley in Yosemite. "Wise use" conservation won the case when Congress approved the project in 1913, but in a gesture to preservation, Congress established the National Park system in 1916. Among early

U.S. civil society conservation organizations are the American Forestry Association (1875), the Society of American Foresters (1900), and the National Parks Conservation Society (1919).

The **Public Health Movement** also had roots in the mid-nineteenth century, with advances in the science of infectious diseases, airborne and waterborne pathogens, sanitation, and clean water, and a growing understanding of the relationship between environmental quality and human health. Sanitation and drinking water treatment became major imperatives of the early twentieth century. By the middle of the twentieth century, epidemiological science linked toxic substances and air, water, and land pollutants to acute and chronic human illness, especially respiratory diseases and cancer. Principal among related civic society organizations are the American Public Health Association (1872) and the United Nations World Health Organization (1948).

The **Environmental Protection Movement** merged preservation, conservation, and public health concerns in the protection of environmental health and resources. Forester Aldo Leopold's *Sand County Almanac* (1949) and biologist Rachel Carson's *Silent Spring* (1962) were influential in merging these values, and many regard their works as signaling the birth of the modern environmental movement. Leopold's land ethic was simply put: "A thing is right when it tends to preserve the integrity, stability, and beauty of the biotic community. It is wrong when it tends to do otherwise" (1949, 224). Carson documented the effects of pesticides on the ecological systems, warned of pests developing bio-resistance, advocated biotic controls of pests, and generally questioned the paradigm of technological progress. Both Leopold and Carson died shortly after their publications, and unfortunately they did not witness the profound effect they had on the environmental movement.

In the 1960s, their influence was strengthened by major pollution problems that people were witnessing firsthand, including urban air pollution episodes; polluted waters; open dumps; oil spills; and the filling of lake, bay, and marine shores for development. In 1969, two events brought public attention to a head: the Santa Barbara oil spill and Cleveland's Cuyahoga River catching on fire. Although neither episode was a true disaster, they helped make the environmental movement a political mandate. The National Environmental Policy Act (NEPA) passed the Senate unanimously(!) in 1969 and the Environmental Protection Agency (EPA) was created in 1970. This began the "environmental decade" of major environmental pollution control legislation, including the Clean Air Act (CAA, 1970); the Clean Water Act (CWA, 1972); the Safe Drinking Water Act (1974); the Toxic Substances Control Act (1976); the Resource Conservation and Recovery Act for hazardous and solid waste (1976); and Superfund (CERCLA for toxic dump cleanup, 1980). The Air Pollution Control Association (originally the Smoke Prevention Association, 1905) and the Water Pollution Control Federation (1928) were early civil society groups advocating pollution control, and later the Environmental Defense Fund (1967), the Natural Resources Defense Council (1970), and other environmental groups used the courts to help steer the EPA and other agencies in implementing pollution laws. By the early 1980s, the environmental movement had become mainstream public policy.

After the 1970s, the Reagan administration had designs on weakening environmental policies, but the laws survived intact. They were even strengthened by 1987 CWA and 1990 CAA amendments, both of which incorporated market-based pollution allocation trading for more cost-effective pollution control. While command and control pollution laws are necessary to abate major pollution problems, many consider their top-down approach insufficient to manage the environment because of limits on implementation and enforcement.

In the late 1980s, the **Industrial Ecology Movement** emerged within industry to improve operating efficiency, reduce costs, and go beyond minimum pollution control standards by taking a systems approach to managing raw materials, processing, and residuals like an ecosystem. The movement incorporated international protocols for environmental management systems (EMSs), such as the International Organization for Standardization (ISO) 14001, Europe's EMAS, and U.S. EPA's Environmental Performance Track. The movement also encouraged voluntary action on the part of industries, facilitated by flexibility in pollution control requirements. The International Society of Industrial Ecology (2001) and its *Journal of Industrial Ecology* advanced the movement.

In the late 1980s, an **Ecosystem Movement** was emerging. With its roots in the Preservation Movement and the writings of Leopold and Carson, it was first manifested in NEPA, the Clean Water Act, the Wilderness Act (1964), the Wild and Scenic Rivers Act (1968), the Endangered Species Act (1973), and three public lands management laws: the Resources Planning Act (1974), the National Forest Management Act (1976), and the Federal Lands Policy and Management Act (1976). By 1990, holistic, science-based ecosystem management principles were replacing previous commodity-based approaches in planning and managing public and private forestlands, parklands, and watersheds. Professional foresters and watershed managers advanced this ecosystem approach, and principal civil society organizations in this movement were the American Forestry Association, the International Union for the Conservation of Nature (1948), and the Society for Ecological Restoration (1988).

The environmental movement was certainly not restricted to the United States. Many countries had their own social movements and responding public policies. In Germany, for example, industrial pollution, the 1970s forest die-off due to acid rain from coal, the 1986 USSR Chernobyl nuclear accident, and other events spawned a strong environmental movement and Europe's first Green Party. The Green Party had political success in the 1990s and helped usher in the world's most aggressive renewable energy policies. Germany's lead affected the entire European Union, which became a world leader in environmental policies by the late 1990s. Other developed countries and many developing countries had their own movements.

As environmentalism spread widely, it also became diverse and somewhat splintered. Healthy debates developed and continue within the movement. Paul Ehrlich pronounced in *The Population Bomb* (1968) that human population growth would outstrip our capacity to provide for future generations. In *The Closing Circle* (1971), Barry Commoner argued that runaway technology and affluence were the principal drivers of environmental destruction. Garrett Hardin surmised, in "The

Tragedy of the Commons" (1969), that individual freedom to use common resources (atmosphere, waters, ecosystems) would bring ruin to all unless we adopted "mutual coercion, mutually agreed upon" to control human nature, propagation, and consumption to protect the commons.

These and other debates continue within the environmental community, over the pros and cons of technology; the relative problems of population growth and overconsumption; reconciling often conflicting objectives for economic growth, social equity, and environmental protection; and the environmental merits and impacts of genetically modified crops, industrial agriculture, urbanization, nuclear power, clean coal, and ecosystem engineering. On one side of many of these debates are the more cautious "don't tamper with mother nature" purists who question many engineered solutions to environmental problems under a "precautionary principle" that assumes a technological advance is guilty until proven innocent. On the other side are the more pragmatic environmentalists who believe that solving our daunting environmental challenges requires every and all tools available to human ingenuity, including the best science; creative design and engineering; and advanced information technology, energy technology, and biotechnology—all tempered by vigilance to prevent unanticipated effects.

A positive outcome of this dialogue has been a **Global Environment Movement**. Within just a few years of the first dramatic pictures of Earth from outer space, the United Nations Conference on the Human Environment, held in 1972 in Stockholm, marked a turning point in international environmental discussion and cooperation. The conference addressed one of the first recognized global-scale environmental impacts, the depletion of the atmospheric ozone layer by human emissions of chlorofluorocarbons (CFCs). The conference and subsequent scientific evidence led to arguably the most successful international accord ever, the 1987 Montreal Protocol, which resulted in the phasing out of ozone-depleting chemicals within a decade. In 1983, the U.N. convened the World Commission on Environment and Development, later called the Brundtland Commission after chairman Gro Harlem Brundtland. Its 1987 report, *Our Common Future*, was instrumental in articulating the concept of "sustainable development," which captured the broad ideals of the Global Environmental Movement.

Subsequent Earth Summits in 1992 (Rio de Janeiro) and 2002 (Johannesburg) built on this theme. The Rio Earth Summit "Agenda 21" spelled out sustainable development guidelines for the twenty-first century. This global perspective trickled down to the community level through "Local Agenda 21," which has been adopted in many cities around the world. The Rio Summit also established the Convention on Biological Diversity and the U.N. Framework Convention on Climate Change (UNFCCC). A large number of environmental organizations have continued to focus on global issues, principally the World Wildlife Fund (1961), the United Nations Environment Program (UNEP), and other U.N. agencies.

The agenda for sustainable development raised awareness about environmentally related socioeconomic issues, especially with regard to disadvantaged populations. In the early 1980s, it became evident that the poor and disadvantaged are often relegated to live in areas of high environmental impact. These vulnerable areas include urban slums; locations that are near polluting industry sites, toxic landfills, and highway corridors; and those that are susceptible to natural hazards.

The **Environmental Justice Movement** emerged from publicity about contamination cases in Houston (TX), Warren County (NC), Triana (AL), West Harlem (NY), Hinckley (CA), and "Cancer Alley" between Baton Rouge and New Orleans (LA). The movement took up the cause of vulnerable populations to improve their safety and livelihood, and to enhance human rights by providing more equitable distribution of environmental burdens and benefits. Robert Bullard's writings, from *Dumping in Dixie* (1990) to *The Quest for Environmental Justice: Human Rights and the Politics of Pollution* (2005), were important rallying cries for the movement. The U.S. EPA established an environmental justice office in 1992, and the Center for Health Environment and Justice, the Coalition Against Environmental Racism, and the Foundation for Environmental Justice (U.K.) are active civil society organizations in the movement. Many of the organizations touted in Hawken's *Blessed Unrest* (2008) focus on environmental justice issues (see Box 1.1).

In the late 1990s, concerns over environmental and social justice attracted religious organizations to the environmental movement, and their involvement expanded to other environmental issues. Environmentalists had long criticized Judeo-Christian tradition based on Biblical guidance for human "dominion over nature," but by the mid-2000s, many groups embraced sustainability concerns as a religious duty for "Creation Protection."

Also in the 1990s, the **Climate Protection Movement** gained ground as a result of the work of the Intergovernmental Panel on Climate Change (IPCC) and the UNFCCC. The World Meteorological Organization and the U.N. established the IPCC in 1988 as a consensus-based body charged with synthesizing scientific research on climate change science, impacts, and mitigation and adaptation strategies. The IPCC's first Assessment Report (1990) recommended establishing the UNFCCC to develop international agreements and action strategies to mitigate and adapt to climate change. The UNFCCC fifth conference of parties (COP) in Kyoto led to the first international climate protection agreement in 1997 (which the U.S. never ratified). The IPCC's fourth Assessment Report (2007) stated "unequivocally" that humans are the major factor in causing climate change induced by global warming. Although the Kyoto Protocol and subsequent COPs, including the 2009 Copenhagen COP15, have fallen short of a comprehensive global climate protection strategy, the work of the IPCC and the UNFCCC led to the Climate Protection Movement, which recognizes climate change as the most important sustainability imperative of the century.

Climate change has been forced largely by human emissions of carbon dioxide from the combustion of fossil fuels, which still accounts for more than 80% of commercial energy use in the world. Annual emissions range from about 18 metric tons per capita (mt/c) in North America to 1 mt/c in most of Africa. One twist on the Climate Protection Movement is an emphasis on "carbon justice," with a goal of attaining comparable carbon emissions per capita around the world.

Despite the lack of a comprehensive global agreement at COP15, the movement has prompted action across the globe—from international organizations to nations to states to local communities. The European Union has been a leader in climate change policy, including its implementation of a carbon cap-and-trade program that is emulated by other regional organizations. More than 1,000

American cities have signed the U.S. Council of Mayors Climate Agreement and are developing local climate action plans to meet the goals put forth by Kyoto. Civil society organizations advancing the Climate Protection Movement include the Pew Center on Climate Change, ICLEI—Local Governments for Sustainability,[1] the Clinton Climate Initiative, the Al Gore–founded Alliance for Climate Protection, and many others. Gore has been instrumental in the movement by raising public awareness about climate change through his slideshow, documentary, and books, *An Inconvenient Truth* (2006) and *Our Choice: A Plan to Solve the Climate Crisis* (2009).

Although the energy-efficient building technology and design movement began in the 1970s with innovations in California, Austin (TX) started the first Green Building program in 1992, and the **Green Building Movement** began to take off. The movement grew largely from within the building and design profession. The U.S. Green Building Council (USGBC) was established in 1993, and its LEED (Leadership in Energy and Environmental Design) protocol has become the industry standard for green new and renovated buildings. Green building design and construction adopts an environmental life cycle approach to materials, energy, and waste, while improving occupant safety and health. The green building market grew from 2% of nonresidential construction starts in 2005 to 12% in 2008 and 25% by 2010; despite the poor economy, the value of green building construction was up 50% during 2008–2010 (MHC 2010). The U.S. EPA, Department of Energy (DOE), and Department of Housing and Urban Development (HUD), as well as USGBC, the Sustainable Building Industry Council, and many other organizations, are all active in advancing green buildings.

Concerns about climate change and the economic, environmental, and security impacts of our dependence on imported oil have led to a **Clean Energy Movement** emphasizing energy efficiency and renewable energy. It aims to apply technology to improve the energy efficiency of buildings, transportation vehicles, equipment, lighting, and community heat and power systems, and to develop wind, solar, and geothermal power projects, as well as biofuels and other alternative fuels. Since the 1970s, Amory Lovins of the Rocky Mountain Institute has been the leading advocate for the Clean Energy Movement, but many others have been involved. The Union of Concerned Scientists and many renewable energy industries and trade associations, as well as the U.S. EPA and DOE and its national laboratories, and the International Energy Agency, have advanced energy as a critical environmental issue.

With the economic downturn in 2009, the Clean Energy Movement merged with goals for economic and jobs recovery into a **Green Economy Movement** as an alternative to the current "black" economy based on fossil fuels. The movement began with the emergence of ecological economics in the 1970s, based on microeconomic principles. It has recently taken a macroeconomic turn, with advocates arguing that economic success for firms and nations in the twenty-first century will come to those that develop green products, plus a workforce and an

---

1. Founded in 1997, ICLEI used to stand for International Council for Local Environmental Initiatives; in 2003, it changed its charter and its official name to ICLEI—Local Governments for Sustainability.

infrastructure that advance clean energy and environmental technologies, including environmental design, low-impact products, renewable energy, efficiency, and possibly clean coal and a renaissance of nuclear power. The Obama administration and many countries, including Germany, other European Union (EU) nations, China, Japan, and Brazil, have adopted the Green Economy as a key part of the economic recovery and the main economic driver of the twenty-first century. "Sustainable prosperity" has found its way into the lexicon of leading business schools, as well as international organizations like the UNEP.

There has been a recent convergence of objectives for preservation, conservation, public health, environmental protection, justice, and climate change, as applied to cities in the **Sustainable Communities Movement**. The movement recognizes that the world is growing more urban. More than half of the world's population now lives in cities, and the number may reach 80% by 2050. The movement aims to create alternatives to unsustainable patterns of automobile-dependent and resource-intensive sprawling development in the U.S. and other countries. Its goal is to make cities more green, livable, healthy, economically vibrant, socially equitable, and resilient to adverse change. It is an integration of the science of urban ecology and the design of livable and affordable neighborhoods. The physical manifestation of the sustainable community emphasizes density, community and neighborhood design, mixed land uses, walkable neighborhoods, effective transit, affordable housing, green infrastructure, natural drainage, urban forestry, urban agriculture, and green building. The movement combines good urban design borrowed from Europe and traditional neighborhoods in the U.S., as well as new designs and technologies for green building and infrastructure.

While physical design is necessary, it is not sufficient for a sustainable community. The socioeconomic-political manifestation of community sustainability includes a vibrant green economy and job creation, a social support system, and a collaborative and inclusive political process. That process and the solutions it develops should be **place-based**: emerging from the history, natural setting, culture, and values of the community. Randolph Hester, in his *Design for Ecological Democracy* (2006), merges physical design and public involvement to preserve and enhance a community's important cultural and natural spaces, which he calls "sacred places." These elements are critical to building community social capital and the capacity for resilience to change.

Beginning in the 1980s, a number of American architects and planners helped advance the Sustainable Communities Movement through their writings and designs, including Michael Corbett (*A Better Place to Live*, 1980); Peter Calthorpe (*Sustainable Communities*, with van der Ryn, 1986; *Urbanism in the Age of Climate Change*, 2011); and Andres Duany et al. (*Suburban Nation: The Rise of Sprawl and the Decline of the American Dream*, 2001; *The Smart Growth Manual*, 2010). In 1991, they and a few others met in Yosemite Park and wrote the Ahwahnee Principles, a set of guidelines for well-designed, mixed-use, and walkable neighborhoods integrated from the site to the regional scale. These principles became the basis of the 1993 Charter of New Urbanism. Also in the 1990s, Smart Growth emerged as a concept for controlling sprawl by emphasizing development and redevelopment in areas of existing infrastructure to revitalize and densify those existing communities, and deemphasizing development in outlying undeveloped agricultural and habitat lands. Urban ecology emerged as a distinct discipline after 2000, advanced by Marina Alberti (2008), Fritz Steiner (2004), and others.

The Sustainable Communities Movement combines the science of urban ecology, Smart Growth concepts of regional development, New Urbanism principles of neighborhood design, and green building techniques of site and building design and construction, to foster dense, green, low-impact, and walkable communities. Sustainable communities are characterized by access to effective transit, mixed use and income, affordable housing, and clean energy. Since the mid-1990s, development projects incorporating these principles have had market success, due to their attractive physical design features and, more importantly, the sense of community they provide. Like green buildings, new rating and certification programs have been developed for green neighborhood development (LEED-ND) and sustainable communities (STAR Communities). In 2009, three U.S. agencies—HUD, the Department of Transportation, and the EPA—announced a collaborative Sustainable Communities Program. Leading advocate organizations of the Sustainable Communities Movement in the U.S. include the Congress for New Urbanism, Smart Growth America, the U.S. Green Building Council, ICLEI—Local Governments for Sustainability, and many others.

Table 1.1 summarizes the many dimensions of the environmental movement, identifying the separate movements, period of origin, and core values, and listing examples of leading champions, agencies, and NGOs, as well as subsequent chapters that explore these topics further. All of these separate movements are part of the evolving environmental movement today.

What's next for environmentalism? As the environmental movement has expanded in scope and numbers, it has also matured—from identifying and protesting problems to formulating and implementing solutions. Stewart Brand (2009) prescribes a positive redirection of the environmental movement, calling for a more "pragmatic environmentalism" that focuses on problem solving using the best tools we have available, including science, technology, design, and bioengineering. Although some disagree with Brand's support for nuclear power and genetic engineering among those tools, future environmentalism clearly must become less problem-oriented and more solution-oriented.

Others believe that even when solving problems, today's environmentalism is too incremental and focuses on single objectives. Gus Speth (2008) and others suggest a more comprehensive, integrative, interdisciplinary perspective: Our problems are interrelated and complex, so must be our solutions. Nobel laureate Murray Gell-Mann (2010) argues that the great transformation to sustainability requires holistic and interdisciplinary perspectives, what he calls a Crude Look at the Whole (CLAW). Geoffrey West (2010) goes on to suggest that the essence of the long-term sustainability challenge is the pervasive interdependency of energy, resources, environmental, ecological, economic, social, and political systems. He believes that instead of treating these factors as independent, we need to apply emerging tools for complexity analysis to understand interactions and formulate sustainable solutions.

Those solutions must go beyond science and technology to include "social solutions" that influence consumer and investor choice for green products and technologies, and individual and community behavior for more conserving and healthy

TABLE 1.1 The Evolving Nature of the Environmental Movement

Movement	Period	Core Values	U.S. Laws, U.N. Actions (examples)	Champion	Agencies (examples)	NGOs (examples)	Looking Ahead (Chapters)
Preservation	1850s	Natural wonders	National Park system 1916 Wilderness Act 1964 Wild Scenic Rivers 1968	Muir, Thoreau	U.S. National Park Service	Sierra Club	16
Conservation	1890s	Wise use of resources	Forest Service 1891 Sustained Yield Act 1956	Pinchott	U.S. Forest Service	American Forestry Assn	16
Public Health	1920s	Human health	Food & Drug Act 1906 Public Health Service 1944 Safe Drinking Water 1974	Winslow	U.S. Public Health Service, CDC, WHO	American Public Health Assn	17, 7, 9, 12
Environmental Protection	1960s	Control pollution for health of people, environment	National Environmental Policy 1970 Clean Air 1963, 1970 Clean Water 1958, 1972 Resource Cons/Rec. 1976	Carson	U.S. EPA	Environmental Defense Fund	7, 8, 9, 12
Industrial Ecology	1970s	Voluntary EMS systems approach in industry	Toxic Substances CA 1976 RCRA 1976 CERCLA (Superfund) 1980	Ayres	U.S. EPA, ISO	International Society for Industrial Ecology	
Ecosystem	1970s	Ecosystem functions, multispecies habitats	NEPA 1970 Endangered Species 1973 Forest Management 1976 U.N. Law of the Sea 1982 U.N. Biological Diversity 1992	Leopold, Holling	U.S. Fish & Wildlife Service Endangered Species	Nature Conservancy	10, 11, 15, 16
Global Environment	1970s	Sustainable development	U.N. Human Environment 1972 Montreal Protocol 1987 Brundtland Commission 1987 Rio Earth Summit 1992	Speth, Brown	U.N. Environment Program Worldwatch	World Resources. Institute Institute	
Environmental Justice	1980s	Equitable distribution of environmental burdens and benefits		Bullard	U.S. EPA	Foundation for Environmental Justice	4
Climate Protection	1990s	Mitigate climate change by reducing GHG emissions	U.N. IPCC 1988 UNFCCC 1992 Kyoto Protocol 1997	Gore	IPCC, UNFCCC	Pew Center for Climate Change	12
Green Building	1990s	Healthy, life-cycle efficient buildings		Watson	U.S. EPA	USGBC	12, 17
Clean Energy	2000s	Efficiency, renewables to reduce oil imports and GHG emissions	Energy Policy Acts 1970s, 1992, 2005	Lovins	U.S.DOE, IEA	Union of Concerned Scientists	12, 17
Green Economy	2000s	Environmental, clean energy jobs and low-carbon economy		Daly	UNEP	Sustainable Prosperity	12
Sustainable Communities	1990s	Livable, mixed-use, walkable, transit, dense, green cities	U.S. HUD	Calthorpe, Duany	Congress for Department of Transportation, EPA	New Urbanism, USGBC, ICLEI	12, 16, 17, 18, 19

patterns of living. These social solutions are critical for building the capacity for sustainability and flexibility in response to changing conditions. They emerge from the adoption of sustainability values, which can be fostered by education, collaboration, and community initiative.

Worldviews of Sustainability

In the midst of the movements that shaped environmentalism, additional elements have competed for society's attention, including social, economic, and political values, as well as ethics, philosophies, and other kinds of movements. Political inclinations, religious beliefs, and concerns about national and personal security, social needs, and personal livelihood—all of these affect the priorities and perspectives people have about long-term environmental and global sustainability. Despite libraries of scientific and technical research, universally held truths about many controversial environmental issues are elusive. People's attitudes and values about the environment filter scientific information to create an interpretation that conforms to those long-held values.

In the early 1970s, when I began to understand the different perspectives people had on environmental issues and the future, I wrote a short essay, "Visions of Paradise." In it I discussed the following five different points of view.

Says the "Optimist": Look how far we have come as a civilization. Imagine how far we can go. Human ingenuity and technology will continue to meet whatever challenges we face. The visions of environmental doomsayers, from Malthus to Carson to Ehrlich, have always been met by society's and technology's innovative solutions. There will always be advantaged and disadvantaged people, but only by advancing technology and growing the economy can we provide opportunities for the less advantaged by increasing the size of the pie. Increasing energy demand will be met by new technologies, carbon capture and storage, a recovery of nuclear power, and perhaps the ultimate source, nuclear fusion. Carbon-free affordable energy will help us meet pollution challenges by improved treatment of pollutant discharges. It will also allow us to cope with climate change that will be less daunting than the doomsayers warn. Human-managed ecosystems will continue to benefit society. Exploiting the frontiers, technology-enhanced recovery, substituting for depleted minerals, and perhaps exploiting extraterrestrial sources will meet resource demands. For the only limits to our future are those we invent. Paradise is our destiny!

Says the "Concerned Optimist": Although we do have some major problems, we have the capacity to solve them. Poverty, population, climate change, energy, species extinction, and sprawling land development pose significant challenges. However, with considerable effort and investment, technology and social adaptation will rise to the occasion. Paradise is within our grasp!

Says the "Hopeful Pessimist": The challenges we face will seriously affect our quality of life, our collective ability to meet the needs of increasing numbers of the world's poor, and the natural systems on which we depend. Global warming–induced climatic change and the resulting sea-level rise, extreme weather events,

ecosystem damage and species extinction, energy constraints, abject poverty, and political tensions stand in the way of a sustainable future. Environmental technologies, such as efficient and renewable energy systems and sustainable agriculture and forestry, must be developed and implemented on a massive scale. Any kind of "Paradise" will require major shifts in social consciousness and economic systems, which are needed to arrest overconsumption by the rich and the false economic imperatives of material growth. This may be asking too much, but we must try, and try together.

Says the "Pessimist": Our dependence on high levels of material economic growth cannot be sustained. Our pitiful efforts to manage the global environmental problems of climate change, energy, and species extinction are grossly inadequate for preventing major impacts and social disruptions, constraining economic advancement, and widening the gap between the rich and poor. Entrenched political ideologies will paralyze government action. If widespread climate change, environmental catastrophes, and destruction of natural ecosystems do not threaten our survival, resulting social tensions will create continuous global security problems and regional wars. Paradise lost!

Says the "Self-Absorbed": Global problems? I've got my own problems to worry about. I have enough difficulty providing for me and mine to be concerned about global people and the planet's environment. Life is hard. I care about me, my family, my property, my liberty, my job and livelihood, and my community and nation only as they affect me and mine. I can't afford to worry beyond that. Let someone else worry about it. Global Paradise? Let's talk about *my* Paradise.

Box 1.2 gives another perspective on worldviews captured in colors by Donella Meadows (1994). The traditional environmental Greens are evolving, so much so that Stewart Brand suggests a new color, Blue-Green or Turquoise, and calls these "enlightened Greens" the Turqs.

Although it is helpful to characterize these different worldviews, it is important to understand that all people do not fit neatly into one or the other. I often debate with myself about my own worldview. Different views are not simply a matter of political ideology, and they are neither constant nor purely defined for anyone. People learn. As they do, their mind-sets, positions, perceptions, tolerance for other views, and fundamental values can also change. Learning is fundamental to environmental management for sustainability.

Just as these mind-sets are variable for individuals, they are also dynamic for society. Cultural and social norms, political systems, and government policies are (or should be) a reflection of a society's values. As society's views about the environment have changed over time, so have the approaches taken to manage the interactions of humans and nature.

From Movement to Management

How do these worldviews manifest themselves in approaches to environmental management? Michael Colby (1991) provides a useful characterization of evolving paradigms of environmental management, including their ethical, political,

BOX 1.2—Colorful Worldviews

The Blues are free marketers, have a positive bias, and are technological optimists. They believe conventional economic approaches are on track because they fuel the essential ingredients for positive change: individual freedom and liberty, innovation, and investment. As a result, they are risk takers and believe that trying new and creative solutions is necessary for tapping human ingenuity to achieve sustainability. They see economic growth as the key to increasing material well-being for all, and market mechanisms as the key to mitigating environmental impact. Therefore, sustainability is all about sustainable economic growth.

The Reds hold various forms of socialism. They believe "bandit capitalism" benefits a minority at the expense of a materially and socially disadvantaged majority (witness the growing worldwide gap between the rich and poor). The environmental issues are a distraction from social issues, and sustainability must have social equity as its primary metric.

The Greens see the world in terms of ecosystems. The major threats are climate change, species extinction, resource depletion, pollution damage, and population growth. Ecological carrying capacity is the key operating concept for sustainability. They are cautious and not risk takers, for there is too much at stake. They are neither antitechnology nor antimarket, because they see technology and market forces as useful tools for environmental protection, but they view both with skepticism: Technology can lead to further impacts, and profits can corrupt. The Greens often appear to be less caring for people than animals. Generally they are a diverse group, and their bold views are often splintered and self-canceling. They tend to unite enemies and divide friends, which is not a recipe for political success. Sustainability is environmental protection.

The Blue-Greens or Turqs are an emerging faction of the Greens. While Brand suggests the "blue" addition represents water, it also represents a bit of Blue-thinking liberty and risk taking applied to problem solving. The Turqs are pragmatic Greens; less romantic, more practical and realistic, less focused on preservation and precaution, more focused on managing and even engineering nature to solve environmental problems. They replace the Greens's "precautionary principle," which constrains innovation, with "precautionary vigilance," which fosters experimentation with careful monitoring of effects. Turqs apply the best science and technology to free human ingenuity to achieve environmental sustainability.

The Whites are synthesists who do not openly oppose or agree with any of the preceding. They are optimistic, not necessarily about technology, but about people and process, for it is "process" that will win the day. Whites often reject Blues, Reds, Greens, and Turqs because they think people who tell others what is right (or wrong) lead society astray. Therefore, they reject ideologies based solely on markets, class, or nature. Whites are in a better position to provide a Crude Look at the Whole (CLAW). They seek a middle way of integration, reform, respect, and reliance. On the environment, they think all issues are local. On business, they think there is no "level playing field" because of imperfect markets, lobbying, subsidies, and capital concentration. On social issues, they believe solutions will naturally arise from place and culture, not from ideology. They want to appear like Taoist leaders, whose "subjects" feel like they succeeded by themselves. To Whites, sustainability is all about democratic engagement.

economic, policy, technological, and methodological dimensions. Colby labels his five paradigms frontier economics, environmental protection, resource management, ecodevelopment, and deep ecology. See the book website (www.envirolanduse.org) for a table (from this book's first edition) comparing various dimensions of these paradigms.

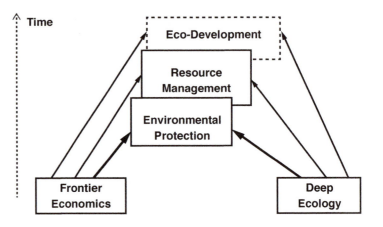

Figure 1.2 Colby's Paradigms of Environmental Management. We are evolving toward ecodevelopment between frontier economics and deep ecology. (*Source:* Adapted from Colby 1991.)

Frontier economics (FE) is characterized by an anthropocentric view that resources are limitless and progress is defined by economic growth. Under FE, property owners have primary management responsibility; strategies include pollution dispersal, industrial agriculture, and fossil energy; and planning methods include economic cost-benefit analysis and net present value maximization.

At the other end of the ideological spectrum is **deep ecology (DE)**, the back-to-nature "biocentric" view that reveres all nature, often at the expense of economic growth. Deep ecology has roots in the Preservation Movement. Under DE, management is largely decentralized; strategies include indigenous low technologies, and simple material needs; and planning emphasizes grassroots bioregionalism, autonomy, and conservation of biodiversity. Colby argues that subsequent approaches to environmental management have evolved partly in reaction to the tension between FE and DE (Figure 1.2).

Environmental protection (EP) is characteristic of U.S. policy in the 1970s and is best represented by the Environmental Protection Movement described earlier. Colby's EP recognizes environmental impacts and aims to lessen them, but generally without significant sacrifice in an economic-growth objective. EP is "business as usual plus a treatment plant" and utilizes command-and-control laws to address severe environmental impacts. Planning approaches include environmental impact assessment after design, optimal pollution levels, and willingness to pay.

Colby's **resource management (RM)** paradigm is more characteristic of U.S. policy in the 1980s and 1990s and is best aligned with the Ecosystem Management Movement described earlier. RM recognizes that today's nonsustainable practices will constrain long-term economic growth. RM also aims to modify traditional economic accounts to include environmental values by internalizing externalities and "getting the prices right" (i.e., "economizing ecology"). Pollution reduction, energy efficiency, population stabilization, and risk assessment are all management strategies under RM. Planning emphasizes ecosystem and social health and the linking of population, poverty, and environment.

Finally, **ecodevelopment (ED)** is a paradigm toward which Colby suggests we are evolving. Although Colby does not fully define it, ED is characterized by an

"ecocentric" view of the world, codeveloping human society and nature, steward-ship and pollution prevention, and a restructured economic system that does not simply give economic value to environmental resources but considers economic values in ecological terms ("ecologizing the economy"). Management requires a blend of public-private-NGO institutional innovation and strategies that embrace uncertainty, resilience, and ecotechnologies like renewable energy and sustain-able forestry. Ecodevelopment is consistent with the concepts of sustainable devel-opment and may be represented in the recent environmental movements of Indus-trial Ecology, Climate Protection, Green Economy, and Sustainable Communities. It does imply a fundamental shifting of values from monetary to natural capital.

Colby argues that an evolution over time toward ecodevelopment is occurring (see Figure 1.2). However, to a large extent all five paradigms are active today in practice and theory, and in the worldviews described above. Shades of FE are alive and well among the Optimists, many Blues, and perhaps the Self-Absorbed. The Greens have a corner on the DE paradigm. Environmental protection and RM include some mix of Concerned Optimists, Blues, Greens, and Turqs. The Turqs would also see their science and technology solution-based approach as a critical element of ecodevelopment, while the Whites seem anchored in RM and would argue their "process" is the key to defining ED. The social and economic transfor-mation implied by ED is consistent with the imperatives of the Hopeful Pessimist.

Toward Sustainability

It is obvious that humans have become an environmental force on planet Earth, affecting localized environments and major atmospheric and ecological systems. The goal of environmental management for sustainability is to stabilize environ-mental conditions and also to foster societal development. This dual goal is char-acterized in Figure 1.3, developed by Wolfgang Lucht (2010) using ideas from Hans Joachim Schellnhuber (1999). The concept assumes that sustainability transition requires both environmental stabilization and societal development, which are interdependent. The figure implies that we are currently advancing societal development, but at the expense of environmental conditions. Further decay of environmental systems could lead to both societal and environmental col-lapse. Our current environmental degrading path of societal development pre-cludes a healthy environment, while further environmental degradation, espe-cially climate impacts, will preclude further societal development. We need to find not only a path to environmental stabilization but a sustainability transition to environmental improvement.

What are the elements of this sustainability transition? Gell-Mann (2010) lists seven required for what the Nobel laureate Potsdam, London, and Stockholm memoranda call the Great Transformation to global sustainability:

1. The demographic transition to a stable population.
2. The technological transition to supplying human needs and desires with lower impact per person.

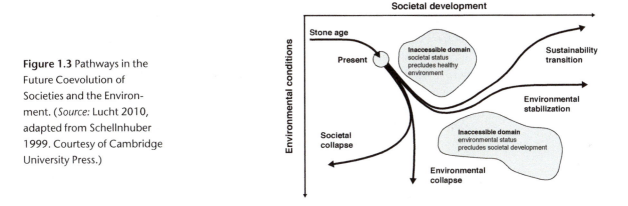

Figure 1.3 Pathways in the Future Coevolution of Societies and the Environment. (*Source:* Lucht 2010, adapted from Schellnhuber 1999. Courtesy of Cambridge University Press.)

3. The economic transition where growth in quality replaces growth in quantity while extreme poverty is alleviated.
4. The social transition to less inequality.
5. The institutional transition to more effectively manage the biosphere and cope with conflict.
6. The informational transition in the acquisition and dissemination of knowledge.
7. The ideological transition to a worldview that combines local, sectarian, national, and regional loyalties with a planetary consciousness and a sense of solidarity with all human beings and with all living things.

Our work is cut out for us. We have made progress on low-impacting technologies and on global information systems that will help. But the transformation must achieve, for the first time in human history, a stable population, a positive decline in the material quantity of economic growth, a closing of the gap between rich and poor, and a planetary consciousness. We are not alone in this quest. We can see emerging change driven by the rapidly evolving and expanding environmental movement, its manifestation in policy and practice, and the million or more organizations working hard in communities and countries and on the global stage to realize this transformation.

Summary and Next Steps

Environmental management for sustainability is a fast-moving and complex field. It is complicated not only by the complexities and uncertainties of natural systems, but also by the wide range of people and institutions involved and their different perspectives on how to manage the environment. It is highly interdisciplinary, involving the latest scientific discoveries, the newest technological advances, analysis and communication of reams of data and information, innovative policy prescriptions, creative institutional arrangements, evolving social values, and new political and collaborative processes.

The environmental movement has driven the advance of environmental management, because how we manage the environment depends on fundamental societal values. The environmental movement has evolved, with new and distinct movements emerging every decade. Thirteen such movements have been described in this chapter, from the Preservation Movement to the Sustainable Communities Movement, and there may be more next year. The environmental movement is still evolving.

The remainder of this book explores the details of how this movement is operationalized in the practice of environmental planning and management. The focus is on land use, but the interconnectedness of sustainability and natural and human systems means that to discuss land use we must also address water, energy, air, climate, biodiversity, human health, justice and equity, and democratic processes, as well as property values and real estate.

2 ■ Environmental Planning for Sustainability

To formulate effective strategies, environmental management for sustainability must integrate scientific, engineering, economic, and demographic information and analysis as well as stakeholder values. Therefore, it requires a unique approach, and planning provides the necessary interdisciplinary perspective, analytical tools, and participatory process. Planning is a critical part of environmental management. This chapter introduces environmental planning, including its range of disciplinary perspectives, the generic planning process, and the multiple roles of the planner.

As introduced in Chapter 1, planning is essentially a matter of figuring out what needs to be done and how to do it. It is basic problem solving or "applying knowledge to action" (Friedmann 1987). It requires determining ends-and-means relationships. Simply stated, planning involves setting objectives, gathering and analyzing information, and formulating and evaluating alternative policies, projects, and designs to meet the objectives. Its future orientation sometimes requires a crystal ball, but good analysis and effective collaboration can help clarify the vision.

Environmental planning applies the process of planning to environmental protection and problem solving. This may entail any of the human–environment interactions discussed in Chapter 1: natural hazards, human and environmental health, natural resource use, productive natural systems and ecosystems, and sustainable communities.

Historical Perspectives on Urban and Environmental Planning

Planning human settlements began when agriculture allowed people to aggregate in permanent communities. Old Jericho is said to have been the first city, but ancient cities in the Middle East, China, Greece, Italy, India, Central America, and Africa all date from 7000 BC to 200 BC. While urban planning was practiced in some form in succeeding centuries, modern urban planning emerged in the last part of the nineteenth century in response to rapidly growing, polluted, and chaotic cities in Western Europe brought about by the industrial revolution (UNHSP 2009).

After 1850, planning was directed at protecting public health through sanitation and separating land use activities, especially residential zones from polluting industry. But planning also had ideological goals of the ruling class to exclude low-income residents and other lower classes from their areas. **Master planning** emerged as the basis for urban planning. It was an exercise in the physical planning and design of settlements that responded to the social, economic, and political issues but did not intervene directly in these matters. This physical master planning was anchored in design and became manifest in large-scale projects and government control of land use through zoning, which varied according to how vested property rights were determined. In the United States, for example, private property rights enjoyed more legal protection than in the United Kingdom, where rights were subject to more government control. The U.K.'s 1932 Town and Country Planning Act established its approach to master planning and development controls, which diffused around the world through colonialism (UNHSP 2009).

In the United States, planning evolved from a design profession applied to urban form to a broader skill set applied to a range of problems and objectives, including environmental quality, as shown in Table 2.1. In the late nineteenth and early twentieth centuries, the master planning tradition was well established, as noted urban designers laid out large-scale master plans for cities. During the 1920s through the 1940s, with the growing use of zoning, urban planning became more regulatory. With the growth of government planning in the 1930s (e.g., the federal New Deal), planning became more bureaucratic, fact-finding, and analytical, in both scientific and economic terms.

The U.S. postwar housing, highway, and development boom of the 1950s and 1960s brought further physical development challenges, but the social movements of the 1960s also made planning more political. As a result, public partici-

TABLE 2.1 **The Evolution of Planning in the United States**

Emphasis	Era	Description
Planning as Design	1850–1950	Urban designers/planners create our cities.
Planning as Regulation	1925→	Zoning/command/control is core of government action.
Planning as Applied Science	1940→	Scientific/economic/policy analysis is problem solving.
Planning as Politics	1965→	Social movements and political action affect decisions.
Planning as Communication	1975→	Public information/participation broadens perspectives.
Planning as Collaboration	1990→	Stakeholders are engaged to reason together.
Planning as Integration of Policy, Science, Collaboration, and Design	2000→	Information revolution and rebirth of design innovation is informed by science, policy, and collaboration.
Planning Sustainable and Livable Communities	2010→	Science, design, collaboration, and policy are applied to community ecology, economy, equity, and livability.

pation grew in the 1970s, "communication" became the emphasis in the 1980s, and the 1990s and first decade of the twenty-first century saw more collaborative approaches involving stakeholders and partners reasoning together using social networks and other emerging means. In the 1990s, planning critics began to lament the loss of the earlier design emphasis of urban planning and its future orientation, and they suggested that the character of our communities had suffered. In the past decade, urban design has reemerged as an important element of urban planning. Today, the evolving skill set for planning integrates all of these approaches and includes technical and policy analysis, collaborative communication and process, and innovation and creative design—all of which are necessary in planning for sustainable and livable communities.

In 2009 planners celebrated the ceremonial 100th anniversary of urban planning in the United States, dating back to the first National Conference on City Planning held in New York in 1909. For the occasion, Birch and Silver (2009), Daniels (2009), and Berke (2008) provided retrospective looks at urban and environmental planning. Birch and Silver note the demographics of America have changed considerably in 100 years, from a population of less than 100 million to more than 300 million, from less than 50% urban to more than 80%, from about 50 cities with a population of more than 100,000 to 250. Of course, the spatial coverage of American cities has expanded far more than the population, as automobile mobility has extended the reach of the city. And the ethnic complexion of the U.S. and its cities has become far more diverse, and life expectancies and aging populations have increased. Domestic migration and shifting economic hubs have created rapid growth in some regions and shrinking cities in others. New imperatives for infrastructure and environmental protection resulting from these changing demographics have created continuing challenges for urban planners.

The progression of environmental planning links the history of planning with the history of environmentalism presented in Chapter 1. We will discuss the evolution of the many components of environmental planning in subsequent chapters, including land conservation, environmental design, stormwater management, urban ecology, urban forestry, watershed management, and ecosystem management. Tom Daniels (2009) provides a nice conceptual overview of the history of environmental planning in five labeled eras, which are summarized below, along with Philip Berke's (2008) historical focus on **green community planning**.

1. **Nineteenth and Early Twentieth Century: Getting on the Green Path**. This period includes the Preservation and Conservation Movements, as well as the City Beautiful Movement, urban parks, and garden cities. Frederick Law Olmstead's plans for Central Park in New York (1857), Boston's Emerald Necklace (1878), Chicago's World Exhibition (1982), and San Francisco's Golden Gate Park exemplified this era in cities. Ebenezer Howard's Garden City design concepts in London (1902) for small, mixed-use, work-live-recreate cities designed in harmony with nature share design characteristics of contemporary New Urbanism and are what Register (2006) refers to as the first "ecocities."

Berke's "Early Utopian Visions" period (1898–1930s) of green community planning distinguishes the polycentric form of Howard's independent cities, from the centrist urban form of Le Corbusier's radiant city, and from the decentrist suburban form of Frank Lloyd Wright's broadacre city.

2. **1920–1969: Regional Ecological Planning and Putting Science in Environmental Planning.** Clarence Stein, Patrick Geddes, Benton MacKaye, and Lewis Mumford (1961) were instrumental in advancing a regional environmental perspective to city planning. In the 1930s, the birth of cost-benefit analysis brought economic science to planning, and by 1969, land suitability analysis popularized by Ian McHarg (1969), ecological studies, engineering technology, and environmental impact assessment established by the National Environmental Policy Act (NEPA) enhanced scientific analysis in environmental planning.

3. **1970–1981: The Birth of Modern Environmental Planning.** Daniels sees the environmental decade of the 1970s and its plethora of federal environmental laws as the birth of modern environmental planning, at least at the federal level (see Chapter 1). This period was a culmination of prior movements, so it may be considered more the "adolescence" than the "birth" of the field. In addition to this federal action, in the 1960s and 1970s, several states experimented with state (e.g., Hawaii, Vermont, Maine, Oregon) and regional (e.g., San Francisco Bay, Twin Cities, Pinelands, Adirondack Park, Lake Tahoe) growth management programs with clear environmental objectives (Bosselman and Callies, 1971). Berke's "Design with Nature and the Environmental Movement" period (1940s–1970s) conforms to Daniels's eras 2 and 3.

4. **1982–2011: Backlash or a Bridge to Sustainability.** Daniels argues that the Reagan (1981–1988) and George W. Bush (2001–2008) administrations created a political backlash against federal environmental programs, especially environmental regulations and federal expenditures for environmental protection. But during this period, most laws prevailed against efforts to weaken them, and some innovative provisions were added to integrate economic mechanisms into regulations, such as the very successful cap-and-trade program for sulfur emissions in the 1990 Clean Air Act amendments, and wetland mitigation banking and water effluent trading in the 1987 Clean Water Act. The George H. W. Bush and Clinton administrations worked to advance the environmental agenda through no-net-loss wetlands policy, habitat conservation planning, energy policy, and voluntary and negotiated regulation to exceed emissions standards. Still, the federal inertia for environmental protection slowed during this period, and this led many states, localities, and NGOs to advance their own environmental planning and policy initiatives for land conservation, water and wetland protection, natural hazard mitigation, growth management, energy planning, and climate change mitigation. By 2005, nongovernmental land trusts numbered 1,667 and conserved more than 37 million acres in the U.S., double the

2000 acreage (LTA 2005). Although these nonfederal activities and the first years of the Obama administration seemed to be building a strong bridge to sustainability, a new backlash against federal environmental programs emerged in 2011 within the U.S. House of Representatives (after the 2010 midterm election) and among several states that adopted a strong political stance for states rights.

5. **1992–Present: Sustainability and the Global Environment**. As discussed in Chapter 1, sustainability at both global and local scales became a tenet of environmental planning with the 1987 United Nations Brundtland Commission report "Our Common Future," and subsequent Earth Summits in Rio and Johannesburg. The growing emphasis on climate change in the past twenty years elevated energy and climate as critical environmental planning objectives. These emerging global, energy, and climate concerns, along with advances in urban ecology, community design, watershed protection, and environmental justice, have created an integrated perspective in environmental planning for sustainable and livable communities.

Berke's "Linking Local Actions to Regional and Global Solutions" era (1980s–2008) starts with a critique of decentralized urban form as socially, economically, and environmentally nonsustainable urban sprawl, and advances more compact centrist and polycentrist forms with regional integration. Berke suggests this current green community planning movement for compact, mixed-use, walkable, transit-oriented, regionally connected, and green infrastructure designs fosters the ideals of harmony with nature, human health, spiritual well-being, livability, and low-impact, fair-share communities.

To achieve the multiple objectives of sustainability, planners must resolve tensions among competing objectives and values. Scott Campbell (1996) suggested that sustainability's 3-E objectives create three potential conflicts in community planning:

1. The **property conflict** between economic growth and equitable distribution of opportunities (e.g., government intervention requiring affordable housing in private development).
2. The **resource conflict** between economic development and environmental values (e.g., land development for profit versus land conservation for ecological protection).
3. The **development conflict** between equity and environment (e.g., affordable housing and commercial development versus nondevelopment environmental interests).

David Godschalk (2004) elaborates on this theme adding "livability" to make a four-objective **sustainability prism**. His prism shows three additional potential conflicts:

4. The **growth management conflict** between livability and unmanaged economic growth.

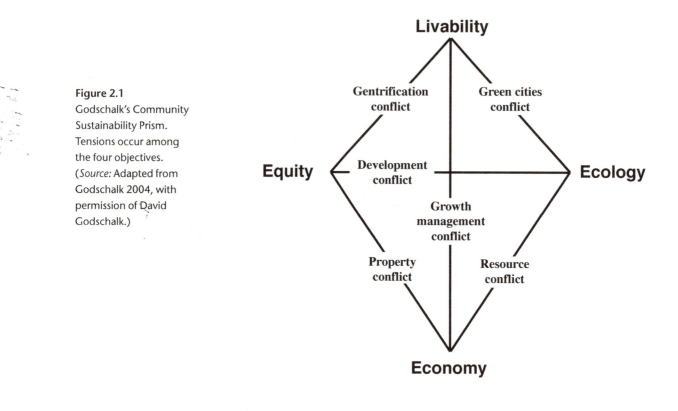

Figure 2.1
Godschalk's Community
Sustainability Prism.
Tensions occur among
the four objectives.
(*Source:* Adapted from
Godschalk 2004, with
permission of David
Godschalk.)

5. The **green cities conflict** between livability and ecology, between the primacy of natural factors and the primacy of built environment design in determining urban form.
6. The **gentrification conflict** between livability and equity, between redevelopment and existing neighborhood preservation.

Figure 2.1 illustrates Godschalk's sustainability prism, containing Campbell's triangle, and shows the six conflicts along the axes of the prism. While these tensions are real, the challenge for environmental and urban planning is to seek common solutions that provide multiple benefits for the four objectives and avoid conflicts between them.

Keep in mind Godschalk's and Campbell's sustainability tensions, as well as Daniels's and Berke's views of the current state of environmental planning for sustainable communities, as you read through the detailed analytical techniques, design principles, planning processes, and policy approaches presented in later chapters. Also remember that although environmental planning has come a long way, its evolution is not complete. It will continue to adapt to changing conditions, both environmental and cultural. It is up to you to continue this evolution and improve the next generation of environmental planning for sustainability.

Approaches to Environmental Planning and the Planning Process

Environmental planning and management can be reactive, proactive, or integrative.

- **Reactive measures** try to correct prior environmental damages, like cleaning up the British Petroleum oil blowout in the Gulf of Mexico or remediating old toxic waste dumps.
- **Proactive measures** are taken explicitly to enhance or protect environmental quality, like banning deep-water oil drilling or land use controls to preserve wildlife habitats and wetlands, protect aquifer recharge areas, or restrict future floodplain development.
- **Integrative measures** involve early and substantive consideration of environmental, social, and contingency factors in the formulation of development plans and projects, like offshore oil operations, a new highway, or a new subdivision. Not only is it less costly and more effective to consider environmental factors early in the development process, but this integration is also essential to achieve the multiple objectives of sustainable development.

Environmental planners usually have specialized expertise in one or more subareas, such as land use and development, air quality, water quality, energy and water resources, waste management, wildlife, or forestry. But they are also generalists, applying planning and problem-solving skills and a wide range of disciplinary perspectives to a variety of environmental concerns.

Although "figuring out what needs to be done and how to do it" is a simple definition of planning, the process is, of course, not quite that straightforward. There is an extensive literature on the theory of planning, and a scholarly debate continues about the merits and needs for different planning approaches. Like environmental management, planning has and is evolving in efforts to better meet society's needs.

Four Classic Approaches to Environmental Planning

There are many conceptions of the theory of planning, which can be summarized in four basic planning approaches: rational-comprehensive, incremental, participatory, and advocacy. Environmental planning generally requires a rational-comprehensive and participatory framework, with elements of adaptive-incremental management and advocacy planning as appropriate (Braisoulis 1989).

- The **rational-comprehensive approach** is based on the scientific method and has five basic steps that focus on objectives, information, alternatives, impact assessment, and evaluation.

- The **incremental approach**, or what Lindblom (1959) called the "science of muddling through," accepts limitations in human knowledge and understanding, and as a result, focuses on short-term goals and objectives and small sequential actions. Adaptive planning is a modern-day form of incrementalism. It recognizes limitations on knowledge and aims to learn by doing: Develop the best plan within limits, implement the plan, monitor the results, and make changes based on monitoring.
- The **participatory approach** suggests that neither the rational-comprehensive nor the incremental approach deals explicitly with the diverse stakeholder perspectives and conflicting values. The participatory approach aims to inform and involve the public in planning and decision making.
- The **advocacy approach** recognizes that interested stakeholders do not speak with one voice but often line up in entrenched camps and fight for their special interests. This situation often requires some advocacy of the underrepresented groups (such as the poor) and values (such as nature) and mediation to resolve differences.

Box 2.1 contains a generic planning process that fits most environmental planning applications. It begins with scoping, a preliminary step to scope out stakeholders and issues and develop a work plan. It continues with the key steps of identifying important issues and objectives, analyzing the planning situation, formulating alternatives, assessing impacts, and evaluating impacts—all of which are elements of the rational-comprehensive process, but with strong stakeholder participation. It concludes with an adaptive element: implementation, monitoring, evaluation, and modification. This basic process can be applied in a simple form (Box 2.2).

The details of the process, the range of issues, the depth of analysis, and the comprehensiveness of the alternatives and impacts all depend on the planning context, which includes the needs and objectives, the political climate, and the available data, resources, and time (Braisoulis 1989). As discussed in the next section, many environmental problems and planning issues are complex and require a variety of disciplinary perspectives, and each step may involve considerable effort. On the other hand, in a focused or incremental application, all the basic steps will occur but in an abbreviated way. Many processes start with a rapid assessment, which is a quick look at problems and available information, and for the purpose of moving quickly from assessment to action (Sayre et al. 2000).

Although the environmental planning process appears as a sequential process, in reality it is somewhat iterative, as all steps are considered simultaneously, with changing emphasis as the process proceeds. The process is always open to new information about subsequent or previous steps at any time. Several of the planning tools highlighted in the process for participation, negotiation, assessment, and evaluation are discussed later in this chapter and in subsequent chapters.

BOX 2.1—A General Process for Environmental Planning

0. Scoping

Stakeholder Issues

- Scope out fundamental issues, stakeholders, opportunities for participation, needs for conflict resolution, and needs for data and analysis
- Draft preliminary work plan for process
- Draft preliminary design for stakeholder involvement and participation

1. Identification of Issues, Opportunities, Concerns, Objectives, Criteria, Uncertainties

Stakeholder Criteria

- Identify IOC (issues, opportunities, concerns), evaluative factors, including institutional, legal, technical criteria
- Participation tools (advisory committees, meetings, workshops, surveys) determined by scoping
- Conflict resolution and negotiation tools (advocacy) depending on degree of controversy

2. Analysis of Planning Situation

Stakeholder Local Knowledge

- Scope of data gathering and analysis determined by evaluative factors
- Identify data limitations and uncertainties
- Participation tools (workshops, surveys)
- Conflict resolution and negotiation tools (advocacy) depending on degree of controversy

3. Formulation of Alternatives

Stakeholder Alternatives

- Scope of alternatives (comprehensive vs. incremental) determined by IOC, planning situation, degree of uncertainty (adaptive)

- Participation tools (workshops, workbooks, surveys)

4. Assessment of Impacts

Stakeholder Assessment

- Economic, environmental, and social effects
- Scope of assessment (comprehensive vs. incremental) depends on evaluative factors, planning situation, and alternatives
- Impact assessment tools (cost-benefit analysis, environmental impact assessment [EIA], social impact assessment [SIA])
- Organization and evaluation tools (matrices, indices, etc.)
- Participation tools (workshops, surveys)

5. Evaluation and Selection of Plan

Stakeholder Evaluation

- Organization and evaluation tools (matrices, etc.)
- Participation tools (workshops, surveys, review and comment)
- Conflict resolution and negotiation tools (advocacy) depending on degree of controversy

6. Implementation, Monitoring, Postimplementation Evaluation, Modification (Adaptive)

Stakeholder Implementation

- Timing and extent of monitoring and modification (adaptive) determined by level of uncertainty and degree of controversy
- Participation tools (citizen monitoring, workshops, annual conferences) determined by level of uncertainty and degree of controversy

BOX 2.2—A Simplified Planning Process

1. Inventory (steps 0, 2) — What do we have?
2. Needs Assessment (steps 1, 2) — What are our problems, objectives, priorities?
3. Management Strategies, Plans, Programs (steps 3, 4, 5) — What should we do?
4. Implementation and Monitoring (step 6) — Let's do it! (and learn from it)

Interdisciplinary Considerations of Environmental Planning and Management

The complexity of environmental problems requires interdisciplinary solutions. Environmental management is an exceptionally diverse field, borrowing heavily from several disciplines, including natural science and engineering, economics, law, politics, and ethics. Growing interest in environmental and sustainability issues has added to the participants and disciplinary perspectives, which have further increased the diversity and complexity of the field. Environmental planners are often grounded in a discipline, but as generalists, they must understand and apply a range of disciplinary perspectives to the planning process, including the ones described below.

Environmental Science and Engineering

Though interdisciplinary, at its roots environmental planning and management are based on scientific and engineering principles. Achieving sustainability requires an understanding of how natural systems work and how designed systems and technologies can lessen the adverse impacts of the built environment. For example:

- Soil erosion control requires a basic understanding of soil mechanics, available soils information, erodibility analysis, and the effectiveness of various land use practices in reducing erosion potential.
- Management of air quality requires knowledge of the effects on human health of pollutant levels, obtained from laboratory and epidemiological studies; the cost and effectiveness of various engineering treatment systems; and the relationship between levels of emissions at the stack and the quality of air people breathe.
- Watershed management requires knowledge of hydrology, climatology, topography, and soil properties; assessment of land cover effects on runoff; and engineering design of conveyance, storage, and infiltration.
- Mitigating climate change requires reducing greenhouse gas emissions by reducing fossil energy consumption through energy efficiency in buildings, transportation, and electrical systems, and by developing non-carbon energy sources with as little environmental impact as possible.

Environmental planning applies science-based technical knowledge to problem solving, and as such, it aspires to approach Brand's (2009) less romantic and more pragmatic environmentalism. Much of Part II of this book describes in detail the scientific and engineering principles of environmental land analysis and technologies for mitigating environmental impacts.

Environmental Design

The technical aspects of environmental planning make a transition from natural and physical sciences and engineering to the design of the built environment, for the purpose of enhancing environmental quality, human health, livability, and overall sustainability. This book details the applications of environmental design, especially in Part II and Chapter 16.

Sustainable environmental design principles are adopted from architecture, landscape architecture, horticulture, civil engineering, and urban design. For example:

- Transit and pedestrian developments and mixed-use neighborhoods require urban design that accounts for people and the environment, creating more livable, walkable, and healthy communities.
- Low-impact development requires knowledge of onsite engineering hydrology, but also landscape design that mimics natural drainage and infiltration of stormwater.
- Adapting to natural hazards and climate change requires understanding the impacts of uncertain events, such as extreme weather, drought, sea-level rise, excessive heat, and water supply disruptions, as well as designing adaptive means to lessen their impact.

Environmental Economics

Economics play a significant role in any public and private decisions, and environmental planners need to understand basic microeconomics, economic efficiency, cost-effectiveness, welfare economics, and market failure. Public policy decisions have long been based on the theory of welfare economics and economic efficiency. This largely utilitarian theory states that social welfare is improved if the total gains among those who benefit exceed the total losses by those adversely affected. The price and exchange mechanisms of the free market generally fail to effectively allocate resources according to this social welfare test of economic efficiency.

Many effects of market activity occur as **market externalities**: These are goods (positive) or damages (negative) that flow from the market to individuals or firms whether they want them or not, and without their paying for them or being able to avoid them by making a payment. Many environmental impacts, such as pollution, wetland destruction, groundwater overdraft, and overgrazing, are negative externalities.

As a result of externalities and other market failures, public policy decisions determining natural resource use and pollution control have relied on more than the dictates of the free market. In many cases, they have been based on the explicit comparison of benefits and costs, including certain nonmarket effects. Economic **cost-benefit analysis** is limited to the costs and benefits that can be measured or estimated in dollar terms. Requirements such as those set forth in NEPA broadened the objectives and definitions of costs and benefits in resource planning, but federal decisions are still based primarily on the economic efficiency test of net dollar benefits.

Cost-benefit analysis makes sense conceptually, but it is plagued with some basic problems in practice. One concerns *equity*, or the distribution of costs and benefits. The comparison of costs and benefits "to whomsoever they may accrue" does not consider who benefits and who loses. A second problem is that many costs and benefits involve considerable *risk or uncertainty*, and these are not well considered in cost-benefit analysis. A third problem is *how effects are valued over time*. The time value of money tells us a dollar today is worth more than a dollar tomorrow, because it can be invested. Future dollar effects are therefore "discounted" to a present value to be compared with today's dollars. But how do we treat environmental and human health effects? Do we discount the value of a future wilderness preserved or destroyed by today's decisions, or of future cancers resulting from today's management of toxic substances, or of the devastating effects of climate change?

Finally, it is difficult to place economic value on *noneconomic effects*, such as habitat destruction. In recent years, the field of **ecological economics** has emerged to improve the economic valuation of environmental resources so that they can be better accounted for in cost-benefit analysis and in planning and decision making. Environmental resource and amenity values are usually measured in terms of their use and option value. In this context, **use** can be consumptive (e.g., cut and use a tree), nonconsumptive (e.g., look at a tree), or functional (e.g., ecological carbon sequestration of a tree). **Option value** refers to the value that nonusers place on a resource, simply to know it exists (*existence value*), for future generations (*bequest value*), or for unforeseen future purposes (*insurance value*, say for a now unknown floral species that might be a cure for cancer).

However, the methods used to quantify these values, such as contingent valuation to measure the willingness of people to pay to protect a resource or the cost of replacing the ecological function with an engineering work, have limitations, and many analysts and economists admit that some societal values cannot be put in economic terms. The evaluation methods discussed in the next sections provide a broader perspective.

Other economic issues in environmental planning include using **market mechanisms** to advance environmental protection (such as emission cap-and-trade programs), **cost-effectiveness** of environmental measures (getting the most environmental benefit for the least cost), and **financing** environmental projects (who pays and how to pay).

Despite the analytical limitations already discussed, economic market forces remain among the most important determinants of consumer and producer decisions. Market mechanisms can work in concert with regulatory approaches to protect the environment. For example, stricter regulations on land-filling of wastes raise the cost of disposal so that recycling programs become more cost-effective. Higher fuel efficiency standards on vehicles not only reduce fuel consumption but also reduce carbon dioxide emissions. Carbon cap-and-trade programs put a price on carbon, which many believe is necessary to adjust the market toward clean energy.

Financing involves how to pay for environmental improvement. Private industry and land development generally must obtain private financing and venture capital. Local government programs have long relied on general obligation (tax-based) or revenue (user-fee-based) bonds to finance such programs as waste management, greenways, and parks. Innovative programs, such as development rights transfers and partnerships with private firms, have enhanced the financial resources available for environmental preservation. Land trusts have been especially innovative in stretching their financial resources through the use of conservation easements, bargain sales, and associated landowner tax benefits.

Environmental Evaluation

Evaluation involves using objective assessment to assign values to options, compare trade-offs, resolve conflicts, and make choices. It is perhaps the most important, yet most difficult, element of environmental planning. Economics alone cannot provide the basis for making decisions because of analytical limitations and, more importantly, the failure of economic assessment to fully capture nonuser and nonutilitarian environmental values.

Assessing and evaluating environmental data are both complicated by the frequent need to combine and compare information that is often subjective and noncommensurable. How do you determine a measure of the visual quality of a wetland, the habitat value of a woodland, or an acceptable level of risk from a hazardous waste facility? How do you compare these measures with one another and with more quantifiable factors, such as economic costs and benefits, to compare and select from alternative courses of action?

Evaluation uses a number of assessment methods. It is useful to distinguish between the following:

- *Partial techniques*, for determining the relative importance, quality, or value of a specific environmental component, such as wildlife habitat, visual amenity, or agricultural land.
- *Comprehensive techniques*, for assessing a wide range of economic, cultural, and environmental effects of alternatives, plus comparing and often combining them to rank alternatives on their relative social worth.

Partial evaluation techniques are used to evaluate changes in specific environmental conditions and thus can compare the effects of alternatives on that specific factor (e.g., comparing habitat conditions A and B predicted to result from alternatives A and B). As such, partial techniques are used in impact assessment and as inputs to more comprehensive methods. Alternatively, partial evaluation techniques can be used to rank specific areas as, for example, habitats, views, agricultural land, historic buildings, or potential recreation areas, to prioritize them for protection programs or for specific uses.

Many of the partial techniques use a sum-of-weighted-factors approach to evaluate and combine environmental information into an index. Examples of these methods are the Land Evaluation and Site Assessment (LESA) procedure for agricultural land evaluation (see Chapter 6), the DRASTIC method for assessing groundwater contamination potential (see Chapter 9), wetland and habitat evaluation (see Chapters 10 and 11), land suitability analysis (see Chapter 14), and certain environmental impact evaluation techniques (see Chapter 14). The sum-of-weighted-factors evaluation method, hypothetically shown in Table 2.2, involves four steps:

1. Selecting a number of factors deemed relevant to the assessment.
2. Measuring the factors and assigning a value to that measurement on a common scale (e.g., 0–10).
3. Assigning weights to each factor based on its relative importance in the assessment (e.g., 1–5).
4. Combining the products of the factor value and weight to produce a final score.

Although it is often appropriate to try to combine information to provide such a final score that gives a synthesis or integrated view of various impacts or factors, these aggregating techniques require distinct value judgments by the analyst. The hypothetical sum-of-weighted-factors example in Table 2.2 shows that the first three steps involve value judgments. In most cases professional planners and technical specialists can supply appropriate values, as long as the assessment is sufficiently bounded to fall within a specific area of expertise (e.g., forest habitat quality). Still, such techniques are often criticized for including arbitrary or hidden value judgments. Usually a broader range of perceptions than those of specialists should be tapped. For example, the LESA procedure includes a local committee to provide a broader community perspective in the assignment of weights and values to site assessment factors.

Whereas partial techniques are normally constrained to one or a small set of environmental components, **comprehensive evaluation techniques** consider a broad range of effects so that alternative solutions can be compared and ranked in terms of their relative overall merits or social worth. Thus, comprehensive techniques are intended to guide decision making and are used in the key step 5 of the planning process given in Box 2.1. Traditional cost-benefit analysis was designed as such a method. However, because of its limitations discussed earlier, its practice is usually relegated to a partial technique.

A number of other comprehensive techniques for comparing impacts have been developed. Loomis (1993) describes several ways to integrate evaluation criteria. The first step in evaluating alternatives to assist decision making is the selection of evaluation criteria or the factors that should determine the best choice. Like choosing factors for the sum-of-weighted-factors method, selecting criteria involves judgment. Loomis suggests five generic criteria for public lands manage-

TABLE 2.2 **A Hypothetical Example of the Sum-of-Weighted-Factors Method**

Factor	Scale	Unweighted Factor Values Area 1	Area 2	Area 3		Weights		Weighted Factor Values Area 1	Area 2	Area 3
Factor A	1–10	7	4	1	×	1	=	7	4	1
Factor B	1–10	3	8	5	×	3	=	9	24	15
Factor C	1–10	1	4	3	×	4	=	4	16	12
						Final Scores		20	44	28

TABLE 2.3 **Evaluating Alternatives Based on a Set of Criteria**

	Alternative A	*Alternative B*	*Alternative C*	*Alternative D*
Criterion 1	*	*	*	*
Criterion 2	*	*	*	*
Criterion 3	*	*	*	*
Criterion 4	*	*	*	*
Result	**	**	**	**

    * Boxes are filled with a description, indicator, or index score (resulting from a partial evaluation technique) of the alternative's effect on the criterion.
    ** Result indicates selection, ranking, or score of the alternative based on the decision method.

    Source: Adapted from Loomis 1993.

ment: physical and biological feasibility, economic efficiency, distributional equity, social and cultural acceptability, and administrative feasibility.

In practice, the evaluation criteria are case-specific and based on professional expertise and the planning process, especially step 1 in Box 2.1. Table 2.3 shows the evaluation framework, using a matrix of four alternatives and four criteria.

The alternative evaluation and selection process (step 5 in Box 2.1) depends on the method used to integrate criteria to provide a basis for the decision. Here are six different methods or decision rules (Loomis 1993):

1. *Maximize one criterion.* One criterion supersedes all others as the basis for selection.
2. *Meet minimum levels of all criteria.* Set minimum thresholds for each criterion, and select the alternative(s) that meet all of these thresholds.
3. *Maximize one criterion while meeting minimum levels of others.* Select the most important criterion, set minimum thresholds for all other criteria, then select the alternative that meets all thresholds and provides the greatest contribution to the most important criterion. This approach often uses linear programming or other optimization techniques.
4. *Rank criteria and maximize from high rank to low.* Prioritize the criteria and select the alternative that provides the best combination of contributions to the most important criteria.
5. *Numerically weight each criterion, rate each alternative's contribution to each criterion, and use the sum-of-weighted-factors method to score each alternative.* This produces an aggregate score or "grand index" for each alternative.
6. *Use the matrix approach.* Fill in the matrix with the best description, indicator, or index of each alternative's contribution to or effect on each criterion, then let reviewers, stakeholders, and/or decision makers apply their own judgments to rank the alternatives.

The choice of integration method depends on the planning situation and needs identified in steps 0–4 of the process (see Box 2.1). Methods 1–5 all require judgments for setting thresholds and/or ranking or weighting criteria. If the criteria are very broad (such as Loomis's, listed above), it is difficult to come up with a universally acceptable ranking or weighting of criteria.

Method 5 aims to aggregate estimates of effects to produce a "grand index" to rank alternatives and help guide decisions. Techniques that use this approach require that effects be measured on a common scale to permit aggregation. This requires some type of sum-of-weighted-factors approach. The comprehensive techniques that aggregate factors thus involve the same problems of value judgments and mathematical manipulations that the partial techniques do. In most cases, the problems are more substantial because the comprehensive "grand index" methods attempt to combine a far broader set of criteria than do the partial techniques. In general, the broader and more diverse the factors or effects to be combined, the more arbitrary and judgmental the choice, measurement, and weighting of the factors become.

Method 6 includes a broad range of factors but does not attempt to aggregate them into a grand index (e.g., the Simple Trade-Off Matrix; see Westman 1985). Instead, the matrix approach displays the effects and trade-offs of alternatives concisely to help reviewers and decision makers reach their own conclusions based on their own values, without the judgments of analysts. This method asks more of reviewers and decision makers than the aggregation methods, but perhaps this is the way it should be. As McAllister argues: "The central purpose of evaluation should be to help individuals—both citizens and public officials—reach personal judgments regarding the desirability of plans on the basis of the best obtainable information, not to compute grand index scores that seem to tell people what their attitudes ought to be. Transforming personal judgments into group decisions is a political problem that should remain within the realm of accepted democratic procedures" (1980, 277). It is the public forum, not an analytical formula, that should decide on how best to manage the environment.

Environmental Politics

That public forum is the political process. Despite requisite scientific, engineering, economic, and evaluative analysis, planning and decision making still end up being a competition of ideas and alternatives. Certainly, technical analysis is essential in that competition, sort of like the quality of the team "on paper" in a sports match. But how the match is actually played determines the outcome, and not always does the best team on paper win. Often utilitarian values of economic growth and development win the analytical competition; for effective decisions, other values need to be represented in the political process.

Although it is sometimes referred to as political science, politics is often more art than science, especially in the give-and-take legislative process of adopting effective environmental action. Compromise is often the name of the game in efforts to pass incremental policies that may not be perfect, but that provide some progress toward sustainability goals. Pragmatism in environmental politics may require giving in on one issue to advance a larger cause. For example, in the spring of 2010, President Obama issued orders for federal support of new nuclear power plants and for relaxing the federal ban on offshore oil and gas development, much to the ire of many romantic environmentalists. But these political acts were designed to win support for a larger initiative for green energy and climate change policies that stood no chance of passage without the support of nuclear and oil and gas advocates. Events often influence the political debate. The 2010 Gulf of Mexico Deepwater Horizon oil spill and the 2011 Fukushima nuclear power plant disaster in the wake of the Japanese tsunami both cast new shadows on the political discussion of U.S. energy policy.

Case studies of local political processes have repeatedly shown that there are three ingredients for success in the political process of environmental decision making: *good technical information* provided often by a dedicated planner, a *strong constituency* provided by advocacy groups, and a *champion* provided by an elected or appointed official (Corbett and Hayden 1981). This formula holds true in land use decisions and environmental protection program/policy adoption, as well as state and federal agency decisions.

The effectiveness of the political process also depends on the "level of democracy" applied to the decision making. The spectrum of democracy ranges from nondemocratic authoritative decision making to representative democracy (often called "weak" democracy) to participatory or "strong" democracy. While we pride ourselves in the United States on our democratic principles, too often public decision making is more authoritative or democratically weak than democratically strong.

Participatory, strong democracy depends on an open planning process and the engagement of the public. The process shown in Box 2.1 incorporates opportunities for engagement at each step. For effective engagement, the stakeholders need to care and to believe that their political participation will affect decisions.

Participation, Collaboration, and Conflict Resolution

The democratic political process is manifested in the planning process through mechanisms for public participation. Environmental planning requires difficult public policy decisions, such as the extent to which natural resources are to be developed or preserved, at what levels and through what means pollution is to be controlled, where major facilities are to be located, and what levels of risk are acceptable. Since most of these determinations are based not only on expert judgment but also on perceptions and values, effective environmental decisions require considerable participation of interested parties.

The rationale for public participation is both philosophical and pragmatic. As discussed previously, in our participatory democracy, decisions affecting the public and public resources, like the environment, should be made in the public forum, in consultation with public stakeholders. More importantly, the implementation success of projects and programs depends on their public acceptability. Collaborative decision making and public-private partnerships have enhanced public and political acceptability by giving stakeholders not only input into planning but also a more active role in decisions and implementation.

The spectrum of public involvement ranges from nonparticipation and manipulation to citizen control and power, as described in Susan Arnstein's (1969) well-known ladder of citizen participation (for a variation of the ladder, see Figure 4.1).

Although different situations may call for different levels of participation, most environmental planning cases demand higher levels of involvement. This tendency toward citizen power is what Barber (1984) refers to as "strong democracy" and King et al. (1998) call "authentic participation."

The nature of participation has changed over the past 30 years. Just a few decades ago, participation by public agencies was characterized by "Tell us what you want, and we'll go away and decide what to do." This approach did much to breed contempt and conflict between agencies and their constituents. It also wrongly assumed that publics speak with one voice. Planners often found themselves having to resolve conflicts among competing interests. A decade or two ago, conflict resolution stressed compromise, which often left competing interests dissatisfied.

More recent advances in collaboration and stakeholder involvement go beyond traditional modes of participation and conflict resolution. Collaborative approaches, characterized by "Tell us what you want and we'll all figure out what to do together," involve stakeholders in a deliberative process of collective understanding and learning, in order to develop innovative solutions to conflicts and problems that serve multiple interests (Forester 1999).

Box 2.1 shows stakeholder involvement occurring throughout the planning process. A number of participation techniques can be used, including public hearings, advisory committees, interactive workshops, collaborative partnerships, and Internet social networking. These methods are discussed in Chapter 4, with special attention to collaborative planning.

Although collaborative methods can resolve many conflicts, often more sophisticated alternative dispute resolution (ADR) methods, negotiation and mediation, are necessary for major environmental disputes. The objectives of conflict resolution are to reach an agreement efficiently, satisfy the interests of those involved, ensure the legitimacy of the process, and improve relationships.

Environmental Law

Environmental planning and management are based on technical principles and public values, but the processes operate through the legal system. **Environmental law** encompasses those legal principles and prescripts that have been used through the judicial system to protect human health and environmental quality. It is a composite discipline drawing from a number of legal subjects, including common law, property law, torts, constitutional law, administrative law, and the writing and interpretation of legislation (Salzman and Thompson 2006).

In the United States, prior to 1970 and the plethora of federal environmental protection legislation, environmental recourse through the courts relied primarily on the principles of common law and property law. Under **common law**, the doctrines of nuisance and public trust have served as the focus of efforts to control pollution and protect natural areas, respectively. A **nuisance** is a substantial and unreasonable interference of the use of one's property without a physical trespass and is often used to stop or seek damages from a polluting source. There are private and public nuisances, and these are addressed through state courts, which vary considerably. A private nuisance involves effects on the property of one individual, or a small number of people, and is judged by a balancing of the interests presented. A public nuisance involves effects on the community at large, but to claim a public nuisance in court, a private claimant must show special damages beyond those borne by the general public.

The **public trust** doctrine, dating to Roman and English law, holds that the government has a duty as a trustee to protect publicly owned resources. Besides specific public land holdings, these resources include navigable waters and tidelands, and it is in these areas that the doctrine has been used for environmental protection, albeit rarely. Like nuisance, public trust is addressed in state courts, and there is high variability from state to state. To constitute a violation of the public trust, the land or resource must be transferred from public to private use, and there must be consequences that impair the public interest. In California, courts have extended the trust to lands other than tidelands by ruling that all navigable waters plus nonnavigable tributaries affecting navigable waters are subject to the trust. In the landmark 1984 public trust case *National Audubon Society v. Superior Court*, the state was required to revoke some previously granted water rights to Los Angeles Water & Power for the withdrawal of Owens River water to the Los Angeles Aqueduct because it caused lowering of water levels in Mono Lake, with resulting increases in salinity and ecological impacts. A final settlement in 1994 provided for restricted withdrawals that would return the lake to nearly historic levels (Hart 1996).

Property law also provides a basis for environmental law. While the U.S. Constitution provides significant **property rights** to private landowners, it also provides government with the power of **eminent domain**, to take or condemn property for a public purpose without the consent of the owner as long as just compensation is provided. Specific applications of eminent domain are a matter of states' jurisdiction and have often been controversial. In 2005, the U.S. Supreme Court ruled in *Kelo v. City of New London* (CT) that the City had authority to take property with compensation and transfer it (for $1 per year) to private use for development. The political backlash from this decision caused some states to restrict such uses of eminent domain.

In addition, governments also are granted **police power** to regulate private activities, including the use of private land property, to protect public health and welfare. Under the Tenth Amendment to the U.S. Constitution, most police powers are reserved to the states. The federal government does not have general police power, except for its military authority for national security and its authority to regulate interstate commerce under the Commerce Clause of the Constitution. It is within this latter authority that most federal environmental laws and regulations fit. States delegate their police powers to localities. In some so-called Dillon Rule states, localities only have authority that is specifically enabled by the state. In other so-called Home Rule states, localities have police power authority unless specifically excluded by the state. Not all states fit neatly into either category.

Due to the property rights provided by the Fifth and Fourteenth Amendments, however, this police power has limits. Indeed, property owners frequently file **inverse condemnation** suits against local governments, alleging that land use restrictions unjustly "take" or diminish the value of their property without compensation. Based on the standard of review established by the Supreme Court in

1922—"while property may be regulated to a certain extent, if regulation goes too far, it will be recognized as a taking" (*Penn. Coal Co. v. Mahon* [260 U.S. 393, 415])—courts have since debated at what point regulations go too far.

The **takings issue** is extremely important to environmental and land regulation, and it has affected local land use controls and federal regulatory programs for wetlands and endangered species. Several Supreme Court cases in the 1980s and 1990s helped clarify the issue, although it remains a moving target and depends on the specifics of the case. Property law remains one of the most important legal principles for land use planning, which has remained largely a state and local enterprise since Congress failed to pass a comprehensive National Land Use Policy Act in 1974 (Nolon 1996; Nolon and Salkin 2011; see Chapters 17 and 18).

A large number of judicial actions to protect the environment have used the principles of **administrative law** and **legislative review**, particularly since the passage of federal environmental laws in the 1970s and innumerable state and local environmental laws since. The federal National Environmental Policy Act, Clean Air Act, Clean Water Act, Safe Drinking Water Act, Endangered Species Act, Surface Mine Control and Reclamation Act, Resource Conservation and Recovery Act, and many other detailed environmental statutes are subject to judicial interpretation. Both environmentalists and regulated industries have used the courts effectively to challenge federal agency decisions and influence judicial review of the laws, thereby fine-tuning their implementation. This judicial oversight is guided by the Administrative Procedures Act of 1966, which states that federal agency actions are subject to judicial review except where clearly precluded by law. For example, NEPA has been the subject of thousands of lawsuits since its passage in 1970. The court cases have focused primarily on the administrative or procedural requirements of the Act, particularly the preparation of environmental impact statements by federal agencies.

The U.S. environmental laws of the 1970s, in addition to providing the statutory basis for judicial argument, have also enhanced the "standing" of citizens and environmental groups in court. To bring a lawsuit, the claimant or plaintiff must demonstrate specific injury or other adverse effect (which may be aesthetic, conservational, or recreational). Despite arguments made for people to represent the rights of nature in court (e.g., *Sierra Club v. Morton* 1972; Stone 1974), standing in court still requires human plaintiffs to show human injury in fact.

Most of the federal pollution control laws call for state administration of their provisions under the primacy principle, and state laws have thus been passed to conform to federal minimum standards. Many states and localities have gone further with innovative laws and programs for land use regulations, wetlands, stormwater, floodplain management, aquifer protection, wildlife habitat protection, natural hazards mitigation, tree preservation, and other initiatives (Nolan 2002).

The above discussion has focused on environmental and land use law in the United States, but legal structures vary around the world. Box 2.3 gives a brief comparative view of environmental and land use planning law in other countries.

BOX 2.3—Environmental and Land Use Planning Law Around the World

Most nations followed the lead of the United States in 1970s pollution control legislation and environmental impact assessment requirements. However, many nations have caught up, and in some cases surpassed the U.S., in environmental law. For example, in 1969 Congress debated the National Environmental Policy Act with its original call that citizens "have a right to a healthy environment" and ultimately replaced it with "should have a healthy environment." Several countries have included that "right," although it is unclear what effect that wording actually has in practice and in judicial rulings. In addition, many countries have responding more substantively than the U.S. to global agreements fashioned by the United Nations. While the 1992 Rio Earth Summit's Agenda 21 has been a guide for environmental laws in many countries, it had little influence at the federal level in the U.S., and the 1997 Kyoto Protocol for reducing greenhouse gases was ratified by every developed nation in the world except the United States.

With regard to land use law, John Nolan (2005) reviewed the historical background and more than 100 laws related to land use and sustainability from countries across the globe, albeit a sample from the world's 200 independent nations. These legal frameworks, summarized below, determine how land use planning is done in these countries.

- European comprehensive town planning dates back to Sweden's 1874 town planning law. Germany's long tradition of top-down state, regional, and local planning has evolved to give localities authority to adopt plans and zoning to control development around preserved historic centers with open space at the perimeter. In France, city infrastructure planning was conducted at the national level until 1982 when a new law transferred significant authority to the nation's 35,000 municipalities. The formation of the European Union (EU) made environmental laws and standards far more uniform in Europe, and the 1999 European Spatial Development Perspective pro-

vided a voluntary strategic plan to guide national, regional, and local authorities in economic development, transportation, and natural and cultural heritage. Still, legal and regulatory authority remains in the national governments of the EU.

- The United Kingdom practiced town and country planning since 1909, but the 1947 Town and Country Planning Act delegated authority to local governments to control all land development, while the central government retained power to approve local plans after public inquiry. The UK's town and country planning traditions had a far-reaching influence on its commonwealth in Asia, Africa, and the Caribbean. The Town and Country Planning Act was amended in 1990 and consolidated with the 1999 Building and Conservation Areas Planning Act and the 1990 Hazardous Substances Planning Act.

- China's 1989 Environmental Protection Law indicated that targets and tasks for protecting and improving the environment must be defined in urban planning.

- Australia's 1991 Land Act established a nationwide system of planning and regulation designed to balance development and environmental protection.

- Environmental and land use laws in many emerging nations were heavily influenced by the 1972 Stockholm Conference on the Human Environment and the 1992 Rio Earth Summit. The latter established Agenda 21, which emphasized the relevance of land use law and regulation to achieving sustainable development. Argentina amended its constitution two years after Rio recognizing the right of all citizens to a healthy environment. Brazil's 2001 Statute of the City gave significant authority to municipalities to regulate the use of urban property for safety and well-being, environmental equilibrium, and the good of the community. Mexico's 2004 General Law of Social Development declares citizens have a right to a healthy environment.

The Role of the Planner

Planners must play a variety of roles in integrating these disciplinary perspectives into the activities involved in the planning process. Figure 1.1 presented environmental management as the interaction of people and institutions in the private sector, government, and civil society. Where does the planner fit into this scheme? Many environmental planners work in the government sector for local, regional, state, or federal agencies. However, professional planners also work in the private sector for development firms and consultants, and in the civil society sector for land trusts and other environmental groups. Although the planner's role varies according to the context, it is always influenced by growing democratization, increasing public value for the environment, the information revolution, and the movement toward more ecological, equitable, and sustainable forms of development. The following overview of the diverse roles of the planner was inspired by John Forester's classic treatise *Planning in the Face of Power* (1989).

The Planner as Technician, as Information Source

Perhaps the most traditional and fundamental role of the planner is as a source of information. If nothing else, the planner is a technician, providing data and information that serve as a basis for decisions. Information is a source of power for planners because their specialized knowledge and technical expertise make them what Forester (1989) calls the gatekeeper of information and access.

Information has continued to be a critical part of planning, especially as planning evolved from design to "applied science" in the 1960s and to political communication during the 1970s through the 1990s. It is difficult for decision makers to ignore good information. Yet misinformation abounds, often presented by certain interests in support of their case. Planners must not only provide information but also manage misinformation that inhibits informed and participatory planning.

As a result of the information revolution, there has been a huge increase in the quantity and quality of environmental and planning data. The Internet provides instant access to data previously unavailable. The planner must convert this expansive data into information, analyze information into knowledge, and translate knowledge into intelligence to develop the best technical understanding of problems and potential solutions.

Advanced information technologies have helped planning meet this challenge. Spreadsheets, statistical software, and computer models have eased data analysis and enhanced the presentation and communication of information. Geographic information systems (GIS) facilitate spatial data collection, storage, retrieval, and analysis. GIS amplifies the visualization of information, alternative actions and scenarios, and impacts to elected officials and citizens. The geospatial revolution, represented by Google Earth and global positioning systems (GPS), and the social network revolution, represented by Facebook, Twitter, and mobile devices, have increased access to more and better information and enhanced communication and dialogue. In turn, improved information and communication make possible a direct basis for decisions and inform citizens of problems and possibilities, thereby indirectly advancing decisions politically by building community support (see Chapter 5).

The Planner as Facilitator of Public Involvement, Builder of Community Support, Champion of Citizen Empowerment

Although it is grounded in technical and economic information, environmental planning is political. Market forces, powerful development interests, and even many elected officials have long been biased toward development at the expense of the environment and underrepresented groups.

Community action runs counter to this so-called growth machine, trying to compensate for the social imbalance of the market. Action by civil society is viewed as a third system of political power in the democratic competition of ideas, join-»ing governments (the state) and economic powers (the market) (see Figure 1.1). Environmental planning enlists citizen action and encourages a process of citizen empowerment. **Collaborative environmental planning** has emerged as an approach for the engagement of citizens and other stakeholders. It begins with participatory planning and joint decision making, but also includes environmental education, encouragement of counterplanning by citizen groups, and citizen involvement in program implementation (see Chapter 4).

The Planner as Regulator

Many government planners spend more time enforcing regulations—permitting and approving, negotiating, or denying development proposals—than they do in actual planning. In this position as the gatekeepers for development projects, planners have been accused of accommodating development rather than managing it. It is true that planners must react to the proposals submitted, often performing little more than ministerial review and approval. And when development plans do not conform to existing regulations, variances and rezonings are commonplace.

All enforcement officials should exercise what discretion they have in a consistent and equitable manner, to improve the quality of projects and reduce their impacts. Enforcing regulations gives planners some authority in negotiations with resource developers. Therefore, planners need to have communicative and argumentative skills to utilize this regulatory authority to its fullest. They need to represent the interests of the community, to counter misinformation, and to foster inquiry.

The Planner as Negotiator Among Interests, Mediator of Conflicts

As regulators, planners must take a position in negotiations with developers. However, planners must also play a more neutral negotiation and mediation role in resolving conflicts among interests in the advocacy planning or development process. Conflict abounds in environmental decisions. The objective of negotiation and mediation is to involve disputing parties in developing agreements that benefit both sides. As citizen involvement increases, so does the need for conflict resolution.

Negotiation and mediation are necessary skills in the planner's quest for the best alternative. Some planning scholars, especially proponents of advocacy planning, argue that the public interest cannot be captured in one unitary statement, and the planner must give voice to the many "publics" who are affected by any public resource allocation decision. Planning can then be looked at as a competitive marketplace of ideas and alternatives (Susskind and Ozawa 1984). In such a context, an alternative reflecting a negotiated agreement between conflicting parties stands the best chance of winning the competition for acceptance, and therefore potentially being politically adopted and successfully implemented.

The Planner as Political Adviser, as Politician

Environmental planning has become increasingly political, as controversy surrounding particular issues escalates, as the process becomes more open, and as elected officials turn to planners for advice. As Forester points out: "If planners ignore those in power, they insure their own powerlessness. Alternatively, if planners understand how relations of power shape the planning process, they can improve the quality of their analyses and empower citizen and community action" (1989, 27). To be most effective, planners must recognize the political context in which they operate and adapt their strategies accordingly.

The Planner as Designer, as Visionary

It is planning's future orientation, the "vision thing," that lured most prospective planners into the field. There is a long tradition of utopianism in environmental planning, and despite all the mundane daily activities planners must engage in, it is their potential contribution to the future that keeps them going. These day-to-day planning actions do cumulatively affect the future, but the development of community comprehensive or management plans offers the best opportunity for planners to help design a community's future. The reemergence of environmental and urban design in planning during the past two decades, along with the synthesis of design with rational science and political participation in planning, enable the development of future scenarios necessary for creating sustainable communities.

Although greater emphasis on design and visual images is needed in planning today, it should not replicate the utopian planning of the past. Rather than designing their own creative vision for the community, planners help the community discover its vision of the future and explore means to achieve it. In this context, as Forester puts it, "designing is making sense together" (1989, 119). It is a collective process, and the vision represented by a comprehensive plan should represent the community's values.

Plan development is a participatory exercise, but this does not mean that planners are just facilitators. By providing good information, by offering creative and visual alternatives, and by clarifying opportunities, planners play a principal role in "organizing attention to possibilities" (Forester 1989, 17). This is no less creative a task than that of the utopian. Developing scenarios, good and bad, has become an important planning tool to characterize alternative futures, articulate the possibilities, and prompt discussion and action to assist communities in shaping their own destiny; forewarned is forearmed (see Chapters 3, 4, and 17).

The Planner as Advocate

The planner should be an agent of change, working through political and participatory democratic channels to empower the community to improve society. The interest of environmental planners in promoting equitable development in harmony with nature implies an advocacy for sustainability, as well as environmental protection, health, and justice.

All planners can use their authority as regulators, as gatekeepers of information, as negotiators and political advisers, and as designers to promote certain programs, plans, and patterns of development or nondevelopment. However, the degree to which a planner can overtly advocate positions depends on the type of planner he or she is, and the position he or she holds. For example, county and city planners, as part of local government administration, are often constrained in their ability to openly promote new initiatives. Their actions need to be more discreet, working with community organizations and sympathetic elected officials. On the other hand, citizen planners, or counterplanning community groups, are the strongest advocates. However, they have less authority, and their influence depends on building a constituency and using information and community support to affect decisions.

Environmental Planning in the Twenty-First Century

In the twenty-first century, we have new environmental planning imperatives, including energy and climate change, environmental justice, human health, and livable and sustainable communities. These issues are complex, and solutions are constrained by uncertainties, political controversy and disputes, limited government budgets, and countering movements for deregulation and property rights protection.

Despite these constraints, a quiet revolution has been under way in environmental planning and management. As discussed in Chapter 1, the many social movements throughout the world have converged toward the quest for sustainability, which combines objectives for environmental protection, human health, energy efficiency, climate protection, economic development, social equity, and community livability. With growing urbanization, that quest is not more apparent than in our cities where environmental planners must work to create more sustainable communities.

We used to think that planning is knowing; now we realize that planning is learning. We are learning to face new challenges and opportunities through emerging approaches for environmental and community planning, design, and management. Over the past two decades, planners, designers, engineers, managers, and

NGOs have experimented with new ways of synthesizing the broad objectives of sustainability and collaboration. These approaches carry different labels—civic environmentalism, integrated resource management, negotiated agreements, learning networks, community-based environmental protection, active living, ecosystem management, watershed management, New Urbanism, and livable communities, to name a few—but they all share common objectives for engaging people in determining the destiny of their communities, living in harmony with the natural environment, and providing for human health and justice.

Here are five basic elements of these emerging approaches to environmental planning for this century:

1. **Science-based sustainability analysis**. Good decisions require good information, and planning must be based on the best science and research in sustainability, which involves environmental, economic, and human factor analysis, including long-term and global impacts.

2. **Adaptive management or scientific learning**. Despite the best science and research, we cannot know everything. We must learn. Rational-comprehensive approaches, which simply "study and do" and deny uncertainties, are insufficient. Rather, learn and adapt: Study and do and monitor and evaluate and learn and study and do and monitor, and embrace uncertainties along the way. Adaptive management follows the learning-by-doing process. The cyclical process involves not only planning, but also action, monitoring, and evaluation. Learning from results is the basis for further planning.

3. **Collaborative planning, design, and decision making or social learning**. Science and economics do not capture all values, so environmental planning needs participation, consensus building, stakeholder involvement, collaborative design, and learning networks. Collaborative environmental planning builds partnerships, social capital (networks), intellectual capital (mutual understanding), and political capital (constituencies), all of which develop the capacity for learning and resiliency.

4. **Seeking common solutions to multiple objectives**. Sustainability implies broad objectives for the economy, the environment, social justice, and livability. Campbell (1996) and Godschalk (2004) argue that planners must manage the conflicts between these often competing objectives. But the quest for sustainability needs to find the solutions that consider all objectives. Plans and designs for sustainable communities can protect water *and* reduce carbon and air pollutant emissions *and* set aside habitat and open space *and* access affordable mobility *and* provide affordable housing *and* support the economy with green jobs *and* foster human health through active living *and* provide greater livability. Seeking common solutions to multiple objectives enhances cobenefits and cost-benefit analysis and gathers diverse constituents to provide political support.

5. **Link local action to both local needs and global issues**. Many of the vast array of programs for sustainable communities are driven not only by the desire to enhance their local community, but also by the need

to contribute to the sustainability of their region, nation, and planet. Such is the case for the thousands of communities developing climate change mitigation plans. Berke (2008) and others view this linkage of local to global as a common thread tying together communities around the world in their common quest for sustainability.

Summary

Planning, especially in the public context, is a diverse and interdisciplinary field that is continuing to evolve as society changes, as democracy matures, and as methods of knowledge generation improve. This is particularly true in an environmental context, which is heavily influenced by both science and human and societal values, as well as the interdisciplinary influences of engineering, economics, politics, communication, law, and ethics.

Making sense of it all can be fun but challenging. Planners have modified their quest to know everything before making decisions by engaging in a process of learning. Although this takes the pressure off the search for the "best and only" solution, it raises different problems of process and communication. When applied to scientific learning through adaptive management, additional challenges for monitoring and evaluation are required for learning by doing.

Environmental planning continues to evolve as we improve our capacity to make smarter decisions based on the best information available and the broadest range of public values. We aim to foster more livable and sustainable communities, and this requires a wide range of skills, including information management, technical analysis, urban and environmental design, communication, and conflict resolution. Chapter 3 discusses a framework for applying those skills to land use planning, and subsequent chapters address specific methods of analysis, communication, and design.

Figure 3.1 Juxtaposed Informal and Formal Land Development Areas in Caracas, Venezuela. (*Source:* Photo by Alfredo Brillembourg, Urban Think Tank. Used with permission.)

Improved Institutional and Regulatory Frameworks

Improved legal systems help clarify both property rights and regulatory authority. They can foster flexibility and interaction among stakeholders. New government, private, and nonprofit agencies—from local to metropolitan to regional and national scales—enhance coordination and communication to produce more effective plans.

Participation and Collaboration in Planning

Engaging stakeholders in plan making and implementation has become a necessary component of planning in most developed countries and is slowly emerging in many developing countries. While political systems in many developing regions have not welcomed democratic engagement, social electronic networks and other communication means have rallied people of diverse interests to be heard and involved in determining their destiny. The 2011 Arab Spring demonstrations in Africa and the Middle East are an extreme version of the demands for democracy that are being voiced throughout the world.

Strategic Spatial Planning to Manage Land Use and Infrastructure

Strategic spatial planning, which has emerged in many developed countries, is generally made possible by strong and well-resourced governments with a strong tax base. It has occurred in stable social democracies, where land use management systems are made possible through state control over how development rights are used (UNHSP 2009). These conditions are not all present in most developing countries.

Strategic spatial planning can occur at a variety of scales. This type of planning recognizes that road networks, transportation systems, and water and sewer infrastructure shape the spatial organization of communities, as well as the opportunities for lower income groups. Therefore, the most effective community plans coor-

to contribute to the sustainability of their region, nation, and planet. Such is the case for the thousands of communities developing climate change mitigation plans. Berke (2008) and others view this linkage of local to global as a common thread tying together communities around the world in their common quest for sustainability.

Summary

Planning, especially in the public context, is a diverse and interdisciplinary field that is continuing to evolve as society changes, as democracy matures, and as methods of knowledge generation improve. This is particularly true in an environmental context, which is heavily influenced by both science and human and societal values, as well as the interdisciplinary influences of engineering, economics, politics, communication, law, and ethics.

Making sense of it all can be fun but challenging. Planners have modified their quest to know everything before making decisions by engaging in a process of learning. Although this takes the pressure off the search for the "best and only" solution, it raises different problems of process and communication. When applied to scientific learning through adaptive management, additional challenges for monitoring and evaluation are required for learning by doing.

Environmental planning continues to evolve as we improve our capacity to make smarter decisions based on the best information available and the broadest range of public values. We aim to foster more livable and sustainable communities, and this requires a wide range of skills, including information management, technical analysis, urban and environmental design, communication, and conflict resolution. Chapter 3 discusses a framework for applying those skills to land use planning, and subsequent chapters address specific methods of analysis, communication, and design.

3 ■ Comprehensive and Strategic Land Use Planning for Sustainability

We now turn the discussion from the concepts of environmental management to land use planning. The use of the land, and the resources required for it, are perhaps the most significant forces driving the impact of humans on the natural environment. Land development for human settlement and resource production causes critical impacts on the land itself, but also on water, air, and materials and energy use, as well as human livability.

The chapter begins with a description of current land use and related planning challenges facing cities and communities around the world and in the United States, and discusses some emerging responses to these challenges. It then characterizes the relationship of land use to environmental protection and sustainability, from climate change to water resource impacts to environmental justice concerns. A framework for comprehensive and strategic community land use planning is presented that will serve to guide subsequent chapters. The chapter concludes by introducing some current and emerging approaches to environmental land use planning, including community-based environmental protection, watershed protection, ecosystem management, Smart Growth and New Urbanism, and sustainable and livable community planning.

Planning Challenges and Responses Around the World

In 2008, the world reached a major milestone when humans living in cities accounted for half of the global population of 6.3 billion. That proportion is expected to grow to 70–80% by 2050, when the population will likely reach 9 billion. Thus, cities will have to accommodate at least a doubling of the urban population from 2008 (3.15 billion) to 2050 (6.3–7.2 billion). In a major 2009 report,

Planning Sustainable Cities, the United Nations Human Settlement Programme characterized the immense planning challenges posed by this demographic change, as well as the emerging and potential responses to it (UNHSP 2009).

Among the challenges is the sheer number of people to be accommodated in cities, especially in developing countries where more than 50 million people will be added to urban populations each year through 2025. These demographics exacerbate a range of other existing and expected problems in the world's cities.

Environmental Challenges

In terms of water and sanitation, the U.N. estimates that half the population of developing countries—2.5 billion people—do not have access to safe drinking water and sanitation.

Regarding air pollution and human health effects, half of the world's urban populations are exposed to unsafe air pollution.

The impact of climate change on water supply, sea-level rise, and coastal flooding will be significant, since most of the world's major cities are in coastal areas, and the poorest people in the poorest countries are the most vulnerable.

Relating to oil depletion, impacts on oil-based economies, and access to clean energy, 40% dependency on oil for energy, along with prospects for peak oil production and resulting peak prices, spell trouble for the global economy, especially developing countries and their cities.

Socioeconomic Spatial Challenges

In developing countries, squatter communities, slums, and ghettos are often the entry point of migrants to the city (Figure 3.1). Government efforts to eliminate or improve these areas have largely failed, yet the informal economies that have developed in them are often vibrant. The challenge now is not to eliminate them but to transition them to appropriate land regularization and management, and to provide basic infrastructure. In both developed and developing countries, there continue to be social inequities across spatial scales from upscale gentrified and suburban areas on one side and tenement zones and environmental risk areas on the other.

The UNHSP study found that among the important responses to these demographic, environmental, and socioeconomic challenges has been the growing application of urban planning, especially in developing countries. The following planning innovations have enhanced the capacity to address these problems.

Bridging the Green (Natural) and Brown (Built) Environmental Agendas

Many cities around the world have adopted sustainability as a community goal and are applying innovative technologies and designs that meet physical needs and improve environmental quality. These include renewable energy, distributed power and water systems, green infrastructure to protect waters and natural areas, mixed-use and compact development, and sustainable transportation systems (Newman 2009).

Figure 3.1 Juxtaposed Informal and Formal Land Development Areas in Caracas, Venezuela. (*Source:* Photo by Alfredo Brillembourg, Urban Think Tank. Used with permission.)

Improved Institutional and Regulatory Frameworks

Improved legal systems help clarify both property rights and regulatory authority. They can foster flexibility and interaction among stakeholders. New government, private, and nonprofit agencies—from local to metropolitan to regional and national scales—enhance coordination and communication to produce more effective plans.

Participation and Collaboration in Planning

Engaging stakeholders in plan making and implementation has become a necessary component of planning in most developed countries and is slowly emerging in many developing countries. While political systems in many developing regions have not welcomed democratic engagement, social electronic networks and other communication means have rallied people of diverse interests to be heard and involved in determining their destiny. The 2011 Arab Spring demonstrations in Africa and the Middle East are an extreme version of the demands for democracy that are being voiced throughout the world.

Strategic Spatial Planning to Manage Land Use and Infrastructure

Strategic spatial planning, which has emerged in many developed countries, is generally made possible by strong and well-resourced governments with a strong tax base. It has occurred in stable social democracies, where land use management systems are made possible through state control over how development rights are used (UNHSP 2009). These conditions are not all present in most developing countries.

Strategic spatial planning can occur at a variety of scales. This type of planning recognizes that road networks, transportation systems, and water and sewer infrastructure shape the spatial organization of communities, as well as the opportunities for lower income groups. Therefore, the most effective community plans coor-

dinate the timing and location of water and sewer infrastructure, transportation, and land use planning.

Monitoring and Evaluating Plans

In the master planning traditions, plans are made for an eternity. In truth, times change, conditions change, and values change, and it is important to monitor and evaluate the effectiveness of plans on a periodic basis to validate, update, and/or revise them.

Planning Challenges and Responses in the United States

The urban planning profession in the United States prides itself on its planning traditions. Indeed, many of the planning innovations cited in the UNHSP report are well established in the U.S. However, there remain significant urban and metropolitan challenges, and some critics suggest that many of them result from ineffective urban plans that are too often influenced by profit-seeking development interests at the expense of community livability, the poor, and the natural environment (e.g., Kunstler 1994).

The fact is that urban and regional planning in a market-driven democracy like the U.S. is not easy. Berke et al. (2006) characterize land use planning as a complex, turbulent, competitive, high-stakes game over a community's future development. And old and new challenges abound for both urban and rural lands. Along with the need to accommodate 100 million more people during the next 40 years, the U.S. must address the following planning objectives to enhance quality of life and natural resources:

- Creating green, healthy, safe, just, livable, and sustainable communities.
- Arresting unsustainable sprawling land development.
- Managing and greening shrinking cities.
- Managing small towns and rural landscapes.
- Protecting ecosystems, waters, air quality, and climate.

Creating Green, Healthy, Safe, Just, Livable, and Sustainable Communities

Green, healthy, safe, just, livable, and sustainable are all adjectives that characterize the current urban planning movement in the U.S. to create communities that work for both people and the environment. Easier said than done. Most agree that the patterns of land use and development prevalent in the last half of the twentieth century lacked many of these attributes. These sprawling patterns are land consumptive, automobile dependent, congestion generating, energy and oil inefficient, carbon emitting, and air and water polluting. They breed physical inactivity and obesity. They have fostered a middle-class flight to the suburbs that left the poor behind in polluted, hazardous, and crime-ridden cities. With climate change, oil depletion, an obesity epidemic, social inequity, and many other looming problems, these patterns are not sustainable.

During the past decade, many planners, designers, and policy makers have realized that there must be a better and more sustainable way, and they have responded to the range of challenges associated with achieving more sustainable and livable communities in the U.S. The responses include better urban and development design; improved energy, water, and transport technologies; more effective government management of development and redevelopment; burgeoning land conservation investments; and the integration of social equity and environmental justice concerns into urban plans.

Arresting Unsustainable Sprawling Land Development

Many of these responses emphasize efforts to arrest urban sprawl and revitalize existing communities. **Sprawl** is land-consumptive, dispersed, auto-dependent land development made up of homogeneous segregated uses: housing subdivisions, shopping centers, office/business parks, large civic institutions, and roadways heavily dependent on collector roads. Box 3.1 presents some of the causes and critiques of sprawl.

Efforts to arrest urban sprawl come from government through Smart Growth management and from the market through compact, mixed-use development designs. Ultimately, arresting sprawl requires a multiscale, multisector, and multijurisdictional approach from neighborhood to region, what Calthorpe and Fulton (2001) call the Regional City.

The Government Response to Sprawl: Smart Growth Management

Uncontrolled sprawl development has prompted many communities and states to adopt more aggressive growth controls to manage the associated impacts. **Growth management** is defined as those policies, plans, investments, incentives, and regulations that guide the type, amount, location, timing, and cost of development to achieve a responsible balance between the protection of the natural environment and the development efforts that support growth, a responsible fit between development and necessary infrastructure, and quality of life. **Smart Growth** emphasizes development and redevelopment in areas of existing infrastructure and discourages development in areas less suitable for environmental, fiscal, livability, or spatial reasons. By doing so, Smart Growth aims to support and enhance existing communities, preserve natural and agricultural lands and resources, and save the cost of new infrastructure.

Using an array of management tools, including innovative zoning regulations, urban growth boundaries, infrastructure investments, community planning procedures, tax policies, and land acquisitions, many rapidly growing localities have tried to control the pace and location of development. Where individual localities have not been able to manage regional growth effectively, several states have adopted state-level guidance and requirements for growth management (see Chapters 17 and 18).

BOX 3.1—Urban Sprawl in the United States

After World War II, a major shift in urban development occurred in the U.S.: outward movement, suburban growth, and urban sprawl. Several forces combined in the 1950s and later to bring about sprawling patterns of land development:

- Population growth spurred by the baby boom and immigration.
- Unprecedented economic prosperity.
- Widespread use of the automobile.
- Massive highway construction, led by the federally subsidized interstate system and other highways, creating convenient access to former hinterlands.
- Social decay, crime, and racial tensions of central cities, which caused an exodus.
- Urban freeway construction that disrupted many central urban neighborhoods, forcing people to look for alternatives.
- Federal policies for subsidized mortgages for single-family homes (e.g., FHA, VA) that led to a construction boom, as more people could afford the "American dream."
- Local zoning laws that segregated uses, creating separated residential subdivisions, commercial shopping centers, and employment centers.

Scholars have been critical of suburban sprawl for more than a quarter-century (e.g., USCEQ 1974). Sprawl's greatest triumph has been the creation of the personal and family "private realm," be it home, yard, or personal car. As a result, there are advocates of sprawl and critics of Smart Growth, including conservative groups and bloggers who argue that people ought to live where they want, and that government Smart Growth gives people and property owners not only fewer choices, but more costly ones (see www.Demographia.com).

But many argue that along with this private triumph has come a public or civic failure. Land uses have separated, and as people have become more segregated—by age, by income, by culture, by race—they have retreated from a more public life, from **communities of place**, to a more controlled life, to **communities of interest**. A landscape of isolated land uses has become a landscape of isolated kids, bored teenagers, chauffeur moms, stranded elderly, weary commuters, and immobile poor (Calthorpe and Fulton 2001; Duany et al. 2000).

Sprawling development has spoiled the visual and cultural diversity of communities, as suburban areas in all parts of the country now look the same. Keith Charters, mayor of Traverse City, Michigan, once said that if development doesn't go somewhere, it goes everywhere; and if it goes everywhere, you look like anywhere.

The physical, economic, and environmental impacts of sprawl are perhaps more significant than the social ones. Land use has spread out. Development density until 1920 averaged more than 6,000 people per square mile; after 1960 it was four times less dense, at 1,500 people per square mile. The development of houses and roads consumed an average half-acre per person in the 1950s and 1960s; that grew by nearly four times (to 1.83 acres per person) by 1985 (Benfield et al. 1999).

In most sprawling developments everyone is forced to drive everywhere. Collector road designs and long commuting distances increase vehicle miles traveled, congestion, and air pollution. Sprawl consumes agricultural land, open space, and natural wildlife habitats at a rapid rate, converting them to subdivisions, shopping centers, and roads. Local governments struggle financially to provide urban infrastructure, services, and schools in response to rapidly growing, dispersed developments.

The Design Response to Sprawl: Compact, Mixed-Use, and Ecological Development

The critique of sprawl prompted creative experiments with new development patterns by several planners, designers, and developers in the 1990s. These designers contend that suburban sprawl is not only ecologically but also socially destructive and that dense, compact, mixed-use, pedestrian- and transit-oriented communities are more sustainable. These designs are inspired by European cities and traditional urban neighborhoods in the United States. Density and mixed residential/commercial/employment/education uses support public transit and nonmotorized transport, which can reduce dependency on the automobile. Walkability promotes public health and social interaction. Mixed-use and mixed-income housing provides diversity in neighborhoods. Density and design allow land set-asides for open space, natural drainage, and other environmental amenities.

The **New Urbanist** Movement has been working to capture these ideas. It synthesizes innovations from a number of American architect planners, including neo-traditional compactness and aesthetics (Andres Duany), ecological compatibility (Michael Corbett), rural character (Randall Arendt), regionalism, pedestrian and transit orientation (Peter Calthorpe), and social engagement (all of the above). All have become party to the Congress for New Urbanism (CNU), a movement being reflected in hundreds of development plans across the country.

Many have joined this larger design movement, and there is an expanding literature of applications at a variety of scales, referred to generally as sustainable urban design (e.g., Duany and Speck 2009; Farr 2208; Hester 2006; Newman and Jennings 2008; Ritchie and Thomas 2009). Following the lead of the Green Building Movement, new certification systems are emerging for sustainable neighborhood design, including the LEED-Neighborhood Development (ND) created by the U.S. Green Building Council in partnership with CNU and the Natural Resources Defense Council (NRDC) and launched in 2010, and the STAR Community Index being developed by USGBC, ICLEI, and the Center for American Progress (see Chapters 14 and 16).

The Metropolitan Response to Sprawl: The Regional City

It has become obvious, in metropolitan areas, that sprawl development is not a local but a regional issue and that its management requires regional solutions. However, local governments have long had difficulty forging multijurisdictional solutions to regional problems because of the lack of regional authority and the competitive, political, parochial, and often petty differences that constrain cooperation. Many opportunities exist for economies of scale and efficiency in regional solutions for water supply, wastewater treatment, air quality management, transportation, and solid waste management; and many metropolitan areas have taken advantage of them or have been required to do so by state or federal law.

But regional governance is still rare in the U.S., especially with regard to land use management. Calthorpe and Fulton (2001) argue that the end of sprawl requires a regional approach. They envision the Regional City, containing effective regional transit, affordable housing fairly distributed, environmental preserves, walkable communities, urban reinvestments, and infill redevelopment. They see the region providing social identity, economic interconnectedness, and the ecological fabric relating urban centers to bioregional habitats and protected farmland. Regions depend on neighborhoods and vice versa. The region is the superstructure, and the neighborhood is the substructure. The region is the scale at which large metropolitan economic, ecological, and social systems operate; neighborhoods are a region's ground-level social fabric and community identity. Andres Duany's Urban Transect is a useful concept in the progression from the center city to the rural hinterlands and from the neighborhood to the region (see Figure 16.12). Effective neighborhood plans must recognize their place among adjacent land uses and the regional context, and effective regional plans must recognize their smaller-scale urban and rural elements (Duany and Speck 2009; see Chapters 16 and17).

Bringing about the vision of the Regional City and the end of sprawl is complicated. Calthorpe and Fulton see physical design policies as a key element, using the building blocks of village, town, and urban centers; districts; preserves; and corridors. They also argue for regional growth boundaries, federal transportation and open space investments, and environmental policies consistent with regional goals. Urban center reinvestment is critical to focus development and redevelopment within urban areas (vacant properties and brownfields) and away from outlying natural areas (greenfields; Box 3.2).

Still, these regional solutions require regional government, or at least a high level of regional cooperation, and effective regional governance is rare in the U.S. However, there are some good examples of regional approaches, including the Twin Cities Metro Council, Tahoe Regional Planning Agency, and Portland Metro, described in Chapter 18. The Regional Plan Association (RPA) in the tri-state New York metropolitan area was established in 1922 to take a regional approach to land use, transportation, environmental, and other planning issues. The New York Metro is already the most transit-oriented region in the country (New York's 14.4

BOX 3.2—Brownfields, Greenfields, and Other Fields

Smart Growth, New Urbanism, and regional approaches aim to accommodate development within urbanized centers and to conserve natural environmental and agricultural lands outside developed areas. Planners have coined a number of clever labels or "fields" to characterize the appropriateness for development within this objective. *Brownfields* are defined as vacant, potentially contaminated areas within urban centers that are difficult to develop because of suspected financial and environmental risk. Brownfield redevelopment is beneficial because it cleans up suspected contamination, improves central urban property values, and avoids development on greenfields outside the city.

Greenfields are open, natural, or agricultural lands that provide natural amenities, wildlife habitat, natural system benefits, resource production, and community character. New development often converts greenfields to urban uses. Environmental planning and design emphasize development that minimizes impact on greenfield benefits or avoids them altogether.

In-fields, like brownfields, are vacant urban areas available for infill development and redevelopment, but they do not pose environmental risk. With existing development infrastructure and little risk of environmental impact, they are far more desirable for development than greenfields. *Greyfields* are vacant or nonprofitable older suburban commercial centers and parking lots that are prime for redevelopment. Converting such sites to community centers can bring much-needed civic space to suburbs. Finally, *brightfields* describe parking lots and other large asphalt expanses available for energy production using solar photovoltaic systems that double as shading devices.

Figure 3.2 The RPA Greensward. The Metropolitan Greensward Campaign is the Regional Plan Association's tri-state plan for protecting public water sources, outdoor recreation, fresh produce, and important habitat in the New York metropolitan area. (*Source:* Copyright Regional Plan Association, Inc., New York, NY. Adapted from "A Region at Risk: The Third Regional Plan For The New York–New Jersey–Connecticut Metropolitan Area," Island Press, 1996. Used with permission.)

vehicle miles traveled [VMT] per capita per day in 2005 was 42% less than the U.S. metro area average of 24.6). The region is planning to expand transit coverage and service to guide development and avoid sprawl, VMT, and related impacts from the expected population growth of 4 million people by 2030. Figure 3.2 shows RPA's Metropolitan Greensward Campaign to protect public water, outdoor recreation, fresh produce, and important habitat. The Greensward open space system provides a regional growth boundary and also a natural amenity for cities and neighborhoods at the region's core.

Managing and Greening Shrinking Cities

Sprawl occurred in most U.S. metropolitan areas during the 1960s through the 1980s as a result of both flight from the central city and new growth from in-migration. Fast-growing cities and suburban "Boomburgs" in the south and western U.S. faced significant growth management challenges (Lang and Lefurgy 2007). Although northern cities witnessed sprawl from flight to the suburbs, many saw their people relocate to the Sunbelt and witnessed sustained population loss. Between 1960 and 2000, St. Louis, Missouri, and Youngstown, Ohio, lost more than half of their populations, and Cleveland, Pittsburgh, Buffalo, and Detroit lost more than 40%. A few of these cities, like Chicago and Minneapolis, have seen some revitalization of their central business districts with redevelopment and new denser residential development, the so-called downtown rebound.

But others have not. These **shrinking cities** are characterized as older industrial cities with significant and sustained population loss and increasing levels of vacant and abandoned properties, including blighted buildings and brownfields. Revitalizing these shrinking cities is a major planning challenge. Schilling and

Logan (2008) describe a number of planning responses to "right-size" these shrinking cities based on experience in several communities (see Chapter 17). Right-sizing strategies include:

- Limiting services or providing them more efficiently through deannexation, decommissioning of surplus infrastructure, or transferring services to private entities.
- Stabilizing dysfunctional markets and distressed neighborhoods by replacing vacant and abandoned properties with green infrastructure and land banks, converting blighted land into community green space.
- Building community consensus through collaborative neighborhood planning.

Managing Small Towns and Rural Landscapes

The considerable attention given to urban and suburban development is appropriate because those locations are where most people live. However, rural and small-town land use and development are also important for three reasons. (1) These greenfield areas are home to important ecological, cultural, and agricultural resources. (2) The inherent use of rural land for resource production of agriculture, forestry, and mineral extraction has significant environmental impact. (3) Rural places are increasingly attractive, as people grow weary of the congestion and lifestyle of the city and suburbs.

Sprawling patterns of rural development occur as more retirees and telecommuters not dependent on urban jobs are choosing small-town and rural living. Many of the same environmental planning issues arise in these areas as in the outer suburbs: conversion of productive agricultural lands to nonproductive estates and subdivisions, and impacts to natural habitats. Also, in the face of change, there are local concerns about preserving the cultural heritage, social character, and economic viability of these communities, as residential development is followed by superstores that impact the visual character and the commercial vitality of historic Main Streets.

Planners have responded with environmental planning approaches specific to small towns and rural communities. Duany's Urban Transect, introduced earlier and discussed in Chapters 16 and 17, identifies natural and rural zones, the latter having its own transect from small town to village to hamlet. The Transect aims to apply community design and planning elements appropriate to place, and for rural zones, the elements include natural area protection, rural growth boundaries, and clustered conservation development. Arendt (1996, 1999) and Yaro et al. (1988) popularized conservation residential design techniques to protect rural and small-town values (see Chapter 16). Knox and Mayer (2009) drew lessons from Europe to articulate small-town sustainability concepts. Sargent et al. (1991) adapted the conventional planning process to rural planning, focusing on the resource base of natural areas, agricultural lands, lakes and rivers, and cultural heritage. They all agree that achieving sustainable development in small towns and rural areas is different from urban and suburban planning. It emphasizes local self-reliance, community economic and social vitality, and natural resource management.

Rural areas are home to many public lands and land trust properties that have their own planning and management challenges. Watershed and ecosystem management principles are most applicable in these areas. Public lands include federal, state, and regional forest, park, refuge, and range lands. These are important environmental lands, and their planning and management provide useful lessons for private land use. Federally owned land makes up about 30% of the total area of the United States, and 90% of these holdings are in resource lands administered by the Forest Service, National Park Service, Fish and Wildlife Service, and Bureau of Land Management. These lands include the premier natural lands of the nation, including prime core wildlife habitats, wilderness areas, and the natural jewels of the national parks. However, these are also productive resource lands providing timber, grazing, energy, and hard minerals, and a wide range of recreational uses. The main planning and management challenge for the administering agencies is determining the appropriate balance among these competing multiple uses.

The public land agencies have long prepared management plans for these lands, applying the general planning process presented in Box 2.1. In fact, these agencies developed some of the traditional and emerging approaches for environmental land use planning, including sustained yield and sustainability, public participation and conflict resolution, carrying capacity studies, environmental impact assessment of land uses, riparian buffers, watershed management, and ecosystem management.

Finally, increasing amounts of rural lands are being placed in conservation easements and land trusts, intended to provide permanent protection from development. Land conservation is a critical part of environmental land management and has become a multi-billion-dollar business largely administered by nonprofits and public agencies. Establishing land trusts and conservation easements is an important start, but achieving the environmental values of these lands over time requires monitoring and land management (see Chapter 15).

Protecting Ecosystems, Waters, Air Quality, and Climate

Among the most critical challenges in planning for sustainability are those related to environmental protection, especially protecting natural waters, air quality, and ecosystems; mitigating climate change by reducing fossil energy and other sources of greenhouse gas emissions; and adapting to the prospective impacts of climate change. These environmental challenges of land use and development, and the planning responses to them, are the focus of this book. The next section describes the relationship of land use and the environment and its many dimensions, and subsequent chapters provide greater detail on these impacts and their solutions.

Land Use and Environmental Protection

The use of land has significant impacts on the natural and human environment. The conversion of natural and productive lands to human use, sprawling patterns and inappropriate location of development, road and building construction, and land use practices following development—all of these have broad impacts on human environmental health and the natural environment. Land use decisions can exacerbate natural hazards and soil erosion, alter the hydrologic balance, pollute surface water and groundwater, destroy wildlife habitats, increase energy use and air pollution, escalate carbon emissions and climate change, further disadvantage poor populations, and diminish community character and quality of life. This section introduces several of these effects. Subsequent chapters discuss these impacts in greater detail, as well as the analytical, planning, engineering, and policy measures to avoid or mitigate them.

Land Use and Climate Change

Climate change is perhaps the most critical environmental problem of the century, with its expected impacts on sea-level rise, coastal flooding, extreme weather events, drought, water supply disruption, ecosystem change, and many secondary effects. Climate change is being caused by global atmospheric warming, forced largely by human emissions of carbon dioxide from the combustion of fossil fuels, which still account for more than 80% of commercial energy in the world. Annual emissions range from about 18 metric tons per capita (mt/c) in the U.S., to 8 mt/c in Europe, to 6 mt/c in China, to 1 mt/c in Africa.

What is the land use connection? Higher emissions per capita in the U.S. relative to other countries result from greater consumption of fossil fuel energy for household, commercial, and transportation needs. Larger houses and commercial buildings, more electricity, greater automobile dependency, more vehicle miles traveled, and less-efficient vehicles all contribute to greater carbon emissions. Sprawling land use patterns are a main cause of more reliance on automobile transport, less transit use, and less nonmotorized transport. Kenworthy (2003) found that U.S. urban transport CO_2 emissions per capita were 3.5 times more than in Western Europe, largely the result of less urban density and far less use of public transit and nonmotorized walking and bicycling (11% of passenger trips in the U.S. versus 50% in Western Europe). (See also Cambridge Systematics 2009; Ewing et al. 2007; and Chapter 12.)

Land Use and Natural Hazards

People are subject to the risks of natural hazards, but these risks can be exacerbated by poor location and design of land developments. In 2003, FEMA estimated that during each decade of the last century worldwide natural disasters killed 1 million people and caused hundreds of billions of dollars of damage (FEMA 2003). These do not include the millions of daily incidents of damage and injury from natural hazards not classified as disasters. There is a difference between hazard and risk. **Hazard** refers to the inherent danger associated with a potential problem; **risk** is the probability of harm caused by that hazard. Risk is increased by human exposure and vulnerability to the hazard. People can sometimes increase the degree of hazard, but more often, people increase the risk by placing themselves in harm's way by building, for example, in the floodplain, seismic, or wildfire area, without proper design to reduce vulnerability.

Natural hazards include the following:

- *Weather-related problems*, such as flooding, stormwater, snowfall, hurricane and tornado wind damage, drought, excessive heat (historically the biggest killer of all natural hazards), and lightning. Climate change is expected to exacerbate extreme weather events and increase these hazards.
- *Geologic hazards*, such as earthquakes, tsunamis, volcanic eruptions, landslides, avalanches, erosion, and support problems. Earthquakes in Haiti (2010) and China (2008) and tsunamis in the Indian Ocean (2004) and Japan (2011) killed more than 550,000 people. On a lesser, but still significant scale, landslides in the United States cause about $1.5 billion in damages and 25 fatalities each year.
- *Wildfire damage*, which has increased considerably in recent years as residential development has spread to more remote areas.
- *Beach erosion*, measured at 2–3 ft per year along the East Coast, which threatens 86,000 existing and planned structures over the next 60 years.
- *Ecological hazards*, including nuisance, pestilent, and disease-carrying wildlife.

All natural hazards cannot be avoided by planning, but the intelligent location and design of structures and land uses can reduce the risks. Natural hazard mitigation requires understanding the hazard, reducing exposure by appropriately locating development, reducing land use effects that increase the hazard, minimizing vulnerability through effective design measures, and preparing for the hazard with emergency preparedness plans (see Chapter 13).

Land Use and Human Environmental Health

Land use affects human health directly and indirectly. **Environmental health** is concerned with the impacts of ambient conditions and exposures on physical and mental well-being. It refers specifically to exposure to toxic contaminants of the air, water, and food, as well as noise. It can also include quality-of-life issues, such as a healthy, active lifestyle, and mental health issues relating to crowding, congestion, and unpleasant surroundings. Many local sustainability programs are labeled Healthy Communities.

Important environmental health issues related to land use include the following:

- *Land use and active living.* Sprawling, auto-dependent land use patterns contribute to the sedentary American lifestyle that has caused a significant increase in obesity. Health advocates are supporting compact, mixed-use, and pedestrian-oriented community design to foster more active and healthy living to enhance cardiovascular activity and reduce obesity (see www.activelivingresearch.org/).

- *Air quality.* More than half the U.S. population still lives in areas that exceed ozone air quality standards. Ozone is produced by photochemical smog mostly from vehicle emissions. Sprawling land use patterns increase vehicle use, miles traveled, and air pollution (see www.epa.gov /airtrends). Indoor air pollution from combustion emissions, volatile chemicals and furnishings, mold, and other sources is increasingly recognized as a health hazard.

- *Drinking water quality.* Sources of drinking water, including groundwater, rivers, and surface reservoirs, are susceptible to contamination from nonpoint source pollution from stormwater runoff from urban areas and farmland. Because groundwater is often untreated, it poses the greatest risk of health effects (see www.epa.gov/safewater).

- *Fish and swimming advisories.* Water pollution from land runoff, discharge, and atmospheric deposition also affects human health through direct contact and contamination of fish (see www.epa.gov /fishadvisories).

- *Toxic and hazardous waste sites.* In the three decades of the federal Superfund program, designed to identify and clean up old waste sites posing threats to human health, more than 1,300 sites have been added to the EPA's National Priority List. Most of the sites have been remediated through the multi-billion-dollar fund, but about 50 sites are added to the list each year (see www.epa.gov/superfund).

- *Toxic pollution releases.* Residential proximity to polluting industry is a less pervasive land use problem in the U.S. than in past decades, but people, usually the poor, still live close to sites that release toxic chemicals. This is a major environmental justice issue. The Toxics Release Inventory estimates that industry releases almost 4 billion pounds, including 2 billion pounds of air releases, mostly from power plants and the manufacturing industry, and 4.75 billion pounds of land releases, mostly from metal mining (see www.epa.gov/tri).

Land Use Impacts on Hydrologic Systems

Land use and development have major impacts on the hydrologic system and pollute surface and groundwater by altering water flows and runoff and land source pollution. These impacts affect drinking water sources, water-based recreation, and stormwater management (see Chapters 7–9).

- *Impervious surfaces* (roads, parking lots, rooftops) associated with urban development increase and speed runoff from storms, thereby increasing downstream flooding; they also reduce the infiltration of water, thereby lowering groundwater recharge and diminishing stream low- and baseflows that are dependent on seepage of subsurface water.

- Agricultural, urban, forestry, and mining land uses increase erosion and sedimentation and *runoff pollution* into rivers, lakes, and estuaries. Runoff nonpoint source pollution is now the largest source of surface water pollution in the U.S.

- Land use–related sources of pollution, like septic drainfields, underground storage tanks of petroleum products, and landfills and waste lagoons, are the biggest sources of *groundwater contamination.*

Land Use Impacts on Agricultural and Other Productive Lands

Development converts economically productive lands, such as agricultural lands, forestlands, and aquifer recharge areas, to urban uses. This conversion diminishes the ecological services and economic productivity of these lands for food and fiber, carbon sequestration, forest canopy, and water supply. The National Resources Inventory (NRI) documents land use change in the United States every 5 years. The latest U.S. Department of Agriculture report covers the period 1982–2007 (USDA 2009).

While the 111 million acres of developed land in 2007 made up only 6% of non-federal land, development has increased dramatically. During the 1982–2007 period it increased by 40 million acres per year, a 56% increase. More than one-third of all land that has ever been developed in the contiguous 48 states was developed in the last quarter century. Forestland and cultivated cropland made up more than 68% of the acreage developed between 1982 and 2007 (USDA, NRCS 2009) (see Chapter 6).

Land Use and Ecological Resources

Land-consuming, sprawling development has a significant impact on natural ecosystems, productive wetlands, and habitats of wildlife, including threatened and endangered species (see Chapters 10 and 11). The net loss for wetlands has been arrested in recent years. Total wetland loss was about 468,000 acres per year in the 1950s–1970s, 290,000 acres per year in the 1970s–1980s, and 59,000 acres per year in the 1980s–1990s. But during 1998–2004, there was actually a net gain of 32,000 wetland acres per year due to wetland mitigation efforts. However, there was a net loss of freshwater vegetated wetlands of 82,000 acres per year, essentially all from urban and rural development. In most cases, new wetland acres from mitigation are of less quality than lost acres.

Land conversion impacts wildlife by destroying and fragmenting habitat. The acceleration of land development in the late 1990s and early 2000s has had a considerable impact that has not been adequately measured. Most attention is given to the habitats of the 1,100 species listed as endangered or threatened under the Endangered Species Act (ESA). The ESA provides for incidental impact of development on listed species's habitats with an approved habitat conservation plan (HCP). While HCPs aim to provide habitat protection, the activity also demonstrates the increasing encroachment of development on critical wildlife habitat.

Land Use Impacts on Energy and Material Consumption

Patterns of land use and construction affect resource consumption. Energy use is the major cause of climate change, because humans are 80% dependent on fossil carbon fuels. And that carbon energy use is high because of inefficient building design and construction, our dependence on automobile transport, and the length of commuting distances. The Green Building Movement has tried to address the material and energy intensiveness of buildings, while Smart Growth and New Urbanism development efforts aim to affect transportation energy requirements through compact, infill, and transit-oriented development (see Chapters 12 and 16).

Land Use and Community Character, Conflict, and Environmental Justice

Land development, characterized by open space conversion to roads, subdivisions, and superstores and large shopping centers, can significantly change the character of communities. Although some change is inevitable, shaping that change within local context and culture can ease the impacts for local residents and preserve the social heritage. This is especially important in older rural and agricultural communities that find themselves in the path of suburban sprawl or exurban development.

Because of these many environmental impacts, conflicts over land use and development are common. Few people welcome the change and disruption they experience as a result of new land development in their neighborhoods and communities. Many uses bring actual or perceived potential impact, and residents often respond with "Not in my backyard." These NIMBY conflicts take the form of angry residents, litigation, and civil disobedience. If a new development requires public agency approval, such as a permit or rezoning, the conflict will likely come to a public stage. When making such a decision, local planners and elected officials must consider the merits and the controversy generated by the development proposal. This is particularly true of locally unwanted land uses, or LULUs. Examples include solid waste transfer facilities, wastewater treatment facilities, wind energy systems, and other uses that are perceived to pose a hazard or reduction in property values.

Historically, these LULUs have been sited in areas lacking the capacity to object. Often these were poor or minority communities that were excluded from the siting process and were victims of the environmental impact. The Environmental Justice Movement emerged in response, to ensure that all people are protected from the disproportionate impacts of environmental hazards. Planners must often play both negotiation and mediation roles in trying to resolve land use disputes; they must engage stakeholders in order to achieve environmental justice through inclusiveness and the assessment of unfair impacts.

A Framework for Comprehensive and Strategic Land Use Planning

Community planning combines analysis, participation, and design to formulate strategies for achieving the objectives of sustainability and livability. It serves as the basis for policies and programs to implement those strategies. Planners produce a network of plans with various scales and purposes, such as comprehensive, regional areawide, community-wide, small area, topical functional, and implementation plans (Berke et al. 2006). All of them should be based on data gathering and analysis (intelligence) and stakeholder and public involvement, as well as implementation feasibility tempered by regulatory authority, budgetary constraints, and political context.

Most U.S. states require municipalities and counties to produce a **comprehensive plan** (also called a general plan) that describes a broad vision for the community. The plan presents a set of goals, objectives, policies, and strategies dealing with various aspects of the community—land use, housing, transportation, utilities, natural environment, parks and recreation, economic development—that aim to guide physical development and community services. The vision, strategies, and policies are based on detailed analysis and public participation, so the comprehensive plan provides both the technical and political basis for local government programs, including growth management, land use regulations, infrastructure investments, and other services. The plan usually has a 10- to 50-year time horizon and is prepared and revised every 4–10 years, requiring monitoring and evaluation. Some recent plans have a 100-year horizon.

The most important manifestation of the comprehensive plan is the spatial land use plan, which characterizes the community's future in visual map form. The spatial plan must consider the various functions of land use systems: as a critical part of environmental systems, as functional spaces for uses, as settings for community activities, as visual features of social symbolism, as publicly planned services and regulated spaces, and as the key element of real estate value and exchange (Berke et al. 2006). A spatial land use plan should be strategic. Rather than presenting a "master plan" in the European tradition or detailed project plans, the land use plan should provide general spatial arrangements.

In perhaps the best reference on the subject, *Urban Land Use Planning* (which has been in print since 1965 and is now in its fifth edition), the authors contend that planning is recognized as the legitimate authority for managing land use change within the constraints of democratic governance (Berke et al. 2006). They characterize land use planning as a high-stakes, competitive game with rules (planning and development procedures) and a number of players or actors (developers and the market, government, citizen interests, and planners). The game develops as sequential interactions among the players, and it results in a product—a land use plan and implementing mechanisms to guide future land development. Land use planning integrates population and economic forecasting, environmental and land analysis, urban and development design, engineering infrastructure, stakeholder perspectives, and implementing policies, regulations, and programs. Planners are the principal game managers who control the process, procedures, and information; gather and analyze intelligence; and mediate conflicts.

Fundamentally, planning is done for places and people, and these vary. Plans for shrinking Rust Belt cities are different from plans for fast-growing Sunbelt cities and suburbs. To touch people and become real, plans need to focus on places within places, like mixed-use neighborhoods, business districts, parks, and conservation areas. And plans vary with the needs of people—their culture, their age, and ethnicity. Plans must be built within the context of places and people (Hoch et al. 2000).

The following framework for planning is synthesized from the primary literature sources (Anderson 1995; Berke et al. 2006; Hoch et al. 2000). Preparing community plans should follow the basic planning process presented in Box 2.1. The framework below focuses on five activities and outcomes critical to land use planning and management: intelligence, the network of plans and plan making, implementation, monitoring and evaluation, and building community consensus.

1. Intelligence: Background Data and Planning Analysis

Comprehensive, land use, and other functional plans require a broad range of information, including census and population data, economic data, engineering data on infrastructure, environmental data, and citizen perspectives. Much of this information is obtained from primary and secondary sources, field investigation, and/or the local knowledge of citizens. Computerized information systems, such as GIS, spreadsheets, and statistical software, are used to analyze, synthesize, and present information. Land use intelligence involves environmental inventorying and mapping, suitability and carrying capacity analysis, and assessment of land use perceptions and community values (livability, attractiveness, symbolism, and quality of life).

A useful exercise is the preparation of a **State of the Community (SOC)** report, which combines information analysis and consensus building (Berke et al. 2006). It involves a community-based assessment of current conditions and trends, as well as future options. Some tasks and outcomes of the SOC report are listed below. Subsequent chapters (indicated) describe methods used for the inventories and assessments. This intelligence is the foundation for effective plan making.

- Assess land use threats, opportunities, forces of change, and other issues.
- Critically review existing programs and ordinances (Chapter 17).
- Inventory and classify land supply (Chapters 6, 10, and 14).
- Inventory and analyze environmental resources and land suitability (Chapter 14).
- Select and measure sustainability indicators (Chapter 14).
- Develop population and land use forecasts and scenarios (Box 3.3).

2. The Network of Plans and Plan Making

Each plan must delineate its focus or bounds (either spatial or functional), lay out its organization and procedures, and show its connection to other plans and programs. It must articulate a direction-setting framework derived from the state of the community and community consensus (see item 5 below). The network of plans may include one or more of the types of plans described next.

Regional or Areawide Plan

This type of plan is usually prepared by a regional or metropolitan agency, such as a designated metropolitan planning organization (MPO) or a specially convened

BOX 3.3—Envisioning Alternative Futures

The heart of the planning process is formulating alternatives and strategies (see Box 2.1, steps 3, 4, and 5). For project planning, alternatives include optional scales, designs, and technologies applied to meet plan objectives. For land use planning, alternatives include spatial configurations and urban designs. For comprehensive planning, alternatives take the shape of different visions of a community's future. For program planning, alternatives may be optional regulations, financing, organizational arrangements, or institutional structures. While the quest may be for the desired future condition (DFC), the best way to identify the DFC is to formulate a range of alternative future conditions and evaluate them through a community involvement process.

Randolph and Masters (2008) present four approaches to developing and assessing future conditions:

- Projecting and forecasting emphasize trend analysis.
- Road mapping seeks to maximize the development of a specific objective.
- Developing "solution wedges" begins with needs assessment and then investigates the various means of meeting a portion, or wedge, of those needs.
- Developing scenarios embraces the uncertainties of any future visioning, identifies driving forces, and uses storylines to articulate different possible futures.

In all types of planning, developing scenarios is a practical tool for articulating future possibilities. It embraces the uncertainties that cannot easily be modeled in forecast models and expands the discussion from just quantitative analysis to include qualitative considerations. Scenarios are simply different visions of the future based on different assumptions. They can capture the imagination and thus can be a tool to generate discussion and creativity about the future. Storylines and visualization, like photo-simulation, are useful for characterizing scenarios. In recent years, the approach has become more systematic and is being applied increasingly to a wide range of business, industry, government policy, and community issues.

Because of expanding interest, Global Business Network (GBN), a firm that specializes in this approach, has made scenario development services a lucrative business. The systematic approach uses a participatory process that has several steps:

1. Pose a key focus question about the future.
2. Identify drivers or factors that will affect the answer to that question.
3. Prioritize, cluster, and ultimately combine the drivers into two critical uncertainties that serve as the axes of a two-by-two scenario matrix.
4. Develop scenario storylines describing the future associated with each of the four pairs of drivers in the four quadrants of the matrix. To the extent possible, the storylines should reflect accurate technical information.
5. Label each quadrant scenario.

Once the scenarios and storylines are developed, they can be used to generate discussion and identify challenges and opportunities that need to be addressed in achieving a desirable scenario, or preventing an undesirable one. Scenario planning can help organize perceptions about the future, remove biases in visioning, focus debates about technology needs, challenge the view that little will change, enable the development of different technology portfolios, and foster a probabilistic rather than a deterministic view of the future.

A good example of scenario development using this model is a participatory planning process used by the Great Valley Center in the Valleys Futures Project for the Great Valley of California. With the focused question of "what will be the future of the Great Valley?" scenarios were developed for three subregions. In the North Valley workshop, participants brainstormed a long list of key factors and environmental forces. They then prioritized the list to identify a few clusters of closely related issues.

BOX 3.3—Envisioning Alternative Futures (cont.)

Finally, several of those clusters were combined and two critical uncertainties were selected to serve as the axes of a two-by-two scenario matrix: resources (from improving to decreasing) and external forces (from positive to negative). The four labeled scenarios in Figure 3.3 galvanized considerable discussion in the region, and the program provides tools for conveners and teachers who wish to use the scenarios for their own purposes. They beg for action so that people can determine their destiny, with the motto: Forewarned = Forearmed. The best part is the storylines that creatively articulate plausible futures—some good, some bad. You can read the storylines at http://www.greatvalley.org/valley_futures/stories/north/index.aspx.

Increasing

GREEN RUSH
Tourists, then new residents, are attracted to the natural beauty of the area, but the fragile natural resources that lured many are spoiled by unplanned growth and the area becomes like urban-California with more trees.

THE GOOD LIFE
Deliberative planning that includes everyone creates a collaborative region that leads to an enviable economic, social, and natural resource balance.

Resources

Negative ← **External Influences** → **Positive**

GHOST TOWN
Global events, drought, and bickering paralyze the North Valley. Instead of pulling together, the North Valley retreats to defenses of localism until residents are forced to leave the area.

BURNT BACK TO BASICS
In exchange for investment, the region trades its water, and when fires spread through the North Valley, a leadership vacuum is revealed that is filled by an inward-looking spiritual awakening.

Decreasing

Figure 3.3 Four Scenarios for the North Valley, California. (*Source:* Adapted from the Great Valley Center, Valley Futures Project, http://www.greatvalley.org/valley_futures/.)

BOX 3.4—Blacksburg, Virginia's 2006–2046 Comprehensive Plan

Introduction

Part I—The Natural Environment
Environment
Parks and Recreation
Part II—The Built Environment
Economic Development
Information Technology
Transportation
Utility Services
Part III—The Human Environment
Public Safety
Public Facilities/Government
Relations
Extraterritorial Area

Part IV—The Planned Environment
Community Planning
Land Use
Downtown Planning Sector
Northwest Planning Sector
North End Planning Sector
Midtown North Planning Sector
Midtown South Planning Sector
South End Planning Sector
Southwest Planning Sector
University Planning

Source: Blacksburg 2007.

group of represented local jurisdictions. The areawide plan should establish general guidelines for land use and development, and specific policies for functional topics such as transportation and water/wastewater/solid waste.

Long-Range Comprehensive Community-wide Plan

This is usually the only plan required of local governments, so it often is broad and inclusive. Box 3.4 contains the contents of the Blacksburg (VA) 2006–2046 comprehensive plan, which addresses most community issues. It is essential to engage the public and stakeholders in the development of the comprehensive plan, especially if this is the only or primary plan making activity.

Community-wide Land Use Plan

This may be part of the comprehensive plan or a separate plan. The spatial plan is best represented in map form, and Figure 3.4 shows the Blacksburg land use plan map. But there is more to it than simply map making. The land use plan should be based on location principles, including suitability, space requirements, holding capacity, and urban design and form. Berke et al. (2006) suggest addressing land use categories in the following order: open space, general urban uses, community activity centers, residential habitats, and specific small areas.

The land use plan often simply classifies land into segregated uses—residential of different densities, commercial, industrial, agriculture and open space, and so on—when livable and sustainable community design prescribes less prescriptive and more creative mixed use, blending housing densities, open space, commerce, and employment to promote walkability and greater neighborhood

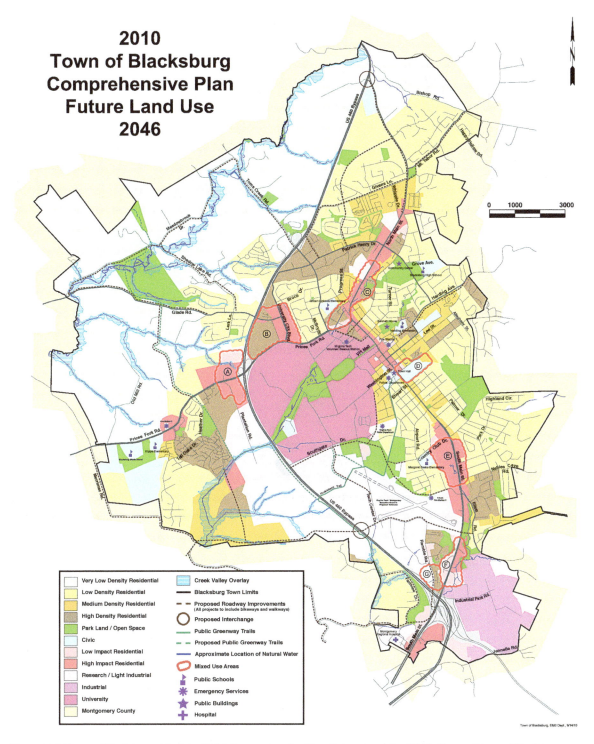

Figure 3.4 Town of Blacksburg, Virginia, 2006 Comprehensive Plan, Future Land Use 2046. (*Source:* Town of Blacksburg 2007.)

diversity. Figure 3.4 shows a very small mixed use area designated in Blacksburg's 2006–2046 plan.

Community-wide Functional Plan

Part II of the Blacksburg comprehensive plan includes several community-wide topics or plan elements, each of which is essentially a functional plan (see Box 3.4). Functional plans may also be conducted outside of the comprehensive planning process and stand alone. If so, they should still be incorporated into the comprehensive plan, because it often has more political and sometimes legal clout than an independent plan. Some of the important functional plans for community sustainability include:

- Green Infrastructure/Urban Forestry/Open Space Plan
- Energy and Climate Action Plan
- Watershed and Stormwater Management Plan
- Vacant/Brownfield Property Plan
- Pedestrian/Bicycle Plan
- Transportation and Transit Plan
- Water and Sewer Infrastructure Plan

District and Small-Area Plans

Land use plans come to life at the living scale, which is in the neighborhood and smaller areas where people live, work, shop, and play. Part III of the Blacksburg comprehensive plan includes district plans for five main sectors of the town. Like functional plans, these small-area spatial plans can be part of the comprehensive plan or stand alone. Several examples of small area plans are in Chapter 16 (see, for example, Figures 16.14 and 16.18).

It is important to include sufficient design detail at this smaller scale to characterize future development patterns. Too often planners use "bubble" plans and "broad felt markers" to distinguish classes that lead to segregated land uses much like the larger-scale community-wide plan. Duany et al. (2000) suggest a "fine pencil" level of detail at this district and small-area scale to represent future land use more completely and to articulate mixed use and creative design. It is quite important to engage the public in this design exercise using visioning workshops, design charrettes, and other participatory techniques. It is also important to involve property owners, developers, and investors in this plan making, because they are usually critical for implementation.

These small-area plans are often conducted for the following specific areas:

- Downtown or Central Business District
- Commercial Centers and Corridors
- Redevelopment Areas
- Residential Habitats and Mixed-Use Neighborhoods

3. Implementation Plans and Programs

Implementation plans and programs address the actions necessary for realizing the vision, objectives, and strategies of comprehensive, land use, functional, and small-area plans. Actions include zoning and development regulations, capital improvement plans and budgets, financing plans, tax policies, infrastructure plans, and other programs. Collectively, several actions may form a comprehensive growth and development management program to provide orderly development, redevelopment, infrastructure, and land conservation to meet the community vision and objectives of the comprehensive plan.

4. Monitoring and Evaluation

The network of plans is not intended to provide master plans for eternity, but is the community's best attempt today to articulate a future vision and the means to get there. Both the vision and the means can change over time, as community values change and as new opportunities, technologies, designs, and policies develop. It is important to monitor plans to see whether they achieved what they intended, whether they reflect the emerging state of the art and science of planning and development, and whether they are consistent with evolving community values. Community comprehensive plans in Virginia must be revisited and updated every 5 years. This iterative step in the planning process is important for keeping plans current.

5. Building Community Consensus

Building community consensus through stakeholder involvement and collaborative planning is part of each of the preceding planning activities, including gathering intelligence, developing scenarios, articulating a community vision, formulating objectives and strategies, and making spatial, functional, and implementation plans. Perspectives and values, as well as local knowledge of citizens, property owners, and businesses, contribute to planning intelligence, and public input provides a foundation for effective and politically acceptable plans. The next chapter is dedicated to this important component of the process of planning for sustainable communities.

Summary, Conclusions, and Emerging Practices

Urban land use and environmental planning face significant challenges, both worldwide and in the United States. These challenges stem from increasing urbanization. Half the world's population is now urban, with prospects of more than 50 million people flooding into the cities of developing countries each year until 2025. The U.S. population, now 80% urban, is expected to increase by 100 million over the next 40 years. Cities around the world will have to accommodate 3–4 billion additional residents by 2050. Beyond simple demographics, planners face environmental challenges from energy and water constraints, the conversion of agricultural and natural lands, and the impacts of climate change, to name a few.

In developing countries, a major challenge is transitioning squatter communities and their informal economies into the urban fabric without major social and economic disruption. Planning has come a long way around the world, but necessary responses to these planning challenges require higher levels of democratization and participation, stronger legal frameworks for property rights and land regulation and management, and resources to improve basic infrastructure.

In the United States, there is a strong planning tradition, but sprawling patterns of urban land use and their resulting impacts on natural land, energy use, and climate change are not sustainable. Some cities have difficulty managing rapid growth and development, while others are plagued by declining populations and vast amounts of vacant and abandoned properties left behind.

The significant impacts of land use and development on the human and natural environment include human health, air and water quality, climate change, watersheds, ecosystems, productive resources lands, natural hazard risk, and environmental justice. Although these impacts and challenges seem daunting, new approaches and practices in urban, land use, and environmental planning are emerging to address them. These emerging practices include the following.

- *Planning for green, healthy, safe, just, livable, and sustainable communities.* Cities and counties across the U.S., large and small, are adopting goals and strategies to achieve measures of sustainability to improve the livability of their communities and to reduce their ecological and carbon footprint on the global environment.
- *Comprehensive and strategic land use planning.* Communities continue to improve processes and procedures for comprehensive and strategic land use planning, stressing multiscalar approaches from metropolitan regions to small areas, participatory approaches engaging the community, and design-oriented community development strategies.
- *Smart Growth Management.* These strategies are being adopted at the local level throughout the U.S. to promote dense infill and redevelopment in areas of existing infrastructure and to discourage sprawling exurban development. Among these strategies for livability and sustainability are compact, mixed-use, diverse, walkable, and transit-oriented neighborhoods that reduce automobile dependency, vehicle miles, and carbon emissions, and that enhance community interaction. These designs are increasingly common in redevelopments and reflected in development regulations such as form-based codes and other growth management programs (see Chapters 17 and 18).
- *Climate action plans.* These practices are being developed in thousands of communities in the U.S. and abroad. They include plans to reduce community carbon emissions and plans to prepare for and adapt to the impacts of climate change (see Chapter 12).
- *Community-based environmental protection (CBEP).* Climate action plans are examples of this emerging practice, in which localities and

their citizens have stopped waiting for national and state government solutions to their environmental problems and have taken the initiative to find their own through local action. CBEP supplements and complements traditional approaches. It is place-based and has some basic principles: focusing on a definable geographic place; working collaboratively with stakeholders through partnerships; assessing, protecting, and restoring the place's environmental quality, including environmental, economic, health, and quality-of-life objectives; integrating private actions and public management to forge effective solutions; and monitoring and redirecting efforts through adaptive management.

- *Watershed management*. This focuses on the drainage catchment, recognizing that managing a water body requires managing the land in its watershed. Science-based watershed management, when coupled with collaborative planning, has become an effective approach for managing land and water resources. It has four basic principles: targeting priority problems, promoting a high level of stakeholder involvement, integrating solutions from multiple agencies and private parties, and measuring success through monitoring and other data gathering (see Chapters 8 and 19).

- *Ecosystem management*. Focusing on ecosystem integrity and health, ecosystem management was developed to promote resource sustainability in response to concerns over biodiversity and limitations of species-specific wildlife management and commodity-based resource management. The ecosystem approach has been applied as various scales for environmental management national, regional, and local agencies and land trusts. Ecosystem management has the following basic principles: primary objective for ecosystem health and biodiversity; long-term time horizon and ecosystem scale; scientific assessment and analysis; stakeholder involvement since humans and society are part of ecosystems; integrated public and private solutions; and adaptive management (see Chapters 10 and 19).

All of these approaches to environmental land planning and management are place-based, aim to achieve environmental and social sustainability, are grounded in scientific analysis, and engage a range of stakeholders. The next chapter focuses on this latter component, collaborative environmental planning.

4 ■ Collaborative Environmental Planning and Learning for Sustainability

A quiet revolution has been occurring over the past two decades—engaging people in efforts to manage the environment and enhance sustainability. Driven primarily by increasing democratization, the environmental movement, the growth of community-based organizations, and the need to integrate diverse values, resolve conflicts, build consensus, and generate knowledge and creative solutions, this evolving practice is referred to as **collaborative environmental planning (CEP)**. The rationale for CEP is well stated in this 1996 policy statement by the U.S. Forest Service:

> Most of us are familiar with top-down planning, in which the few decide for the many and change comes from the outside. Collaborative planning is different. It emerges locally—bringing together communities of place and interest. It honors a full spectrum of values, holds everyone responsible for success, and begins with educating one another and discovering common ground. There is no one leader and no one is excluded from sitting at the table. Together, the group envisions the future and creates a plan to get there. For those paralyzed by resource use conflicts, collaboration may be a way to help defuse polarization and start discussing issues in conference rooms instead of courtrooms. Collaboration works, but it is not always quick or easy. It means taking the time to reach out to people, to build trust, seek common ground and compromise, and forge integrated solutions. (USDA, Forest Service website 1996)

Collaborative environmental planning is the basis for some of the emerging practices introduced in previous chapters, including civic environmentalism, community-based environmental protection, ecosystem and watershed management, and planning for sustainable and livable communities. The role of public participation

80

and collaboration in planning was discussed in Chapters 1–3 (see Figure 1.1, Table 2.1, Box 2.1). Increasing participation in planning is cited by the UNHSP report, *Planning Sustainable Cities*, as one of the ongoing positive responses to the world's urban planning challenges (UNHSP 2009). Collaboration is the means required for greater public and political engagement, in order to achieve sustainability and community resilience (Goldstein 2011).

Like environmental planning generally, CEP itself has evolved over the past five decades. This chapter begins with some concepts related to the role of participation in democratic processes and then describes the evolution of collaborative planning from pre-1960s nonparticipation to 2010s collaborative learning. It addresses some key questions in establishing a collaborative planning program, and describes traditional and emerging approaches and tools used for collaboration and learning.

Strong Democracy, Shared and Social Capital, Informality, and Power

Achieving the next level of environmental improvement and sustainable communities will depend less on the mandates of government and more on the actions of people, communities, industries, nongovernmental organizations, landowners, and others, working together, often voluntarily. Environmental planners and managers often work to design participatory processes to bring together **stakeholders**, defined here simply as those who effect change as well as those who are affected by it. To engage these stakeholders in planning, learning, and acting requires a common sense of community, effective formal and informal collaborative processes, and the sharing of power and authority.

As introduced in Chapter 2, the spectrum of democracy ranges from nondemocratic authoritative decision making to representative democracy (often called weak democracy) to participatory democracy. Although in the United States we pride ourselves on our democratic principles, too often public decision making has been more authoritative or democratically weak than democratically strong. The progression toward greater collaboration and more citizen power is referred to as strong democracy (Barber 1984).

One of the key ingredients of a strong participatory democracy and an effective civil community is its social capital. **Social capital** is a community's stock of social trust, networks, and civic experience, upon which people draw to solve problems collectively. It is normally built on a history of formal and informal interactions, usually through community activities and in public spaces where people interact, such as walkable neighborhoods, community centers, and schools. When planning issues and problems occur, people and groups can rely on their "bank" of social capital not only to help one another, but also to work together to solve problems (Dryzek 1990; Forester 1999; Gray 1989; Healey 1997; Innes 1996).

Social capital is a critical element of a community's resilience to catastrophe, disaster, or major change. A system's **capacity for resilience** is its ability to absorb perturbations without being undermined or becoming unable to adapt, self organize, and learn. The characteristics of bonding, bridging, linking, and reciprocity inherent in social capital create a latent capacity that can be relied on to bind a community in times of distress, making it more resilient to change (Adger 2001; Randolph 2011).

Social capital is one of three components of shared capital (Innes et al. 1994). In addition to social capital, successful collaboration requires intellectual capital, or the collective knowledge of problems and potential solutions, and political capital, the capacity for organization and influence necessary to achieve results in the political process. Intellectual capital is enhanced by collaborative learning, and political capital is about power.

Without social capital, it is difficult to achieve collective knowledge or a common sense of purpose. Some scholars lamented the decline in civic engagement and the deterioration of social capital in the United States during the 1990s (e.g., Putnam 1996, 2000). They argue that people retreated from community activities to their private realms due to suburbanization, sprawl, and dependency on the automobile; increased job mobility, reducing the stability of local populations; demographic changes, including more single-person households, child-bearing later in life, two-career families, and rising divorce rates; and advances in technology, from television to computers, which took people from social space to Myspace.

These social forces continue, but more recently there appears to be an increasing desire for community; a louder cry for more input from affected parties in public and private decisions that affect neighborhoods, communities, and the environment; and the use of the same technologies that isolated people in the 1990s to connect them today through electronic social networks. These trends have created both **communities of place** for more informal interaction in neighborhoods and public spaces, and **communities of practice** for more organized interaction about a topic or issue of common interest. Both types of communities are represented in the million or more environmental and social justice NGOs, praised by Hawken (2007). As a result, more people have engaged in collective efforts to help shape better decisions, and more governmental, nongovernmental, and private agencies and firms have embraced participation and collaboration as part of their way of doing business (Daniels and Walker 1996; John 1994; Keuhl 2001; London 1995; Porter and Salvesen 1995).

Collaborative processes can increase all three elements of shared capital. The process of working together for a common goal strengthens social capital. Collaborative planning creates a forum for interaction among stakeholders. By its nature, collaboration is informal relative to the traditional formal bureaucratic structures of government master planning and rational-comprehensive planning. These mechanistic formal structures tend to ratify existing authority, routinize interaction and procedures, differentiate status, and ignore social emotion. **Informality**, on the other hand, is unregulated organic behavior that is more chaotic than formal structures, but it embraces affective involvement, has a freer flow of information, and tends to level status and be more creative. In collaborative planning, these formal and informal systems are interdependent, and planners must operate at their interface and manage the tensions between them (Innes, Connick, and Booher 2007).

Collaborative learning develops intellectual capital by tapping local knowledge, mutual education, and discovery. The common constituency created by social networks, and the shared knowledge developed by collaborative social and scientific learning, are all sources of political capital—the power to affect decisions and actions.

Power is thus enhanced by both good, accepted information and public stakeholder support, two desired products of collaborative planning. In our Information Age and the resulting Age of the Network Society (Castells 1996), collaborative planning can result in **network power**—the shared ability of linked agents to alter their environment in ways that are advantageous to them both individually and collectively. Network power can emerge if the agents or stakeholders represent a diverse range of interests and knowledge relevant to the issues at hand; they are interdependent in that their ability to fulfill their interests depends on each other's actions; and they are able to engage in authentic dialogue (Booher and Innes 2002). The collective power of networks, along with their capacity to enable effective communication, learning, and consensus building, have made them an important part of the emerging generation of collaborative planning. The power of electronic social networks was evident in the role they played in the democratic unrest in the 2011 Arab Spring in Africa and the Middle East.

The Evolution of Collaborative Planning: From Nonparticipation to Collaborative Learning

Like environmental management and planning, collaborative planning has evolved and continues to mature as we experiment, learn, and develop new processes and approaches to engage stakeholders. We can characterize this evolution as five periods, or generations, of public participation and collaborative planning in the United States (Table 4.1). Figure 4.1 shows this simple characterization in an extension of Susan Arnstein's (1969) well-known ladder of participation.

In the pre-1960s **dormant generation of nonparticipation** in the U.S., citizens had little access to decisions except through the ballot box. Social movements had some effect, but the real power of influence laid in development-oriented special interests, and the "capture" of public land agencies and local elected officials was common. The **first-generation public information** period (1960s–1970s) came with the social unrest of the 1960s, demanding greater public participation in government decisions. Laws like NEPA codified public comment requirements. Agencies produced many information brochures and held lots of public meetings, but elected officials were under little obligation to act on public comment, and citizens were often discouraged and alienated by the lack of response. Toward the end of this period, new techniques, such as public advisory committees and focus groups, began to improve opportunities for public input.

As new techniques began to generate useful public comment, agencies became more committed to **public involvement** in the **second generation**, 1970s–1980s. Still, participation was characterized by: "Tell us what you want and

TABLE 4.1 **The Evolution of Collaborative Planning**

Generation	Period	Name	Characterization	Power	Outcomes
Dormant	Pre-1960s	Nonparticipation, passive participation	Special interest influence/capture, manipulation of public, citizen voter	Elected officials, agencies, special interests	Agency capture by special interests
1st	1960s–1970s	Public information, notification	Public meetings, notification, surveys, special interests	Elected officials, agencies, focus groups	Agency decision making, informed publics
2nd	1970s–1980s	Public involvement	Public input workshops, advisory committees, conflict resolution	Elected officials, agencies, public as special interest	Agency decision making, public consultant
3rd	1990s–2000s	Collaborative planning and decision making	Stakeholder involvement, consensus building, public partnerships	Elected officials, agencies, public as partner	Collaborative and communicative values-based decision making
4th	2000s–2010s	Collaborative learning and collaborative management	Social networks, learning networks, joint fact-finding, comanagement, consensus building, communities of practice	Elected officials, agencies, network power, consensus power, information as power	Collaborative fact-based and values-based decision making, creative solutions, new knowledge, collaborative implementation

we'll go away and decide what to do." This approach did not endear constituents, and it wrongly assumed that diverse publics speak with one voice. Opposition to plans was common, and participants offered conflicting demands and opinions. Resolving conflicts stressed compromise, which often left competing interests dissatisfied. Emerging methods for conflict resolution and mediation focused on win-win solutions and became part of participatory planning. Other useful techniques for involvement included interactive workshops and task forces.

In the early 1990s, public involvement experience began showing that more collaborative means of engaging stakeholders in resolving conflicts, building consensus, and developing options could lead to more acceptable decisions. Planning and elected officials began to realize that giving some authority to stakeholder groups could pay off in plans and decisions that had less opposition. The 1996 Forest Service statement that began this chapter illustrates this realization. This **third generation of collaborative planning and decision making** was characterized by "Tell us what you want and we'll all figure out what to do together." At the same time, citizens and groups became more organized and functioned as forces "to be reckoned with" by agencies and developers alike. Collaborative planning creates a forum in which diverse and interdependent participants

Collaborative Learning and Co-management
Network Power
Communities of Place
Communities of Practice
Networks as Decision Maker
Learning Networks
Joint Adaptive Management

Stakeholders take part in networks and communities of place and practice to learn and develop new knowledge and build consensus for creative solutions. Beyond decisions, stakeholders engage in joint implementation and learn from adaptive management.

Collaborative Decision-making
Collaboration
Delegated Power
Shared Decision Making
Consensus Building
Partnerships

Stakeholders have the clearest and most accurate perception of needs and priorities of their community and should make decisions themselves. They must be given the means and opportunity to engage in dialogue to resolve conflict and reach consensus, and the shared authority to make decisions.

Active Involvement
Citizen as Consultant
Conflict Resolution

Citizens should be consulted to contribute their opinions during the decision-making process. When given adequate information, citizens can make educated decisions. Conflicts among citizens and between citizens and decision makers should be resolved.

Passive Participation
Citizen as Respondent
Informing
Citizen as Constituent
Citizen as Voter

Experts and elected representatives have the right to make decisions on behalf of citizens. Citizens vote for their representatives, but public decision-making is a complex pursuit and should be left to skilled experts and policymakers. Citizens do not necessarily know what is needed or what is the best approach, but their opinions should be surveyed and used in decision-making.

Non-participation
Citizens Left Out
Manipulation
Special Interest Capture

Citizens are not part of the decision-making process, but special interests are, and elected officials are not held accountable for their actions. Citizens may be manipulated into thinking their interests are being served.

Figure 4.1 Evolving Levels of Citizen Participation. (*Source:* Adapted from Arnstein 1969.)

can develop a shared vision, resolve conflict, build consensus, and formulate creative solutions.

The latest **fourth generation of collaborative learning and comanagement** recognizes that simply tapping the values and knowledge of stakeholders, resolving conflicts, and building consensus to inform decisions are still limited efforts in the quest for better and more creative solutions and effective implementation. This emerging approach focuses on the generation of new knowledge through joint learning and on stakeholder involvement in implementation or comanagement.

The Fourth Generation: Collaborative Learning and Comanagement

Learning characterizes the latest generation of collaborative planning. As stated in Chapter 2, we used to think planning is knowing; now we know planning is learning. In our quest to advance planning to address our environmental challenges and achieve sustainability, we must continue to learn. Emerging approaches like learning networks, joint fact-finding, and communities of practice take collaborative processes into a dedicated learning mode, which can synthesize diverse information, develop new knowledge, and build consensus for creative values-based and fact-based solutions to environmental and community problems.

This emerging generation of collaborative planning also goes beyond decision making to collaborative management, in which community groups and NGOs, private businesses, and citizens, often acting in partnership with government agencies, are actively involved in implementing plans, projects, and programs to improve the environment and the community.

Comanagement, or joint implementation, is usually place-based and involves a community of place. Collaborative learning uses a variety of methods and can operate within a community of place or a community of practice. Recall that a community of place is bounded by a location like a neighborhood or a watershed, and common interest in that place is the glue that holds the group together and the focus of the group's attention. Participants are members of that place. A community of practice, on the other hand, developed for private firm collaboration, is not bound by location and focuses on a common interest or issue, as specific as a production process or as complex as mitigating climate change. Members are not from the same place, but they share the common interest in the subject at hand. Members may be diverse in their perspectives on the subject, but they may also have similar views and are interested in advancing the cause. They do not necessarily seek consensus but rather expertise, good collective practice, and problem-solving capacity (Wenger 1998, 2000).

Collaborative Learning

Collaborative planning has long sought to promote learning among stakeholders to share knowledge and understanding. In practice, stakeholders have often discovered that their disagreements result from limited knowledge and faulty assumptions. **Collaborative learning** allows them to investigate data and information together, thus creating a common knowledge base and new assumptions that can lead to consensus and new solutions (Daniels and Walker 1996). Several methods of collaborative learning are described below.

Learning Networks

A learning network integrates a community of practice with multiple-stakeholder collaboration to nurture collective, topical expertise among members. Networks can operate at different scales, and the collective expertise can flow up to inform national and regional policy and down to affect local plans.

Goldstein and Butler (2010) describe their work with the national Fire Learning Network (FLN) supported by the U.S. Forest Service and The Nature Conservancy. About 150 landscape collaboratives have participated in the FLN, with the common goal of restoring ecosystems that depend on fire. FLN participants learn about and create innovative restoration practices at landscape levels, share innovations, and develop collaborative expertise to enable them more effectively to engage in collaborative processes at regional levels, thereby influencing fire management policy at the national level. Goldstein and Butler (2009) found that through the use of a mix of communication technologies, media, and face-to-face interaction, participants strengthened relationships, built trust, shared skills and ideas, and developed a common language and shared perspective across the entire network. In some cases, the participants never met one another in person. Although this large national, multiscalar learning network is complex and long term, it illustrates the potential of learning networks to develop new knowledge and scientific consensus, experiment with new practices in the field, and improve regional and national policy.

Joint Fact-Finding

Joint fact-finding (JFF) was developed as a collaborative exercise that promotes shared learning to create a credible, legitimate, and relevant knowledge base for environmental decision making. The approach helps resolve scientific disputes, build consensus about information and assumptions, and ensure that science and politics are appropriately balanced in decisions.

Advanced by the Consensus Building Institute, founded by Larry Susskind at MIT, joint fact-finding is a key element of a consensus-building process in cases involving complex scientific and technical questions. To be successful, JFF must involve key stakeholders, including scientists, to legitimize knowledge, employ a professional neutrality to facilitate face-to-face dialogue among stakeholders, and result in written agreements. JFF is more formal than the learning network, but its formal structure keeps the process on track and is necessary for controversial problems. Still, JFF applies the collaborative skills of dialogue and conversation to channel people who hold opposing viewpoints into civil discourse, in order to discover common ground, mutual understanding, and consensus about scientific issues (Karl et al. 2007).

Participatory Appraisal

Participatory appraisal is based on the **participatory rural appraisal (PRA)** method developed in the 1980s in international development projects to engage people in assessing realities of their own lives and conditions as a basis for plans and actions (Chambers 1994). In the participatory appraisal method of collaborative learning, stakeholders develop and share information and learn together. It is especially useful in gathering, assessing, and mapping local knowledge. The information is generally drawn on maps that help clarify information, identify problems, foster discussion, and suggest possible solutions. The process generates dialogue and learning. Group visualization through graphical mapping of the community and its resources is an important step in participatory appraisal. Hand-drawn maps are helpful, but advances in public participation geographic information systems (PP-GIS) have enhanced this kind of mapping exercise (see Chapter 5).

A variation of PRA is **participatory vulnerability assessment (PVA)**. This approach requires the active involvement of community stakeholders to identify and map natural hazard vulnerabilities and mitigation strategies that are feasible and practical (Smit and Wandel 2006).

Digital Democracy and Electronic Networks

Experience with learning networks, joint fact-finding, and participatory appraisal shows that nothing beats face-to-face dialogue to achieve trust building, consensus building, and mutual understanding. However, the information and network revolution provides new means of information access and communication that can complement these methods. The Internet offers the capacity for "one-to-many," "many-to-one," and "many-to-many" types of communication that were not possible before (Castells 2007).

Electronic social networks have become an integral part of American and global culture. E-mail, Facebook, Twitter, YouTube, blogs, and other social networking sites and methods are creating new opportunities for communication and engagement. Traditional participation methods have benefited simply by using websites to disseminate information, along with e-mail, interactive sites, and surveys to get public feedback. While these methods are limited in promoting dialogue, blogs can serve this purpose through interactive discussion threads that can gather participant opinion, tap participant knowledge, and manage misinformation (Gil de Zúñiga et al. 2010).

Open Source Planning and Crowdsourcing

Most people are familiar with open source software and file-sharing networks, and there is an open source movement to enhance free access to a wide range of interactive information and tools. The movement has spread to urban planning, in efforts to shift its traditional top-down culture to greater public interaction using free-access data libraries, web forums, crowdsourcing methods, and interactive mapping software like *GeoServer*. *GeoServer* is an open source software server, developed by the nonprofit The Open Planning Project (TOPP), that allows anyone to view and edit geospatial data (see Chapter 5).

Communities and agencies are using Internet citizen science projects to gather information and local knowledge. Websites like EveryBlock (to track and discuss what's new in your neighborhood, now operating in 16 cities) and SeeClickFix (to promote eyes-on-the-street empowerment, efficiency, and engagement by logging and mapping neighborhood problems) allow people to log information to inventory conditions and seek solutions. In 2010, San Francisco launched *The Urban Forest*

Not all people have access to the Internet, and relying on electronic networks for collaborative learning and participation will automatically leave some people out, especially the poor. But this so-called digital divide is closing. In 2010, 74% of all Americans had access to the Internet, up from 54% in 2002. Both the racial and the income divides have closed, as 70% of African American and 60% of low-income households (below $30,000 per year) now have access. And an increasing number of Americans use mobile devices (cell phones and Wi-Fi laptops) to access the Internet (59% in 2010, compared to 51% in 2009). African Americans (64%) and Hispanics (63%) now have greater wireless Internet use than Whites (57%), and wireless use by low-income households increased from 35% in 2009 to 46% in 2010.

The divide is also closing globally. At the end of 2009, 67% of the world's population had cell phones (up from 49% in 2007) and 26% had access to the Internet (up from 22% in 2007). Access by the world's poor is still limited, but there is a global movement (called 50 x 15) to increase access to 50% of the world's people by 2015.

Sources: International Telecommunication Union 2010; Pew Research Center 2010.

Map project, to use the public to identify and map every tree in the city through an interactive open source Internet site (see Chapter 10).

The term "crowdsourcing" was coined by Jeff Howe in *Wired* magazine in 2006 as a web-based model that harnesses the creative solutions of a distributed network of individuals through an open call for proposals. Intended initially for use by private sector firms for their own employees, the model has been used successfully for broad marketing. Planning scholars now see the potential for crowdsourcing to harness collective intellect and creative solutions from a network of citizens to serve planning needs. Tapping this "crowd wisdom" has great potential for participation and collaborative learning, but there remain challenges for the use of crowdsourcing in planning. These include constrained access posed by the "digital divide" (Box 4.1), sustaining an online community, and managing users (Brabham 2009).

Collaborative Community Design

Growing interest in collaborative planning has led to tools and applications for collaborative design. By its nature the design process is a creative one, and a collaborative approach aims to integrate the perceptions and insights of the participants to develop innovative and acceptable results. Perhaps the most ardent advocate of collaborative community design is Randolph Hester (2006). He defines his "Ecological Democracy" as governance by the people emphasizing direct, hands-on involvement in actions guided by understanding natural processes and social relationships to produce enabling, resilient, and impelling communities (see Chapter 16).

Tools for collaborative community design include visual surveys, computer photo simulations, design charrettes, scenario development, and participatory mapping.

Figure 4.2 People Involved in a Participatory Mapping Exercise. (*Source:* Calthorpe Associates. Used with permission.)

- Visual surveys are used to obtain a community response to different designs using slide images. Participants are asked to rate each image on a positive-to-negative scale. Photo simulations on the computer support visual surveys by showing the design potential for familiar areas (see Figure 16.22 for photo simulations by Steve Price of Urban Advantage).
- Design charrettes are workshops in which participants are given a design problem and small groups work to develop their collective design. The practice of design charrettes owes much to Douglas Kelbaugh of the University of Michigan and Bill Lennertz of the National Charrette Institute.
- Scenario development is an important community-wide exercise (see Chapter 3), and it can take on a design approach through future participatory mapping and assessment of development options. Both of these techniques were popularized by Calthorpe Associates in their envisioning projects in Salt Lake City (Utah), Austin (Texas), and Twin Cities (Minnesota) metropolitan areas (Figure 4.2; see Chapter 16).

Adaptive Collaborative Management

Too often, collaborative planning efforts conclude with a decision on a plan, and participants congratulate one another and go home. The plan then flounders in the political process of adoption or in the implementation phase. Rich Margerum (1999) posed the challenge of "Getting Past Yes," his play on words of the well-used books on participation and mediation, *Getting to Yes* (Fisher et al. 1991) and *Getting Past No* (Ury 1993). Both of these books deal with the important process of reaching a positive consensus. Margerum's point is that getting to a positive decision is just winning a battle. Getting that decision adopted and implemented is winning the war.

Collaborative efforts must tap not only social and intellectual capital to reach collective decisions, but also political capital to push the decision or plan through the political process of approval or adoption. The process does not end there. Stakeholder groups should also oversee, and in some cases play a role in, the implementation of plans to ensure completion and accountability. Volunteer groups often play important roles in implementing watershed improvement plans, water quality monitoring, stream restoration projects, habitat and trail improvements, and other environmental projects. These efforts assist with implementation but also promote learning. Participants develop expertise, learn what is working and what is not, and can contribute to improving the plan through adaptive management. Recall from Chapter 2 that adaptive management follows a learning-by-doing process. Implementation is monitored and evaluated, lessons are learned, and plans are modified accordingly.

Such stakeholder implementation is referred to here as **collaborative management**, or **comanagement**, and it has become a key element of the fourth generation of collaborative environmental planning. Comanagement is based largely on the common pool resource management theories of Elinor Ostrom, 2009 Nobel laureate in economics. Based on her fieldwork in Africa and Nepal, in her seminal work, *Governing the Commons* (Ostrom 1990), she gives eight critical elements of effective common pool resource management: (1) clearly defined boundaries, (2) resource appropriation rules adapted to local conditions, (3) collective-choice arrangements to enhance collaboration, (4) effective monitoring for accountability, (5) sanctions for those who violate community rules, (6) conflict resolution procedures, (7) recognition of community self-determination by higher authorities, and (8) multiple layers of nested management with local managers at the base level. Three related approaches for collaborative management are presented below.

Natural Resource Comanagement

Resource comanagement is collective action by stakeholders working together with a government agency to undertake resource management or plan implementation. Comanagement can promote learning, develop shared capital, and build both community and ecosystem resilience. Using a case study of coastal comanagement in Trinidad and Tobago, Tompkins and Adger (2004) suggest that working together consolidates what they call spaces of dependence, such as social support networks and local bonding relationships, and that working with government expands what they call spaces of engagement, such as outward-reaching networks.

Comanagement was developed in an international development context and has been applied to forestry, fisheries, and coastal management. But many collaborative community projects in the U.S. are variations of comanagement.

Community-Based Sustainability Programs

Chapter 3 introduced community-based sustainability programs (CBSPs), in which localities, often led by citizens, community groups, and local universities, take the initiative for environmental protection and community development (Shandas and Messer 2008). Beginning in the 1990s, the movement has risen organically in cities and towns where citizens have taken their own initiative. The most successful projects have occurred when community groups partner with local government and private businesses. The EPA chronicled early community experiences under the label community-based environmental protection (CBEP) (EPA 1999). The EPA and other federal agencies have developed funding programs using this CBEP model of partnering community groups and local governments. These community-based sustainability programs take different forms, and many are presented in subsequent chapters. Three examples illustrate the diversity of CBSPs.

The Washington, DC, Anacostia Watershed Restoration Committee was established in 1987 and has worked steadily with the District of Columbia, Maryland counties, and the Metropolitan Washington Council of Governments to raise citizen awareness, conduct stream restoration projects, and monitor progress. Ultimately the State of Maryland and the U.S. Army Corps of Engineers became partners, and the effort led to the 2005 federal Anacostia Watershed Initiative Act and the 2010 Anacostia Watershed Restoration Plan, a 2-year, $2.8-million planning effort (see Chapter 19).

In a 6-week period in 2004, a series of four major hurricanes hit land in Florida. This series of disastrous storms was unthinkable, and they stressed communities beyond anyone's expectations. However, unlike the dysfunctional response to Hurricane Katrina in New Orleans, Florida dealt with the 2004 hurricanes with relative control and composure. In what Kapucu (2008) refers to as collaborative emergency management, the capacity to respond is largely determined by the community's social structures and processes in place when a disaster occurs. In Florida, this capacity was developed through community coordination involving a complex interaction among multiple agencies, nonprofits, private businesses, and citizens that built trust and relationships before disaster hits. Public managers and citizens navigated the maze of response and recovery. Managers struggled to find funds to meet unexpected expenses, and residents banded together to rebuild severely damaged communities. Although these storms affected millions and killed 117, residents were able to go to multiple, coordinated sources to help rebuild their lives and the lives of their neighbors.

Community development programs led by local groups and NGOs are prevalent through the U.S., and many focus on sustainability and livability in neighborhoods. The Local Initiatives Support Corporation (LISC) and Enterprise Community Partners are examples of national organizations with a community focus, dedicated to assisting local community development corporations and nonprofit organizations transform distressed neighborhoods into healthy and sustainable communities.

Citizen Environmental and Sustainability Monitoring

Increasingly, individual citizens and organized groups have participated in environmental program implementation through volunteer monitoring of environmental data. Local birding groups, and lake and stream assessment groups, have long monitored and recorded information. Other applications include tracking well and spring water quality, land use change, wetland conditions, health concerns, wildlife conditions, and pollutant releases. Citizen monitoring programs provide free labor, local knowledge, K–12 and adult education, and improved communication between agencies, the regulated community, and the public, while building a constituency for community-based environmental protection and sustainability programs.

Perhaps the best examples of citizen monitoring programs are in stream and lake water quality monitoring. Since 1969, the Izaak Walton League of America's Save Our Streams (SOS) has engaged hundreds of groups in water quality monitoring, wetland protection, and watershed restoration to inspire stewardship and conservation through education and technical support. The SOS Stream Doctor program, launched in 1993, goes beyond monitoring to help people diagnose stream problems and initiate "wellness care" for their stream. SOS has spawned a multitude of other volunteer water programs throughout the country. Thousands of volunteers operating in all the states are monitoring thousands of streams, lakes, wetlands, and estuaries. State and federal environmental agencies accept volunteer-gathered data in their water quality databases. This citizen-generated information adds greatly to the knowledge of local water quality conditions.

The use of citizens as data sources has expanded to other issues, and online networks have helped. The San Francisco Urban Forest Map project (mentioned earlier) is a good example of using open source Internet methods to get citizens to collect and input data to contribute to a community database. Another example is the Green Map System. It uses citizen volunteers to locate and map environmentally significant sites throughout a community. It shows the array of natural, built, and cultural features and the connections between them (www.greenmap.org).

Considerations in Developing a Collaborative Planning Program

With this theoretical and historic perspective on collaborative environmental planning, we are ready to look at the nuts and bolts of implementing a CEP program. We first look at some definitions, objectives, and issues involved in designing a program. Then we review some elements of stakeholder involvement and the range of participatory and collaboration tools used to achieve it.

Collaborative Environmental Planning Types and Objectives

The previous discussion makes clear that CEP is broadly applied and involves a wide variety of methods and approaches. Margerum (2008) differentiates three types of collaboratives. *Action collaboratives* seek change through action projects; focus on direct on-the-ground activities, such as monitoring, education, and restoration; and involve citizens and community groups. *Organizational collaboratives* seek change through organizations; focus on programs and budgets; and involve government agencies, local stakeholders, and interest groups. *Policy collaboratives* seek change through policy initiatives; focus on new management approaches; and involve policy makers, government agencies, and regional stakeholders.

While the type of collaborative may vary, they all have some common motivations and objectives. Wondolleck and Yaffee (2000) list these desirable outcomes of collaboration:

- Sharing information and building an understanding by educating and learning from the public and engaging in joint fact-finding.
- Making wise decisions and building support for them by addressing common problems and resolving disputes.
- Getting the work done by mobilizing resources and sharing management responsibilities.
- Developing agencies, organizations, and communities by building staff capacities and enhancing social capital and community.

Table 4.2 gives three basic objectives of CEP. Many collaboratives involve some conflicts among stakeholders, and a key objective is to resolve them. If the process begins too late, after conflicts have become entrenched, it is difficult for the stakeholders to find consensus. If begun early, however, the group can look beyond their own positions to find shared values. If conflict has not become entrenched, the process can result in a shared vision of the future. Perhaps most important for planning, participants in the collaborative process can engage in a learning process to formulate creative solutions to solve problems and achieve their shared vision.

Collaboratives apply some basic elements to achieve these objectives. They aim to involve a wide range of stakeholders, to strike the appropriate balance between technical information and political factors, to take a broad holistic approach, and to seek integrated and creative solutions (Table 4.3).

The process and procedures for CEP must be developed to fit the situation. Table 4.4 gives two critical components: a planning framework and stakeholder involvement. CEP follows the basic planning process (see Box 2.1), incorporating adaptive and participatory elements to integrate stakeholder issues and allow for new information.

TABLE 4.2 **Objectives of Collaborative Environmental Planning**

Resolve conflict	Some collaborative efforts aim to engage stakeholders in a process of resolving conflicts among them through negotiation and mediation.
Develop a shared vision	Some collaborative efforts intend for the stakeholders to come up with a vision or direction that they can agree to and buy into.
Formulate creative solutions	All collaborative efforts hope to use dialogue and group processes to develop creative solutions that may not have emerged from traditional planning exercises.

TABLE 4.3 Elements of Collaborative Environmental Planning and Decision Making

Stakeholder involvement	Early and extensive engagement of stakeholders in the process of planning, decision making, and implementation. Stakeholders are those effecting change in the environment and those affected by it.
Scientific basis	Strong and sound scientific information and analysis on whichto base decisions.
Holistic, proactive approach	Holistic understanding of environmental problems and their contexts, and proactive efforts to resolve and prevent them.
Integrated solutions	Integration of a wide range of creative solutions to problems, such as flexible regulation, economic incentives and compensation, negotiated agreements, voluntary actions, and educational programs.

TABLE 4.4 Critical Components in Conducting CEP

Planning framework	An adaptive, iterative, and open process that balances scientific information and stakeholder participation to achieve objectives: 1. Scoping the problem and the stakeholders 2. Gathering and analyzing scientific and other information 3. Formulating alternatives 4. Assessing effects of the alternatives 5. Evaluating and selecting alternatives
Stakeholder involvement	Process of inclusive and open dialogue to resolve conflicts, develop a shared vision, and formulate creative solutions.

Stakeholder Involvement

Stakeholder involvement is the heart of collaboration. The practice of collaboration can be enhanced through a number of procedural and substantive elements, including the following:

- *Building on common ground* associated with a sense of place or community, shared fears or aspirations, and compatible interests.
- *Creating effective and enduring processes and opportunities for interaction* by sharing information; establishing structures such as advisory committees; facilitating well-managed meetings that are inclusive and representative; and using consensus decision making and early, often, and ongoing involvement.

- *Focusing on the problem in new ways* by being willing to be flexible and positive; viewing the problem holistically; framing issues by problem, not positions; focusing on the factual and knowledge basis of the problem; learning together through joint fact-finding and discovery; and inventing options together.
- *Fostering a sense of responsibility and commitment* by transforming "them" to "us"; developing ownership of the problem, process, and decision; developing commitment to the collaborative process; and being fair.
- *Understanding that partnerships are people and social interactions are essential* by focusing on individuals, not organizations; fostering understanding; building sustainable relationships by fostering trust and respect; motivating involvement by a sense of fun and hands-on experiences; embracing cultural and community differences; and acknowledging and rewarding success.
- *Practicing a proactive and entrepreneurial approach* by enlisting community leaders and local champions; being willing to take risks; taking advantage of existing opportunities like community social networks; building on small successes; and being persistent (Wondolleck and Yaffee 2000).

Some of these elements are included in Table 4.5, which highlights six basic tasks involved in effective stakeholder involvement (Randolph and Bauer 1999). The aim of inclusiveness makes the identification of stakeholders important; excluding an important stakeholder can undermine the process. Stakeholder groups lacking authority or responsibility are rarely successful. The process should be well structured, with a clear schedule, explicit milestones, and the use of small working groups. Collaboration works best in small subgroups with a limit of about 15 people.

One of the greatest challenges of a stakeholder group is achieving trust among participants, especially with a group of diverse interests. The respect and understanding necessary for trust can be facilitated by getting to know one another through social functions (usually involving food and beverages). Collaboration is a process in which the group as a whole must be self-governing and in which all participants are equally represented in the making of joint decisions. Still, an effective leader must guide and coordinate that decision-making process.

The main goal of stakeholder involvement is collaborative learning. Through commitment, trust, openness, and responsibility, groups can rise above initial perceptions to learn from one another and develop creative solutions to problems. Articulating perceptions and hidden agendas can lead to the identification of shared values, a new problem statement, and creative solutions (Bauer and Randolph 2000).

Opportunities and Barriers in Collaborative Environmental Planning

Implementing collaborative approaches is easier said than done. There are several challenges and barriers confronting collaborative approaches, including:

TABLE 4.5 Stakeholder Involvement: The Heart of Collaborative Environmental Planning

Identify stakeholders	A critical first step is to identify all stakeholders and give them an opportunity to participate; additional stakeholders may be identified during the process and should be included.
Establish authority	To foster commitment and engagement, the stakeholder group must be given some authority for action and responsibility for implementation.
Structure the process	Care must be taken to design a process that: • Gives stakeholders the opportunity to participate. • Has accepted milestones and deadlines. • Divides the group into subgroups of 10–15 to achieve a working scale.
Achieve trust	Trust is critical to the success of the effort and should be established early; trust is built on respect and understanding, and social functions can be useful to get stakeholders to know one another.
Share authority and assign roles	Although stakeholders should have shared authority so that each has the opportunity to affect decisions, some "quiet leadership" is required in the form of facilitator, convener, or negotiator, depending on the situation.
Engage in collaborative learning	Collaborative learning is the goal of stakeholder involvement. Through learning, stakeholders can begin to understand one another, resolve conflicts, and develop shared visions and creative solutions. Possible steps in the process: 1. State issues, perceptions, and values. 2. Identify hidden agendas. 3. Develop shared values. 4. Restate the problem. 5. Seek creative solutions.

- The basic dilemma of *self-interest and competition.*
- *Institutional and structural barriers*, such as conflicting goals and missions, inflexible policies and procedures, constrained resources, and lack of incentives.
- *Barriers due to attitudes and perceptions*, including mistrust and misconceptions, and organizational norms and culture.
- *Problems with the process of collaboration*, such as lack of process skills or unfamiliarity with the process.

To achieve effective collaboration, a number of conditions or prerequisites are needed to overcome these barriers. They include sufficient time, effective communication, and building understanding, relationships, trust, and reciprocity. As highlighted in Table 4.6, good information is fundamental. Collaboration takes considerable time and often financial resources to support participants. More important is the commitment of participants to sustain the often lengthy process. Participants must be willing to learn, to be adaptable in their perceptions and positions. As a group they must take responsibility for their actions. They must be given sufficient authority so that they know that what they do will have an effect. That authority must be shared within the group.

TABLE 4.6 **Prerequisites and Barriers in Collaborative Environmental Planning**

Prerequisites for CEP	Barriers to CEP
• Good information	• Missing or misleading information
• Time to participate, to build trust, to learn, to resolve disputes, to create solutions	• Immediate problem, no time to deliberate
	• Lack of commitment by participants
• Commitment of participants	• High level of advocacy; entrenched positions by stakeholders
• Willingness to learn	
• Responsibility to affect and implement decisions	• No responsibility given to stakeholders
• Shared authority	• Uneven or hierarchical authority
	• The goal of litigation or precedent

Conversely, the lack of any of these conditions serves as a barrier to collaboration. Misinformation, insufficient time, lack of commitment and responsibility, entrenched positions, or uneven authority can undermine the collaborative process. In addition, if litigation or legal precedent is a goal of certain stakeholders, collaboration clearly will not work.

A critical issue for collaborative approaches to decision making is accountability (Weber 1998). The principal concerns among critics include vested authority, exclusion, and lack of expertise. In other words, as Wondolleck and Yaffee ask, is the resulting collaborative planning decision *legitimate*, is it *fair*, and is it *wise*? Regarding authority, legal authority is usually vested in elected officials or delegated to agency leaders who are accountable for decisions. Although it is desirable to provide some authority to collaborative groups, legal authority should remain with the appropriate party. Regarding fairness, the assumption is that collaborative processes are inclusive and representative, but that is not always the case. And regarding expertise, collaborative processes must be grounded in good science so that group decision making is not based solely on perceptions and emotions. To promote greater accountability, process reporting, performance standards, appeal procedures, independent scientific review, and monitoring and evaluation should be built into the structure and procedures of collaborative processes (Wondolleck and Yaffee 2000).

Considerations in Designing a Participation/Collaboration Process

Most planning situations call for some form of public participation. Since each is unique with regard to its context, objectives, and audience, the participation program must consider these specific circumstances. Careful program design is critical for success; in fact, a poorly designed program may be worse than no participation at all (Zahm and Randolph 1999). An effective participation program cannot be constructed unless the following key questions are answered:

- What are the motivations and objectives for participation?
- What level of participation is appropriate?
- Who should be involved?
- When should participation occur?
- What obstacles and opportunities are present?
- How should participation be evaluated?
- What tools should be used?

What Are the Motivations and Objectives for Participation/Collaboration?

The motivation and objectives for participation affects the design of the process. Some are general, others more specific to the planning situation.

1. *Participation is a good idea.* It is the foundation of a strong democracy. Collaboration expands local know-how, makes more efficient and effective use of scarce resources, and has a greater potential for success and change.
2. *Collaborative decision making is an idea that works.* It encourages an open exchange of information and ideas, establishes a collective vision for the future, can be accomplished with less confrontation, and seeks solutions that are tailored to local needs.
3. *Public participation is often required by state or federal law or regulation.*
4. *The planning situation presents specific motivations and objectives for participation.*

What Level of Participation/Collaboration Is Appropriate?

Schedules, budgets, and staffing may place limits on the types of interactions and the number of stakeholders in the process. Even with unlimited time and resources, there are still trade-offs between the number of citizens that can be involved in planning and the degree to which they actually become part of the process.

Figure 4.1 shows the different roles citizens can play. The higher forms of participation (collaborative learning, comanagement, and collaborative decision making) require a significant commitment of time and resources by both planners and stakeholders. Active and sometimes passive participation may be appropriate when public information is available, there is little controversy, and citizens are satisfied and trust elected officials.

Who Should Be Involved?

The number and selection of participants will depend on the objectives of the program, budget, schedule, and level of participation. A list and profile of interested parties should be developed that includes key decision makers and important stakeholders. Particular attention should be made to identify underrepresented stakeholders. It is important to err on the side of inclusiveness because groups and individuals who are excluded can raise questions about the representativeness and legitimacy of the process.

When Should Participation Occur?

Opportunities for public involvement can be identified in each phase of a program or project planning, implementation, and evaluation. Initiating the process early is important in nearly all cases, especially for controversial and complex planning issues.

What Obstacles and Opportunities Are Present?

When planners are designing the participation process, they must consider four common factors that deter stakeholders from long-term involvement and participation in planning and decision making:

1. *No matter what you do, not everyone who needs to participate, or wants to participate, will participate* for a variety of reasons: They are not identified as stakeholders, meeting times and places are inconvenient or inaccessible, the topic or information is too technical, language is a barrier for non–English-speaking communities, and/or some people prefer to complain! To maximize participation, an organized outreach program may be necessary.
2. *History of past mistakes has resulted in cynicism and mistrust that cannot be overcome.*
3. *The time between decision and action is too long and people give up.* Planners should consider how best to become part of the more informal conversations that take place within neighborhoods and communities, rather than tie participation to government decision cycles that are often delayed. Taking some early action and showing some success help carry the process, engage participants, and build community, civic, and social capital.
4. *The group attempts to tackle issues that are too complex.* Regardless of the scope of the problem, it may be more important to complete a small but certain task where the collaboration virtually guarantees success over the short term. Once several small successes have been achieved, the collaborators may be organized and informed enough to take on larger and more complex issues.

How Should Participation Be Evaluated?

Evaluation is an important part of participation and should be considered in the design of the process.

A *process evaluation* examines the information and other opportunities that were made available to citizens. This type of evaluation focuses on "counting," for example, the number of public hearings held and how many citizens attended.

An *outcomes or impact evaluation* seeks to understand how the participation process actually influenced decision making. The evaluation might attempt to determine whether stakeholders believe they played a role in decision making and how satisfied participants were with the way the process was conducted.

What Tools Should Be Used?

The results of the preceding activities will determine the tools and practices to use in the participation program. These tools can help organize the community and build its capacity for problem solving; inform stakeholders of problems, processes, and decisions; involve stakeholders in planning and problem solving; and create new partnerships and new processes for decision making. The next section reviews a variety of participation and collaboration tools.

Tools for Participation and Collaboration

A variety of techniques are used in participatory and collaborative planning, and they are summarized in Table 4.7. The table links the tools to our evolving generations of collaborative planning, but most of the methods listed for early generations still have their place today in stakeholder collaboration and participation.

These methods have both advantages and limitations. For example, media notices and feature stories can inform the public but are not designed to elicit feedback to involve stakeholders. Public meetings and hearings are usually too formal to allow a wide range of stakeholders to give meaningful input. Review and comment on draft documents, like hearings, are important components of "formal" participation requirements, but they are often too late in the process and are more useful for other agencies and organized groups rather than individual stakeholders. Public brochures, surveys, and polls can get a "pulse" of the public and can both inform the public and obtain feedback. However, none of these methods are interactive or provide a forum for participants to explore issues in "give-and-take" dialogue.

Workshops and other stakeholder meetings are designed to provide discourse among participants. With less formality than the preceding methods, workshops can be flexible and creative in their exploration of issues, information, and ideas. Workshops can be used for brainstorming and visioning, assessing alternatives, or designing features through a charrette format. Charrettes are problem-solving sessions where participants immerse themselves in an intensive daylong or weekend experience to develop a plan or design.

Focus groups can be used to get public reaction to alternative actions or plans, but they are a snapshot in time and tend not to be fully representative of a wide range of stakeholders. Advisory committees are more useful for providing ongoing participation by selected stakeholders. Committees can be effective in providing technical expertise (e.g., technical advisory committee) as well as value-based information (e.g., citizen advisory committee). It is often difficult for advisory committees to be representative of all stakeholders.

Table 4.7 Participation/Collaboration Techniques

Technique	Description	Strengths	Weaknesses
First Generation: Public Information, Notification			
Media	Public announcements, press releases, feature stories	Efficient distribution of information: "informing"	No "involving"; can be biased
Public meeting/ hearings	Often information meetings or formal hearings lacking substantive interaction	Part of "formal" participation opportunity for public to speak, if not to be heard; to vent	Tends to cater to the extremes; "loudest" tend to be heard; question of representativenes
Review and comment	Opportunity for external agencies, groups, and publics to review draft documents and offer comments before plans and decisions are finalized	Part of "formal" participation; opportunity for structured documented comments; good for well-organized, well-staffed groups	Too late in process to be effective; not interactive; not good for individuals or less well-organized groups; thus question of representativeness
Surveys, polls, brochures	Newsletters, brochures, mail-back surveys, polls, workbooks designed to inform	Can provide two-way flow of information; surveys can reach large and diverse population	Often not interactive; expensive; response rate often low; can be misused; requires staff expertise
Second Generation: Public Involvement			
Workshops: brainstorming and visioning	More interactive meetings with stakeholders using exercises or games to enhance involvement and creative thinking	More interactive and two-way communication than formal hearings; very useful if well-designed	Representativeness and effectiveness depend on good design and implementation
Advisory committee	Small appointed representative group called on throughout the process to advise planners and decision makers	Can build constituency and provide continuity in participation process; well-informed participants provide technical and value-based informatiion	Question of representativeness, often elitist; requires commitment of participants
Focus group	One-time meeting of a cross-sectional group of people, to get their reaction to ideas, actions, or plans	Can reach a variety of interests and can focus on issues; tends to be interactive	Question of representativeness
Conflict resolution techniques	Negotiation, mediation, arbitration, alternative dispute resolution (ADR)	Can resolve differences and lead to win-win solutions; can save time and legal fees	Often result from ineffective participation; may focus on compromise, not consensus
Third Generation: Collaborative Planning			
Stakeholder collaboration	Collaborative program with interest groups, firms, agencies, citizens to develop common vision and solutions in plans and decisions	Builds shared capital and builds consensus; often creates innovative solutions	Not easy; needs to be started early in process; often lengthy process requiring openness and adaptation by participants

TABLE 4.7 **Participation/Collaboration Techniques (cont.)**

Technique	Description	Strengths	Weaknesses
Third Generation: Collaborative Planning (cont.)			
Partnership	Longer-term relationship among active stakeholders to facilitate decisions and action	Establishes social capital and the foundation for continuing collaboration	Often difficult to sustain over long term; often elitist and nonrepresentative
Consensus building	Combines conflict resolution and stakeholder collaboration to bring consensus to controversial issues	Helps resolve conflict and identify common ground and acceptable solutions	Not easy to resolve entrenched conflicts
Fourth Generation: Collaborative Learning and Collaborative Management			
Learning networks	Community of practice to nurture collaborative and topical expertise among members	Can operate at multiple scales at once; can develop new knowledge	Require long-term commitment of participants
Joint fact-finding	Collaborative exercise of diverse stakeholders to create credible, legitimate, relevant knowledge	Helps resolve conflict and develops fact-based information accepted by all parties	Often hard to deal with scientific uncertainty in conflictual cases
Participatory appraisal	Use of citizens to assess their environment, usually in map form	Gathers local knowledge and engages citizens	Need to keep simple and translate local knowledge into spatial form
Electronic networks	Using information technology and Internet to foster communication and dialogue among participants	Complement other methods by providing asynchronous means of communicating	Digital divide: not all people have access to needed technology
Open source and crowdsourcing	Using open Internet tools to gather ideas, information, problems, and solutions	Can tap "crowd wisdom" and assist information gathering	Digital divide issue; quality control needed to monitor information and misuse
Design charrette, scenario workshop	Focused activity workshop to tap participant and group creativity in designing living spaces and the future community	Promotes learning of participants and gathers local knowledge and perceptions in visual design form	Time consuming and requires good program design
Comanage-ment	Partnerships of public, nonprofit, private firms, and/or citizens to implement and monitor plans	Engages partners, including resource users and residents, in action programs, enhancing learning, knowledge, and involvement	Often complex arrangements required to ensure quality control

A number of methods are designed specifically for resolving conflicts. Negotiation, mediation, and alternative dispute resolution (ADR) methods are applied according to the level of conflict. If these methods fail, conflicting parties may be forced to seek arbitration or litigation. Such extreme conflicts are beyond the assistance of participation and collaboration methods, but conflict resolution methods of facilitation, negotiation, and mediation are important elements of collaborative processes where some conflicts, misunderstandings, and preexisting disputes need to be resolved if effective collaboration is to occur.

Electronic networks can enhance the work of advisory committees. The Internet can help not only disseminate information but also elicit feedback and dialogue in an asynchronous format, where group members can log in and participate at different times. Online networks use e-mail, threaded discussions, and blogs to promote discourse among committee members or stakeholder groups between meetings. Such methods as open sourcing and crowdsourcing contribute to the new world of digital democracy, which is likely to further impact collaborative planning in the future, especially as the digital divide continues to close.

Additional tools include emerging methods used in collaborative learning and comanagement. Learning networks and joint fact-finding engage communities of practice in discovery, enhancing learning and building knowledge, to achieve consensus and solve problems. Participatory appraisal and collaborative design can involve and educate citizens through data gathering, problem identification, and design solutions, while they also tap local knowledge and build social capital. Comanagement of natural resources and community development, as well as citizen monitoring, provide learning opportunities for participants and involve stakeholders in implementing plans, allowing them to take action to affect their future community sustainability.

Summary

Environmental planning in the United States has evolved to embrace participatory and collaborative approaches to enhance public acceptability, resolve conflicts, and develop creative solutions to problems. In many cases, it has improved public involvement in environmental decision making and provided increased opportunities for dialogue and discourse among stakeholders. Stakeholders include those who are creating change (e.g., developers, industry members, government agencies), as well as those who are affected by it (e.g., citizens, neighborhoods, communities, and groups representing them and the environment).

Like environmental planning, collaborative planning continues to evolve. From a dormancy of participation prior to 1960 in the United States, public involvement is now in a fourth generation of collaborative learning and collaborative management. Various methods of communication and participation involve stakeholders not only in decision making, but also in generating new knowledge on which those decisions are made and in implementing those decisions. This new level of involvement builds shared and social capital and strengthens our participatory democracy.

Environmental Planning: Technical Principles and Analysis

5 ■ Environmental Data and Geospatial Analysis

This chapter begins Part II, which focuses on the scientific principles and technical analysis involved in environmental land use planning and management. Environmental science and engineering principles and data analysis are critical to the methods presented in the chapters on soils, geology, hydrology, ecology, natural hazards, and climate change (Chapters 6–13). Chapter 14 addresses the integration of environmental and spatial information, including measurable indicators that clarify and compare community sustainability and track change and progress.

First we must introduce fundamental concepts, sources, and analysis of information, especially geospatial data. This chapter presents some general considerations in information gathering and data analysis and then reviews the exploding field of geospatial analysis, remote sensing, and geographic information systems: **the geospatial revolution**. We begin with a vision statement presented by then Vice President Al Gore in his now famous January 1998 speech on "The Digital Earth" at the California Science Center in Los Angeles, a time when few conceived of even Google Earth, which was launched 7 years later. Our current geospatial revolution has progressed far closer to Al Gore's vision of the Digital Earth than anyone would have predicted in 1998.

> Imagine a young child going to a Digital Earth exhibit at a local museum. After donning a head-mounted display, she sees Earth as it appears from space. Using a data glove, she zooms in, using higher and higher levels of resolution, to see continents, then regions, countries, cities, and finally individual houses, trees, and other natural and man-made objects. Having found an area of the planet she is interested in exploring, she takes the equivalent of a "magic carpet ride" through a 3-D visualization of the terrain. Of course, terrain is only one of the many kinds of data with which she can interact. Using the systems' voice recognition capabilities, she is able to request information on land cover, distribution of plant and animal species, real-time weather, roads, political boundaries, and population. She can also visualize the environmental information that she and other students all over

the world have collected as part of the GLOBE project. This information can be seamlessly fused with the digital map or terrain data. She can get more information on many of the objects she sees by using her data glove to click on a hyperlink. To prepare for her family's vacation to Yellowstone National Park, for example, she plans the perfect hike to the geysers, bison, and big-horn sheep that she has just read about. In fact, she can follow the trail visually from start to finish before she ever leaves the museum in her hometown.

She is not limited to moving through space, but can also travel through time. After taking a virtual field-trip to Paris to visit the Louvre, she moves backward in time to learn about French history, perusing digitized maps overlaid on the surface of the Digital Earth, newsreel footage, oral history, newspapers and other primary sources. She sends some of this information to her personal e-mail address to study later. The time-line, which stretches off in the distance, can be set for days, years, centuries, or even geological epochs, for those occasions when she wants to learn more about dinosaurs [or forward in time to view scenarios for those occasions when she wants to see what the future may hold and what she can do about it]. (Gore 1998)

Information and Data Analysis in Environmental Planning

Pragmatic environmental problem solving requires science- and fact-based technical information on which to base decisions and actions. Environmental planners are generally the gatekeepers of information (as well as managers of misinformation), and they must be adept at gathering, analyzing, interpreting, integrating, and presenting information. In a land use context, much of this information is spatial and is best represented in maps and spatial images.

The integration of spatial, scientific, engineering, and economic information with normative perceptions and values is challenging because of the wide range of both quantitative and qualitative information. The planning process determines the type and specificity of information needed. As shown in Box 2.1, Scoping (Step 0) identifies data needs and develops a work plan for collecting and analyzing data. Analysis (Step 2) focuses on information gathering and analysis. This activity continues throughout the planning process.

A Tiered Process

Information gathering and assessment often follow a tiered process, first by looking at readily available and general information, followed by increasing levels of detail (Table 5.1). Many studies start with **rapid assessment**, which takes a quick look at problems and available information and moves quickly to initial action (Sayre et al. 2000). Although moving to action quickly has advantages, rapid assessment should also identify needs for more detailed analysis to follow. This is sometimes referred to as **data gap analysis**, or the identification of data gaps in need of filling.

Intermediate and advanced assessment involves increasing levels of detail, more analysis, and more sophisticated data products. The first step is gath-

TABLE 5.1 **Tiered Approach to Information Gathering and Analysis**

	Level of Detail	*Information Sources*	*Products*
Rapid assessment	General, coarse scale; little analysis	Readily available information, available maps, secondary sources, Internet sources	Hand-drawn working maps, Internet map, lists
Intermediate assessment	More specific data, more analysis	Remote sensing images, detailed secondary data sources	Information matrices, more detailed map displays
Advanced assessment	Detailed, refined, targeted information; detailed analysis	Primary data sources, field surveys, local maps, local knowledge	Integration of data and analysis

ering basic data, such as maps or remotely sensed information on topography, soils, geology, and land use/land cover. This inventory may also include more specific information on wetlands, habitats, and culturally significant areas acquired from field monitoring or the local knowledge of citizens.

Analytical studies prioritize and interpret the data, and generally aim to make sense of the information. Specific data and mapped products are determined by the planning objectives. For example, assessing environmentally sensitive and critical areas may require information on land use, land ownership, development infrastructure, population growth, and other factors influencing land use change. Methods such as build-out and environmental impact assessment can clarify possible future effects.

Subsequent chapters describe specific data gathering, analysis, and display methods used for planning studies involving soils (Chapter 6), stormwater quantity and quality (Chapters 7 and 8), groundwater (Chapter 9), watersheds (Chapters 7 and 19), landscape and urban ecology (Chapters 10 and 19), urban forestry (Chapter 10), wetlands (Chapter 10), wildlife habitat (Chapter 11), energy and climate change (Chapter 12), natural hazards (Chapter 13), and land suitability (Chapter 14).

Considerations and Pitfalls in Using Data and Information

The proper use, the accuracy, and the documentation of land-related information depend on several data issues that should be considered throughout the planning and analysis processes, especially in the early stages. These issues include data form, scale, accuracy, coverage, completeness, age, confidentiality, maintenance, paper-trail-to-sources, communication, and appropriateness (Hirschman et al. 1992).

1. *Form.* Are the data digital (e.g., georeferenced in a database), spatial (e.g., on a map), temporal (e.g., plotted on a graph with a time dimension), or a combination of these? Are data qualitative (e.g., groundwater moves rapidly) or quantitative (e.g., flow is 50 ft per day)?

2. *Scale.* How large or small is the mapped representation of a given land area? If two maps are the same size, the large-scale map will represent less land than the small-scale map. Accordingly, the large-scale map is more detailed. This is important when overlaying maps of different scale.

3. *Accuracy.* How well do the data and/or the mapped locations of features reflect their actual existence or location on the land surface (or how much "slop" is there in the mapped representation)? For example, map units in a soil survey (see Chapter 6) are commonly accurate to 2 acres. Differing accuracies of data sets become important when comparing or overlaying information. Note that accuracy is the degree of agreement between sample or map data and reality, and precision is how well you can reproduce the data values that you measure, monitor, or map.

4. *Coverage.* What states, counties, and/or tax parcels are included in a data set? For example, detailed geology maps have been published for only one of the nine quadrangle maps covering Montgomery County, Virginia. It's best to find out what is available before counting on the data.

5. *Completeness.* What percentage or number of a given feature is actually presented in a data set? Not every incidence of an endangered species, sinkhole, cave, land use practice, or other feature in the real world is represented on a map or in a database. Likewise, factors such as water quality, slope, and soil permeability are based on a limited number of sample points.

6. *Age.* How old are the data? The age of data is more important for factors such as land use and tax parcel boundaries, which can change in short periods of time, than for factors like geology.

7. *Confidentiality.* Should there be restrictions on the dissemination, use, and communication of certain data? This is an issue with data on endangered species, caves, and archaeological sites where widespread dissemination of the data may lead to adverse impacts to the resource.

8. *Maintenance.* What must be done to keep the data up to date and otherwise useful? Data should be maintained as new information becomes available and existing data become obsolete. This is a particularly important consideration for data that can change, such as tax parcel boundaries.

9. *Paper trail to sources.* This involves documenting the source agency, original scale, age, and accuracy for each data source. This documentation, known as metadata, is especially important if data products are to be used for regulatory purposes.

10. *Communication with the public and decision makers.* Are the data in a form that is understandable to laypeople and elected officials, or does the information require repackaging and interpretation for effective communication?

11. *Appropriateness.* How relevant are the data to planning needs and applications? How can important qualitative data be used with quantitative data? What data and analytical methods will be most appropriate, accessible, and cost-effective for achieving program objectives?

Information Sources and Field Data

Where do you get the needed information for environmental analysis? We rely on a wide array of secondary information, especially for rapid and intermediate assessment applied to planning studies for large geographic areas. **Secondary data** are sets of information gathered and analyzed by others and presented in map, tabular, or report form. The reliability of secondary data depends on the reliability of the source. Agencies and firms that have provided time-tested information are generally reliable, but it is still important to address some of the secondary data issues listed above. Most of the geospatial data discussed in this chapter, and indeed in this book, are secondary data.

For local environmental planning, these sources are very useful, especially for rapid and intermediate assessment, but they do not replace local knowledge and field observation and monitoring of environmental conditions. **Primary data** are those gathered by the analyst by observation, sample survey, or measurement.

Field studies can move the level of analysis beyond rapid assessment to intermediate and advanced assessment. They complement government monitoring and remote sensing data in four ways:

1. Field studies verify or "ground-truth" the secondary sources of information.
2. They "fill in the blanks" of information not available from secondary sources.
3. They can focus on site and neighborhood scale better than secondary data, which are often limited to community scale.
4. Field studies tap local knowledge and monitoring conducted by groups, landowners, and residents who often know more about their local environment than government sources.

Many secondary sources of information are often not provided at sufficient accuracy or currency for specific applications. Field studies can check specific locations, measurements, and changing conditions that may not be reflected in secondary data. Secondary sources are often limited in scale or do not focus on the location or data needed for a specific planning application. Government stream-water quality monitoring stations, for example, are located several miles apart on rivers and not available at all on many tributaries. They may not monitor the water contaminants that are needed for a planning study. Field monitoring can complement secondary sources by focusing on specific study locations and necessary data.

Increasingly, planners realize that secondary and professional sources of information often miss detailed information that is readily apparent to those living in an area. This local knowledge can contribute greatly to planning intelligence. Surveys, interviews, focus groups, workshops, and other participatory methods are all used to acquire local knowledge and ethnographic information from residents and landowners. These methods may be the only source of historical information about changing environmental conditions.

In addition, agencies are constrained by budgets and personnel, and they often cannot monitor environmental conditions at the scale, accuracy, or frequency needed for informed decisions. Local voluntary monitoring programs can contribute greatly to agency databases and educate local groups about environmental conditions at the same time. There are three basic approaches to field observation:

1. Monitoring: measuring and recording quantitative environmental data.
2. Visual surveys: simple observation and recording of visual environmental conditions.
3. Mapping: spatially recording environmental conditions.

In Chapter 4, we discussed the use of participatory appraisal and volunteer monitoring as ways to engage local residents in environmental assessment. These activities can involve stakeholders, but they also provide useful geospatial data. Later in this chapter we discuss how public participation can be enhanced with the information capacity and visualization of geographic information systems.

The **global positioning system (GPS)** has greatly improved the collection of geospatial field data, whether done by professionals or by volunteers. GPS is a navigation system operated by the U.S. Department of Defense that uses 30 satellites (and another 36 planned) to provide positioning data to a growing market of mobile devices. You know a GPS device can help you find your way to the pub by showing the location of the device (and you) on an overlay map that also shows the location of the pub. For data collection, the device can georeference a data entry, photo image, or other information, so you know exactly where you took it; you can later retrieve it as georeferenced data in a geographic information system.

Geospatial Information and Analysis

We are in the midst of a geospatial revolution. To get a sense of the magnitude and implications of this revolution, check out the Public Broadcasting Service (PBS) series, produced by Penn State's Geospatial Revolution Project (http://geospatial revolution.psu.edu). Land use and environmental planning have benefited from this revolution, spurred by better quality and availability of geospatial data, user-friendly geographic information systems (GIS), and growing public use of maps and spatial data. Before discussing these systems, it is important to understand some of the fundamentals of geospatial information that describes the topography or surface features of the land. We begin with an overview of maps, remote sensing, and land information systems, then turn to GIS and growing access to geospatial data and analysis on the Internet.

Maps

A map is a "masterpiece of false simplicity . . . (whose) secret meanings must be mulled upon, yet all the world is open to a glance" (Muehrcke and Muehrcke 1998, x). Less poetically, maps are graphic descriptions of the surface features of the land drawn to scale. *Map scale* is the relationship of distance on the map to distance on the land. It can be represented as a graphical scale, or as a fraction or ratio. For example, 1:24,000 means 1 inch on the map equals 24,000 inches or 2,000 feet on the land. The smaller the ratio or fraction value, the smaller the scale. The ratio value is smaller when the second number (the land distance) of the ratio is larger. Although somewhat counterintuitive, a map of smaller scale shows a larger area. Remember: Smaller scale = larger area; larger scale = smaller area. Only the graphical scale is accurate when the map is enlarged or reduced.

Map Scale:

Graphical: /————/————/
            0   1 km   2 km

Ratio: 1:24,000

Equation: 1 inch = 2,000 feet

Figure 5.1 gives the map scales typically used in various planning studies. The scales range from very large for project planning (e.g., 1:1,200 or 1 inch = 100 feet) to very small for state or regional planning (e.g., 1:1,000,000 or 1 inch = 16 miles). Figure 5.2 shows maps of four scales of the same area. The top map of larger scale shows a smaller area and more detail and accuracy.

Figure 5.1 Scales of Maps Typically Used in Planning Studies.

Application	Ratio Scale	Equation Scale
Project Planning, Planning Regulations	1:600	1" = 50'
Neighborhoods	1:1,200	1" = 100'
Towns	1:2,400	1" = 200'
Small Cities	1:6,000	1" = 500'
Large Cities	1:12,000	1" = 1,000'
	1:24,000	1" = 2,000'
Counties	1:62,500	1" = 1 mile
Metropolitan Areas	1:125,000	1" = 2 miles
Regions	1:250,000	1" = 4 miles
States	1:500,000	1" = 8 miles
Small Nations	1:1,000,000	1" = 16 miles

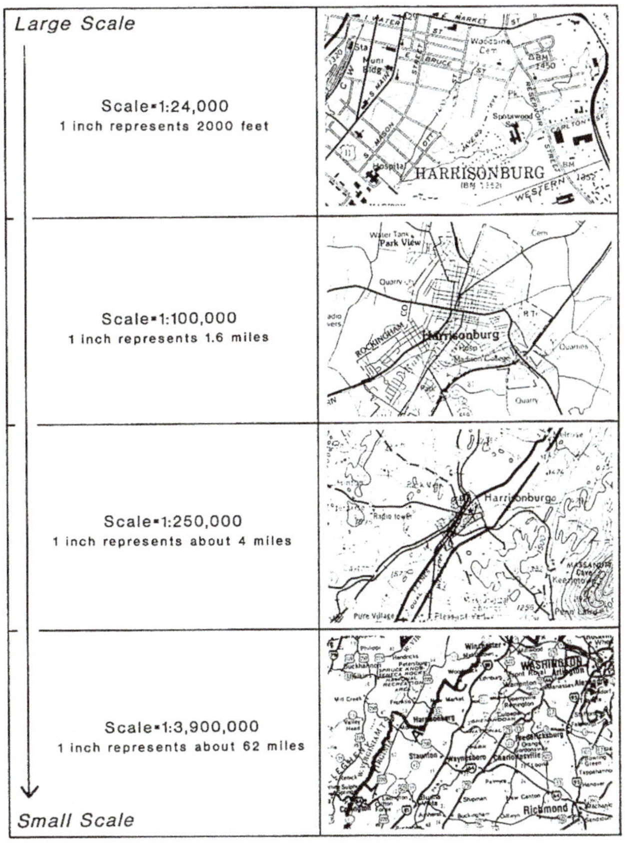

Figure 5.2 Maps Showing Various Scales of the Same Area. Large-scale maps represent less and show more detail than small scale maps. (*Source:* Hirschman, Randolph, and Flynn 1992.)

Large Scale

Scale=1:24,000
1 inch represents 2000 feet

Scale=1:100,000
1 inch represents 1.6 miles

Scale=1:250,000
1 inch represents about 4 miles

Scale=1:3,900,000
1 inch represents about 62 miles

Small Scale

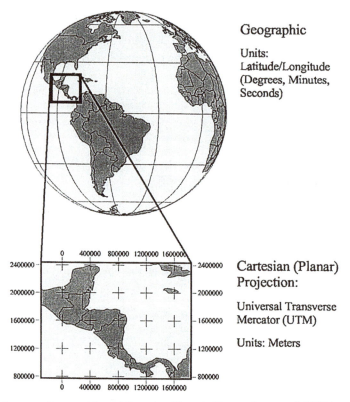

Figure 5.3 Coordinate Systems: Geographic and Cartesian (Planar). (*Source:* Sayre et al. 2000.)

Maps are two-dimensional, which creates a challenge for accurately representing the scale for locations on the round Earth. *Geographic spherical coordinate referencing* uses longitude and latitude to accurately identify location. However, for flat maps representing scale in length, a grid coordinate system can identify location by using the *Cartesian planar coordinate system* (Figure 5.3). The most used international plane grid system is the Universal Transverse Mercator (UTM) grid, which divides Earth into 60 longitudinal zones. A separate grid is made for each of the 60 zones. The method achieves an accuracy level of 1 part in 2,500 maximum error (Muehrcke and Muehrcke 1998).

Topographic Maps

We are all familiar with U.S. Geological Survey (USGS) **topographic maps**, produced, and occasionally updated, at various scales for the entire U.S. (see Figure 5.2). The most popular and useful of these are the 7.5-minute quadrangle (quad) series, which show areas 7.5 minutes latitude by 7.5 minutes longitude in size at a scale of 1:24,000 (1 inch = 2,000 feet) and also 1:25,000 (1 cm = 250 m). The top map in Figure 5.2 and Figure 5.4 show portions of maps from this series. The Blacksburg map in Figure 5.4 was produced in 1965 and was last updated (with changes shown in red) in 1983.

These quad maps show a variety of land features, including water and forested land, and human-made features, such as roads, railroads, buildings, and commu-

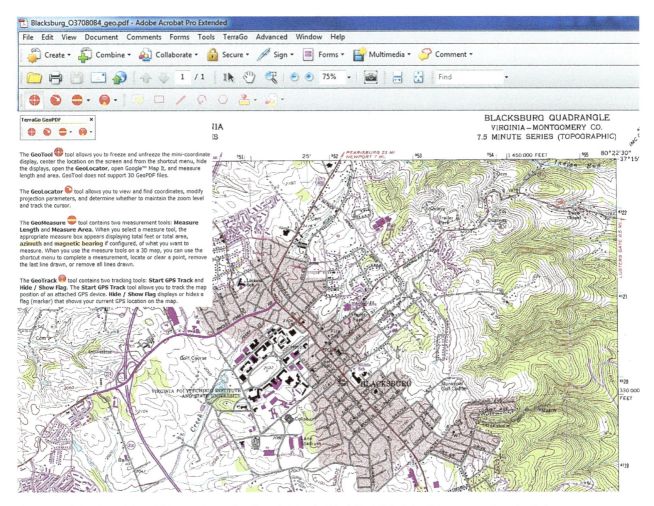

Figure 5.4 A Portion of the USGS 7.5-Minute Quadrangle Map for Blacksburg, Virginia. This map was downloaded as a GeoPDF from the USGS Store using the simple Map Locator. It is shown in an Adobe Acrobat window with TerraGo GeoPDF toolbar and inset explanation of functions.

nities. The topographic map also shows the area's vertical relief with **elevation contour lines**. These lines connect points on the land surface having the same elevation. The contour interval is the vertical distance between adjacent contour lines. The elevation above sea level is usually printed on every fifth contour line. The closer together the contour lines are, the steeper the terrain. The steepness, or *slope*, of the land is an important characteristic in determining its suitability for various uses and its susceptibility to erosion and landslides. (A method from the first edition using elevation map contour lines to measure the slope of the terrain is presented on the book website, www.envirolanduse.org). The terrain also affects drainage, and Chapter 7 shows how to use elevation contours to delineate drainage basin or watershed boundaries.

The USGS makes available all of its topographic maps from its USGS Store, which offers print-on-demand service not for only its maps but for many other maps, including international maps. But the world of maps from the USGS and other sources is changing rapidly, from purchased printed maps to online interactive map viewing to new digital map products. The growing familiarity of consumers with Internet mapping sites (e.g., Google Maps, Google Earth, and Microsoft Earth Explorer) and GPS has taken maps and map making from the domain of cartographers to everyone's daily lives.

Butler (2006) suggests that Google Earth amounts to the "democratization of GIS." Although this characterization is not quite right, Google Earth has enhanced cartographic understanding, as well as democratized maps and map making. So have other Internet-based map access systems, including interactive online travel maps, tax parcel maps, and spatial environmental maps of soils (Chapter 6), vegetation (Chapter 10), wetlands (Chapter 10), floodplains (Chapter 7), and natural hazards (Chapter 13). The USGS advances in online map access are worth elaboration here.

The USGS National Geospatial Program has many components. A cornerstone of the Program is **The National Map (TNM)**, a collaborative project to improve and deliver topographic information. TNM provides easy access to downloadable maps and digital data layers, including orthoimagery (aerial photographs), elevation, geographic names, hydrography, boundaries, transportation, structures, and land cover. Maps and data are easily accessible for any location and scale using TNM Viewer (http://viewer.nationalmap.gov/viewer/). Selected data, maps, and images are ordered and delivered by e-mail. Figure 5.5 shows a map of the town of Blacksburg, Virginia, with a land cover overlay, forest cover, and an imperious surface overlay, all downloaded from TNM Viewer.

The National Map portal offers great access to maps and data, but the USGS is also advancing its basic products to fit this digital world. In October 2009, it unveiled the latest generation of digital topographic maps, the **US Topo maps**. Following the traditional 7.5-minute quadrangle format in order to look and feel like the paper maps, they support better public distribution through the Internet, and more importantly, they enable basic, on-screen geographic analysis for any user. The US Topo maps are downloadable free via the Internet and are constructed in a *GeoPDF format* from the data layers in the National Map, except for land cover, which is planned to be added in 2011. Each quadrangle file is about 15–20 megabytes. Users can turn data layers on and off, zoom in and out, print customized maps, and perform additional analysis with free software developed by TerraGo Technologies. (Figure 5.4 shows a traditional quadrangle as GeoPDF.) The orthographic imagery comes from the National Agricultural Imagery Program, which covers the 48 contiguous states every 3 years; thus, the US Topo data will follow a 3-year cycle, an improvement on the decades-long cycles of the old quadrangle series. Figure 5.6 is an example of the latest US Topo map in the TerraGo and data layer edit screen.

Planimetric/Thematic Maps: Land Use/Land Cover Maps

Planimetric maps, or **thematic maps**, differ from topographic maps in that they do not show elevation contours. They are usually used to highlight specific thematic information, such as geology or land use and land cover. **Land use/land cover (LULC) maps** show vegetation type and how the land is used. The USGS

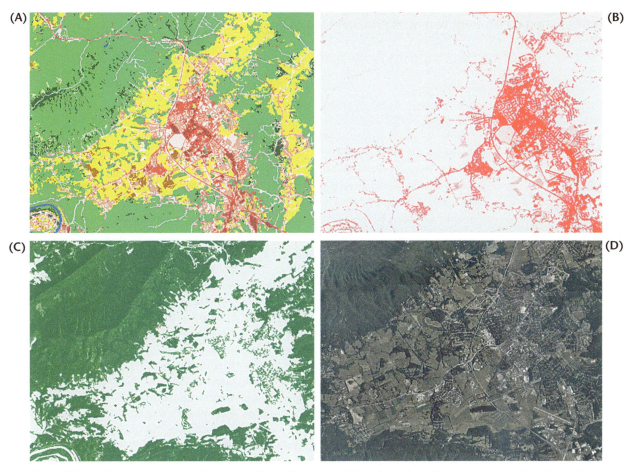

Figure 5.5 Four Blacksburg Images Downloaded from The National Map. A: Land use/land cover (red-pink = urban, yellow-brown = agriculture, green = forest). B: Impervious surface. C: Forest canopy (darker = higher percentage). D: Orthoimagery.

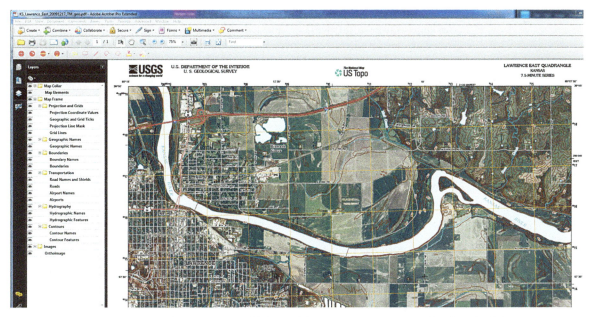

Figure 5.6 The Next Generation of US Topo Map, with Data of the Lawrence, Kansas, East Quadrangle. This map was downloaded as a GeoPDF from the USGS Map Store using Map Locator and viewed in Adobe Reader, showing data layers and TerraGo toolbar.

TABLE 5.2 **USGS Level I and II Land Use and Land Cover Classification System**

Level I Classes	Level II Classes
1 Water	11 Open Water
	12 Perennial Ice/Snow
2 Developed	21 Low-Intensity Residential
	22 High-Intensity Residential
	23 Commercial/Industrial/Transportation
3 Barren	31 Bare Rock/Sand/Clay
	32 Quarries/Strip Mines/Gravel Pits
	33 Transitional
4 Forested Upland	41 Deciduous Forest
	42 Evergreen Forest
	43 Mixed Forest
5 Shrubland	51 Shrubland
6 Non-Natural Woody	61 Orchards/Vineyards/Other
7 Herbaceous Upland Natural/ Semi-Natural Vegetation	71 Grasslands/Herbaceous
8 Herbaceous Planted/Cultivated	81 Pasture/Hay
	82 Row Crops
	83 Small Grains
	84 Fallow
	85 Urban/Recreational Grasses
9 Wetlands	91 Woody Wetlands
	92 Emergent Herbaceous Wetlands

has produced land use/land cover maps since the 1960s, but they were not standardized until the development of a classification code by Anderson et al. (1976). Based on aerial photos and satellite data, LULC information was compiled at 1:100,000 and 1:250,000 scales, so the resulting maps were small in scale. The code was later modified, and the current version is summarized in Table 5.2, which lists the level I and II classes. Anderson et al. (1976) included detail to level III (e.g., commercial retail) and level IV (e.g., commercial food/grocery) that are useful for neighborhood- or community-scale LULC maps.

LULC maps are derived from aerial photos and satellite data. Before exploring the major advances in the National Land Cover Database, we will introduce remote sensing.

Remote Sensing Information: Aerial Photos and Satellite Imagery

Remote sensing is essentially the observation and/or measurement of data from a distance. Advances in remote sensing technologies in the last few decades have greatly improved our observation of the environment. Just as the first images of Earth from space raised global consciousness, digital photographic images and satellite data have expanded our capabilities in monitoring, analyzing, and understanding the Earth's processes and our impacts on them.

Remote Sensing Fundamentals

Remote sensing technologies detect electromagnetic radiant energy reflected by or emitted from objects and land surfaces. This radiation can be interpreted and analyzed to reveal practical information about those objects and surfaces. Figure 5.7 shows the electromagnetic spectrum, the range of frequencies or wavelengths of radiation, from very shortwave gamma rays and X-rays (0.0001 micrometer, or micron), to visible light (0.4–0.7 micron), near-infrared (0.7–0.9 micron), shortwave infrared (1.6–2.5 microns), thermal infrared (8–12 microns), to microwaves (1,000 microns) and radio waves (1,000,000 microns).

All objects emit radiation. In addition, emitted radiation from the sun reflects off surfaces and objects. The reflected radiation is determined by the characteristics of the object, that is, its color, orientation, and thermal properties. Figure 5.8 gives the reflectance, or spectral signatures, of different objects or surfaces in the visible and near-infrared wavelengths. In the visible range, the reflected radiation is a function of the object's color. In the near-infrared range, it is a function of its temperature and thermal properties. *Passive remote sensing devices*, such as photographic and video cameras and thermal and multispectral scanners, simply detect the radiation reflected and emitted by surface objects. *Active sensors*, such

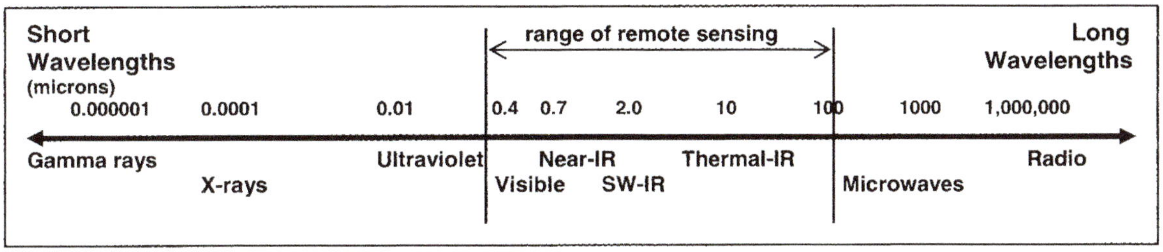

Short Wavelengths (microns)			range of remote sensing				Long Wavelengths
0.000001	0.0001	0.01	0.4 0.7	2.0	10	100 1000	1,000,000
Gamma rays	X-rays	Ultraviolet	Visible Near-IR SW-IR	Thermal-IR		Microwaves	Radio

Figure 5.7 The Electromagnetic Spectrum and the Wavelength Range of Remote Sensing.

Figure 5.8 The Spectral Reflectance of Dry Bare Soil, Vegetation, and Water. (*Source:* Thomas Lillesand and Ralph Kiefer, 2004 Remote Sensing and Image Interpretation, 4th ed. New York: John Wiley and Sons. Used with permission of Thomas Lillesand.)

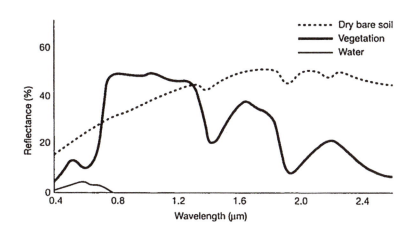

as radar, sonar, and LiDAR (light detection and ranging), emit their own waves to illuminate features of interest, then measure the reflected wavelengths that return.

Photographic cameras use film emulsions that are sensitive to visible or infrared wavelengths and produce an image. Multispectral scanners, on the other hand, actually measure radiation data separately in several spectral or wavelength bands. Having digital data in different wavelengths for the same object or surface permits more sophisticated computer analysis and interpretation.

Aerial Photos

Well established as a key source of topographic information, **aerial photos** vary in scale, view angle, and spectral characteristics, all of which determine the type and usefulness of information they display. Most aerial photographs show a *vertical view angle*. *Oblique photos* are those taken at an angle less than perpendicular to the surface; they are often used by planners for visual assessments. Scale depends on the elevation from which photos are taken and the lenses used. Only vertical photos are accurate in scale, and their accuracy depends on the elevation of the sensor. Vertical views taken from low to medium elevations are often distorted in scale toward the edges of the image. Objects at the edges are a greater distance from the sensor than those at the center of the image and will appear relatively smaller than they actually are.

Photographic film can detect different wavelengths of electromagnetic radiation. Normal black-and-white and color films both try to replicate what we see and are designed to be sensitive to visible wavelengths detected by the human eye. Infrared film senses slightly beyond the visible into the infrared range (see Figure 5.7). Satellite sensors (discussed below) have multispectral scanners that measure radiation data in several spectral bands.

Analysts can interpret a great deal of topographic information from the characteristics of aerial photos, based on an image's texture, tone, the size and shape of objects, their site and association with other objects, and the terrain. Terrain can be visualized from photographs by viewing them stereoscopically. Using a stereo-viewer, the observer focuses each eye on the same location in photo pairs, and a three-dimensional image emerges.

Spectral factors can also aid in interpretation. **Near-infrared photos** provide several distinct contrasts: wet areas (lakes, streams, wetlands) are very dark, dry meadows and woodlands are light, and conifers are darker than deciduous trees. In color infrared photos, healthy deciduous trees and lawns appear red, while conifers are a darker purple. **Thermal infrared photos** can reveal surface temperatures.

Microwave radar imagery differs from conventional photography in two ways. First, rather than a passive system sensing natural radiation, it uses an active sensing system, generating waves that bounce off objects on the land and are detected by the sensor. Second, it uses wavelengths well outside the visible spectrum, enabling the sensing of surface features not detectable from natural radiation. Side-looking airborne radar (SLAR) produces images resembling air photos with a low-angle sun and shadow effects. LiDAR emits visible and laser wavelengths and provides high-resolution imagery for many applications.

Aerial photos are used by planners for map making, for identifying and interpreting terrain features, for environmental inventories and monitoring, and as a source of data and digital images for GIS. The USGS has used vertical aerial photographs to produce and update its topographic maps since 1928. And with TNM and the new US topo map, the agency has continued to better integrate imagery and maps.

These improvements began in the 1970s, when the USGS first produced **orthophotoquads**, or nondistorted photomaps, at the scale of the 7.5-minute quadrangle series. Using a photomechanical process, the USGS can eliminate the scale distortion of vertical photographs. Information from the 7.5-minute map could then be superimposed onto the orthophotograph. To produce the photomap images, the USGS first used the National High-Altitude Aerial Photography (NHAP) program, later reconfigured as the National Aerial Photography Program (NAPP). That program produced images on a 5- to 7-year cycle. The new US Topo maps will rely on the National Agricultural Imagery Program, which produces aerial photos of the contiguous 48 states on a 3-year cycle.

Since 1990, orthophotoquad images have been taken in both black-and-white and color infrared. Figure 5.9 shows a color infrared digital orthophoto quarter quad (DOQQ) for Blacksburg, Virginia.

Satellite Imagery and Data

Satellite remote sensing has revolutionized environmental monitoring and data collection. It has two distinct advantages over traditional aerial photos: (1) using a multispectral scanner, it produces digital data in different wavelength bands for use in computer imaging and GIS; and (2) whereas aerial photos are a "snapshot in time," satellites provide recurring data of the same location at frequent intervals (e.g., 16 days for Landsat 7, one day for Terra's MODIS sensor), thereby providing continual monitoring.

Satellite digital imagery measures the amount of radiation received from a specific location on the ground. The images are produced as *pixels*, or picture elements, of a given resolution grid-cell size. The finer the resolution, the more spatially detailed the resulting data. The Landsat 4 multispectral scanner (MSS) had a resolution of about 80 meters square (an area of 6400 m^2 or 1.5 acres). The Thematic Mapper (TM) sensor on Landsat 5 (launched in 1984) improved this resolution to about 30 meters or 0.2 acre. Landsat 7 (launched in April 1999) has the Enhanced Thematic Mapper Plus (ETMP), which has the same resolution of the TM but adds a panchromatic band with a 15-m (0.05 acre or 2400 ft^2) resolution.

The Terra satellite was launched in December 1999 and contains five sensor systems. The most practical data to date have come from the *ASTER (advanced spaceborne thermal emission and reflection radiometer) sensor*, which senses 14 spectral bands at varying resolutions: 4 in the visible and near-infrared (VNIR: 0.52–0.86 micron), 6 in the shortwave infrared (1.6–2.4 microns), and 5 in the thermal infrared (8.1–11.6 microns). At 15 m in the VNIR range, ASTER provides

Figure 5.9 A Color Infrared Digital Orthophoto Quarter Quad Aerial Photograph of Blacksburg, Virginia. (*Source:* Image downloaded from TNM portal.)

four times the resolution of Landsat 7. The MODIS sensor, also aboard the Terra, provides near daily repeat coverage of the entire globe. Commercial satellites are producing even finer resolution. The IKONOS satellite, designed by Lockheed Martin and launched by Space Imaging (now owned by ORBIMAGE), was launched in 2000 and has a sensor with 0.82-m to 4-m resolution for panchromatic images and 4-m to 10-m range for multispectral data. *GeoEye-1*, launched in 2008, has 41-cm (16-in) resolution for panchromatic and 4-m multispectral imagery in an 8-km swath. GeoEye-2, planned for a 2011–2012 launch, will have 25-cm resolution. Figure 5.10 shows images from the ASTER and GeoEye from

Figure 5.10 High-Resolution ASTER and GeoEye Satellite Remote Sensing Images for Monitoring Natural Disasters. A: Galveston (Texas) before and after the 2008 Hurricane Ike. B: Banda Aceh, Sumatra, after the 2004 tsumani. C: New Orleans (Louisiana) before and after the 2005 Hurricane Katrina. (*Source:* A: GeoEye. B, C: NASA/GSFC/ METI/ERSDAC/ JAROS, and U.S./ Japan ASTER Science Team.)

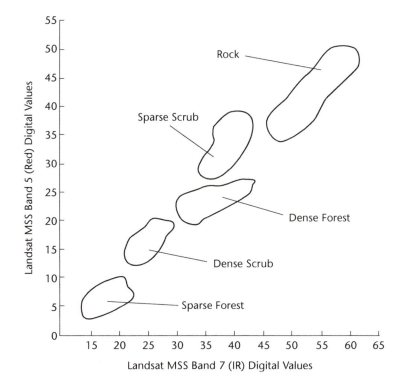

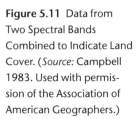

Figure 5.11 Data from Two Spectral Bands Combined to Indicate Land Cover. (*Source:* Campbell 1983. Used with permission of the Association of American Geographers.)

recent natural disasters. For more images, see GeoEye (www.geoeye.com) or NASA websites (http://visibleearth.nasa.gov/, http://asterweb.jpl.nasa.gov/).

The value of the satellite data is that sensors record values in different spectral wavelength bands for each pixel. The data can be entered into computer programs, and the digital values for different bands can be retrieved individually or in combination for interpretation. Figure 5.11 shows how values from two bands can be interpreted to distinguish types of land cover. For example, areas with a Landsat band 7 value of 30–40 and band 5 value of 20–25 are dense forests. Pixels having specific digital values or combinations of values can be assigned certain colors and can be displayed on a monitor and photographed or printed. The real usefulness of these data is that they are in digital form and can be used in combination with other spatial information in geographic information systems. Recurring data for the same location can be used to monitor changing conditions, as the experience described next demonstrates.

Land Use/Land Cover Revisited: The National Land Cover Database

In 1993, the system for land use and land cover mapping changed dramatically. The Multi-Resolution Land Characteristics (MRLC) Consortium of federal agencies pooled its resources to purchase Landsat-5 satellite data for the entire country, in order to create a National Land Cover Database with 1992 data (the NLCD

1992). The Consortium includes the EPA, the National Oceanic and Atmospheric Administration (NOAA), the U.S. Forest Service (USFS), the USGS, the National Aeronautics and Space Administration (NASA), the National Park Service (NPS), the Fish and Wildlife Service (USFWS), the Bureau of Land Management (BLM), and the Natural Resources Conservation Service (NRCS), with the USGS EROS Data Center taking the lead. The Consortium repeated this effort and purchased Landsat-7 2001 data to produce the NLCD 2001, which followed a protocol consistent with NLCD 1992 (Homer et al. 2007).

The NLCD allowed consistent land cover mapping for the entire nation, using the method described above of combining the different band data for a pixel to interpret its land cover. But the second 2001 iteration has provided a powerful tool for comparative analysis (Chandler 2009). By overlaying the two geographic data sets, it is possible to identify land use change. The National Land Cover Change Retrofit Product was prepared by the MRLC Consortium at 30-m resolution for the country (Fry et al. 2008). The product revealed a 3% change is U.S. land cover from 1992 to 2001, with a large net loss of forest and agriculture and large net gains in grass/shrub and urban. The real value of the analysis became apparent at smaller areas (larger scale).

Figure 5.12 shows two examples of these study subsets, the top set for a mountaintop coal mining area near Beckley, West Virginia, and the bottom set for rapid urban development in suburban Las Vegas. For each, the left and middle images show enhanced Landsat reflectance in a 6-4-2 band combination for 1992 and 2001, respectively. The right image and legend indicate 2001 land cover and change since 1992. In the top West Virginia set, 40 km^2 in large patches changed from forest to barren or grass/shrub. In the bottom Las Vegas set, 80 km^2 or 20% of the subset area changed from grass/shrub or barren to urban. The barren areas were already prepared for development in 1992.

Geographic Information Systems

The real power of digital data has been realized with advances in **geographic information systems (GIS)**. GIS has emerged as one of the most widely used and fundamental computer systems for any application requiring spatial information. It has revolutionized the field of cartographic analysis and map making, rendering virtually obsolete the cartographic artisan with pen in hand. Here are the primary advances:

- *Improved computer software.* Improved analytical capabilities, graphic display, user-friendliness, and affordability during the past decade have expanded GIS users from sophisticated experts to every local government to home users.
- *Improved computer hardware.* From the 1970s to as recently as the early 1990s, GIS software had to run on mainframe computers, and the results were blocky plotted maps that took considerable imagination to interpret. Improved software required improved hardware, including

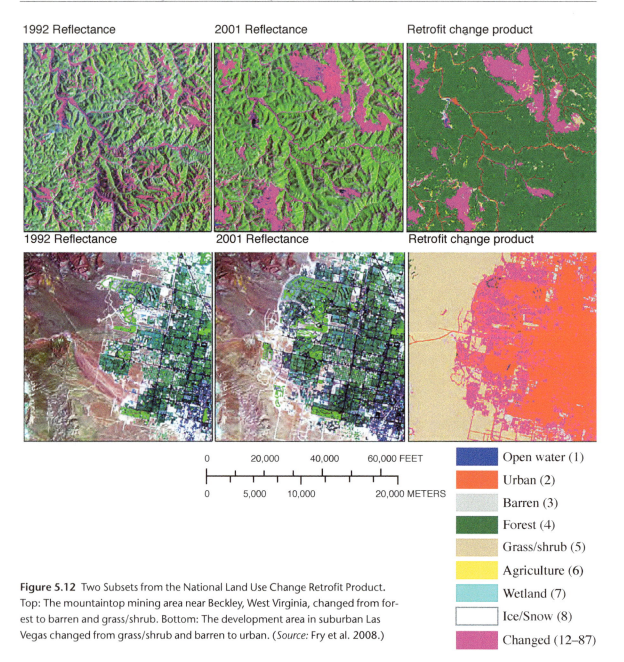

Figure 5.12 Two Subsets from the National Land Use Change Retrofit Product. Top: The mountaintop mining area near Beckley, West Virginia, changed from forest to barren and grass/shrub. Bottom: The development area in suburban Las Vegas changed from grass/shrub and barren to urban. (*Source:* Fry et al. 2008.)

faster and larger-memory computers, higher-resolution monitors, and faster and higher-quality printers and plotters. As these hardware devices became readily available, GIS moved from mainframe to desktop to laptop computers, and printed map products outpaced manual cartographic capabilities. At the same time, GIS accessibility became more affordable, thus attracting increasing numbers of users.

- *Improved spatial databases.* As software and hardware improved, the limiting factor in the use of GIS was digital data. Spatial data were available from maps and aerial photos, but they were not in digital form. Digitizing these data manually was tedious and costly. As we have already seen, the scope, resolution, and availability of digital spatial data have exploded during the past decade. Like hardware and software, the increased quality, availability and affordability of data have expanded usability to a wide range of users. Finally, increased availability and affordability of global positioning systems (GPS) have enhanced the gathering and monitoring of digital field data for use in GIS.

- *Improved applications.* Success begets success. Increased and innovative uses of GIS have illustrated the possibilities and led to additional applications. These include new clients (e.g., the uses for commercial marketing are endless), new fields (e.g., bioinformatics), new dimensions (e.g., 3-D, fly-by, and fly-through projections), and new forms of product delivery (e.g., Internet mapping systems).

As a result of these advances, GIS services, software, and hardware sales grew tenfold from an industry valued at $0.76 million in 1994 to a $7.7-billion industry in 2001. According to industry tracker Daratech, the GIS industry has grown at an average annual rate of 11% over the past decade, despite a slowdown to 1% in 2009 due to the global recession. Earth Systems Research Institute (Esri), makers of the Arc suite of products, including ArcGIS, ArcMap, ArcIMS, and others, now dominates the worldwide GIS software market with a 30–35% share.

Fundamentals of GIS

A GIS is a set of interrelated computer technologies that achieve the entry, storage, processing, retrieval, and generation of spatial data. As discussed, advances in software, hardware, data, and training have brought GIS from the domain of the geographic specialist to that of any computer user. GIS is used to make and update maps, integrate maps and other information from a variety of sources, analyze spatial information, and inform decisions about land use, natural resources, demographics, commercial markets, and innumerable other applications with spatial dimensions.

GIS is often characterized as consisting of four components: (1) *hardware*, or the computer's processing, memory, digitizing, and printing components; (2) *software* for data management, input, and manipulation, and for geographic querying, analysis, and visualization; (3) *data* from various sources, including digitized maps, satellite imagery, geographic data in tabular form, field data with GPS coordinates, and digitized aerial photos, all of which are entered into a consistent coordinate system; and (4) *people*, to manage systems, design systems, and interpret results.

Data Layers and Formats

As shown in Figure 5.13, GIS stores spatial data in **layers**, or themes. Each layer contains information that is "geocoded" in geographic coordinates indicating location. A variety of geographic coordinates can be used (e.g., longitude/latitude, address, census block, Cartesian grids from map projections). All layers must be

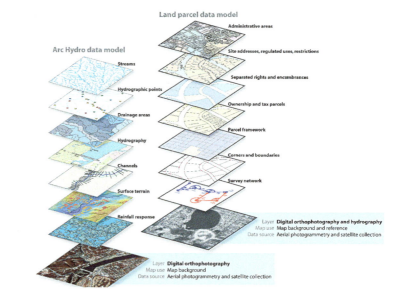

Figure 5.13 The Storage of GIS Data in Layers. (*Source:* Copyright © 2004 Esri. All rights reserved.)

represented in the same coordinate system so they can be combined and manipulated to generate new spatial data products. By linking information to geographic coordinates, a GIS user can access information for any location (what are the soils on my building site?) as well as locate specific information (where are the wetlands in my community?).

Three types of geographic information are represented in GIS: **points** (e.g., buildings); **lines** (e.g., roads and streams); and **polygons** (e.g., soils and wetlands). GIS works with two formats to store and manipulate this information. The **vector format** stores point, line, and polygon boundaries in x-y coordinates, such as the hydrographic points, streams, and drainage areas in Figure 5.13. The vector format describes discrete features, like points and lines, very well, but it is not as useful in describing continuously varying features, such as soils or imagery.

Raster datasets, the second type of format, are based on a grid model providing continuous pixel-based data for each point or grid cell in the data layer, such as surface terrain and orthophotography layers in Figure 5.13. The raster format is especially useful for overlay analysis, since each data layer has the same grid system and layers can combine information for each grid cell. Raster datasets are also referred to as imagery, because the overlay combination of pixel data is fundamental to analyzing remote sensing data in different wavelength bands. GIS information is stored as **attribute tabular information**, which describes the features and values in each data layer.

Operations and Analysis in GIS

Many tasks and processes are involved in GIS operations, including data input, manipulation, management, query, analysis, visualization, and map serving. **Data input** used to require digitizing paper maps, but now digital spatial data are readily available and accessible. GPS and related software applications have enabled automated data input of field data into GIS.

All geographic data are not in the same scale or format, and **data manipulation** is required to provide compatibility so that data can be overlain and integrated. Manipulation includes projection changes, data aggregation, filtering, scaling, and stretching. **Data management** includes storage, organization, and access in a database management system, in which data are stored in a collection of tables. Common fields are used to link the different tables together (Esri 2002).

GIS operations use queries and spatial analysis. **Queries** simply ask questions that can be answered by using or combining information from different data layers. For example, "What is the dominant soil in a county's existing agricultural zones?" Answering this query requires use of the soils layer and the county zoning layer. A query used in the example on the book website (www.envirolanduse.org) is "What is the value of property impacted by a 50-foot buffer creek overlay district in Blacksburg in its Rural Residential zone?" This requires layers on streams, zoning, property parcel boundaries, and parcel value.

More sophisticated **spatial analysis** can assess patterns and trends, perform scenario development, incorporate statistical analysis, and develop spatial models. Two important examples of spatial analytical tools are proximity analysis and overlay analysis. **Proximity analysis** takes advantage of the horizontal spatial scale of GIS layers and measures data within a specified distance from a point, line, or polygon boundary. The example query above requires proximity analysis to identify the stream buffer area. Proximity analysis can determine the population (potential customers) located within a mile of a store, the number of septic systems located within 200 yards of a lake, the boundary of a 100-yard buffer around wetlands, and so on.

Overlay analysis integrates different data layers to provide composite maps. The birth of GIS was based on this operation, dating back to Ian McHarg's (1969) manual overlay transparencies and David Tomlinson (2003), the so-called father of GIS, who used thematic data layers and overlays as the cornerstone of GIS. Figure 5.14 illustrates how the overlay method is used to analyze satellite wavelength band data to produce a composite image of land cover (see Figure 5.12). Data layers are overlaid to produce a composite map. Figure 5.15A shows how data layers on foundation soils, utility availability, and wetland impacts can be rated and combined to produce a new composite layer on residential suitability. Figure 5.15B illustrates how overlay operations are used to produce output overlays that become part of the stored database.

Figures 5.15A and 5.16 are examples of **spatial modeling**, which combines operations to answer a query and produce a new map product. The Figure 5.16 query is "Where are the most suitable sites for a new park that serves the most people and does not duplicate existing parks?" New overlays are produced for

Figure 5.14 Overlay Analysis. This technology combines data layers to produce a composite map, image, or new data layer. Satellite wavelength band data layers are combined to produce a composite of land cover. (*Source:* Copyright © Esri. All rights reserved.)

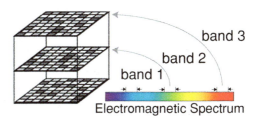

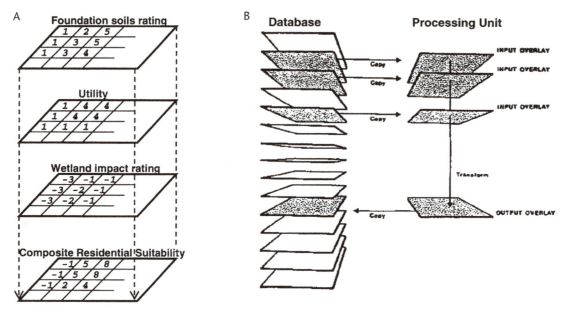

Figure 5.15 The Use of Overlay Analysis to Combine Weighted Data Layers to Produce Composite Maps. The maps are then added as new layers in the database. (*Source:* Adapted from Tomlin 1983.)

Figure 5.16 Simple Spatial Modeling. This technique is used to find the best locations for a new park that is closest to population densities (top) but does not duplicate existing parks (bottom proximity). The result (right) shows the best potential in darker purple. (*Source:* Copyright © Esri. All rights reserved.)

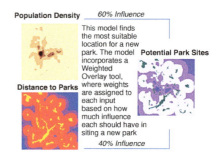

population density and distance from existing parks (by proximity analysis), the two overlays are weighted for relative importance, and they are overlaid to produce locations maximizing proximity to population density, with an appropriate distance to existing parks.

Additional GIS analytical capabilities include the following:

- Spatial statistical analysis ("What is the average property value in a land preservation zone?")
- Network analysis and routing ("What is the best route between points A and B?")
- Computer-assisted design (CAD) (drawing capabilities and 3-D models)
- Land information systems (combined mapping and database capabilities for parcels, including location, size, and land records)
- Multimedia, hypertext, and hot links (use of sound, photos, video, links to text and other media)
- Simulation modeling ("How would build-out according to current zoning affect traffic congestion and runoff pollution loading in an undeveloped area?")

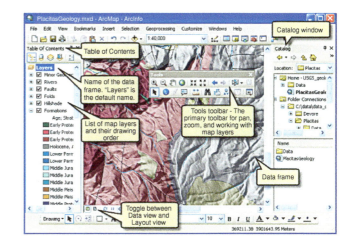

Figure 5.17 An Esri ArcMap Window, Showing Data Frame, Layers, Data Catalog, and Toolbars. (*Source:* Copyright © Esri. All rights reserved.)

Spatial visualization is an important objective of GIS. GIS map-making capabilities provide visual representations of land use, land use change, environmental resource problems, and opportunities. Because of the visualization capabilities, GIS has become a useful tool in public communication. Visualization is enhanced by photo and satellite imagery and three-dimensional characterizations enabled by digital elevation data.

It is not the purpose of this text to instruct you how to use GIS, but rather to explain some of the basic language and especially the capabilities and opportunities GIS provides for environmental planning. Still, it is useful to understand that GIS software, although sophisticated, is another piece of software for which most computer users can become proficient, like Microsoft Word, Powerpoint, and Excel. It takes some instruction, and then use and practice. Figure 5.17 shows the basic window of Esri's ArcGIS version 10.0 for a sample geologic map. There are callouts on various toolbars and contents, including the map or data frame, the layers that can be shown on the map or hidden, and the catalog of data. If you have access to ArcGIS or other software and data layers for your community, you can learn the basics of GIS map making. Esri has excellent online tutorials that can get you started.

Examples of GIS Products

We are more interested here in getting a feel for the capabilities of GIS, which are best conveyed by examples of GIS products. Esri publishes a Map Book gallery each year that includes maps produced by users of its suite of software. The three parts of Figure 5.18 show some map excerpts relevant to our discussion. Figure 5.18A uses 3-D display and digital elevation model (DEM) data to show the impact of a 2-m rise in sea level due to climate change on Broward County, Florida. Figure 5.18B shows the growth of the urban edge in Phoenix and Maricopa Counties over time. Figure 5.18C shows a 3-D land use map of downtown Portland, a mashup of ArcGIS and SketchUp using Lidar elevation data.

Subsequent chapters contain many other maps and images that are products of GIS, including inventory and suitability maps on soils, geology, slope, watersheds,

Broward County, Florida, today

Broward County, Florida, 2 meter sea level rise

Figure 5.18A The Impact of Climate Change on Sea-Level Rise, Broward County, Florida. Fort Lauderdale, Miramar, Pembroke Pines, and Cooper City would be underwater. (*Source:* Craig et al. 2007; Esri Map Book 23. Used with permission.)

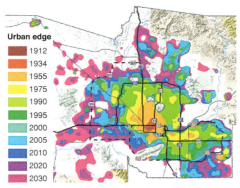

Figure 5.18B Historic and Projected Urban Edge in Phoenix and Maricopa Counties, Arizona. (*Source:* Bagley 2007; Esri Map Book 23. Used with permission.)

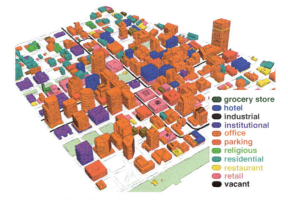

Figure 5.18C Three-Dimensional Land Use Inventory of Portland, Oregon, Central City. The model calculates the area by use and building floor. (*Source:* Martin 2008; Esri Map Book 24. Used with permission.)

floodplains, groundwater, vegetation, urban forestry, wetlands, habitats, air quality, carbon emissions, land conservation, green infrastructure, gray infrastructure, brownfields, urban design, and Smart Growth Management. It would be a challenge to do environmental planning (and to write this book!) without maps and the GIS that produced them.

Web Map Serving

As mentioned earlier, Internet travel mapping, Google Earth, and other spatial imaging websites, as well as daily GPS use in mobile devices, have increased the average person's geospatial awareness through instant access to geographic maps and images. Interactive online mapping through **web map serving** is increasingly used to provide portals for geospatial information. Following a protocol developed by the Open Geospatial Consortium, web map serving can use a variety of software, such as open source MapServer and Esri's ArcGIS Server and ArcIMS.

We will rely on many of these portals for data and information used in environmental planning studies discussed in subsequent chapters. Of primary interest to us are web map services provided by government sources. Local government websites allow users to map parcels and neighborhoods and view and print parcel data, imagery, and maps from the community scale to the site scale. Some regional and state agencies also provide web map services. We will use a variety of federal agency map serving sites, including The National Map from the USGS discussed earlier. Listed below are some relevant federal map serving websites, most of which are participants in the Esri Federal User Community.

- EPA EnviroMapper for Water
  (http://www.epa.gov/waters/enviromapper/)
- EPA EnviroMapper for Envirofacts
  (http://www.epa.gov/emefdata/em4ef.home)
- FEMA Flood Map Viewer
  (https://hazards.fema.gov/wps/portal/mapviewer)
- FWS Critical Habitat Mapper
  (http://criticalhabitat.fws.gov/flex/crithabMapper.jsp?)
- FWS Wetlands Inventory Mapper
  (http://www.fws.gov/wetlands/Data/Mapper.html)
- FWS Gulf of Mexico oil spill mapper
  (http://137.227.242.82/GulfSpill/GulfSpillMapper.html)
- NOAA nowCOAST (real time observations and forecasts)
  (http://nowcoast.noaa.gov/)
- USDA NRCS Web Soil Survey
  (http://websoilsurvey.nrcs.usda.gov/app/HomePage.htm)
- USDA Food Environment Atlas (http://maps.ers.usda.gov/FoodAtlas/)
- USGS Natural Hazards Support System (current natural hazards)
  (http://nhss.cr.usgs.gov/)
- USGS The National Map Viewer (http://nationalmap.gov/viewers.html)

GIS Data Access

Downloading web-served interactive maps is useful for rapid and intermediate environmental assessment, but detailed assessment requires GIS analysis. The heart of a GIS is the geodatabase, and one of the keys to advancing the use, application, and benefits of GIS is access to quality geospatial data. The geospatial revolution has been spurred by the availability of downloadable data from the Internet that is supported by federal, state, and local agencies and private vendors. Box 5.1 lists major federal data sites.

Several websites provide portals to these resources, such as the Geo Community's GIS Data Depot (data.geocomm.com), Geodata.gov (which hosts government source data), and the USDA's Geospatial Data Gateway. Specific federal agencies are making their geospatial information available not only in map form but in data files to be used in GIS programs. These data are available in an extensive variety of formats. A common format for data layers is shapefiles, which have the extension .shp. For large image files, a format is MrSid (multiresolution seamless image database, propriety of LizardTech), with the extension .sid.

Many of the federal agencies listed above, as well as state and local agencies, offer downloadable GIS data files. In addition, the U.S. Census Bureau offers

---

BOX 5.1—U.S. Federal Sources of Geospatial Maps, Data, and Imagery

A key element of the geospatial revolution is ready access to geospatial data, maps, and imagery. The number of Internet sources grows daily, and you can Google search "geospatial data sources" to find up-to-date lists and links. There are university, U.S. state and local government, commercial, and international data sources, too numerous to list here. The following list gives major U.S. federal government websites for viewing and downloading geospatial maps, images, and data, including GIS-ready data files. (See also the list in the text giving federal environmental agency mapper sites.)

- **Geodata.gov**
  (http://gos2.geodata.gov/wps/portal/gos):
  A one-stop portal for finding and using federal, state, and local geospatial data.
- **National Atlas** (http://nationalatlas.gov/):
  Assemble, view, and print your own maps using National Atlas map layers.
- **NASA LP DAAC** (Land Processes Distributed Active Archive Center)
  (https://lpdaac.usgs.gov/lpdaac/get_data):
  Search and order earth science data from all NASA datacenters.
- **USDA NAIP** (National Agriculture Imagery Program):
  (http://www.fsa.usda.gov/FSA/apfoapp?area=home&subject=prog&topic=nai):
  National aerial photo imagery on a 3-year cycle.
- **USGS National Geospatial Program**
  (http://www.usgs.gov/ngpo/): A portal for USGS geospatial data coordination.
- **USGS Store**
  (http://store.usgs.gov/b2c_usgs/b2c/start/%28xcm=r3standardpitrex_prd%29/.do): Maps for purchase and download using a map locator.

- **USGS Earth Explorer**
  (http://edcsns17.cr.usgs.gov/EarthExplorer/),
  New Earth Explorer (http://edcsns17.cr.usgs.gov/NewEarthExplorer/):
  A complete search and order tool for aerial photos, elevation data, and satellite products from USGS.
- **USGS The National Map**
  (http://nationalmap.gov/viewers.html) and
  Seamless Server (http://seamless.usgs.gov/index.php): View and download map and data files.
- **USGS GLOVIS** (global visualization) Viewer
  (http://glovis.usgs.gov/): A quick and easy search and order tool for USGS and NASA global satellite and aerial images.
- **USGS EROS** (Earth Resources Observation and Science) Center (http://eros.usgs.gov/):
  A portal for finding science and remote sensing data, with an image gallery.
- **USGS Web Mapping Portal** (http://cumulus.cr.usgs.gov/): A developmental website that allows metadata searches for multiple USGS datasets.
- **USGS Emergency Operations Portal**
  (http://eoportal.cr.usgs.gov/EO/): Provides critical pre- and post-disaster images and datasets for immediate viewing and downloading.
- **USGS Natural Hazards Support System**
  (http://nhss.cr.usgs.gov/): A portal for current natural hazard events.
- **USGS Geographic Data Download**
  (http://edc2.usgs.gov/geodata/): Download GIS digital elevation model (DEM), digital line graphs (DLG), and LULC datafiles.
- **US Census TIGER file portal** (http://www.census.gov/geo/www/tiger/): Census district shape (.shp) line and data files.

TIGER (Topologically Integrated Geographic Encoding and Referencing system) census line boundary and demographic data.

Public Participation GIS

As mentioned earlier, Butler (2006) says that Google Earth has led to a democratization of GIS. While it is true that online mapping and geospatial visualization have provided access and geospatial data to anyone with an Internet connection, Google Earth does not have the analytical capabilities of GIS. So a better statement would be that Google Earth has led to a democratization of geospatial information.

Public participation GIS (PP-GIS), on the other hand, does aim to democratize the analytic capabilities of GIS. PP-GIS uses GIS and other geospatial information technologies in a participatory setting to support integrated conservation and development and sustainable natural resource management. It provides community empowerment through measured, demand-driven, user-friendly, and integrated applications of geospatial maps and spatial analysis (Rambaldi et al. 2006). It basically takes the experience of participatory appraisal and comanagement (see Chapter 4), and applies the latest geospatial technologies to enhance the process and the product. Its most dramatic applications are in developing countries.

PPgis.net is an open forum on participatory information systems and technologies, and posts case studies of hundreds of participatory mapping projects. While providing skills training, each project develops local capacity for planning and analysis, builds local confidence to manage resources, and acquires historic information, local knowledge, and detailed field data.

Access to technology and training has inhibited applications in many poor countries, but this is changing with the availability of simpler and cheaper technologies and better data, including satellite imagery and Google Earth. Box 5.2 describes a project in Mexico designed to provide community verification of forest

---

BOX 5.2—Using PP-GIS to Baseline Forest Management for Carbon Sequestration Credits

To manage carbon in a climate changing world, there are opportunities for forest management and resulting carbon sequestration in developing countries that can be rewarded with financial carbon credits under the UNFCCC REDD+ program (reduced emissions from deforestation and degradation in developing countries + sequestration). However, it is difficult to provide the measuring and monitoring of carbon services within the community, and bringing in high-cost specialists is prohibitive. A recent project in Mexico's Michoacan State used simple geospatial technologies and community members to assess and map community forest carbon to qualify for credits. Using open source freeware for GIS (ILWIS Open), spatial images (Google Earth), and field data capture (CyberTracker); a smart phone or PDA with GPS capabilities; and a laptop computer with Internet access, the project developed the baseline data necessary to participate in a carbon sequestration credit program.

The final map of carbon forest management for San Juan Baustista was produced after exporting CyberTracker .shp files into ILWIS and using the class domain procedure to create vector linear elements. The map gave pilot and permanent sample plots, the carbon pools, community forest management systems, and sources of degradation, all of which were needed for the REDD+ program.

The project showed the potential to engage local communities to gather field data and their local knowledge, and to build local capacity for other community projects. It was conducted under the KTGAL programme at the University of Twente, Netherlands.

Source: Peters-Guarin and McCall 2010.

Figure 5.19 Some PDA Touch-Screen Icons Used in CyberTracker to Monitor Field Observations. (*Source:* Cybertracker, www.cyberTracker.co.za.)

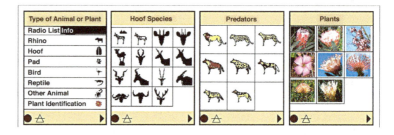

management carbon sequestration credits through a PP-GIS project. Using open source freeware CyberTracker and ILWIS Open GIS, Google Earth, a GPS-enabled smart phone, and a laptop computer with Internet access, the project developed the baseline data necessary to participate in a carbon sequestration credit program.

CyberTracker deserves further mention. It is a user-friendly data collection tool developed in South Africa to tap the unique knowledge and expertise of illiterate and innumerate South African bushmen to monitor the movements and behavior of wildlife. It has been further adapted for fauna identification. Programmed into a PDA with a GPS unit, bushmen simply point at an icon on the screen when they see a species, tracks, or other indicator (Figure 5.19), and the data and GPS georeferenced location are automatically stored. The software allows adaptation and design of screens that facilitate the collection of any field data in a systematic way. Data are stored and later downloaded to spreadsheets and as shape (.shp) files to GIS (see www.cyberTracker.co.za).

PP-GIS is not just an approach for international development. Open source and affordable access to software and data has enabled citizens and groups in the U.S. and other developed countries to participate on a more level-information-playing-field with development interests. Planners can better engage citizens in the business of data gathering and analysis, once thought too complex for the average Joe. It has also enabled counterplanning by environmental groups, for providing alternative plans and assessments.

The first edition of this book highlighted examples of PP-GIS use in counterplanning and data monitoring. The Chattooga River Watershed Conservation Plan, a scenario developed by the Chattooga Conservancy using GIS, contributed to the management planning of three national forests. (See the book website, www.envirolanduse.org, for this short case study.) A second example is a technique developed in 2001 for digital field monitoring of visual stream problems in Virginia, using CyberTracker, GIS, a PDA with GPS, and a digital camera (Box 5.3).

GIS Mashups: Integrating and Networking Geospatial Imagery

A useful tool for PP-GIS, as well as any simple map display project, is a **geospatial mashup**, which combines data or functions from one or more sources using an open application programming interface (API). This technique lets users add their own content to web-based maps. Google Maps, Google Earth, and other web-mapping tools use a format called keyhole markup language (KML) for mapping mashups. Many sources of geospatial data and products support KML so that their

Stream assessment field monitoring by volunteer groups often relies on paper forms for recording information, but these forms are not optimal for efficient data collection, entry, and display. Recently, accepted protocols have been adapted for the digital entry and storage of data using handheld computers or personal digital assistants (PDAs), GPS, digital water quality sensors, and digital cameras (for visual assessments). These tools, and software like CyberTracker, provide an efficient means of collecting, recording, storing, analyzing, and mapping stream, watershed, habitat, and wildlife data, then presenting the results in an interactive format on the Internet.

Jason Anderson (2001) adapted the programmable CyberTracker software for stream survey data collection. Data monitored in the field are entered onto the PDA touchpad. The GPS automatically enters into the PDA the spatial location of the data and any digital photos taken. Back in the office, the data are downloaded into a spreadsheet, checked, and then transferred to a GIS, complete with location coordinates. Figure 5.20 shows the GIS project window with digital topographic map on which red pluses indicate the data collection locations. By clicking the mouse on a location, the data and photo pop up. Anderson (2001) tested the tools and protocol using both experienced stream surveyors and schoolchildren with great success.

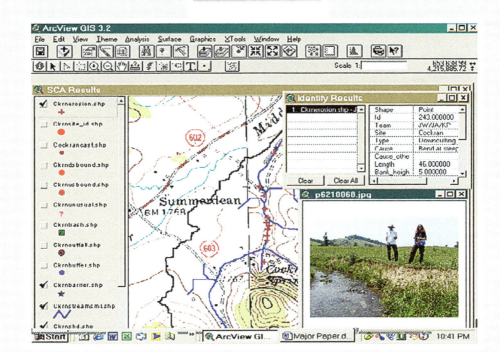

Figure 5.20 The Use of CyberTracker for a Stream Survey. Top: PDA/GPS was used with CyberTracker software to record data and geo-reference digital images. Bottom: This GIS project window shows stream survey results. When you click on map locations (red pluses), stream data and images pop up. (*Source:* Anderson 2001.)

Figure 5.21 A U.S. Forest Service Mashup of 2007 Southern California Wildfires into Google Earth. (*Source:* U.S. Forest Service, MODIS Active Fire Mapping Program, 2007.)

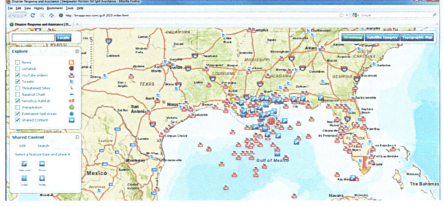

Figure 5.22 The ESRI Gulf of Mexico Oil Spill Social Network Map. This image shows the Deep Water Horizon oil blowout site and spatial links to shared content (YouTube videos, Tweets, web links, and notes posted by users). (*Source:* Copyright © Esri and its data processors. All rights reserved. http://www.esri.com/services/disaster-response/gulf-oil-spill-2010/index.html.)

data and products can be integrated into Google Earth images and vice versa. In Figure 5-18C, the 3-D image of downtown Portland is a mashup of ArcGIS and SketchUp. Figure 5-21 shows a USFS mashup giving a visual image of 2007 Southern California forest fires.

Mashups into Google Earth are popular on the evening TV news, but they are also useful for planners and citizens to display their own data and provide geospatial visualization without an elaborate GIS or geospatial experience. They are particularly useful in PP-GIS inventory studies. They can also be used to display social networking content in a spatial form, for facilitating dialogue and information sharing. Figure 5.22 shows an image from an interactive map site that displays links to photo, video, and document content relating to specific locations impacted by the BP Gulf of Mexico Deep Water Horizon oil spill. Users can both view and post content. As useful as mashups are, it is important to remember that mapping mashups do not support spatial analysis (at least for now), and they can be subject to error, misinterpretation, and other pitfalls.

The Power and Pitfalls of GIS

Geographic information systems have emerged as one of the most useful tools in environmental land planning—in fact, in all applications that have a spatial dimension. Advances in software, hardware, data availability, and user training have been accompanied by ever-increasing applications.

In environmental land planning, GIS facilitates land inventories, land analysis, visioning and scenario building, visualization and presentation, and participation. The ease of producing maps has enabled more analysis, alternatives, and planning scenarios—more ideas and possibilities—than previously possible. As GIS has become more affordable and accessible, it has moved from the domain of the expert to that of any computer user. Through PP-GIS, it has enhanced the involvement of residents in assessing the present and planning for the future of their communities. Community and environmental groups are now using GIS to produce their own plans, rivaling the sophistication of the plans of agencies and consultants, while incorporating their own values.

Although this penetration of the technology has largely been a good thing, it has also raised concerns, as people who have little or no cartographic knowledge are becoming mapmakers. Kent and Klosterman (2000) identified common mistakes made by GIS users that reduce the effectiveness of their products. These pitfalls include:

- Failing to understand the purpose of the map.
- Trying to improve accuracy by zooming in.
- Neglecting map projections and coordinate systems.
- Failing to evaluate and document map sources.
- Neglecting to include necessary map elements, such as title, scale, or legend.
- Presenting too much information.
- Misrepresenting quantitative and qualitative data.

What does the current geospatial revolution mean for environmental and urban planning? William Drummond and Steve French (2008) address this question, providing an excellent history of GIS and planning and addressing some future prospects as well. They lament the possibility that the current geospatial revolution will leave planners on the sidelines in a field they helped develop. On the one hand, GIS software development has become increasingly sophisticated and beyond the technical reach of planners. On the other hand, the mass marketing of geospatial technologies (including GPS and wireless devices), along with Internet mapping and open source GIS software, has brought capacity to almost anyone with computer savvy. Here are a few suggestions (Drummond and French 2008):

1. Planners should take full advantage of the opportunity provided by the growing mass geospatial market and work to marry Internet mapping and mashups with PP-GIS.
2. Planners should retain some fundamental programming skills to understand the functioning of commercial GIS software, but also take advantage of the GIS wing of the open source software movement (www .opensourcegis.org).
3. Planners can partner with allied disciplines and departments, which also are developing and using geospatial data and technologies.

In addition, planners should understand that GIS is a powerful spatial analysis and visualization tool, but its effectiveness depends heavily on the data quality and an appropriate analytical procedure for problems at hand. Despite the greater access to open source data and software and improved mapping capabilities, there are still barriers to GIS use in planning. Based on surveys of practicing planners, these challenges are more organizational and institutional than technological; they could be addressed by improved training in Internet-based GIS tools and applications for public participation and visualization, and by better networking in order to share experiences (Gôçmen and Ventura 2010).

The Promise and Prospects of Geospatial Data and Technology

Al Gore's 1998 vision of the Digital Earth, presented at the beginning of the chapter, was thought of at the time as a dream that would take 100 years to realize. Yet the speed with which the geospatial revolution has progressed since that speech has led many to believe that we are moving toward its realization. On the occasion of the tenth anniversary of the speech, analysts reviewed the progress so far and the steps ahead. Indeed, a new journal, *The International Journal of Digital Earth*, was inaugurated in 2008.

Gore's Digital Earth envisioned a multiresolution, three-dimensional representation of the planet that could be accessed to find, visualize, and make sense of vast amounts of georeferenced information on the physical and social environment. It would allow users to navigate through space and time, enable access to historical data as well as future predictions based on environmental models, and support access and use by everyone from scientists to policy makers to children. The system would support not only viewing but also the uploading of information to continually add to the database.

This chapter has reviewed the considerable progress made toward this vision. Many of the following key developments toward Digital Earth were barely on the drawing board in 1998 (Craglia et al. 2008; Goodchild 2008):

- *Spatial data infrastructures (SDI)*, to standardize the organization of geographic information.
- *Geo-browser development*, using geography to organize information. These include Google Earth, Microsoft Virtual Earth, and Esri ArcGIS Explorer.
- *Geo-sensing* at finer resolution from satellite and airplane sensors, including multispectral, panometric, and active sensors, such as LiDAR.
- *GPS data* and the mass marketing of GPS devices.
- *Innovative computer technologies*, including data storage capacity, wireless access, and mobile devices.
- *Interoperability*, to integrate data from multiple sources, such as mashups, PP-GIS, and crowdsourcing techniques.

Despite the progress made, many of these achievements are still not developed to the extent envisioned by the Digital Earth, and other developments are necessary. For example:

- *Limited interoperability:* Interoperability is still in its infancy in terms of uploading a wide range of local knowledge, the technical integration of mashup data into databases, and quality control.
- *Analytical capability:* Geobrowsers still lack GIS analytical tools to perform simple queries, find spatial anomalies, and otherwise analyze spatial data to meet user needs.
- *Modeling and simulation*: Digital Earth envisions a historical perspective and future scenarios based on scientific models. Historical data are emerging in Google Earth, for example, from past spatial datasets and mashups with historical imagery and data. But opportunities for querying future scenarios across multiple disciplines to envision the future are still lacking.

What needs to happen in order to resolve these limitations and achieve the dream of the Digital Earth? To enhance problem-solving capacity, Craglia et al. (2008) suggest developing a better search and query capability, improved access to future scenarios, and enhanced visualization of abstract concepts, like human and ecosystem health. Goodchild (2008) says that geobrowsers must develop more analytical tools to provide these functions. Better open access for data uploading, such as GeoServer and Wikimapia methods, must be developed to crowdsource information and knowledge.

Paul Zwick (2010) suggests that the emerging approach of GeoDesign could address some of these limitations. GeoDesign is a set of geospatial techniques and technologies that integrate multiple disciplines and stakeholders in an interactive problem-solving format. An early example of GeoDesign is FEMA's HAZUS program (see Chapter 13).

Summary

This chapter has addressed the important topic of information and data in environmental planning. Informed and knowledgeable planning decisions depend on the proper collection, analysis, and presentation of information. A planner's role is to help decision makers, elected officials, members of the public, and other stakeholders make sense of the huge volume of potentially conflicting information.

For environmental issues relating to land use, geospatial information is critical. We are in the midst of a geospatial revolution. Geobrowsers such as Google Earth, developed as recently as 2005, now have hundreds of millions of users. GPS devices little known a decade ago are now an essential need of millions of travelers. Satellite data and imagery have improved from 30-m to 0.41-m resolution. Access to digital data has never been better, and it improves daily. Analytical and visualization capabilities also continue to improve. Open source data, software, and interoperability provide not only new access to data and GIS, but they create a two-way street with the Internet for uploading local data. It's a whole new geospatial world, and it is hard to keep up. While this chapter has tried to explain it, the information becomes outdated quickly in this fast-moving field, and you should check with cited sources for the latest updates.

The geospatial revolution creates both opportunities and challenges for planners. They have far greater access to geospatial data and analysis, and we will discuss many examples in subsequent chapters. They also have additional tools for engaging the public and stakeholders in the planning process through geospatial visualization, and by acquiring local knowledge through online geospatial technologies and PP-GIS techniques. However, planners are also challenged to keep pace with this fast-changing field, amidst their other daily demands.

Al Gore's 1998 vision of the Digital Earth would provide access for everyone to an interactive, multiresolution, three-dimensional representation of the planet. Most believed this vision was a pipedream, but geospatial technology and data developments over the past dozen years have taken us far closer to achieving the goals of the Digital Earth than anyone, even Al Gore, would have thought at the time of his speech in 1998.

6 ■ Soils, Agriculture, and Land Use

To understand the natural processes of the land, and to plan land use in accordance with them, there is no more fundamental place to start than the soil. Soil is a living dynamic resource that supports plant life by providing a physical matrix, biological setting, and chemical environment for water, nutrient, air, and heat exchange. Soil also controls decomposition of organic matter and biogeochemical cycles; affects surface and subsurface hydrology; determines inherent vegetation, habitat type, and agricultural potential; and supports human habitation and structures. As a result, many disciplines are interested in soils: the agronomist, the hydrologist, the wildlife biologist, the farmer, the gardener, the builder, the engineer, and the environmental land use planner, to name a few.

This chapter introduces some land use properties of soils, discusses soil surveys and interpretation, and addresses major issues and assessment for agricultural lands and urban soils. It describes techniques for evaluation of soils used by planners, including soil quality indicators, soil suitability mapping, agricultural land assessment, and erosion prediction and sedimentation control. The chapter also addresses land application of wastes and concludes with a discussion of the growing interest and opportunities in urban agriculture and its implications for planning.

Land Use Properties and Soil Quality

Soils are made up of *inorganic minerals* (rock, clay, silt, and sand), which provide structure; *organic matter* (living and decomposing plant and animal material), which supplies nutrients and holds moisture; and *air, water, and dissolved nutrients*, all of which are essential for living organisms. Box 6.1 provides some soil fundamentals, including soil formation processes and soil profiles (Figure 6.1), soil taxonomy, and principal characteristics, including texture, bulk density, soil

BOX 6.1—Basic Soil Fundamentals

The process of soil formation and depletion is a complex combination of physical, chemical, and biological processes (Figure 6.1). Underlying rock provides the *parent material* that, through physical and chemical **weathering,** produces the fine-grained minerals of soil. Overlying vegetation and animals provide organic matter (litter), and through various stages of biological **decomposition**, this material produces the soil's humus. Physical processes of **deposition** and **erosion** continually remove and replace surface materials. **Percolation**, the downward movement of water, leaches materials from the surface to lower depths. It takes 100–400 years to form 1 centimeter of soil through these processes.

The vertical cross section of the soil, or **soil profile,** contains distinguishable *zones or horizons.* The O horizon is the organic litter above the A horizon or topsoil. A contains the most organic matter and has the greatest biological activity. Between A and B is the E or leached horizon, which is the source of the downward removal of materials by **leaching** (the process of eluviation). B and C horizons are the subsoil. B has greatest accumulation of leached materials from above through the process of illuviation (leachate accumulation in Figure 6.1), and C contains weathered parent material.

Soil Taxonomy

The contiguous United States is dominated by ten soil classes, which are subdivided into subclasses. See the NRCS Soil Taxonomy website for information on the classification system and location of classes and subclasses at http://soils.usda.gov /technical/classification/taxonomy/.

Soil Characteristics

Texture is the relative proportion of particles of different sizes. Here are particle definitions by diameter:

Cobbles > 75 mm
Gravel 2.0–75 mm
Sand 0.05–2.0 mm
Silt 0.002–0.05 mm
Clay < 0.002 mm

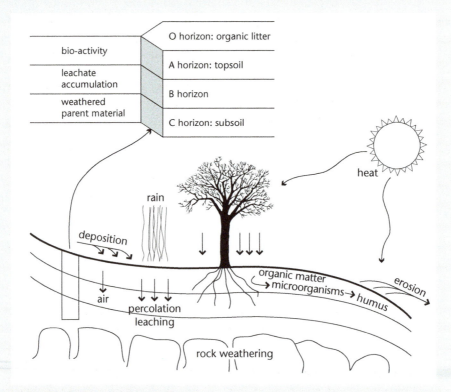

Figure 6.1 Soil Processes and Profiles.

BOX 6.1—Basic Soil Fundamentals (cont.)

Of course, soils are generally mixtures of different-sized particles, so the U.S. Department of Agriculture (USDA) has devised textural classes of soils depending on their composition of sand, silt, and clay. The texture of the soil has a great effect on its drainability, erodibility, bearing strength, and stability.

Bulk density is the unit volume weight of the soil. An ideal density is 1.33 megagrams per cubic meter (Mg/m^3). Values over 1.6 Mg/m^3 tend to inhibit plant root penetration. **Compacted soil** is compressed to a bulk density greater than 1.6 Mg/m^3.

Structure is determined by the shape of particle clusters, called *peds*. Peds can provide openings for percolation, even in clay-rich soils.

Soil color can indicate the types of minerals present, the organic content, and seasonal water fluctuations. *Organic content* is the amount of humus, leaf mold, sawdust, and other organic material in the soil, indicating better nutrient cycling. Reddish soils are highly weathered with a high content of oxidized iron; dark or black soils indicate high organic matter; gray soils have permanently high and stagnant water tables. Mottled soils showing spots of different colors indicate a fluctuating water table or poor drainage, and thus can reflect seasonal wetness even when examined in dry periods.

Soil ecology broadly describes the biological activities of the soil. In most vegetated soils, there is a complex soil ecosystem involving plants and organic residue, and several trophic levels of bacteria, algae, fungi, protozoa, nemotodes (worms), anthropods, and more complex animals (gophers, mice, shrews, moles, woodchucks). Soils play a critical role in biogeochemical cycles.

Consistence, the degree and kind of adhesion and cohesion of the soil, is described under dry, moist, and wet conditions. Under dry and moist conditions, the hardness of the peds or the difficulty in crushing the ped by hand is noted. Under wet conditions, the stickiness and plasticity of the soil are noted. Consistence affects the workability of the soil, its ability to support loads, and its tendency to shrink and swell.

Plasticity is determined by seeing how well the soil can be shaped into a "spaghetti wire" and then how well the wire can be manipulated. It is quantitatively defined in terms of the Atterberg limits, which are a soil's *plastic limit* (the water content, in percent water, at which the soil begins to deform) and its *liquid limit* (the water content at which the soil cannot retain its shape and begins to flow). The soil's plasticity index is the liquid limit minus the plastic limit. Shrink-swell soils generally have a high plasticity index.

Permeability (or **hydraulic conductivity**) is the ease with which gases and liquids pass through a given volume of soil. It can be measured by a *percolation test* in which a 2 ft x 2 ft x 2 ft hole is filled with water and allowed to drain; the hole is filled with water again. The permeability is the distance the water drops in 1 hour; the percolation rate is the time it takes the water to drop 1 inch. Permeability is rated on a scale from rapid (greater than 6 in./hr) to slow (less than 0.2 in./hr). Coarse-grained soils (sands) have relatively large spaces between particles and thus have rapid permeability rates, whereas fine-grained soils (clays) have slow rates. The structure of fine-grained soils can affect permeability rate; the rate can be higher if there are avenues between peds for infiltration. **Soil porosity** is the percentage of the total soil volume not occupied by soil particles and indicates its water-holding capacity.

Hydric soils are those that are often saturated due to high water tables, and they exhibit the coloration and mottling typical of poorly drained soils. They are a good indicator of the presence of wetland conditions.

Reaction indicates its pH or degree of acidity or alkalinity, affecting crop production and corrosion of materials. **Salinity**, the salt content of soil, can inhibit vegetative growth.

Fertility, measured by a chemical analysis of plant nutrients, indicates the soil's fertilizer needs for supporting crop growth. *Productivity* of the soil is a measurement of the yield of a specific crop. It depends on fertility, texture, structure, and other factors, such as slope.

The **stoniness** of the soil is the amount of course fragments 10–24 inches in diameter in or on the soil. Stoniness is classified on a 0–5 scale: 0 indicates no or few stones, 4 indicates that stones make the use of machinery impractical.

The **rockiness** of the soil is the amount of the soil surface occupied by bedrock outcrops. A 0–5 scale similar to the stoniness scale is used to classify rockiness.

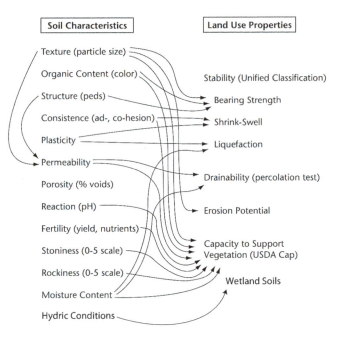

Figure 6.2 Land Use Properties of Soil.

ecology, plasticity, and permeability. These characteristics affect the soil's quality and land use potential.

Land Use Properties of Soil

Soils exhibit properties that have a significant influence on land capabilities, and they are an important consideration when planning land use. Figure 6.2 displays five important land use properties of soils and the types of soils and soil characteristics affecting their use in agricultural and urban settings. Certain soils may compress, shrink, swell, or shift, causing problems for structures. Others may drain surface water or septic effluent poorly, or they might be highly susceptible to erosion. Still others may have productive resource value—for example, as prime agricultural soils, simply to support urban vegetation, or as a property of productive wetlands.

Soil Stability: Strength and Movement

The stability of the soil involves its susceptibility to compression or settling, shrinking and swelling, and spontaneous flow. Stability determines how well the soil can support built environment structures and infrastructure. A soil's potential for settling or compression when subjected to a load depends on its **bearing strength**, which is related to the soil's bulk density or its dry weight per unit of bulk volume. In general, coarse soils, such as gravelly soils, have better bearing strength than loosely consolidated fill, water-saturated, clayey, or highly organic soils. Soil **settlement** is a particular problem on land reclaimed from lakeshores or bayshores by filling in with dredge spoils, municipal wastes, or other materials. Especially when not properly compacted and when placed on soft saturated muds, these materials will settle when supporting a load, due to their own low strength and/or the low internal cohesion. The potential settling of low-strength soils generally does not preclude construction but requires special engineering measures, such as compaction, surcharging, or the use of bearing or friction piles, to mitigate potential problems.

Shrink-swell potential depends on the soil's plasticity or water-bearing characteristics. Some clay soils (made up of such minerals as smectite or montmorillomite) will expand excessively when wetted and shrink when dried. These expansions and contractions can exert extreme pressures, sufficient to crack foundations and roadways and dislodge structures. Other soils may also expand when frozen; these *frost-heave soils* are generally fine soils that retain water. Spontaneous flow, or **liquefaction** potential, may be high where soil is made up of loosely packed, well-sorted fine-grained sands and silts, and where high water tables are prevalent. When these soils are saturated, only a portion of the load of the overlying soil and structures is carried by the grain-to-grain contact of the soil particles. The remainder of the load is supported by the buoyant force of water between the particles. When shaken by an earthquake or other impulse, the contact between the grains may be lost, and the saturated soil will behave like a liquid. Any structure resting on the soil will also move.

The Unified Soil Classification system rates soils in terms of their properties for structures and foundations, based on bearing strength and potential expansion (Table 6.1). The most important soil characteristic affecting these properties is texture, categorized by letters G (gravel), S (sand), and C (clay). Also important is the content of plastic clay and organic matter. The best engineering soils are uniformly large-particle soils without plastic clay and organic material. Clayey and organic soils rate the worst.

Drainability

The Unified Soil Classification system also rates the drainability of the soil, which is important not only for buildings and roads, but also for other land uses, such as crop production, septic and infiltration drainfields, and waste containment facilities. **Drainability** depends primarily on soil *permeability* (the ease with which fluids pass through the soil; see Box 6.1). It also depends on soil depth and the depth to the groundwater table. Generally, coarse-grained soils that have relatively large spaces between particles have rapid permeability rates, whereas fine-grained soils have slow permeability rates. Soil compaction reduces permeability and impedes drainability. Good drainage of soils is desirable for most land uses except waste or chemical containment facilities, such as sanitary landfills, lagoons, or underground storage tanks. In such cases, compacted clay or artificial liners are used to contain water drainage, which is often contaminated by waste leachate.

Onsite wastewater or septic systems and drainfields require construction permits and are usually designed by public health engineers based on soil drainability. Septic drainfields can create water quality problems in two ways. First, soil drainability is often insufficient to drain effluents, and surface seepage occurs. Second, when soil drainability is too high and/or drainfields are too close to receiving waters, insufficient filtration and biodegradation occur before effluent ends up in

TABLE 6.1 **The Unified Soil Classification System**

Soil Group	USCS Symbol	Soil Description	Allowable Bearing (lb/ft²) with Medium Compaction	Drainage* Characteristics	Frost Heave Potential	Shrink-Swell Potential
Group I Excellent	GW	Well-graded gravels, gravel sand mixtures, little or no fines	8,000	Good	Low	Low
	GP	Poorly graded gravels, gravel-sand mixtures, little or no fines	8,000	Good	Low	Low
	SW	Well-graded sands, gravelly sands, little or no fines	6,000	Good	Low	Low
	SP	Poorly graded sands, gravelly sands, little or no fines	5,000	Good	Low	Low
	GM	Silty gravels, gravel-sand-silt mixtures	4,000	Good	Medium	Low
	SM	Silty sands, sand-silt mixtures	4,000	Good	Medium	Low
Group II Fair to Good	GC	Clayey gravels, gravel-sand-clay mixtures	4,000	Medium	Medium	Low
	SC	Clayey sands, sand-clay mixtures	4,000	Medium	Medium	Low
	ML	Inorganic silts and very fine sands, rock flour, silty or clayey fine sands, or clayey silts with slight plasticity	2,000	Medium	High	Low
	CL	Inorganic clays of low to medium plasticity, gravelly clays, sandy clays, silty clays, lean clays	2,000	Medium	Medium	Medium
Group III Poor	CH	Inorganic clays of high plasticity, fat clays	2,000	Poor	Medium	High
	MH	Inorganic silts, micaceous or diatomaceous fine sandy or silty soils, elastic silts	2,000	Poor	High	High
Group IV	OL	Organic silts and organic silty clays of low plasticity	400	Poor	Medium	Medium
Unsatisfactory	OH	Organic clays of medium to high plasticity, organic silts	0	Unsatisfactory	Medium	High
	PT	Peat and other highly organic soils	0	Unsatisfactory	Medium	High

* Percolation rate for good drainage is > 4 inches/hour, medium drainage is 2–4 inches/hour, poor is < 2 inches/hour

G—gravelly soils > 2 mm
S—sandy soils
M—fine inorganic sand and silt
C—inorganic clay
O—organic silts and clays
PT—peat, highly organic soils

W—uniform particle size, absence of clay
C—uniform particle size, binding clay fraction
P—non-uniform particle size, absence of clay
L—low placticity (liquid limit < 50)
H—high plasticity (liquid limit > 50)

surface waters or groundwater. (Onsite wastewater systems and soils are discussed later.)

Erodibility

A soil's **erodibility** is another important land use property. Soil loss through erosion on agricultural and silvicultural lands can reduce productivity; erosion from

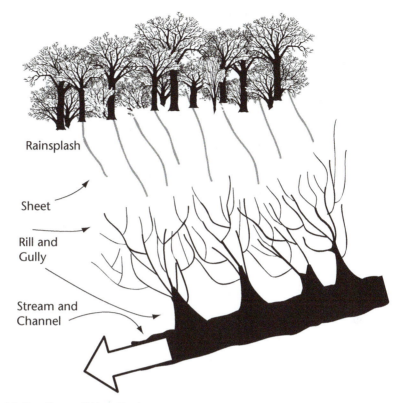

Figure 6.3 Four Types of Water Erosion.

these lands and from construction sites often leads to sedimentation of water bodies. The four types of water erosion are schematically depicted in Figure 6.3:

- **Rainsplash erosion** results from the direct impact of falling drops of rain on soil particles. The impact dislodges soil particles and splashes them into the air. The dislodged particles can then be easily transported by surface runoff.
- **Sheet erosion** removes a layer of exposed surface soil by the action of rainfall splash and runoff. The water moves in broad sheets over the land and is not confined to small depressions.
- **Rill and gully erosion** develops as flowing runoff concentrates in grooves, called rills, which cut several inches into the soil surface. Rills grow to deeper and wider gullies, where concentrated water flow moves over the soil.
- **Stream and channel erosion** involves increased volume and velocity of runoff , which can cause erosion of the stream bottom, especially channel banks.

The loss of soil depends on soil type and, more importantly, on the surface slope (which affects the speed and erosive force of the runoff) and the vegetative cover (which intercepts raindrops, decreases runoff by increasing infiltration, and slows

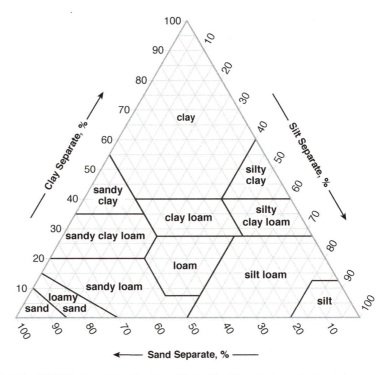

Figure 6.4 The USDA Textural Classification of Soils. The triangle shows textural classes graphically depending on composition of sand, silt, and clay. (*Source:* USDA, http://soils.usda.gov/).

what runoff remains). Figure 6.4 shows the U.S. Department of Agriculture (USDA) Textural Triangle, for classifying soil texture according to the composition of sand, silt, and clay. The most erodible soils are unvegetated silt loams, because of their high surface runoff potential due to their clay content, and a low resistance to erosion due to their sand and silt content. The soil erodibility factor and index, as well as the use of the Universal Soil Loss Equation (USLE) to estimate annual loss of soil from a parcel of land, are discussed later in this chapter.

Capacity to Support Vegetation

The capacity of a type of soil to support agriculture, silviculture, and urban vegetation is another land use property. The top horizons are critical for vegetation, as roots for even large trees extend only about 18 inches in depth (see Figure 6.1). A number of factors affect the agricultural capability of soils, including fertility, reaction, texture, bulk density, drainability, hydric conditions, stoniness, rockiness, and erodibility (see Box 6.1). Prime agricultural soils are fertile, well-drained soils on level or gently sloping lands; these areas generally include floodplains, river valleys, and certain grassy plains. Flood deposit plains have the best potential with their alluvial (water-deposited) soils, flat topography, and limited utility for other uses. The USDA Agricultural Land Capability system considers these factors in rating cropland (Box 6.2). Urban uses of soil, including landscaping, park and

BOX 6.2—The USDA Agricultural Capability Classification

The USDA classifies lands based on the capacity of their soils to produce crops without deterioration. The system takes into account soil types, slope and drainage of the land, the erodibility and rockiness of the soil, and other factors. Land is classified into the eight categories. The higher the number, the more severe are the limitations for agricultural use. Often, specific limitations are identified by a letter following the number: e = erosion, w = wetness, s = internal soil problems, and c = climatic limitations. Classes 1 and 2 are "prime agricultural lands." The capability classification is an important input in the Land Evaluation and Site Assessment (LESA) system. Here are the categories:

Class 1: Few limitations for crop production

Class 2: Moderate limitations that reduce crop choice

Class 3: Severe limitations that reduce crop choice

Class 4: Very severe limitations that reduce crop choice

Class 5: Moderate limitations that make soils unsuitable for cultivation

Class 6: Severe limitations that make soils unsuitable

Class 7: Very severe limitations that make soils unsuitable

Class 8: Limitations that preclude commercial crop production

street boulevard management, community gardens, and urban forestry, must also address soil quality. The removal, compaction, filling, and contamination of urban soils all affect productive use.

During the past several decades, suburban sprawl has converted millions of acres of prime farmland soils to development. Farmland preservation programs aim to protect agricultural lands, and they use the Land Evaluation and Site Assessment (LESA) system to evaluate farmland. Agricultural lands, LESA, urban soils, and urban agriculture are discussed in later sections.

Wetland Soils

As explained in Box 6.1, hydric soils indicate poor drainability. These soils are formed under conditions of saturation, flooding, or ponding long enough to develop anaerobic (without oxygen) conditions in the A and B horizons. Most soils are aerated and contain oxygen, which is important for aerobic microorganisms critical for certain crop production and waste assimilation. In hydric soils, water saturation forces out air, thus creating anaerobic conditions. A combination of the hydric soil, hydrophytic vegetation, and hydrology properties defines wetlands under federal and state wetland conservation regulations (see Chapter 10). The NRCS has produced manuals to help identify hydric soil conditions in the field (USDA, NRSC, 2010).

Soil Quality and Soil Degradation

Soil quality is the fitness of a soil to function within its surroundings, support plant and animal productivity, maintain or enhance water and air quality, and support human health and habitation. The quality of a specific soil depends on the use to which it is put. Soil quality is evaluated by monitoring several indicators chosen

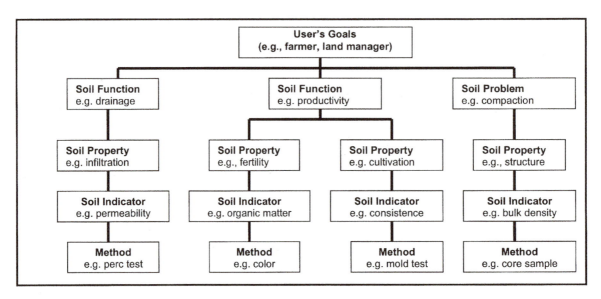

Figure 6.5 Chart for selecting Soil Quality Indicators.

to reflect the specific function and use of the soil. Indicators can show the health or degradation of the soil, point to improvement strategies, and provide the focus for monitoring change.

Soil degradation occurs in many ways. Most causes are initiated or exacerbated by human activities. Erosion is probably the most important soil degradation process, removing potentially tons per acre per year from sites denuded of vegetation, either for crop production or land development. Grading for land development, mining, and other activities often removes valuable topsoil. Soil can be contaminated with pollutants, salts, or acidic or alkaline conditions that limit their useful functions. Soil can be compacted by human use, increasing bulk density and reducing drainability and capacity for root growth.

Soil quality indicators should be measurable, meaningful, and manageable, and should be determined by the user's objectives. Figure 6.5 is a flowchart for selecting soil quality indicators based on a user's goals. Many of these indicators can be measured and monitored in the field. There are several field methods for measuring biological, chemical, and physical soil quality indicators. For example, an organic smell and visual inspection of the soil for such fauna as earthworms, fungi, and larvae indicates a biologically healthy soil. Soil pH (acidity and alkalinity), salinity, and nitrate content are common chemical indicators. Infiltration rates, bulk density, and visual signs of erosion are physical characteristics.

Indicators should be used to identify soil degradation problems and to formulate plans for soil improvement. Monitoring indicators over time shows the effectiveness of improvement plans. For example, low organic matter reduces fertility and indicates poor structure. Soil amendments can increase organic matter, thereby improving soil functions. Bulk density indicates soil compaction, which limits drainage, root growth, and gas exchange. Aeration methods can counter the impacts of compaction. Monitoring bulk density can show the effectiveness of aeration methods and frequency. For more information on soil quality, see http://soils.usda.gov/sqi/.

Soil Surveys and Interpretive Soils Mapping

Soil surveys provide the best available information on soils for land planning. The USDA Natural Resources Conservation Service (NRCS, formerly the Soil Conservation Service, SCS) has been producing soil surveys since the turn of the last century, and the process is continuous. Every year surveys are being revised to meet current needs, and new areas are being surveyed. Although soil surveys in the United States date back to 1896, the modern soil survey dates from about 1956 and reflects improved and standardized mapping and interpretation techniques. For a list of all current and historic soil surveys by state, see http://soils.usda.gov /survey/printed_surveys/. They were available only in print form until the 1990s. Figure 6.6 shows not only that coverage is nearly complete across the contiguous 48 states, but also that the form has changed from print to spatial and tabular data. The print soil survey is becoming quickly obsolete. The NRCS Web Soil Survey now provides interactive access to local soil data and maps, and its Soil Data Mart provides downloadable soil survey spatial and tabular data for use in GIS.

To get a feel for the soil survey, let's first look at the contents of print version of the modern soil survey. Then we'll turn to the Web Soil Survey and its use for interpretive soils mapping.

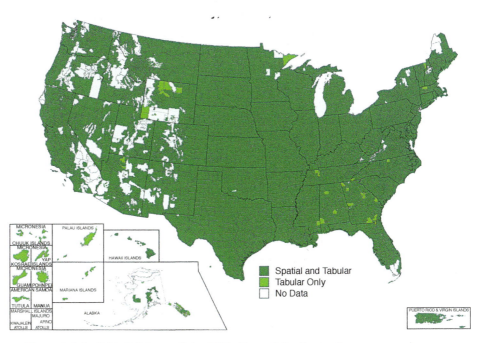

Figure 6.6 Available Soil Survey Data, 2011. (*Source:* http://websoilsurvey.nrcs.usda.gov /DataAvailability/SoilDataAvailabilityMap.pdf.)

The modern print soil surveys include three useful components:

- *Text* describes the county, its general 5–10 types of soils (called *associations*), the 15–20 more specific types of soils (called *series*), and the 40–60 soil series-slope combinations (called *map units*).
- *Maps* show the location of the soils by map units or symbols, which denote soil series and complexes at different slopes. The maps are usually produced at a scale of 1:15,840 or 1:24,000. As shown in Figure 6.7, aerial photographs are used as the base map, and the soils polygons and surface features, like roads and drainages, are included in the soils overlay. The polygon symbols on the soils overlay refer to the map units; the number denotes the soils series or complex, the letter denotes the slope.
- *Tables* provide detailed information for each series and map unit. The tables include engineering, physical, and chemical properties and water characteristics, as well as interpretive suitability and limitation information, such as expected yields for various crops, woodland productivity and limitations, wildlife habitat potential, potential sources of construction materials, and limitations for building site development and sanitary facilities (e.g., septic systems, landfills, etc.). In the Montgomery County, Virginia, Soil Survey, there are 55 map units rated under each table heading, which is fairly typical (USDA, SCS 1985).

Although soil surveys are the best source of soils and related information, they have some limitations. They are accurate only to about 2 acres. As a result, for site-level work, it is necessary to investigate soil conditions in the field.

The Web Soil Survey and Interpretive Soil Suitability Mapping

This book's first edition described a method for using the soil survey to produce interpretive soil suitability maps. By combining the base map of map units (without reference aerial photo) and the tables on soil properties and limitations, one could produce interpretive maps for any factor included in the tables. The book website (www.envirolanduse.org) describes that manual method.

All of this changed, however, with NRCS's development of the **Web Soil Survey (WSS)** in 2008. The website allows users to zoom in on an area of interest (AOI), map the soil units of the AOI, access detailed information on those units, create interpretive maps for any of the suitability and property factors included for that survey, and produce instantaneous detailed PDF documents reporting on that analysis, including scaled maps and explanatory text.

There are three basic steps in using the Web Soil Survey (USDA, NRCS 2010; see http://websoilsurvey.nrcs.usda.gov and tutorial):

1. Identify an area of interest (AOI) by first using Search for the location (state, county, address, etc.) (Figure 6.8A). Then use the zoom function to find your site. Use the AOI tool to set the boundaries of your AOI (Figure 6.8B). Once the AOI is set, subsequent viewing and exploring

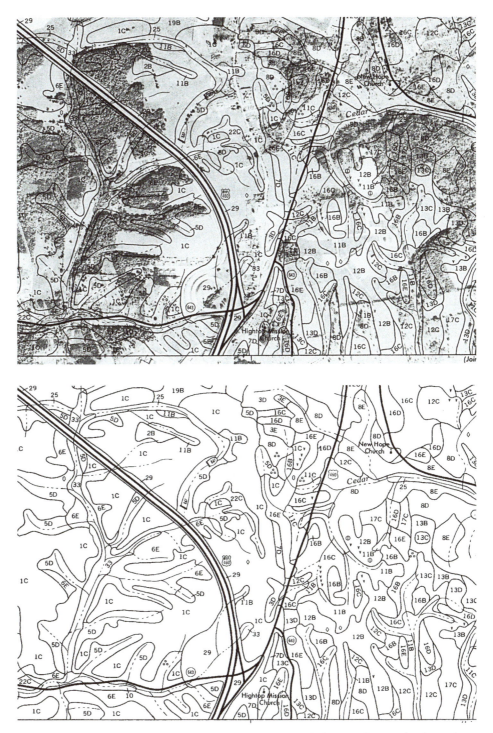

Figure 6.7 A Print Soil Survey Map. The base map is an aerial photo, and an overlay shows the map units, roads, and drainage. (*Source:* USDA, SCS 1985.)

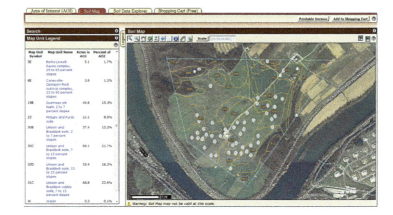

(A)

(B)

Figure 6.8 Using the Web Soil Survey. A: The search page. B: Area of interest designator with Whitethorne site AOI in Montgomery County, Virginia. (*Source:* NRCS Web Soil Survey, http://websoilsurvey.nrcs.usda.gov/app /HomePage.htm.)

Figure 6.9 A WSS Soil Map for the Whitethorne, Virginia, Site AOI.

will focus on this AOI. View the soil map units and their descriptions for the AOI by clicking the Soil Map button (Figure 6.9).

2. Explore soil data by clicking the Soil Data Explorer button, then either the Soil Suitabilities and Limitations button or the Soil Properties button. Figure 6.10 shows all the pull-down menus and lists of suitability and property categories available to explore for the AOI.

3. Select the suitability/property category of interest, and the WSS will automatically map the AOI with category data, replacing the map unit designations with colors representing the suitability/property category (Figure 6.11).

4. Decide which categories you wish to include in the soils report, and click Add to Shopping Cart. Once you have added the analyses you wish, click Shopping Cart (Free) and the WSS immediately produces a professional Soil Report for the AOI, including the analyses you have selected. Figure 6.12 shows the custom report map of limitations for dwellings with basements for the Whitethorne property AOI.

Suitabilities and Limitations Ratings ②

Open All | Close All ⑦

- Building Site Development ⑦ ⑧
- Construction Materials ⑦ ⑧
- Disaster Recovery Planning ⑦ ⑧
- Land Classifications ⑦ ⑧
- Land Management ⑦ ⑧
- Military Operations ⑦ ⑧
- Recreational Development ⑦ ⑧
- Sanitary Facilities ⑦ ⑧
- Vegetative Productivity ⑦ ⑧
- Waste Management ⑦ ⑧
- Water Management ⑦ ⑧

Properties and Qualities Ratings ②

Open All | Close All ⑦

- Soil Chemical Properties ⑦ ⑧
- Soil Erosion Factors ⑦ ⑧
- Soil Physical Properties ⑦ ⑧
- Soil Qualities and Features ⑦ ⑧
- Water Features ⑦ ⑧

Soil Chemical Properties ⑦ ⑧
- Calcium Carbonate (CaCO3)
- Cation-Exchange Capacity (CEC-7)
- Effective Cation-Exchange Capacity (ECEC)
- Electrical Conductivity (EC)
- Gypsum
- pH (1 to 1 Water)
- Sodium Adsorption Ratio (SAR)

Building Site Development ⑦ ⑧
- Corrosion of Concrete
- Corrosion of Steel
- Dwellings With Basements
- Dwellings Without Basements
- Lawns, Landscaping, and Golf Fairways
- Local Roads and Streets
- Shallow Excavations
- Small Commercial Buildings

Construction Materials ⑦ ⑧
- Gravel Source
- Roadfill Source
- Sand Source
- Source of Reclamation Material
- Topsoil Source

Disaster Recovery Planning ⑦ ⑧
- Catastrophic Mortality, Large Animal Disposal, Pit
- Catastrophic Mortality, Large Animal Disposal, Trench
- Clay Liner Material Source
- Composting Facility - Subsurface
- Composting Facility - Surface
- Composting Medium and Final Cover
- Rubble and Debris Disposal, Large-Scale Event

Land Classifications ⑦ ⑧
- Conservation Tree and Shrub Group
- Ecological Site ID
- Ecological Site Name
- Farmland Classification
- Forage Suitability Group ID (Component Table)
- Hydric Rating by Map Unit
- Irrigated Capability Class
- Irrigated Capability Subclass
- Nonirrigated Capability Class
- Nonirrigated Capability Subclass
- Soil Taxonomy Classification

Land Management ⑦ ⑧
- Construction Limitations for Haul Roads and Log Landings
- Erosion Hazard (Off-Road, Off-Trail)
- Erosion Hazard (Road, Trail)
- Harvest Equipment Operability
- Mechanical Site Preparation (Deep)
- Mechanical Site Preparation (Surface)
- Potential for Damage by Fire
- Potential for Seedling Mortality
- Soil Rutting Hazard
- Suitability for Hand Planting
- Suitability for Log Landings
- Suitability for Mechanical Planting
- Suitability for Roads (Natural Surface)

Military Operations ⑦ ⑧

Recreational Development ⑦ ⑧
- Camp Areas
- Off-Road Motorcycle Trails
- Paths and Trails
- Picnic Areas
- Playgrounds

Sanitary Facilities ⑦ ⑧
- Daily Cover for Landfill
- Sanitary Landfill (Area)
- Sanitary Landfill (Trench)
- Septic Tank Absorption Fields
- Sewage Lagoons

Vegetative Productivity ⑦ ⑧
- Crop Productivity Index
- Forest Productivity (Cubic Feet per Acre per Year)
- Forest Productivity (Tree Site Index)
- Iowa Corn Suitability Rating
- Range Production (Favorable Year)
- Range Production (Normal Year)
- Range Production (Unfavorable Year)
- Yields of Irrigated Crops (Component)
- Yields of Irrigated Crops (Map Unit)
- Yields of Non-Irrigated Crops (Component)
- Yields of Non-Irrigated Crops (Map Unit)

Waste Management ⑦ ⑧
- Disposal of Wastewater by Rapid Infiltration
- Land Application of Municipal Sewage Sludge
- Manure and Food-Processing Waste
- Overland Flow Treatment of Wastewater
- Slow Rate Treatment of Wastewater

Water Management ⑦ ⑧
- Embankments, Dikes, and Levees
- Excavated Ponds (Aquifer-Fed)
- Pond Reservoir Areas

Soil Erosion Factors ⑦ ⑧
- K Factor, Rock Free
- K Factor, Whole Soil
- T Factor
- Wind Erodibility Group
- Wind Erodibility Index

Soil Physical Properties ⑦ ⑧
- Available Water Capacity
- Available Water Supply, 0 to 100 cm
- Available Water Supply, 0 to 150 cm
- Available Water Supply, 0 to 25 cm
- Available Water Supply, 0 to 50 cm
- Bulk Density, 15 Bar
- Bulk Density, One-Tenth Bar
- Bulk Density, One-Third Bar
- Linear Extensibility
- Liquid Limit
- Organic Matter
- Percent Clay
- Percent Sand
- Percent Silt
- Plasticity Index
- Saturated Hydraulic Conductivity (Ksat)
- Saturated Hydraulic Conductivity (Ksat), Standard Classes
- Surface Texture
- Water Content, 15 Bar
- Water Content, One-Third Bar

Soil Qualities and Features ⑦ ⑧
- AASHTO Group Classification (Surface)
- Depth to a Selected Soil Restrictive Layer
- Depth to Any Soil Restrictive Layer
- Drainage Class
- Frost Action
- Frost-Free Days
- Hydrologic Soil Group
- Map Unit Name
- Parent Material Name
- Representative Slope
- Unified Soil Classification (Surface)

Water Features ⑦ ⑧
- Depth to Water Table
- Flooding Frequency Class
- Ponding Frequency Class

Figure 6.10 WSS Full Listing of Soil Suitabilities and Limitations Ratings and Properties and Qualities Ratings Under Data Explorer.

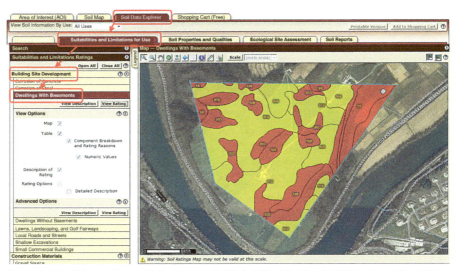

Figure 6.11 WSS Dwellings with Basements Soil Suitability Map for the Whitethorne Site AOI.

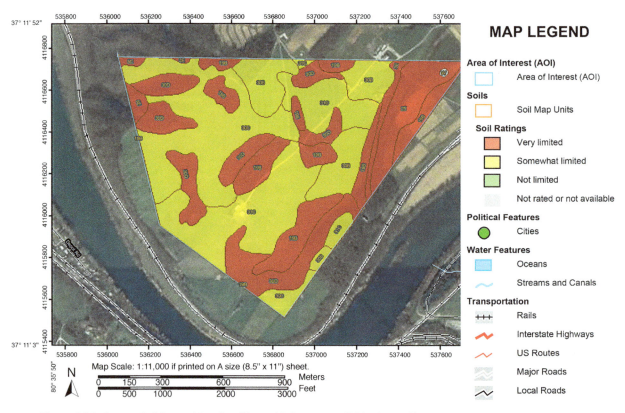

Figure 6.12 Custom Soil Report Map, Dwellings with Basements, Whitethorne Site.

Geospatial Soil Survey Data

The Web Soil Survey has transformed access to soils maps and information in the U.S. However, the most important use of soils information is in land analysis, which integrates soils and other spatial information. As we know, this is best done in geographic information systems (GIS), which require geospatial data to form soils data layers. The WSS not only provides detailed soil reports for the specific area of interest, but the Download Soils Data button lets users order spatial and tabular data for the AOI. Data are ordered, and then the user receives an e-mail with a link to the processed data.

In addition, the NRCS provides free downloadable county-level spatial and tabular soil survey data from the Soil Survey Geographic Database (SSURGO) through its Soil Data Mart (http://soildatamart.nrcs.usda.gov/). Data are available for most counties of the country (see Figure 6.6). Users identify their county, select the data format (shapefiles, coverage, or interchange) and coordinate system, and submit the data request. As with the WSS, requests are processed and the user receives an e-mail with a link to the downloaded data files.

Soil Factors for Onsite Wastewater and Land Application of Wastes

Soil considerations are very important in land disposal and the application of wastes. Soil drainability, ability to absorb and treat wastes, and other soil factors affect a site's capacity for onsite wastewater systems, waste lagoons, waste landfills, and land application of manure fertilizer and biosolids.

Waste Landfills

Sanitary landfills for municipal wastes are designed to contain waste materials and leached liquids. Therefore, they are designed for zero drainage from the contained landfill. In the past, this was achieved by using low-permeability compacted clay as a landfill lining material. However, continued leaching problems led to federal landfill standards (U.S. EPA 1993a, 1993b), requiring the following:

- **Location restrictions** to avoid faults, wetlands, floodplains, and unsuitable soils.
- **Composite flexible impervious liners** overlaying 2 ft of compacted clay soil to protect groundwater and underlying soil.
- **Leachate collection and removal systems**, sitting on top of the liner and removing leachate for treatment and disposal.
- **Operating practices**, including compacting and covering waste frequently with several inches of soil to control odors, litter, and pests, and protect public health.
- **Groundwater monitoring** with wells to determine whether wastes escape from landfill.
- **Closure and postclosure care**, including covering landfill and maintaining site.
- **Financial assurance** for operation, corrective action, closure, and postclosure care.

Table 6.2 shows that despite increased recycling, composting, and combustion of wastes through the years, landfills were still used for 54% of municipal wastes in 2009 (U.S. EPA 2009). The good news is that despite growing population, discards to landfills have declined since 1990. Net material waste generation per capita is measured in pounds per person-day (lb/p-d). In 2009, at 2.88 lb/p-d, it was the lowest since 1960, even lower than 1960 if energy recovery is taken into account (2.36 lb/p-d).

Land Application of Wastes

In addition to landfilling municipal solid wastes, there are other practices for land application of wastes and wastewaters. These include stabilized sludge from

TABLE 6.2 U.S. Generation, Recovery, and Landfill Discard of Municipal Solid Waste, 1960–2009

Activity	1960	1970	1980	1990	2000	2005	2007	2009
Generation, million tons (Mt)	88.1	121.1	151.6	208.3	242.5	252.4	255.0	243.0
Generation, pounds/person-day	2.68	3.25	3.66	4.57	4.72	4.67	4.63	4.34
Recovery for recycling, Mt	5.6	8.0	14.5	29.0	53.0	59.3	63.1	61.3
Recovery for composting*, Mt	~ 0	~ 0	~ 0	4.2	16.5	20.6	21.7	20.8
Total materials recovery, Mt	5.6	8.0	14.5	33.2	69.5	79.9	84.8	82.0
Recovery, pounds/person-day	0.17	0.22	0.35	0.73	1.35	1.48	1.54	1.46
Percent of generation recycled	6.4%	6.6%	9.6%	16.0%	28.6%	31.6%	33.3%	33.8%
Combustion w/ energy recovery[†]	0.0	0.4	2.7	29.7	33.7	31.6	32.0	29.0
Discards to landfill, other[‡]	82.5	112.7	134.4	145.3	139.4	140.9	138.2	131.9

* Composting of yard trimmings, food scraps, and other MSW organic material. Does not include backyard composting.
† Includes combustion of MSW in mass burn or refuse-derived fuel form, and combustion with energy recovery of source separated materials in MSW (e.g., wood pallets, tire-derived fuel).
‡ Discards after recovery minus combustion with energy recovery. Discards include combustion without energy recovery.
Source: U.S. EPA 2010.

municipal sewage treatment plants, manure wastes from confined animal facilities, and other wastes and wastewaters. Of course, we still have an environmental legacy from past sins of illegal land disposal of wastes and hazardous materials, which continues to be a focus of remediation and recovery programs, such as the EPA's Superfund cleanup program. But land application of organic wastes from sewage treatment and animal waste treatment are legal and regulated.

Sewage Sludge Biosolids

The EPA regulates land application of stabilized sludge from municipal sewage treatment facilities under section 503 of the Clean Water Act, according to rules promulgated in the 1990s after Congress banned ocean dumping of sewage sludges. At least 60% of biosolids generated by sewage treatment are applied to the land as fertilizer and soil amendment to promote soil productivity. These biosolids must meet EPA criteria for treating disease-carrying organisms and stabilizing organic materials. Since anything flushed down the toilet can end up in sewage biosolids, there have been concerns about risks of soil contamination with heavy metals and toxic chemicals.

In 2002, the National Research Council (2002) concluded that there was continuing uncertainty about adverse effects, even though there was little documented evidence of a problem. In an assessment study, the EPA was itself critical of current practices, including a reduction in enforcement of the regulations. By 2007, it became clear that the capacity of the land to absorb biosolids depends on the soil's capacity to absorb potential toxins, and this varies by soil composition. In 2007, a research committee representing northeastern states issued guidelines for land application of biosolids tailored to soils in the Northeast (Northeast Research Committee on Land Application 2007).

Animal Manures and Nutrient Management Plans

It is common practice for farmers to apply animal manures to the land as a fertilizer and soil amendment, but the process must be managed, in order to prevent excessive application and resulting contamination of soil and runoff. This is especially true for large confined animal facilities, like feedlots, that generate huge quantities of waste. These wastes must first be stabilized, usually in collection and treatment lagoons. It is critical for the application of stabilized waste fertilizer to be determined by a Nutrient Management Plan (NMP) based on the yields of the crop (and thus the uptake of the fertilizer) and the type of soil. In Virginia, nutrient management standards and criteria require that NMPs be specific to the soil types and conditions given in the soil survey (Virginia Department of Conservation and Recreation 2005).

Onsite Wastewater Systems

Onsite wastewater or septic systems are used by about 26 million, or 20%, of all U.S. housing units (U.S. EPA 2008). This ranges from more than 50% of Vermont households to 10% of California's. Nearly half of all septic systems are in southern states. Figure 6.13 shows a conventional onsite system. There are two main components: (1) a septic tank, which provides primary treatment by removing most settlable and floatable material, as well as some digestion of organic matter, although this is limited by the oxygen-poor (anaerobic) conditions; and (2) a subsurface wastewater infiltration system (SWIS), a drainfield or leachfield that uses soils to absorb, filter, and biologically process the septic tank effluent under

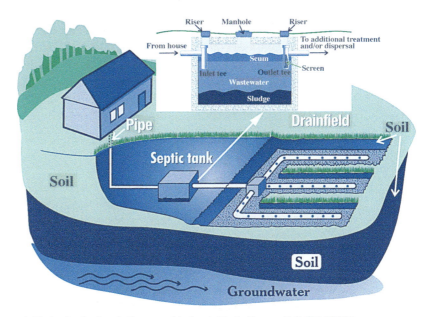

Figure 6.13 An Onsite Septic System with Septic Tank. (*Source:* U.S. EPA 2008.)

aerobic conditions. The effluent contains remaining organic matter, nitrogen and phosphorus nutrients, and possibly pathogens (disease-causing organisms).

These systems have advantages in areas not served by central sewers because they are simple and inexpensive, they are relatively low-maintenance, and they return nutrients to the soil. They can remove 90–99% of organics, pathogenic organisms, suspended solids, toxic chemicals and metals, and phosphorus (but only 10–20% of nitrogen). They can work effectively for more than 20 years placed in areas with appropriate soils and hydraulic capacities; when located an appropriate distance from wells and water bodies; and properly designed, installed, and maintained. However, this is not always the case.

Septic System Failure

A 1997 U.S. Census survey estimated that more than 400,000 homes had septic system breakdowns during a 3-month period in 1997. The EPA estimates failure rates at 10–20%, not including undetected systems that may be contaminating surface and groundwater. States with the highest failure rates include Minnesota (50–70%), West Virginia (60%), Louisiana (50%), and Missouri (30–50%) (Angoli 2001; U.S. EPA 2002).

Ineffective and failed septic systems result in contaminated ground and surface waters and public health problems. In 1996, the EPA estimated that 500 communities had public health problems caused by failed septic systems. Septic systems are cited as the third most common source of groundwater contamination. Systems contribute to surface water contamination as well, especially where they are located close to riparian, lake, and coastal waters. A study of Buttermilk Bay in Massachusetts found that 74% of the nitrogen entering the bay came from ineffective and failing septic systems (U.S. EPA 2002).

Because of the level of use and rates of failure, onsite wastewater septic systems are a major environmental problem in urbanizing areas, as well as recreation areas. Nationally, they are second only to underground storage tanks as a source of groundwater pollution. In some urbanizing areas, onsite systems were thought of as a temporary measure until centralized sewage systems were built. However, the high costs of service extension and other factors have made these systems more permanent. As a result, public management of these systems has not been effective, and many communities have suffered the consequences.

Siting and System Design

The proper siting and design of new conventional systems require an estimate of wastewater flow and a site and soils assessment. Soils are the heart of the treatment system. They must have sufficient permeability, hydraulic capacity, and depth to bedrock and water table to provide the time for biological digestion and dispersal of the septic tank effluent. Other important characteristics include topography, surface drainage, vegetation, and proximity to surface waters, wells, wetlands, rock outcrops, and property lines. Soil investigations usually employ test pits or borings to determine soil depth, horizons, texture, structure, color, consistence, and redoximorphic features. Redoximorphic features are iron modules and mottles that form in seasonally saturated soils, which obviously are not good for absorption fields.

Finally, soil investigation measures infiltration, or the rate water is accepted by the soil, and hydraulic conductivity, or the rate water is transmitted through the soil. These measurements are not easy to obtain. The long-used percolation test measures the rate at which water drops in a 2-ft-square hole (see Box 6.1). However, the test is flawed primarily because it is a snapshot in time, and it has been replaced by detailed descriptions of the soil profile that indicate longer-term conditions.

Improved designs and new technologies have enhanced the effectiveness and longevity of onsite systems. These include redundant or reserve drainfields, sand/media filters, enhanced nutrient removal, sequenced batch reactors, and disinfection (see Fieden and Winkler 2006). Decentralized community-scaled systems, such as cluster systems or septic tank effluent pumping (STEP) or gravity (STEG) systems, offer attractive alternatives to both onsite systems and centralized sewers. STEP systems have conventional septic tanks, but effluent is collected and piped to central or package plant treatment rather than discharged to the soil (English and Yaeger 2002; U.S. EPA 2000).

Decentralized Wastewater Systems and Land Use

Construction of onsite wastewater systems is generally permitted by local public health departments on a site-by-site basis. However, these systems have environmental and land use implications. Onsite wastewater systems not only *allow* dispersed development where centralized sewer extensions are not cost-effective (usually less than 50 housing units per sewer mile), but these systems often *require* dispersed development to provide the land area necessary for the size and soil requirements of effluent drainfields. As a result, they can inhibit denser and more walkable rural-cluster developments. As a major source of groundwater and shoreline pollution, decentralized systems must be planned for and managed for environmental protection.

The allowance, location, construction, and management of decentralized wastewater systems should be controlled not only by public health requirements, but also by land use and watershed planning conditions. This is especially true where development sites are some distance from central sewers and walkable densities are desired, where soils are unfavorable for drainfields, and/or where there the quality of proximate receiving waters is nitrogen limiting (see Chapter 7). Watershed planning goes beyond a site-by-site approach and provides a broader geographic perspective for the collective decentralized wastewater system, including cumulative impacts on ground and surface waters. Land use development plans should incorporate infrastructure requirements, including centralized wastewater systems and decentralized systems only as needed. Dependence on decentralized systems should not preclude more livable mixed-use and clustered development. Innovative designs, like cluster and STEP systems, allow denser development.

Figure 6.14 shows the Village at Tom's Creek, a walkable cluster development in Blacksburg (VA) that is served by an effective STEP/STEG system. In such

Figure 6.14 The Village at Tom's Creek, Blacksburg, Virginia. This is a walkable cluster development with a septic tank effluent pump and gravity (STEP/STEG) system. Effluent is pumped to a central sewer or package plant in small pipes. (*Source:* Gay and Neel, Inc.; The Village at Tom's Creek, http://www.villageattomscreek.com. Used with permission.)

systems, each unit has a septic tank, but no soil drainfield. Septic tank effluent is pumped to a package treatment plant or a central sewer. Because solids are removed in the tanks, the pipes, pumping requirements, and package plant requirements are much smaller than conventional sewerage, and their location does not depend on gravity flow.

Managing Decentralized Systems

An effective community management program for onsite systems includes clear program goals, public education, technical standards, monitoring and maintenance, certification of providers, enforcement mechanisms, funding mechanisms, and program evaluation (U.S. EPA 2002). Feiden and Winkler (2006) describe different management models, from more laissez-faire reliance on private landowners, to technical assistance and education, to government inspection with land owner response, to government ownership and maintenance of onsite and decentralized systems. In this last approach, landowners would pay a wastewater service fee similar to what users of central sewerage pay.

Soil Erosion and Assessment

Soil erosion is a worldwide problem, caused by wind or water and accelerated by the removal of vegetation. Erosion threatens agricultural production capacity, and it is the major source of damaging sediment in rivers, lakes, and estuaries. Figure 6.15, from the National Resources Inventory (NRI), shows that wind erosion and sheet and rill erosion estimates declined from 3.06 billion tons per year in 1982 to 1.73 billion tons in 2007 (USDA, NRCS 2009). Most of this reduction came from a drop in erosion on highly erodible land (HEL), much of which was taken out of production by the federal Conservation Reserve Program (CRP). Under this program, farmers are paid a benefit not to farm highly erodible lands (see Chapter 15).

Soil Erosion Assessment Using the Revised Universal Soil Loss Equation

The basis for most assessments of soil erosion is the **Universal Soil Loss Equation (USLE)**, originally developed by W. H. Wischmeier and D. D. Smith (1960) from decades of data measured on experimental agricultural plots in several states. In the early 1990s, the USLE was revised (RUSLE), fine-tuning some of the parameter values and improving applications on nonagricultural lands. It was further revised in 2001 (RUSLE2) and converted to a software package. It went through further refinements in 2005, 2008, and 2010 and now better represents the effects of perennial vegetation and the sequence of runoff events.

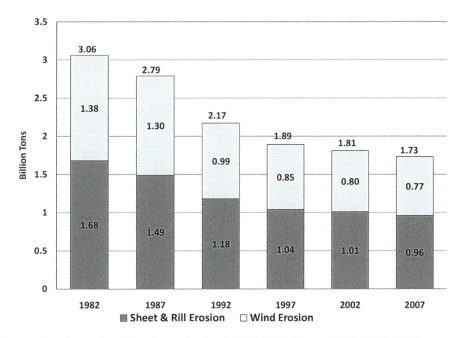

Figure 6.15 The Decline of Erosion on Cropland, 1982–2007. (*Source:* USDA, NRCS 2009.)

The RUSLE calculates the expected annual potential interill-rill soil loss per acre, based on climate, soil, topography, and land use, the latter including cover-management practices and supporting practices like conservation tillage. This is the RUSLE equation:

$$A = r \times k \times l \times s \times c \times p$$

where
A = average annual soil loss in tons per acre ($t/a/y$)
r = rainfall/runoff erosivity
k = soil erodibility
l = slope length = at 72.6 ft
s = slope steepness = 1 at 9% slope
c = cover-management = 1 for continuous cultivated fallow condition
p = supporting practices = 1 for no supporting practices

The ($r \times k$) factor is the unit plot soil loss in tons/acre-year for a standard topography (l = 76.6 ft, s = 9%), continuous cultivated fallow field condition, and no supporting practices. The other factors are dimensionless, with values of 1 for assumed standard conditions.

The erosivity factor r depends on local climatic rainfall patterns and ranges from 6 in arid Las Vegas to 120 in Minneapolis to 270 in Dallas to 630 in tropical storm-prone New Orleans. The assessment yields best results for areas with annual rainfall greater than 20 inches. The erodibility k depends on soil texture, structure, organic matter, and permeability or runoff rate. Typical k values are:

- 0.1–0.2 for clay (although it has high runoff rate, it is tightly bound)
- 0.05–0.15 for sand (low runoff rate and heavy texture size)
- 0.3–0.5 for silt loam
- 0.4–0.6 for silt (the most erodible combination of runoff rate, binding, and particle size)

Medium texture soils yield the best results. RUSLE should not be used for highly organic soils.

Combined factors s and l range in value from about 0.1 for flatter, shorter slopes to 6.0 for steeper, longer slopes. The RUSLE assessment is most reliable for 3–20% slopes 50–300 ft long. It is not reliable for slopes >100% (45 degrees) and >1000 ft long.

Factor c is the most dominant, ranging from 1 for cultivated fallow conditions to 0.004 for established grass meadow to 0.0001 for undisturbed forest with 75–100% canopy and 90–100% litter. For cultivated cropland, it incorporates management methods like conservation tillage. Construction sites with no mulch have a c = 1.0, but can be reduced to 0.2 with 1 ton per acre straw mulch and to 0.08 with 7 tons/acre wood chips. The assessment yields best results for cultivated cropland, moderately good results for disturbed sites (like construction, deforested, or mined sites), and acceptable results for hay pasture.

Factor p ranges from about 0.1 to 1.0 and includes the use of contouring or strips, buffers, and barriers.

RUSLE2 Computer Software

The U.S. Department of Agriculture has helped advance the precision and use of the RUSLE equation by developing software and databases that can perform the assessment for most locations and applicable land uses. The first edition of this book presented information to perform a manual calculation of the equation for given conditions. The relevant tables and graphs for factor values, and an example of the manual calculation, are reproduced on the book website (www.enviroland use.org). First-time users should try this manual method, because it more transparently steps through the calculation and the factors influencing soil loss, even though it is more tedious and less consistent than the software version described below.

The latest version of the RUSLE2 is available for download from http://www .ars.usda.gov/Research/docs.htm?docid=6038 (or Google RUSLE2). There are five simple steps:

1. Chose a location to set the climate. Use the pull-down menu of states, then the general area within the state. Pick the nearest location to your site, and the program will set the r value.
2. Choose the soil type. This is done by textural class and high-medium-low organic matter and permeability, all of which can be gleaned from the soil survey for the site.
3. Set the slope topography. Enter the length and steepness.
4. Select and modify management. This sets the c value by selecting from an extensive pull-down menu of values specific to land use, cover, and management.
5. Set supporting practices. This sets the p value from pull-down choices under contouring, strips/barriers, and diversion/sediment basin.

Figure 6.16 shows three examples for three different land cover management schemes in the Minneapolis region, all other factors held constant. Results are shown at the bottom left as soil loss (t/a/y) and sediment delivery (t/a):

A: Dense grass cover has a loss of only 0.015 t/a/y.
B: Continuous cropping corn without conservation management has a loss of 8.2 t/a/y
C: Disturbed construction site without mitigation has a loss of 13 t/a/y.

The software has many more functions and capabilities than described here. For example, you can tailor the assessment to the specific conditions of the site, including complex slope geometries. You can compare the effect of different cover management practices on soil loss without having to rerun the five-step procedure. Download the software and try it out.

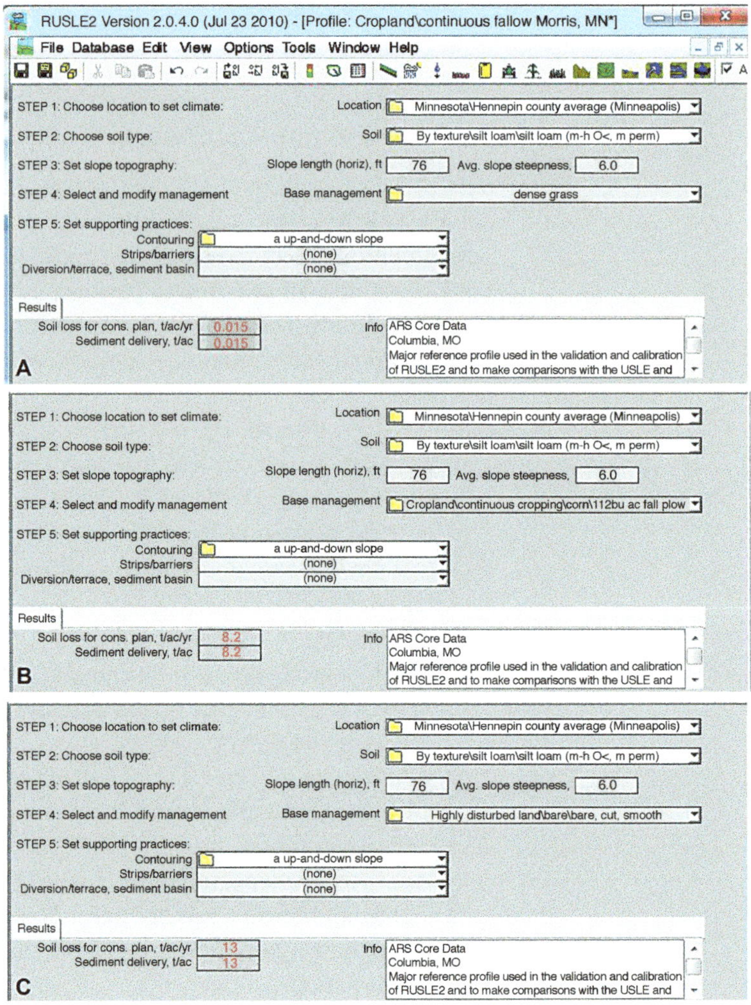

Figure 6.16 Three Examples of RUSLE2 Software Calculations. A: An undisturbed site with dense grass. B: Cropland, continuous cultivated, fall plow. C: A highly disturbed construction site cut bare and smooth.

The Erodibility Index and Highly Erodible Soil

The erodibility index (EI) is defined by the inherent erosion properties of the site (r, k, l, and s), and a tolerance (T) value of soil loss, usually 3–5 tons per acre. The values of k and T are given in soil surveys (see Soil Erosion Factors on lists in Figure 6.10).

$$Erodibility\ Index: \frac{r \times k \times l \times s}{T}$$

Highly erodible lands (HEL) are defined as lands with EI greater than 8. The Conservation Reserve Program (CRP) provides benefits to farmers to keep certain lands out of production. Since the early 1980s the CRP has focused on HEL, and thousands of these areas have been taken out of cultivation. This is a main reason for the significant reduction in soil erosion from 1982 to 2007 estimated by the NRI (see Figure 6.15).

Mitigating Soil Erosion

Understanding the basics of the USLE helps us envision strategies to reduce soil erosion and sedimentation. We can't do much about the general location of the land activity (which determines r) and the soils (k) and perhaps not much about the topography of the site (l and s), but we can employ land cover management (c) and supporting practices (p), which have a significant impact on soil loss and sedimentation. Box 6.3 lists some practices for mitigating erosion from disturbed sites. They all aim to cover or bind exposed soils, reduce runoff, and/or protect receiving waters. You can find many more practices in the pull-down menus and assess their impact when you download and use the RUSLE2 software.

Urban Erosion and Sediment Control

Construction grading and filling are processes that remove vegetation, thereby leading to erosion. In Figure 6.16, the RUSLE showed that a graded construction site without mitigation has almost 60% more soil loss than a cultivated cornfield with any conservation management, and 1,000 times more soil loss than a dense grass cover. After construction, such projects produce impervious surfaces on roads, parking lots, and the building footprint, taking soils out of use. The exposure of unvegetated soil during construction, disruption of drainage patterns, and the impervious surfaces that increase runoff all contribute to removing eroded soil from the site, as well as the offsite deposition of sediments in receiving waters. Sediment reduces water quality, increasing turbidity and nutrients, and lowering flow capacity. As a result, most states and localities implement erosion and sediment (E & S) control regulations for land construction and development.

The regulations often require temporary measures during construction, as well as long-term design measures to control erosion and runoff. Before construction

BOX 6.3—Erosion and Sedimentation Practices for Various Land-Disturbing Activities

Crop Production
Conservation tillage, contour and/or strip cropping
Cover and green manure cropping
Mulching

Pasture and Grazing
Fencing for grazing management
Streambank protection (see Chapter 8)
Filter strips, buffers (see Chapters 8, 10)

Forest Products Harvesting
Filter strips, buffers
Road and trail access system design
Revegetation

Mining
Bench drainage, toe berms
Filter strips
Revegetation
Check dams
Stream protection

Construction
Site design (see Chapter 8)
Minimize extent of area exposed at one time
Mulching
Filter strips, buffers (see Chapters 8, 10)
Sediment barriers
Revegetation

BOX 6.4—Erosion and Sediment Control Principles and Planning

Design Phase

1. Evaluate the site: topography, drainage, vegetation, soils, rainfall patterns.
2. Divide the site into the natural drainage areas.
3. Plan the development to fit the site.
4. Determine the limits of clearing and grading. Divide the project into sections, clearing small amounts of vegetation at a time.
5. Divert water from disturbed areas, minimize the length and steepness of slopes, avoid soil compaction by restricting heavy equipment to limited areas.
6. Select temporary and permanent E & S control practices.
   a. Soil stabilization (soil cover: vegetative and nonvegetative covers)
   b. Sediment control (sediment filters, basins)
   c. Runoff control (diversion, check dams)

Construction Phase

7. Temporary structure practices
   a. Erosion control blankets
   b. Straw bale dike
   c. Silt fence
   d. Temporary swale
   e. Many others

Operation Phase

8. Maintain installed E & S practices (e.g., vegetative cover, diversion works, detention basins).

Source: Craul 1999; USDA, NRCS 2000.

begins, the owner or contractor must prepare an erosion and sediment control plan incorporating E & S principles into the development's design, construction, and operation (Box 6.4).

Good erosion and sediment control planning can avoid considerable problems and costs later in the process. Key considerations are topography, drainage ways, soils, and natural vegetation. A combination of slope gradient and length pose erosion hazards. Generally, slopes of 0–7% are a low erosion hazard (unless greater than 300 ft); 7–15% presents a moderate hazard (unless greater than 150 ft); and above 15% is a high erosion hazard.

E & S control practices include three types of measures:

- *Soil stabilization:* Vegetation stabilization, topsoiling, erosion control matting, mulching, and tree protection.
- *Runoff control:* Reduction, diversion, detention, infiltration (see Chapter 8).
- *Sediment control*: Vegetated buffers, sediment catchments, sediment traps. The amount of sediment removed depends on the speed of water, the time water is detained, and the size of the sediment particles.

Box 6.5 outlines an erosion and sediment control project. The construction of the building, access road, and parking lot has potential impact on the sedimentation of Pine Creek. Eight control measures are described in the list and shown in Figure 6.17. They include grading, runoff diversion, vegetation, filter fence, and detention pond.

BOX 6.5—An E & S Control Project

1. Grassed diversion swale is constructed above the hillside cut for the building. It will drain in opposite directions.
2. The cut made for the building is stabilized with grasses and other slope erosion control measures.
3. Clearing of the forest and grass vegetation is done only where construction is necessary. The remaining vegetation is maintained.
4. A pond is constructed on the lower terrace next to No Name Brook before land clearing begins for the cut slope, building pad, and parking lot. It is a permanent sediment and runoff control basin during and after construction.
5. A bridge is built over No Name Brook. Filter strips are placed around the abutment areas to prevent siltation of the fill. The abutments are stabilized after construction with grasses and erosion control blankets.
6. A grassed diversion swale is constructed above the proposed cut for the access road. It drains into No Name Brook well above the bridge abutment to minimize erosion at the abutment.
7. The access road entrance is stabilized so that sediment does not enter the lateral ditches for Sweet Road and Pine Creek.
8. A filter fence is constructed along the access road and parallel to Pine Creek to prevent sediment from entering Pine Creek.

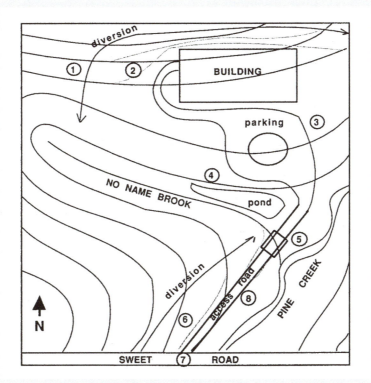

Figure 6.17 A Hypothetical Erosion and Sediment Control Project. The development is superimposed on the physical site. The numbered elements correspond to the list. The dark lines represent original contours; the lighter lines represent modified contour lines.

Urban Soils

Except for E & S control, soils in urban areas do not receive the attention that agricultural soils do. But urban soils are also important for urban forestry, landscaping, urban agriculture, and land development. As discussed earlier, soil strength and stability are important considerations for building and road construction. In addition, many of the same factors affecting agricultural land use are important for vegetation in urban areas, including urban woodlands, parklands, street boulevard trees, riparian buffers, and community gardens.

Here are the most common urban soil problems:

- *Soil compaction:* Increased bulk density caused by any weight on land surface, such as construction equipment, vehicles, and pedestrians. Compaction inhibits drainage, aeration, and root growth. Compacted soil often behaves like impervious surfaces, such as concrete and asphalt.
- *Impervious surfaces:* Surfaces like roads and parking lots interrupt the exchange of gases, alter drainage, and increase soil temperature.
- *Soil erosion and stream sedimentation:* Land development and construction remove vegetative cover and disrupt natural hydrology, creating short- and long-term erosion and sedimentation problems.
- *Moving soils:* Moving soil through grading and clearing eliminates topsoil, increases erosion, and affects drainage and aeration.
- *Soil contamination:* Road salts, chemical spills, waste dumping, excessive fertilizer and pesticide use, and runoff pollution contaminate soils.
- *Elevated soil temperatures:* Removal of tree canopy and vegetation exposes soils, raises temperature, and reduces moisture.
- *Fill dirt:* The use of fill dirt affects drainage, aeration, and compaction.

A common concern is soil compaction that affects root growth and drainage on parklands, recreation fields, and landscaping, especially tree propagation in central urban areas dominated by impervious surfaces (Craul 1999). Signs of soil compaction include very hard soil, standing water, excessive runoff, high bulk density, and poor plant growth.

Compaction can be prevented by avoiding wet areas, limiting travel routes and parking, and applying mulch. For new planting sites, soil compaction problems can be resolved by tilling and mixing soil and mulching. For existing planted sites where tilling is not possible, core aeration, vertical mulching, and radial trenching can reduce soil compaction.

Urban soils are also subject to contamination by petroleum products from surface runoff and leaking underground storage tanks, heavy metals, and other chemicals, including excessive use of pesticides. One of the biggest challenges for brownfields redevelopment in urban areas is contaminated soils. Restoration of urban soils can improve conditions, reduce impacts, and enhance productivity. **Phytoremediation** is the use of green plants to remove contaminants from soils.

It is especially effective in removing heavy metals (U.S. EPA 1998). Aeration methods can help relieve the compaction of heavily used areas, such as recreation fields and lawns. Soils for community gardens and landscaping can be improved by adding organic materials like compost to reduce density, diversify texture, and enhance fertility.

Agricultural Lands and Food Systems

Perhaps the most important contribution of soil to human society is its capacity to support vegetation and the terrestrial food supply. This section focuses on agricultural soils and farmland and discusses the loss of agricultural land, especially prime soils, to development, the land evaluation and site assessment method for rating farmland suitability for preservation, and the emerging interests in urban agriculture and community and regional food planning.

Agricultural Land Conversion

The conversion of prime agricultural lands to nonagricultural uses, such as highways and suburban development, has been an issue of concern in the U.S. for four decades. Although converting agricultural areas may result in a higher economic return from the land, at least in the short term, it can also irreversibly remove highly productive agricultural soils that have taken centuries to develop. In many areas, agricultural land use is an important contribution to the local economy and to the agrarian character that many communities would like to maintain.

Prime farmland is rural land with the best combination of physical and chemical characteristics for producing food, feed, forage, fiber, and oilseed crops. It has USDA capability class 1 or 2 soils (see Box 6.2). In the United States, prime farmland is 64% cropland, 15% forestland, 11% pastureland, and 6% rangeland. The rest is other rural land not in production. The biggest concentration of prime farmland is in the belt of four midwestern states (Ohio, Indiana, Illinois, and Iowa); in that region, more than half the nonfederal rural land is prime farmland (USDA 2009).

The NRI documents land use changes in the United States every 5 years. The latest report covers the period 2002–2007 (USDA 2009). As shown in Figure 6.18, the estimated 325.6 million acres of prime farmland in 2007 was down 13.8 million acres from the 1982 total—mostly converted to urban developed land, which grew 56% from 1982 (71 million acres) to 2007 (111 million acres). About 30% of newly developed land was converted from prime farmland. Total cropland declined 15% from 420 to 357 million acres; about half of that reduction was due to enrollments in the Conservation Reserve Program, which took millions of highly erodible land out of production (USDA 2009).

In response to these trends, several states and localities in the United States have developed programs to preserve agricultural lands. These programs include tax incentives, regulations, and the purchase or transfer of development rights. (Specific programs are discussed in Chapters 15, 17, and 18.) A first step for

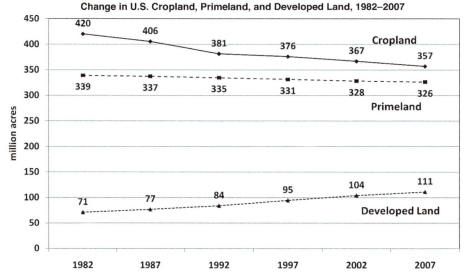

Figure 6.18 Changes in U.S. Cropland, Primeland, and Developed Land, 1982–2007. (*Source:* Data from USDA, NRCS 2009.)

planners, however, is to assess farmlands to see which areas are most suitable for retention in agricultural use to qualify for these programs and which ones may be more suitable for development. The LESA system was developed for that purpose.

Land Evaluation and Site Assessment

In response to the Farmlands Protection Act of 1981, the SCS (now the NRCS) developed the LESA system to help planners judge the relative agricultural suitability of lands near urban areas (USDA, SCS 1983). County planners throughout the country have implemented the procedure. It involves two parts:

1. **Land evaluation (LE)** rates the soils of the area, usually a county, for cropland.
2. **Site assessment (SA)** identifies factors other than soils that are important to the quality of a site for agricultural use and rates specific sites based on those factors.

Variations of the system can also be used to evaluate forestland and rangeland. Implementing the LESA system requires first establishing the rules of the system and then applying the system to individual sites.

Establishing the LESA System in a County

Although some states have developed statewide LESA programs (e.g., California Department of Conservation 1997), most applications are in individual counties. Since a number of subjective decisions are required to establish the system's rules, the procedure calls for a local LESA committee representing different agricultural, conservation, and development interests.

The first part of the system, the land evaluation (LE), involves an interpretation of information in the county soil survey. NRCS staff works with the county to generate the 10 LE groupings of soil series based on their productivity or potential for growing an indicator crop selected by the local LESA committee. The indicator crop is usually the most important crop in the county. Soil productivity indicates the expected yield for the indicator crop under a high level of management; soil potential adjusts the productivity by considering the costs of measures to overcome capability limitations such as erosion or wetness and the continuing limitations after measures are taken. The soil groupings are also influenced by the USDA Land Capability classifications (see Box 6.2) and an "important farmland" classification. This latter rating includes four categories (prime, statewide importance, local importance, and other) and can emphasize the importance of certain farmlands or uses regardless of their soil types, such as for specialty crops or animal production.

Given the indicator crop, NRCS staff provides counties with the LE groupings. In a worksheet, the NRCS groups all soil map units according to their Land Capability classification, important farmland designation, yield of the indicator crop in tons per acre, and productivity index (as given in the soil survey tables; see the Vegetative Productivity category in the Figure 6.10 tables). The index simply normalizes the yields to a 0–100 scale, where 100 corresponds to the yield of the highest-yield soils. Each of these ratings can affect the group into which the map unit is placed. Table 6.3 shows LESA Worksheet #2 for Montgomery County, Virginia, which summarizes this information and computes a relative value for each group, from 0 to 100.

TABLE 6.3   **Land Evaluation Groups and Relative LE Values: LESA Worksheet #2 for Montgomery County, Virginia**

LE Group	Land Capability Class	Important Farmland Class	Soil Potential Index	Soil Map Units	Acres in County	Percentage of County	Relative Value
1	2e/2w	Prime	100	28, 30B, 16B, 12B, 20B	10,105	3.9	100
2	2e/2w	Prime	84–96	13B, 15B, 19B, 33	7,695	3.0	90
3	2e/3e	Statewide	81–92	11B, 12C, 15C, 21C, 30C	11,881	4.6	87
4	3e/3w	Statewide	69–77	11C, 13C, 14, 17C, 31C	12,676	4.9	74
5	2e/3e/4w	Local	61–76	2B, 25, 2C	12,177	4.7	64
6	3e/3s	Local	48–57	1C, 26C, 10	11,102	4.3	55
7	3e	Statewide	45–53	22C, 16C	9,964	3.8	47
8	4e	Statewide	21–33	30D, 15D, 16D, 13D	12,668	4.9	22
9	4e	Local	13–17	9C, 3D, 26D	10,290	4.0	16
10	6e/6s/7s	—	—	3E, 4E, 5D, 6E, 7D, 8D, 8E, 9D, 29, 16E, 18B, 18C, 18D, 23C, 24D, 26E, 27E, 32B, 32C, 32D, 34E		61.8	0

Source: Montgomery County (VA) Planning Department 1984.

The LE thus provides a fairly objective means for assigning agricultural value to the soils of the county. The 50 or so soil series and map units are aggregated to 10 groups of common agricultural *capability* for growing a specific indicator crop.

However, the *suitability* of land for agricultural use also depends on factors other than soils. The site assessment (SA) portion of LESA investigates these non-soil factors that contribute to the suitability of specific parcels for retention in agricultural use. The procedure calls for a sum-of-weighted-factors approach. As discussed in Chapter 2, identifying and evaluating the factors using this approach is a value-laden process. It requires broad local participation to be fair in the eyes of local citizens, and to be responsive to local, areawide, and national needs. Therefore, the procedure calls for the local LESA committee to determine and weight the factors to be used in the site assessment, thus establishing the "rules" of the process.

Examples of these rules, that is, the factors and weights, are shown in Table 6.4. Table 6.4 lists 12 factors selected by the LESA committee in Montgomery County. They range from "percentage of land in agriculture within 1/2 mile" of the site to "zoning" for the site to "central sewerage system availability"—each has some bearing on the suitability of the site for agriculture and alternative uses. Each factor has a maximum score of 10 and an assigned weight between 1 and 10 (in this case between 4 and 8). Multiplying the maximum score for each factor by its weight and summing the products yield a maximum total (770). Because the procedure calls for a maximum SA score of 200, the weights are adjusted by multiplying by 0.26 (or 200/770). Multiplying the adjusted weights (e.g., 2.1 instead of 8) by the maximum scores for each factor and summing the products yield the desired maximum total of 200. Individual sites are assessed by assigning the site values for these factors; a sum of the products of these factor values multiplied by their adjusted weights will give a total site assessment value between 0 and 200.

A total LESA score combines the LE and SA scores for a value between 0 and 300. Normally, the committee will determine a cutoff score, such as 200, which roughly separates higher and lower suitability agricultural sites.

The Montgomery County (VA) LESA program dates back to 1984. Figure 6.19 gives another example of a LESA system, this one for Fulton, Wisconsin, adopted in 2010. The establishment of the system followed the same procedure, except that the rating system is based on a total maximum score of 10 rather than 300. This is simply done by adjusting weights to produce a 10-point scale. LE scores still account for one-third of the total, but instead of 100 out of 300, they are given a weight of 0.34. Fulton's SA criteria are nicely grouped into three categories: the agricultural group, development group, and natural resources group.

Applying LESA to Specific Sites

Once the rules of the LESA procedure are established, it can be applied to specific parcels of land. Box 6.6 illustrates the process for a site in Montgomery County. Table 6.5 shows that the Land Evaluation component assigns to each soil map unit on the site, the LE value (0–100) for the agricultural soil group that includes that series. The average Land Evaluation value for the site is computed by multiplying

TABLE 6.4 LESA Site Assessment Factors, Scoring, Weights (W), and Adjusted Weights (AW) for Montgomery County, Virginia

		W	AW
1. Percent of Area in Agriculture within Radius of the Property Boundary		7	1.8

10	95–100%
8	75–95%
6	50–75%
4	24–50%
2	10–25%
0	0–10%

2. Land Use Adjacent to Site   7   1.8

10	All sides of Site in Agriculture
8	One Side of Site Adjacent to Nonagricultural Land
5	Two Sides of Site Adjacent to Nonagricultural Land
2	Three Sides of Site Adjacent to Nonagricultural Land
0	Site Surrounded by Nonagricultural Land

3. Zoning   8   2.1

10	Site and All Surrounding Sides Zoned for Agricultural Use
8	Site and Three Sides Zoned for Agricultural Use
5	Site and Two Sides Zoned for Agricultural Use
2	Site and One Side Zoned for Agricultural Use
0	Site Zoned for Nonagricultural Use and/or Site Zoned on All Sides for Nonagricultural Use

4. Availability of Less Productive Land   8   2.1

10	More Than 2/3 of the Land within a 2-Mile Travel Distance Is Less Productive
5	1/3 to 2/3 of the Land within a 2-Mile Travel Distance Is Less Productive
0	Less than 1/3 of the Land within a 2-Mile Travel Distance Is Less Productive

5. Compatibility with Comprehensive Plan   8   2.1

10	Agriculture Use Compatible with Plan
0	Agriculture Use Incompatible with Plan

6. Central Water Distribution System   6   1.6

10	No Public Water within 1 Mile
7	Public Water within 2,000 Feet
4	Public Water within 500 Feet
0	Public Water at or Adjacent to Site

7. Central Sanitary Sewerage System   6   1.6

10	No Public Sewer Line within 1 Mile
7	Public Sewer Line within 2,000 Feet
4	Public Sewer Line within 500 Feet
0	Public Sewer Line at or Adjacent to Site

8. Transportation   4   1.0

10	Site Access to Unimproved Road
5	Site Access to Secondary Road
0	Site Access to Primary Road

9. Compatibility of Proposed Use with Surrounding Existing Land Use   8   2.1

10	Incompatibility
0	Compatibility

	W	AW
10. Site in Agricultural & Forestal District AFD	5	1.3
10 In AFD		
0 Not in AFD		
11. Soil Conservation District Plan Filed	5	1.3
10 Active Plan		
5 Inactive Plan		
0 No Plan		
12. Family Farm Value	5	1.3
10 Three or More Generations		
5 Two Generations		
0 One Generation		

Source: Montgomery County (VA) Planning Department 1984.

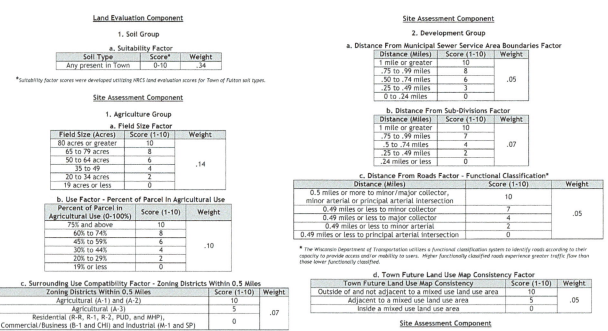

Figure 6.19 The LESA System in Fulton, Rock County, Wisconsin. LESA is scored on a 10-point scale instead of the customary 300-point scale. (*Source:* Rock County Planning, Economic & Community Development Agency 2010.)

BOX 6.6—LESA

TABLE 6.5 **Land Evaluation for Whitethorne**

Map Unit	Soil Name	Slope	Acres	Agricultural Group
30B	Unison and Braddock Soils	2–7%	64.2	1
30C	Unison and Braddock Soils	7–15%	128.4	3
30D	Unison and Braddock Soils	15–25%	124.0	8
19B	Guernsey Silt Loam	2–7%	125.6	2
31C	Unison and Braddock Cobbly Soils	7–15%	101.8	4
28	Ross Soils	0–2%	27.8	1
33	Weaver Soils	0–2%	21.3	2
25	McGary and Purdy Soils	0–2%	13.3	5
10	Craigsville Soils	0–2%	21.6	6
20B	Hayter Loam	2–7%	47.1	1
3E	Berks-Lowell-Rayne Complex	25–65%	25.6	10
8E	Caneyville-Opaquon-Rock Outcrop Complex	25–65%	55.1	10

Map Unit	Agricultural Group	Relative Value	Acres	Acres % Relative Value
30B	1	100	64.2	6,420.0
30C	3	87	128.4	11,170.8
30D	8	22	124.0	2,728.0
19B	2	90	125.6	11,304.0
31C	4	74	101.8	7,533.2
28	1	100	27.8	2,780.0
33	2	90	21.3	1,917.0
25	5	64	33.3	2,132.2
10	6	55	21.6	1,188.0
20B	1	100	47.1	4,710.0
3E	10	0	25.6	0.0
8E	10	0	55.1	0.0
			775.8	51,883.2

$$\text{Land evaluation site score} = \frac{51,883.2}{775.8} = 67.0$$

BOX 6.6—LESA (cont.)

TABLE 6.6 **Site Assessment for Whitethorne Site**

Factor	Assigned Points	Adjusted Weight	Adjusted Weight Assigned Points
1. % of Area in Agriculture	6	1.8	10.8
2. Land Use Adjacent to Site	8	1.8	14.4
3. Zoning	0	2.1	0.0
4. Availability of Less Productive Land	10	2.1	21.0
5. Compatibility with Comprehensive Plan	10	2.1	21.0
6. Central Water	10	1.6	16.0
7. Central Sewer	10	1.6	16.0
8. Transportation	10	1.0	10.0
9. Compatibility with Existing Surrounding Land Use	10	2.1	21.0
10. AFU	0	1.1	0.0
11. Soil Conservation Plan	0	1.1	0.0
12. Family Farm Value	0	1.3	0.0
Site assessment value			130.2

Total LESA score = 67.0 + 130.2 = 197.2

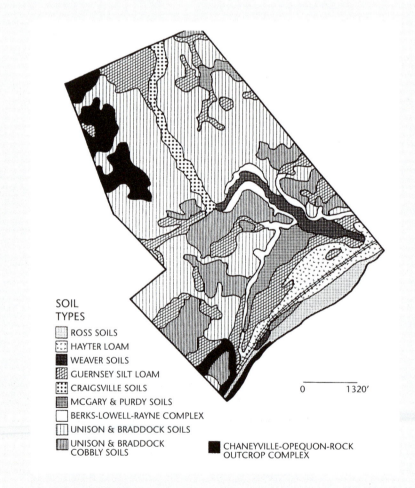

Figure 6.20 The Whitethorne Site, Montgomery County, Virginia. (*Source:* Montgomery County Planning Department 1984.)

SOIL TYPES

ROSS SOILS
HAYTER LOAM
WEAVER SOILS
GUERNSEY SILT LOAM
CRAIGSVILLE SOILS
MCGARY & PURDY SOILS
BERKS-LOWELL-RAYNE COMPLEX
UNISON & BRADDOCK SOILS
UNISON & BRADDOCK COBBLY SOILS
CHANEYVILLE-OPEQUON-ROCK OUTCROP COMPLEX

0   1320'

map units and dividing by the total acres. The average LE value for the White-thorne site is 67. Recall that the best soils in *that* county for producing corn (the LESA committee's choice as the indicator crop) are rated 100.

The site assessment table (Table 6.6) gives the 12 factors and their adjusted importance weights chosen by the committee in Table 6.4. The product of the factor ratings (0–10) assigned to the site and the adjusted weights gives the "adjusted weights assigned points," which are summed to give the total SA score. This site has a value of 130.2. Recall that the maximum value is 200. The LE value of 67 and the SA value of 130.2 combine to give a LESA total of 197.2 on the 300-point scale (Montgomery County Planning Department 1984).

Using LESA

The implementation of LESA for agricultural lands by rural and urbanizing counties has increased steadily since it was established in the mid-1980s. Applications have included the following:

- Evaluating rezoning and other development applications for sites currently zoned for agriculture.
- Impact assessment.
- Prioritizing or qualifying sites for inclusion in land protection programs, such as agricultural districts, agricultural zones, and development rights transfer or purchase areas.
- Comprehensive land use plans where community growth should be encouraged and discouraged based on agricultural suitability.

A Critique of LESA

Since LESA has become the basic planning tool for evaluating agricultural lands throughout the country, some comments on its strengths and weaknesses are appropriate. LESA goes well beyond previous measures of agricultural land value (e.g., land capability classes) by incorporating nonsoil factors. LESA is designed to be flexible so that individual counties can tailor key factors in the process (i.e., indicator crop, SA factors and weights) to meet the county's needs and perceptions. Although the nature of the sum-of-weighted-factors process is value-laden (e.g., what is an appropriate indicator crop, what are the appropriate weights to assign to SA factors), the values are chosen by a committee of members representing diverse interests in the community.

Although it takes some time and participation to establish the rules of the process by the local committee, once the rules are established, applying the procedure to individual sites is straightforward. Some have questioned the relative weights assigned by the LESA procedure to soil (1/3) and nonsoil (2/3) factors; in many cases, they argue, soil factors should be given greater weight. Although LESA is designed to be flexible, flexibility may lead to misuse of the procedures. Preconceived notions, even existing programs for land protection, can bias the choice of factors to justify those notions or programs. Finally, whereas flexibility may serve individual counties, it does not serve regional or statewide interests since LESA values from one county cannot be compared with another. Some states have had to develop a statewide LESA system separate from the county system, to produce comparative values for setting priorities for state farmland protection programs.

Urban Agriculture and Food Systems Planning

The increasing interest in protecting agricultural land from development pressures in metropolitan areas stems in part from the growing movement for food security, access to healthy food from local sources, and urban agriculture. Participants in urban agriculture include backyard gardeners, community gardeners, and commercial farmers who grow food for themselves and others. Urban agriculture is practiced in yards, on balconies and rooftops, and in greenhouses, schoolyards, community gardens in inner-city vacant lots and dedicated parks, and small farms at the city's edge, as well as in greenbelts around the city. Urban agriculture also includes farmers markets and municipal composting facilities.

The USDA estimates that 15% of the world's food is now grown in urban areas. That percentage is lower in the U.S., but it is on the rise. Urban agriculture has become an important part of a new area of urban sustainability planning—planning the community food system. Raja, Born, and Russell (2008) characterize the community food system as a comprehensive system—from food production to processing, to distribution, consumption, and disposal (Figure 6.21).

Several of these components are important planning issues, including farmland preservation (discussed above) and mixed-use neighborhood access to grocery stores. For example, Philadelphia has focused on bringing grocery stores to

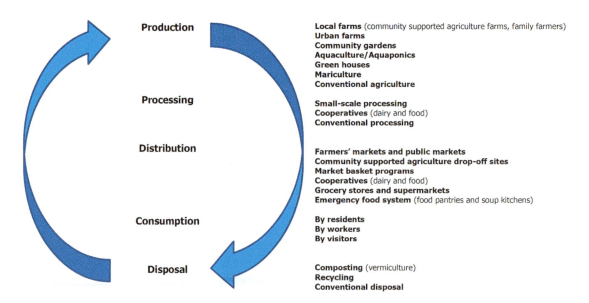

Production
Local farms (community supported agriculture farms, family farmers)
Urban farms
Community gardens
Aquaculture/Aquaponics
Green houses
Mariculture
Conventional agriculture

Processing
Small-scale processing
Cooperatives (dairy and food)
Conventional processing

Distribution
Farmers' markets and public markets
Community supported agriculture drop-off sites
Market basket programs
Cooperatives (dairy and food)
Grocery stores and supermarkets
Emergency food system (food pantries and soup kitchens)

Consumption
By residents
By workers
By visitors

Disposal
Composting (vermiculture)
Recycling
Conventional disposal

Figure 6.21 The Community Food System, from Production to Disposal. (*Source:* Adapted from Raja et al. 2008.)

underserved neighborhoods. Marin County, California, includes "Food" as an element of its comprehensive plan, which incorporates goals for preservation of agricultural land, improving agriculture economic viability, and community food security (County of Marin 2007).

Next we focus on three important issues in urban agriculture and food systems planning: community gardens, farmers markets, and municipal composting.

Community Gardens and Urban Farms

There are an estimated 18,000 community gardens in the U.S. and Canada, but it is difficult to get an accurate number. These gardens are shared open spaces where people grow fruits and vegetables, as well as flowers and plants. These gardens provide not only food, but civic open green space and neighborhood interaction. Although many community gardens are on private land and are managed by community groups, several cities have contributed to developing and maintaining community gardens and farms. Residents and planners in cities with large numbers of vacant properties have found that they can convert them into community gardens, turn an eyesore into community space, and help revitalize neighborhoods. Green Up Pittsburgh, Baltimore Green Space, Philadelphia Green, Greening of Detroit, and many others are all community programs for converting vacant lots into community gardens. Michigan's Garden for Growth Program offers $50 per year per lot for communities and individuals to cultivate and garden vacant lots. Many of these programs are posted by LOTS 2 Green, a national program offering technical assistance to communities to use vacant properties for community gardens (see http://codegreen-usa.org/Lots2Green.htm). Growing Power, Inc., based in Milwaukee, also promotes community gardens and farms (see www.growingpower.org/).

Portland (Oregon) and Madison (Wisconsin) are also noted for their community garden programs. Portland has a Food Policy Council that has developed a number of initiatives. Troy Gardens is Madison's community garden exemplar. The city helped facilitate the purchase of state surplus property by the Madison Area Community Land Trust, which developed five of the 31-acre sites for 30 affordable housing units. The remaining 26 acres are under conservation easement as a 5-acre community supported agriculture (CSA) farm, community gardens, prairie restoration, and nature trails (Figure 6.22). Neighbors care for 330 family garden plots, and 100 households pick up weekly bags of organic vegetables from the CSA farm (http://www.troygardens.org/).

Farmers Markets

Another important component of community food is the distribution of local agriculture products to residents. Community farmers markets are critical for local farmers, and they provide a consistent source of local, fresh food to residents. They give farmers the opportunity to develop a personal relationship with their customers and cultivate consumer loyalty with the farmers who grow the produce. The growth of farmers markets has been explosive. The USDA estimates that there are currently 6,132 operating farmers markets in the U.S., up 16%

Figure 6.22 Troy Gardens Community, Madison, Wisconsin. This 31-acre site includes a 5-acre affordable housing development, 300 community garden plots, a 5-acre CSA farm, and prairie preserve/hiking trails. (*Source:* Madison Area Land Trust. http://www.affordablehome.org, http://www.troygardens.org. Used with permission.)

from 2009 (5,274) and 350% since 1994 (1,755). Many farmers markets take food stamps (EBT cards), thereby increasing the access for lower-income residents to healthy, local food (see http://www.ams.usda.gov/AMSv1.0/FARMERS MARKETS).

Community Composting Programs

Composting brings us back to the soil. Compost is the aerobic decomposition and stabilization of organic material to the point where it is beneficial to plant growth as a soil conditioner and fertilizer. Composting is the best way to recycle food waste. Compost can help revitalize urban soils into rich productive gardens. It improves the soil's physical structure and moisture, chemical acidity-alkalinity (pH) balance, nutrients, and biota.

Composting is a popular backyard project for recycling kitchen vegetable waste for garden compost. Many communities, including Minneapolis, Portland (Oregon), San Francisco, and Vancouver (British Columbia, Canada) are offering or piloting community composting programs, including curbside pickup of organic waste. Commercial composting facilities can operate at much higher temperatures than backyard composters and can process a wider range of organic wastes, including paper waste. Community and commercial composting produces compost products for local gardeners and farmers.

Summary

Soils are a fundamental natural resource of the land; they influence the land's capability of supporting vegetation and development. Land use is affected by soil strength and stability, drainability, erodibility, and agricultural and resource potential. Soil quality is subject to degradation by human activities, including compaction, erosion, and contamination, and can be improved through remediation.

In the U.S., the soil survey is the best source of information for analysis of how these factors can influence agriculture, development, and other uses, from the site scale to the community scale. Soil survey information, especially the new Web Soil Survey, can be used to map soil suitability for land development, onsite wastewater systems and land application of wastes, and a range of other uses. The soil survey also rates soils at the site scale for agricultural capability, used in the LESA evaluation method, and for erosion potential, used in the Revised Universal Soil Loss Equation. Like the Web Soil Survey, the RUSLE2 software simplifies soil erosion analysis. Federal agricultural programs, like the Conservation Reserve Program, have been effective in reducing the nation's cropland soil erosion.

Urban soils are subject to erosion and sedimentation from land development construction practices and are also plagued by contamination and compaction problems. Urban soils have become more important as more and more communities are turning to community gardens and urban farms for local food. This movement toward local and regional food and agriculture planning incorporates farmland preservation programs, conversion of vacant properties to community gardens, the significant growth of farmers markets, and community composting programs to bring food wastes back to the soil from which they came.

7 ■ Water and Land Use: Stream Flow, Flooding, and Runoff Pollution

If we can take care of the waters, we are well on our way to protecting the environment. Fresh, clean water supplies are becoming increasingly precious to humans and ecosystems, especially as we experience the effects of climate change. Severe storm events bring flooding and major damage and loss of life. Precipitation falling on the land runs off or infiltrates, and what's on the land affects the fate of that water—where it goes, how clean or polluted it is, how quickly it accumulates in stormwater flows, how well it recharges groundwater. Water supply, drainage, and stream water quality management used to be solely the domain of the engineer. This has changed, with the recognition that effective water management demands management of the land and engagement of the people on it—and that is the domain of the planner. **Watershed management** is the integration of land and water science, engineering, planning, and policy, and it has become the accepted approach for restoring and protecting the waters, from a small stream in a city to a multistate resource like the Chesapeake Bay.

Water is such an important issue in environmental land use planning that more than three chapters focus on it. This chapter discusses the effects of land use on stream flow, water quality, and stream integrity. Critical issues include storm flows and flooding, which pose natural hazards to property and people; baseflows and low flows, which affect aquatic ecology; and runoff pollution, which affects both natural waters and sources of community water supplies. Chapter 8 discusses emerging approaches for stormwater management and stream restoration to address these impacts. Chapter 9 focuses on groundwater and water supply. Chapters 10, 12, 13, and 19 discuss related issues of wetlands, climate change, natural hazards, and watershed management.

The hydrologic cycle is intimately related to the land (Figure 7.1). Water evaporates from the land and the ocean and ultimately precipitates as rain or snow. Precipitation that does not immediately evaporate and transpire through vegetation

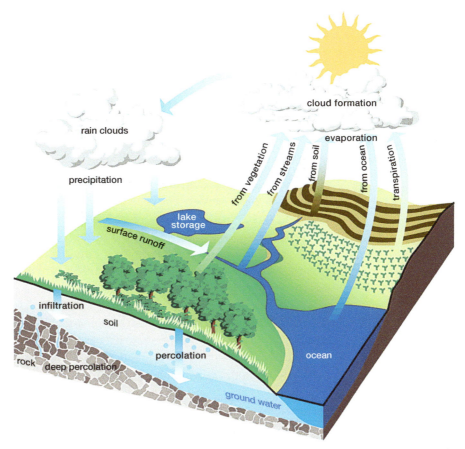

Figure 7.1 The Hydrologic Cycle. The transfer of water from precipitation to surface water and groundwater, to storage and runoff, and eventually evaporating back to the atmosphere as pure water vapor, is an ongoing renewing cycle. (*Source:* Federal Interagency Stream Restoration Working Group 1998.)

back to the atmosphere has one of two fates: (1) It infiltrates the soil and contributes to soil moisture, subsurface flow, and groundwater recharge; or (2) it runs off on the surface, contributing to surface streams, lakes, and rivers. Runoff contributes the most to **stormwater flows**, and much of the infiltrated water finds its way to groundwater aquifers or ends up as subsurface flow, which seeps to the surface and contributes the most to **baseflow** or stream flow between storms. Surface streams and lakes are important ecosystem elements, and they, along with groundwater aquifers, are important existing or future sources of the water supply for people and communities.

Disturbance of the land from natural conditions has an effect on these processes. Agriculture, forestry, and mining remove critical vegetation, exacerbating erosion and sedimentation in streams, and release organic and toxic pollution to runoff. Urbanization and development pave the land with impervious parking lots, streets, and rooftops. This reduces infiltration and increases the rate of accumulation and the amount of stormwater runoff, which in turn exacerbates drainage and flooding problems and **channel erosion** downstream. This urban runoff carries with it **nonpoint source (NPS) water pollution** that now exceeds industrial and municipal "point" discharges in contributing to the pollution of lakes, rivers, and estuaries in the United States.

The Water Balance

Precipitation is the heart of the hydrologic cycle, and the patterns of rain and snowfall in a location determine its distribution of water on and under the ground, as well as its local ecology. The measurement of precipitation is straightforward, and gauging stations have been recording rainfall data throughout the United States for nearly two centuries. These historic data have been analyzed statistically to give average precipitation over a drainage basin or region and the frequency of storms of given intensities that are likely to occur in the future. Most of this analysis was done decades ago (U.S. Weather Bureau 1961). This assumption that the future will resemble the past is a critical one in hydrology, and it assumes relatively constant climatic conditions. Climate change may affect this assumption and our use of long-term historic data as a design basis for the future.

Figure 7.2 gives annual precipitation for the United States averaged for the period 1971–2000. The semihumid eastern United States (30–60 inches per year)

Precipitation: Annual Climatology (1971–2000)

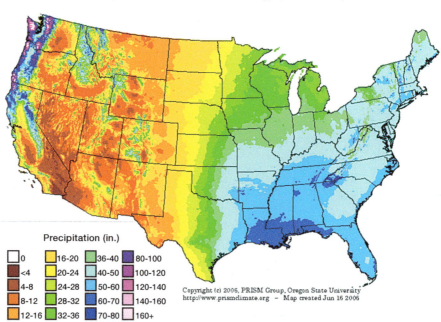

Figure 7.2 Annual Precipitation in the United States, 1971–2000. (*Source:* USDA, NRCS Water and Climate Center, Portland, Oregon. Modeling performed by Christopher Daly using PRISM model based on 1971–2000 data from NOAA Cooperative stations and NRCS Snotel sites.)

is distinguished from the semiarid west (0–30 inches per year). Not only do annual averages vary, but so do the seasonal variations, as well as the intensity and duration of storms. It is this pattern of precipitation that determines runoff and flooding problems and stormwater management needs.

For this reason, historic precipitation data are analyzed in terms of the **frequency**, **intensity**, and **duration** of storms. The map in Figure 7.3 shows the intensity for storms of a specific duration and frequency. These maps are available for many durations and frequencies; see the websites at the U.S. Weather Bureau (USWB 1961) and the National Weather Service (NWS 2002). For a specific location, the intensity-duration-frequency data can be plotted in one curve. Figure 7.4 shows the return interval (frequency) for storms of different intensities (inches/hour) and durations. For the period recorded on the graphs, although Seattle and Miami got about the same annual precipitation on average (48 inches per year), the pattern of rainfall was far different in the two cities. For example, the recurrence of a 1-hour, 1-inch rainfall in Seattle was greater than 100 years, whereas the return interval of such a storm in Miami was less than 2 years.

The frequency or return interval is a simple way of stating the probability of occurrence based on history. A 100-year storm does not mean that if we have such an event this year, we won't see another one for 100 years. It simply means that

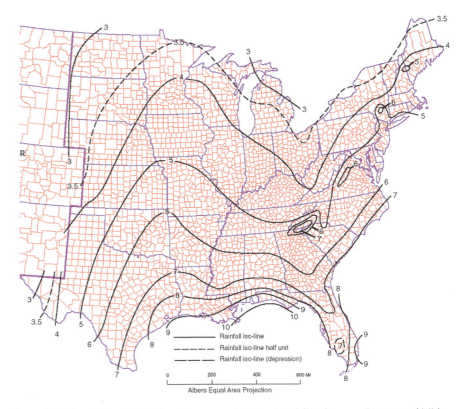

Figure 7.3 Storm Intensity: 10-Year Frequency, 24-Hour Rainfall Inches over Eastern and Midwestern United States. (*Source:* USDA 1986.)

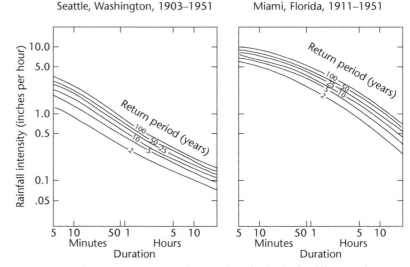

Figure 7.4 Intensity-Duration-Frequency Curves for Seattle and Miami. The differences between the two sets of curves reflect differences in the climates of the two cities. (*Source: Water in Environmental Planning* by Thomas Dunne and Luna Leopold, copyright © 1978. Reprinted with permission of W. H. Freeman.)

based on historic data, the probability of the event occurring in any year is 1 in 100, or 1%. If we get such an event this year, we still have a 1% chance of a similar event next year, and we could get it next month. Because of this misleading nature of recurrence period, hydrologic data are now being referenced more in terms of annual probability.

Watersheds and Channel Processes

Precipitation that does not evaporate either infiltrates the ground or runs off on the surface as overland flow. Much of the infiltrated water ultimately seeps out of the ground, contributing to stream baseflow between storms. The texture of the soil determines its permeability and infiltration rate. But for all soils, as they become saturated from a given storm, a greater percentage of the precipitation will end up as surface runoff. Figure 7.5 shows this water balance between precipitation, infiltration, and runoff.

Overland Drainage: Runoff and Watersheds

Topography determines how surface water drains. It delineates **drainage basins**, also called **watersheds** or **catchments**. Rain falling within the **drainage boundary** (or *divide*) will drain through the basin exit channel. Other basin characteristics include:

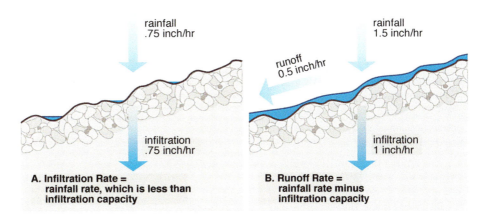

Figure 7.5 Water Balance of Rainfall, Infiltration, and Runoff. The precipitation rate (PR) and infiltration rate (IR) determine the runoff rate (RR). IR depends on soil texture, soil moisture, and vegetative cover. A: If PR ≤ IR, RR = 0. B: If PR ≥ IR, RR = PR − IR. (*Source:* FISRWG 1998.)

- *Basin or watershed area:* The area within the boundary.
- *Basin length:* The distance from the first-order channel farthest upstream to the basin outlet.
- *Drainage density:* The length of all the channels divided by the basin area; generally, the greater the drainage density, the steeper the slopes in the basin and the higher the peak flows for a given rainfall.

Figure 7.6 shows a drainage basin and the convention for stream order classi-fication. First-order channels are highest in the watershed and have no tribu-taries. First-order channels join to form second-order streams, second-order streams join to form third-order streams, and so on. Stream channels are also

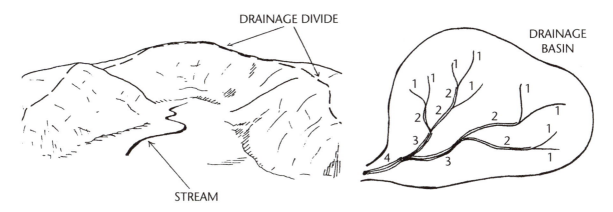

Figure 7.6 The Drainage Basin and Strahler Stream Order Classification. Headwater streams are first-order streams, which combine to form second-order streams, which combine to third-order streams, and so on.

Figure 7.7 GIS Watershed Delineation Using the National Hydrography Dataset Watershed Tool, DEM Data, and Data Preprocessing. Left to right, top to bottom: Box 1: Select the point of interest. Box 2: Upstream navigation is performed on the centerline network, and the program calls drainage catchments that have a 1:1 relation to the NHD reaches. Box 3: The catchment where the selected point of interest falls in is split in two, and the subarea upstream is isolated from the remaining area. Box 4: The subcatchment is combined with all upstream catchments, and internal boundaries are dissolved. (*Source:* USGS 2004.)

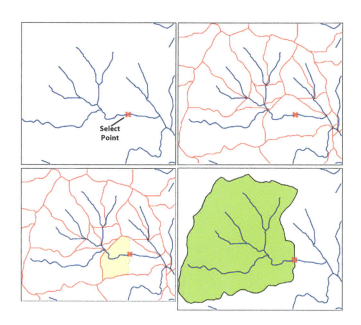

defined by how often water is present. **Perennial streams** (shown as a solid blue line on color topographic maps) normally run all year long. **Intermittent streams** (shown as dashed blue lines on topographic maps) run during the wet season. **Ephemeral streams** (not shown on topo maps) run only during and immediately after storms.

Delineating the drainage basin or watershed boundary is key to understanding the relationship of land and water, and it is the first step of watershed management (see Chapter 19). It is often important to identify critical watersheds, those deserving special attention. These may be watersheds of existing or potential water supply reservoirs, watersheds with potential drainage capacity problems, or those undergoing land development. Like most mapping, watershed delineation is now largely conducted with GIS using spatial analysis extensions and digital elevation model (DEM) data. Figure 7.7 illustrates some steps in a process using the National Hydrography Dataset Watershed, an Esri ArcGIS extension that requires some data preprocessing (USGS 2004).

All environmental planners should know how to delineate watersheds by hand, using topographic maps. Box 7.1 outlines the basic method for doing so, as shown in Figure 7.8. Rain falling within the boundary will drain to the outlet point.

Channel Processes and Geomorphology

Topography obviously affects drainage, but drainage also affects topography through the processes of geomorphology and the formation of landforms by water erosion and deposition. The erosion and deposition processes of the river channel largely determine the landforms of the valley floor, including the floodplain. Channels do not flow uniformly over time; they are dynamic in nature. Channels have a natural tendency to meander or to develop a wavy pattern from a straight

BOX 7.1—Delineating a Watershed Boundary

1. Identify the outlet point on a stream or river that defines the watershed draining to that point.
2. Find and trace drainage channels within the watershed. On a color topo map, they are blue lines. V-shaped elevation contours point upstream.
3. Find and place an X on neighboring channels outside the watershed. The watershed boundary will be between the channels in the basin (step 2) and these outside channels.
4. Consider yourself a drop of water and check the direction of drainage by inspecting the slope direction between the "in" and "out" channels.
5. Find and mark the high points (peaks and saddles) between the in and out channels. These will be on the watershed boundary.
6. Connect these points with light pencil, intersecting the contour lines at roughly a right angle.
7. Consider yourself a drop of water again and check where you would go if you fell inside or outside the line. Make corrections as necessary.
8. Finalize the map.

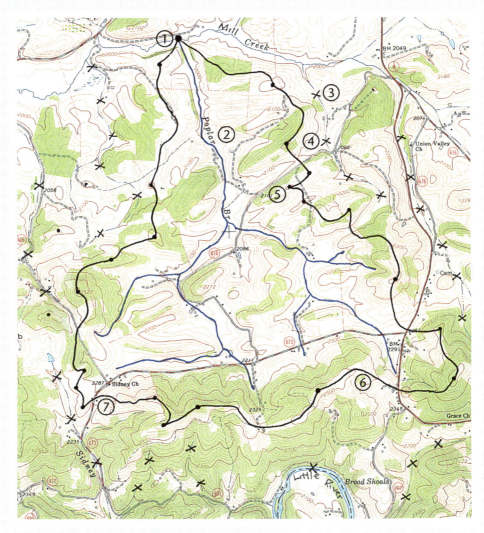

Figure 7.8 Delineating a Watershed on a Topographic Map.

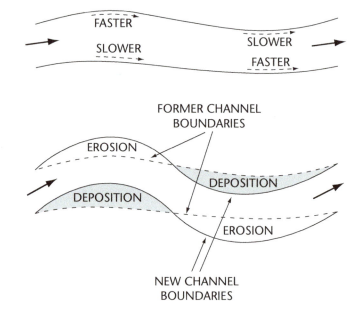

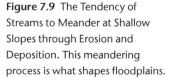

Figure 7.9 The Tendency of Streams to Meander at Shallow Slopes through Erosion and Deposition. This meandering process is what shapes floodplains.

one. Figure 7.9 shows how the varying water velocities in the channel section produce this meandering effect. Faster water on the outside of the stream curves causes more erosion, while slower velocities in the inside cause deposition of sediment. Over time these processes cause the curves to enlarge. This process also contributes to the deep pool, shallow and stony riffle, and unobstructed run sequence in natural stream segments. It is this meandering process, not flooding, that actually causes the development of floodplains and the distinct landforms common to river valleys.

These geomorphic processes create different stream shapes and configurations. Rosgen (1994) created a stream classification system, recognizing that a stream has a **longitudinal transition** along its length and a **lateral transition**, which extends outward from the normal and bankfull channel to the floodplain, to the reach of its riparian vegetation, all the way to its upland watershed boundary. The figure representing these stream shapes from the first edition of this book is on the book website (www.envirolanduse.org).

A typical stream cross section is shown in Figure 7.10, which delineates channel characteristics. **Bankfull depth and width** and the **hydrologic floodplain** are dimensions with the channel at maximum flow, or its bankfull discharge. The **bankfull discharge**, also called the channel-forming or dominant flow, is defined as the flow that fills a stable alluvial channel to the elevation of the active or hydrologic floodplain. Greater flows will overtop the channel and spread out onto the topographic floodplain. (Flooding and floodplain delineation are discussed later in the chapter.)

Streams and river channels change from headwaters to discharge to another receiving water body. Three zones vary in slope, stream discharge and mean flow velocity, channel width and depth, channel bed material grain size, and rela-

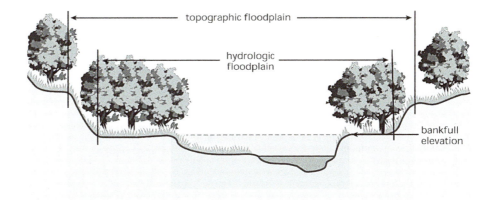

Figure 7.10 Characteristics of Stream Channels: Bankfull Dimensions and Floodplain Definitions. (*Source:* FISRWG 1998.)

tive volume of stored alluvium or deposited materials from upstream. The three zones are:

- *Headwater zone*, with steeper slopes, higher velocity, larger bed material, and lower discharge, channel width and depth, and stored alluvium.
- *Transfer zone*, between headwater and deposition zones.
- *Deposition zone*, with flat slope, lower velocity, smaller bed material, and higher discharge, channel width and depth, and stored alluvium.

Land Use, Stream Flow, and Predicting Peak Discharge

A **hydrograph** shows how the flow rate, measured in cubic feet per second (cfs) or cubic meters per second, at a specific point on a stream will change over time after a rainstorm event in its watershed. A hypothetical hydrograph is shown in Figure 7.11. The rainfall is generally given in a histogram showing the depth of rainfall for each hour of the storm. The curve that follows shows the channel discharge response as a flow rate that builds up to a peak, then drops back to the original baseflow. Important to note are the timing and magnitude of the peak. The peak will occur at some time after the center of mass of the storm, called the **lag time.**

The **peak flow** is the maximum flow that occurs when the water flow elevation is highest and the potential for flooding is the greatest. The hydrograph relationship of rainfall to discharge depends on several characteristics of the watershed, including soil type, land cover, slope, channel length, and ponding. Given the relationship, hydrologists can generate a peak discharge frequency and a flood elevation frequency based on rainfall frequency.

Land cover and drainage characteristics affect the accumulation of stormwater flow, as well as the amount of baseflow between storms. Figure 7.12 depicts how

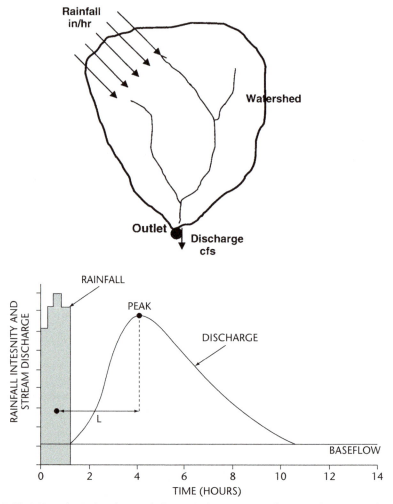

Figure 7.11 A Hypothetical Hydrograph Showing the Response of Stream Flow. L is the lag time to peak discharge. Baseflow is stream flow without storm event.

the process of urbanization—paving and covering the land with impervious surfaces and constructing drainage pipes and lined channels—increases the peak discharge from a given storm event by (1) reducing the amount of water that infiltrates the ground, thus *increasing the volume* of surface runoff, and, more importantly, (2) *increasing the rate* at which the runoff accumulates, thereby reducing the hydrograph lag time. Because of impervious surfaces, less water infiltrates the ground, and, thus, less is available for groundwater-contributed baseflow between storms, especially in dry weather periods. As a result, urban streams run faster and higher during storms, and often run dry between storms.

The peak flows from a given storm event will be greater from a watershed after it has experienced land development than before, and the baseflow between storms will be much less (Figure 7.13). Baseflow and summer low flows are critical to supporting stream ecology and riparian vegetation. Figure 7.14 shows that downstream stream geometry exhibits higher flood flows and a broader floodplain

Figure 7.12 The Effects of Urbanization and Impervious Cover on Water Balance. (*Source:* FISRWG 1998.)

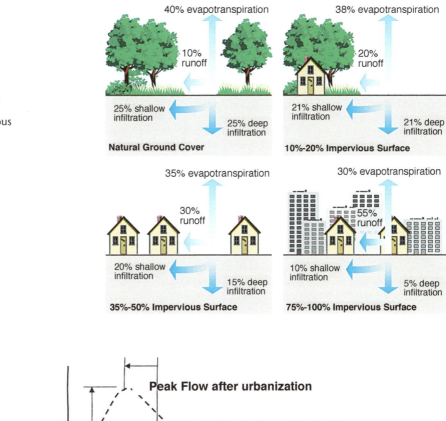

Figure 7.13 The Effects of Urbanization on Hydrograph Peak Flows and Baseflow.

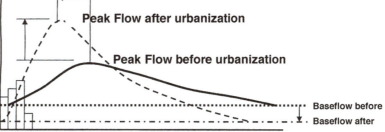

Figure 7.14 Changes in Flood Elevation as from Urbanization. (*Source: Controlling Urban Runoff: A Practical Manual for Planning and Designing Urban BMPs*, by Tom Schueler, 1987. Reprinted with permission of Metropolitan Washington Council of Governments.)

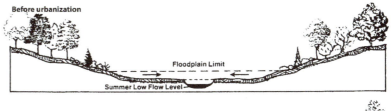
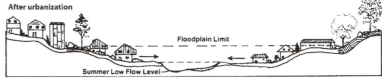

after urbanization upstream. Land development and urbanization cause significant hydrologic changes, which have the following detrimental effects:

- *Downstream flooding:* The increased flows caused by land development can exacerbate flooding downstream.
- *Contaminated water:* Urban runoff carries water contaminants that compromise the quality of receiving water; generally, as urban runoff increases, so does the pollution it carries.
- *Diminished baseflow and recharge:* Reduced infiltration reduces groundwater storage and dry weather stream flows.
- *Damage to creeks and streams:* Natural creeks and streams are directly affected by erosion caused by more frequent higher flows, and indirectly by pressure to channelize or pipe the channels.

Urban hydrologists suggest that **impervious surface coverage** in a watershed is a good indicator of potential impact on stream health. Table 7.1 shows the water cycle changes associated with impervious surfaces. The increased density of urbanization results in more impervious surfaces, which in turn reduce infiltration and increase runoff. Urban stormwater management measures aim to increase infiltration and reduce and detain runoff (see Chapter 8).

Predicting Peak Discharge

Planning and designing these measures and stormwater drainage systems, as well as understanding land use effects on runoff, require the ability to predict runoff flows from storm events. Planners and engineers also need to be able to assess the capacity of channels to carry stormwater flows and to design mitigation measures to reduce peak flows. In the past 40 years, a number of computer simulation and other methods have been developed that model stormwater responses to precipitation and estimate the effects of land use and control measures on flows.

Table 7.2 compares some of the more popular approaches to modeling rainfall-runoff-stream flow events. Many of the newer models also assess water quality, the subject of our next section, as well as mitigation measures, discussed in Chapter 8. The models are introduced here, as a preview.

TABLE 7.1 **Hydrologic Cycle Changes of Impervious Surface Associated with Urbanization**

Land Use/Cover	Imperviousness (%)	Evapotranspiration (%)	Infiltration (%)	Runoff (%)
Natural cover	0	40	50	10
Low-density residential	10–20	35	42	23
Urban residential	35–50	35	35	30
Urban center	75–100	30	15	55

Source: U.S. EPA 1993.

TABLE 7.2 **Stormwater Model Attributes and Functions**

Attribute	Rational Method	HSPF	HEC Models	SWMM	TR-55/ TR-20	BASINS ·	SUSTAIN	Watershed Treatment Model
Sponsoring agency		U.S. EPA	U.S. COE	U.S. EPA	NRCS (SCS)	U.S. EPA	U.S. EPA	CWP
When developed	1860	1960s	1970s	1971	1986	1996	2009	2010
Latest version	Modified	1997	2010 (RAS 4.1)	2004 (5.0) 2009 (5.018)	2003 WinTR55 2007 (1.00.09)	2007	2009	2010
GIS	None	None	HEC GeoRAS	No: Export to GIS	None	Yes: Map Window	Yes: ArcGIS	None
Simulation type	Single	Continuous	Single event	Continuous	Single event	Continuous	Continuous	Single event
Water quality analysis	None	Yes	Yes	Yes	None	Yes	Yes	Yes
Rainfall/runoff analysis	Yes	Yes	Yes	Yes	Yes	Yes	Yes	None
Sewer system flow routing	None	None	Yes	Yes	Yes	Yes	Yes	None
Dynamic flow routing eqn.	None	None	None	Yes	Yes	Yes	Yes	None
Regulators, overflow struct	None	None	None	Yes	None	Yes	Yes	Yes
Storage analysis	None	Yes	Yes	Yes	Yes	Yes	Yes	None
Treatment analysis	None	Yes	Yes	Yes	None	Yes	Yes	Yes
Data and personnel needs	Low	High	High	High	Medium	Medium	High	Low
Overall model complexity	Low	High	High	High	Low	High	High	Low

Source: Adapted and updated from Prince George's County 1999b; Caraco 2010.

The Rational Method

This is the grandfather of runoff assessment techniques. In the 1860s, Emil Kuichling suggested the simple relationship for assessing land use and peak discharge, based on Mubraney's formula developed in 1851:

$$Q = CiA \qquad \text{(Eq. 7.1)}$$

where

Q = peak discharge (cubic ft per second)
C = rational runoff coefficient, based on land cover
i = rainfall intensity (inches/hour)
A = drainage area (acres)

The runoff coefficient (C) is a dimensionless factor ranging between 0.05 for woodlands to 0.95 for concrete. The rainfall intensity (i) is derived from the intensity-frequency-duration curve (see Figure 7.4) for the desired frequency and the duration set at the time of concentration (Tc). The Tc is time of flow from the most remote point in the basin to the outlet point and depends on the length of travel, the drainage slope, the land cover, and channel type.

An example calculation using the Rational Method from the first edition is on the book website (www.envirolanduse.org). Incredibly, the Rational Method was used in the design of most urban stormwater drainage systems until the 1960s, when the Stanford Watershed Model was developed by Ray Linsley and his colleagues. The use of computerized simulation models to predict watershed effects on runoff had begun.

The Win TR-55 Method: Urban Hydrology for Small Watersheds

In the mid-1970s, the Soil Conservation Service (now the NRCS) issued Technical Release No. 55 (TR-55), *Urban Hydrology for Small Watersheds* (USDA, SCS 1986). The TR-55 model is considered more accurate than the Rational Method for larger urban drainage areas (up to about 2,000 acres), because it takes into account more factors and involves less judgment on the part of the user (particularly in the choice of the time of concentration). The peak discharge method can also be used to produce hydrographs for larger areas (up to 20 mi^2) using a tabular hydrograph method. Although it is less sophisticated than many simulation models, TR-55 is heavily used in state and local stormwater and erosion and sediment control programs and land analysis software like CITYgreen (see Chapter 10).

The first edition of this book presented the TR-55 tabular and graphical peak discharge method. That discussion and examples are posted for reference on the book website (www.envirolanduse.org).

In 2003, the NRCS reconfigured the method in a Microsoft Windows software version called Win TR-55, which is downloadable from the NRCS website; see http://www.wcc.nrcs.usda.gov/hydro/hydro-tools-models-wintr55.html. Win TR-55 is a single-event rainfall-runoff small watershed hydrologic model that generates hydrographs from both urban and agricultural areas and subareas and at selected points along the stream system. Hydrographs are routed downstream through channels and/or reservoirs. It has certain limitations, including being restricted to modeling only 24-hour storms and maximum watershed size (< 25 mi^2), number of watersheds (< 10), and number of stream reaches (< 10). Figure 7.15 consists of twelve parts that demonstrate using the Win TR-55 software. Figure 7.15A–C shows the example, an agricultural site with three subareas of drainage, and a small storage reservoir. The opening main window for Win TR-55 is shown in Figure 7.15D.

The Win TR-55 method involves the following steps, keyed to Figure 7.15:

1. Sketch the watershed configuration, including subareas, storage, and stream reaches (see Figure 7.15C).

2. In the Win TR-55 Main window, enter the user's identification information and choose the location with the drop-down menu. This location automatically sets the Storm Data Source and Rainfall Distribution Identifier.

3. Click the Land Use icon (1), which opens the Land Use Details window (Figure 7.15E). For each subarea, enter acres for each land cover and hydrologic soil group. This window calculates the total area and weighted average **runoff curve number (CN)** for the subarea, and automatically enters the subarea data on the Main window.

   • CN is a measure of the land cover influence on infiltration and runoff, similar to the C factor in the Rational Method. It ranges in value from about 30 (good woods, HSG A) to 98 (impervious cover). It depends on the vegetative or impervious cover, land use practice, and hydrologic soil group (HSG). Based on their texture and infiltration rates, soils are classified in HSG A (high-infiltration sands and sandy loams), B (silt loam and loam), C (sandy clay loam), and D (low-infiltration clay, clay loam, sandy clay, silty clay). Other factors, like soil compaction or high water table, can supercede the effect of texture. Soil surveys list HSG for different soils and map units.

4. From the Main window, click the T_c icon (2), which opens the Time of Concentration window (Figure 7.15F). For each subarea, enter the length, slope, and other data for sheet, shallow concentrated, and channel flow. This window computes the time of travel (T_t) for each type of flow and sums them to give the subarea time of concentration.

   • **Sheet flow** is flow over plane surfaces, and it usually occurs in the headwaters of streams. It depends on frictional resistance to flow, measured by the Manning's roughness coefficient, n. The value for n depends on surface conditions and is chosen from a drop-down menu in the sheet flow line.

   • **Shallow concentrated flow** is the fate of sheet flow after a maximum of 300 ft. Velocity depends on channel slope; it is estimated for paved or unpaved channels selected from a drop-down menu on the shallow flow line.

   • **Open channel flow** applies to intermittent and perennial channels. Flow velocity (V) is determined by Manning's equation (Eq. 7-2, below); this requires information on channel's hydraulic parameters (Figure 7.16), slope, and roughness. (Appendix 7A describes a method for estimating channel roughness for use in testing channel capacity.) Once values are entered, the software calculates V from Manning's equation (Eq. 7.2) and T_t from Equation 7.3 below.

5. Click the Main window's Storage Structure icon (3), which opens the Storage Structure window (Figure 7.15H). Enter the Storage Structure data for as many as three trials.

6. Click the Reach Data icon (4) to open the Reach Data window (Figure 7.15G). Enter data for each reach and identify the storage structure.

(A)

(B)

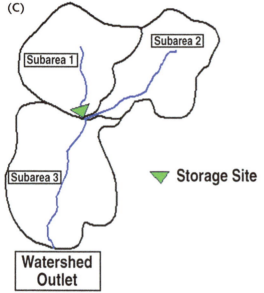

(C)

Subarea 1

Subarea 2

Subarea 3

▼ **Storage Site**

**Watershed
Outlet**

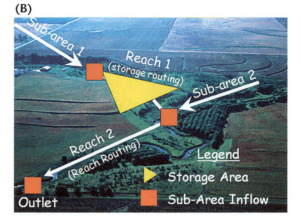

(D)

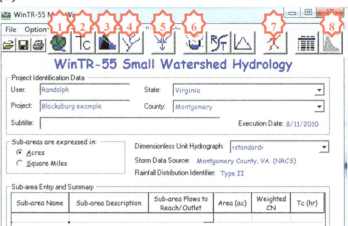

(E)

Land Use Details

Sub-area Name

Sub-area 1   Rename   Clear   **Land Use Details**

Land Use Categories

○ Urban Area   ○ Developing Urban   ● Cultivated Agriculture   ○ Other Agriculture   ○ Arid Rangeland

Area (Square Miles) for Hydrologic Soil

Cover Description		A	CN	B	CN	C	CN	D	CN
SR + Crop residue	poor		71	1.100	80		87		90
SR + Crop residue	good		64		75		92		65
Contoured (C)	poor		70		79		64		66
Contoured (C)	good		65		75		82		88
C + Crop residue	poor		69		78		83		87
C 0+ Crop residue	good		64	0.180	74		81		85
Cont & terraced (C&T)	poor		66		74		80		82
Cont & terraced (C&T)	good		62		71		78		81
C&T + crop residue	poor		66		73		79		81
C&T + crop residue	good		61		70		77		80
Small grain Straight row (SR)	poor		55	0.100	76		84		88
Straight row (SR)	good		63	0.500	75		83		87
SR + Crop residue	poor		54		72		83		88
SR + Crop residue	good		60		72		80		84

Project Area (Mi²)   Summary Screen   Sub-Area

3.93   ● Off ○ On   Area (mi²) 1.88   Weighted CN: 78   Help   Cancel   Accept

File: C:\Program Files\WinTR55\tutorial_sample.w55   8/28/01   10:21 AM

(F)

Time of Concentration Details

Sub-area Name

sub-area 1   Rename   Clear   2-Year Rainfall (in) 3   **Time of Concentration Details**

Flow Type	Length (ft)	Slope (ft/ft)	Surface (Manning's n)	n	Area (ft²)	WP (ft)	Velocity (f/s)	Time (hr)
Sheet	100	0.0050	Grass-Range Short (0.15)					0.294
Shallow Concentrated	1800	0.0500	Unpaved					0.139
Shallow Concentrated								
Channel	12590						5.000	0.699
Channel								
Total	14.490						3.5557	1.132

Help   Cancel   Accept

File: <new file>   8/11/2010   1:08 PM

(G)

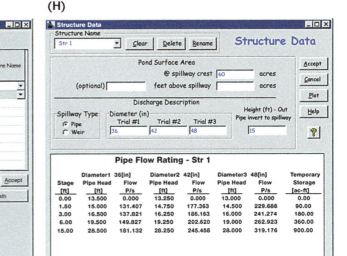

(H)

(I)

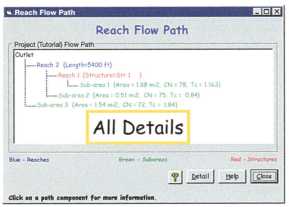

(J)

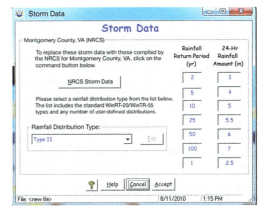

(K)

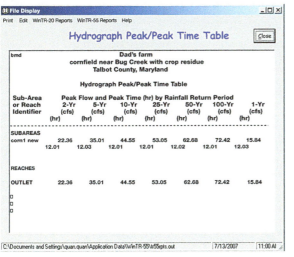

(L)

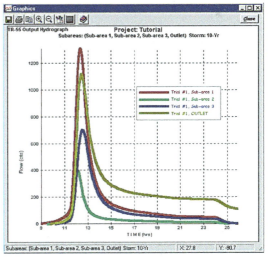

Figure 7.15 A Summary of Win TR-55 Software. A–C: Visualizing watershed configuration. D: Main window. E: Land Use Details window. F: Time of Concentration window. G: Reach Data window. H: Storage Data window. I: Reach Flow Path window. J: Storm Data window. K: Run Display window. L: Output Hydrograph window. (Source: USDA, NRCS 2008.)

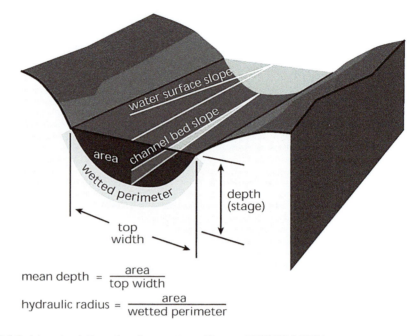

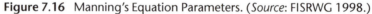

$$\text{mean depth} = \frac{\text{area}}{\text{top width}}$$

$$\text{hydraulic radius} = \frac{\text{area}}{\text{wetted perimeter}}$$

Figure 7.16 Manning's Equation Parameters. (*Source*: FISRWG 1998.)

$$V = \frac{1.49 r^{2/3} s^{1/2}}{n} \quad \text{(Manning's equation)} \quad \text{(Eq. 7.2)}$$

where

V = average velocity (ft/s)
r = channel full hydraulic radius (ft)
$r = a/p_w$, where a = cross-sectional flow area (ft²)
p_w = wetted perimeter (ft) (see Figure 7.16)
s = slope of hydraulic grade line (channel slope, ft/ft)
n = Manning's roughness coefficient for open channel flow

$$T_t = \frac{L}{3600V} \quad \text{(Eq. 7.3)}$$

where T_t = travel time (hr)
L = flow length (ft)

V = average velocity (ft/s)

3600 = conversion factor from seconds to hours

7. Click the Reach Flow Path button on the Reach Data page or icon (5) on the Main page to check that the reach flow path conforms to the watershed configuration (Figure 7.15I).

8. Click the Storm Data icon (6) and select the storm frequencies to run (Figure 7.15J).
9. Click the Run TR-55 icon (7) to see the results of peak discharge in cubic feet per second (Figure 7.15K). Click the Hydrograph icon (8) for the hydrograph data and graph (Figure 7.15L).

The Win TR-55 software is user-friendly and is helpful for running different scenarios to see the effects of changing land use.

Watershed Simulation Models

Win TR-55 is useful for site planning purposes, but larger watershed studies require more sophisticated models. Several of the models listed in Table 7.2 are summarized here.

HSPF. The Stanford Watershed Model of the 1960s ushered in the age of simulation models for stream flow response to watershed rainfall events. In the 1970s, the EPA sponsored a FORTRAN version of the Stanford model, and water-quality processes were added to what was awkwardly renamed the Hydrological Simulation Program— FORTRAN (HSPF). The USGS helped sponsor software improvements in the 1980s, and an interactive version 11 was developed in 1997. HSPF is now a lumped watershed model that simulates runoff and pollutant loadings, integrates them with point source contributions, and analyzes hydrologic and water quality in reaches.

HEC-1, HEC-2, HEC-RAS. The Army Corps of Engineers Hydrology Engineering Center (HEC) has produced a number of simulation models for use in its hydrologic studies. HEC-1 was developed as a single-event watershed model and has been used less than the EPA models, which have continuous simulation with more water quality parameters. HEC-2 was a river hydraulics model and was superceded in 2002 by HEC-RAS (River Analysis System), which is now in version 4.1, with a GIS extension HEC-GeoRAS for ArcGIS 9.3. HEC-RAS is the principal model used in developing floodplain maps for FEMA.

SWMM. Meanwhile, in 1971 the EPA developed the Storm Water Management Model (SWMM), a dynamic rainfall-runoff simulation model that computes runoff quantity and quality from primarily urban areas. The model can collect runoff from several subcatchments and can route flows through pipes, pumps, channels, and storage/treatment devices. SWMM was rewritten as version 5 in 2005 and has had a number of revisions since. The EPA does not provide technical support, but there is a healthy SWMM users group that shares experience and self-developed improvements, such as integrating results into GIS.

Gironás et al. (2009) developed for the EPA a useful manual of SWMM applications. Figure 7.17 shows three applications from that manual, comparing hydrographs for three site scenarios: an undeveloped site, a developed site, and a developed site with some low-impact development (LID) measures (infiltration trenches and filter strips). The hydrographs record storms of various magnitudes

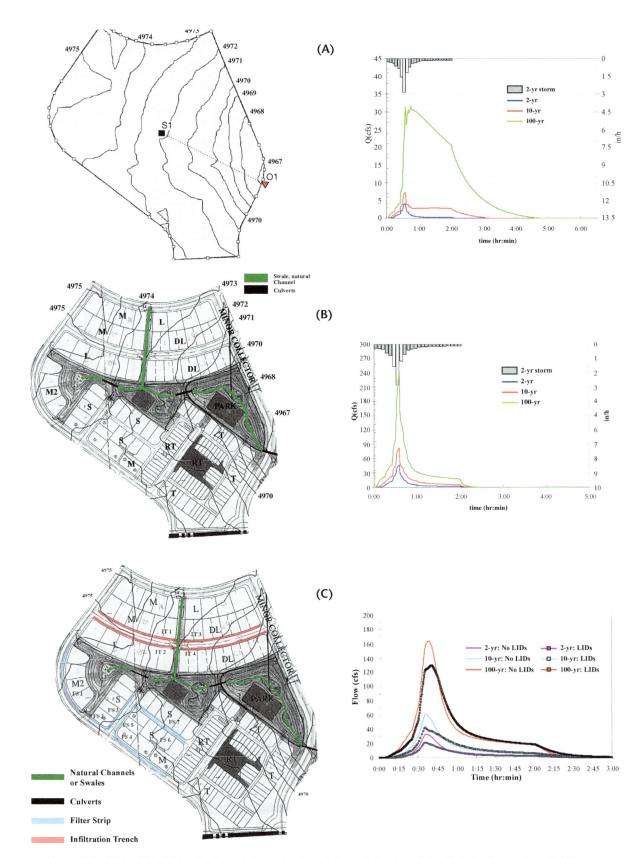

Figure 7.17 SWMM Model Applications. A: An undeveloped site. B: A developed site. C: A developed site with LID measures. (*Source:* Gironás et al. 2009.)

(frequencies/probabilities). Site development increased the peak discharge from 32 to 240 cubic feet per second. With the LID measures, SWMM predicts the outlet discharge would be 20% lower than without the LID.

BASINS. By the 1990s, HSFP and SWMM were well accepted models used by engineering hydrologists. The EPA recognized a need for an easier-to-use, multipurpose watershed model with GIS capabilities to support the development of total daily maximum loads (TMDLs). BASINS (Better Assessment Science Integrating Point and Nonpoint Sources) was developed for that objective in 1996. It uses two watershed models for nonpoint source assessment, HSPF for urban stormwater and SWAT (Soil and Water Assessment Tool) for agricultural runoff. The USDA developed SWAT to predict the effects of land management on water, sediment, and agricultural chemical yields in a complex watershed. To better meet the objectives of open access and wide use of BASINS, the 2007 version 4.0 shifted from Esri GIS software to open source GIS (MapWindow).

SUSTAIN. Although these increasingly sophisticated models integrate water quantity and quality, and runoff and point discharges, to assist water and land management, they are silent on an important factor—the cost of managing stormwater. Since 2003, the EPA has been working to develop a watershed-scale decision-support system based on cost optimization. Released in November 2009, the System for Urban Stormwater Treatment and Analysis Integration (SUSTAIN) is a public domain tool for evaluating the optimal location, type, and cost of stormwater best-management practices (BMPs) at multiple scales to meet water quality goals in urban watersheds. It uses algorithms from SWMM and HSPF and runs in conjunction with ArcGIS. For an illustration of SUSTAIN used to evaluate four BMPs for reducing total suspended solids (TSS) in an urban watershed in Milwaukee, see Shoemaker, et al. (2009). That example is summarized on the book website (www.envirolanduse.org).

CWP Watershed Treatment Model. The Center for Watershed Protection developed a spreadsheet-based model that analyzes runoff volumes and pollutant loads from existing conditions; application of future land, runoff, and pollutant management practices; and future land development. The model does not calculate runoff peak discharge, but instead focuses on pollutant loads from the "water quality volume" or the first flush of rainfall. The spreadsheet model and user's guide are downloadable from the CWP website (http://www.cwp.org/).

Peak Discharge, Flooding, and Flood Hazard Maps

One of the chief concerns of the peak discharge shown on a hydrograph is that this flow of water can overtop streambanks and spread out, flooding the landscape and everything in its path. Massive flooding events are recurring and appear to be on the rise with more frequent extreme weather. Chapter 13 on natural hazards will discuss in detail the options available to mitigate damage from floods. While we are

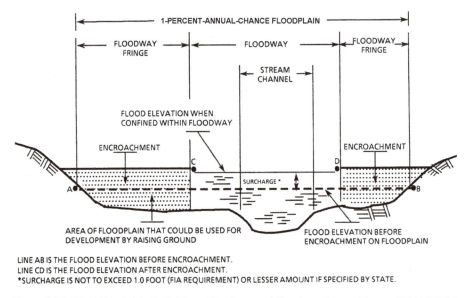

LINE AB IS THE FLOOD ELEVATION BEFORE ENCROACHMENT.
LINE CD IS THE FLOOD ELEVATION AFTER ENCROACHMENT.
*SURCHARGE IS NOT TO EXCEED 1.0 FOOT (FIA REQUIREMENT) OR LESSER AMOUNT IF SPECIFIED BY STATE.

Figure 7.18 FEMA Floodplain Definitions: Floodway and Floodway Fringe. (*Source:* FEMA 2009.)

discussing peak discharge in this chapter, it is useful to describe its effects and how we assess them.

Figure 7.9 showed the *hydrologic* and *topographic floodplains*. The former is the area inundated by the bankfull flow, the latter is the extent of floods outside the banks to the first major rise in ground elevation. Figure 7.13 showed the effect of peak flow on discharge height and the spread of water over the floodplain. For the developed land cover, the peak discharge, height of water, and spread of flooding are much more than for the natural land cover. The relationship between peak discharge and water elevation is given by a rating curve that plots discharge on the horizontal axis and stage height on the vertical axis. Knowing the peak discharge response to storms of different frequencies from hydrologic models and the stage or elevation of those events, floodplain maps of different storm frequencies can be plotted on topographic maps or with digital elevation model (DEM) data in a GIS.

Figure 7.18 gives additional floodplain definitions. These are important for regulatory purposes associated with the Federal Emergency Management Agency (FEMA) and its National Flood Insurance Program (see Chapter 13). To qualify for this program, communities must implement floodplain management and zoning rules linked to those definitions.

- **Floodway:** A fairly narrow area close to the stream that must remain open so that floodwaters can pass through.
- **Floodway fringe:** The area within the 100-year (or the 1% annual chance) floodplain that can be subject to encroachment or filling without causing more than a 1-ft surcharge in the height of the 1% flood carried by the floodway.

Floodplain zoning must, at minimum, prohibit development in the floodway, but it may allow development with floodproofing in the 1% floodway fringe. Note that FEMA is moving away from the recurrence-year (e.g., 500-year) designation of flood magnitude and adopting the more accurate and less misleading annual probability (e.g., 0.2%) of occurrence. Floodproofing usually involves elevating structures or portions of structures prone to damage above the 1% annual chance flood elevation plus the 1-ft surcharge.

Floodplain maps and data are available for nearly all flood-prone areas in the U.S. through FEMA. This floodplain map service is closely tied to the National Flood Insurance Program (NFIP). In addition to providing community flood hazard maps, FEMA issues flood insurance rate maps (FIRMs), which show degrees of hazard for establishing insurance rates. Although FEMA no longer issues printed flood plain maps, they are available as PDF and image digital files, and FEMA provides access in four ways through its Flood Map Service Center (http://msc.fema.gov):

1. Flood maps provide access to current FEMA-issued flood maps by location. Available maps and the Flood Insurance Study can be viewed and/or purchased on CD or as a downloadable file.
2. FIRMettes allow users to produce a zoomed-in FIRM for a small area of interest using the Current FEMA Maps finder. Following a simple process, users create a free and downloadable PDF or image file. Figure 7.19 shows a FIRMette for a portion of Blacksburg (VA).
3. MapViewer-Web provides access to National Flood Hazard Layer (NFHL) maps for a specific location. Figure 7.20 shows a Flood Hazard Layer map for the same portion of Blacksburg. The NFHL is a database that contains the flood hazard map information from FEMA's Flood Map Modernization program, including data from Digital Flood Insurance Rate Map (DFIRM) databases and Letters of Map Revision (LOMRs). There are utility files to view the NFHL in Google Earth, a Web Map Service, and NFHL GIS data.
4. DFIRM database (where available) can be accessed by inputting a location.

Figures 7.19 and 7.20 identify the floodway and the 1% and 0.2% floodplains. The maps show Flood Hazard Zones. Zone A is within the 1% annual probability (or 100-year) floodplain, and subcategories of Zone A are used if there are specific flood hazards or information (e.g., AE indicates Zone A areas for which there are baseflow data). Zone B is between the 1% and 0.2% flood boundary, Zone C is outside the 0.2% boundary, and Zone D is undetermined. Zone V applies to coastal flooding wave surges (see Chapter 13).

The Flood Insurance Study includes **flood profile** graphs and **floodway data** tables to accompany the maps. Figure 7.21 gives the flood profile and floodway data for the floodplain shown in Figures 7.19 and 7.20. The profile plots the water elevations (y-axis) for floods of various annual probabilities (10%, 2%, 1%, and 0.2%) against stream distance above its outlet (x-axis). For example, in

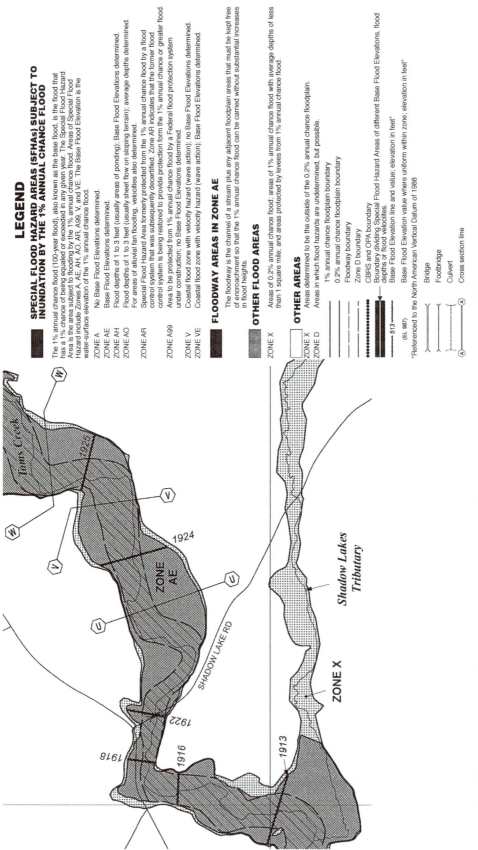

Figure 7.19 A FIRMette for a Portion of Tom's Creek, Blacksburg, Virginia. This image was produced from the current FEMA Maps finder website.

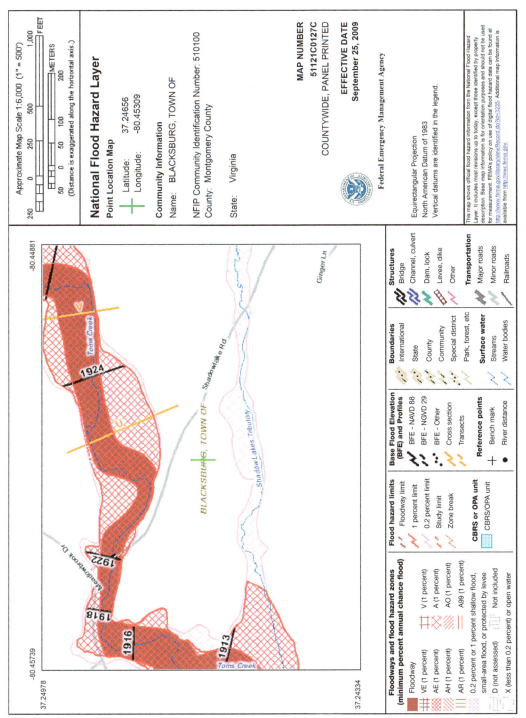

Figure 7.20 A Flood Hazard Layer Map for the Same Portion of Tom's Creek. This piece was produced from FEMA's MapViewer-Web website.

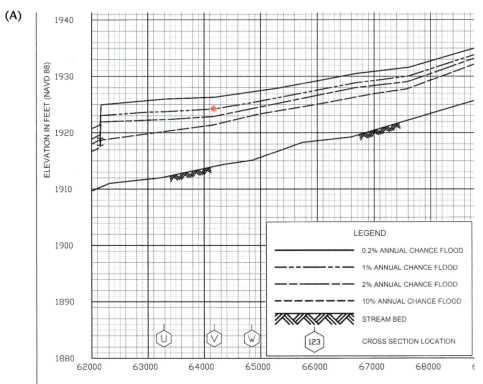

(A)

(B)

FEDERAL EMERGENCY MANAGEMENT AGENCY

FLOODING SOURCE		FLOODWAY			BASE FLOOD WATER SURFACE ELEVATION (FEET NAVD)			
CROSS SECTION	DISTANCE	WIDTH (FEET)	SECTION AREA (SQUARE FEET)	MEAN VELOCITY (FEET PER SECOND)	REGULATORY	WITHOUT FLOODWAY	WITH FLOODWAY	INCREASE
Toms Creek (continued)								
R	56,475[1]	200	1,124	4.5	1,905.7	1,905.7	1,905.7	0.0
S	58,090[1]	230	1,287	4.0	1,908.1	1,908.1	1,908.3	0.2
T	59,890[1]	270	1,148	4.4	1,911.1	1,911.1	1,911.5	0.4
U	63,280[1]	200	1,357	3.4	1,923.7	1,923.7	1,924.3	0.6
✳V	64,175[1]	280	1,398	3.3	1,924.2	1,924.2	1,925.2	1.0
W	64,840[1]	200	1,123	3.8	1,925.3	1,925.3	1,926.0	0.7
X	68,890[1]	320	1,001	4.0	1,934.2	1,934.2	1,934.2	0.0

[1] FEET ABOVE NEW RIVER

MONTGOMERY COUNTY, VA

(AND INCORPORATED AREAS)

FLOODWAY DATA

TOMS CREEK AND TOWN BRANCH

Figure 7.21 Tom's Creek Flood Profile and Floodway Data. The section letters U, V, and W on (A) the profile graph and (B) the floodway table correspond to the cross sections on the maps in Figures 7.19 and 7.20. The red stars on the graph and table refer to the example in the text. (*Source:* FEMA 2009.)

Figure 7.21A, you can read from the graph the elevation of the 1% flood at point (or cross section) V along the stream (stream distance 64,175 ft). The elevation is about 1,924.2 ft above sea level (see red star). This datum is also given on the floodway data table (Figure 7.21B). Note that the maps show cross sections U, V, and W. These cross sections link together the maps, flood profile graph, and floodway data table. Planners and landowners can determine the regulatory floodway elevation below which building or filling is not allowed.

If you have a building site near a stream—for example, along the V cross section in Figure 7.19—you have to survey the site to determine the site's elevation above sea level (Let's say 1,923.2 ft). To determine whether you can get a building permit for the site, the local planner or building inspector will identify the site on the flood profile and floodplain map. If the site elevation is above the base floodwater elevation (1% annual chance flood elevation plus 1 ft surcharge, in this case 1,925.2 ft), the site passes the FEMA test (this one does not); if not, the site elevation must be compared with the regulatory elevation (1,924.2 ft) to see whether it is within the floodway (it is, and a permit will likely be denied). However, the local jurisdiction may have stricter standards; Blacksburg, for example, protects the entire 1% floodplain plus a creek overlay depending on the riparian slope (see Chapter 17).

Land Use and Water Quality

In addition to affecting runoff quantity, land use also impacts water quality, because the surface runoff from cultivated, disturbed, and developed land carries water contaminants to receiving waters. Before focusing on land use and nonpoint source pollution, we first focus on some water quality fundamentals. Subsequent sections review stream quality assessment, and the sources and impacts of NPS. (Measures and programs for controlling stormwater quality problems are presented in Chapter 8.)

Water Quality Fundamentals

In the United States, we have made considerable progress cleaning up our waterways and improving the safety of water for human and aquatic life, primarily through improved engineering treatment at municipal sewage treatment plants and industrial facilities.

Between 1970 and 2000, we have doubled the number of waterways that are safe for fishing and swimming, doubled the number of Americans served by adequate sewage treatment, and reduced soil erosion from cropland by one-third. However, indicators of stream and lake impairment have worsened since 1998. In the latest national water quality assessment, the EPA found that 45% of assessed rivers and streams and 64% of assessed lakes were impaired, meaning they do not meet water quality standards (U.S. EPA 2009).

The primary focus has shifted from municipal and industrial discharges to runoff pollution from nonpoint sources (NPS). Indeed, national water quality assessments indicate that 60–70% of the nation's waters not meeting water quality standards are impaired by NPS pollution. Therefore, the remaining work in improving natural water quality requires land use measures to control runoff and pollutants it carries from urban, agricultural, and other land-disturbing activities.

Water Pollutants

Water quality is a complex subject, and it is useful to understand some basic scientific concepts. Table 7.3 summarizes the major categories of water pollutants carried by surface runoff:

- *Organic oxygen-demanding wastes.* Biological decomposition of these pollutants depletes the water's **dissolved oxygen (DO)**, which is essential for supporting aquatic life. Water bodies gain oxygen from atmospheric aeration and photosynthesizing plants. But they also consume oxygen through respiration by aquatic life, decomposition, and various chemical reactions. Wastewater from runoff or treatment plants contains organic materials that are decomposed by microorganisms, using oxygen in the process. The strength of the wastes is measured by the oxygen required to decompose them, known as biochemical oxygen demand (BOD). Biological treatment uses the natural decomposition process at an accelerated rate to stabilize organic waste.
- *Plant nutrients.* Inorganic plant nutrients, such as phosphorus and nitrogen, contribute to the excessive growth of algae and other undesirable aquatic vegetation in water bodies. Phosphorus is the limiting nutrient in most fresh waters, so even a modest increase in phosphorus can set off a chain of undesirable events in a stream, including accelerated plant growth, algae blooms, low DO, and the death of certain aquatic animals. Nitrogen, another essential nutrient, is present in organic form as well as inorganic ammonia (NH_3), nitrates (NO_3), and nitrites (NO_2). Total Kjeldahl nitrogen (TKN) is the sum of ammonia and organic nitrogen. Together with phosphorus, nitrates and ammonia in excess amounts can accelerate aquatic plant growth, thus changing the types of plants and animals that live in the stream. This, in turn, affects DO, temperature, and other indicators. Nutrients can be removed by advanced physical and chemical treatment, but biological treatment using vegetation uptake is also effective.
- *Thermal pollution.* The cooling capacity of natural waters makes them attractive for power plants and industry needing to discharge heat. Cooling water is returned to receiving waters much hotter and heats up these waters, impairing their ability to support cold-water species and depleting dissolved oxygen. Runoff on impervious surfaces, especially black asphalt, also contributes heated water to streams.
- *Sediment and suspended particles.* Suspended solids cause sedimentation in receiving waters. They include particles that will not pass through a 2-micron filter, including silt and clay, plankton, algae, fine organic debris, and other particulate matter. They can serve as carriers of toxics

TABLE 7.3 **Water Pollutants, Sources, and Effects**

Water Pollutant	Sources	Effects	Measurement	Controls
Organic oxygen-demanding wastes	Sewage, industry, runoff	Depletes DO, alters life-forms, kills fish	BOD_5	Biological treatment
Plant nutrients	Sewage, agricultural and urban runoff, industry	Algae growth, waterweeds	Nitrogen, phosphorus	Advanced treatment, biological treatment
Thermal effluent	Power plants, industry, impervious surfaces	Accelerates decomposition, biological activity; reduces DO solubility	Temperature	Cooling towers, ponds
Sediments and suspended particles	Runoff	Reduce clarity; smother bottom life	Turbidity	Settling
Dissolved solids: minerals and salts	Agricultural runoff	Taste; inhibit freshwater plants	Total dissolved solids (TDS)	Desalination; chemical treatment
Synthetic, volatile organic chemicals (e.g., oil, pesticides)	Industry, oil spills, agricultural runoff, air pollution	May be toxic to aquatic life, humans; subject to biomagnification	Chemical analysis	Filtration
Inorganic chemicals (e.g., acids, heavy metals)	Industry, mining runoff, air pollution	May be toxic to aquatic life, humans; subject to biomagnification	Chemical analysis	Chemical treatment
Radioactive substances	Nuclear fuel cycle, medical wastes, industry	Toxic to aquatic life, humans	Chemical analysis, beta count	Isolation, chemical treatment
Bacterial contamination	Sewage, runoff, bacterial sources	Disease transmission, pathogenic organisms	Fecal coliform count	Disinfection

like pesticides, which readily cling to suspended particles. Solids are removed by settling in detention facilities.

- *Dissolved solids*. Dissolved minerals and salts include calcium, chlorides, nitrate, phosphates, iron, sulfur, and other ion particles that will pass through a filter with pores of around 2 microns (0.0002 cm). Dissolved solids affect the water balance in the cells of aquatic organisms. Removal requires advanced physical treatment, such as reverse osmosis or desalination.

- *Acidity and alkalinity*. These are measured by pH on a scale from 1.0 (very acidic) to 14.0 (very alkaline), with 7.0 being neutral. The pH level affects many chemical and biological processes in the water. For example, different organisms flourish within different ranges of pH. Most aquatic animals prefer a range of 6.5–8.0, and pH level outside this range reduces the diversity in the stream. Low pH can also allow toxic compounds to become available for uptake by aquatic plants and animals. Alkalinity is a measure of the capacity of water to neutralize acids.

Water Bodies and Beneficial Uses

The effects of these pollutants depend on the quality of the receiving waters and their beneficial uses. The major types of water bodies are freshwater streams and rivers, freshwater lakes and wetlands, mixed freshwater and saltwater estuaries, coastal and marine waters, and groundwater.

Streams. The self-flushing and aerating action of streams gives them some assimilative capacity for conventional pollutants, such as organic matter, nutrients, suspended particles, and waste heat. However, the natural quality of streams varies widely from pristine headwaters to more nutrient-enriched downstream waters. Streams and rivers have a wide range of beneficial uses, including water supply, recreation, fish propagation, agricultural and industrial applications, and waste assimilation.

Lakes. Lakes have much lower assimilative capacity than streams, because of poor flushing. As a result, pollutants tend to accumulate in lakes; sediments fill up lake bottoms, nutrients contribute to the excessive growth of algae and other undesirable vegetation, and organics consume DO. This natural process, known as **eutrophication**, or the aging of lakes, will ultimately reduce a lake's beneficial uses for water supply, fish propagation, recreation, and aesthetics. Under normal conditions, eutrophication can take centuries, but runoff pollution containing nutrients and sediments can accelerate the process. This human-induced "cultural" eutrophication can occur in decades. Natural lakes and human-made reservoirs are both subject to the same process of aging. Lakes have a much longer residence time (so pollutants will accumulate more) but have a smaller watershed (which may be easier to manage). Reservoirs have a shorter residence time and more through-flow and flushing, but their much larger watersheds can contribute more pollutants and be more difficult to control.

Estuaries, Coastal Waters, Marine Waters. Estuaries are subject to some of the same processes as lakes and rivers, since some have flows and flushing (including intertidal mixing) like rivers, and others are more stagnant bays that behave like lakes. As important breeding and development habitats for fish and shellfish, estuaries have special needs, because pollution can easily disrupt fish growth or contaminate populations with resulting economic impacts. Coastal waters, and especially marine waters, have the largest assimilative capacity for water pollutants, but pollution can impact coastal waters for recreation and fishing.

Groundwater. As we shall see in Chapter 9, groundwater encounters complex patterns of flow and filtering, and it undergoes various chemical processes. Because groundwater from private wells is often used for domestic water supply without treatment, groundwater quality concerns relate more to human health than to ecological health.

Water Quality Criteria and Standards

The 1972 federal Clean Water Act (CWA), as amended in 1977 and 1987, provides the framework for the management of water quality in the U.S. The CWA sets forth a national goal of achieving a level of quality in all waters to support recreation and fish consumption; this standard is referred to as *fishable and swimmable*. To define this threshold, the CWA, and its administering agency the U.S. EPA, called on the states to establish water quality standards for their water bodies, monitor compliance, and manage pollutant discharges to meet these standards. (The CWA's management programs for nonpoint sources are discussed in Chapter 8.)

The process of establishing water quality standards begins by each state designating the beneficial uses of individual water bodies. The CWA's goals call for minimum standards for recreation and the propagation of aquatic life, but certain water bodies or reaches of streams may have beneficial uses (e.g., sources of community water supply or trout waters) that require higher standards. The state then determines criteria, such as chemical-specific thresholds or descriptive conditions, that aim to protect the beneficial uses. In addition, the CWA provides an antidegradation policy to prevent waters that meet the standards from deteriorating from current conditions. Natural surface waters are classified based on their natural quality and their beneficial uses, and water quality standards are assigned to different classifications.

Tables 7.4 and 7.5 illustrate the system used in Washington state to designate beneficial uses to fresh water bodies and the water quality standards for those uses. Table 7.4 is part of a long table that shows the designated uses for each

TABLE 7.4 **Sample Designations of Beneficial Uses to Stream Reaches, Washington State**

TABLE 602	Aquatic Life Uses						Recreation Uses			Water Supply Uses				Misc. Uses				
Use Designations for Fresh Waters by Water Resource Inventory Area (WRIA)	Char Spawning /Rearing	Core Summer Habitat	Spawning/Rearing	Rearing/Migration Only	Redband Trout	Warm Water Species	Ex Primary Cont	Primary Cont	Secondary Cont	Domestic Water	Industrial Water	Agricultural Water	Stock Water	Wildlife Habitat	Harvesting	Commerce/Navigation	Boating	Aesthetics
WRIA 18 Elwha-Dungeness																		
Boulder Creek and Deep Creek: All waters (including tributaries) above the junction.	✓						✓			✓	✓	✓	✓	✓	✓	✓	✓	✓
Dungeness River mainstem from mouth to Canyon Creek (river mile 10.8)		✓						✓		✓	✓	✓	✓	✓	✓	✓	✓	✓
Dungeness River, tributaries to mainstem, above and between confluence with Matriotti Creek to Canyon Creek (river mile 10.8)			✓					✓		✓	✓	✓	✓	✓	✓	✓	✓	✓
Dungeness River and Canyon Creek: All waters (including tributaries) above the junction.	✓						✓			✓	✓	✓	✓	✓	✓	✓	✓	✓
Elwha River and tributaries from mouth to Cat Creek, except where designated Char		✓					✓			✓	✓	✓	✓	✓	✓	✓	✓	✓
Elwha River and Cat Creek: All waters (including tributaries) above the junction	✓						✓			✓	✓	✓	✓	✓	✓	✓	✓	✓

Source: Adapted from WDOE 2006. (Full table is available at http://www.ecy.wa.gov/pubs/0610091.pdf.)

TABLE 7.5 **Sample Water Quality Criteria for Beneficial Uses, Washington State**

Beneficial Uses	Temperature 7-DADMax	DO-low 1-day min	Turbidity NTU	pH	Bacteria	Toxics, Radioactive	Aesthetics
Aquatic Life							
Char spawn	9°C (48.2°F)	9.5 mg/l	+5 NTU above	6.5 to 8.5±0.2		< criteria for 29 chemicals	No impairment
Core salmon	12°C (53.6°F)	9.5 mg/l	+5 NTU above	6.5 to 8.5±0.2		< criteria for 29 chemicals	No impairment
Salmon spawn	13°C (55.4°F)	8.0 mg/l	+5 NTU above	6.5 to 8.5±0.5		< criteria for 29 chemicals	No impairment
Recreation							
Extraordinary					< 50 col/100	< criteria for 29 chemicals	No impairment
Primary contact					< 100 col/100	< criteria for 29 chemicals	No impairment
Water Supply						< criteria for 29 chemicals	No impairment
Misc. Uses						< criteria for 29 chemicals	No impairment

Source: WDOE 2006.

stream reach and water body segment in the state. The beneficial use categories include aquatic life, recreation, water supply, and miscellaneous. Table 7.5 lists the water quality standards for some of those designated uses. Toxic and aesthetic criteria apply to all uses. Note the quantitative standards for "fishable and swimmable" waters, given as aquatic life and recreation uses. Aquatic life standards are the most specific and include temperature, DO, turbidity (increase in nephelometric turbidity units), and pH. Recreation standards include a bacterial contamination standard. Washington also has separate standards for marine waters and an antidegradation policy to protect high- quality waters that exceed the standards. The management goals of both point and nonpoint sources of water pollution are to achieve and maintain these water quality standards (WDOE 2006). For water quality standards for each state, see http://www.epa.gov/ost/wqs/.

Impaired Waters in the United States

Section 305(b) of the CWA calls on the states to assess, every 2 years, the health of their waters and to demonstrate progress toward meeting the standards and goals. In addition, section 303(d) requires the states to identify and prioritize all of their impaired waters, or those that do not meet their water quality standards (WQS). States group their assessed waters into the following categories:

TABLE 7.6 **The Quality of the U.S. Waters, 2004**

Water Body	Total Length or Area	Assessed (%)	Good (%)	Good, but Threatened (%)	Impaired 2004 (%)	Impaired 2000 (%)	Impaired 1998 (%)
Rivers, streams	3.53 million miles	16	53	3	44	39	35
Lakes, ponds, reservoirs	41.7 million acres	39	33	1	64	45	45
Estuaries	87,791 square miles	29	70	1	30	51	44
Great Lakes shoreline waters	5,521 miles	20	0	7	93	78	96

Source: U.S. EPA 2000a, 2002, 2009.

1. Attaining WQS
   a. Good/Fully Supporting: Meets WQS
   b. Good/Threatened: Meets WQS but may degrade in near future
2. Impaired, Not Attaining WQS
   a. Fair/Partially Supporting: Meets WQS most of the time but occasionally exceeds them
   b. Poor/Not Supporting: Does not meet WQS
3. WQS Not Attainable
   a. Use-attainability analysis shows that one or more designated uses is not attainable because of specific conditions.

Table 7.6 summarizes the 2004 National Water Quality Inventory results for the various types of surface water bodies, their total length or area, the percentage that was assessed, and the assessment ratings (U.S. EPA 2009). Although the national network of monitoring is extensive, only 16% of rivers and stream miles; 39% of lake, pond, and reservoir acres; 29% of estuary miles; and 20% of Great Lakes shoreline waters were included in the 2004 assessment. Percent impairment increased from 35% in 1998 to 44% in 2004 for assessed river and stream miles, and from 45% in 1998 to 64% in 2004 for assessed lake, pond, and reservoir areas. Impairment of assessed estuaries improved from 51% in 2000 to 30% in 2004. Great Lakes shoreline waters continue to be significantly impaired (93% of assessed miles) by the legacy of polluted sediments from past industrial and municipal discharges.

Table 7.7 lists the uses that are impaired, the major pollutants (stressors), and sources causing the impairment for rivers and streams; lakes, ponds, and reservoirs; and estuaries. Common uses impaired for all three categories are aquatic life, fish consumption, and swimming. Some 40% of assessed rivers and streams are impaired for safe fish consumption, 36% for aquatic life, 28% for primary contact like swimming, and 18% for drinking water supply. Several pollutants are problematic, led by pathogenic bacteria, habitat alteration, oxygen-demanding organics, nutrients, and sediments. Main sources of impairment are agricultural and urban runoff and stream modification. The story is much the same for lakes

TABLE 7.7 **Causes and Sources of Impaired Waters in United States, 2004**

	Rivers and Streams		*Lakes, Ponds, and Reservoirs*		*Estuaries*	
Uses	Fish consumption	40%	Fish consumption	73%	Aquatic life	27%
Impaired	Aquatic life	36%	Aquatic life	30%	Fish consumption	19%
(% miles/acres	Swimming	28%	Swimming	26%	Swimming	13%
assessed)	Drinking water	18%	Drinking water	20%		
Stressors	Pathogenic bacteria	72,305 mi.	Mercury	5,890,915 ac.	Pathogens	2,845 sq.mi
(assessed	Habitat alterations	57,577	PCBs	2,344,542	Toxic organic + pest	2,481
miles/acres/	Oxygen demanding	42,177	Nutrients	1,952,386	Oxygen demanding	2,180
sq. miles	Nutrients	38,632	Metals	1,517,163	Mercury	1,700
impaired)	Sediment	35,177	Oxygen demanding	1,214,301	Nutrients	1,047
Sources	Agriculture	94,182	Atmoshperic depos	2,009,363	Atmospheric deposit	3,260
(assessed	Urban runoff + NPS	68,115	Agriculture	1,670,513	Urban runoff + NPS	2,940
miles/acres	Hydromodification	61,748	Hydromodification	1,248,432	Muni. point source	2,487
impaired)	Habitat modification	42,752	Urban runoff+NPS	1,186,609	Industrial discharges	1,343

Source: U.S. EPA 2009.

and estuaries, except toxic organics, mercury, and other metals are added to the major stressors, and atmospheric deposition of mercury and metals is the major source of impairment.

National aggregation and summary of state 305(b) reports lag by about 4 years, so the best current water quality assessments come from the states themselves. For example, Figure 7.22 maps Virginia's distribution of water impairment from its 2010 water assessment: 84% of the state's 1,247 watersheds had at least one impaired stream segments, and 61 watersheds had 10 or more. Figure 7.23 zooms in on the Potomac River Basin in northern Virginia, showing impaired waters in red, as well as the basin's 450 monitoring stations (including 125 citizen monitoring locations) and major dischargers. Figure 7.24 shows advancing stream impairment in Fairfax County in the northeast portion of Virginia's Potomac Basin. The 2004 assessment found 24 total impaired waters, which grew to 52 impaired waters in 2006, and 67 in 2008.

Stream Flow and Water Quality Data

Tens of thousands of monitoring stations throughout the country operated by federal, state, and local agencies measure water flow and many water quality constituents and biological indicators. The USGS's National Streamflow Information Program operates 7,663 active continuous stream gauges, with at least 355 daily values per year and more than additional 1000 partial record gauges. Data are readily accessible from its website (http://water.usgs.gov/nsip/), and real-time stream flow and some water quality data are posted. Figure 7.25A shows a national

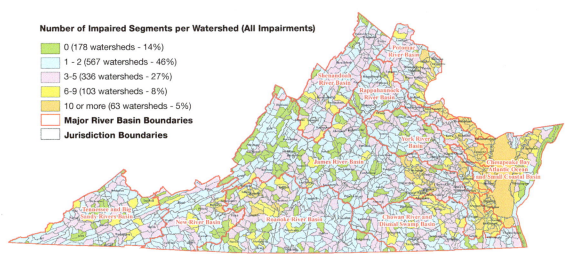

Number of Impaired Segments per Watershed (All Impairments)

- 0 (178 watersheds - 14%)
- 1 - 2 (567 watersheds - 46%)
- 3-5 (336 watersheds - 27%)
- 6-9 (103 watersheds - 8%)
- 10 or more (63 watersheds - 5%)
- Major River Basin Boundaries
- Jurisdiction Boundaries

Figure 7.22 Virginia 2010 Water Assessment Distribution of Impaired Waters by Watershed. (*Source:* Virginia DEQ 2010.)

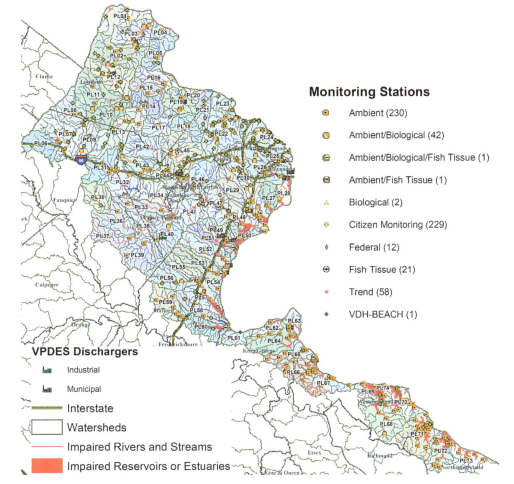

Monitoring Stations

- Ambient (230)
- Ambient/Biological (42)
- Ambient/Biological/Fish Tissue (1)
- Ambient/Fish Tissue (1)
- Biological (2)
- Citizen Monitoring (229)
- Federal (12)
- Fish Tissue (21)
- Trend (58)
- VDH-BEACH (1)

VPDES Dischargers

- Industrial
- Municipal
- Interstate
- Watersheds
- Impaired Rivers and Streams
- Impaired Reservoirs or Estuaries

Figure 7.23 Virginia 2010 Water Assessment, Potomac River Watershed, Impaired Waters, Monitoring Stations, and Dischargers. (*Source:* Virginia DEQ 2010.)

Figure 7.24 Fairfax County, Virginia, Impaired Waters, 2004, 2006, 2008. From 2004 to 2008, the number of impaired waters in Fairfax County grew from 24 to 67. (*Source:* Rose 2010. Used with permission of Fairfax County, Virginia.)

real-time stream flow for August 17, 2010. You can zoom in to get real-time data for specific gauging stations shown in Google Maps, such as the data for Roanoke River stream gauge in Roanoke (VA) in Figure 7.25B.

Water quality data comes from a wide range of monitoring sources. The EPA manages the **National STORET Data Warehouse** as a repository for water quality monitoring data collected by federal agencies, states and territories, tribes, volunteer monitoring organizations, and universities. It contains more than 70 million records of water quality data that are used by many agencies, planners, and scientists in water quality reporting (such as biennial 303 assessments), research, and decision making through mapping applications and water quality models. The data-sharing system not only provides access to data, but also facilitates the consistent and systematic uploading of monitored data from the diverse sources. The EPA has developed a Water Quality Exchange (WQX Web) system (http://www .epa.gov/storet/wqx.html) to simplify submitting data to the STORET Warehouse.

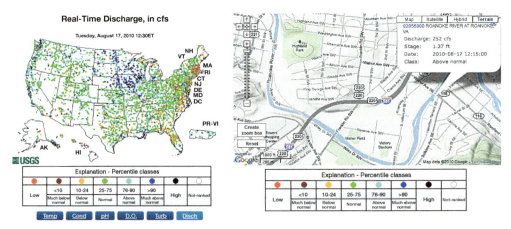

Figure 7.25 Stream Flow Data. Left: Real-time discharge at USGS gauging stations relative to normal. Right: Real-time discharge and stage, Roanoke River, Roanoke, Virgina. (*Source:* http://waterwatch.usgs.gov/.)

Figure 7.26 EPA EnviroMapper for Water Display for the Washington, DC, Metropolitan Area. This image shows STORET data sites (green dots) and impaired waters (red lines). (*Source:* http://map24.epa.gov/emr/.)

STORET monitoring sites and data are viewable at EPA's EnviroMapper for Water website (http://map24.epa.gov/emr/). Figure 7.26 is an image from Enviro Mapper of the northern Virginia/Washington, DC/Maryland area (including Fairfax County from Figure 7.24), showing STORET data sites in green, impaired streams in red, and nonimpaired sites in blue. On the interactive website, clicking on each green dot opens a window giving the monitoring and access to data.

The monitored data in the STORET system include a number of water quality parameters, such as temperature, dissolved oxygen, pH, turbidity, bacteria, and, increasingly, biological data. The overall health and integrity of water to support aquatic life is best measured by these biological indicators, obtained from sample fish and macroinvertebrate species. Appendix 7B describes a streamside method using a biosurvey of macroinvertebrates to indicate water quality.

Land Use Practices and Nonpoint Sources (NPS) Pollution

Well over half of the pollutants entering the nation's waters comes from runoff. The most pervasive problems affecting freshwater streams and lakes are agricultural runoff (affecting about 60% of water impairment), urban sources (runoff, hydromodification, and discharges, affecting about 50%), and mining runoff and silvicultural runoff (each affecting about 10%). Figure 7.27 gives an overview of land use practices that cause runoff pollution (first column), the results and consequences to receiving waters (second and third columns), and potential controls (fourth column). The figure is divided into the major land uses and practices causing NPS pollution: agriculture—animal production, agriculture—crop production, forestry, mining, and urban land use.

The land use practices generating runoff pollution include the following:

Major Nonpoint Sources, Consequences and Controls

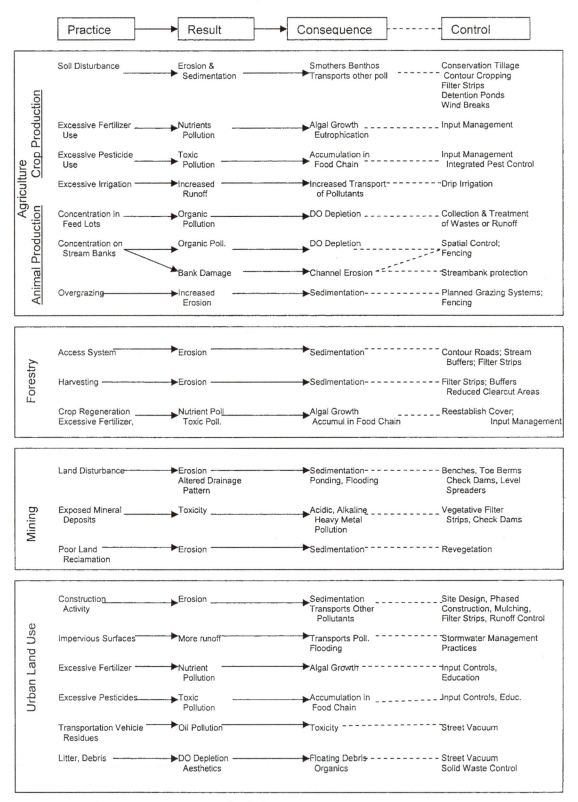

Figure 7.27 Land Use Practices Causing Runoff Pollution.

- **Soil disturbance** caused by agricultural cultivation and land development can result in erosion, leading to sedimentation of streams, lakes, or estuaries, which can smother bottom-feeding or benthic organisms. Conservation tillage (which leaves some crop residue to reduce erosion), contour cropping, and filter strips aim to control agricultural erosion at the source, while level spreaders, filters strips, ponds, and wetlands can remove suspended solids before they enter waterways.
- **Excessive use of fertilizer** for agricultural or urban development can result in runoff laden with plant nutrients, which can lead to algal growth in lakes and estuaries. Nutrient management programs aim to control excess fertilizer application by calculating fertilizer loading to match plant uptake. Filter strips and vegetative buffers can absorb nutrients before they enter waterways.
- **Pesticides** used in agriculture, silviculture, and urban land development can be carried by runoff, thereby contributing to toxic pollution of receiving waters. Input management and integrated pest control (which relies on nonchemical means of pest management and selective chemical use) can reduce pesticide pollution.
- **Animal concentration in feedlots** produces large amounts of organic wastes that can be carried by runoff and overload receiving waters, depleting the water's DO and causing fish kills. For such concentrated facilities, the collection and treatment of runoff is generally required.
- **Animal overgrazing in open pasture** can deplete available grass, exposing soil and creating erosion problems. In addition, animals tend to occupy streambanks, the so-called cows-in-creeks syndrome, which causes organic pollution and destroys channel banks. Spatial control through fencing is necessary to reduce these impacts.
- **Mining** disturbs the land, not only creating conditions for erosion, but also often altering drainage patterns. Benches cut into slopes, check dams, and level spreaders can help alleviate runoff and pollution problems during operations. Extensive reclamation and revegetation of mined lands are necessary to solve long-term erosion and NPS problems.
- **Cutting access roads and harvesting methods** in forestry operations increase erosion, particularly in proximity to stream channels and with greater land disturbance. Controls include building roads and trails along contours and providing vegetated or artificial filter strips to intercept runoff, and maintaining natural buffers along water bodies.
- **Urban runoff** carries sediment from construction activities; nutrients and pesticides from excessive uses on lawns, gardens, and golf courses; organic material and floating debris from roadside litter; and petrochemicals and toxic substances from transportation residues and air pollution desposition. More than half of the substances on the EPA's list of 129 priority toxic chemicals have been found in urban runoff.
- **Hydraulic modification** of channels, shorelines, and riparian areas for drainage or land development is another source of pollution into waterways, causing channel and habitat destruction.

Urban Runoff and the First Flush Effect

Urban runoff pollutants are carried in the highest concentrations during the first part of a storm event, referred to as the **first flush effect**. Monitoring and modeling research in the early to mid-1970s established a simple standard that was adopted by many communities trying to control stormwater pollution: Size the stormwater control measure to capture the runoff from the first portion of a storm, and 90% of the annual pollutant load will be treated. As a result, urban stormwater pollution control strategies normally focus on a storm's initial runoff, or they use a lower-frequency or smaller design storm. For example, an area's 1-year 24-hour storm may be 2 inches and its 10-year 24-hour storm is 5 inches. Although planners may wish to control stormwater from the larger storm to mitigate flooding, controlling runoff from the smaller storm may be sufficient to manage water quality.

For many years it was believed that this 90% objective could be achieved by capturing and treating the first half-inch of runoff in any storm. This "half-inch rule" was adopted in many ordinances, but field studies showed that though it was effective in areas of 30% and less impervious cover, the half-inch runoff carried less than 90% at greater imperviousness. One study showed that at 50% impervious cover, the first half-inch carried 75% of TSS (total suspended solids), and at 70% it carried only 53% (Chang, Parrish, and Souer 1990). As a result, rather than assuming the first half-inch rule, stormwater controls now calculate the **water quality volume** (WQv), or the volume of storage needed to capture and treat 90% of the average annual stormwater pollutant load, based on impervious surface. (These calculations are discussed in Chapter 8.)

Watershed planner Tom Schueler (1987) developed what he called the Simple Method to estimate pollutant loads from an urban site of catchment. The method yielded reasonable results compared with more complex models (Ohrel 1996). Most planning studies rely on more sophisticated methods, but the Simple Method is useful for starting to understand the parameters involved in mass balance calculations of pollutant loads. For a description of the Simple Method and an example calculation, see the book website www.envirolanduse.org.

Effects of Land Use on Stream Health and Integrity

Land use alters natural vegetative cover and increases runoff, peak flows, erosion and sedimentation, and nonpoint source pollution—all of which damage the physical and biological integrity of natural channels. Higher storm flows cause channel erosion and increase pressures for channel modifications that help drain stormwater through culverts, pipes, and channels, but destroy streambeds and streamside riparian vegetation. In addition, increased runoff lowers infiltration rates, reducing groundwater recharge and subsurface interflow and baseflow, causing streams to run dry in drought or dry months, thereby impacting stream ecology and riparian vegetation.

Any land-disturbing practice can create these impacts, but urbanization has the biggest effect, resulting from its permanent alteration of land cover by replac-

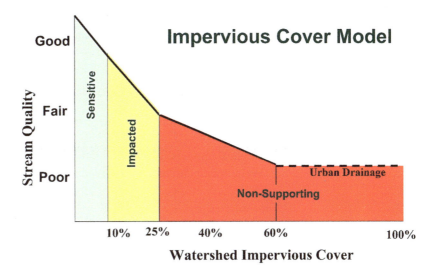

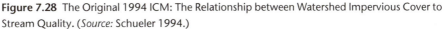

Figure 7.28 The Original 1994 ICM: The Relationship between Watershed Impervious Cover to Stream Quality. (*Source:* Schueler 1994.)

ing natural cover with impervious roadways, parking lots, and rooftops. This section expands on the effect of urban land use on stream quality, and describes some means of assessing the integrity of natural channels.

Stream Integrity and Impervious Surfaces

Many analysts have argued that impervious surface coverage, or **impervious cover (IC)**, in a watershed is a good indicator of impact on stream health. Leading the charge is Schueler, who in 1992 founded the Center for Watershed Protection (CWP) in Ellicott, Maryland, and developed it into a national leader in the watershed research and management practice. In 1994, using scatter plots from recent research on land use and stream quality indicators, Schueler introduced the Impervious Cover Model (ICM) to describe the strong negative relationship between subwatershed impervious cover and stream health. Figure 7.28 shows the simple original ICM. If there is more than 10% impervious cover in the subwatershed, receiving streams begin to be impacted, and above 25% imperviousness, streams begin to become nonsupporting of beneficial uses.

In an extensive 2003 synthesis of 225 research studies, CWP documented the profound effects of impervious cover on aquatic systems (Center for Watershed Protection 2003). It used the project to assess the validity of the ICM for the following stream quality indicators:

Largely confirmed ICM for:
- Hydrologic impacts: Increased runoff volume, increased peak discharge.
- Physical impacts: Stream channel enlargement, increased channel modification, reduced large woody debris, increased stream temperature, changes in pool riffle/structure, decline in streambed quality,

- Water quality impacts: Violations of bacterial standards.
- Biological impacts: Loss of riparian continuity, decline in stream habitat quality, reduced fish spawning, loss of coldwater species, decline in fish diversity, decline in aquatic insect diversity, decline in amphibian community.

Inconclusive for:

- Hydrologic impacts: Increased frequency of bankfull flow, diminished baseflow
- Physical impacts: Increased road crossings.
- Water quality impacts: Increased nutrient load, increased sediment load, increased pesticide levels, increased chlorine levels.

Contradicted for:

- Biological impacts: Decline in wetland plant diversity.

The model has been controversial, and many are dissatisfied with it. Stream ecologists think the ICM is a gross oversimplification, Smart Growth advocates complain that it rewards low-density sprawl, river advocates contend it sacrifices urban streams; it is loathed by developers, new urbanists, economists, and paving contractors (Schueler 2008). Among the critiques is that imperviousness alone may be too simplistic to capture the effects of urban development on stream quality. First, the effects of impervious surfaces will depend on whether they are *hydraulically connected* to the stormwater drainage system. Second, there are land use practices and measures, such as detention, infiltration, and treatment, that can lessen the effects of imperviousness on runoff, NPS pollution, and other stream impacts.

In 2008, Scheuler and his CWP colleagues conducted a new study of 65 peer-reviewed stream research studies released since the 2003 CWP study was completed. In all, 72% of the research confirmed or reinforced ICM and 28% were inconclusive or contradicting, and most of the latter were for large watersheds with legacy problems. The research that confirmed the ICM sampled small sub-watersheds (first-order to third-order streams) and tested them over a range of measured impervious cover. The researchers largely found a strong linear negative relationship for the stream indicator and IC, with a detectable shift in quality in the 5–15% IC range and a shift to fair or poor quality in the 20–30% range. Schueler et al. (2009) found from this study that:

- The impacts of land development are now detected as low as 5–10% IC.
- Riparian forest buffers have a mitigating effect on the ICM up to about 15% IC.
- Stormwater and watershed treatment did not have much of a mitigating effect on the ICM.
- The ICM does not apply everywhere, such as large watersheds degraded by legacy water diversions.
- Pollutant concentrations and loads do not follow the ICM.

To better fit the growing and more specific evidence about the impact of the ICM on stream quality, Schueler reformulated the model, as shown in Figure 7.29.

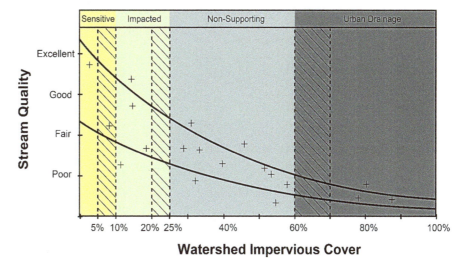

Figure 7.29 The Reformulated 2008 ICM. This version of the model shows the relationship of watershed impervious cover to stream quality as a band rather than a straight line. (*Source:* Schueler et al. 2009.)

Rather than a linear relationship, it expresses the effect of impervious cover on stream quality as a band that is widest at lower IC levels and progressively narrows at higher IC. It reflects subwatershed variability observed in research studies, as well as expected improvement that could be attributed to stormwater and watershed treatment. It shows that stream quality can be impacted down to "fair" rating for IC < 10%, and up to "fair" rating for IC in the 30–40% range, to account for mitigating measures. Schueler suggests that there are a range of responses to mitigate the impact of land development and the ICM, including land planning, design, and zoning; water quality regulations; engineered systems; and economic policies (see Chapter 8).

Stream Assessment

Stream assessment is important for monitoring stream integrity and identifying restoration problems and opportunities, as well as evaluating stream or watershed projects. A monitoring program should follow a clear strategy with defined objectives, an assessment design including sampling and data interpretation, and a reporting program. The evaluation objectives will determine the assessment tools and indicators (Table 7.8).

There are four approaches to stream monitoring:

1. *Watershed survey:* To identify watershed boundaries, upland land use, pollution sources, and stream corridor physical dimensions and conditions.
2. *Habitat assessment:* To determine riparian conditions, including vegetation, erosion, and other impairments.

TABLE 7.8 **Stream Assessment Objectives and Evaluation Tools and Indicators**

General Objectives	Evaluation Tools and Indicators
Assess watershed trends	Land use/land cover Land management Topography and soil types
Evaluate hydrologic changes	Channel dimensions Water depth and velocity Rates of bank and bed erosion Flood stage surveys
Improve riparian habitat	Percent vegetative cover Buffer width and condition Wildlife use, species diversity
Improve aquatic habitat	Pool/riffle composition, water depth Percent cover and shading Bed material composition Biological assessments
Improve water quality	Dissolved oxygen Priority pollutants Turbidity, suspended solids, floating matter Biological assessments

Source: Adapted from U.S. EPA, Watershed Academy 2000.

3. *Macroinvertebrate sampling:* To indicate aquatic habitat and water quality integrity and impairment.
4. *Water quality sampling:* To measure water quality and identify water pollution.

The tiered framework for doing stream assessments includes four progressively more complex activities: a stream or watershed walk to gather visual and dimensional data, a streamside biosurvey to collect and evaluate macroinvertebrates at the side of the stream, a channel capacity and erosion assessment, and an intensive biosurvey to collect biotic species and water samples and analyze them in the laboratory.

Visual surveys and streamside biosurveys are described here based on EPA and NRCS protocols (U.S. EPA 1997; USDA, NRCS 1998). They draw heavily from other procedures (e.g., California Department of Fish and Game 1996; Izaak Walton League of America 1994). Most of these approaches modify professional assessment protocols for volunteer implementation. Thus, they are made to be straightforward, simple, and quite appropriate for our discussion.

The Watershed Survey

The watershed survey begins by delineating the watershed of the stream reach being assessed. This procedure, using a topographic map, was described in

Box 7.1. Quite often the causes of stream impairment are upland uses and nonpoint pollution sources. Walking the land of the watershed and sketching onto the watershed map land uses, impervious cover, potential runoff pollution sources, drainage characteristics, vegetative cover, and other characteristics can reveal watershed improvements needed for stream restoration. Existing maps, aerial photos, and other available information can be very useful in watershed assessments.

Stream Walk and Visual Assessment

A systematic stream walk using an accepted protocol provides a useful assessment of the conditions of the riparian habitat and stream banks. Channel dimensions can also be measured for use in channel capacity calculations. The NRCS visual assessment protocol gives a good illustration of procedures and results (USDA, NRCS 1998), but other methods are also available. Some of the useful measures gathered in the stream walk include stream channel and bank characteristics relating to width and depth, pools and riffles, substrate (channel bottom), shading, and cover. Also included are water characteristics, such as appearance, odor, and temperature. Some of these dimensions are used for assessing channel capacity, velocity, and erosion. A box from the first edition gives some useful guidelines for stream walks, and it is posted on the book website (www.envirolanduse.org).

The NRCS protocol assesses up to 15 indicators that are combined into an index score of overall stream condition. The indicators include the following:

- Channel condition
- Hydrologic alteration
- Riparian zone
- Bank stability
- Water appearance
- Nutrient enrichment
- Instream fish cover
- Barriers to fish movement
- Pools
- Insect/invertebrate habitat
- Canopy cover: coldwater or warmwater fishery (if applicable)
- Manure presence (if applicable)
- Salinity (if applicable)
- Riffle embeddedness (if applicable)
- Macroinvertebrates observed (if applicable)

An appendix in the first edition, now posted on the book website, gives the assessment form and the scoring procedure for each indicator. Assessment scores are logged on the form, and an average score (the sum of the scores divided by the number of indicators used) is calculated.

A visual biological survey notes the presence of fish, fish barriers, aquatic vegetation, and algae. Fish can indicate stream quality sufficient for other organisms. Aquatic plants provide food and cover for aquatic organisms. Algae are simple, unrooted plants that mainly live in water and provide food for the food chain. Excessive algal growth may indicate excessive nutrients (organic matter or a pollutant such as fertilizer) in the stream.

The Streamside Biosurvey

The streamside biosurvey assesses stream macroinvertebrates or nonfish species. The presence, absence, and abundance of both sensitive and tolerant species serve as a useful indicator of stream health and water quality. Biosurvey methods have been used by water quality agencies and volunteer monitoring programs for two decades. The Izaak Walton League of America institutionalized the method in its Save Our Streams (SOS) program, and variations have been used throughout the United States. Several thousand monitoring groups now assess streams, and the results have proven to be so reliable that they are included in state and federal databases, including STORET.

A biosurvey protocol is discussed in Appendix 7B. Based on the EPA's *Volunteer Stream Monitoring: A Methods Manual* (1997), the method gathers, sorts, and counts macroinvertebrates present in a sampling reach and computes a stream health indicator based on the abundance and distribution of species.

Digital Field Monitoring

Field monitoring by volunteer groups relies on paper forms for recording information, but these forms are not optimal for efficient data collection, entry, and display. Recently, these accepted protocols have been adapted to allow the digital entry and storage of data using handheld computers or PDAs, GPS, digital water quality sensors, and digital cameras (for visual assessments) (see Figure 5.20). The use of these tools, along with other emerging software applications (e.g., CyberTracker, Excel, ArcGIS, and ArcIMS), allows an efficient means of collecing, recording, storing, analyzing, and mapping stream, watershed, habitat, and wildlife data, then presenting the results in an interactive format on the Internet.

Assessing Channel Capacity and Excessive Channel Erosion

Urban streams face a survival challenge as a result of the increase in upstream impervious cover. More frequent and higher stormflows reach and exceed the bankfull capacity of channels more often, resulting in excessive flooding and channel erosion. The typical remedy is to improve the drainage characteristics of the channel by straightening, widening, and lining. Unfortunately, this destroys the ecological, aesthetic, and other environmental benefits of natural creeks. Efforts to preserve and restore natural streams must consider the flow capacity and erosive forces of the channels. Stream preservation efforts must assess hydraulic characteristics of the channel, including its flow capacity and erosion problems.

Assessment methods for channel capacity use open channel flow calculations based on two equations. (1) Manning's equation calculates flow velocity based on the shape of the channel (its hydraulic radius), slope, and roughness (estimated from an assessment of channel vegetation, obstructions, meandering, and other factors). The equation was presented earlier as Equation 7.2, along with Figure 7.15. (2) The Continuity Equation calculates channel flow based on channel velocity from Manning's equation and cross-sectional area:

$$Q = AV \qquad \text{(Eq. 7.4)}$$

where

Q = flow in the channel (cfs)
A = cross-sectional area of the channel (sq ft)
V = average velocity in the channel (ft/sec)

This method is used to determine **bankfull velocity** and **bankfull capacity** (see Figure 7.10). A channel is considered to be "adequate" if its capacity is greater than the stream flow of a design frequency storm and the channel is resistant to the erosion from the bankfull flow velocities. If the assessment of a natural channel fails the first test (i.e., insufficient capacity), measures must be considered to reduce runoff flows in the watershed; or the channel may have to be modified to increase its capacity. If the channel fails the velocity test, the segments of the stream susceptible to erosion can be treated with vegetation and/or rocks to reduce the erosion potential (see Chapter 8).

The procedure for assessing natural streams and designing human-made or restored channels is essentially the same. For channel design, you assess an assumed channel size using the procedure; if it is too big or small, you adjust the size and test it again. The procedure has three main steps:

1. Determine the "required" flow capacity (i.e., the peak discharge from the design storm) and the "permissible" velocity of the channel (i.e., the maximum velocity without erosion for the channel lining or banks).
2. Calculate the channel velocity using the Manning equation and the channel capacity using the continuity equation.
3. Compare the results from (1) to those from (2): If the channel velocity is greater than the permissible velocity, excessive erosion is likely; if the channel capacity is less than the required capacity, excessive flooding is likely. Remedial action or a modified design is required.

To solve Manning's equation and the continuity equation, you need stream data from a stream walk survey, as well as some design tables (see Appendix 7A).

Summary

Water has a major effect on the landform, shaping the land through dynamic processes of erosion and deposition, creating alluvial floodplains and river valleys. Likewise, land use has a significant influence on water balance, affecting infiltration and runoff, peak and baseflows, and water quality and aquatic ecology. Although any land disturbance changes the water balance and aquatic ecosystem, land development and urbanization, and their associated impervious surfaces, have hydrologic, physical, water quality, and biological impacts on streams. These effects combine to cause higher peak discharges and greater stormwater and flooding problems during major storm events, reduced baseflows and low flows between storms and during droughts, and major changes in stream morphology and water quality due to erosive flows and nonpoint source pollution. This chapter provided a primer on water quality that will aid discussion in later chapters.

There are several methods for analyzing this relationship between land use and hydrology, water quality, and stream integrity. They include watershed delineation, peak discharge analysis using computer software such as Win TR-55 and simulation models, interpreting floodplain maps, characterizing nonpoint source pollution, modeling the effect of impervious surface on stream health, and conducting stream assessments, including testing channel capacity. Managing stormwater and natural channels involves applying these and other analytical methods to inform land development and design, as well as preservation and restoration decisions. The next chapter presents engineering, design, planning, and policy approaches to stormwater management and stream restoration, including a range of stormwater management land use practices.

Appendix 7A

Testing Channel Capacity

From a stream walk survey, obtain the following information needed for computing the channel capacity:

1. Draw a typical profile of the channel bottom.
2. Select control points along the channel for making measurements; select enough points so that data will adequately describe the stream.
3. Measure the shape and dimensions of the stream's cross section at the control points, and at other points as necessary, to determine an average.
4. Describe the channel between control points, including the material of the channel bed and banks, vegetation, meander, and obstructions to flow.

This information is used in a three-step procedure:

Step 1
- Determine the required peak flow (Q_r) the channel must carry from peak discharge calculations for a design storm (e.g., 2-year or 10-year storm).
- Determine the permissible velocity (V_p) for erodible channels. For human-made grass-lined channels, V_p values are given in Table 7A.1; for natural channels, V_p should be determined for the most erodible section of the stream, that is, areas of exposed soil. Values for various earthen channels are given in Table 7A.2. These values may be increased by 50% where dense vegetation exists naturally or is applied; or the erosion potential can be nearly eliminated by applying riprap (rocks) to highly erodible sections.

Step 2
- Determine the channel velocity (V) using Manning's equation.

$$V = \frac{1.49R^{2/3}S^{1/2}}{n}$$

This is the most complicated part of the procedure. The channel geometry must be approximated for natural channels. As shown in Figure 7A.1, the channel geometry will determine the cross-sectional area (A) and the hydraulic radius (R). The slope (S) of the channel comes from the channel profile.

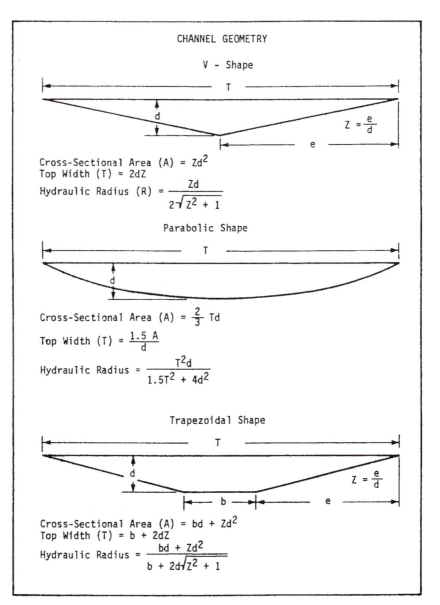

Figure 7A.1 Channel Geometry. (*Source:* VDCR 1992.)

All that remains to solve Manning's equation is the roughness coefficient (n), which depends on the channel lining. For riprap linings, $n = 0.0395\,D$, where D = the median stone size in feet in the riprap mixture.

For natural channels, several factors affect n. The procedure involves assuming a basic n for the channel bottom material (n_b), shown in Table 7A.3, then modifying the basic n. Modifying factors include the irregularity of the channel surfaces (n_1), the variations in channel shape or size

TABLE 7A.1 **Permissible Velocities for Unlined Earthen Channels**

Soil Types	Permissible Velocity
Fine Sand (noncolloidal)	2.5 ft/sec
Sandy Loam (noncolloidal)	2.5 ft/sec
Silt Loam (noncolloidal)	2.5 ft/sec
Ordinary Firm Loam	3.5 ft/sec
Fine Gravel	5.0 ft/sec
Stiff Clay (very colloidal)	5.0 ft/sec
Graded, Loam to Cobbles (noncolloidal)	5.0 ft/sec
Graded, Silt to Cobbles (colloidal)	5.5 ft/sec
Alluvial Silts (noncolloidal)	3.5 ft/sec
Alluvial Silts (colloidal)	5.0 ft/sec
Coarse Gravel (noncolloidal)	6.0 ft/sec
Cobbles and Shingles	5.5 ft/sec
Shales and Hard Pans	6.0 ft/sec

TABLE 7A.2 **Permissible Velocities for Grass-lined Channels**

Channel Slope	Lining	Permissible Velocity
0–5%	Bermudagrass	6 ft/sec
	Reed canarygrass	5 ft/sec
	Tall fescue	
	Kentucky bluegrass	
	Grass-legume mixture	4 ft/sec
	Red fescue	2.5 ft/sec
	Redtop	
	Sericea lespedeza	
	Annual lespedeza	
	Small grains	
	(temporary)	
5–10%	Bermudagrass	5 ft/sec
	Reed canarygrass	4 ft/sec
	Tall fescue	
	Kentucky bluegrass	
	Grass-legume mixture	3 ft/sec
Greater than 10%	Bermudagrass	4 ft/sec
	Reed canarygrass	3 ft/sec
	Tall fescue	
	Kentucky bluegrass	

TABLE 7A.3 **Roughness Coefficients for Man-made (*n*) and Selected Natural Channels (*n*ᵦ)**

Boundary	Manning Roughness, n Coefficient
Smooth concrete	0.012
Ordinary concrete lining	0.013
Vitrified clay	0.015
Shot concrete, untroweled, and earth channels in best condition	0.017
Straight unlined earth canals in good condition	0.020
Rivers and earth canals in fair condition—some growth	0.025
Winding natural streams and canals in poor condition—considerable moss growth	0.035
Mountain streams with rocky beds and rivers with variable sections and some vegetation along banks	0.040–0.050

(n_2), obstructions in the channel (n_3), vegetation in the channel (n_4), and channel meandering (m). Values for these modifiers are also listed in Table 7A.4. The total roughness coefficient is given by

$$n = (n_b + n_1 + n_2 + n_3 + n_4) \times (m)$$

With the input values (R, S, and n), the channel velocity (V) can be determined by Manning's equation.

- Determine the channel capacity using the continuity equation:

$$Q = AV$$

Step 3
- Compare the channel capacity to the required capacity:
  If $Q < Q_r$, the channel capacity is inadequate.
- Compare the channel velocity to the permissible velocity:
  If $V > V_p$, sections of the channel will be subject to excessive erosion.

Example of the Procedure for Testing Channel Capacity

Given the following characteristics of a stream, test its capacity to carry a 2-year peak flow of 400 cfs without overtopping or without excessive channel bank erosion.

TABLE 7A.4 **Roughness Coefficient *n* Value Adjustments for Natural Channels**

	Channel Conditions	n Value Adjustment	Example
n_1: Degree of irregularity	Smooth	0.000	Compares to the smoothest channel attainable in a given bed material.
	Minor	0.001–0.005	Compares to carefully dredged channels in good condition but having slightly eroded or scoured side slopes.
	Moderate	0.006–0.010	Compares to dredged channels having moderate to considerable bed roughness and moderately sloughed or eroded side slopes.
	Severe	0.011–0.020	Badly sloughed or scalloped banks of natural streams; badly eroded or sloughed sides of canals or drainage channels; unshaped, jagged, and irregular surfaces of channels in rock.
n_2: Variation in channel cross section	Gradual	0.000	Size and shape of channel cross sections change gradually.
	Alternating occasionally	0.001–0.005	Large and small cross sections alternate occasionally, or the main flow occasionally shifts from side to side owing to changes in cross-sectional shape.
	Alternating frequently	0.010–0.015	Large and small cross sections alternate frequently, or the main flow frequently shifts from side to side owing to changes in cross-sectional shape.
n_3: Effect of obstruction	Negligible	0.000–0.004	A few scattered obstructions, which include debris deposits, stumps, exposed roots, logs, piers, or isolated boulders, that occupy less than 5 percent of the cross-sectional area.
	Minor	0.005–0.015	Obstructions occupy less than 15 percent of the cross-sectional area and the spacing between obstructions is such that the sphere of influence around one obstruction does not extend to the sphere of influence around another obstruction. Smaller adjustments are used for curved smooth-surfaced objects than are used for sharp-edged angular objects.
	Appreciable	0.020–0.030	Obstructions occupy from 15 to 20 percent of the cross-sectional area or the space between obstructions is small enough to cause the effects of several obstructions to be additive, thereby blocking an equivalent part of a cross section.
	Severe	0.040–0.050	Obstructions occupy more than 50 percent of the cross-sectional area or the space between obstructions is small enough to cause turbulence across most of the cross section.
n_4: Amount of vegetation	Small	0.002–0.010	Dense growths of flexible turf grass, such as Bermuda, or weeds growing where the average depth of flow is at least two times the height of the vegetation; supple tree seedlings such as willow, cottonwood, arrowweed, or saltcedar growing where the average depth of flow is at least three times the height of the vegetation.
	Medium	0.010–0.025	Turf grass growing where the average depth of flow is from one to two times the height of the vegetation; moderately dense stemmy grass, weeds, or tree seedlings growing where the average depth of the flow is from two to three times the height of the vegetation; brushy, moderately dense vegetation, similar to 1- to 2-year-old willow trees in the dormant season, growing along the banks and no significant vegetation along the channel bottoms where the hydraulic radius exceeds 2 feet.

TABLE 7A.4 Roughness Coefficient *n* Value Adjustments for Natural Channels (cont.)

	Channel Conditions	n Value Adjustment	Example
	Large	0.025–0.050	Turf grass growing where the average depth of flow is about equal to the height of vegetation; 8- to 10-year-old willow or cottonwood trees intergrown with some weeds and brush (none of the vegetation in foliage) where the hydraulic radius exceeds 2 feet; bushy willows about 1 year old intergrown with some weeds along side slopes (all vegetation in full foliage) and no significant vegetation along channel bottoms where the hydraulic radius is greater than 2 feet.
	Very Large	0.050–0.100	Turf grass growing where the average depth of flow is less than half the height of the vegetation; bushy willow trees about 1 year old intergrown with weeds along side slopes (all vegetation in full foliage) or dense cattails growing along channel bottom; trees intergrown with weeds and brush (all vegetation in full foliage).
m: Degree of meandering	Minor	1.00	Ratio of the channel length to valley length is 1.0 to 1.2.
	Appreciable	1.15	Ratio of the channel length to valley length is 1.2 to 1.5.
	Severe	1.30	Ratio of the channel length to valley length is greater than 1.5.

Note: Adjustment values apply to flow confined in the channel and do not apply where down-valley flow crosses meanders.

- Cross section: trapezoidal: T = 25'; d = 4'; b = 9'; e = 8'.
- Stream profile slope: 0.015 ft per foot.
- Channel is earthen in fair condition.
- Channel banks are 1/3 shales, 1/3 fine gravel, and 1/3 firm loam.
- Channel size changes occur gradually, its surface has moderate irregularity, there are minor obstructions, and for each 20 ft of straight channel length there are 25 ft of meander length.
- Vegetative growth has a moderate influence on channel roughness.

Example Solution

Step 1: Required peak flow: Q_r = 400 cfs

Permissible velocity: V_p = 3.5 ft/sec (from Table 7A.1 for the most erodible section, firm loam)

Step 2: Determine channel velocity V:

a. Channel cross section:
$A = bd + zd^2$, $z = e/d = 8/4 = 2$
$A = (9)(4) + (2)(4)^2 = 36 + 32 = 68 \text{ ft}^2 = A$

b. Hydraulic radius:

$$R = \frac{bd + 2d^2}{b + 2d(z^2+1)^{1/2}} = \frac{(9)(4) + 2(4)^2}{9 + (2)(4)(2^2+1)^{1/2}} = 2.53$$

c. Roughness:

$$n = (n_b + n_1 + n_2 + n_3 + n_4) \times (m)$$

n_b: earthen, fair condition = 0.025 (from Table 7A.3)

n_1: moderate irregularity = 0.010

n_2: gradual size changes = 0.000

n_3: minor obstructions = 0.012

n_4: vegetation = 0.015

m: *meander* = 25/20 = 1.25 = 1.15

$$n = (0.025 + 0.010 + 0.000 + 0.012 + 0.015)(1.15) = (0.062)(1.15) = 0.070 = n$$

Manning's equation:

$$V = \frac{1.49 R^{2/3} S^{1/2}}{n} = \frac{1.49(2.53)^{2/3}(0.015)^{1/2}}{0.07} = 4.5 = \frac{ft}{sec} = V$$

Channel capacity = $Q = AV = (68)(4.5) = 306$ cfs = Q

Step 3:

Q (306) < Q_r (400) → capacity inadequate

V (4.5) > V_r (3.5) → excessive erosion of firm loam banks

Appendix 7B

A Streamside Biosurvey

The streamside biosurvey assesses stream macroinvertabrates or nonfish species. The presence, absence, and abundance of both sensitive and tolerant species serve as a useful indicator of stream health and water quality. Biosurvey methods have been used by water quality agencies and volunteer monitoring programs for two decades. The Izaak Walton League of America institutionalized the method in its Save Our Streams (SOS) program, and variations have been used throughout the United States. Several thousand monitoring groups now assess streams, and the results have proven to be so reliable that state and federal agencies accept them in their water quality databases. The protocol discussed below is drawn from the EPA's *Volunteer Stream Monitoring: A Methods Manual* (1997). The monitor collects, sorts, and counts macroinvertebrates present in a sampling reach, and then computes a stream health indicator based on the abundance and distribution of species.

To do a streamside biosurvey, you need the necessary tools and equipment. This includes a kick net with a #30 or #35 mesh for sampling substrates, a D-frame net for gathering samples under logs, a bucket, and waders or creek shoes. Recording forms are useful for entering data and calculating index scores. In planning a survey, you must determine the stream habitats present (e.g., substrates, snags and logs, vegetated beds and banks), select sampling sites (Figure 7B.1), and determine the number of jabs or samples to take from each site (with a goal of 20 total). Using the kick-net and D-frame net methods shown in Figure 7B.2, you collect macroinvertebrate organisms. The collected organisms are sorted, identified, counted, and released.

You group the macroinvertebrates into three categories based on pollution tolerance and sensitivity. The three categories are given in Box 7B. Group I (sensitive organisms) includes pollution-sensitive organisms, like mayflies and stoneflies, typically found in good-quality water. Group II (somewhat sensitive organisms) includes somewhat pollution-tolerant organisms, such as crayfish, sowbugs, and clams, found in fair-quality water. Group III (tolerant organisms) includes pollution-tolerant organisms, like worms and leeches, found in poor-quality water (Figure 7B.3).

Figure 7B.1 Stream Sample Points. Stream ruffles visible at the top and bottom of this photograph are good sample points for benthic macro-invertebrates. (*Source:* U.S. EPA 1999.)

(A)

Figure 7B.2 Sampling Techniques for Gathering Benthic Organisms. A: Kick net. B: Dip net or D-frame net. (*Source:* U.S. EPA 1999.)

(B)

You count the specimens found in each sensitivity category and determine whether they are rare (R: 1–9 organisms found in a sample), common (C: 10–99 organisms), or dominant (D: 100 or more organisms). You then add the numbers of Rs, Cs, and Ds in each category and multiply each by the appropriate weighting factor (Table 7B.2). You add the scores to a total score and compare it to the water quality rating scale (Table 7B.2).

Tables 7B.3 and 7B.4 show the scoring system for a hypothetical site. Three species were found in Group I; two were common, and one was rare. Six species were found in Group II; three were rare, one common, and two dominant. Two species were in Group III, one rare and one common. The number of Rs, Cs, and Ds in each group are multiplied by the weights and summed to a total index of 37.7 or a fair rating.

Group I Taxa

Pollution-sensitive organisms found in good-quality water.

1 **Stonefly: Order Plecoptera.** 1/2" to 1 1/2", 6 legs with hooked tips, antennae, 2 hairline tails. Smooth (no gills) on lower half of body.

2 **Caddisfly: Order Trichoptera.** Up to 1", 6 hooked legs on upper third of body, 2 hooks at back end. May be in a stick, rock, or leaf case with its head sticking out. May have fluffy gill tufts on underside.

3 **Water Penny: Order Coleoptera.** 1/4", flat saucer-shaped body, 6 tiny legs and fluffy gills on the other side. Immature beetle.

4 **Riffle Beetle: Order Coleoptera.** 1/4", oval body with tiny hairs, 6 legs, antennae. Walks slowly underwater. Does not swim on surface.

5 **Mayfly: Order Ephemeroptera.** 1/4" to 1", brown, moving, platelike or feathery gills on the sides of lower body, 6 largehooked legs, antennae, 2 or 3 long hairlike tails. Tails may be webbed together.

6 **Gilled Snail: Class Gastropoda.** Shell opening covered by thin plate called operculum. As opening faces you, shell usually opens on right.

7 **Dobsonfly (Hellgrammite): Family Corydalidae.** 3/4" to 4", dark colored, 6 legs, large pinching jaws, 8 pairs feelers on lower half of body with paired cottonlike gill tufts along underside, short antennae, 2 tails, and 2 pairs of hooks at back end.

Group II Taxa

Somewhat pollution-tolerant organisms found in good-/fair-quality water.

8 **Crayfish: Order Decapoda.** Up to 6", 2 large claws, 8 legs, resembles small lobster.

9 **Sowbug: Order Isopoda.** 1/4" to 3/4", gray oblong body wider than it is high, more than 6 legs, long antennae.

10 **Scud: Order Amphipoda.** 1/4", white to gray, body higher than it is wide, swims sideways, more than 6 legs, resembles small shrimp.

11 **Alderfly Larva: Family Sialedae.** 1" long. Looks like small hellgramite but long, branched tail at back end (no hooks).

12 **Fishfly Larva: Family Cordalidae.** Up to 1-1/2" long. Looks like small hellgrammite but often a lighter reddish-tan color, or with yellowish streaks. No gill tufts underneath.

13 **Damselfly: Suborder Zygoptera.** 1/2" to 1", large eyes, 6 thin hooked legs, 3 broad oar-shaped tails, positioned like a tripod. Smooth (no gills) on sides of lower half of body. (See arrow.)

14 **Watersnipe Fly Larva: Family Athericidae (Atherix).** 1/4" to 1", pale green, tapered body, caterpillar-like legs, conical head, feathery "horns" at back.

15 **Crane Fly: Suborder Nematocera.** 1/3" to 2", milky, green, or light brown, plump caterpillar-like body, 4 fingerlike lobes at back end.

16 **Beetle Larva: Order Coleoptera.** 1/4" to 1", light-colored, 6 legs on upper half of body, feelers, antennae.

17 **Dragonfly: Suborder Anisoptera.** 1/2" to 2", large eyes, 6 hooked legs. Wide oval to round abdomen.

18 **Clam: Class Bivalvia.**

Group III Taxa

Pollution-tolerant organisms found in any quality of water.

19 **Aquatic Worm: Class Oligochaeta.** 1/4" to 2", can be very tiny, thin wormlike body.

20 **Midge Fly Larva: Suborder Nematocera.** Up to 1/4", dark head, wormlike segmented body, 2 tiny legs on each side.

21 **Blackfly Larva: Family Simulidae.** Up to 1/4", one end of body wider. Black head, suction pad on other end.

22 **Leech: Order Hirudinea.** 1/4" to 2", brown, slimy body, ends with suction pads.

23 **Pouch Snail and Pond Snails: Class Gastropoda.** No operculum. Breathe air. When opening is facing you, shell usually open to left.

24 **Other Snails: Class Gastropoda.** No operculum. Breathe air. Snail shell coils in one plane.

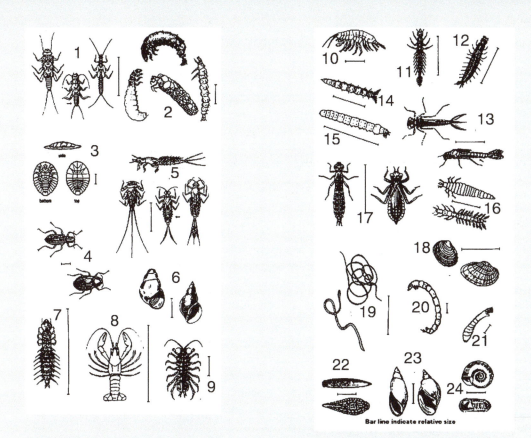

Figure 7B.3 Stream Macroinvertebrates. Lower numbers are more pollution-sensitive and are found in higher-quality water. (*Source:* Izaak Walton League of America 1994; USDA, NRCS 1998.)

Source: Izaak Walton League 1994; USDA, NRCS 1998.

TABLE 7B.1 **Weighting Factors Used in Calculating Stream Water Quality Ratings**

	Weighting Factor		
Abundance	Group I Sensitive	Group II Somewhat Sensitive	Group III Tolerant
Rare (R)	5.0	3.2	1.2
Common (C)	5.6	3.4	1,1
Dominant (D)	5.3	3.0	1.0

TABLE 7B.2 Rating Scale for Streams in Maryland

Score	Rating
> 40	Good
20–40	Fair
< 20	Poor

TABLE 7B.3 Example: Macroinvertebrate Count

Identify the macroinvertebrates in your sample and assign them letter codes based on their abundance: R (rare) 4 1–9 organisms; C (common) 4 10–99 organisms; and D (dominant) 4 100 plus organisms.

Group I Sensitive	Group II Somewhat-Sensitive	Group III Tolerant
C (50) Water penny larvae	R (4) Beetle larvae	R (5) Aquatic worms
R (2) Hellgrammites	_____ Clams	_____ Blackfly larvae
_____ Mayfly nymphs	_____ Crane fly larvae	_____ Leeches
_____ Gilled snails	R (6) Crayfish	_____ Midge larvae
_____ Riffle beetle adult	_____ Damselfly nymphs	C (50) Snails
C (25) Stonefly nymphs	D (100) Scuds	
_____ Non net-spinning caddisfly larvae	D (150) Sowbugs	
	R (8) Fishfly larvae	
	_____ Alderfly larvae	
	C (27) Net-spinning caddisfly larvae	

TABLE 7B.4 Example Sample Calculations of Index Values for Volunteer Creek

Group I Sensitive	Group II Somewhat Sensitive	Group III Tolerant
1 (No. of R's) $\times$ 5.0 = 5.0	3 (No. of R's) $\times$ 3.2 = 9.6	1 (No. of R's) $\times$ 1.2 = 1.2
2 (No. of C's) $\times$ 5.6 = 11.2	1 (No. of C's) $\times$ 3.4 = 3.4	1 (No of C's) $\times$ 1.1 = 1.1
	2 (No. of D's) $\times$ 3.0 = 6.0	
Index Value for Group I = 16.2	Index Value for Group II = 19.20	Index Value for Group III = 2.3

Total Index = 16.2 + 19.2 + 2.3 = 37.7 (Fair)

8 ■ Stormwater Management and Watershed Restoration

Stormwater management epitomizes the evolution of environmental planning discussed in earlier chapters. It has shifted from the sole domain of engineers to an interdisciplinary field of hydrologists, soil scientists, ecologists, engineers, designers, and planners. The range of stakeholders may also include landowners and citizen volunteers. Once thought merely as the means to get the water out, it has become the art and science of mimicking nature to counter the effects of land disturbance and impervious cover by conveying, retaining, infiltrating, and treating stormwater where the runoff originates, and using vegetation to slow and treat the water. Nature knows best. Rather than burying or destroying natural channels for the sake of "good drainage," this evolving approach to stormwater management embraces natural water features and relies on vegetative cover to counter impervious cover, thereby contributing to community green infrastructure, natural aesthetics, and livability.

This chapter summarizes the state-of-the-art practice of stormwater management by first reflecting on its evolution over the past few decades in the United States. We will explore the emerging comprehensive approach for integrative management of runoff quantity (integrating stormwater control and flood damage mitigation), water quality (integrating point and nonpoint source pollution), multiscale restoration (from the stream reach to the watershed), and development design (integrating stormwater control and community livability). The approach has required an institutionalization of stormwater management at all government levels.

A review of emerging measures and practices used in stormwater management follows, including land use design and onsite and neighborhood-scale low-impact development techniques, with methods for sizing and selecting these measures for specific applications. Stream and watershed restoration methods are introduced next, and the chapter concludes with policies and programs for realizing comprehensive stormwater management.

Toward Integrated Stormwater Management

The way stormwater is managed has changed significantly in recent decades, as practitioners have broadened their objectives and improved engineering, design, and planning methods. Table 8.1 summarizes the changing nature of **stormwater management (SWM)** in the United States. Historically, managing stormwater meant building drainage works to get the water out more quickly so it would not accumulate and flood the land. These works include gutters, pipes, culverts, and widened and straightened channels with concrete or rock "armor." Although such drainage measures got the water out, they destroyed natural channels, and by accelerating the drainage of water from one area, they often increased storm flows downstream, carried more pollution to waterways, and created higher velocity flows and more erosive forces on downstream channels.

Beginning in the 1970s, engineers and planners began to understand better the effects of impervious surfaces on storm flows, the pollution carried by stormwater, the public's desire to maintain natural drainage systems, the limitations of traditional engineering works, and the range of new measures available. As a result, SWM has become more complex and more comprehensive in addressing storm flows and baseflows, water quality, flood damage mitigation, natural drainage, and stream restoration.

Control measures have evolved from centralized structures to distributed and onsite practices and from structural methods to natural and biological, so-called low-impact development (LID) measures. Management previously focused on tax-supported public works, but now it emphasizes onsite development ordinances and stormwater impact fees. In the past few years, this emphasis on decentralized LID measures has become part of new livable neighborhood design criteria, and onsite and natural drainage has become an integral part of new and redevelopment land projects.

This comprehensive and integrative approach has five components:

1. Integrating stormwater quantity control and flood damage mitigation.
2. Integrating water quality nonpoint and point source permitting.
3. Restoring streams and watersheds.
4. Incorporating onsite stormwater controls in sustainable community design.
5. Institutionalizing stormwater management.

Integrating Stormwater Quantity Control and Flood Damage Mitigation

A prime objective of stormwater management is to reduce flooding, but too often the emphasis has been local and does not consider downstream effects. Mitigating the negative effects of local "good drainage" practices on downstream areas requires a shift to close-to-the-source controls, in order to detain, store, and infiltrate stormwater runoff onsite rather than to get it out.

TABLE 8.1 **The Increasing Complexity and Effectiveness of Stormwater Management in the U.S.**

	Before 1970 *Structural SWM*	*1970s–1980s* *Good Drainage*	*1990s–2000s* *Low-Impact SWM*	*2010s* → *Sustainable SWM*
Objectives	Provide adequate stormwater drainage from developed land; try to control flood flows.	Provide adequate drainage, manage new floodplain development, mitigate storm flows closer to the source, apply erosion and sediment controls and best-management practices for runoff pollution.	Adequate drainage by onsite mitigation of stormwater flows; infiltration to support baseflows and low flows; runoff treatment; non-erosive channel velocities; protect/restore natural drainage channels; floodplain management.	Use watershed and subwatershed approach to integrate stormwater management, flood damage mitigation, water quality, stream restoration, and sustainable and livable community design.
Control measures	Increase drainage capacity; gutter streets, enlarge/line channels; pipes/culverts; "armor" natural channels with concrete/rocks to prevent channel erosion; use stormwater detention.	Mitigate storm flows by onsite and offsite detention; increase drainage capacity as necessary.	More effective onsite and other decentralized runoff control and treatment; encouraging or mandating "low-impact" development designs and integrated stormwater control practices; infiltration; bioengineering to restore natural channels.	Land use planning and design to manage development density, minimize and mitigate impervious cover; low-impact and light-imprint methods to achieve desired densities and onsite controls. Daylight buried streams.
Design methods	Size capacities based on Rational Method and other rudimentary techniques.	Analyze effects of land use change on stormwater quantity and quality and size capacities using sophisticated computer modeling techniques.	Use of both computer models and simpler sizing and design methods to estimate land use impacts and apply appropriate on site measures.	Integrative models (BASINS, SUSTAIN) for multiple objectives; landscape design, new urbanist, Smart Growth land development principles.
Programs, ordinances, financing	Public works funded by tax dollars.	Stormwater ordinances require developers bear costs in projects, stormwater fees, and tax dollars.	Stormwater utilities; more effective prescriptive and performance-based stormwater ordinances; impact fees; citizen volunteers (stream monitoring and restoration).	Stronger federal/state oversight; stormwater integrated with sustainable community planning; ordinances reflect best practices for new and redeveloped sites.

Table 8.2 compares the effects of the conventional good drainage approach and close-to-the-source low-impact approach. Good drainage controls in upstream development can exacerbate downstream flooding and invalidate floodplain maps and zoning boundaries. The low-impact approach employs detention and infiltration to approximate predevelopment hydrology for runoff peak discharge, time of concentration, frequency, duration, infiltration, and groundwater recharge. By controlling to predevelopment conditions, the low-impact approach reduces downstream flooding effects and maintains the integrity of floodplain maps and zoning.

Table 8.2 **Effects of Conventional "Good Drainage" and "Low-Impact" Approaches**

Hydrologic Parameter	Good Drainage	Close-to-the-Source Low-Impact Control
Onsite		
Impervious cover	Encouraged to achieve effective drainage	Minimized to reduce impacts
Vegetation/natural cover	Reduced to improve efficient site drainage	Maximized to maintain predevelopment hydrology
Time of concentration	Shortened, reduced as a by-product of drainage efficiency	Maximized and increased to about predevelopment conditions
Runoff volume	Large increases in runoff volume not controlled	Controlled to predevelopment conditions
Peak discharge	Controlled to predevelopment conditions for 2-year storm	Controlled to predevelopment conditions for all storms
Runoff frequency	Greatly increased, especially for small, frequent storms	Controlled to predevelopment conditions for all storms
Runoff duration	Increased for all storms because volume is not controlled	Controlled to predevelopment conditions
Rainfall abstractions (interception, infiltration, depression storage)	Large reduction in all elements	Maintained to predevelopment conditions
Groundwater recharge	Reduction in recharge	Maintained to predevelopment conditions
Offsite		
Water quality	Reduction in pollutant loadings but limited control for storm events that are less than design discharge	Reduced pollutant loading; full control for storm events less than design discharge
Receiving streams	Documented impacts: channel erosion and degradation; sediment deposition; reduced baseflow; habitat suitability decreased, or eliminated	Stream ecology maintained to predevelopment
Downstream flooding	Peak discharge control can reduce flooding immediately below control structure but increase flooding downstream	Controlled to predevelopment conditions

Integrating Water Quality Nonpoint and Point Source Permitting

The 1972 Clean Water Act (CWA) established lofty goals of "fishable and swimmable" waters and "pollutant discharge elimination," and set up a policy and regulatory framework to try to achieve them. The foundation of the program was the establishment of water quality standards (WQS) for all of the nation's waters that met these goals for aquatic life (fishable) and recreation contact (swimmable) (see Chapter 7). The primary regulatory tool for achieving the WQS was the use of permits for all pollutant discharges, so-called National Pollutant Discharge Elimination System (NPDES) permits. If the wastewater discharge were to be released into a receiving water meeting the WQS, the permit effluent limit would be "technology-based," meaning the discharger must apply an EPA-specified "best available technology economically achievable" for that discharger category (e.g., municipal sewage treatment or an industrial steel plant). However, if the discharge were to be released into waters not meeting the WQS (impaired waters; see Chapter 7), the permit effluent limit should be "water-quality-based," meaning the discharger must apply controls beyond the technology standards to meet the WQS.

In the first two decades of the CWA, the NPDES program made significant strides to control point-source dischargers using technology-based permits. But half of our assessed waters still do not meet the WQS, because the Act has been less effective at (1) controlling nonpoint runoff pollution sources, including urban stormwater; and (2) improving water-quality-based impaired waters. After the 1987 CWA amendments, programs for these two areas have improved, but as we saw in Chapter 7, our water quality impairment continues, and much work remains to be done.

Nonpoint Source Pollution Control and MS4 Stormwater Permits.

The CWA recognized the importance of runoff pollution, but its diffuse nature complicated efforts to control it. The original Act's section 208, and the 1987 amendment's section 319, set up a planning, funding, and largely voluntary implementation program for primarily agricultural nonpoint sources. The amendments were more specific on urban and industrial stormwater, and in the early 1990s, the EPA brought these sources into the section 402 NPDES permit program. Under Phase I of the program, municipal separate stormwater systems (called MS4) in cities greater than 100,000 in population and certain industrial site runoff (including construction sites greater than 5 acres) were subject to NPDES stormwater discharge permits.

In 2003, the EPA implemented Phase II, which expanded these requirements to communities larger than 50,000 in population, construction sites greater than 1 acre, and institutional categories. Many states now include smaller localities, populations of 10,000–50,000, so nearly all communities with stormwater systems must obtain an MS4 permit. To do so, localities must develop a stormwater management plan (SWMP) that meets EPA criteria addressing outreach, education, construction projects, post-construction operations, illicit discharges, and pollution prevention.

The MS4 program has increased NPDES permitting by nearly tenfold. Between 1972 and 1992, some 60,000 point source permits were issued to industry and municipal sewage treatment plants. MS4 Phase I issued 300,000 permits by the mid-1990s, and Phase II added 200,000 permits after 2003. The EPA has been plagued not only by the magnitude of the program, but also by the complexity of effective management of stormwater quantity and quality. State and local governments are also constrained by insufficient funding and expertise to respond effectively.

In 2007, the Government Accountability Office (GAO) issued a report on the impact of the EPA stormwater program. The report noted delays in EPA implementation, inconsistent community reporting, and lack of a system to gauge the program's overall effectiveness. In response, the EPA issued an evaluation guidance document, but it also requested the National Research Council (NRC) to review the permitting program and offer suggestions for improvement. The resulting 2009 NRC report, *Urban Stormwater Management in the United States*, was also critical of the EPA's program, saying it did not recognize the extent of the problem and that it is unlikely to control stormwater's contribution to water impairment (National Research Council 2009).

The report provides a comprehensive review of the state of urban SWM in the U.S., but it could not offer the EPA a silver bullet to resolve the complexities and challenges of the national permitting program. Box 8.1 summarizes the key findings from the study. We discussed the second and third topics, land use effects on water and watershed models, in Chapter 7 and will describe stormwater control measures (SCM) shortly below.

One of the NRC's critical recommendations is listed last (and paraphrased here): *The greatest improvement to the EPA's Stormwater Program, and the one most likely to check and reverse degradation of the nation's aquatic resources, would be to convert the current piecemeal system into a watershed-based permitting system.* This is occurring in some states, and some communities have banded together and established an MS4 permitting program on a watershed basis. The River Network (2009) highlights one such watershed-based effort in Michigan's 760-square-mile Clinton River watershed, home to 60 jurisdictions and 1.4 million people.

Integrating Point and Nonpoint Sources in TMDL and Watershed Implementation Plans

In addition to the MS4 program, the EPA's implementation of the CWA incorporated a second significant change in the past decade: the major application of the TMDL process.

Total Maximum Daily Load Planning. Applying technology-based permits to municipal and industrial dischargers in the 1970s and 1980s did much to clean up major pollution of U.S. waters. However, as discussed in Chapter 7, 44% of our assessed rivers and streams and 64% of assessed lakes are impaired, or fail to meet WQS for their designated uses. For such impaired waters, the CWA called for a

BOX 8.1—Urban Stormwater Management in the United States: Summary of NRC Findings and Recommendations

EPA Role: The MS4 Permit Program

- The EPA's current approach to regulating stormwater is unlikely to produce an accurate or complete picture of the extent of the problem, nor is it likely to adequately control stormwater's contribution to water body impairment.
- The EPA should engage in much more vigilant regulatory oversight in the national licensing of products that contribute significantly to stormwater pollution.
- The federal government should provide more financial support to state and local efforts to regulate stormwater.

Effect of Land Use on Receiving Waters

- There is a direct relationship between land cover and the biological condition of downstream receiving waters.
- Flow and related parameters like impervious cover should be considered for use as proxies for stormwater pollutant loading.
- Roads and parking lots can be the most significant type of land cover with respect to stormwater.
- The protection of aquatic life in urban streams requires an approach that incorporates all stressors.

Monitoring and Modeling

- Although the quality of stormwater from urbanized areas is well characterized from monitoring data from MS4s nationwide over 10 years, more stormwater monitoring is needed from certain industrial sectors, and continuous sampling methods should replace grab sampling of storm - water data.
- Watershed models are useful tools for predicting downstream impacts from urbanization and designing mitigation to reduce those impacts, but they are incomplete in scope and do not offer definitive causal links between polluted discharges and downstream degradation.

Stormwater Control Measures

- Individual controls on stormwater discharges are inadequate as the sole solution to stormwater in urban watersheds and integrated controls are needed over sub-watersheds.
- Nonstructural SCMs, such as pollution prevention from product substitution, better site design, downspout disconnection, conservation of natural areas, and watershed and land use planning, can dramatically reduce the volume of runoff and pollutant load from a new development.
- SCMs that harvest, infiltrate, and evapotranspirate stormwater are critical to reducing the volume and pollutant loading of small storms.
- Performance characteristics are starting to be established for most structural and some nonstructural SCMs, but additional research is needed on the relevant hydrologic and water quality processes within SCMs across different climates and soil conditions.
- The retrofitting of urban areas presents both unique opportunities and challenges.
- The greatest improvement to the EPA's Stormwater Program would be to convert the current piecemeal system into a watershed-based permitting system that would encompass coordinated regulation and management of all discharges having the potential to modify the hydrology and water quality of the watershed's receiving waters. These discharges include existing wastewater, stormwater and other diffuse sources, and those anticipated from future growth.

Source: Adapted from NCR 2009.

process to determine the discharge limits, or **total maximum daily load (TMDL)**, of each violated pollutant that could be discharged into a water body and still attain the WQS. TMDLs are then allocated to the various sources, including industrial and municipal dischargers (waste load allocation, WLA), human-caused nonpoint sources (NPS) load allocations (LA), and natural NPS. The allocated load to point dischargers serve as the basis for their NPDES effluent permits. The human-caused NPS LA serve as a basis for NPS reduction. For impaired waters, the TMDL is the basis for permits:

Total discharge allocations to regulated sources = WLA + LA = TMDL – Natural NPS

The TMDL process is complicated and involves the following steps:

1. Determining the TMDL to achieve WQS often requires complex modeling and monitoring, in order to understand the relationship between discharge concentration and quantity of a pollutant and its ambient concentration in a receiving water.
2. Allocating TMDL to sources requires considering equity and economic factors.
3. Permits for regulated sources must be based on TMDL allocations.
4. Unregulated sources must be managed to achieve TMDL allocations.

Because of these complexities, the EPA and the states were slow to respond until a series of lawsuits in the 1990s forced them to act. The EPA issued initial rules in 1995, and the process began. But, like the MS4 permit program, early implementation of the process was criticized by GAO reports, and the NRC weighed in with a 2001 report. The EPA considered the NRC comments and finally issued TMDL rules in 2003. The program is well under way.

The EPA's tally of TMDL plans is impressive. There are about 40,000 impaired waters in the U.S., led by Pennsylvania (6,957), Virginia (2,534), and Washington (2,419). The top pollutants causing impairment are pathogens, metals, nutrients, organics, and sediment. As of August 2010, the EPA lists 41,960 TMDL plans addressing more than 44,000 causes, led by pathogens, metals, mercury, and nutrients. Top TMDL states are Pennsylvania (6,686) and New Hampshire (5,518) (U.S. EPA 2010b).

In a 2004 report, the EPA highlighted 17 TMDLs that incorporated permitted MS4 dischargers. However, in its 2009 report, the NRC commented on the difficulty of incorporating MS4 permits into the TMDL process because of the dual problems of uncertainty and limited monitoring.

Watershed Implementation Plans. Establishing a TMDL plan is one thing; implementing it is another. **Watershed implementation plans (WIPs)** are emerging as a critical tool for implementing the most complex TMDL plan yet developed: the Chesapeake Bay TMDL. Completed in late 2010, the plan's goal is to ensure that all pollution controls needed to restore Chesapeake Bay and its tidal rivers are in place by 2025, with 60% of them in place by 2017. The WIPs prepared by each of the six bay states and the District of Columbia (DC) detail how and when the jurisdictions will meet the pollution allocations for the watershed's 92 TMDL segments. Phase I WIPs prepared in late 2009 contributed to the final TMDL and its final target load allocations for each jurisdiction. Phase II WIPs are required by late 2011 and provide finer-scale detail to strategies at the local level to meet 2017 objectives. Phase III WIPS are due in 2017 and will detail further strategies needed to meet 2025 goals (U.S EPA Chesapeake Bay Program, 2010, 2011). The Chesapeake Bay TMDL and WIPs are discussed further in Chapter 19.

Water Quality Trading.   Yet another development in TMDL water quality management under the CWA that shows promise is **water quality trading**, which has the potential to achieve WQS at lower cost, apply a watershed approach to permitting, coordinate point and nonpoint source controls, and provide compensation to farmers to control their runoff pollution. Box 8.2 introduces the approach and uses a hypothetical example from the EPA's *Water Quality Trading Assessment Handbook* (2004) to illustrate the procedure and the potential benefits. Several states have experimented with trading programs.

Restoring Streams and Watersheds

Stream and watershed restoration is the third component of comprehensive and integrated stormwater management. Most urban areas have a legacy of impervious land cover and degraded streams, known as the **urban stream syndrome (USS)**, reflecting the range of effects caused by altered hydrology, altered geomorphology, altered habitat, and polluted runoff (Walsh et al. 2005). Effective remediation and restoration cannot just patch the problem by treating the stream; they must address the causes or stressors on the system. A watershed approach is needed, moving from the water to the land, for it is the land cover and land use practices that create the problem. This approach requires retrofitting the land uses and the stormwater system to counter this legacy, thereby reducing the stressors on the watershed and its streams.

The exciting prospect of comprehensively treating the stressors that cause the USS is that it re-creates conditions under which urban streams can recover and maintain their hydrologic, ecological, recreational, educational, and aesthetic qualities. These improved land use and hydrologic conditions enable the daylighting and recovery of streams previously buried, armored, or channelized to counter the prior conditions of excessive urban runoff. (Stream and watershed restoration is covered at length in the last section of this chapter.)

Incorporating Onsite Stormwater Controls in Sustainable Community Design

The fourth component of comprehensive stormwater management includes the wide range of onsite and neighborhood-scale stormwater controls and designs. These measures can be applied to retrofit, redevelopment, and new development efforts, and they have become important design features for creating green and livable neighborhoods. Because of their reliance on vegetative cover and natural

BOX 8.2—Water Quality Trading Under TMDL

Designated impaired waters not meeting water quality standards (WQS) require a total maximum daily load (TMDL) plan to determine necessary pollutant load reductions and allocate them to point and nonpoint dischargers. Water quality trading has gained increasing attention as an innovative approach for achieving water quality goals at lower cost; it allows dischargers with high abatement costs to meet their allocated reductions by compensating those with lower costs to overcontrol beyond their allocations and provide credit to compensating dischargers. An example from U.S. EPA (2004) illustrates the process.

Figure 8.1 shows a hypothetical case of Happy River that is impaired for phosphorus in the reach about Easyville Dam. The figure shows the major dischargers, including five industrial and two community POTW (publicly owned treatment works) point sources and one agricultural non-point source (Herb's Farm). The TMDL sets load targets for each source to meet the phosphorus WQS and needed reductions, as shown in Table 8.3. Several steps are involved in determining the opportunities for water quality trading among the sources:

- *Pollutant suitability:* Compares the type/form of the pollutant and the timing and alignment of the discharge within the watershed, the supply and demand of pollutant reduction credits, the uncertainty of nonpoint source controls, and the relative **water quality (WQ) equivalence** of each discharger's pollutant reduction.
- *Financial attractiveness:* Based on relative incremental cost of control and WQ equivalence.
- *Market infrastructure:* To ensure compliance with WQS and executing and monitoring trades.
- *Stakeholder readiness:* To inform and engage dischargers and other stakeholders.

Table 8.3 shows the results for the trading assessment for this hypothetical example. Incremental cost of control of phosphorus for each source is given in column 6. WQ equivalences are given in column 7. For example, Herb's Farm and

Pleasantville have 1:1 equivalence since they are in the same reach, but Herb's NPS has 50% uncertainty. Pleasantville has a 5:1 equivalence with Hopeville because of the major diversion between the two. That means it takes 5 lb reduction from Pleasantville to credit Hopeville with 1 lb reduction. Pleasantville and Production Co. have a 3:1 equivalence because of their relative influence on Lake Content. Chem Co.'s reduction requirement exceeds all of the other discharges, so it needs to control its effluent outside of the trading scheme. Laughing Larry's Trout Farm is outside the TMDL reach and is not involved. The last column shows promising WQ trades from this assessment. For more detail, see U.S EPA (2004).

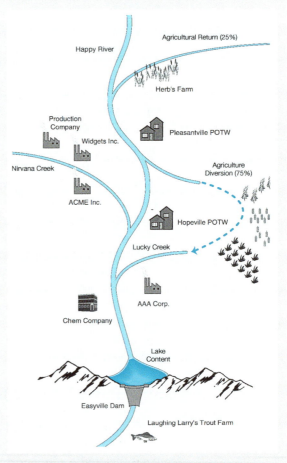

Figure 8.1 A TMDL and Water Quality Trading Example. (*Source:* U.S. EPA 2004.)

BOX 8.2—Water Quality Trading Under TMDL (cont.)

TABLE 8.3 **Hypothetical TMDL and Water Quality Trading Assessment Results**

		Phosphorus TMDL Results			*Water Quality Trading Assessment*			
Source	*Form: soluble/ non-soluble*	*Current load (lb/da)*	*TMDL target (lb/da)*	*Reduc-tion (lb/da)*	*Incremental control cost/lb*	*WQ equivalent ratios*	*Uncer-tainty*	*Financial attractiveness of trades: (x) compensates (➤)(y)*
(1) Herb's Farm	30/70	753	527	225	$5	1:1(2) 5:1 (6)	50%	
(2) Pleasantville POTW	90/10	791	633	158	$20	1:1 (1) 1:3 (4) 5:1(6)		(2)➤(1):$5×1/0.5 = $10 < $20 yes (2)➤(4):$36×1/3 = $12 < $20 yes
(3) Acme, Inc.	100/0	547	410	137	$60	1:1(4,5)		(3)➤(4): $36×1 = $36 < $60 yes
(4) Production Co.	100/0	228	171	57	$36	1:1(3,5)		
(5) Widgets, Inc.	100/0	165	124	41	$49	1:1(3,4)		(5)➤(4): $49×1 = $49 < $60 yes
(6) Hopeville POTW	90/10	62	50	12	$100	1:5(1) 1:5(2)		(6)➤(1):$5×5/0.5 = $50 < $100 yes (6)➤(2): $20×5 = $100 = $100 ??
(7) AAA Corps.	100/0	195	166	29	$15			None: Lucky Creek compliance
(8) Chem Co.	100/0	1,645	493	1,151				None: reduction >> supply
(9) Laughing Larry's Trout Farm	N/A	N/A	N/A	N/A	N/A	N/A		None: outside of TMDL reach

drainage and related water features, these controls enhance green infrastructure and related wildlife habitat, recreation, and aesthetic benefits.

Institutionalizing Stormwater Management

Greater emphasis on stormwater quantity, quality, restoration, and design has elevated the issue of stormwater management at all levels of government in the U.S. During the 1990s, SWM became a federal regulatory program implemented by the states under MS4 NPDES permitting. State oversight of MS4 permitting expanded states' interests in stormwater, and most have developed statewide standards and design manuals to be implemented by localities. As the technical approaches to stormwater have changed to emphasize low-impact, nonstructural measures and a watershed approach, these standards and manuals have been revised to reflect them. Localities have implemented state and federal requirements, and many have responded with their own programs for stormwater utilities and fees, as well as the development of ordinances and codes.

State Stormwater Control Standards and Design Manuals

Many states developed stormwater management standards in the late 1990s and early 2000s, partially in response to the federal MS4 program. Some states have continued to upgrade their standards and design manuals in response to new approaches and practices tested in the field. Two states with major estuaries, Maryland and Washington, offer good examples of the changing nature of these standards. Their stormwater manuals have three basic parts: standards and requirements, design criteria and details for SCM, and hydrologic and sizing analysis methods.

The Maryland Stormwater Management Program. Maryland got an early start in stormwater management as part of its Chesapeake Bay initiatives in 1984. These early rules emphasized runoff flow control. Maryland is home to Tom Schueler's Center for Watershed Protection in Ellicott City and to Prince George's County, one of the early adopters of LID designs, so the state was a leader in stormwater management. By 2000, the Maryland Department of the Environment (MDE) had proposed new regulations to promote environmentally sustainable techniques for controlling the quantity and quality of runoff from new development. The MDE also developed the *Maryland Stormwater Design Manual*, which establishes specific design criteria and procedures for localities. They emphasize total site design and incentives for green development techniques so that sites would more closely mimic natural processes and reduce reliance on structural measures to manage runoff (Comstock et al. 2000).

The program got a major upgrade with the enactment of the Stormwater Management Act of 2007, which requires that environmental site design be implemented to the maximum extent practicable through the use of better site design techniques, alternative surfaces, nonstructural measures, and microscale practices. Specific standards for development areas greater than 5,000 sq ft include qualitative provisions (e.g., minimize the generation of stormwater and maximize pervious areas, use environmental site design practices) and quantitative requirements (e.g., maintain groundwater recharge rates, control the 2- and 10-year frequency storm event onsite, capture water quality volume to remove 80% of annual TSS and 40% of annual phosphorus loads, provide channel protection storage volume from 1-year storm event). The MDE manual provides sizing techniques to determine volumes for water quality, recharge, and channel protection and discharge rates for overbank and extreme flood protection. The Maryland program includes incentives by giving credits for such methods in these sizing calculations for required water quality, recharge, and channel protection volumes (Maryland Department of the Environment 2009).

In addition to the manual, the MDE developed a model SWM ordinance to help localities comply with the requirements. Excerpts from the ordinance are on the book website (www.envirolanduse.org), and the full ordinance is linked to the MDE manual at http://www.mde.state.md.us/assets/document/sediment stormwater/model_ordinance.pdf.

Washington Stormwater Management. Washington state's Department of Ecology (WDOE) initiated its oversight of stormwater in response to the 1987

Puget Sound Water Quality Management Plan, which called on the agency to develop guidance for stormwater quality improvement. The *Puget Sound Manual* was updated in 2005 to apply to all of western Washington (Washington DOE 2005). While the manual is not a regulation, its content becomes required through local MS4 and stormwater programs, which must comply because the WDOE issues the Phase I and Phase II permits.

The manual provides ten minimum requirements (MR) for new and redevelopment. All development must comply with MR 2; smaller new and redevelopment (>2,000 sq ft of new/replaced impervious surface or disturbed area >7,000 sq ft) must comply with MR 1–5; larger new and redevelopment (>5,000 sq ft of new/replaced impervious surface, converts >0.75 acre of native vegetation to lawn or landscaped, or converts >2.5 acres of native vegetation to pasture) must comply with MR 1–10. Here are the ten minimum requirements:

1. Preparation of Stormwater Site Plans
2. Construction Stormwater Pollution Prevention (SWPP) (includes 12 specific elements)
3. Source Control of Pollution (MR may be more stringent if TMDL plan)
4. Preservation of Natural Drainage Systems and Outfalls
5. Onsite Stormwater Management
6. Runoff Treatment (sized for volume of 6-month, 24-hour storm)
7. Flow Control
8. Wetlands Protection
9. Basin/Watershed Planning (MR may be more or less stringent if watershed plan)
10. Operation and Maintenance.

In 2008, the state's Pollution Control Hearing Board ruled that the MS4 Phase I permit had to be modified to require use of low-impact development (LID) where feasible to meet the federal and state law "maximum extent feasible" requirement. The WDOE reissued permits to Phase I localities in 2007 and stipulated that their local stormwater regulations and manuals must be revised and made equivalent to the WDOE Manual. Pierce and King Counties revised their ordinances and manuals in 2008 (King County 2008; Pierce County 2008), with Seattle completing its revision in 2009. It includes a provision requiring the use of "green stormwater infrastructure"—best-management practices (BMPs) using infiltration, evapotranspiration, or stormwater reuse—to the maximum extent feasible for meeting the minimum requirement. To support its revisions, the city planners prepared a *Best Available Science Review* report on stormwater flow control and quality treatment, including green stormwater infrastructure measures (Seattle 2009).

Local Stormwater Programs, Ordinances, Utilities, Fees

Like these Washington cities and counties, many localities have been driven by their state to adopt stormwater management programs and ordinances. Others have acted on their own. Bellevue (WA), for example, established one of the nation's first local stormwater utilities in 1984. It assessed fees on landowners based on parcel impervious surface area and used the resulting fund to support community SWM projects. Fairfax County (VA) has an extensive program that includes detailed development ordinances, stream restoration, and watershed planning, which goes well beyond state mandates. (See Boxes 8.5 and 8.6 describing the Fairfax County program in sizing and stream restoration sections later in this chapter.)

Perhaps the nation's most sophisticated local stormwater management program is in Portland, Oregon. Portland is well regarded as one of the most sustainable cities in the U.S., and it is highlighted elsewhere in this book. Its stormwater management program has strict requirements linked to its MS4 permit, a manual to support implementation, a well-funded stormwater utility with retrofit incentives, significant public green street and green roof projects, and a comprehensive watershed management plan of which its stormwater program is part. Box 8.3 gives an overview of Portland's program.

Stormwater Control Measures

Over the past two decades, there has been a large body of research and resulting literature on land use practices for mitigating the effects of runoff on receiving waters. They are referred to as best-management practices in nonpoint source pollution engineering, integrated management practices in low-impact development, and stormwater management practices in urban stormwater. Not to take away from these terms (especially BMPs), we will capture all of these methods in the term adopted by the 2009 NRC urban stormwater report: **stormwater control measures (SCMs)**.

SCMs can be categorized in different ways. They vary in *scale*, from a development site to a watershed. They vary in *timing* in the runoff regime, meaning they are placed at different points from sheet flow to concentrated flow. They have different primary *objectives* or benefits, such as runoff storage, detention, conveyance, infiltration, and treatment. They may be *structural* or *nonstructural*. They may be applicable along different points of the *urban transect*, from ultra-urban to suburban to rural. We will distinguish the SCM strategies and measures by these different factors and organize them in the following groups:

- Land use design and management
- Pollution prevention and product substitution
- Onsite and neighborhood infiltration, storage, and conveyance measures
- Concentrated flow measures

There is a growing body of resource literature on SCMs, especially low-impact measures. There are some nice graphical guides and design manuals, including the City of Portland's Bureau of Environmental Services' *Stormwater Solutions* (Portland 2010), the *Low Impact Development Approaches Handbook* (Clean Water Services 2009), the *Low-Impact Development: Technical Guidance Manual for Puget Sound* (PS Partnership 2005), and *Stormwater Management Handbook: Implementing Green Infrastructure in Northern Kentucky Communities* (Nevue

BOX 8.3—Portland's Stormwater Management Program

Portland is well known as a sustainable city, but it has a legacy of watershed problems, including an old combined sewer system, endangered salmon and trout habitats, the Portland Harbor superfund site, and seven TMDLs for impaired waters. Table 8.4 shows how significant investment has reversed this trend. The city's watershed management plan is at the center of this change, and its stormwater management program is the primary means of implementation.

Stormwater Utility

In operation since 1977, the utility now has an $80 million annual budget, 85% supported by user fees. All landowners pay a stormwater fee based on impervious cover, now about $8/month per 1000 sq ft, or almost $20/mo for a typical household. In 2006, the utility split the fee into onsite (35%) and offsite (65%) services and offered discounts on the onsite portion for private onsite measures to control flow rate, pollutants, and disposal. Some 33,000 have registered for discounts.

Stormwater Ordinance and Manual

Portland's sustainable stormwater management principles are: (1) Manage runoff as close as possible to its source, (2) mimic natural hydrologic functions, (3) integrate runoff into the built environment, (4) design for multiple sustainable benefits, and (5) act early to avoid costly mitigation and restoration. The stormwater ordinance and manual were first adopted in 1999 and last revised in 2008. The ordinance applies to projects that develop or redevelop more than 500 sq ft of impervious surface or propose new offsite discharges.

- *Infiltration and discharge* are based on the hierarchy in which the top priority is total infiltration, second is discharge to infiltration trench or dry well, third is discharge to stream or storm-only pipe, and fourth is to combined sewer. Surface infiltration facilities must be able to infiltrate the 10-year, 24-hour storm.
- *Flow control* must maintain predevelopment, undeveloped peak flow for 2-, 5-, and 10-year, 24-hour storms.
- *Pollution reduction* requires 70% removal of TSS from 90% of annual runoff.

The manual provides more detailed guidelines for these rules, as well as simplified prescriptive and performance analysis methods, including spreadsheet tools. It also has excellent design schematics of infiltration and discharge, flow control, and pollution reduction measures.

Stormwater Plans, Strategies, and Projects

Portland has been innovative in engaging people and the private sector in its watershed and stormwater initiatives. It experimented with parking lot swales (1990), green roofs (starting density bonuses in 2001), clean river (2000) and watershed (2005) plans, stormwater user fee discounts (2006), a green streets policy (2007), and a $50 million gray-to-green strategy to plant trees, construct green ecoroofs, install green street facilities, and purchase priority natural areas.

Source: Portland 2008; U.S. EPA 2010b; Vizzini 2010.

Table 8.4 **A Chronology of Portland's Water Woes and Recovery**

Era	Population	Sewer and Stormwater Initiatives and Watershed Conditions
1860	10,000	First sewer constructed
1890	50,000	Decision to build combined sewer system
1890–1950s		**Steady decline in watershed health**
1950s	375,000	Interceptor sewers and treatment plant completed
1970s	375,000	Sewer system improvements and secondary treatment completed
1950s–1990s		**Minor improvement in watershed health**
1990s	450,000	Court-ordered Combined Sewer Overflow Program begins
2000	530,000	Stormwater manual adopted
2009	580,000	Grey-2-Green Initiatives launched
1990–2010		**Rapid improvement in watershed health**

Source: Adapted from Vizzini 2010.

Ngan Associates et al. 2009a). Of course, the state and local manuals discussed above provide design details and sizing methods (e.g., King County 2008; MDE 2009; Portland 2008; Washington DOE 2005).

Before describing specific measures, it is important to address some design concepts. A useful place to start is Portland's sustainable stormwater principles: Manage runoff close to the source, mimic natural hydrology, integrate runoff into the built environment, design for multiple benefits, and act early to avoid costly mitigation. The close-to-the-source methods to minimize impervious cover, and effectively convey, store, and infiltrate, have collectively been referred to as low-impact development (LID) measures since Maryland's Prince George's County developed its LID manual in 1999. Seattle refers to them as green stormwater infrastructure.

Low-Impact Development and Light-Imprint Design

The LID stormwater movement took hold during the past decade, and its onsite protection of existing vegetation and bioretention of runoff fit well in low-density, large-lot suburban development. But large-lot development runs counter to emerging sustainable development designs for compact, mixed-use, walkable places and the social connectivity they foster. Tom Low, a planner and architect at Duany Plater-Zyberk and Company (DPZ), recognized the disconnect and developed a new "LID"—**light-imprint design**, which integrates sustainable stormwater and New Urbanism design principles. His critique of the original LID is threefold:

- LID onsite stormwater storage and infiltration work for low-density development, and LID standards may discourage more compact forms of development.
- LID is stormwater-centric and may ignore other environmental and social considerations in environmentally sustainable community design.
- LID measures rely on landscape and vegetation, but often use costly infrastructure conveyance and high-maintenance filtration methods, rather than lower-tech design solutions, which can be as effective, less costly, and more attractive. For example, crushed and washed stone and pea gravel can be used as alternatives to pervious asphalt or concrete.

Low's highly illustrated *Light Imprint Handbook* (2008) describes sustainable stormwater designs for paving, channeling, storage, and filtration applied at different scales along Duany's urban transect, from the urban core to the rural natural. Figure 8.2 shows the transect of filtration measures, including ponds and wetlands, bioretention swales and rain gardens, and green roofs. It has an example of a "green finger" from Habersham (South Carolina), an extension or preservation of a natural landscape into an urbanized area that maintains natural vegetation, drainage, and filtration.

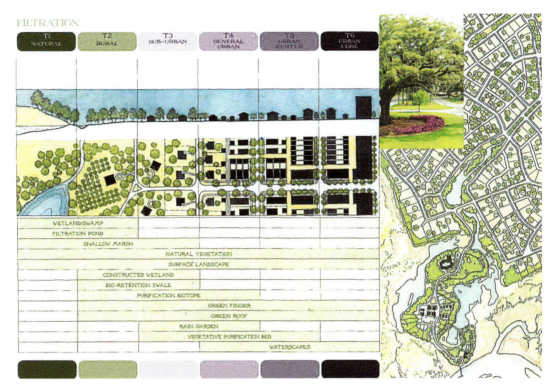

Figure 8.2 A Light-Imprint Transect for Filtration with Habersham (SC) Green Finger. This is an example of extension or preservation of a natural landscape into an urbanized area, maintaining natural vegetation, drainage, and filtration. (*Source:* Low 2008. DPZ Architects and Town Planners. Used with permission of Tom Low.)

Land Use Planning and Management SCM

Low's light-imprint approach emphasizes onsite design details, but its reliance on the urban transect and community design places those onsite measures in a larger-scale context, as shown in the Habersham green finger example. Land use design affects both new development and redevelopment, and includes three strategies: integrating SCMs across the watershed, green infrastructure, and neighborhood design.

Integrating SCMs Across the Watershed

Planning land use for water begins with the watershed, and all stormwater management practices should be informed by watershed assessments and plans. The NRC's 2009 stormwater report recommended that the EPA adopt a watershed approach for stormwater management to provide necessary monitoring and assessment, along with management flexibility. This holds true for state and local programs as well, and we have seen programs in Maryland, Portland, the Chesapeake Bay, and Michigan's Clinton River that use a watershed approach.

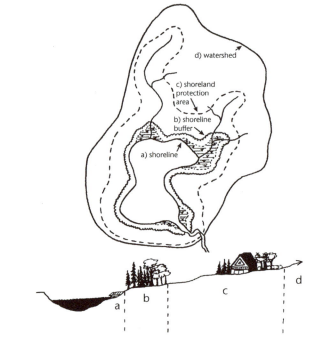

Figure 8.3 Four Zones of Lake Protection. (*Source:* Cappriella and Schueler 2001. Used with permission.)

Green Infrastructure Land Conservation

Managing development and redevelopment is the focus of most stormwater management programs, but managing new site impacts must be complemented by watershed preservation and restoration efforts. For example, protecting, restoring, and planting forested riparian buffers are collectively perhaps the most important measures for maintaining stream and watershed health. Buffering lake and bay shores is also critical (see below; see also Chapters 10, 14, and 15). Figure 8.3 shows lake protection zones with unbuildable shoreline and shoreline buffer zones, and conditionally buildable shoreland protection and watershed areas. For development criteria for these zones, see the book website (www .envirolanduse.org).

Neighborhood Design

Four important stormwater issues in neighborhood design are minimizing impervious surface, mitigating developed impervious surface, retaining natural vegetation and drainage, and development density. Low's light imprint tries to integrate these with livable community design. Low argues that LID low-density solutions work against design objectives for walkability and social connectivity. Low density can also exacerbate stormwater runoff, runoff controls being equal. The EPA's report (2005) of Smart Growth solutions to stormwater compares three development scenarios for 80,000 houses. Higher density reduces runoff per household:

- At 1 house/acre, 80,000 houses would take 80,000 acres (or 8 watersheds) at 20% impervious cover and produce 1,500 million cu ft of stormwater runoff.

Figure 8.4 Density in Neighborhood Design. Left: A conventional site plan for 103 house lots. Right: A cluster site plan with open space to retain vegetation and natural drainage. (*Source:* PS Partnership and WSU Extension 2005. Images by AHBL, Inc. courtesy of Puget Sound Partnership.)

- At 4 houses/acre, 80,000 houses would take 20,000 acres (or 2 watersheds) at 38% impervious cover and produce 500 million cu ft of stormwater runoff each year.
- At 8 houses/acre, 80,000 houses would take 10,000 acres (or 1 watershed) at 65% impervious cover and produce 400 million cu ft of stormwater runoff each year.

Density matters. And the configuration of that density also matters. Figure 8.4 from the Puget Sound LID Manual compares a conventional site plan for 103 lots and a compact design with the same number of units clustered on smaller lots with narrower streets, retention of vegetation and natural drainage, and bioretention areas integrated into the neighborhood design (PS Partnership 2005). Figure 8.5 zooms in to show potential site measures for both large lots and compact lots.

Pollution Prevention, Source Control, and Product Substitution

This category includes a group of measures intended to remove pollutants before they become part of runoff pollutants. In an agricultural setting, these BMPs include nutrient management plans and integrated pest management to mitigate the excessive use of fertilizer and pesticides, which end up in the stormwater runoff. For urban stormwater, these measures include litter control and street vacuuming. At the state and national levels, policies for reducing phosphorus in detergents or fuel additives are effective, as these materials ultimately wash off from the land and pollute runoff and receiving waters.

Onsite and Neighborhood SCM: Primarily Storage

There are many onsite and neighborhood-scale SCMs that provide onsite water storage, infiltration, conveyance, and treatment. Many of them provide two or more

Figure 8.5 Site Design. Left: Large-lot stormwater control measures. Right: Small-lot control measures. (*Source:* PS Partnership and WSU Extension 2005. Images by AHBL, Inc. courtesy of Puget Sound Partnership.)

of these functions. For ease of presentation, we will look at their primary function. Among the SCMs that provide primarily storage are rainwater harvesting, green roofs, bioretention rain gardens, parking lot storage, and underground tanks.

Downspout Disconnect and Rainwater Harvesting

Rainwater collection has been practiced for millennia in arid climates for water supply purposes. In more humid climates, other sources of water supply are used, and under the "good drainage" approach, roof gutters and downspouts are typically used to collect rainfall in order to get it out. One means of reducing the connectivity of impervious rooftops to stormwater drainage systems is simply to disconnect gutter downspouts from storm drains and let rainwater drain to pervious surfaces. Figure 8.6 combines a disconnect with a "raintainer" rain barrel to enhance storage and capacity for watering the garden. Larger-volume collection tanks can be used above the ground or buried, for the purpose of using rainwater for other nonpotable functions, such as toilet flushing, thereby reducing the consumption of precious drinking-quality water. The cistern is back! Figure 8.7 shows the design and installation of a buried cistern tank in St. Paul, Minnesota.

Green Roofs, Ecoroofs, and Roof Gardens

Roofs contribute a significant amount of impervious surface in cities, and one way to mitigate their effect is to detain and absorb water on the roof through vegetation. Chicago, Portland, New York, Seattle, and other cities provide incentives, and in some cases mandates, for vegetated flat roofs. **Green roofs** require several layers to provide structural support, moisture sealing, insulation, water drainage and storage, growing medium, and the vegetation itself (Figure 8.8A). There are two primary types of green roofs, depending on depth of soil, which affects use and

Figure 8.6 Raintainer and Downspout Disconnect. A simple downspout disconnect with a "raintainer" rain barrel. (*Source:* SD1, Wright, Kentucky, http://www.sd1.org/. Used with permission.)

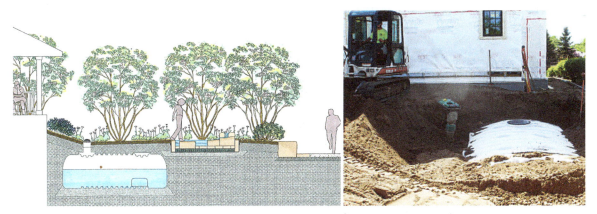

Figure 8.7 Harvesting Rainwater. Left: The design for a buried cistern. Right: Installation of that design. (*Source:* Landscape Architecture, Inc., St. Paul, Minnesota, www.landarcinc.com. Used with permission.)

vegetation. Intensive green roofs, or **roof gardens**, have thicker soil and can grow deeper rooted plants. Extensive green roofs, or **ecoroofs**, have a thinner layer of soil and shallow roots for sedum and grasses. These often cover large roof areas. The green roof at New York's Calhoun School is a turf-covered ecoroof with roof garden boxes on the perimeter (Figure 8.8B). While green roofs have some energy insulating value, their primary benefit is their ability to absorb, detain, and evapotranspire stormwater.

Figure 8.8 Vegetated Flat Roofs. Left: Typical green roof profile contains several layers to provide a variety of functions. Right: This extensive green roof on Calhoun School in New York has intensive garden boxes. (*Source:* Left: AMERGREEN. Illustration used with permission from American Wick Drain Corp. Right: Courtesy www.designshare.com © DesignShare.)

Bioretention Basins and Rain Gardens

One of the most practical onsite low-impact measures is the bioretention basin. Called rain gardens in a residential application, the basins have versatile applications for mitigating impervious surfaces along roadways and parking lots. While bioretention provides storage and slow release, with appropriate design and vegetation, they have infiltration and treatment benefits as well. Figure 8.9 shows the materials and dimensions for a typical rain garden. Figure 8.10A shows a residential rain garden, one of many installed under Stewardship Partners' 12,000 Rain Gardens campaign in Puget Sound. This September 2010 photograph was taken after a very heavy rain, and the storage capacity of the bioretention basin is evident. The rain garden drained completely within 24 hours. This installation also solved the problem of a constantly wet foundation and crawlspace during the rainy season. Figure 8.10B shows an ultra-urban application as a green alley.

In bioretention, landscaping features are usually located in parking lot islands or residential land depressions, where there is likely to be mulch, soil, and vegetation to provide natural pollutant removal mechanisms. After filtering through the mulch and soil bed, runoff that does not infiltrate is usually collected in a perforated underdrain and returned to the storm drain system. Design variations produce **bioretention swales**, providing conveyance as well as storage and infiltration, and **bioretention benches**, in which deposited soil bed, mulch, and vegetation act as a bench on slopes to slow, store, and filter runoff.

Onsite and Neighborhood SCM: Primarily Infiltration

Infiltration of runoff is a critical objective of stormwater management, to reduce runoff volume and to achieve predevelopment groundwater recharge. Con-

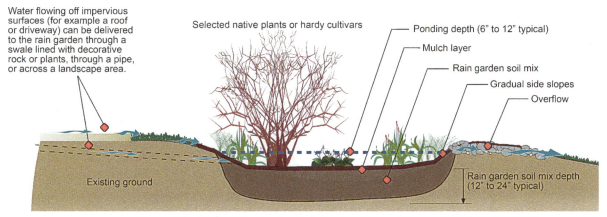

Water flowing off impervious surfaces (for example a roof or driveway) can be delivered to the rain garden through a swale lined with decorative rock or plants, through a pipe, or across a landscape area.

Selected native plants or hardy cultivars

Ponding depth (6" to 12" typical)

Mulch layer

Rain garden soil mix

Gradual side slopes

Overflow

Existing ground

Rain garden soil mix depth (12" to 24" typical)

Figure 8.9 A Typical Bioretention Rain Garden. (*Source:* Hinman, WSU Extension 2007. Graphic by AnderDesigns. Used with permission.)

(A)

(B)

Figure 8.10 Rain Gardens. A: A residential bioretention rain garden after heavy rain. Inset: Before installation. B: A bioretention green alley. (*Source:* A: Photo by Stacey Gianas, Stewardship Partners. Design and construction by Rain Dog Designs. Used with permission. B: Virginia DCR 1999.)

trol measures that enhance infiltration are bioretention infiltration basins and planters, infiltration trenches, and pervious and porous pavement.

Infiltration Basins, Planters, and Trenches

Infiltration basins are common parking lot mitigation measures, while **planters** are often used to collect and infiltrate building roof runoff. Infiltration basins require good drainable soils, although an underlying gravel trench can be used if soil conditions are not ideal. Like a bioretention basin, a vegetated infiltration basin drains water from impervious surfaces and uses vegetation for both water treatment and aesthetic appearance; but unlike bioretention, additional

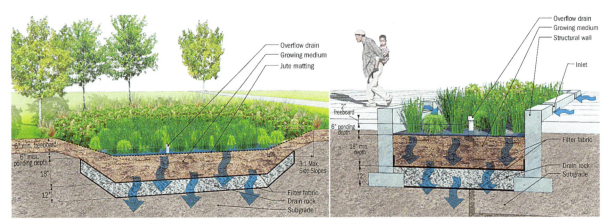

Figure 8.11 Enhancing Infiltration by Biorentention. Left: A vegetated infiltration basin. Right: A vegetated infiltration planter. Both measures are intended to infiltrate all runoff input and have only overflow outlets. (*Source:* Clean Water Solutions, LIDA Approaches, 2009. Used with permission.)

underlying gravel material enhances infiltration, and there is usually no outlet except for an optional overflow (Figure 8.11A). The design is similar for an infiltration planter, which can be applied in dense urban areas to mitigate impervious surface and provide vegetative cover (Figure 8.11B). Figure 8.12 shows a series of infiltration planters in downtown Portland. Infiltration trenches are generally topped with gravel and not vegetated, and while they infiltrate runoff, they do not provide the added "green" amenity and ecological value of vegetated basins.

Pervious Pavements

Asphalt and concrete pavement for roads, parking lots, driveways, and sidewalks are a major cause of impervious cover (IC) and resulting stormwater runoff problems. Although more pervious alternatives have been on the market for 30 years, cost and maintenance requirements have inhibited wide adoption. However, new technologies and designs, along with new regulatory encouragement of pervious pavements, have increased the market and lowered the cost.

There are four main design alternatives for pervious pavements:

1. **Concrete grid pavers** allow drainage through openings filled with gravel (Figure 8.13A). Although they are about 90% impervious, they have less effective IC due to distributed infiltration channels. The cost is about $5/sq ft (Portland 2006).
2. **Porous concrete and asphalt** are mixed with more coarse and little fine aggregate to provide infiltration, and underlain with permeable gravel. Properly installed pervious concrete can absorb as much as 200 inches of water every hour (Figure 8.13B). The product lifetime is more than 20 years. The cost is about $10/sq ft, including base rock (Portland 2006).

Figure 8.12 Infiltration planters on Portland's 12th Avenue Green Street. The planters drain street runoff and provide an attractive buffer between sidewalk and street. (Photo by Kevin Robert Perry, Nevue Ngan Assoc. Used with permission.)

3. **Reinforced grass pavement** uses turf blocks (Figure 8.14A) or hard plastic honeycombs (Figure 8.14B) underlain with gravel and filled with soil and planted with grass. These provide structural strength for driveways and parking areas, infiltration, and attractive green appearance. Turf blocks cost $4–$6/sq ft (Portland 2006).
4. **Reinorced gravel paving**, like grass pavement, uses blocks or plastic honeycombs and fills the voids with gravel instead of grass.

Onsite and Neighborhood SCM: Primarily Conveyance

Conveyance involves moving runoff where you want it. Since water flows with gravity, effective conveyance assists natural drainage to move water into storage and infiltration control measures.

Swales

Vegetated channels that drain stormwater ultimately to natural channels without pipes and concrete are known as **swales**. They can be grass or vegetated, and steeper swales may have small rock check dams to slow the flow. Vegetated swales have infiltration, detention, and treatment properties similar to bioretention, except their primary purpose is to give water the opportunity to move along. Figure 8.15 illustrates vegetated swales along parking lots. Figure 8.16A shows the construction of a grassed swale and its result in the High Point development in Seattle. High Point's integrated drainage plan has swales on every street—3 miles of swales in all (Figure 8.16B).

Figure 8.13 Pervious Pavements. Left: Grid pavers for parking lots. Right: Pervious concrete driveways, parking, and side-walks in High Point, Seattle, Washington. (*Source:* Left: Photo by Lynn Betts, USDA, NRCS. Right: Pervious Concrete, Inc. www.perviouscrete.com. Used with permission.)

Figure 8.14 Reinforced Grass Pavement. Left: A turf block grass paver. Right: BodPave85 plastic honeycomb-reinforced paver for turf or gravel. (*Source:* Left: Exterior Designs of Alexandria, Minnesota, Bio Builder, Inc., http://www.exterior designsof alexandria.com, used with permission; inset photo by Titus Tscharntke, http://www.public-domain-image.com.) Right: Boddingtons Inc., http://www.boddingtons.us/ground-reinforcement/porous-grass-pavers.htm, used with permission.

Curb Cuts and Curb Extension Bioretention Swales

In most urban areas, stormwater drainage is dominated by curb and gutter systems. Initially believed to provide good drainage, these systems inhibit conveying stormwater to detention and infiltration. **Curb cuts** allow the passage of water to bioretention swales and infiltration basins (see Figure 8.12). It is often difficult to

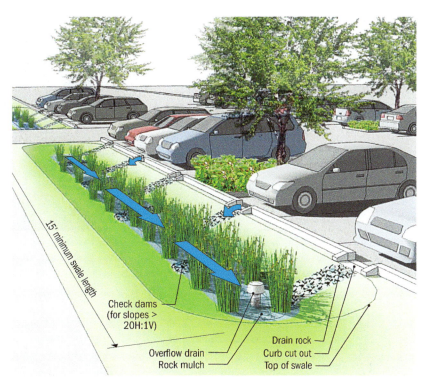

Figure 8.15 Parking Lot Vegetated Swales. (*Source:* Clean Water Solutions, LIDA Approaches, 2009. Used with permission.)

Figure 8.16 Vegetated Swales. Left: This grassed swale is being constructed in Seattle's High Point neighborhood. Right: Here are some of the 3 miles of swales on the streets of High Point. (*Source:* Phillips 2010, Seattle Housing Authority. SvR Design Company, Seattle. www.svrdesign.com. Used with permission.)

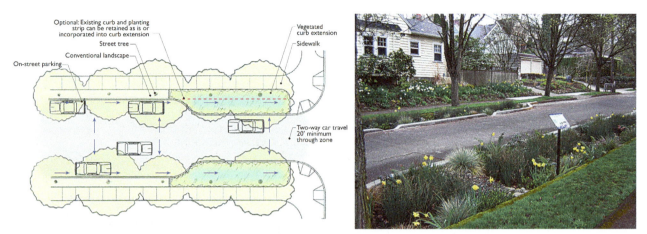

Figure 8.17 A Curb Extension Bioretention Swale. Left: Concept plan for street intersection curb extension in Kentucky. Right: A retrofit curb extension in Portland's Green Street program. (*Source:* Left: Nevue Ngan Assoc. et al. 2009. Used with permission. Right: © 2011 Environmental Services, City of Portland Oregon. Used with permission.)

retrofit curb and gutter systems, but **curb extension bioretention swales** are an effective means of channeling gutter runoff into bioretention.

Creating a curb extension bioretention swale is a prominent strategy in the Green Streets programs; they replace impervious roadway with green space, provide bioretention of gutter runoff, and calm traffic. Figure 8.17 illustrates the design, used in Portland and Kentucky. Gutter flow is captured at the upflow inlet, and runoff is captured in the vegetated basin. Excess flow exits at the overflow outlet.

Onsite and Neighborhood SCM: Primarily Filtration and Treatment

All of the vegetated measures discussed above provide treatment, and we will compare the effectiveness of various treatment practices shortly. Some measures, including sand filters, sediment tanks, and filter strips, are designed primarily for runoff quality treatment. They are used where there is pollution concentration, such as ultra-urban and industrial areas.

- The widely used **surface sand filter** has an aboveground sediment basin and filter chamber (Figure 8.18). It is usually employed offline to capture the water quality volume (WQv). Treated runoff is collected for exfiltration or discharge. Organic matter (e.g., peat, compost, charcoal) can be used instead of, or mixed with, sand to enhance the filtering of nutrients or trace metals.
- A **perimeter underground filter** has a sediment chamber and filter, designed on the perimeter of parking lots. Figure 8.19 shows the installation of such a system. Runoff flows from the parking lot into the chamber via perimeter curb cuts or grating drains.
- A **filter strip** is a grass or vegetated slope onto which a level spreader evenly distributes runoff to be filtered and treated by vegetation (Figure 8.20). A level spreader bard or curb is required at the collection trough to spread the flow evenly.

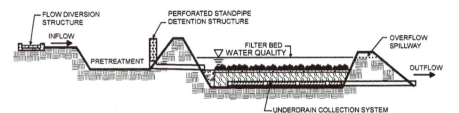

Figure 8.18 A Surface Sand Filter Diagram. (*Source:* Virginia DCR 1999.)

Figure 8.19 Installing a Perimeter Sand Filter. (*Source:* Virginia DCR 1999.)

Concentrated Flow SCMs

A traditional means of stormwater control under the good drainage approach is the use of detention ponds to capture concentrated flow from gutters and pipes and slowly release it downstream. Even with improved onsite and neighborhood storage and infiltration, there is still a place for containment of concentrated flow. Such measures should still be placed as close to the source as possible and scaled appropriately. Among many design variations, including extended ponds, smaller pocket ponds, and multiple pond systems, there are three basic types of containment of concentrated flow:

- **Dry detention ponds** have no permanent storage. They fill during storms and slowly release water over time. Dry ponds reduce peak discharge and erosive velocities but provide minimal water quality treatment. Figure 8.21 shows a dry pond before and after a storm.

Figure 8.20 Filter Strips. Top: A grass filter strip diagram. Bottom: A completed filter strip along a roadway. (*Source:* Top: Clean Water Solutions, LIDA Approaches, 2009. Bottom: California Storm - water Quality Association, California Stormwater BMP Handbook, TC-31, 2003.)

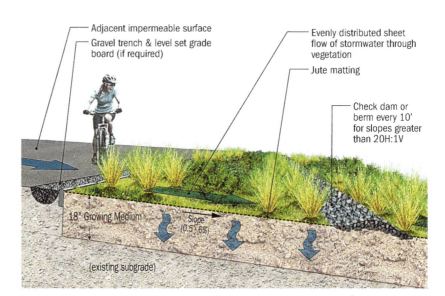

Adjacent impermeable surface

Gravel trench & level set grade board (if required)

Evenly distributed sheet flow of stormwater through vegetation

Jute matting

Check dam or berm every 10' for slopes greater than 20H:1V

18" Growing Medium

Slope (0.5–6%)

(existing subgrade)

Figure 8.21 Containment of Concentrated Flow. Left: A dry detention pond before a storm. Right: The same area following a storm. (*Source:* Virginia DCR 1999.)

Figure 8.22 A Wet Retention Pond. In High Point, Seattle, this wet retention pond adds community value. (*Source:* SvR Design Company, Seattle, www.svrdesign.com. Used with permission.)

- **Wet retention ponds** (Figure 8.22) can provide all WQv in a permanent pool; they are cost-effective and widely used. While they are limited in highly urbanized areas and arid climates, they provide a community amenity.
- **Stormwater wetlands** are constructed wetlands similar to wet ponds that also incorporate wetland plants. Pollutants are removed by settling and biological uptake. These created wetlands are the most effective ponds in removing pollutants (Figure 8.23). Box 8.4 describes the CWP's design for the "next generation" of stormwater wetlands (Capriella et al. 2008).

The Effectiveness of Stormwater Control Measures

The effectiveness of urban SCMs depends on the functional goals of the application. As discussed earlier, stormwater management objectives include improving stormwater quality, controlling stream channel erosion, reducing flooding, and enhancing groundwater recharge. Controls can reduce flooding and channel erosion by slowing runoff and reducing peak storm flows. Controls that increase infiltration will enhance groundwater recharge. Improving water quality through stormwater treatment is more difficult.

Figure 8.23 Stormwater Wetlands. This is a new stormwater wetland with first growth. (*Source: Virginia DCR 1999.*)

Table 8.5 compares stormwater control and treatment practices, based on data from several sources. Each measure is rated for its capability to remove pollutants, recharge groundwater through infiltration, reduce erosive velocities of runoff to protect natural channels, and reduce peak discharge to provide flood protection. In addition, the table gives pollutant removal values, drainage area limitations, and a rating of cost, maintenance, and acceptability. As the table shows, bioretention practices provide good pollutant removal and infiltration for small drainage areas at reasonable cost and public acceptability. As a result, they are a primary measure for onsite application. Ponds and wetlands provide good detention volume and therefore reduce flooding and channel erosion. Wet ponds and wetlands also have good pollutant removal, but dry ponds do not. Because ponds and wetlands are effective for drainage areas greater than 25 acres, they are primary measures for large properties or concentrated flow. Generally they are sized to store at a minimum the water quality volume (WQv). Filtering and infiltration measures provide very good treatment, and infiltration also improves recharge, but these practices are more expensive and higher maintenance than others. Both wet and dry swales have good treatment capabilities.

Effective measures can capture and treat the full WQv and are capable of removing 80% of total suspended solids (TSS) and 40% of total phosphorus. The WQv is the volume of storage needed to capture and treat 90% of the average annual stormwater pollutant load.

The Center for Watershed Protection (CWP) provides useful guidelines for selecting the appropriate treatment measure. Stormwater ponds, wetlands, infil-

BOX 8.4—The Next Generation of Stormwater Wetlands

n one of a series of articles prepared for the U.S. EPA, the Center for Watershed Protection (CWP) proposed the next generation of stormwater wetlands. Objectives for the new emergent wetland/pond design include improving pollutant removal; reducing runoff volume and peak flows; minimizing construction, maintenance costs, and land consumption; and creating a diverse plant community, valuable wildlife habitat, and a safe and attractive amenity for residents. The design is illustrated in Figure 8.24. It includes an online wet pond cell that supplies a steady supply of water to an offline shallow wetland cell, which reduces water level fluctuations in the wetland cell that can impact plant diversity and habitat value. The wetland/pond system can be sized at 3% or less of the contributing drainage area, with a minimum length-to-width ratio of 3:1, although 5:1 is preferred.

The numbers below correspond to the circled numbers in Figure 8.24 for the design elements:

1. *Pretreatment* by downspout disconnection, bioretention, or dry swales reduces runoff volume, velocity, and pollutant load.
2. *Sediment forebay* with volume = 10% of WQv reduces velocity and promotes sediment removal.
3. *Wet pond cell* with volume = 70% of WQv in permanent pool provides additional pretreatment, a steady flow of water to the wetland, and additional detention for channel protection and overbank and extreme flood storage from larger storm events. The *wetland riser* contains feeder pipes to the lower-elevation wetland cell, and the *dissipation riser* provides overflow from larger storm storage to the dissipation pool (5).
4. *Wetland cell* provides treatment of soluble pollutants and native plant and habitat diversity. The four cells are equal in area. Cell 1 is 18–24 inches deep and should be able to support emergent plant species that live 3–18 in. below water level. Cell 2 is 2–4 in. deep and can support species that live 1–3 in. above the water. Cell 3 is 12–18 in.

deep, and cell 4 is 2–4 in. deep. The alternating deep and shallow cells create a diversity of landscape and vegetation and a sequence of aerobic and anaerobic zones that enhance nitrogen removal.
5. *Dissipation pool* is 3–4 ft deep with volume = 10% of WQv and has adjustable weir/riser to regulate levels and releases.
6. *Transitional cell* receives inflow from both the wetland cells and the wet pond prior to receiving water.
7. *Wetland buffer* of vegetated cover extends at least 50 ft from the outward edge of the water surface.

Source: Capriella et al. 2008.

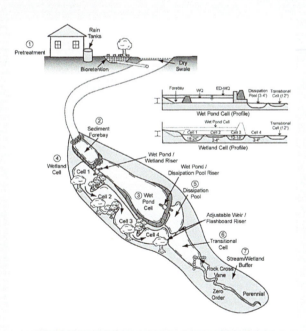

Figure 8.24 Next Generation Stormwater Wetlands. The design combines wet pond retention and consistent flow through wetland cells to maximize storage, pollutant removal, and vegetative and habitat diversity, while minimizing land area and cost. (*Source:* Capriella et al. 2008. Center for Watershed Protection. Used with permission.)

TABLE 8.5 Urban Stormwater Control and Treatment Practices Compared

Practice	Capabilities				% Pollutant Reduction				Cost/ Acceptance		
	Pollutant Removal Capability	Ground-water Recharge Capability	Channel Protection Capability	Overbank Flood Protection	TSS	TP	TN	DA	Initial Cost	Main-tenance	Community Acceptance
Bioretention	G	G	L	L	NA	65	49	<2	$2^1/_2$	2	2
Ponds											
Dry	L	L	G	G	7	19	5	—	—	—	—
Wet	G	L	G	G	79	49	32	>25	2	$1^1/_2$	$1^1/_2$
Wet ED	G	L	G	G	80	55	35	>25	2	2	2
Multiple	G	L	G	G	91	76	na	>25	3	2	$1^1/_2$
Pocket pond	G	L	G	G	87	78	28	<5	$1^1/_2$	4	3
Wetlands											
Shallow	G	L	G	G	83	43	26	>25	3	$3^1/_2$	2
ED wetland	G	L	G	G	69	39	55	>25	3	3	$2^1/_2$
Pond/wetland	G	L	G	G	71	56	19	>25	3	2	$1^1/_2$
Pocket marsh	G	L	L	M	57	57	44	<5	2	4	3
Filtering											
Surface sand	G	G	M	L	87	59	32	<10	4	$3^1/_2$	$2^1/_2$
Underground sand	G	L	L	L	80	50	35	<2	$4^1/_2$	4	1
Perimeter sand	G	L	L	L	79	41	47	<2	4	$3^1/_2$	1
Organic	G	L	L	L	88	61	41	<10	4	$3^1/_2$	$2^1/_2$
Infiltration											
Trench	G	G	M	M	100	42	42	<5	$3^1/_2$	5	2
Basin	G	G	M	M	90	65	50	<10	3	5	4
Porous pavement	G	G	M	M	95	65	83	<5	3	5	1
Open channels											
Dry swale	G	G	L	L	93	83	92	<5	$2^1/_2$	2	$1^1/_2$
Wet swale	G	L	L	L	74	28	40	<5	2	2	$1^1/_2$
Grass channel	L	L	L	L	81	34	31	—	—	—	—

TSS: Total suspended solids removal. Initial cost: 1 = low, 5 = high
TP: Total phosphorus. Maintenance: 1 = low, 5 = high.
TN: Total nitrogen. Community acceptance: 1 = high, 5 = low.
DA: Maximim drainage area, acres. Ratings, depending on design: G = Good, M = Marginal, L = Little or none.
ED: Extended detention

Source: Adapted from CWP 2000; New York 2001; Prince George's County 2002; Schueler 2000; Winer 2000.

TABLE 8.6 **Pollutant Removal Capabilities of Stormwater Treatment Practices**

Practice	n	TSS	TP	TN	Carbon	Bacteria	HC	Metals
Stormwater ponds*	44	80	51	33	43	70	81	50–74
Stormwater wetlands	39	76	49	30	18	78	85	40–69
Infiltration	6	95	70	51	54	ND	ND	98–99
Filters†	19	86	59	38	54	37	84	49–88
Swales‡	9	81	34	84	69	(25)	62	42–71
Ditches	11	31	(16)	(9)	18	5	ND	0–38

Values are median percentage removal before and after treatment practice.
n = number of performance studies.
TSS = total suspended solids; TP = total phosphorus; TN = total nitrogen.
Carbon = organic carbon (BOD, COD, or TOC).
Bacteria = mean removal rates of fecal coliform bacteria.
HC = total petroleum hydrocarbons.
Metals = range for cadmium, copper, lead, and zinc.
ND = not determined.
*Includes wet ponds and excludes conventional dry detention ponds.
† Includes a variety of sand filters and bioretention; excludes vertical sand filters and vegetated filter strips.
‡ Includes biofilters, wet swales, and dry swales.

Source: Schueler 2000; Winer 2000.

tration, bioretention, filtration, and swales can meet these treatment criteria if they are designed to store and treat the full WQv (Table 8.6). As a result, these are the only measures recommended by the CWP. It does not recommend filter strips, dry wells, ditches, and grass channels that do not store the full volume. It also discourages using oil/grit chambers and dry detention because of limited treatment capabilities, and porous pavements because of high maintenance and failure rates. While these recommendations are nearly a decade old, they still hold up, although there have been improvement in some measures, such as porous pavements (CWP 2000).

In 2010, the CWP developed the Watershed Treatment Model that was introduced in Chapter 7. The spreadsheet model analyzes annual pollutant loads, accounting for the benefits of the full suite of stormwater control measures and programs. The model assesses existing conditions and practices and evaluates future practices and retrofits, as well as projects future land use and development. The straightforward, easy-to-use spreadsheet and user's guide can be downloaded for free from the CWP website (http://www.cwp.org) (Caraco 2010).

Selecting and Sizing Stormwater Controls

The selection and sizing of SCMs depends on various factors, including management objectives and applications. Based on CWP criteria, Table 8.7 provides a selection matrix for categories of SCMs. Hotspots are areas of potentially high pollution, like industrial areas, and ultra-urban are areas where space is limited and original soils have been disturbed. The N and ? ratings are based on ability to

TABLE 8.7 **Stormwater Management Control Selection Matrix for Various Land Uses**

SMC	Rural	Residential	Roads and Highways	Commercial High-Density	Hotspots	Ultra- Urban
Bioretention	?	?	Y	Y	A2	Y
Wet pond	Y	Y	Y	?	A1	N
Pond/wetland	Y	Y	N	?	A1	N
Infiltration trench	?	?	Y	Y	N	?
Dry well*	?	Y	N	?	N	?
Surface sand filter	N	?	Y	Y	A2	Y
Underground sand filter	N	N	?	Y	Y	Y
Perimeter sand filter	N	N	?	Y	Y	Y
Dry swale	Y	?	Y	?	A2	?

Y = Yes. Good option in most cases.
? = Depends. Suitable under certain conditions, or may be used to treat a portion of the site.
N = No. Seldom or never suitable.
A1 = Acceptable option, but may require a pond liner to reduce risk of groundwater contamination.
A2 = Acceptable option, if not designed as an ex-filter.
*The dry well can only be used to treat rooftop runoff.

Source: Adapted from State of New York, CWP, 2001.

achieve needed water quality volume, required land area, and cost/maintenance compared with other options.

Table 8.8 describes the sizing criteria for stormwater management practices developed by the CWP and used by New York state, Maryland, Virginia, and other states. Individual or a combination of measures are sized to meet design volumes for water quality treatment (WQv), channel erosion protection (CPv), peak discharge reduction to reduce overbank flooding (Q_o), and extreme flooding (Q_f). The formulas for WQv are given in the table. CPv is the runoff volume from the 1-year 24-hour storm, as determined by the TR-55 method (see Chapter 7). The volumes for peak discharge mitigation for the 10- and 100-year storm are determined by TR-55.

Box 8.5 provides a case example used in Fairfax County (Virginia), and three additional case examples are given at http://www.fairfaxcounty.gov/dpwes/stormwater/.

Stream and Watershed Restoration

The emerging comprehensive approach to urban stormwater in the U.S., presented in this chapter, has institutionalized SWM from the federal to the local level for integrated solutions to runoff quantity, flood mitigation, water quality, and stormwater's human and ecological dimensions. This approach has dramatically improved stormwater management, but our urban streams continue to be impaired, as we are confronted with the legacy of excessive impervious surface

TABLE 8.8 **Stormwater Management Practice Sizing**

WQv Water Quality Volume	**90% Rule:** $WQv = [(P)(R_v)(A)]/12$ (acre-feet) $\quad R_v = 0.05 \times 0.009(I)$ $\quad I$ = Impervious cover (percent) $\quad$ Minimum $R_v = 0.2$ $\quad P$ = 90% rainfall event number (about 1 inch, may vary with location) $\quad A$ = site area in acres
CPv Channel Protection Volume	**Default Criterion:** CPv = 24-hour extended detention of post-developed 1-year, 24-hour $\quad$ storm event **Option for Sites Larger Than 50 Acres:** Distributed runoff control—geomorphic assessment to determine the $\quad$ bankfull channel characteristics and thresholds for channel stability and $\quad$ bedload movement.
Q_o Overbank Flood	Control the peak discharge from the 10-year storm to 10-year $\quad$ predevelopment rates. Control the peak discharge from the 100-year storm to 100-year $\quad$ predevelopment rates Safely pass the 100-year storm event
Q_f Extreme Storm	**Example:** Size the storm pool volume of a wet retention pond based on WQv for a 5-acre development site being converted from meadow to a 30% average impervious surface development. Assume P = 1 inch. Selection: retention basin (wet pond). $\quad WQv: \quad R_v = 0.05 + 0.009(30) = 0.32$ $\quad WQv = (1)(0.32)(5)/12 = 0.133$ acre-feet

and seemingly "good drainage" practices that led to the urban stream syndrome (USS) of altered hydrology, eroded channels, degraded riparian and aquatic habitat, and polluted runoff.

We have not yet taken the next step, which is fully integrating water management on a watershed basis. However, we see signs of hope in efforts so far and recognize that this increasingly comprehensive approach is yielding positive effects. In addition, applications of watershed management in places like Portland (Oregon) and Fairfax County (Virginia) show promise. Perhaps the most exciting trend is the realization that urban streams have benefits, and with better onsite and neighborhood SCMs using good design and vegetated conveyance, storage, and infiltration, natural urban streams can better handle resulting lower flows, velocities, and pollutant loads, and recover from their urban stream syndrome.

This case study is one of four provided by Fairfax County to illustrate how to size SMC detention and water quality volume to meet the county's stormwater ordinance (Figure 8.25). It is a residential tear-down redevelopment project that will replace a 1,500 sq ft house with a new 2,900 sq ft house on a 12,000 sq ft lot. Since there is an existing dwelling on the site, the ordinance requires a SMC BMP to store the WQv. Fairfax simplifies the WQv calculation by assuming WQv to be 0.5 in. over the impervious cover (IC) of the site. In other words:

WQv (cu ft) = (0.5"/12" per ft) x IC (sq ft)

WQv = 0.5"/12" per ft x 5,100 sq ft = 213 cu ft

There are two options for meeting this requirement:

- Option A: Add a 213 sq ft bioretention basin in the southeast drainage corner, assuming 1 ft deep from 6" surface storage and 6" sub-surface storage.

- Option B: Use 213 sq ft of permeable pavement in the southeast drainage corner, assuming 1 ft deep storage in gravel bed below pavement.

Existing Conditions	Post-Development Conditions
Woods = 3,800 sq ft	Woods = 1,300 sq ft
Roof + pavement = 2,500 sq ft	Roof + pavement = 5,100 sq ft
Lawn = 5,700 sq ft	Lawn = 5,600 sq ft
Site drains to southeast corner	Roof leaders drain to driveway
	Drainage pattern is unchanged

Source: Adapted from Fairfax County, Virginia 2005.

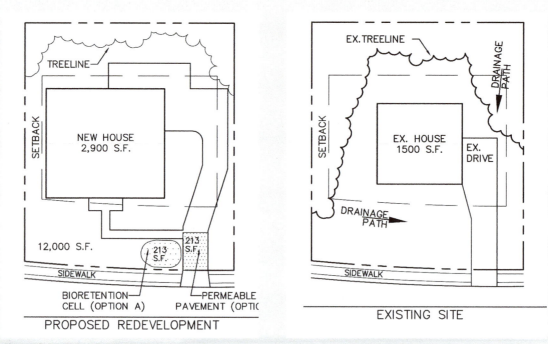

Figure 8.25 Sizing Onsite SMCs in Fairfax County, Virginia: A Single-Family Residence Case Study. (*Source:* Fairfax County, Virginia 2005. Used with permission.)

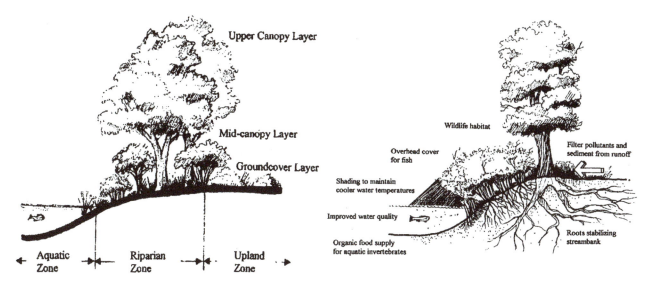

Figure 8.26 The Riparian Zone. Left: The riparian zone lies between the aquatic and upland zones. Right: The zone provides significant water quality, runoff control, aquatic ecology, and wildlife habitat benefits. (*Source:* USDA, NRCS, undated.)

Most of the control measures and practices presented above affect new development and redevelopment, and it is obvious that we are not going to "develop our way" out of our USS legacy. We must take proactive steps to retrofit existing developments and to remediate existing streams and riparian corridors. Many communities are doing just that—some with volunteer groups restoring streambanks one reach at a time, and others with comprehensive watershed restoration plans and significant investment. Some are daylighting and restoring streams previously buried in pipes and culverts or running in concrete channels.

Riparian Zones

Although all land use in the watershed contributes to stream impairment, the most important and sensitive areas in the watershed are where the land meets the water in the riparian zone. Figure 8.26 shows the zone and the benefits it provides for water quality, aquatic ecology, and wildlife habitat. Riparian vegetation, especially forested buffers, are critical to protection and restoration in watershed management. Figure 8.27 and Table 8.9 show buffer zones and their functions and appropriate width, vegetation, and land uses. Restoration efforts generally focus on the streamside zone, stabilizing streambanks and planting trees and other vegetation.

Stream and Corridor Restoration

The first edition of this book described principles and procedures for stream and corridor restoration, including sections on (1) designing restored stream channels, meanders, and floodplains; and (2) bioengineering measures for restoring stream corridors and controlling bank erosion. Because of the new material in this chapter and space constraints, those sections are now posted at the book website (www.envirolanduse.org).

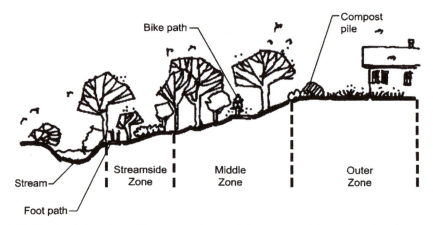

Figure 8.27 Riparian Buffer Zones. The streamside zone is the most sensitive, and land use is restricted (see Table 8.9). (*Source:* USDA, NRCS, undated.)

TABLE 8.9 **Characteristics of Riparian Buffer Zones**

	Streamside Zone	*Middle Zone*	*Outer Zone*
Function	Protect the physical integrity of the stream ecosystem.	Provide distance between upland development and streamside zone.	Prevent encroachment and filter backyard runoff.
Width	Minimum of 25 ft plus wetlands and critical habitat.	50–100 ft depending on stream order, slope, and 100-year floodplain.	25-ft minimum setback to structures.
Vegetative target	Undisturbed mature forest; reforest if grass.	Managed forest, protect 100-yr flood plain + 4 ft per % slope + adjacent wetlands.	Forest encouraged, but usually turfgrass.
Allowable uses	Very restricted (e.g., flood control, footpaths, etc.).	Restricted (e.g., some recreational uses, some stormwater BMPs, bike paths).	Unrestricted (e.g., residential uses, including lawn, garden, yard wastes, most BMPs).

Watershed Restoration and Management Plans

Watershed management plans are a critical tool for coordinating the diverse programs and projects for stormwater management of new construction, complying with MS4 and other federal and state regulations, retrofitting measures to mitigate existing impervious surfaces and USS, and restoring urban creeks and riparian areas. Many communities and metropolitan areas are beginning to take a watershed approach (see examples in Box 8.3 and Box 8.6).

The planning process involves gathering detailed stream assessment data, doing watershed modeling, and inviting extensive community involvement to

BOX 8.6—Fairfax County Watershed Restoration

airfax County, Virginia, is a large, urbanized county of 400 sq mi and more than 1 million people. It suffers from the typical legacy of USS, resulting from the suburban explosion in 1950–1970 and no stormwater control requirements. The county began requiring erosion and sediment control onsite detention by the 1970s and water quality BMPs in the water supply Occoquan watershed in the 1980s. This was extended to all new development in 1993, when Chesapeake Bay ordinances were adopted, which also designated Resource Protection Areas (RPA) along streams. In 1997, the County adopted MS4 Phase I requirements. In 1999, it initiated a Stream Protection Strategy (SPS) with a benthic macroinver-

tebrate assessment (see Appendix 7B) of 114 sites that showed 45% rated poor or very poor (a 2008 assessment of 40 sites showed 60% poor or very poor). In 2003, it conducted a Stream Physical Assessment of riparian buffers that showed considerable deficiency throughout the county (Figure 8.28A). In 2004, it extended RPA protection upstream beyond state requirements (Figure 8.28B). Despite these efforts, its stream impairment has increased (see Figure 7.24). It has 10 completed TMDL plans and is negotiating its MS4 permit renewal. In addition, it is likely to face new requirements is response to Chesapeake Bay programs.

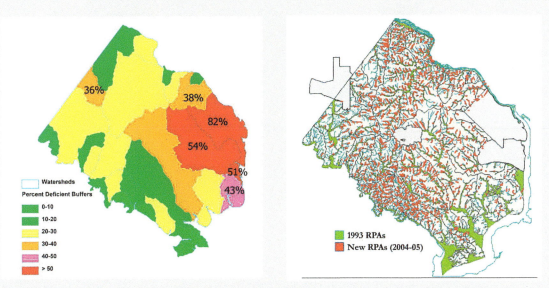

Figure 8.28 Fairfax County, Virginia, Stream Assessment and Response. Left: A stream physical assessment: percentage of stream miles with deficient buffers. Right: Resource Protection Areas, 1993, and new RPA extensions, 2004–2005. (*Source:* Fairfax County, Virginia, 2010; Rose 2010. Used with permission.)

In 2003, Fairfax initiated the Watershed Management Program (WMP) to develop a 25-year prioritized list of improvement projects based on ranked conditions of its 800 miles of streams below 50-acre catchment. It has used watershed models, assessment data, and extensive community involvement to identify structural and nonstructural BMP and stream restoration retrofits. Figure 8.29 shows three of the 30 site-scale water-

shed improvement projects identified for the Belle Haven Watershed. Figure 8.29A shows a stream restoration project, Figure 8.29B shows an extended detention retrofit, and Figure 8.29C shows a parking lot bioretention retrofit. The county has completed plans for 11 of its 30 watersheds, with the remainder in process. It is integrating the plans into its MS4 permit, TMDL plans, and Chesapeake Bay response.

BOX 8.6—Fairfax County Watershed Restoration (cont.)

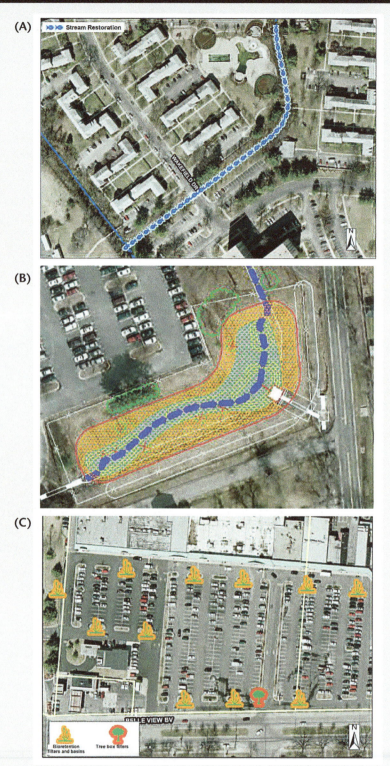

Figure 8.29 Three WMP Projects for Belle Haven Watershed, Fairfax County, Virginia. A: Stream restoration. B: Extended detention pond. C: Bioretention and tree box filters. (*Source:* Fairfax County 2010.)

Source: Fairfax County 2010; Rose 2010.

identify structural and nonstructural BMP and stream restoration retrofits to be implemented on a 25-year schedule. In the Fairfax County example (see Box 8.6), the first six plans covering 11 watersheds contained 300 policy and action recommendations (Fairfax County 2010). Watershed management is a continuing topic in subsequent chapters, especially Chapter 19.

Summary

Planning for and managing the interaction of land use and water is one of the most important jobs for environmental planners. Like many planning activities, planning and managing urban stormwater have changed dramatically over the past two decades. What has emerged is a more comprehensive approach that integrates objectives for runoff flow control, flood damage mitigation, water quality, urban ecology, development design, and community livability. Stormwater management has become increasingly institutionalized by more structured federal and state permitting for municipal separate stormwater systems (MS4), TMDL planning integrating point and nonpoint water pollution control, watershed implementation plans, water quality trading, and detailed state regulations and manuals for stormwater systems.

Urban design and technology have contributed to the development of those systems. Research is showing that onsite and neighborhood stormwater management controls for storage, infiltration, and treatment reduce runoff volume, peak flows, and velocities; treat runoff pollution; and enhance groundwater recharge.

Many localities are responding to these requirements and moving beyond them to correct the legacy of urban stream syndrome of altered hydrology, eroded channels, degraded riparian and aquatic habitat, and polluted runoff. By better controlling runoff and pollution close to the source, they are realizing that urban streams once restored can better handle the newly reduced flows and loads without erosion and degradation. The urban stream restoration movement is advancing throughout the country.

The next step in stormwater management requires integrating these various regulations, programs, and projects on a watershed basis. The watershed is the spatial umbrella over all stream and stormwater issues. We will never correct our urban stream syndrome and impaired waters by piecemeal efforts to install a BMP here and plant a tree there. We need watershed management plans to coordinate and guide all activities for both cost-saving efficiency and environment-saving effectiveness. Chapter 19 explores watershed management planning in greater detail.

9 ■ Groundwater and Source Water Protection

We now have a better understanding of how land use affects the hydrologic water balance. Impervious surfaces increase surface runoff by stealing water and sending it down its slippery slopes when it would otherwise infiltrate the ground. Reduced infiltration means less interflow and baseflow to support stream flow between storms, and it also means less recharge of groundwater aquifers. Aquifers serve as important sources of water supply, as do many surface reservoirs and streams. Pollutants from the land can run off, infiltrate, and contaminate these water supply sources. Before exploring these impacts and discussing how to manage groundwater and sources of water supply, we review some concepts and terminology related to hydrogeology and groundwater use.

Groundwater Hydrology Fundamentals

Figure 9.1 summarizes groundwater relationships and introduces some terminology associated with **groundwater** (also called phreatic water). Subsurface water must occupy the voids or interstices within soil and rocks that are not occupied by solid material. The degree of voids existing in soil or rock material is measured by its **porosity**, or the ratio of the volume of voids to the total volume of soil or rock. If the interstices are connected so that a fluid can move from one to another, the material is said to be permeable. Recall from Chapter 6 that **permeability** is the capacity to transmit fluids under pressure. (The coefficient of permeability is measured in volume of water transmitted through an area under a standard pressure and temperature.) Generally, subsurface materials having high porosity and permeability make good water-bearing formations.

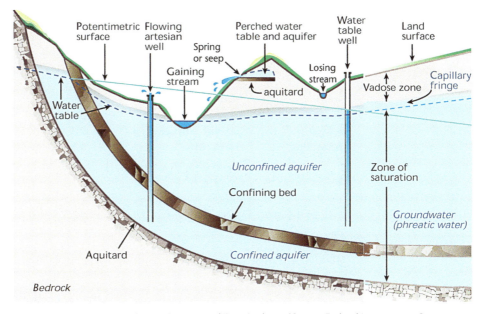

Figure 9.1 The Groundwater System and Terminology. (*Source:* Federal Interagency Stream Restoration Working Group 1998; USGS 1972.)

Aquifers and Recharge

Formations that contain enough water and have sufficient permeability to be used as water supply sources are called **aquifers**. An **aquiclude**, such as clay, is usually porous and may contain groundwater but transmits it slowly and is not a good water supply source. An **aquifuge**, such as rock, neither stores nor transmits water. Aquicludes and aquifuges can serve as confining **aquitards**, or layers, above or below aquifers. The occurrence of aquifers, their recharge, and the movement of groundwater are determined by geologic factors, including surface and subsurface materials, stratigraphy, and structure. Porosity and permeability of materials determine their water-bearing potential. The potential of unconsolidated materials depends on texture and degree of sorting. Some rock materials, such as sandstones and limestones, may have sufficient voids and permeability to provide good aquifer potential. Other rock materials (e.g., igneous and metamorphic rock, shale) have poor potential unless a high degree of weathering and fracturing has produced voids. Table 9.1 gives porosities and permeabilities for selected materials and types of openings in water-bearing rocks.

   Unconfined aquifers (also called free aquifers) have direct vertical contact with the atmosphere through the open pores in the soil, and recharge comes from infiltration above. The top of an unconfined aquifer is the ground **water table** (see Figure 9.1). Below the water table is the saturated zone, and above it is the **vadose zone**, also called the unsaturated or aeration zone. The **capillary fringe** is the moisture zone above the water table. The level of the water table fluctuates with periods of rainy and dry weather. Unconfined **perched aquifers**

TABLE 9.1 **Porosities and Coefficients of Permeability for Common Materials**

		Porosity (%)	Permeability (gal/ft²/da)
	Clay	45	0.01
Good	**Sand**	**35**	**1,000**
water-	**Gravel**	**25**	**100,000**
bearing	**Gravel and sand**	**20**	**10,000**
materials	**Sandstone**	**15**	**100**
	Shale	5	1.0
	Granite	1	0.01

produce **springs** or **seeps**, where underlying layers force water to spill out of the ground.

Figure 9.2 shows aquifer recharge areas for a typical unconfined aquifer in a river valley made up of unconsolidated alluvial and colluvial deposits having good porosity and permeability. The primary recharge area is directly above the aquifer. Secondary recharge comes from runoff from mountain flanks, which flows into the primary area. Tertiary recharge comes from runoff higher up the watershed, which contributes to stream flow in the river.

If the aquifer is overlain by a geologic layer through which water cannot move, it is said to be a **confined aquifer**. Stratigraphy and structure influence the recharge of confined aquifers. **Stratigraphy** is the study of layered rock material in Earth's crust. Layers of different types of geologic material may fold and bend, occasionally cropping out to the surface, occasionally dropping to significant depths. As shown in Figure 9.1, a confined aquifer is a layer of good water-bearing material bounded by confining layers or materials of low permeability. Thus, a confined aquifer is recharged where its permeable stratum intercepts the ground or by connection to another aquifer or surface water sources. Connection to such sources can result from **subsurface structure** or faults and fractures, which provide avenues for water movement. **Semiconfined aquifers** are those that are recharged at their interception with the ground surface and by fractures through their confining layer that may extend to the ground surface. Figure 9.3 shows the semiconfined Edwards Aquifer in Texas. Runoff and stream flow from the drainage area flow into the recharge area; faults and fractures in the recharge area provide the principal avenues for aquifer recharge from the stream flow.

Piezometric (Potentimetric) Surface and the Cone of Depression

When a well is drilled or pipe sunk into an aquifer, the water in it will rise to a certain level. The height of that water above some arbitrary datum, usually sea level, is called the head or **piezometric (potentimetric) surface**. For an unconfined aquifer, this level will be the water table. As shown in Figure 9.1, for confined aquifers this level is determined by the height of water in the confined column below its recharge area. It may be above the water table, an **artesian well**, or

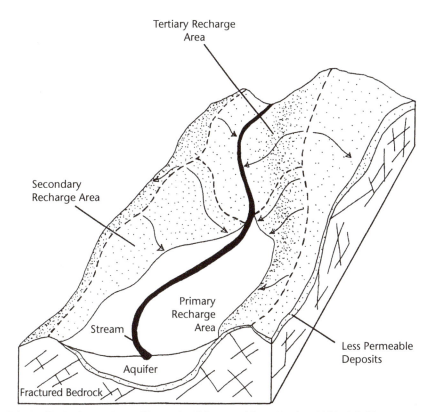

Figure 9.2 Aquifer Recharge Areas. (*Source:* Jon Witten and Scott Horsley. 1995. *A Guide to Wellhead Protection.* Planning Advisory Service Report 457/458. Used with permission of the American Planning Association.)

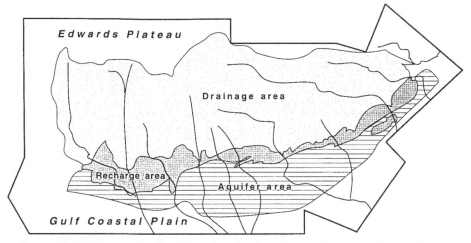

Figure 9.3 The Edwards Aquifer. This semiconfined aquifer supplies most of the water for central Texas. (*Source:* Jon Witten and Scott Horsley. 1995. *A Guide to Wellhead Protection.* Planning Advisory Service Report 457/458. Used with permission of the American Planning Association.)

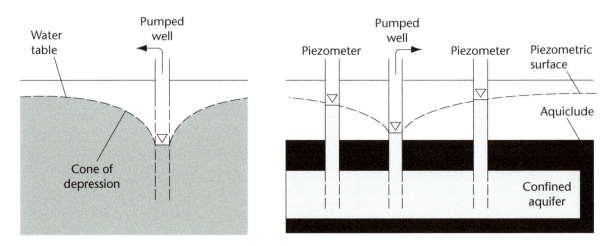

Figure 9.4 Cones of Depression. Pumping from a well lowers the piezometric surface. In unconfined aquifers (left), this lowers the water table. In confined aquifers (right), it lowers the piezometric surface, which can be measured with piezometers. For large aquifers, the cone can extend for several miles and take years to recover, even after adequate recharge. (*Source: Water in Environmental Planning* by Thomas Dunne and Luna Leopold, copyright © 1978. Reprinted with permission of W. H. Freeman and Company.)

below the water table, a **subartesian well**. If the pressure is great enough for the water to actually rise above the ground surface and flow freely, it is called a **flowing artesian well**.

Pumped wells can dramatically affect the piezometric potential and cause adverse effects. As shown in Figure 9.4, pumping causes a **cone of depression** that lowers the potentimetric surface not only at the well but also in the surrounding area. With several wells tapping the same aquifer, competition can result, as one deep well can lower the surface below neighboring shallower wells. The piezometric depressions in Tidewater Virginia, where large industrial wells are used by pulp and paper mills in Franklin and West Point, have caused a drop in the piezometric surface of 100–160 feet that extend as far as 50 miles from the wellhead.

Figure 9.5 shows that along a stream, a cone of depression can lead to surface-to-groundwater flow. In times of drought, the stream can be completely drained in this way. Along the coast, heavy pumping of groundwater can lead to **saltwater intrusion**. Lighter fresh groundwater occurs as a wedge above heavier saline groundwater. The height of the wedge above sea level is 1/40 of its depth below. Pumping fresh water raises saltwater 40 times faster than it depresses the cone of fresh water. If the cone is depressed to sea level, saltwater intrudes into the well, reducing water quality, even though there is adjacent fresh water.

Groundwater Flow and Relationship to Surface Water

Groundwater flow is determined by piezometric pressure and aquifer materials. Shallow groundwater generally conforms to surface topography. This is not always true for confined aquifers. In the recharge-discharge process of a typical groundwater system, subsurface movement may be relatively rapid in shallow systems,

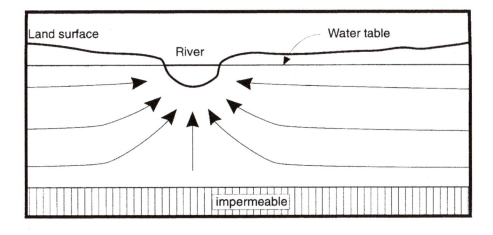

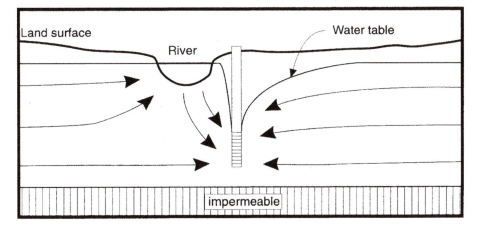

Figure 9.5 Surface-to-Groundwater Flow. A cone of depression can turn a gaining stream into a losing stream. (*Source:* Jon Witten and Scott Horsley. 1995. *A Guide to Wellhead Protection.* Planning Advisory Service Report 457/458. Used with permission of the American Planning Association.)

whereas the groundwater in deep confined aquifers may take decades to move from recharge to discharge.

Discharge from shallow groundwater flow is an important component of stream flow between storms. The effluent or gaining stream, shown in Figures 9.1 and 9.5 (top), gains surface flow from subsurface flow when the water table is above the surface water. An influent or losing stream loses surface flow to groundwater when the water table is below the surface water. Figure 9.5 (bottom) shows that a well's cone of depression can turn a gaining stream into a losing stream.

Figure 9.6 shows the karst hydrologic system and the interaction of surface and groundwater movement. **Karst** refers to limestone-dominated geology susceptible to solution weathering that creates sinkholes and caves. Not only does karst provide direct avenues for unfiltered flow from surface to groundwater, but landowners often try to fill sinkholes associated with karst with wastes that contribute toxic materials to the groundwater.

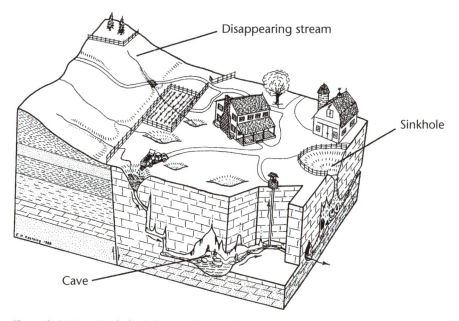

Figure 9.6 A Karst Hydrologic System. (*Source:* Virginia Cave Board. Drawing by E. H. Kastening, 1988.)

A graduate student's study near Blacksburg, Virginia, demonstrated the rapid movement of groundwater flow (and the contaminants it may carry) in karst systems. He injected a dye tracer into two sinkholes in the Lusters Gate area. He intended to monitor the possible release of the dye into surface seeps near the Roanoke River 3 miles away by inspecting the seeps at daily intervals for several months. To his surprise, the dyes were present on his first inspection of the seeps the next day, within 24 hours of the dye injection (Hayman 1972).

Land Use, Groundwater Recharge, and Contamination

Land use impacts the groundwater in much the same way as it affects surface waters. All groundwater originates on the land. Impervious surfaces inhibit infiltration, subsurface water flow, and groundwater recharge. Most groundwater contaminants originate from land activities and seep into groundwater by subsurface flow. Managing groundwater quantity and quality requires understanding the groundwater system, maintaining recharge, and controlling sources of contamination. This requires managing land use development and land use practices.

Impervious Surface and Groundwater Recharge

As discussed in Chapters 7 and 8, impervious surfaces have a critical impact on surface water flows and quality. Since they inhibit infiltration, they reduce shallow groundwater flow that contributes to stream flow between storms. They also reduce deeper groundwater flow that contributes to aquifer recharge. Communities dependent on groundwater for water supply have a special challenge to understand their groundwater system and to manage development to protect recharge areas. The first step is to delineate recharge areas. Figure 9.3 shows the important Edwards Aquifer in Texas and the location of its recharge area, as well as the drainage area that contributes to that recharge. The next step is to control land use development and practices that can potentially impact aquifer recharge.

Groundwater Contamination

Although land use can affect groundwater recharge, especially through the construction of impervious surfaces, its more significant impact is groundwater contamination. Concerns over groundwater contamination stem from three factors:

1. Groundwater is out of sight and therefore generally out of mind. It is difficult to monitor, and problems are usually not discovered until damage has occurred.
2. Groundwater contamination is far more difficult to treat and remediate than surface water pollution.
3. Groundwater in private wells is generally used for domestic and drinking water needs without treatment.

Because groundwater is used for drinking water, contaminants of concern are those related to human health effects. These are distinguished between those causing acute health effects and those resulting in chronic effects. *Acute health effects* are immediate effects, appearing within hours or days. They can result from exposure to pathogens (disease-causing organisms) or nitrates in drinking water. Pathogens are waterborne bacteria, viruses, protozoa, and parasites that cause gastrointestinal illness and, in extreme cases, death. Protozoa *Giardia lamblia* and *Cryptosporidium* have caused several disease outbreaks in the United States in recent years. Nitrates in drinking water can cause acute health effects in infants, such as methemoglobinemia, or "blue baby syndrome."

Chronic health effects result from exposure to a drinking water contaminant over many years. These include birth defects, cancer, and other illnesses from long-term exposure. Contaminants that cause chronic health effects are lead and other metals, and volatile organic chemicals, such as pesticides, solvents, and other petrochemicals.

Groundwater contamination comes from several sources introduced on the land surface (e.g., liquid or solid wastes, road salt, animal feedlots, fertilizer and pesticides, airborne particulates), above the water table (e.g., leaching landfills, septic systems, leaking underground storage tanks, leaking pipelines, stormwater dry wells), or below the water table (e.g., abandoned wells, exploratory wells, waste injection wells, mines, saltwater intrusion). Land use involves the first two categories. Here are the primary sources of groundwater contamination from land use:

- **Septic systems** can be a problem when located too close to wells in soils having very high permeability or structural avenues for rapid wastewater movement (see Chapter 6).

- **Leaking underground storage tanks** containing petroleum products have caused considerable contamination and abandonment of wells.
- Contamination from **landfills** and **lagoons** has led to stricter standards and controls, including dual liners and groundwater monitoring.
- **Surface runoff** from agricultural, urban, mining, and industrial lands have all contributed to contamination. Nitrogen fertilizers and pesticides on agricultural lands have created human health-related problems.

The movement of contaminants depends on the groundwater flow regime discussed previously. It also depends on the characteristics of the pollutant, including its density and its chemical and physical properties that may affect its reaction and filtration when in contact with subsurface materials. Pollutants having the same density as water will follow the groundwater flow path. Those denser will sink and not migrate laterally as quickly. Those less dense may actually float on top of the water table.

Assessing Groundwater

Managing groundwater, preventing groundwater contamination, and protecting water supplies at the local level involve four components:

1. Understanding the groundwater system
   a. Hydrogeologic and groundwater investigations
   b. Groundwater modeling
   c. DRASTIC studies
2. Assessing and protecting source water
   a. Source water assessment
   b. Wellhead protection area (WHPA) delineation
   c. Sole source aquifer delineation
3. Inventorying and assessing threats and potential sources of contamination
4. Monitoring groundwater
5. Developing a groundwater management program
   a. Remediation
   b. Prevention
      i. Regulatory measures
      ii. Nonregulatory measures

Improved groundwater assessment methods have helped communities better understand their groundwater systems. Hydrogeologic investigations and modeling and DRASTIC studies help communities gain a better scientific understanding of their groundwater system, opportunities for aquifer water supply, and susceptibility to contamination. In an effort to protect water supplies, the 1986 federal Safe Drinking Water Act called for assessment for surface and ground source waters, establishment of wellhead protection areas, and identification of sole-source aquifers for special attention.

Understanding the Groundwater System: Hydrogeologic Investigations

Community groundwater investigations can assess groundwater potential and problems. They describe the physical setting of the community (i.e., physiography, hydrology, and soils), the hydrogeology (geologic formations and aquifer systems), groundwater quality, groundwater problems, and groundwater development potential. The location of recharge areas is important to apply land use strategies for groundwater protection.

The first edition of this book included two maps from the Roanoke County Groundwater Study (Breeder and Dawson 1976). These maps are now included on the book website (www.envirolanduse.org). The study describes the hydrogeology of the county, giving the geologic formations and their water-bearing characteristics; both aerial and sectional views are given to show the stratigraphy and structure as well as the surface materials. One map identifies the main aquifer recharge areas. In Roanoke's case, they are associated with the fault lines and river valleys. This map also identifies where urbanization has interfered with recharge through the construction of impervious surfaces and where artificial recharge is provided. The other map denotes specific groundwater problem areas. It shows land subsidence areas and where poorly sited developments (landfills and industrial operations) have caused groundwater contamination; included is the Dixie Caverns Landfill. The name advertises the waste landfill's inappropriate location in a karst and cave area. Not surprisingly, this site became a national Superfund site.

The study concluded that the aquifers could safely yield 50–60 million gallons per day (mgd) in addition to current withdrawals of 10 mgd; but to protect this resource, the study recommended that groundwater recharge zones be maintained as open space areas (Virginia State Water Control Board 1976). Despite this potential, Roanoke County determined in the late 1980s that groundwater contamination in this urbanizing area posed too great a risk and decided to develop surface water for long-term water supply.

DRASTIC: Mapping Groundwater Contamination Susceptibility

In the late 1980s, the U.S. EPA, in conjunction with the American Water Well Association, developed a method to help counties assess and map susceptibility to groundwater contamination based on hydrogeologic factors (Aller et al. 1987). The DRASTIC method is a sum-of-weighted-factors technique that considers the following seven factors:

D: Depth to Water (feet): greater D → less susceptibility
R: Net Recharge (inches): greater R → greater susceptibility

A: Aquifer Media (material): more porous/permeable → greater susceptibility

S: Soil Media (material): more porous/permeable → greater susceptibility

T: Topography (slope): greater T → less susceptibility

I: Impact of the Vadose Zone (material): more porous/permeable → greater susceptibility

C: Hydraulic Conductivity (gallons per day per ft^2): greater C → greater susceptibility

The calculation of a DRASTIC score for a specific area involves adding together the products of the factor ratings (r) and the factor weights (w):

$$DRASTIC\ score = D_rD_w + R_rR_w + A_rA_w + S_rS_w + T_rT_w + I_rI_w + C_rC_w$$

The factor weights between 1 and 5 are given in Table 9.2. The basic DRASTIC weights are used in normal applications. Where agricultural use and pesticides are a concern, the agricultural or pesticide weights should be used. Factor ratings on a 1–10 scale are described in Table 9.3.

The data necessary to perform DRASTIC calculations are fairly complex. Soil surveys, geologic maps, county government information, and local industry and university studies are especially useful sources of data. However, data on all of the DRASTIC factors are not available for many areas. To help implement DRASTIC where detailed data may not be available, the method provides information on **hydrogeologic settings** for different groundwater regions of the country. Figure 9.7 shows the 11 groundwater regions. For each region, different hydrogeologic settings are identified, and for each setting, DRASTIC factor values are estimated and DRASTIC scores are calculated. A table listing all the hydrogeologic settings and their DRASTIC scores is on the book website (www.envirolanduse.org). Values range from 65 for GW region 1 Western Mountain slopes to 103 for GW region 7 Glaciated Central glacial till over bedded sedimentary rock to 218 GW region 11 Coastal Plain solution limestone and shallow surficial aquifers. All GW regions have a wide range of DRASTIC values for their different hydrogeologic settings.

TABLE 9.2 **DRASTIC Weights**

Factor	Basic Weight	Agricultural Weight
D	5	5
R	4	4
A	3	3
S	2	5
T	1	3
I	5	4
C	3	2

TABLE 9.3 DRASTIC Factors, Ranges, Ratings, and Weights

D Depth To Water (*Feet*)

Range	Rating
0–5	10
5–15	9
15–30	7
30–50	5
50–75	3
75–100	2
100+	1

Weight: 5   Pesticide Weight: 5

R — Net Recharge (*Inches*)

Range	Rating
0–2	1
2–4	3
4–7	6
7–10	8
10+	9

Weight: 4   Pesticide Weight: 4

A — Aquifer Media

Range	Rating	Typical Rating
Massive Shale	1–3	2
Metamorphic/Igneous	2–5	3
Weathered Metamorphic/Igneous	3–5	4
Glacial Till	4–6	5
Bedded Sandstone, Limestone, and Shale Sequences	5–9	6
Massive Sandstone	4–9	6
Massive Limestone	4–9	6
Sand and Gravel	4–9	8
Basalt	2–10	9
Karst Limestone	9–10	10

Weight: 3   Pesticide Weight: 3

S— Soil Media

Range	Rating
Thin or Absent	10
Gravel	10
Sand	9
Peat	8
Shrinking and/or Aggregated Clay	7
Sandy Loam	6
Loam	5
Silty Loam	4
Clay Loam	3
Muck	2
Nonshrinking and Nonaggregated Clay	1

Weight: 2   Pesticide Weight: 5

T — Topography (*Percent Slope*)

Range	Rating
0–2	10
2–6	9
6–12	5
12–18	3
18+	1

Weight: 1   Pesticide Weight: 3

C — Hydraulic Conductivity (*GPD/ft²*)

Range	Rating
1–100	1
100–300	2
300–700	4
700–1000	6
1000–2000	8
2000+	10

Weight: 3   Pesticide Weight: 2

I — Impact of the Vadose Zone Media

Range	Rating	Typical Rating
Confining Layer	1	1
Silt/Clay	2–6	3
Shale	2–5	3
Limestone	2–7	6
Sandstone	4–8	6
Bedded Limestone, Sandstone, Shale	4–8	6
Sand and Gravel with significant Silt and Clay	4–8	6
Metamorphic/Igneous	2–8	4
Sand and Gravel	6–9	8
Basalt	2–10	9
Karst Limestone	8–10	10

Weight: 5   Pesticide Weight: 4

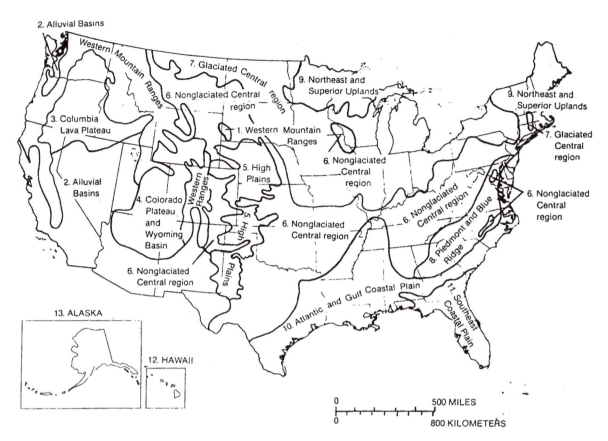

Figure 9.7 Groundwater Regions of the United States. (*Source:* Aller et al. 1987.)

The procedure for conducting a DRASTIC study culminating in a county DRASTIC map involves the following steps:

1. Gather available data on DRASTIC factors from soil surveys, geologic maps and studies, and other sources.
2. For each factor, prepare a map overlay displaying the values for the factor.
3. If data are not available for certain areas or factors, identify the hydrogeologic settings for the areas and consult the provided factor data for these settings. Fill in the gaps in the factor overlays as necessary.
4. Overlay individual factor maps and delineate the boundaries of combined factors.
5. Combine the overlays of all factors and delineate the boundaries of all combinations of factors.
6. Calculate the total DRASTIC scores for each delineated area.
7. Group the areas into 20-point categories (i.e., 0–19, 20–39, 40–59, etc.) and color the map by category.
8. Provide a legend for the map and write an interpretation in the accompanying text.

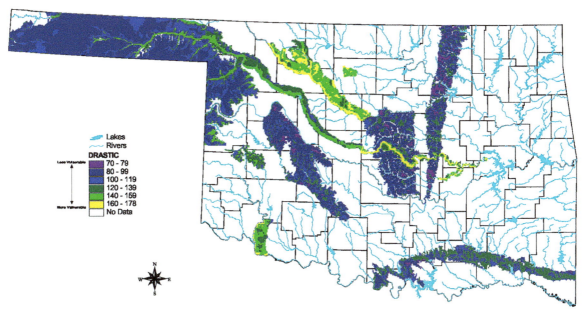

Figure 9.8 Oklahoma DRASTIC Study of Major Aquifers. (*Source:* Osborn et al. 1998.)

Figure 9.8 is an example of a final DRASTIC map for Oklahoma. It shows by color areas the relative susceptibility for groundwater contamination. Efforts continue to improve the DRASTIC method (Fritch et al. 2000; USGS 1999). When producing DRASTIC maps and interpreting their results, it is important to consider the major assumptions used in the development of the procedure:

1. The contaminant is introduced at the ground level.
2. The contaminant is flushed into the groundwater by precipitation.
3. The contaminant has the mobility of water.
4. The area evaluated using DRASTIC is 100 acres or larger.

The final assumption is perhaps the most important. Because of the lack of precision in the method, it cannot be used for small areas. No area on the DRASTIC map should be smaller than 100 acres. As discussed below, DRASTIC maps can be used to target high-potential areas for action or special standards. Still, the 100-acre limitation inhibits the use of the DRASTIC map as the sole basis for overlay zoning.

Groundwater Modeling

Groundwater models represent groundwater flow paths. These modeled flow paths generally show the expected flow direction and extent of movement over one or several time periods, such as 2, 5, and/or 10 years. Flow paths can help predict the flow, dispersal, and treatment of possible contaminants from land use

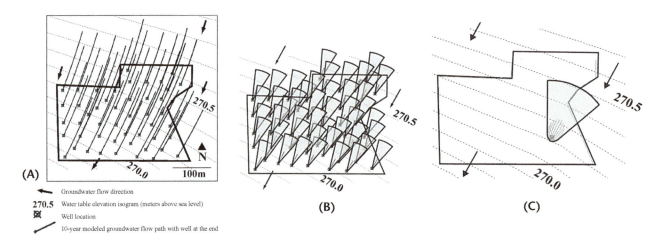

(A)

⬅ Groundwater flow direction

270.5 Water table elevation isogram (meters above sea level)

⊠ Well location

⟋ 10-year modeled groundwater flow path with well at the end

Figure 9.9 Groundwater Modeling. A: Modeled flow paths for individual wells, East Lake Village Estates subdivision. B: Individual well capture area. C: Community well capture area. (*Source:* Reprinted with permission from Wilcox et al. 2010.)

sources and identify the extent of recharge areas that contribute to a well. The models are usually verified in specific applications by monitoring wells or by drillers' well construction reports.

Wilcox et al. (2010) describe the use of groundwater modeling in understanding the flow paths and implications for groundwater source protection, especially in residential developments with onsite wastewater drainfields. Figure 9.9A shows their modeled flow paths for groundwater at typical well depths for a subdivision, East Lake Village Estates, in Sauk County near Madison (Wisconsin), and Figure 9.9B and C shows the probable flow paths for water to planned individual wells and to an alternative community well. Individual well flow paths (Figure 9.9B) are likely to intersect with septic drainfields with the potential for contamination, while the community well would not. Understanding groundwater flows in highly permeable soils can reveal potential problems (such as septic effluent contamination of individual shallow wells) and thereby inform planning decisions.

Despite the availability of useful information, however, institutional factors can inhibit good decision making. Based on model results, Sauk County planners tried to require 100-ft casing for wells at East Lake to reduce the threat of septic and fertilizer contamination. This requirement delayed the project for almost 3 years, and ultimately the planning department relented, because Wisconsin did not specifically grant authority to localities to require well casing depths more restrictive than the state code. Instead, the planners included a statement in the subdivision covenant, informing owners of the permeable soils and susceptibility to septic and nitrate contamination and recommending that well casings be extended to the sandstone aquifer. A review of data on wells drilled in the subdivision between 2004 and 2008 showed that despite this warning, none of the wells met the recommended safety guidelines. The developer did not even follow his own recommendation in four spec houses built in the subdivision. The lesson is that groundwater (and other environmental) protection requires more than good information.

It requires the authority to use that information to control and enforce protection (Wilcox et al. 2010).

Protecting Ground and Surface Source Water

The Safe Drinking Water Act (SDWA), first enacted in 1974 and last amended in 1996, established a better authority for providing safe drinking water supplies and protecting sources of such supplies. It focuses on public water supplies, so it would not affect the private well case described above. The SDWA promulgated detailed community drinking water standards (maximum contaminant levels, MCL) and water supply monitoring and reporting requirements for public water systems. As of 2007 there are 161,000 public water systems (PWSs) in the U.S., which include 52,110 community water systems (CWSs) that serve 286 million; 18,839 nontransient non-community water systems (NTNCWSs), such as schools and factories that serve the same people for more than 6 months but not year-round; and 84,744 transient noncommunity water systems (TNCWSs), like restaurants on wells. All federal regulations apply to CWSs, most requirements apply to NTNCWSs, and only regulations for contaminants that pose immediate health risks (like microbial contamination) apply to TNCWSs, unless they rely on surface sources. In that case they must have filtration and disinfection. Of the CWSs, 85% serve 3,300 or fewer people, and 8% serve more than 10,000 and 81% of the population (U.S. EPA 2010).

The 1996 amendments to the SDWA recognized the limitations of relying on water treatment to ensure safe drinking water supplies and stressed the protection of water sources. Source waters of public drinking water are classified as groundwater, surface water, and groundwater under the influence of surface water. This last category is groundwater subject to surface pollution, such as protozoa and turbidity. Protection of source waters is where the CWA and the SDWA interact.

Source Water Assessments under SDWA

Under the SDWA, states are required to conduct **source water assessment** for every public water system. The source water assessment includes:

- *Delineation* of the source water protection area (the watershed or groundwater recharge area that may contribute pollution).
- *Contamination source inventory*, which identifies potential sources of pollution.
- *Susceptibility determination*, which indicates potential for contamination.
- *Dissemination* of source water assessment results to the public.
- *Management measures* to protect the resource.
- *Contingency planning* in case of accident or contamination. This last step in the framework was reinforced by the 2002 Public Health Security and Bioterrorism Act.

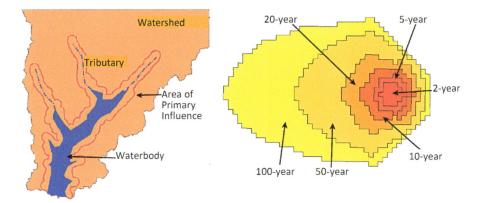

Figure 9.10 Source Water Protection Zones. Left: Surface water. Right: Groundwater, showing chemical flow years to well. (*Source:* Texas CEQ 2010.)

Source water assessments are conducted in order to protect public health, prepare water systems for possible problems, and identify cost-effective ways for communities to achieve safe water standards. For surface water sources, source water protection focuses on the watershed of the source; for groundwater sources, it focuses on wellhead protection.

Considering the number of PWSs, states have been busy conducting source water assessments since the 1996 amendments. It is useful to look at a few examples to understand what is involved in these assessments. Figure 9.10 shows how Texas graphically defines the protection zones included in its assessments. For surface water sources, the zones include:

- The **waterbody**, which serves as the drinking water source for the PWS in question. It may be a lake or reservoir, river, canal, terminal reservoirs, or other tributary.
- The **watershed**, which contributes the rainfall and drainage to the waterbody.
- The **area of primary influence (API)**, an artificial boundary around the waterbody based on a 1,000-ft border from the shoreline plus a 2-hour time of travel upstream.
- The API may extend up **tributaries** feeding a reservoir, or in the absence of a reservoir, they may serve as the surface water source. In such cases, the API will extend 1,000 ft from the tributary shoreline and upstream to approximate a 2-hour travel time.

For the groundwater well (Figure 9.10B), the years indicate the estimated time it would take chemicals released in that zone to reach the well.

The New Jersey Department of Environmental Protection (DEP) performed source water assessments to predict the susceptibility of source water for all community water systems and those noncommunity water systems using surface water, based on hydrogeology and contaminant use intensity within the water-contributing area. It looked at the following contaminants: nutrients (nitrates), pathogens, pesticides, volatile organic compounds (VOCs), inorganics (metals), radionuclides/radon, and disinfection by-product precursors (DBPs, e.g., chlorine compounds). Each source received a susceptibility rating of high, medium, or low to each contaminant category.

- A low rating for the well or intake indicates the source water is not likely to equal or exceed 10% of New Jersey's drinking water maximum contaminant level (MCL).
- A medium rating indicates the source water is not likely to equal or exceed 50% the MCL.
- A high rating includes wells and intakes for which source water contaminants may equal or exceed 50% the MCL; therefore, sources with high susceptibility ratings will not necessarily exceed the drinking water standard.

To determine these ratings, the DEP used a framework that included statistical modeling, evaluation of past studies, and water sample data. The models were developed using water-quality data from groundwater and surface water samples collected and analyzed by the USGS. The results showed that urban and agricultural land use was the most common intensity variable found to determine susceptibility. For surface waters, metals, DBPs, and pathogens were the primary causes of high ratings, and for unconfined groundwater sources, nitrates, VOCs, and radionucleides caused most of the high ratings. The DEP generated detailed source water assessment reports for the 606 community systems. Figure 9.11 shows an example of an assessment map and table for the 22 wells that are part of the Atlantic City water system.

A third example is from Massachusetts, which posts its source water assessments on a web-based GIS application that allows users to zoom in on systems and areas of interest (Massachusetts DEP 2010). Figure 9.12 gives a snapshot of an area around Worcester. The map shows protection zones for surface and groundwater source waters, as well as the location of interim wellhead protection areas (IWPAs), solid waste landfills, wetlands, roads, and pipelines. For surface water sources, Zone A is 400 ft from the water supply reservoir and 200 ft from tributaries, Zone B is 0.5 mile from the reservoir but not beyond the watershed boundary, and Zone C is the remaining area of the watershed. For groundwater wellhead protection, Zone I is 100–400 ft from the well, Zone II is the land area that contributes water to the well, and IWPA is the protection area until Zone II is approved. The protection areas indicate buffer zones around source waters and trigger land use controls to protect them (Massachusetts DEP 2001, 2002).

Sole Source Aquifer Designation

The SDWA also established the Sole Source Aquifer Program to designate important groundwater sources and protect them, especially from the impacts of

Sources	Pathogens			Nutrients			Pesticides			Volatile Organic Compounds			Inorganics			Radio-nuclides			Radon			Disinfection Byproduct Precursors		
	H	M	L	H	M	L	H	M	L	H	M	L	H	M	L	H	M	L	H	M	L	H	M	L
Wells - 22		4	18	16	3	3		8	14	11		11	6	13	3	16	3	3		19	3	7	15	

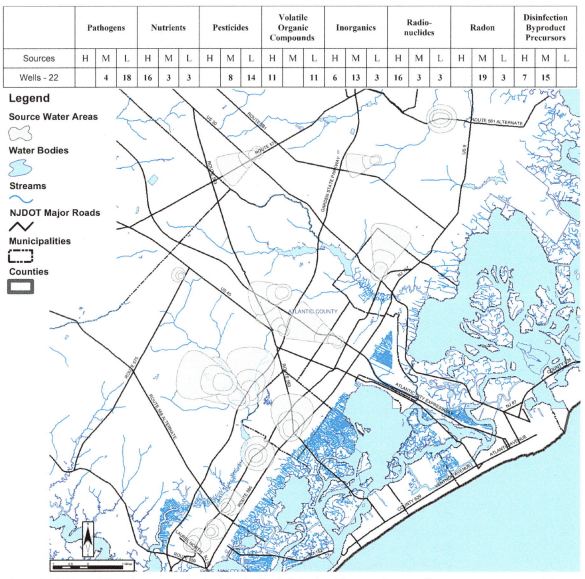

Legend

Source Water Areas

Water Bodies

Streams

NJDOT Major Roads

Municipalities

Counties

Figure 9.11 Source Water Assessment for the Atlantic City (NJ) Region. The map shows well source water zones, and the table gives 22 wells' susceptibility ratings for eight contaminants. (*Source:* New Jersey DEP 2004a.)

federally funded projects. A **sole source aquifer (SSA)**, also called a principal source aquifer, is one that supplies at least 50% of the drinking water consumed in the area overlying the aquifer.

The Edwards Aquifer in Texas (see Figure 9.3) was the first SSA designated in the country. As the major water supply for central Texas, including the cities of San Antonio and Austin, the Edwards Aquifer has become one of the most managed groundwater systems in the country. The coordinated effort is administered by the Texas Natural Resources Conservation Commission and the regional Edwards Aquifer Authority, as well as the cities and counties relying on the water source. Studies showed that major recharge areas are where the limestone reservoir crops

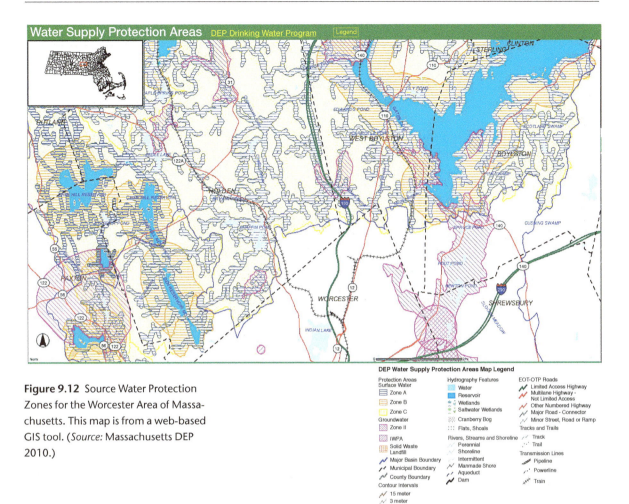

Figure 9.12 Source Water Protection Zones for the Worcester Area of Massachusetts. This map is from a web-based GIS tool. (*Source:* Massachusetts DEP 2010.)

out of the impervious tight clay, and where large crevices and cracks occur in the streambeds along the Balcones Fault zone. The direct recharge by surface flow through this fault zone, and by various solution openings, makes the aquifer susceptible to runoff pollutants. As early as the 1970s, land use control programs were developed to protect the aquifer from runoff pollution, including the requirement of a special permit for development in the area draining to the aquifer. Permits are based on a point system that assesses the risk of a proposed development to contaminate the groundwater.

There are about 70 designated SSAs in the United States. EPA groundwater programs in each of its ten regions include maps of the SSAs, ranging from most of the Fresno (California) metropolitan area to the eastern shore of New Jersey, to several small community aquifers. Development projects having the potential to contaminate designated SSAs are subject to EPA review by a groundwater specialist. For example, these projects might include highways, wastewater or stormwater treatment facilities, agricultural projects, and others. This review can result in requirements for design improvements, groundwater monitoring, and other measures.

Wellhead Protection Area Planning

Section 1428 of the 1986 SDWA amendments established the **Wellhead Protection (WHP) Program**. It aims to help communities protect vulnerable groundwater supplies by controlling land use development and practices around public drinking water wells. All but one of the states have EPA-approved WHP programs. To establish a program, communities must delineate the wellhead protection area, identify sources of contamination, and develop regulatory and nonregulatory measures to manage contamination, filtration, and disinfection.

Delineating Wellhead Protection Areas

The first step in wellhead protection is delineating the protection area. Although DRASTIC provides a countywide view of its hydrogeology, wellhead protection focuses on individual wells and the land area that must be controlled to protect the water supply. The wellhead protection area (WHPA) does not necessarily include the entire aquifer and its recharge area. The WHPA tends to be a smaller part of the total aquifer. A technical challenge is determining the boundaries of that area. Figure 9.13 presents some technical terminology.

- **Zone of influence (ZOI)**: The surface projection of the boundaries of the cone of depression around the well.
- **Zone of contribution (ZOC)**: The surface projection of the boundaries of the portion of the aquifer recharge area that contributes water to the well. This normally extends to a localized groundwater divide on the upflow side and to a portion of the cone of depression on the downflow side. ZOC is Zone II in Massachusetts WHP areas in Figure 9.12.

Delineation of the WHPA can be done in different ways, depending on available data and analysis. Figures 9.14 and 9.15 show two examples of WHPAs. The example in Figure 9.14 has three WHPA zones; the first uses a fixed radius around the well, the second zone is the primary recharge area, and the third is the secondary recharge. Figure 9.15 shows a private well protection zone based on a fixed radius of 100 ft around the well plus a 200-ft buffer up the groundwater flow gradient.

Figures 9.16 and 9.17 show the integration of hydrogeologic studies and WHPA delineation by the Hamilton to New Baltimore (Ohio) Groundwater Consortium (HNBGC). The multijurisdictional consortium used aquifer, DRASTIC, and subsurface time of travel studies to identify critical recharge zones for its groundwater sources (HNBGC 2003).

Inventorying and Assessing Threats and Potential Sources of Contamination

Both DRASTIC and WHPA delineation are based on hydrogeology, but they do not consider what land uses and sources may contribute to contamination. An

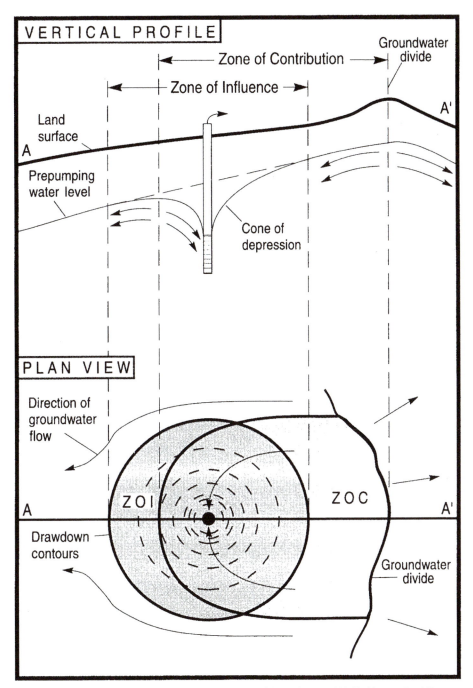

Figure 9.13 The Zone of Influence (ZOI) and Zone of Contribution (ZOC). (*Source:* Jon Witten and Scott Horsley. 1995. *A Guide to Wellhead Protection.* Planning Advisory Service Report 457/458. Used with permission of the American Planning Association.)

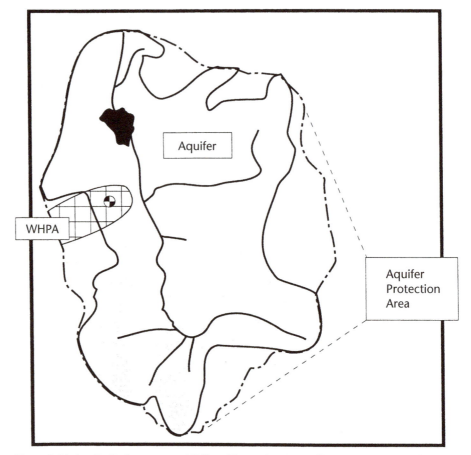

Figure 9.14 Aquifer Recharge versus Wellhead Protection Areas. (*Source:* Jon Witten and Scott Horsley. 1995. *A Guide to Wellhead Protection.* Planning Advisory Service Report 457/458. Used with permission of the American Planning Association.)

Figure 9.15 Private Well Protection. (*Source:* Jon Witten and Scott Horsley. 1995. *A Guide to Wellhead Protection.* Planning Advisory Service Report 457/458. Used with permission of the American Planning Association.)

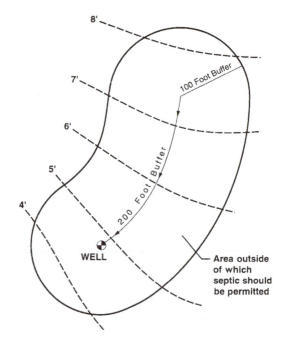

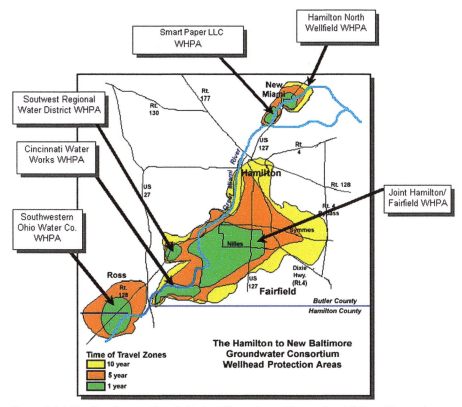

Figure 9.16 The Hamilton to New Baltimore Groundwater Consortium Wellhead Protection Areas. (*Source:* HNBGC 2003.)

inventory of potential sources of contamination is necessary to identify existing and future problems. An inventory includes locations of waste landfills and lagoons, areas of septic system use, gas stations and other underground storage tanks, industrial facilities with hazardous materials, and agricultural areas with extensive pesticide and fertilizer use. These threats can be mapped and overlaid onto DRASTIC and/or WHPA maps (Crowley and Tulloch 2002).

Developing and Implementing Groundwater Protection Measures

EPA programs for groundwater are not regulatory. There are no enforceable national groundwater standards. Federal groundwater programs generally coordinate, facilitate, educate, and assist with the protection of groundwater. Management largely depends on state and local initiatives. Box 9.1 gives examples of regulatory and nonregulatory measures for protecting the source groundwater available to local governments. (Most of these land use control measures are discussed in Chapters 15 and 17.)

Regulatory measures include land use zoning to prevent potentially polluting sources from locating in susceptibility or wellhead protection areas. **Wellhead**

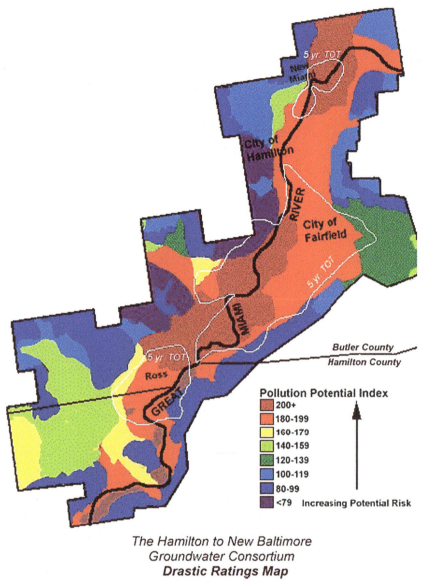

Figure 9.17 Hamilton to New Baltimore DRASTIC Map. (*Source:* HNBGC 2003.)

or groundwater protection overlay zoning is an effective approach that does not require major revision of existing ordinances. The overlay is placed on top of existing zoning. The overlay zone will conform to WHPA boundaries. Within the zone, special conditions or standards are required of proposed land uses. Cluster zoning regulations can also be tailored to wellhead protection by allowing development densities onsite while setting aside sensitive areas, including WHPAs. (Chapter 17 discusses overlay and cluster zoning methods in greater detail.)

Other regulatory measures include local permitting requirements for groundwater sources, such as new wells and springs, and for potential contamination

BOX 9.1—Regulatory and Nonregulatory Measures for Wellhead Protection Areas

Regulatory Tools

Land use controls: Zoning ordinances, subdivision controls, cluster and planned unit development

Prohibitions or conditional permitting of potentially contaminating uses: Gas stations, landfills, industries handling hazardous chemicals

Health regulations: Septic system controls

Nonregulatory Measures

Public education

Land purchase, conservation easements

Groundwater monitoring

sources, such as septic systems, waste lagoons, and other sources. Depending on groundwater protection needs, specific conditions, standards, or restrictions may apply.

Nonregulatory measures include public education, household hazardous waste collection, continuous groundwater monitoring, and land acquisition of protection areas. A good example of land acquisition is the Edwards Aquifer in Texas (see Figure 9.3). Government Canyon is the recharge zone for the Edwards Aquifer. A proposal to build 766 homes and an 18-hole golf course in the canyon sparked the formation of a public-private coalition in San Antonio that purchased the land for $2 million. The City of Austin voted to authorize $20 million in bonds to purchase critical watershed land for open space (U.S. EPA 2001).

Mapping of susceptibility, protection areas, and threats does not indicate whether there is a groundwater problem. **Groundwater monitoring** is necessary for determining whether there is contamination and where it occurs. Comprehensive groundwater monitoring is not available in most areas, so existing well data often must be used to get a snapshot of groundwater conditions. The Virginia Cooperative Extension Service at Virginia Tech implemented an effective household well and spring monitoring program in several Virginia counties, with the dual objectives of providing assistance to households with wells and gathering one-time samples of groundwater quality. The program advertises a public well water quality workshop to which well and spring users are invited to bring water samples from their sources. At the workshop, presenters talk generally about good well and springbox maintenance and water handling. At a second workshop, results of lab testing of the samples and source-specific recommendations are provided to the households. Testing includes bacteria, inorganic chemicals such as iron and sulfur, hardness, nitrates, and in some cases pesticides. The data are also used to provide a baseline of groundwater quality. Knowing the location of the samples, the data can be mapped to show hot spots of well water pollution.

Given the information from susceptibility and protection area mapping, inventory of potential threats, and groundwater monitoring, a locality is prepared to develop a groundwater management program. If monitoring discovers severe problems, some groundwater remediation may be necessary.

Summary

Groundwater is an important source of drinking water. Although most of the population in the United States uses surface water supplies, about 80% of public water systems and nearly all individual systems depend on groundwater sources. Most individual groundwater sources are used without treatment. Groundwater is closely related to the land, since nearly all of it comes from infiltration recharge from the land surface. Impervious cover on the land surface inhibits infiltration and recharge. Unconfined shallow aquifers are closely connected to surface waters. Groundwater contributes baseflows to gaining streams and is recharged by losing streams. In karst geology, there are direct conduits between surface waters and groundwater.

Because of its close connection to the land surface, groundwater is susceptible to contamination from surface sources, including underground storage tanks of petroleum and other chemical products, landfills and other waste areas, polluted stormwater, and septic systems and wastewater lagoons. As a result, management of groundwater requires planning and management of the land. It is important to understand groundwater flow and recharge as well as susceptibility to contamination. In recharge areas, impervious surfaces should be minimized, and potential sources of contamination should be restricted. DRASTIC and other hydrogeological studies can help explain surface-groundwater relationships and guide land use decisions.

Special care should be taken to manage land use in the vicinity of wellheads of public water supplies. Overlay zoning and other land regulations are appropriate for restricting land uses in order to protect public health. The experience of state source water protection programs in the last decade provides a tremendous database to inform land use decisions and their relationship to precious sources of drinking water. Local planners must use this information effectively to formulate groundwater protection plans, and states should provide localities with the necessary authority to implement them.

10 ▪ Landscape and Urban Ecology, Urban Forestry, and Wetlands

Urbanization and other intensive uses of land and related water resources result in significant impacts on natural ecosystems, the habitats and wildlife they support, and the environmental functions they provide to human society. At the same time, people have increasingly recognized the values associated with natural features and the ecological integrity of the landscape. These values have been translated into increased property values and greater public attraction of land use management and development designs that reflect sensitivity to natural ecosystems. At the same time, we understand that urban ecosystems are different, and we need to apply ecological planning principles to manage the coupled human-ecological systems of cities.

This chapter introduces some basic concepts of landscape and urban ecology, to explain and help us understand the complex interrelationship of human and ecological functions in urban and urbanizing areas. We then discuss how this understanding is applied in planning and management strategies for urban forestry, wetlands, and coastal zones. Chapter 11 extends the discussion to wildlife habitats and biodiversity, and Part III (Chapters 15–19) will address land conservation, development design, and growth management to achieve urban ecology objectives.

Fundamentals of Landscape and Urban Ecology

Although the methods and techniques discussed here do not require a detailed background in ecological science, it is important to understand some fundamental ecological principles. **Ecology** is the study of the interrelationships of living organisms with one another and with the physical environment. It can focus on an individual, a species population, an ecological community, or ecosystems of various scales, from a site to a region. **Biodiversity** is the variety of life and all processes that keep life functioning. It is studied at genetic, species, and ecosystem levels. While ecologists have long held that greater diversity leads to greater stability in ecosystems, most now agree that the relationship between diversity and ecosystem resilience depends more on context than a generalized theory. Global efforts to manage biodiversity aim to arrest species extinction and preserve intact natural ecosystems. Box 10.1 provides an overview of several ecological concepts,

---

BOX 10.1—Basic Ecological Concepts: An Overview

Energy and Material Flow in Ecosystems

Simple **food chains**, or food webs, are often used to characterize the flow of energy and minerals in ecosystems. Figure 10.1 shows an aquatic food chain. Through photosynthesis, plants convert radiant solar energy into chemical energy. They store this energy in their biomass for their own use and for the use of all other forms of life. Plants are therefore called **producers** or **autotrophs** ("self-feeding"), as distinguished from the **consumers** or **heterotrophs** ("other-feeding"). The levels of the food chain are called **trophic levels**, where level I is the primary or plant level, level II is the plant eater or herbivore level, level III is the eater of the plant eater or first carnivore level, and so on.

About 80–90% of energy consumed by the various life-forms is required for maintenance and **respiration**, and this energy is ultimately lost as heat. As a result, the carnivorous occupants of higher trophic levels require tremendous quantities of plant biomass to support their food chain. Thus, they usually require very large habitats. This concept of food chain respiration and biomass requirements is also the basis of **biomagnification** of contaminants. Animals must absorb large amounts of food compared to their body weight, since so much of the energy must be expended for respiration. If that food source contains contaminants that do not pass through but tend to be stored in fats and tissues, those contaminants will concentrate quite readily. And as an organism moves up the food chain, it is exposed to food with higher concentrations. This is why Great Lakes fish contain high concentrations of toxins and are subject to human consumption advisories.

Whereas energy flows through ecosystems, minerals cycle around them, changing from organic form in living matter to inorganic form in the nutrient pool and back again. **Decomposers** (fungi, bacteria, and other microorganisms) play the crucial role of converting excrement and other dead organic material into the inorganic nutrients that plants can absorb and reconvert to organic plant material. The important elements of life—carbon, hydrogen, oxygen, nitrogen, phosphorus, potassium, sulfur—all are involved in **biogeochemical cycles**; the name indicates the various forms the elements can take.

Succession and Productivity

Like their respective members, ecosystems develop from a young to a mature state through the

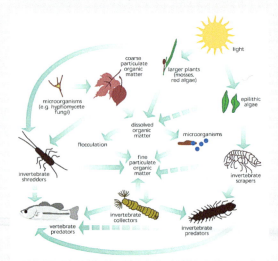

Figure 10.1 An Aquatic Food Chain. (*Source:* Federal Interagency Stream Restoration Working Group 1998.)

BOX 10.1—Basic Ecological Concepts: An Overview (cont.)

1 Arctic Cordillera
2 Tundra
3 Taiga
4 Hudson Plains
5 Northern Forests
6 Northwestern Forested Mountains
7 Marine West Coast Forests
8 Eastern Temperate Forests
9 Great Plains
10 North American Deserts
11 Mediterranean California
12 Southern Semi-Arid Highlands
13 Temperate Sierras
14 Tropical Dry Forests
15 Tropical Humid Forests

Figure 10.2 Major Biotic Regions of North America. (*Source:* Commission for Environmental Cooperation 1997.)

process of **ecological succession**. For example, a shallow lake over time may convert to a swamp, then a meadow, and finally a forest. The mature state is called the **climax community**. The type of vegetation that characterizes it depends largely on the physical parameters of the area, principally its **temperature, sunlight, moisture,** and **soil conditions**. Thus, succession results from the modification of the physical environment by the community, but the physical environment determines the pattern, rate of change, and limits of succession (Odum 1971). Figure 10.2 shows the climax vegetative communities, known as biotic regions or **biomes**, associated with the various environmental conditions of North America.

In the process of maturing, an ecosystem, like an individual organism, enjoys an early period of high growth. This physical growth slows, ultimately ceasing by maturity. Growth is measured by **net community production**, the conversion of sunlight to a net increase in total biomass. Fig-

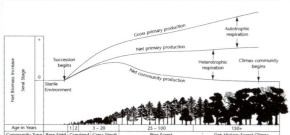

Figure 10.3 Ecological Succession and Productivity. In the early stages of succession, the ecosystem acts like a nutrient sponge, assimilating available nutrients into biomass. The magnitude of the sponge decreases as the climax community is approached. At climax, the same mass of nutrients leaves the ecosystem, primarily by decomposition, as enters it. Net community production drops to zero.

ure 10.3 shows that **gross primary production**, the total photosynthesized primary energy, and **net primary production**, the gross production minus plant respiration, begin low, grow, then level out at a maximum when the climax community is achieved. On the other hand, net community production rises initially to a peak, then falls off to zero at climax. The large net primary production is absorbed by heterotrophic respiration, particularly that of the decomposers. Table 10.1 shows that net primary productivity varies considerably for different ecosystems, topped by salt marshes, freshwater wetlands, and tropical rain forests.

TABLE 10.1 **Net Productivity of Selected Ecosystems***

Salt marsh	2,300
Freshwater wetland	2,000
Tropical rainforest	2,000
Warm temperate mixed forest	1,000
Cold deciduous forest	1,000
Cultivated land	750
Grassland	700
Boreal forest	500
Desert	150

*grams/m^2/year.

BOX 10.1—Basic Ecological Concepts: An Overview (cont.)

Diversity, Habitat, and Ecological Niches

As an ecosystem develops toward maturity, it tends to acquire greater diversity, a broader variety of organisms. **Diversity** can be measured in a number of ways, the simplest being **species richness** or the number of species per 1,000 individuals in an ecosystem. Other measures aim to incorporate species "evenness," or the apportionment of individuals to species. In most cases, diversity is directly correlated with the stability of an ecosystem, its ability to maintain in the presence of some upsetting circumstance like drought or disease. High rates of species extinction have made protecting biodiversity an important objective in land and ecosystem management. It is the basis for the Endangered Species Act (ESA) and other programs that protect diversity at various scales: from the regional landscape to ecological communities, to species populations and habitats to genetic diversity (Wilson 1988, 2002).

An ecosystem provides a **habitat** or **habitat niche** for its member species, thus supplying them with their life needs of food, water, cover, and space. An ecosystem may provide only a limited number of habitat niches. Modifying an ecosystem may alter its ability to supply the needs of its members. Conversely, individual species themselves contribute to the complete fabric of the ecosystem. Each plays a functional role or occupies a special **ecological niche** in the ecosystem. Odum (1971) draws the analogy that a species' habitat niche is its "address," while its ecological niche is its "profession," ecologically speaking. If that species is removed from the ecosystem, either another species must then occupy its niche or the ecosystem will change.

Organism Growth: Liebig's Law

Populations of organisms can grow if conditions are right. Species have specific requirements for food nutrients, sunlight, water, and other factors. Any one of these factors can constrain or limit the growth of an organism or population. This is the basis of **Liebig's Law of the Minimum**. It states that under steady-state conditions, an organism's or population's growth is limited by the essential nutrient or factor present in the least amount relative to the species' needs. If that nutrient or factor is increased, the population will grow; if it is decreased, the population will decline.

The Concept of Carrying Capacity

Although Liebig's Law deals with the influence of specific factors on the population growth of individual species in an area, the concept of carrying capacity deals with the ability of the area to support them. An area's **carrying capacity** is the number or biomass of organisms that can be sustained without adversely affecting that area. The term comes from the study of population dynamics and involves the concepts of **biotic potential**, the maximum reproduction rate, and **environmental resistance**, the sum of environmental limiting factors that prevent the biotic potential from being realized (Odum and Barrett 2004).

The most common growth pattern on populations in nature follows a sigmoid or S-shaped curve. In this case, the environmental resistance to growth does not occur suddenly but increases gradually in response to greater population density. It can take the form of increased competition for food and space (and light for vegetation), increased transmission of disease, and increased predation. The rate of population growth starts slowly in the establishment phase, rises exponentially, then slows as it encounters increasing environmental resistance, and finally levels off at a sustainable population, which defines the area's carrying capacity. In reality, populations may oscillate around the carrying capacity, rising above it in favorable times, only to fall below when conditions are unfavorable. In some cases, exceeding the carrying capacity may result in its reduction. For example, overgrazing can result in excessive erosion, which can reduce grassland productivity and ultimately the grasslands' carrying capacity. (Chapter 14 has more discussion of the application of the carrying capacity concept to managing human settlements.)

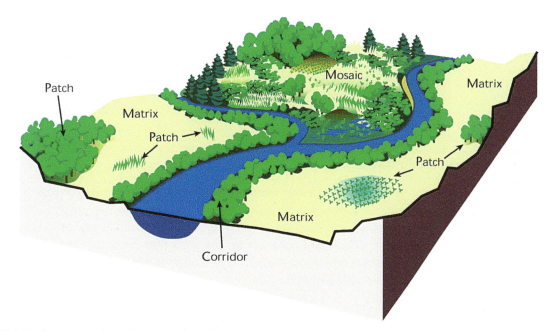

Figure 10.4 Spatial Structure in Landscape Ecology. (*Source:* FISRWG 1998.)

including energy and mineral flow in ecosystems, ecological succession, biodiversity, limiting factors, and carrying capacity.

Landscape Ecology

Ecology addresses a wide range of spatial scales, from a small local area, like a stream section or reach, to a catchment to a larger watershed, to a still larger landscape scale to a regional scale. This "nesting" of scales is a useful way to bound a study area but recognize the area's relationship to smaller and larger ecosystems (see Chapter 19). A **landscape** is defined as an area having a repeated pattern of components, including both natural and human-altered areas (FISRWG 1998). Landscape ecologists organize spatial structure with four basic components that can be applied at multiple scales: mosaic, matrix, patch, and corridor (Figure 10.4).

- **Mosaic** is a collection of patches, none of which are dominant enough to be interconnected throughout landscape.
- **Matrix** is the land cover that is dominant and interconnected over a majority of land surface (e.g., forest, agriculture, urban).
- **Patch** is a nonlinear polygon area less abundant than and different from a matrix.
- **Corridor** is a linear or elongated patch that links other patches in the matrix.

Landscapes are mosaics of patches and can range in size from a few to several thousand square miles. At the landscape scale, patches and corridors can be described as discrete ecosystems. Patches are discrete areas of homogeneous environmental conditions relevant to organism or ecology. Landscape connectivity is the degree to which landscape facilitates or impedes the flow of resources or organisms, and corridors are primary pathways for the movement of energy, materials, and organisms. They connect patches and are conduits between ecosystems and external environments.

Urban Ecology

Some think of cities not as ecosystems but merely as human systems. But cities are still subject to forces of nature (like natural hazards); they require air, water, food, and other resources that depend on natural systems; and they need natural features for their biophysical and metaphysical benefits. Marina Alberti (2008), of the University of Washington, has expanded our understanding of urban ecology and suggests that we not consider "nature in cities" or "cities in nature," but cities as a hybrid, coupled, interdependent human and ecological ecosystem. In *Advances in Urban Ecology*, she synthesized ecological research applied to urban systems toward advancing a theory of urban ecology.

Some of the basic principles of urban ecology are summarized in Box 10.2. Among the principles are urban gradient hypotheses. Along the gradient of urban disturbance from rural natural hinterlands to the urban core, there are specific impacts of urbanization. They include impacts on:

- Ecological functions (biological process rates decrease while human resource inputs increase).
- Biodiversity (native bird species decrease while synanthropic species increase, peak in tree-canopied inner suburbs, then decrease toward the urban core).
- Surface temperatures (creating the urban heat island exacerbated by reduced vegetative cover and increased impervious cover).
- Hydrology and nutrients (runoff quantity increases with more impervious surface, and nutrient loading increases, peaks, then decreases toward the urban core).

The **intermediate disturbance hypothesis** states that higher biodiversity is achieved at an intermediate level of urban disturbance between rural nature and urban core. The peak in biodiversity, however, is achieved by more **synanthropic species**, including birds, rodents, and plants, that are more capable of rapid colonization, adaptive to new conditions, and tolerant of people.

As a planner, Alberti also suggests what these concepts mean for urban and environmental planning, for balancing human and ecological functions in cities. She offers six planning principles: resilience, development diversity, resource efficiency, flexible policies, strategies for learning, and adaptation. She argues that sprawling development works against the hybrid urban ecology and that planned development is essential to support ecological and human functions by applying understanding of the coupled ecosystem, linking scientific research to develop-

BOX 10.2—Alberti's Concepts of Urban Ecology

1. **Urban ecosystems are different**.
   a. Hybrid human-ecological ecosystems are different from natural ecosystems in terms of climate, flow of energy and materials (water, biogeochemical cycles), and species.
   b. Human and ecological functions are inter-dependent in urban ecosystems.
   c. As we replace ecological functions with human functions in urbanizing regions, the processes supporting the ecosystem may reach a threshold and drive the system to a new regime (or to collapse), which may be reversible, irreversible, or effectively irre-versible in a human time scale.
   d. Urban ecosystems are complex, uncertain, and heterogeneous.

2. **Human urbanization is key driver of eco-system change and impact**. It affects natu-ral ecological functions:
   a. Urbanization impacts vegetation, soils, hydrology, atmosphere, species, and bio-geochemical cycles.
   b. Urban development affects ecosystems, changing ecological functions and species, by
      i. fragmenting natural habitat through land conversion,
      ii. modifying biophysical processes (e.g., hydrology),
      iii. imposing barriers (e.g., roads), and
      iv. homogenizing natural patterns of land cover (e.g., converting diverse vegeta-tive cover to lawns).
   c. Urban sprawl shifts land cover from abun-dant, well-connected natural cover to reduced, highly fragmented natural cover.

3. **Urbanization and biodiversity**.
   a. Urban transformation of land cover favors *synanthropic species*, which are capable of rapid colonization, adaptive to new condi-tions, and tolerant of people.
   b. Urbanizing areas have unique combina-tions of organisms, and diversity may peak at intermediate levels of urbanization, where native and non-native species both thrive, but this diversity declines as urban-ization intensifies (Marzluff et al. 2008).

   c. *Edge species* occupy the interfaces between vegetation types, and ecotones increase as the pattern of land cover is changed, such as converting forest to grass cover (see Chapter 11).

4. **Urban landscapes are best characterized by gradients, patches, networks, and hierarchies**. These can be viewed through both human and ecological lenses.
   a. An important gradient is the *urban transect*, or change in natural land cover and imper-vious surface and human land use and den-sity from the urban core to the rural and natural hinterlands.
   b. In human-dominated ecosystems, *patch dynamics* are affected by human and eco-logical factors, creating hydrological, eco-logical, and sociocultural heterogeneity.
   c. Urban landscapes are complex networks of human and natural agents connected by both biogeophysical and socioeconomic processes.
   d. Four hierarchical dimensions of urban landscape pattern are land use form, density, heterogeneity, and connectivity, as measured by both human and ecological metrics.

5. **Planning for complex, uncertain, and heterogeneous urban ecosystems**.
   a. Six principles for planning urban eco-systems (Alberti and Marzluff 2004):
      i. *Maximize resilience*. Resilience in urban ecosystems is the system's ability to maintain human and ecosystem func-tions simultaneously.
      ii. *Maintain diverse development patterns* to enhance resilience.
      iii. *Integrate and minimize resource use* and diversify resource supplies, such as energy and water.
      iv. *Create flexibility in policies* that mimic natural processes and the heterogeneity of human communities.
      v. *Learn* by creating buffers for error and opportunities for experimentation.
      vi. *Employ adaptation*. Plan by designing experiments and monitoring progress.

BOX 10.2—Alberti's Concepts of Urban Ecology (cont.)

b. Planned development can create urban development patterns that simultaneously support ecological and human functions, allowing greater resilience of the coupled urban ecosystem, by:
  i. Applying a shared understanding of the coupled ecosystem.
  ii. Using better indicators of human, ecological, and coupled functions and linkages.

  iii. Linking scientific research to urban development policy.
  iv. Developing alternative scenarios reflecting the complexity, uncertainty, and heterogeneity of urban ecology.

Source: Adapted from Alberti 2008.

ment policy, and using scenarios to reflect the complexity and uncertain of urban ecosystems (Alberti 2008).

Vegetation

Have you thanked a green plant today? Ecologically, plants are the producers of useful energy and materials for all of life. Environmentally, vegetation provides a variety of functions in erosion control, runoff control, slope and dune stabilization, atmospheric purification, and cover for wildlife. And in human settlements, vegetation contributes to the quality of life in its value for forest products, recreation, aesthetics, windbreaks, and sun shading and temperature control.

There are many benefits of urban vegetation, such as the environmental control benefits of erosion, runoff, and NPS pollution control and slope stability. Moreover, vegetation can help control noise and microclimatic conditions. Vegetation helps counter the "urban heat island" effect by increasing cities' albedo (reflected solar radiation) and evapotranspiration cooling. Vegetation provides habitat for wildlife, and the dominant vegetation is used to identify habitat type. In addition to all that, people like "green stuff," and vegetation adds to property values and community livability.

Classifying, Inventorying, and Mapping Vegetation

Vegetation information is usually displayed on maps showing vegetative types, existing woodlands and tree types, open lands, active farmland, wetlands, and other areas. These vegetation inventory maps can provide a base map for urban forestry programs and special studies of visual quality or special ecological zones, such as wetlands, riparian lands along streams and lakes, dune systems along coasts, and habitats of specially classified or desirable wildlife species. They can provide guidance for land use policies and programs to protect vegetative and ecological features.

Vegetation inventory maps can be produced using available map and aerial photograph information. As discussed in Chapter 5, land use and land cover maps and data distinguish types of forests, agricultural lands, rangeland, wetlands, and barren land, as well as developed land (see Figures 5.5 and 5.12). Higher-resolution satellite imagery and data have improved land cover and vegetation mapping. Aerial photographs are useful sources of vegetation information. Vegetative cover types can be distinguished from aerial photographs by investigating differences in tone, texture, and pattern, as shown in the following list.

1. Woodlands and forests are easily distinguished from nonforested lands:
   • Deciduous stands show branched texture in winter photos, show red in summer infrared color, and appear lighter than coniferous stands in infrared black and white.
   • Coniferous stands show fuller and darker than deciduous stands in winter photos and infrared black-and-white summer photos; appear dark purple in infrared color photos.
2. Orchards show a repetitive pattern.
3. Nonforested lands can be further interpreted:
   • Cropland can be distinguished by the presence of plowed furrows or the straight line pattern of the previous season's crop rows.
   • Pastureland has a uniform texture on the photographs.
   • Nonpasture open land appears less uniform as the processes of succession may have begun with shrubs, bushes, and small trees contributing to the mixed texture.

When conducting vegetation studies, it is useful to categorize the existing vegetation. There are a variety of classification schemes; a four-level land cover system is described by Marsh (1978) and shown in Figure 10.5. (1) *Vegetation structure* is indicated by the life-form of the vegetation, such as forest, brush, or wetland. (2) The dominant individual *plant types* are indicated by common name (e.g., oak, cattail, etc.). (3) *Size and density* involve the range of stem diameters and the number of stems per acre, or simply the percent cover for grasses and shrubs. (4) The *site features* list the habitat type, such as greenbelt, farmland, and tidal marsh.

Vegetative inventories are important first steps in rapid ecological assessments and urban forestry. Rapid assessment was described in the first edition of this book, and that material is now posted on the book website (www.envirolanduse .org). Urban forestry inventories are discussed later in this chapter.

Vegetative Buffers

Vegetative buffers use permanent vegetation strategically located to enhance ecological functions and landscape conditions, including:

• Stable and productive soils
• Reduced runoff, more infiltration
• Cleaner water

Level I (vegetative structure)		Level II (dominant plant types)	Level III (size and density)	Level IV (site and habitat or associated use)	Level V (special plant species)
Forest (trees with average height greater than 15 ft with at least 60% canopy cover)		E.g., oak, hickory, willow, cottonwood, elm, basswood, maple, beach, ash	Tree size (diameter at breast height) Density (number of average stems per acre)	E.g., upland (i.e., well-drained terrain), floodplain, slope face, woodlot, greenbelt, parkland, residential land	Rare and endangered species; often ground plants associated with certain forest types
Woodland (trees with average height greater than 15 ft with 20–60% canopy cover)		E.g., pine, spruce, balsam fir, hemlock, douglas fir, cedar	Size range (difference between largest and smallest stems)	E.g., upland (i.e., well-drained terrain), floodplain, slope face, woodlot, greenbelt, parkland, residential land	Rare and endangered species; often ground plants associated with certain forest types
Orchard or plantation (same as woodland or forest but with regular spacing)		E.g., apple, peach, cherry, spruce, pine	Tree size; density	E.g., active farmland, abandoned farmland	Species with potential in landscaping for proposed development
Brush (trees and shrubs generally less than 15 ft high with high density of stems, but variable canopy cover)		E.g., sumac, willow, lilac, hawthorn, tag alder, pin cherry, scrub oak, juniper	Density	E.g., vacant farmland, landfill, disturbed terrain (e.g., former construction site)	Species of significance to landscaping for proposed development
Fencerows (trees and shrubs of mixed forms along borders such as road, fields, yards, playgrounds)		Any trees or shrubs	Tree size; density	E.g., active farmland, road right-of-way, yards, playgrounds	Species of value as animal habitat and utility in screening
Wetland (generally low, dense plant covers in wet areas)		E.g., cattail, tag alder, cedar, cranberry, reeds	Percent cover	E.g., floodplain, bog, tidal marsh, reservoir backwater, river delta	Species and plant communities of special importance ecologically and hydrologically; rare and endangered species
Grassland (herbs, with grasses dominant)	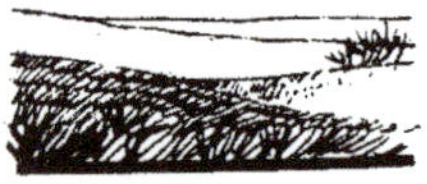	E.g., big blue stem bunch grass, dune grass	Percent cover	E.g., prairie, tundra, pasture, vacant farmland	Species and communities of special ecological significance; rare and endangered species.
Field (tilled or recently tilled farmland)		E.g., corn, soybeans, wheat; also weeds	Field size	E.g., sloping or flat, ditched and drained, muckland, irrigated	Special and unique crops; exceptional levels of productivity in standard crops

Figure 10.5 A Four-Level Vegetation Classification System. (*Source:* William Marsh, *Environmental Analysis: For Land Use and Site Planning*, 1978, McGraw-Hill. Reprinted with permission of McGraw-Hill Companies.)

- Enhanced aquatic and terrestrial wildlife habitat and populations
- Protected crops, livestock, and structures
- Enhanced aesthetics and recreation opportunities
- Sustainable landscapes

Several types of vegetative buffers are used in agricultural and urban applications, including riparian buffers, filter strips, contoured grass strips, grassed waterways, windbreaks, and field cross-wind traps. **Riparian forest buffers** are perhaps the most important and provide the widest range of benefits. These areas of trees and shrubs next to streams, lakes, and wetlands protect water bodies by intercepting surface runoff and the sediment and pollutants it carries. In addition, buffers provide food and cover for wildlife, shade shoreline water to lower temperatures during hot periods, slow flood flows, stabilize streambanks and shorelines, and provide litter and woody debris for aquatic organisms.

We discussed the runoff and water quality benefits of riparian vegetative buffers in Chapter 8, and Figure 8.27 showed the three land use zones:

- The **streamside zone** is the shore plus a minimum 25 ft plus wetlands and critical habitats. It should be undisturbed mature forest or reforested if grass, and it has very restricted use.
- The **middle zone** runs from the streamside zone 50–100 ft plus the 100-year floodplain and steep slopes. It should be managed forest and has restricted use, including some recreation.
- The **outer zone** runs from the middle zone with a 25-ft setback for structures. Forest is encouraged, but turfgrass is allowed, and residential land use is unrestricted.

Figure 10.6A shows a riparian forest buffer, and Figure 10.6B shows Mecklenberg County's network of 32,000 acres of stream buffers, including 22,600 acres of tree canopy in North Carolina. The buffers provide an estimated $350 million annual stormwater management benefit (American Forests 2010).

(A) (B)

Figure 10.6 Riparian Forest Buffers. A: Forest buffers provide many benefits to the riparian and stream ecology. B: A network of riparian buffers in Mecklenberg County (NC) totals 32,000 acres and 22,600 acres of forest canopy. (*Source:* A: USDA, NRCS 1998. B: American Forests 2010. Used with permission.)

Forest Health

Managing the health of forest ecosystems has become an important objective of the U.S. Forest Service (USFS), not only for national forests but also for private and urban forests. The USFS identifies several health concerns (USDA 2003):

- **Wildfire threat**: Fuel buildup and overcrowding from fire suppression and other management practices have increased the threat of catastrophic fire on 39 million acres of the national forests. Ex-urban residential development at the wildland/urban interface has increased the threat to human safety and property (see Chapter 13).
- **Invasion of exotic pests**: Gypsy moth, Asian long-horned beetles, hemlock woolly adelgids, and a wide range of other foliage-feeding, wood-boring, and sapsucking pests have caused extensive damage to forests, woodlands, and urban trees.
- **Forest diseases**: Many root and butt, foliage, stem and cone, and wood decay diseases impact specific species. (See www.forestpests.org.)
- **Air pollution**: Acid rain and ozone pollution can transport long distances and impact forest ecosystems, especially in the eastern United States. Ozone and nitrogen oxide impacts are also prevalent in the southwestern United States.
- **Degraded riparian areas**: High-quality forest riparian areas are critical for runoff and sediment control and wildlife habitat. This has been a serious problem in the southwestern U.S., where 65% of animals depend on riparian habitats during all or part of their life cycles.

Large areas of U.S. forestland are at risk from disease or insect mortality. Almost 10% of the nation's 737 million acres of forests are at risk. About 47% of the at-risk acres are part of the National Forests, and 53% are on other lands. Four groups account for about 70% of the acres at risk: gypsy moths, in the East, root diseases in the interior West, southern pine beetles in the South, and bark beetles in the West.

Urban Forestry

The urban forest includes all woody vegetation within the environs of human populated places. Forested land in urban and metropolitan areas constitutes a surprising 25% of the U.S. forest canopy (McPherson 2003). Although these forests do not yield much timber production, they provide greater benefits to human settlements through climate control, air quality enhancement, watershed protection and runoff control, noise reduction, habitat for urban wildlife, recreation opportunities, and aesthetics. In short, they clean our air and water, protect us from the summer heat and winter winds, and enhance our emotional and spiritual lives (Landauer 2001). Thus, the management of the urban forest is an important local environmental issue. Table 10.2 summarizes the benefits of the urban forest.

TABLE 10.2 **Benefits of the Urban Forest**

Scale	Category	Benefit
Watershed	Environmental	Reduce stormwater runoff
		Improve regional air quality
		Reduce stream channel erosion
		Improve soil and water quality
		Provide habitat for terrestrial and aquatic wildlife
		Reduce summer air and water temperatures
Parcel	Economic	Decrease heating and cooling costs
		Reduce construction and maintenance costs
		Increase property values
		Positively influence consumer behavior
	Environmental	Reduce urban heat island effect
		Enhance function of stormwater control measures
	Community	Increase livability
		Improve health and well-being
		Provide shade and block UV radiation
		Buffer wind and noise
		Increase recreational opportunities
		Provide aesthetic value

Source: Cappiella, Schueler, and Wright 2005.

This increasing understanding of the ecological, economic, and social benefits of the urban forest has occurred at the same time as an epidemic decline in the urban forest canopy resulting from development. Few cities adequately manage their trees and forests. The USFS estimates that 13 southeastern states will lose 30 million acres of prime forestland to urban development over the next four decades. In metropolitan Atlanta, heavy tree cover (where canopy covers more than half the land surface) declined from about 50% of the metro area in 1974 to about 25% in 1996. Areas with less than 20% cover increased from 44% to 71%. Average tree cover dropped from 45% to 29% (American Forests 2001b). The non-profit conservation organization American Forests has demonstrated significant reductions in urban and metropolitan tree canopy, what it calls "the national urban tree deficit," and to achieve an average 40% canopy cover in urban areas would require planting more than 600 million trees. Several cities have initiated aggressive urban tree-planting programs, including Chicago's program, which has planted 600,000 trees since 1989, Los Angeles' Million Tree LA, New York's MillionTreesNYC, and many other U.S. and international city campaigns.

Urban and Regional Forest Canopy Analysis

American Forests (AF) was founded in 1875 with a vision to have healthy forest ecosystems in every community. AF has been conducting studies known as the Urban Ecosystem Analysis for the past decade. As of August 2010, it has done 39 such studies for metropolitan areas. The studies assess land cover change based on USGS National Land Cover Dataset (NLCD) and Landsat data. In recent studies, it is using National Agriculture Imagery Program (NAIP) 1-meter resolution, 4-band data (see Chapter 5).

To analyze the impacts of land cover change and the loss of forest canopy, AF has its own CITYgreen for ArcGIS software for calculating the value of green infrastructure for stormwater runoff reduction, using TR-55 (see Chapter 7); water quality improvement, using EPA's Long-Term Hydrological Impact Assessment spreadsheet model; and air pollution control, using the urban forest effects (UFORE) model, which calculates the carbon sequestered and the amount of ozone, carbon monoxide, sulfur dioxide, and nitrogen dioxide deposited or absorbed by the tree canopy. CITYgreen computes the economic benefits (and losses) from the resulting data on canopy cover (and its decline).

These assessments have followed a similar methodology, involving the following steps:

1. For larger metropolitan or regional-scale analysis, Landsat MSS and TM images (and more recently high-resolution satellite data) are used to quantify tree canopy changes from the 1970s to the 1990s or 2000s.
2. For local area or neighborhood-scale analysis, ground surveys and aerial photos of sample sites representing different land uses are used to assess trees, grass, and impervious surfaces. Most recent studies have shown that high-resolution satellite images can provide similar data detail for an entire area without sampling (American Forests 2010).
3. CITYgreen software is used to calculate ecosystem benefits (stormwater, air quality, and energy) for sample sites, then extrapolate the findings to the entire region based on total area for each land use and tree canopy category.

This book's first edition looked at studies of Atlanta, the Willamette/Lower Columbia (Oregon) area, and Chattanooga (Tennessee). Those materials are posted on the book website (www.envirolanduse.org). The trends for the Willamette area are different from the other areas. Whereas the others have shown a decrease of heavy canopy (> 50% tree cover) from the 1970s to the 1990s, the Willamette area shows a decline to 1986, then an increase to 2000. American Forests believes this trend reversal was the result of Oregon's use of urban growth boundaries to contain sprawling development that impacts forest canopy (see Chapter 18).

Figure 10.7 shows the forest canopy decline in Charlotte–Mecklenberg County (NC) between 1985 and 2008. The county lost 33% of its tree canopy and 3% of its open space, while its urban land cover grew by 60%. Meanwhile, the City of Charlotte lost 49% of its tree canopy and 5% of its open space, and its urban land grew by 39%. The assessment estimated these changes reduced the tree canopy's ability to:

- Naturally manage more than 250 million cu ft of stormwater, valued at more than $500 million using a local engineering cost of $2/cu ft.
- Remove approximately 3.8 million lb of air pollutants annually, valued at $8.8 million per year.
- Sequester 1.5 million lb of carbon annually.

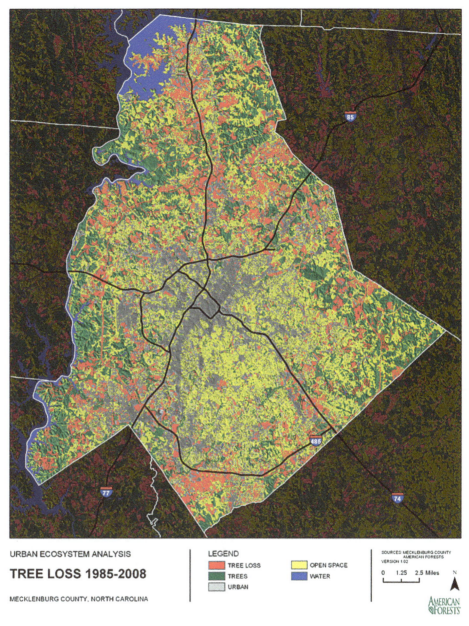

URBAN ECOSYSTEM ANALYSIS

TREE LOSS 1985-2008

MECKLENBURG COUNTY, NORTH CAROLINA

LEGEND

TREE LOSS   OPEN SPACE

TREES   WATER

URBAN

SOURCES: MECKLENBURG COUNTY
AMERICAN FORESTS
VERSION 1.02

0   1.25   2.5 Miles

AMERICAN FORESTS

Figure 10.7 Urban Ecosystem Analysis for Mecklenberg County, North Carolina, based on Satellite Forest Cover Data. (*Source:* American Forests 2010. Used with permission.)

The Charlotte-Mecklenberg Urban Ecosystem Analysis recommends that the county establish tree canopy goals of 50–55% that could be achieved by arresting the current decline trend; identifying critical areas for reforestation, such as riparian stream buffers in the McDowell and Goose Creek Subwatersheds; and engaging local citizen groups in environmental improvements, including tree planting (American Forests 2010).

Developing a Community Forest Management Strategy

Urban forestry has a modest history in the U.S., starting as park and street tree management (about 30% of urban trees are publicly owned), and a reactive response to tree disease and storm damage. By the 1980s and 1990s, communities began adopting tree preservation and landscaping ordinances for new development. However, most localities lack a comprehensive proactive approach for protecting and enhancing existing trees, and for reforesting areas to arrest the decline of the urban forest canopy. Such a proactive approach should employ the basic planning process introduced in Chapter 2 (see Boxes 2.1 and 2.2):

1. ***What do we have?*** A first step is to inventory and assess the forest and tree resources, as well as the current management framework, stakeholders, ordinances, programs, and budgets.
2. ***What do we want?*** Identify needs and goals based on the assessment of resources and management and on stakeholder involvement. Goals and objectives need not be complicated. Table 10.3 lists a simple set of urban forestry goals and objectives:
   - Protect undeveloped forests from human encroachment and impacts of land development through planning techniques, regulatory tools, and incentives.
   - Enhance the health, condition, and function of urban forest fragments, including hydrology, habitat, and tree growth.
   - Reforest open land through active replanting and regeneration to increase forest canopy and cover to regain forest functions and benefits.

Table 10.3 **Urban Forestry Goals and Objectives**

Goal	Objective	Description
Protect	A. Protect Priority Forests	Select large tracts of currently unprotected and undeveloped forest to protect from future development.
	B. Prevent Forest Loss during Development and Redevelopment	Directly or indirectly reduce forest clearing during construction.
	C. Maintain Existing Forest Canopy	Prevent clearing and encroachment on existing protected and unprotected forest fragments on developed land.
Enhance	D. Enhance Forest Fragments	Improve the structure and function of existing protected forests.
Reforest	E. Plant Trees during Development and Redevelopment	Require onsite reforestation as a condition of development.
	F. Reforest Public Land	Systematically reforest feasible planting sites within public land, rights-of-way, or other priority sites.
	G. Reforest Private Land	Encourage tree planting on feasible locations within individual yards or property.

Source: Cappiella, Schueler, and Wright 2005.

Figure 10.8 San Francisco's Urban Forest Map Website. This interactive tool asks residents to add trees and information to the city's forest database. (*Source:* SF Urban Forest Map, http://www.urbanforestmap.org/.)

3. ***How do we get what we want?*** The heart of the planning process is formulating an urban forestry plan and management strategy. This involves establishing organizational structure, adopting ordinances, charging fees, making investments, and other strategies.

4. ***Let's do it! (and learn from it)***. The plan becomes reality through implementation. Monitoring progress is critical to evaluating effectiveness and modifying the plan as necessary.

Inventorying and Evaluating the Urban Forest

The first edition of this book included a section on inventorying the urban forest using sampling methods, photogrammetry, and ground surveys. That material is posted on the book website (www.envirolanduse.org). This section adds to these traditional methods the use of high-resolution remote sensing data and crowdsourcing to involve the public in the tree inventory.

Tree Inventory Mapping with Crowdsourcing. Chapters 4 and 5 introduced San Francisco's efforts to map every tree in its urban forest, using web-based interactive mapping and crowdsourcing for residents to enter tree data (urban forestmap.org). The Urban Forest Map program was launched in August 2010. The web-mapper is shown in Figure 10.8, with an inset of a zoomed-in sector of the city showing trees as green dots; clicking on the dot reveals data about the tree. Users can find a tree, add a tree, edit data for a tree, and post tree photos and comments. The website contains instructions on identifying species and measuring trees.

Forest Canopy Assessment Using High-Resolution Land Cover Data.   One-meter-resolution IKONOS and other satellite data provide a high-quality assessment of forest cover. American Forests uses these data in its Urban Ecosystem Analysis, and the accuracy of those assessments increases with incremental improvement in spatial resolution (see Figure 10.7).

Planning Analysis for Increasing Forest Cover in Urban Areas

As a result of assessments showing the dramatic decline in urban forest canopy, one of the primary objectives of urban forestry programs is increasing forest cover. This requires integrating tree protection and reforestation in the land development process to change the development process from one that destroys forest cover to one that enhances it. In addition, reforestation and tree planting on both public and private lands are needed to fill the urban forest deficit.

In 2005 and 2006, the Center for Watershed Protection (CWP) produced a three-part manual series for the U.S. Forest Service on using trees to protect and restore urban watersheds (Cappiella, Schueler, Tomilson, and Wright 2006; Cappiella, Schueler, and Wright 2005, 2006). This *Urban Watershed Forestry Manual*, the Forest Service Southern Region Urban Forestry Manual (USDA, Forest Service, 2001), and the Planning Advisory Service report on urban forestry (Schwab 2009) provide good references for this important topic. The CWP manual views the urban forest from the holistic perspective of the watershed and focuses on increasing forest cover, conserving and planting trees on development sites, and tree planting at the site and watershed scale.

The CWP's planning method for increasing forest cover includes six steps:

1. Conduct a watershed leaf-out analysis.
2. Develop forest cover goals and objectives.
3. Identify existing forest and reforestation opportunities.
4. Conduct a field assessment of existing forest and reforestation opportunities.
5. Prioritize existing forest and reforestation.
6. Develop recommendations for meeting forest cover goals.

The step 1 **leaf-out analysis** assesses the future forest cover if the site or watershed is built out to the full capacity of existing zoning. Given this baseline, the method investigates goals, objectives, opportunities, priorities, and recommendations for increasing forest cover. There are seven steps:

1.1 Estimate the distribution of current land cover in the watershed.
1.2 Identify protected and unprotected lands in the watershed.
1.3 Determine whether parcels are developed or undeveloped.
1.4 Determine allowable zoning on undeveloped land.
1.5 Summarize watershed data.
1.6 Acquire forest cover coefficients.
1.7 Estimate future forest cover in the watershed.

Figure 10.9 illustrates steps 1–4.

Figure 10.9 Leaf-Out Analysis. Current land cover (1.1), protected (e.g., public or easement land) and unprotected lands (1.2), developed or undeveloped land (1.3), and allowable zoning (1.4). (*Source:* Cappiella, Schueler, and Wright 2005. Used with permission of the Center for Watershed Protection.)

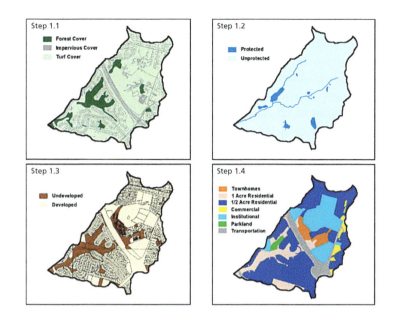

This information is quantified in a summary of watershed data in Figure 10.10. For each zoning category, the figure records current impervious cover, protected/developed forest cover and developed public and private turf cover (all of which are not likely to change), and unprotected/undeveloped buildable forest cover and undeveloped turf cover (both of which are likely to change).

Step 1.6 involves applying forest cover coefficients to future land development, using three forest conservation scenarios:

- NFC, No Forest Conservation: Clearing can proceed anywhere on the site except protected wetlands.
- IFC, Indirect Forest Conservation: Some areas cannot be cleared because of steep slopes, wetland buffers, stream buffers, floodplains, or other restrictions.

| Zoning Category | Current Impervious Cover (acres) | Current Forest Cover (acres) | | Current Turf Cover (acres) | | |
| | | Protected/ Developed | Buildable (unprotected/ undeveloped) | Developed | | Undeveloped |
				Public	Private	
Agriculture	100	1,000	50	0	3,000	50
Open urban land	150	2,000	100	4,000	0	0
2 acre residential	500	500	200	0	4,000	1,000
1 acre residential	1,000	500	2,000	0	2,000	500
½ acre residential	1,000	500	3,000	0	1,500	1,000
¼ acre residential	2,000	500	1,000	0	1,000	500
⅛ acre residential	2,000	0	50	0	150	100
Townhomes	4,000	0	500	0	100	400
Multifamily	3,000	0	100	0	100	0
Institutional	1,000	0	500	3,000	500	0
Light industrial	5,000	0	500	0	50	100
Commercial	5,000	0	2,000	0	500	500
Total	24,750	5,000	10,000	7,000	2,950	4,150

Figure 10.10 Leaf-Out Step 1.5: Watershed Data Summarized by Zoning Category. (*Source:* Cappiella, Schueler, and Wright 2005. Used with permission of the Center for Watershed Protection.)

TABLE 10.4 **Forest Conservation Scenarios for Five Zoning Categories**

Zoning Category	Impervious Cover (%)	Turf Cover (%)			Forest Cover (%)		
		NFC	IFC	DFC	NFC	IFC	DFC
Open urban land	9	86	76	41	5	15	50
1-acre residential	14	81	71	36	5	15	50
1/8-acre residential	33	62	52	47	5	15	20
Townhouses	41	54	44	39	5	15	20
Commercial	72	23	13	13	5	15	15

Source: Cappiella, Schueler, and Wright 2005.

- DFC, Direct Forest Conservation: Additional site areas cannot be cleared because of explicit forest conservation or afforestation requirements at the site.

Table 10.4 gives a hypothetical example of these scenarios for five zoning categories, and Figure 10.11 shows the effect of forest conservation regulations at a development site.

Step 1.7 articulates assumptions for estimating future forest cover:

1. All developed land will remain in its current land cover.
2. All protected land will remain in its current land cover.
3. All impervious cover will remain impervious (e.g., no removal of pavement).
4. All land that is unprotected and undeveloped is considered "buildable" under its allowable zoning category.
5. Full buildout of the watershed will occur based on allowable zoning (e.g., no rezoning).
6. Future cover of buildable land can be estimated by its zoning category's cover coefficients.
7. The land cover coefficients reflect the forest conservation regulations in the watershed.

Figure 10.12 is a leaf-out analysis worksheet for estimating future forest cover for a worst-case scenario in a Maryland watershed (see Figure 10.10) where forest conservation coefficient requirements apply. It is worst case because there are no priority forest acres protected. Section 2 of the worksheet computes the forest conserved during development buildout according to the requirements (2,780 acres). In section 1, this is added to the 5,000 acres protected or developed (step 1.5, Figure 10.10), to total 7,780 acres of future forest cover. In section 3, this is compared to current forest cover of 15,000 acres (5,000 plus 10,000 in step 1.5, Figure 10.10) to show a loss of 7,220 acres or 48% of current forest cover.

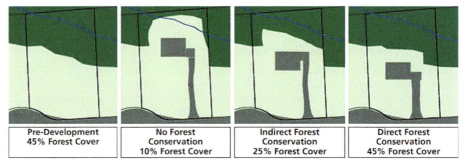

| Pre-Development 45% Forest Cover | No Forest Conservation 10% Forest Cover | Indirect Forest Conservation 25% Forest Cover | Direct Forest Conservation 45% Forest Cover |

Figure 10.11 Forest Cover Regulations at Development Sites. (*Source:* Cappiella, Schueler, and Wright 2005. Used with permission of the Center for Watershed Protection.)

BOX 13. LEAF-OUT ANALYSIS WORKSHEET FOR ESTIMATING FUTURE FOREST COVER IN A WATERSHED--WORST-CASE SCENARIO (e.g., no additional reforestation or conservation efforts)

Section 1. Future Forest Cover

Current Protected or Developed Forest Cover:	*5,000*	acres
From Table 4. All protected or developed forest will remain forested.	+	
Priority Forest Area Protected	*0*	acres
See section 2 of this worksheet. Default value is zero.	+	
Area of Forest Conserved During Development	*2,780*	acres
See section 2 of this worksheet.	+	
Area Reforested	*0*	acres
Default value is zero.	=	
Total Future Forest Cover	*7,780*	acres

Section 2. Forest Conserved During Development

Zoning Category	Buildable Forest (acres)		Priority Forest Protected (acres)		Buildable Forest Remaining (acres)		Forest* Cover Coefficient		Forest Conserved During Development (acres)
Agriculture	50	-	0	=	50	x	.50	=	25
Open urban land	100	-	0	=	100	x	.50	=	50
2 acre residential	200	-	0	=	200	x	.50	=	100
1 acre residential	2,000	-	0	=	2,000	x	.50	=	1,000
½ acre residential	3,000	-	0	=	3,000	x	.25	=	750
¼ acre residential	1,000	-	0	=	1,000	x	.25	=	250
⅛ acre residential	50	-	0	=	50	x	.20	=	10
Townhomes	500	-	0	=	500	x	.20	=	100
Multifamily	100	-	0	=	100	x	.20	=	20
Institutional	500	-	0	=	500	x	.20	=	100
Light industrial	500	-	0	=	500	x	.15	=	75
Commercial	2000	-	0	=	2,000	x	.15	=	300
Total	10,000		0						2,780

* Use forest cover coefficients that represent forest conservation requirements in your area

Section 3. Results Summary

Total Current Forest Cover	*15,000*	acres		
From Table 4.	-			
Total Future Forest Cover	*7,780*	acres		
From Section 1 above.	=			
Future Forest Loss	*7,220*	acres	*48*	%

Figure 10.12 A Leaf-Out Analysis Worksheet. (*Source:* Cappiella, Schueler, and Wright 2005. Used with permission of the Center for Watershed Protection.)

TABLE 10.5 **Sample Future Forest Cover Goals**

Watershed Type	Impervious Cover (%)	Forest Cover Goal	Primary Benefits
Suburban forested	< 25	60% minimum with 70% riparian forest cover	Stream protection, filtering, aquatic ecosystem, habitat
Suburban agricultural	< 25	40–50% minimum	Stream protection, filtering, aquatic ecosystem, habitat
Urban-suburban	26–60	25–40% minimum	Reduce stormwater runoff, urban heat island; increase habitat, aesthetics
Urban	> 60	15–25% minimum	Reduce urban heat island, stormwater runoff; improve air quality, livability

Step 2 of the planning method involves setting future forest cover goals for different watershed and subwatershed types, such as the numerical targets in Table 10.5. To meet these goals, the overall objectives (see Table 10.3) are reviewed and prioritized. For example, is designating and protecting priority forests more apt to achieve the numerical goal than planting trees during development? Or reforesting public land? Or preventing forest loss during development by imposing a higher forest cover coefficient?

These objectives can be tested using the leaf-out analysis worksheet. For example, total future forest cover of 7,780 acres in the worst-case scenario of Figure 10.11 could be increased to 16,000, or an increase of 1,000 acres or 7% above current cover of 15,000 acres (see Figure 10.10), by doing the following:

- Designating and protecting 2,000 acres of priority forest from all zoning categories (sec. 2, col. 3).
- Imposing 0.50 forest cover coefficients for all zoning categories (sec. 2, col. 5), resulting in 5,000 acres conserved during development.
- Reforesting 4,000 acres in the watershed (sec. 1, line 7).

Step 3 explores how these opportunities for protection and reforestation can be achieved, and step 4 involves field assessment of these opportunities. Based on steps 3 and 4, step 5 prioritizes these opportunities, and step 6 develops specific recommendations for meeting forest cover goals.

Conserving and Planting Trees at Development Sites

The process of land development is the major cause of forest canopy depletion now well documented in U.S. metropolitan areas. Land clearing and grading for roads, parking lots, buildings, utilities, and other uses destroys trees, disturbs soils, and increases impervious surface. Can urban forest canopy be increased while land development continues? The answer is yes, but it requires a shift in land develop-

ment and construction practices. Several approaches must be taken to conserve existing trees and plant new ones.

Conserving trees at construction sites requires the following steps (Cappiella, Schueler, and Wright 2006):

- Inventorying the existing forest, including species, size, condition, and location.
- Identifying trees to protect based on the inventory.
- Designing the development with tree conservation in mind, using open space design techniques incorporating existing trees, site fingerprinting that sets a limit of disturbance (LOD) around the building footprint, and setbacks from critical root zones (CRZ).
- Protecting trees and soils during construction using physical barriers to identify CRZ and LOD.
- Protecting them after construction through resident education and homeowner association programs.

Tree Planting to Increase the Urban Forest Cover

Increasing forest cover cannot be achieved solely by conserving existing trees; it requires planting more. In addition to tree planting on construction and development sites, urban tree planting programs are of three types:

1. Planting on public lands, properties, and rights-of-way. These are public investment projects but can engage citizen volunteers. Figure 10.13 shows a few of the many types of public spaces and rights-of-way that can be reforested.

Figure 10.13 Public Tree Planting. Public rights-of-way, highway buffers, and cloverleaves provide great locations for public tree planting campaigns. (*Source:* Cappiella, Schueler, and Wright 2006. Used with permission of the Center for Watershed Protection.)

2. Planting on private property. Land stewardship by home and property owners can enhance tree planting with incentives and education.
3. Tree planting campaigns in cities, such as Chicago's efforts to plant 600,000 trees, the MillionTreeNYC program, and the Million Tree Los Angeles (MTLA) campaign, can engage citizens and create a social movement for urban forestry (Pincetl 2009).

Planting sites should be carefully selected and evaluated. Some basic principles for tree planting include (Cappiella, Schueler, and Wright 2006):

- Providing adequate soil volume to support trees to maturity.
- Preserving and improving soil quality.
- Providing adequate space for the tree to grow.
- Selecting trees for diversity and site suitability.
- Protecting trees from impacts of pedestrian and vehicle traffic, toxic runoff, deer browsing, low water, and high temperatures, among others.

Policies to Increase Forest Cover in Urban Watersheds

Urban forestry management programs can use a range of land use policies to achieve protection and reforestation. Table 10.6 gives a comprehensive list of techniques that localities should consider. Most of these policy options are discussed in later chapters, especially Chapter 15 on land conservation and Chapter 17 on land use requirements.

Urban forestry ordinances are an important category on this list, because they have a direct effect on the forest cover on private property. Ordinances vary widely in form, content, and complexity, but an effective tree ordinance should meet the following criteria (International Society of Arboriculture 2001):

1. *Goals* should be clearly stated and ordinance provisions should address the stated goals.
2. *Responsibility and authority* should be designated to a tree commission to set policy and to a city arborist and other staff to conduct operations and enforcement.
3. *Basic performance standards* should indicate which practices, conditions, and performance are acceptable and which are not. Standards should be specific and quantifiable.
4. *Flexibility* must be maintained in meeting provisions and in enforcement.
5. *Enforcement* methods should be clear.
6. The ordinance should be part of a *comprehensive urban forest management strategy*. The lack of integration between urban forest management and tree ordinances is common.
7. The ordinance should be developed with *community support*.

TABLE 10.6 **Policies and Techniques for Protection, Enhancement, and Reforestation**

Goal	Objective	Description
Protect	A. Protect Priority Forests	1. Conservation easements 2. Land acquisition 3. Transfer of development rights
	B. Prevent Forest Loss during Development and Redevelopment	4. Bonus and incentive zoning 5. Clearing and grading requirements 6. Forest conservation regulations 7. Open space design 8. Overlay zoning 9. Performance-based zoning 10. Stream buffer ordinance
	C. Maintain Existing Forest Canopy	12. Protection of significant trees 13. Tree removal restrictions for developed areas
Enhance	D. Enhance Forest Fragments	14. Increase forest area where possible 15. Increase habitat diversity 16. Manage deer 17. Protect soils from erosion and compaction 18. Provide food, cover, and nesting sites for wildlife 19. Reduce or eliminate invasive species 20. Remove trash and prevent dumping
Reforest	E. Plant Trees during Development and Redevelopment	21. Landscaping requirements 22. Planting trees in stormwater treatment practices 23. Planting trees in other open areas 24. Shading and canopy requirements
	F. Reforest Public Land	25. Allow natural regeneration 26. Actively reforest public lands
	G. Reforest Private Land	27. Education 28. Incentives for tree planting 29. Stewardship and neighborhood action

Source: Cappiella, Schueler, and Wright 2005.

The Role of Urban Forestry

Urban forestry has become the primary mechanism in efforts to arrest the continuing endemic decline of forest cover in metropolitan areas. The benefits of urban forests are significant, and their continued decline creates substantial economic, environmental, and social costs. Urban forestry has evolved from the management of public street and park trees, to a comprehensive program that assesses the trends and causes of canopy cover loss, protects and enhances existing trees and forest cover, conserves and plants trees as part of the land development process, and engages citizens and financial resources in reforestation efforts.

Urban forestry is a key component in more general green infrastructure development that also includes vegetative stormwater practices (see Chapter 8), wildlife habitat and corridors (see Chapter 11), land conservation (see Chapter 15), and watershed and ecosystem management (see Chapter 19).

Wetlands Protection and Management

Like forest canopy, wetlands are regarded as a critical part of urban ecosystems, providing significant environmental, economic, and social benefits. **Wetlands** are defined as areas where saturation with water is the dominant factor, determining the nature of soil development and the types of plant and animal communities living in the soil and on its surface (Cowardin et al. 1979). The Clean Water Act defines wetlands as "those areas that are inundated or saturated by surface or ground water at a frequency and duration sufficient to support, and that under normal circumstances do support, a prevalence of vegetation typically adapted for life in saturated soil conditions. Wetlands generally include swamps, marshes, bogs and similar areas" (40 CFR 230.3[f]).

As part of the National Wetlands Inventory program, the U.S. Fish and Wildlife Service (USFWS) developed a wetlands and deepwater classification system (Figure 10.14). In December 1996, this "Cowardin system" was designated the national standard for wetland mapping (Cowardin et al. 1979). The main subsystems (marine, estuarine, riverine, lacustrine, and palustrine) are further distinguished by class, usually defined as bottom type for deep water and as vegetative type for wetlands. Palustrine or inland, freshwater wetlands account for about 95% of the wetlands in the coterminous United States; the remainder are estuarine wetlands, mostly of the emergent class.

The National Research Council (1995) lists several major vernacular classes of U.S. wetlands and some plants associated with each:

- **Freshwater marsh**: Freshwater-saturated area having aquatic vegetation and grasses, sedges, and herbs.
- **Tidal salt and brackish marsh**: Saltwater-saturated area subject to tidal influence and having aquatic vegetation and salt-tolerant grasses and rushes.
- **Prairie potholes**: Shallow depression occurring in outwash or till plain resulting from glacial retreat, having grasses, sedges, and herbs.
- **Fens**: Peat-accumulating wetland receiving water from surface runoff or seepage, having sedges, grasses, shrubs, and trees.
- **Bogs**: Nutrient-poor, acidic wetland dominated by waterlogged spongy mat of sphagnum moss that forms acidic peat, fed primarily by rainwater and no inflow or outflow; also has shrubs and trees.
- **Swamp bottomland**: Area intermittently or permanently covered with water, having shrubs or trees, usually cypress, gum, and red maple.
- **Mangrove forest**: Water-saturated or submerged area with water-tolerant black, red, and white mangrove trees.

Marine: Open ocean overlying the continental shelf and associated high-energy coastline. Examples of wetland types within this system are subtidal and intertidal aquatic beds, reefs, and rocky shores.

Estuarine: Deep-water tidal habitats and adjacent tidal wetlands that are usually semienclosed by land but have open, partially obstructed, or sporadic access to the ocean and in which ocean water is at least occasionally diluted by freshwater runoff from the land. Examples of estuarine classes are subtidal and intertidal emergent wetlands, forested wetlands, and rock bottom. **Riverine:** Wetlands and deep-water habitats contained within a channel with two exceptions: (1) wetlands dominated by trees, shrubs, persistent emergent plants, emergent mosses, or lichens, and (2) habitat with water containing ocean-derived salts in excess of 5 ppt (parts per thousand). Rivers and streams fall within this system, and subsystems include tidal, perennial, or intermittent watercourses. **Lacustrine:** Wetlands and deep-water habitats with all of the following characteristics: situated in a topographic depression or a dammed river channel; less than 30% area coverage by trees, shrubs, persistent emergent vegetation, emergent mosses, or lichens; and total area exceeding 8 hectares (20 acres). Lakes typify lacustrine wetland systems. **Palustrine:** All nontidal wetlands dominated by trees, shrubs, persistent emergent vegetation, emergent mosses, or lichens, and all such wetlands that occur in tidal areas where salinity due to ocean-derived salts is below 5 ppt. This system also includes wetlands lacking such vegetation if they are less than 8 hectares, lack wave action or bedrock shoreline features, and at the deepest spot are no deeper than 2 m at low water. Examples are ponds, bogs, and prairie potholes.

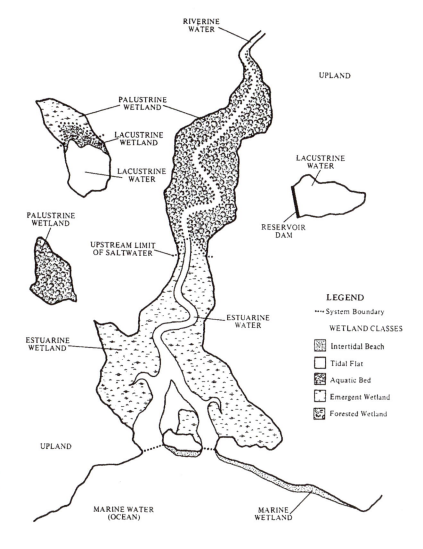

Figure 10.14 Wetland Systems Definitions. (*Source:* Cowardin et al. 1979.)

Wetland types are diverse, but they all possess hydrologic, soil, and biotic characteristics that distinguish them from upland or other aquatic ecosystems. **Hydrological characteristics**—the duration, flow, amount, and frequency of water on a site—are the *primary factors* that determine soil and vegetation elements. Wetland hydrology occurs when a site is wet enough to produce soils that can support hydrophytic ("water-loving") vegetation. Wetland soils are called **hydric soils** and are saturated with water for all or part of the year (see Chapter 6). Saturated soils become anaerobic as water drives the oxygen out of the spaces between soil particles. This changes the soil's structure and chemistry (Somers et al. 2000).

Because of waterlogged and anaerobic conditions, wetlands are hostile to most terrestrial plants. As a result, they are dominated by **hydrophytic plants** that are adapted to these conditions. Wetland plant species include emergent plants (cattails, sedges, and rushes), submerged plants (pondweeds, eelgrass), floating plants (e.g., duckweed), trees (cypress, red maple, and swamp oak), shrubs (willows and bayberry), moss, and other types of vegetation. Because wetlands exist at the land-water interface, they are used by animals from both wet and dry environments. Many invertebrate, fish, reptile, and amphibian species depend on wetland water cycles to survive or complete their life cycles. Nearly all amphibians, approximately 75% of all commercial marine fish species, and at least 50% of migratory birds use wetlands regularly (NRC 1995).

In 2004, wetlands accounted for 5.5% of the coterminous U.S. land area, deep water made up 1%, and the remaining 93.5% was uplands. Of the 107.6 million wetland acres, 90% are freshwater vegetated wetlands, 5% are freshwater non-vegetated ponds, and 5% are estuarine intertidal wetlands. Half of freshwater vegetated wetlands are forested, and half are emergent/shrub.

Benefits of Wetlands

Historically, wetlands have been viewed as wasted land, which could be put into productive use only through draining and earth filling. As a result, well over half of the original 221 million acres of wetlands in the contiguous 48 states have been converted to other uses. However, the values and benefits of wetlands have been better recognized in the past 25 years, and in response, efforts to control wetland conversion have grown considerably.

Box 10.3 summarizes the many benefits of wetlands. Not only do wetlands provide important ecological benefits for wildlife and natural systems, but they also support human activities through flood and erosion control, water quality treatment, groundwater recharge, and recreation. Most wetlands in the United States are located in the southeast coastal plain, lower Mississippi Valley, the prairie potholes region, Great Lakes states, and upper New England. Such lands have been called "the cradle of life" for waterfowl, fisheries, endangered species, countless small birds, mammals, and a wide variety of plant life.

The National Wetlands Inventory

The National Wetlands Inventory (NWI) was established by the USFWS in 1974 to conduct a nationwide inventory to aid in wetlands conservation efforts. The methods for inventorying using remote sensing data have greatly improved through the years and provide information on the status of wetlands change. The NWI serves as the basis for USFWS's periodic Status and Trends report and for its interactive Wetlands Mapper. Like similar web-mapper tools, it lets users locate wetlands and produce location-specific wetlands maps for local inventories or impact studies. Figure 10.15 shows a Wetlands Mapper product map for part of New Orleans (Louisiana) on a local street base map. There are options for a satellite imagery base map and viewing wetlands on Google Earth. Go to http://www.fws.gov/wetlands/Data/Mapper.html and make a wetlands map of your area.

BOX 10.3—Benefits of Wetlands

Flood Damage Reduction

Wetlands often function like natural tubs or sponges, storing water and slowly releasing it. Trees and other wetland vegetation help slow floodwaters. This combined action, storage, and slowing can lower flood heights. A U.S. Army Corps of Engineers study of the Charles River Basin in Massachusetts concluded that the loss of 8,100 acres of forested wetlands would result in millions of dollars of annual flood damages downstream (U.S. Army Corps of Engineers 1976).

Shoreline Erosion Control

Wetlands dissipate wave energy and erosive potential, thus buffering shorelines and upland areas from erosion.

Water Quality Improvement

Wetlands intercept surface runoff and remove nutrients, organic wastes, and sediment before they reach open water, helping to improve water quality, including groundwater and sources of the water supply.

Groundwater Recharge

Since freshwater wetlands occur at the outcrop of the water table, they are an important interface between surface water and groundwater and contribute to the recharge of aquifers.

Healthy Fisheries

About 75% of commercial fish and shellfish depend on estuaries and their wetlands. Most freshwater fish are dependent on marshes and riparian wetlands, where they spawn during spring floods.

Ecological Benefits to Wildlife and Biological Diversity

Wetlands are among the most biologically productive natural ecosystems in the world. They can be compared to tropical rain forests and coral reefs in the diversity of species they support. An estimated 46% of the listed threatened and endangered species rely directly or indirectly on wetlands for their survival. Wetlands provide critical habitats for 50–80% of the continental waterfowl, 80% of North America's breeding birds, and 190 species of amphibians, as well as many mammals, including muskrat, beaver, mink, raccoon, marsh and swamp rabbits.

Recreation, Aesthetics, Education, and Research

Wetlands provide opportunities for such popular activities as hiking, fishing, and boating. For example, an estimated 50 million people spend approximately $10 billion each year observing and photographing wetlands-dependent birds.

Source: Adapted from NRC 1995.

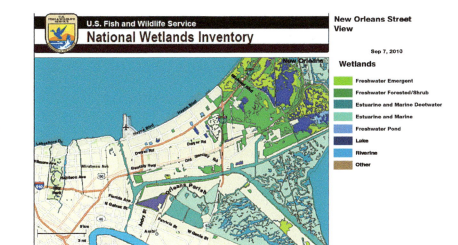

Figure 10.15 A Sample Wetlands Inventory Mapper Product, Showing a Portion of New Orleans, Louisiana. (*Source:* U.S. Fish and Wildlife Service, http://www.fws.gov /wetlands/Data /Mapper.html.)

Wetland Conversion and Alteration

An estimated 52% of the original 221 million acres of wetlands in the United States have been converted to other uses, about 80% of which have been for agricultural purposes. The U.S. is continuing to lose quality wetlands, but the loss has slowed considerably in the last four decades. In fact, the NWI reports net gains in wetland acres since 1998. As shown in Table 10.7, annual wetlands loss of 458,000 acres in the 1950s to the early 1970s slowed to less than 300,000 acres by the 1980s and, from the mid-1980s to the mid-1990s, to about 100,000 acres per year, with a net loss of 58,500 acres as a result of wetland creation and restoration. From 1998 to 2004, the loss was about 38,000 acres per year, but gains of about 70,000 acres per year led to a net gain of 32,000 acres per year. Through the mid-1980s, agricultural activities caused by far the greatest impact on wetlands, but since then, urban and rural land development has been the greatest cause of the loss of wetlands in the U.S.

Reasons for the declining rate of losses include regulation by the federal CWA section 404 wetland permitting, as well as state and local wetlands protection programs; policies for "no net loss" and "net gain" by the last four federal administrations; enactment of the "Swampbuster" provisions of the farm bills since 1985 (see Chapter 15); expansion of federal, state, local, and private restoration programs; and increased public awareness and support for conservation.

Although there has been a recent net gain in wetland acreage, in most cases, new wetland acres are of lower quality than lost acres. Most of the 1998–2004 wetland gain is attributable to the development of open ponds, including agricultural ponds and urban retention ponds for stormwater management. Freshwater ponds are defined as open water less than 20 acres and shallow enough for sunlight to

TABLE 10.7 **Improved U.S. Wetlands Loss Trends, 1950s–2004**

Time Period	Net Wetlands Loss	Net Annual Rate of Loss	Types Lost	Causes of Loss
1950s to 1970s	9.1 million acres	458,000 acres/year	Majority of loss freshwater wetlands	Agriculture: 87% Urban development: 8% Other: 5%
Mid-1970s to mid-1980s	2.6 million acres	290,000 acres/year	98% freshwater wetlands	Agriculture: 54% Other: 41% Urban development: 5%
1986 to 1997	644,000 acres	58,500 acres/year	98% freshwater wetlands	Urban and rural development: 51% Agriculture: 26% Silviculture: 23%
1998 to 2004	229,000 loss – 420,000 gain = –191,000 acres	Net gain of 32,000 acres/year	Net gain due to creation of 695,400 acres of ponds	Urban and rural development: 61% Agriculture: 17% increase Silviculture: 8%

Source: Adapted from Dahl 2006; Wright et al. 2006.

reach the bottom. Without the 695,000 acres of ponds created in the 1998–2004 period, wetland gains would have failed to overcome wetland losses. While these ponds have helped manage stormwater, they do not provide the same ecological and environmental functions as natural wetlands. Wright et al. (2006), the Environmental Law Institute (2008), and others also raise concerns about the USFWS NWI methods that exclude ephemeral wetlands (wetlands that are dry for part of the year) and wetlands smaller than 1–3 acres.

Urban and rural development accounted for 89,000 and 51,000 acres of wetland loss, respectively, for a combined 61% of total losses. Most of these losses have come in small increments of less than 5 acres each. Wright et al. (2006) suggest that this calls for a stronger role for local governments to protect wetlands from the impacts of land development.

Land development and agricultural and silvicultural activities damage wetlands in a number of ways. Most damage is caused by physical alterations, like draining, filling, and dredging, but chemical and biological changes also reduce wetland benefits. Box 10.4 describes several ways land use activities can alter wetlands.

BOX 10.4—Methods of Altering Wetlands

Physical Alterations

Filling: Adding any material to change the bottom level of a wetland or to replace the wetland with dry land.

Draining: Removing water from a wetland by ditching, tiling, or pumping.

Excavating or dredging water away: Preventing the flow of water into a wetland by removing water upstream or lowering groundwater tables.

Flooding: Raising water levels either behind dams, by pumping, or otherwise channeling water into a wetland, often done to create livestock watering ponds, irrigation ponds, detention ponds, or water hazards on golf courses.

Fragmenting: Bisecting wetlands with roads that create barriers to the normal flow of water and normal activity of wildlife, also creating a source of mortality for wetland animals migrating from one portion of the wetland to another.

Shading: Placing pile-supported platforms or bridges over wetlands, causing vegetation to die.

Conducting activities in adjacent areas: Disrupting the interconnectedness between wetlands and adjacent land areas, or incidentally impacting wetlands through activities at adjoining sites.

Chemical Alterations

Changing levels of nutrients: Increasing or decreasing levels of nutrients within the local water and/or soil system, forcing changes in the wetland plant community.

Introducing toxins: Adding toxic compounds to a wetland either intentionally (e.g., herbicides and/or pesticides) or unintentionally (e.g., stormwater runoff from nearby roads containing oils, asbestos, heavy metals), which adversely affects wetland communities.

Biological Alterations

Grazing: Consumption and compaction of vegetation by large numbers of domestic livestock.

Disrupting natural populations: Altering the number or abundance of existing species, introducing exotic or domestic species, or otherwise disturbing resident organisms.

Source: Adapted from Somers et al. 2000.

1. Avoid Impact

2. Minimize Impact   Increasing

3. Mitigate or Compensate Unavoidable Impact: Difficulty

    a. Restore Damaged Wetlands   and Cost

    b. Enhance Existing Wetlands

    c. Create New Wetlands

Figure 10.16 A Wetlands Protection and Mitigation Hierarchy.

Wetland Protection, Mitigation, Restoration, and Creation

With growing awareness of the benefits of wetlands, wetlands advocates and environmental agencies have worked to develop policies and strategies to arrest the alteration, conversion, and destruction of wetlands. The progress made is reflected in the declining rate of wetland loss (see Table 10.7). Since 1990, the federal government has had a policy of "no net loss" of wetlands. The Clinton administration wanted to achieve a net gain of 100,000 wetland acres per year by 2005. In 2004, the Bush administration adopted this net gain policy, calling for restoring, improving, and protecting more than 3 million acres over 5 years. But even a net gain policy does not by itself protect existing wetlands; there was a net gain of 191,000 acres of wetlands from 1998 to 2004, but we still lost 229,000 acres.

Figure 10.16 gives a wetlands protection hierarchy. Given the benefits of wetlands, as well as the inconvenience to the landowner posed by permit requirements, costly mitigation, and negative public opinion, the best action is to avoid wetlands impacts altogether. Next, landowners should minimize impacts and mitigate or compensate for unavoidable impact. Figure 10.17 illustrates wetland avoidance and mitigation in a development project (Salveson 1994).

Under the federal CWA section 404 regulatory program, applicants are permitted to mitigate wetlands impacts only after they have taken every effort to avoid and minimize the impact. Mitigation can be accomplished by restoring previously damaged wetlands, enhancing existing wetlands, or creating new wetlands. Lewis (1990) provides these definitions for the three measures:

- **Restoration**: Returning a degraded or former wetland to as close to the preexisting condition as possible.
- **Enhancement**: Increasing one or more of the functions performed by an existing wetland beyond what currently or previously existed. There may be an accompanying decrease in other functions.
- **Creation**: Converting a nonwetland (either dry land or deep water) to a wetland.

The first measure for renewing functions in mitigation is the *passive approach*, or removing the factors causing wetland degradation or loss and letting nature do

Initial Site Plan   Location of Wetlands   Approved Site Plan

Wetlands

Figure 10.17 Initial and Approved Plans for the Village of Thomas Run, Maryland. (*Source: Wetlands: Mitigating and Regulating Development Impacts* by David Salveson, 1994. Reprinted with permission of the Urban Land Institute.)

the work of restoration. However, an *active approach* may be necessary if passive methods are not enough to restore the natural system. Active methods involve direct control of wetland processes when a wetland is severely degraded, or in the case of wetland creation and most enhancements. Wetland creation is the most difficult mitigation measure. Before wetland vegetation will thrive, hydrologic conditions and hydric soils must be established. Wetland enhancement and restoration are easier because wetland hydrologic or soil conditions may be present. Chapter 8 discussed the benefits of created wetlands for runoff and NPS pollution control, but it is very difficult to replicate the full range of benefits provided by natural wetlands (see Box 8.4).

Federal Wetlands Regulation

The principal federal program to protect wetlands is section 404 of the CWA, which regulates the discharge of dredged and fill material into waters of the United States, including wetlands. A section 404 permit must be obtained from the U.S. Army Corps of Engineers (Corps) or a delegated state agency before a discharge into wetlands can occur. A permit will not be issued if it is determined that the nation's waters would be degraded or a practicable alternative exists that is less damaging. In other words, an applicant must show that he or she has (1) taken steps to avoid wetland impacts where practicable; (2) minimized potential impacts to wetlands; and (3) provided compensation for any remaining, unavoidable impacts through activities to restore, enhance, or create wetlands.

The U.S. EPA jointly administers the program with the Corps, and the USFWS, the National Marine Fisheries Service, and state resource agencies play advisory roles. The Corps administers the day-to-day program, including individual permit decisions; develops policy and guidance; and enforces section 404 provisions. The EPA develops and interprets environmental criteria for evaluating permit applications, has the authority to veto the Corps' permit decisions (section 404[c]), identifies activities that are exempt, and reviews and comments on individual permit applications. Section 404(f) exempts some activities from regulation, including many ongoing farming, ranching, and silviculture practices.

A permit review process controls regulated activities, including discharges, filling, land clearing, ditching, and channeling. An *individual permit* is usually required for potentially significant impacts. However, for most discharges that will have only minimal adverse effects, the Corps often grants up-front *general permits*. These may be issued on a nationwide, regional, or state basis for particular categories of activities (e.g., minor road crossings, utility line backfill, and bedding) as a means to expedite the permitting process. These general permits do not require public notice, and the public, state, and federal agencies do not have the opportunity to comment on individual projects. The vast majority of wetland permits are general permits.

The application of section 404 has been controversial. This is not surprising, as it is one of the few federal programs regulating land use. Major issues include definitions of what constitutes a wetland and regulated land use activity under the program, what can be included in "nationwide" permits, regulation of isolated wetlands, and compensation for landowners whose property values are diminished by the regulation. Even though the CWA has not been reauthorized or amended since 1987, continual policy directives and court cases since have tried to clarify the wetlands program.

For example, several cases have argued the extent of the government's regulation of "isolated" wetlands, or those not physically adjacent to navigable surface waters. In the 2001 Solid Waste Agency of Northern Cook County (SWANCC) decision, the U.S. Supreme Court ruled 5–4 that the Corps' denial of a permit for damage to isolated wetlands, solely on the basis of impact on migratory birds exceeded its authority. Although the EPA and the Corps issued an interpretation of the decision allowing some continuation of federal regulation of isolated wetlands, the future of a strong federal role in this area is uncertain. The Natural Resources Defense Council (NRDC) estimates that perhaps 20 million acres of wetlands could go unregulated as a result of the SWANCC decision (Zinn and Copeland 2003).

In 2006, in the Rapanos decision (named for one of two Michigan property owners the Corps sued for filling in infrequently saturated wetlands without a permit), the Supreme Court ruled that the Corps had to establish a "significant connection" between wetlands and "navigable waters" (the operating authority of the CWA) on a case-by-case basis. This has placed uncertainty about federal jurisdiction over isolated, especially intermittent, wetlands and, perhaps more importantly, ephemeral and intermittent streams under other CWA provisions (e.g., water quality standards, NPDES permits; see Chapter 8). As a result of these uncertainties, the responsibility for isolated wetlands and important ephemeral and intermittent stream headwaters may fall to state and local wetland and watershed protection programs.

The Tulloch Rule is another controversial section 404 permit issue. It allows developers to ditch and drain wetlands, as long as that practice does not cause more than an "incidental fallback" of material back into the wetland. In 2001, the Corps tried to close this loophole by requiring section 404 permits for certain ditching, draining, and in-stream mining that cause more than incidental fallback. Still, the ditching under the Tulloch Rule continues in some parts of the country.

There has also been debate about whether to treat all wetlands equally or to classify them based on size, functions, or values, and how these metrics should be considered when determining compensation for wetland loss. In 2001, the Government Accountability Office questioned the in-lieu fee system of compensation, and the National Research Council suggested the no-net-loss goals could not be met without considering wetland function. Several legislative proposals have called for a three-tier system, from highly valuable wetlands that would have the greatest protection to the least valuable wetlands on which alterations would be allowed. In practice, the Corps and the EPA do not use a tiered system, but they provide flexibility in permit implementation based on the wetland, the size of the project, and the degree of impact (Zinn and Copeland 2003).

Wright et al. (2006) summarize seven limitations of the section 404 permitting program:

1. Wetland contributing drainage areas are not protected.
2. Some isolated wetlands may be outside of the program jurisdiction.
3. Some activities are not subject to regulation, such as drainage; removal of vegetation "incidental fallback" activities; and established agricultural, silvicultural, or ranching activities.
4. Most activities authorized by general permits do not have as extensive a review process and may not require any mitigation.
5. Cumulative impacts to wetlands are not addressed due to the permit-by-permit approach, as opposed to a watershed approach.
6. Mitigation is not based on wetland type or function.
7. Lost wetland acreage is often not replaced due to high failure rates of mitigation wetlands or lack of implementation and enforcement.

In addition to the CWA, the federal farm bills have had a major effect on wetlands conversion. In recognition that agriculture has had a dramatic impact on wetlands, the farm bills established the Swampbuster, Wetlands Reserve, and Conservation Reserve programs to use incentives and disincentives to protect and restore wetlands. The Wetlands Reserve Program gives landowners payments for placing permanent easements on farmed wetlands. Agriculture wetland conversion dropped from more than 87% of all conversion in the 1950s and 1960s to 26% during 1986–1997, to a net gain in wetland acres during 1998–2004.

Wetland Mitigation Banking

The restoration, creation, enhancement, and, in some cases, preservation of wetlands (or other aquatic habitats) for the purpose of providing compensatory mitigation *in advance* of wetland damage permitted under the section 404 regulatory program is known as **mitigation banking**. It creates a market-based program for wetland mitigation, including "sellers" and "buyers." There are wetland mitigation banks operating in 31 states (Environmental Law Institute 2008).

Sellers are any group that restores wetlands and "banks" the mitigation credits with the Corps or delegated state agency. Buyers are landowners needing mitigation to get a wetland permit for their land use activity. By creating a "market" for wetland restoration, this program has prompted many civic-minded groups into entrepreneurial wetland restoration, knowing they will be compensated for their efforts. It has also eased the delays and regulatory burden on land developers who can achieve required wetland mitigation simply by buying credits of wetlands already restored.

This program also solves another problem of mitigation: knowing whether promised mitigation will actually work. Without banking, permits are issued based on mitigation plans by landowners, but there is often some question whether the plans will be fully implemented or if the restoration will work. Under mitigation banking, the project has already been completed, so there is more certainty that the restoration will be successful.

The wetland mitigation banking process involves the following five steps:

1. A group or firm identifies degraded wetlands, documents their conditions, and proposes restoration to the permitting agency under the mitigation banking program.
2. The group or firm restores the wetland, using labor and capital.
3. After restoration, the group or firm and the agency document the restoration and assign wetland mitigation credits to the project.
4. When a landowner in the watershed applies for a wetlands permit for a wetland-disturbing activity, the agency will seek evidence that the applicant has attempted to avoid and minimize impacts. If wetland impacts are deemed unavoidable, the applicant seeks to mitigate the impacts by purchasing wetland mitigation credits.
5. The agency decides what appropriate level of mitigation credits the applicant requires, and it requires a fee from the applicant for the credits. The fee is used to compensate the group or firm who conducted the restoration.

Box 10.5 gives an example, the Springbrook Creek Wetland and Habitat Mitigation Bank in Renton, Washington. The Mitigation Bank Instrument, or detailed proposal, identifies specific mitigation activities for the reestablishment, rehabilitation, and enhancement of wetlands and habitats by the City of Renton, to generate 45 mitigation credits to be available to the city and the Washington Department of Transportation for unavoidable impacts from transportation projects.

State Wetland Programs

Although the federal section 404 program gets the most attention, some of the earliest and most effective wetland programs are in the states. The federal wetland program is limited, and state and local programs are needed to "fill in the gaps" to

BOX 10.5—The Springbrook Creek Wetland and Habitat Mitigation Bank

The purpose of the Springbrook Wetland and Habitat Mitigation Bank, located in the city of Renton, King County, Washington, is to provide compensation for unavoidable impacts to wetlands and other aquatic resources caused by Washington State Department of Transportation (WSDOT) highway construction projects and city mitigation requirements within the service area. The Springbrook Bank is expected to generate 45.12 mitigation credits (1 credit compensates for 1 acre of Category II wetland) on the 129.37-acre site through:

- The reestablishment of 17.79 wetland acres (units C, D, E).
- The rehabilitation of 52.14 wetland acres (units A, B, C).

- The enhancement of 32.54 wetland acres (units C, D).
- The enhancement of 7.80 upland acres and 6.55 riparian upland acres adjacent to Springbrook Creek, for a total of 116.82 acres.

The restoration and enhancement activities will reconnect floodplain wetlands with Springbrook Creek, reestablish wetlands, and may improve water quality, hydrologic, floodplain, habitat, and riparian functions in a highly urbanized area. Figure 10.18 shows the mitigation bank units and locations of reestablishment, rehabilitation, and enhancement.

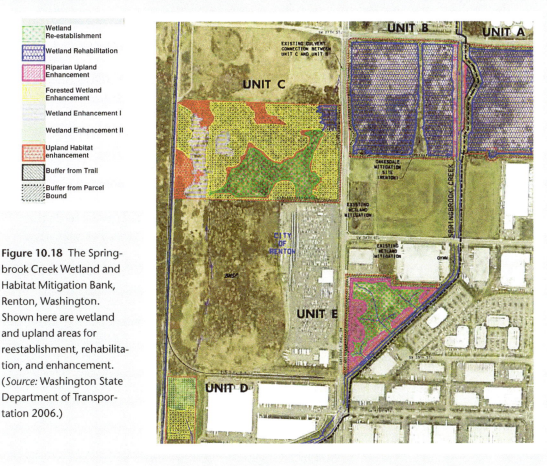

Figure 10.18 The Springbrook Creek Wetland and Habitat Mitigation Bank, Renton, Washington. Shown here are wetland and upland areas for reestablishment, rehabilitation, and enhancement. (*Source:* Washington State Department of Transportation 2006.)

Source: Washington State Department of Transportation 2010.

provide protection for isolated wetlands and ephemeral/intermittent stream head-waters not addressed by federal jurisdiction.

The Environmental Law Institute (ELI 2008) conducted a 50-state assessment of state wetland programs under six areas identified by the EPA as core components of a comprehensive state wetlands program:

1. *Regulation.* Twenty-nine states have adopted regulatory authority to issue section 404 permits, 15 for both tidal and freshwater wetlands and 8 for just tidal wetlands. Six states (Indiana, Ohio, North Carolina, Tennessee, Washington, Wisconsin) regulate activities in geographically isolated wetlands. Wisconsin's 2001 law specifically requires water quality certification for nonnavigable, intrastate, or isolated wetlands not subject to federal regulation due the SWANCC decision.

2. *Water quality standards (WQS).* Including wetlands in surface WQS or developing wetland-specific WQS gives wetlands the same level of protection as other waters under the CWA. Thirteen states have designated uses, criteria, and/or antidegradation policies for wetlands.

3. *Monitoring and assessment.* These are important for evaluating wetlands status and trends, as well as the effectiveness of regulatory and restoration programs. Maine conducts biological monitoring of wetlands as part of its surface water assessments.

4. *Restoration activities through public-private partnerships.* State wetland restoration efforts often rely on partnerships with land conservation groups, landowners, and corporations. The Corporate Wetlands Restoration Partnership operates in many states. It uses corporate contributions and volunteers to support restoration and monitoring projects.

5. *Coordination among state and federal agencies.* Wetlands values cut horizontally across state agencies and vertically to federal and local agencies, so coordination is important to providing effective and efficient wetlands protection. The Minnesota Interagency Wetlands Group, for example, includes state, federal, local, and tribal agencies and meets monthly to coordinate management activities. Twenty-six states have developed Wetland Conservation Plans to develop strategies and improve effectiveness of regulatory and nonregulatory programs. Pennsylvania's Wetlands Net Gain Strategy aims to coordinate all related wetlands programs to achieve a net gain in wetlands acreage.

6. *Education and outreach.* These are important for increasing public awareness about wetland values and functions, and for building political support for wetland program activities.

Local Wetland Programs

Local wetland protection programs are important because local governments are the first line of land use control, and their activities can complement federal and state programs. Most localities with urban forestry, urban wildlife, or riparian protection programs include wetlands. Localities should employ the basic planning

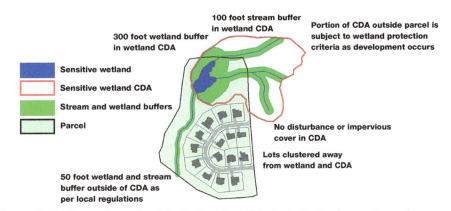

Figure 10.19 Wetland Protection Criteria. Applying WPC directs the development away from the wetland and reduces the need for wetland permits. (*Source:* Strommen et al. 2007. Used with permission of the Center for Watershed Protection.)

process to identify and assess wetlands, develop community objectives for wetland protection/restoration, formulate strategies, and integrate protection/restoration strategies into comprehensive and land use plans.

As part of the Center for Watershed Protection's series on wetlands and watersheds, Strommen et al. (2007) developed a model local ordinance to protect wetland functions. Not surprisingly, they suggest a watershed planning approach. The model is based on three concepts and principles for protecting wetlands:

1. *Identify sensitive wetlands.* A first step is to prioritize which wetlands should be included under the ordinance. Sensitive wetlands have a low tolerance for disturbance and can become degraded with even low-level inputs of urban stormwater. Wetlands that provide a vital community or ecological function (e.g., flood control, protected species habitat) may also be designated as sensitive.
2. *Address wetland contributing drainage areas.* To address indirect impacts from land development and stormwater runoff, the ordinance must apply to all the land that drains to a sensitive wetland through surface flow (and subsurface flow, if known). This regulated area is referred to as the contributing drainage area, or CDA.
3. *Apply wetland protection criteria.* For development projects where some or all of the parcel is located within a sensitive wetland CDA, the ordinance provides performance criteria, termed wetland protection criteria (WPC). The performance criteria intend to reduce indirect impacts to wetlands by locating the development away from the wetlands, providing vegetated buffers, and reducing runoff and pollutants into the wetland through the use of site design, erosion and sediment control, and stormwater management techniques. Figure 10.19 illustrates WPC on a development site and how it can protect the CDA.

Coastal Zone Ecology and Management

Coastal marshes, backbays, and estuaries are the transitional zone between marine and upland ecosystems, and they provide unique conditions for the propagation of fish, shellfish, and wildlife. The diversity of the estuarine environment includes the **marsh and seagrass community** of aquatic, riparian, and land species; the microorganism **plankton community** of both plants (phytoplankton) and animals (zooplankton); the **nekton community** of free-swimming larger species; and the **benthic community** of bottom dwellers. Estuaries play an important role in the life cycle of many species, including shrimp and anadramous fish. Figure 10.20 illustrates unimpacted and impacted temperate seagrass ecosystems. Major threats to important seagrasses are eutrophication, reduced light penetration and algal blooms, physical removal, and invasive species.

The protection of coastal ecology involves protecting both habitat and water quality. Habitat protection requires managing shoreline and marshland activities, including establishing buffer zones between water and development and other intensive human uses. Water quality protection requires the management of development, land uses, and wastewater discharges, not only in the coastal zone but also in the larger watershed draining into the estuary.

Efforts to protect the Chesapeake Bay, for example, illustrate the complexities and the challenges. Initial strategies focused on wastewater discharges into the Bay and its finger estuaries. Attention then turned to land use on its shores, then to uses surrounding the Bay. The comprehensive Chesapeake Bay program now focuses on "tributary strategies," including land uses in all of the basins draining into the Bay (see Chapter 19).

Because of the ecological value of the coastal zone, its management has become a national priority. Although the federal government has largely refrained from regulating private land use, it has recognized the need for coastal zone planning and has provided funds for such activities by state and local governments. The **Coastal Zone Management Act (CZMA)** of 1972 aimed to stimulate land use planning and controls in coastal areas due to the environmental values, natural hazards, and development pressures coincident in these areas. The objectives of the CZMA are to centralize control of development decision making in coastal areas from fragmented local governments to the regional or state level. The program is administered by the Office of Ocean and Coastal Resources Management (OCRM) of the U.S. National Oceanic and Atmospheric Administration (NOAA).

The goals of the CZMA were not to specify how coastal zone lands should be used, but rather to establish state-developed plans, procedures, and institutions through which land use decisions could be made. The program provides two incentives for states to participate voluntarily and develop and implement coastal zone management (CZM) programs. First, under section 306, the CZMA gives grants to the states for program development and operation. Second, once a state program is approved, federal activities must be consistent with the program. In addition, grants are issued to states with approved plans to acquire land to preserve natural areas under the National Estuarine Sanctuary Program and for coastal rehabilitation projects. To qualify for the grants, the state program plans

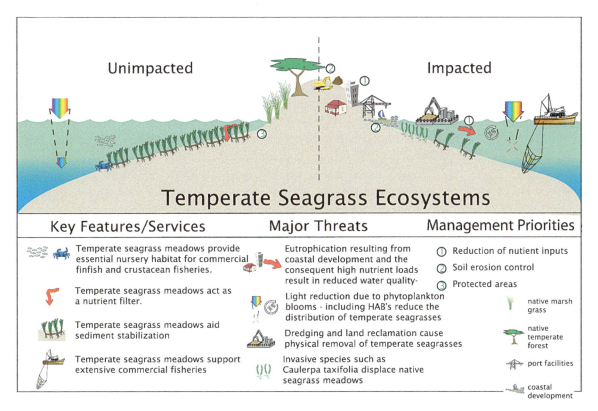

Figure 10.20 Temperate Seagrass Ecosystems: Features, Threats, and Priorities. (*Source:* Integration and Application Network, UMD. http://ian.umces.edu/imagelibrary/displayimage-search-0-790.html.)

must include a number of required items, such as a definition of permissible uses, means by which land and water uses are to be controlled, and an organizational structure for implementation.

In general, CZM planning involves the following process:

1. Delineation of the coastal zone, participating agencies, jurisdictions, and stakeholders.
2. Inventory and analysis of coastal environmental, economic, and social resources.
3. Establishment of management objectives, such as maintaining a high-quality environment, protecting species diversity, conserving critical habitats and ecological processes, controlling pollution, identifying lands for development, protecting against natural hazards, restoring damaged ecosystems, and encouraging participation.
4. Development of integrated strategies by appropriate agencies and stakeholders to achieve objectives, including regulatory programs and nonregulatory programs, such as land trusts, conservation easements, and education.
5. Implementation of strategies and monitoring of progress and effectiveness.

Coastal Zone Management Elements and Measures

The first edition of this book described the results of evaluation studies of the CZM program commissioned by the OCRM in the late 1990s. The three studies focused on protecting beaches, dunes, bluffs, and rocky shores (Bernd-Cohen and Gordon 1998); protecting estuaries and coastal wetlands (Good et al. 1998); and redeveloping urban ports and waterfronts (Goodwin et al. 1997). The studies' results measured progress not only in program implementation, but also of the practice of CZM in the United States. The full discussion from the first edition is posted on the book website (www.envirolanduse.org). The studies identified these key elements of an effective CZM program:

1. For protecting beaches, dunes, bluffs, and rocky shores:
   - Regulation: Coastal setbacks, construction controls, shoreline stabilization, access restrictions, and habitat protection.
   - Planning: Adopted plans and enforceable policies for resources protection, beach nourishment, inlet management, dunes restoration, and so on.
   - Management and acquisition: Inventory of public coastal land holdings, public land management and stewardship, coastal land acquisition.
2. For protecting estuaries and wetlands:
   - Information/research: Wetland inventory, function assessment, monitoring change, mapping.
   - Regulations: Wetland permits, no-net-loss policy, mitigation > 1:1 ratio, evaluation outcomes.
   - Planning: Local land use plans based on state standards for estuary and wetland protection, special area management planning (SAMP), reliable outcome data.
   - Acquisition: Conservation easements for land and wetland protection.
   - Nonregulatory tools: Public and landowner education, wetland restoration to achieve a net gain of wetland area and function.

State programs have continued to improve. Two good examples are innovative development planning, illustrated in Box 10.6, and living shoreline treatment.

Shoreline erosion and loss of emergent vegetation are major problems in the Chesapeake Bay. **Living shoreline treatment (LST)** is a management practice that addresses erosion by providing for long-term protection, restoration, and enhancement of vegetated shoreline habitats. This is achieved by strategic placement of plants, stone, sand fill, and other structural and organic materials. A significant advantage of LSTs is that they do not require structures that sever natural processes and connections between riparian, intertidal, and aquatic areas, such as tidal exchange, sediment movement, plant community transitions, and groundwater flow. Figure 10.22 presents before and after pictures of an LST application and a diagram of the treatment.

BOX 10.6—Alternative Coastal Development Designs

NOAA's Coastal Services Center offers how-to guides on a variety of coastal management issues. The importance of land development impacts and need for innovative land use controls and designs have prompted considerable interest in new practices for conservation subdivisions and New Urbanism designs (see Chapter 16). NOAA's how-to guide on alternative coastal development for three scenarios for a prime coastal Georgia residential site—conventional, conservation, and New Urbanism—is shown in Figure 10.21. As Table 10.8 shows, the conservation and New Urbanist scenarios provide less environmental impact and arguably more livability and developer profit. (For all impacts and assumptions, see http://www.csc.noaa .gov/alternatives/.)

Figure 10.21 NOAA Alternative Coastal Development Scenarios: Conventional, Conservation, New Urbanist. (*Source:* NOAA Coastal Service Center, http://www.csc.noaa.gov/alternatives/.)

TABLE 10.8 Indicators and Impacts for Three Development Scenarios

Design	Maximize	SF/MF Units	% Open	% IC	Docks (ft)	Profit
Conventional	Large waterfront lots, private water access	857/100	15%	26%	43,721	$39 million
Conservation	Environment preservation, cluster development	720/0	71%	14%	1,013	$44 million
New Urbanist	Compact civic-oriented villages, open space	867/100	67%	16%	2,086	$46 million

Source: National Oceanic and Atmospheric Administration 2010.

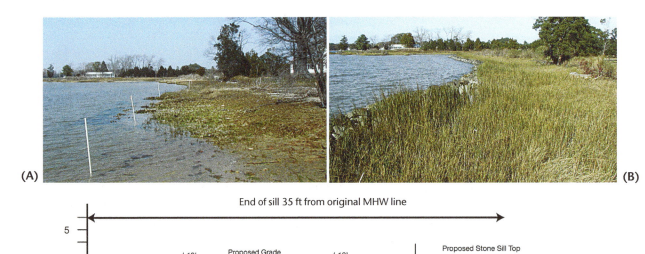

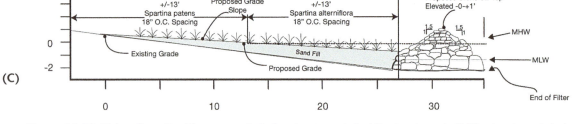

Figure 10.22 Living Shoreline Treatment. A: Before treatment. B: After treatment. C: The treatment design. (*Source:* A, B: Virginia Institute for Marine Science, Center for Coastal Resources Management. C: Maryland Department of the Environment 2008.)

State CZM Programs: The California Coastal Commission

The evaluation studies of the CZM program reviewed state planning and implementation, and provided some examples. Maryland and California were cited for effective programs for protection of wetland and estuarine resources, Washington and Wisconsin were among the exemplary programs for waterfront redevelopment, and California, Oregon, North Carolina, and Maryland were noted for protection of dunes and bluffs. The California program illustrates the breadth of state programs.

The California coastal program was established by public referendum in 1972. The California Coastal Commission (CCC) was modeled after the effective San Francisco Bay Conservation and Development Commission, established by the state legislature in 1965 (see Chapter 18). The CCC oversees the state coastal program, which combines mandatory local planning and permitting, as well as state coastal resource and land acquisition.

The program requires local coastal programs (LCPs) with CCC certification and oversight. Each LCP must identify specific coastal resources, hazard areas, coastal access, use priorities, and significant cumulative development impacts on coastal resources and access; and adopt a land use plan, zoning ordinances, and zoning district maps to reflect the level and pattern of development consistent with the Coastal Act. CCC certification of an LCP results in delegation of coastal development permit authority.

Local Planning and Permitting

There are 126 LCP segments statewide, of which 88 have CCC-certified programs and local permit delegation responsibilities. Certified LCPs vary regarding development of oceanfront property. Some impose rigorous guidelines for any new development and encourage the purchase of remaining undeveloped properties; 24 coastal jurisdictions recognize coastal geologic hazards through designation of special zones, geologic hazard ordinances, or comparable techniques. Regarding blufftop development, some local jurisdictions use predetermined, fixed setbacks that range 10–320 ft. Others employ a cliff retreat rate, usually over a 50-year period. Most communities compromise safe setback considerations in infilling areas. The lack of state guidelines for safe beach-level development has led to some continued development and reconstruction in hazardous locations.

Coastal Land Acquisition

Nearly half (47%) of California's 1,100-mile-long coastline is in public ownership and active public management. The state's Department of Parks and Recreation (DPR) manages more than 375 miles, or 34%, of the ocean shoreline in the state park system. There are 87 bluff-front state parks and 32 rocky shore state parks. The DPR acquisition program for beaches and dunes, through special site-specific legislation and some bond funds, has acquired 26,838 acres of state beaches, 6,000 acres of unclassified beach areas, 27.3 miles of land in five state parks and one state reserve, and 2.8 miles of dunes.

Coastal Zone Restoration

The California State Coastal Conservancy was established in 1976 to award grants to local governments and nonprofit organizations for coastal restoration, coastal resources enhancement projects, resource protection zones, and buffer areas surrounding public beaches, parks, natural areas, and fish and wildlife preserves in the coastal zone. Between 1976 and 2011, 1,800 projects were completed involving access, wetlands protection, trail, recreational pier restoration, and farmlands protection. Between 1976 and 2011, the Conservancy has put more than $1.5 billion to work for coastal zone protection and public access (California State Coastal Conservancy 2011; Good et al. 1998).

Estuarine and Wetland Protection

The San Francisco Bay Conservation and Development Commission (BCDC) preceded and served as a model for the CCC. Wetland loss due to filling has dramatically reversed, from 2,300 acres/year during 1940–1965 (before BCDC), to 20 acres/year during 1965–1986 (post-BCDC and early CZM), to 4 acres/year during 1987–1991 (recent CZM). Mitigation has more than compensated for these losses, with more than 30 acres/year net gain since 1987. The entire Bay is in a high protection zone, and four special area management plans provide for more detailed protection and restoration (Bernd-Cohen and Gordon 1998). (See Chapter 18 for more on the BCDC.)

Summary

This chapter has introduced the principles of landscape and urban ecology and their applications in urban forestry, wetlands protection and enhancement, and coastal management. The field of urban ecology is maturing, thanks to the recent work of Alberti, Marzluff, and others. Urban ecosystems are unique, and as hybrid human and ecological systems, they need to be managed as coupled systems to build resilience to the dynamic change in land cover, hydrology, and habitat typical in urban and metropolitan areas.

Two important resources for effective urban ecosystem management are water and vegetation. (Water was the subject of the preceding three chapters.) Vegetation, especially forest cover, provides significant ecological, environmental, economic, and social benefits in urban areas. But the urban forest canopy has been declining throughout the U.S. over the past four decades. American Forests has done a great service through its Urban Ecosystem Analyses in bringing urban forest canopy decline to light and fostering efforts to reverse these trends.

Urban forestry is a growing field responding to the challenge of managing vegetation and forests in urban environments. Cities throughout the country are developing their programs to protect and enhance existing trees and forests during the land development process and to engage the community in tree planting to increase the declining forest canopy. San Francisco's Urban Forest Map project not only builds a forest and tree inventory, but educates and engages citizens in urban forestry. Guidance developed by the U.S. Forest Service, most recently with the assistance of the Center for Watershed Protection, has helped communities take a systematic approach, and we have relied on that guidance in this chapter.

Riparian forests, wetlands, and coastal areas are critical environmental zones at the land-water interface. By their nature, they are dynamic systems and sensitive to impact, but they provide significant environmental and economic services to communities, by buffering natural hazards, treating pollution, and supporting both terrestrial and aquatic ecosystems. Wetland protection and management have become benchmarks for the environmental movement, and the chapter reviewed the practice of wetland protection and the policy and political dimensions as well. Again, the CWP has provided useful recent guidance (this time for the U.S. EPA) for wetland protection practitioners, linking wetlands to watersheds. There remain limitations in the federal wetland protection program, especially for isolated wetlands and ephemeral and intermittent wetlands and streams, but a few states and localities have filled this gap with their own protection programs. More states need to join in, especially in mountain and western states where most wetlands and streams fit these categories.

The coastal zone overlaps high development pressure (everyone loves the beach) with significant natural hazards from coastal hurricanes and storm surges and with sensitive coastal ecology, the nursery ground for our fisheries. The approach to better management of the coastal zone depends on better regulations to protect sensitive areas, better development design, watershed management of land use and runoff, and restoration of shoreline buffers and dunes and other natural protection mechanisms. Coastal zone management has become more important as development pressure increases and as climate change and its impacts on sea-level rise and extreme coastal weather events become more apparent. Related climate change adaptation and natural hazard mitigation strategies are presented in Chapters 12 and 13.

11 ■ Wildlife Habitats and Urban Biodiversity

During the past four decades, planning for wildlife in the United States has evolved from managing indicator species, usually sport and commercial species, to planning and managing ecosystems and the habitats that support wildlife. Prior to 1970, wildlife was considered secondary to the needs of humans, and impacts on wildlife were one of the costs of progress. Times have changed. With the passage of the Endangered Species Act in 1973, and the advancing environmental movement and policies it spawned, planning for wildlife habitat protection and restoration has emerged not only as an indicator of progress, but a more integral part of land and infrastructure development. It is not just "indicator" wildlife or endangered species that are important, but all forms of wildlife, as they are part of a larger functioning whole—the ecosystem. In the 1990s, **ecosystem management** emerged as the organizing concept for managing wildlife, habitats, and biodiversity on wildlands, and we now see the approach applied to urban and regional environments.

As introduced in Chapter 10, **biodiversity** is defined as the variety of life and all processes that keep life functioning. It is studied at genetic, species, and ecosystem levels. Global efforts to manage biodiversity aim to arrest species extinction and preserve intact natural ecosystems. Local efforts have traditionally focused on wildlands, but the last decade has seen new approaches to biodiversity of working landscapes and urban biodiversity.

This chapter applies the ecological concepts discussed earlier to the management of wildlife and biodiversity. The primary focus is human-modified agricultural and urbanizing landscapes. Special attention is given to wildlife and habitat action planning at the state and local levels, and to habitat conservation planning under the Endangered Species Act.

Wildlife Habitat Fundamentals

A **habitat** is the arrangement of food, water, space, and cover (for protection, hiding, and reproduction) that is required by an individual, a species, or a population. The arrangement determines a limited number of **habitat niches** that animals fill in the ecosystem. Plant communities provide habitat food, water, and cover; therefore, the *plant community type* is used to define the type of habitat. *Habitat types* are defined by plant associations (e.g., woodland, wetland, meadow, pond) and dominant plant species (e.g., pine, oak-hickory).

Although a plant community type is a unique combination of plants that occur in an area, the community is usually defined by the dominant single species of the climax community, even though several community types may exist at that time. The plant community during succession from bare ground to the climax vegetation passes through various **successional stages**, each of which may have different community types and thus different habitats. Figure 11.1 shows forest successional stages and their effect on habitat attributes.

Edges are produced where different plant communities or successional stages come together. **Ecotones** are formed where these different communities and stages overlap or intersperse. Edges and ecotones exhibit attributes of different communities and thus can provide greater plant diversity, more habitat niches, and greater habitat richness (or a greater number of wildlife species residing in an area). Figure 11.2 illustrates a gradual edge and explains the edge effect: Wildlife adapted to plant community A are likely to spill over to ecotone C, where A's influence extends into community B; likewise, the wildlife of community B will likely spill over into ecotone D. In addition, there may be species particularly adapted to the combined ecotone E. Therefore, the edge and overlap can support a greater range and richness of species.

Habitat Variable	Successional Stage (see figure)					
	1-GF	2-SS	3-PS	4-Y	5-M	6-OG
Plant diversity	••	•••••	•••	•	••	•••
Vegetation height		•	••	•••	••••	•••••
Canopy volume		•	••	•••	•••••	••••
Canopy closure	•	••	••••	••••	••••	•••
Structural diversity	•	••••	•	•	••	•••••
Forage potential	•••••	•••	•	•	••	•••
Browse potential	•	•••••	•	•	••	•••
Animal diversity	•••	••••	•	••	•••••	••••

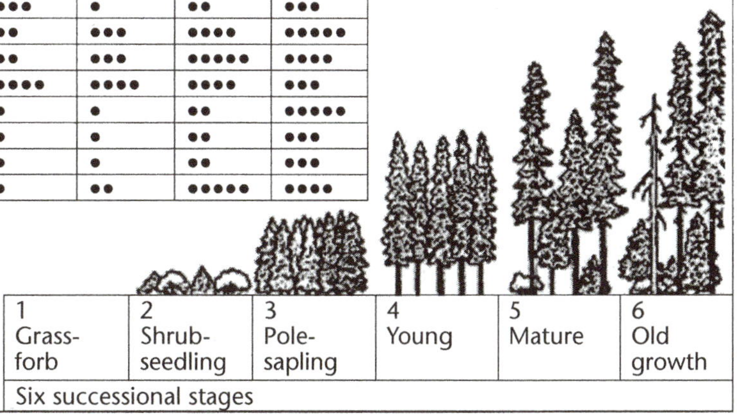

1 Grass-forb	2 Shrub-seedling	3 Pole-sapling	4 Young	5 Mature	6 Old growth

Six successional stages

Figure 11.1 Forest Successional Stages and Their Relationship to Habitat Variables.

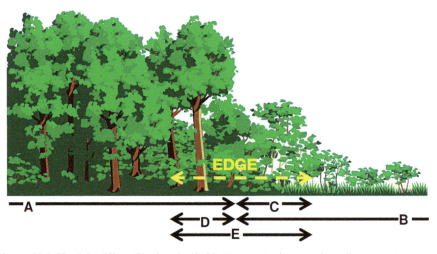

Figure 11.2 The Edge Effect. Overlapping habitat types at edges produce diverse ecotones.

Although edges can enhance diversity, wildlife need **core habitat** (also called interior habitat) for sufficient protected space and cover. Reduction and fragmentation of core habitat has the greatest impact on urban wildlife. Core habitat, edge buffers, and corridors connecting cores are essential habitat elements in agricultural and urbanizing areas. Water is a key for habitat vitality and richness not only as a primary need of wildlife, but also for the unique vegetative types, increased edges, and special habitats that occur near water bodies. This **riparian habitat** zone also provides distinct microclimates and migratory corridors for wildlife.

The shelter and reproductive requirements of wildlife are enhanced by the presence of potential **nesting and den areas**. In terrestrial habitats, dead standing trees (snags), dead and downed logs in various stages of decay, cliffs, caves or talus, and broken rocks at the base of steep slopes provide these habitat elements. In aquatic habitats, pools, underwater live and dead vegetation, and spawning gravels are important elements.

Wildlife studies in agricultural and urban landscapes show that perhaps the major landscape change impacting the viability of wildlife is **habitat fragmentation**, the incremental conversion of natural areas to other uses, reducing and isolating core habitats. Landscape ecology principles have proven useful in efforts to understand and respond to these impacts. Recall from Chapter 10 that landscape ecology views the landscape as a **matrix**, the dominant land use; **patches**, isolated vegetative types or habitats; **corridors**, natural or induced linear areas that link patches; and **mosaic** (also called structure), the overall collection of patches and corridors in the landscape. Figure 11.3 shows agricultural and urban matrixes.

Patches need to be large enough to provide core habitat. For many species, interior habitat begins to develop about 150 ft from the patch edge. Habitat fragmentation reduces the capacity of a landscape to support healthy wildlife populations by diminishing original habitat, reducing patch size, increasing edge, increasing isolation of patches, and modifying natural changes or disturbances (e.g., fire sup-

Figure 11.3 Landscape Elements. Left: Agricultural matrix. Right: Urban matrix. (*Source:* FISRWG 1998.)

pression). Individual effects such as these may be small, but they are cumulative over time and can easily add up to major impacts (USDA, NRCS 1999).

Connectivity becomes a critical issue when movements across landscapes become constricted by fragmentation. Species need connectivity for access to resources in their home range, seasonal migration, immigration and emigration within metapopulations, gene flow to facilitate evolution as the environment changes, recolonization after local extinction, population movement in response to disasters or changing climate, ecological processes such as disturbance, predator-prey interactions, and seed dispersal. In unaltered landscapes, natural species movements and ecological pathways provide connectivity. When wildland is fragmented by land conversion to development, transportation systems, or agriculture, habitats lose their capacity to provide ecological pathways.

In response to problems of habitat fragmentation, landscape ecologists and wildlife managers have recognized the need to provide sufficient undisturbed core reserve habitats, to buffer them from human-disturbed land, and to connect them, as Figure 11.4 shows. The **core reserve** is the key element, providing

Figure 11.4 Habitat Core, Buffers, and Corridors. (*Source:* USDA, NRCS 1999.)

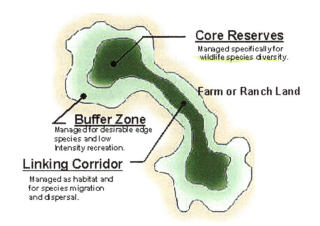

Core Reserves
Managed specifically for wildlife species diversity.

Farm or Ranch Land

Buffer Zone
Managed for desirable edge species and low intensity recreation.

Linking Corridor
Managed as habitat and for species migration and dispersal.

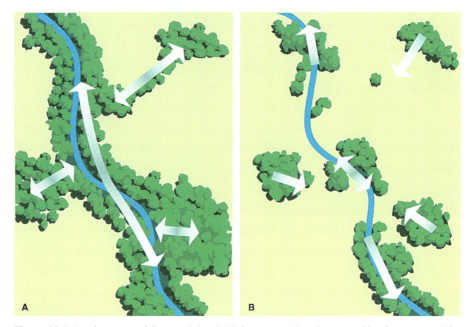

Figure 11.5 Landscapes and Connectivity. A: High connectivity: Connected landscapes provide enhanced ecological functions. B: Low connectivity: Fragmented landscapes are less successful. (*Source:* FISRWG 1998.)

essential space and cover for wildlife. But the effectiveness of core reserves is reduced if they are encroached on or isolated by agriculture or development. Patches need to be large enough to provide interior or core habitat. **Buffers** gradually change habitat conditions from the core reserve to surrounding land use. **Corridors** provide secure habitat conditions for wildlife migration from one core reserve to another. Figure 11.5 illustrates landscapes with high and low levels of connectivity.

Figure 11.6 shows several landscape planning principles for managing habitat. These principles apply to both urbanizing and agricultural landscapes. Patches need to be as large as possible, connected, unified, redundant, and near to one another. Corridors should be continuous, as wide as possible, redundant, and reflective of natural and historic conditions. Landscape structure needs to be horizontally and vertically diverse and must incorporate native vegetation; the matrix other than patches and corridors also needs to be managed with wildlife in mind (USDA, NRCS 1999).

Scott and Allen (undated) argue that effective corridors must provide "functional connectivity." This includes not only opportunities for movement, but also the contribution to (1) population parameters (e.g., growth rate, demographics, genetic structure) and (2) ecological processes (e.g., flows of water and nutrients, trophic/species interactions, recovery from disturbance). Corridor needs are species-dependent. Remnant or remaining natural corridors are more effective at providing these functions than introduced corridors.

PATCHES

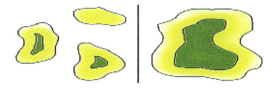

A: Large reserves/patches are better than small reserve/patches.

B: Connected reserves/patches are better than separated reserves/patches.

CORRIDORS

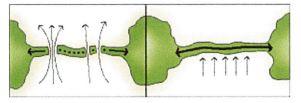

C: Continuous corridors are better than fragmented corridors.

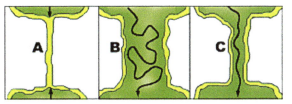

D: Wider corridors are better than narrow corridors.

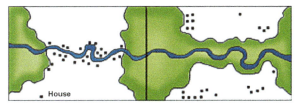

E: Natural connectivity should be maintained or restored.

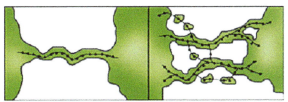

F: Two or more corridor connections between patches (redundancy) are better than one.

STRUCTURE

Vertical Structure

G: Structurally diverse corridors and patches are better than simple structures.

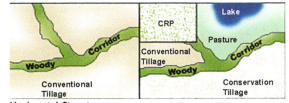

Horizontal Structure

H: Native plants are better than introduced plants.

Figure 11.6 Wildlife Planning Principles for Patches, Corridors, and Structure. (*Source:* USDA, NRCS 1999.)

Functional Connectivity and Habitat Restoration

Although these basic principles are very useful in assessing habitat change and planning for protection and restoration, providing effective habitats in a complex ecosystem is not quite as straightforward. Planners and wildlife specialists may be quick to include patches and corridors, but they rarely assess whether these linkages are optimal or even sufficient for all species, much less for the ecosystem processes needed to sustain them. All corridors are not the same. Some species require more corridor than others. Rather than define wildlife movement by corridors, it may be more prudent to define it by (1) the forces and motivation creating a species' need to move, (2) the possible avenues of movement, and (3) the target or destination of movement. There are cases where the combination of motivation and target overwhelms the obstacles of a pathway, just as there may be cases where a lack of motivation keeps wildlife out of suitable corridors (Scott and Allen, undated).

Scott and Allen (undated) describe many factors that can impede movement and functional connectivity even when corridors exist:

1. Intrinsic characteristics of the corridor (e.g., corridor habitat is inadequate or too heterogeneous to provide unbroken pathways).
2. Diversity of species using corridors (most corridors are justified by large mammal movement, even though fragmentation is more devastating for smaller species and plants).
3. Fragmentation, which alters patterns of ecosystem dynamics.
4. Altered patterns of movement (corridors replace unbroken regions, and thus may alter movement and adversely impact viability).
5. Inadequate corridor width (width is important but does not determine functions).
6. Reliance on introduced rather than remnant corridors.

These factors should be considered in habitat restoration undertaken in response to habitat damage. Most wildlife restoration efforts are *passive approaches*, meaning that habitat is re-created or restored to enhance the natural capacity of wildlife populations to grow and colonize unoccupied areas. Restoration is often done as mitigation for destroyed habitat in an exchange of acres gained for acres lost. *Active approaches* to wildlife restoration involve the manipulation of wildlife movement and demography. Passive approaches are less costly, but they rely on the premise that wildlife will migrate to new habitat conditions ("build it and they will come"). However, this may not always be the case, and habitat restoration is an uncertain means for recovering wildlife populations (Scott et al. 2001).

Passive wildlife restoration assumes that animals (and therefore other populations) will flow down a gradient of density from surrounding habitats onto restoration sites. This is based on island biogeography theory (MacArthur and Wilson 1967) and habitat patches (Diamond 1975; Forman and Godron 1986), which consider patches like islands in a hostile sea of human-dominated landscapes

(Scott et al. 2001). Distance, connectivity, and island or patch size will determine migration. Impediments to movement occur at the landscape scale (the mosaic of patches of varying size, age class, and plant species) and the species scale (motivation, movement needs).

Habitat restoration must be planned to maximize the potential for colonization in challenged landscapes. The probability of restoration site colonization depends on the site's proximity to the target species' geographic distribution, the size of the site relative to the species' needs, the level of patch isolation, and the social or behavioral characteristics of the species. Although evaluating the colonization potential of a target species is difficult, evaluating ecosystem restoration is far more complex. It requires a regional perspective and the careful coordination of restoration projects (Scott et al. 2001).

Another critical issue in habitat restoration is **invasive species**, also referred to as exotic species. These species, especially plants, destroy more habitat each year in the United States than urban growth. The U.S. Fish and Wildlife Service (USFWS) estimates that 4,600 acres of habitat are lost *each day* to invasive species. Removing and managing these invaders is a major component of restoration work (Interagency Workgroup on Wetland Restoration 2002).

Habitat Inventories and Evaluation

An important part of planning for wildlife and biodiversity is the inventory and evaluation of habitats. These range from simple to very complex studies, depending on needs and resources. Habitat assessment and evaluation are useful for management planning, impact assessment, and mitigation. They can compare the habitat value at different locations at the same point in time (e.g., today) or at the same location at different times (e.g., 5 years ago and today). Generally, evaluation procedures are based on two principles: (1) the habitat has a **carrying capacity** to support wildlife populations, and (2) the **suitability** of a habitat for a species can be based on its vegetative, physical, and chemical conditions. Assessment techniques include simple wildlife inventories, GAP analysis, the qualitative species-habitat matrix, indicator species studies, and diversity and habitat indices. More detailed ecological studies are necessary for habitat conservation plans (discussed below).

Habitat inventories can be very useful at a variety of planning scales. They can be used to "red flag" areas of concern to be considered in land use and development. The inventories identify species and groups of organisms, and special natural areas, and display the information on a series of maps, in which symbols and numbers represent species, habitats, and habitat use.

GAP analysis is a "coarse-filter" assessment of the conservation status and potential for species in a region or watershed. It is based on vegetation communities, but also considers land ownership and management practices. The analysis produces a species richness map, which highlights areas with high biodiversity potential, and a GAP map, which compares this potential with existing conservation management practices, showing a "gap" in the protection of wildlife. GAP 1 is highly protected; GAP 4 is not protected. Box 11.1 gives a procedure for GAP analysis, and Figure 11.7 shows a GAP analysis for the Sonoran Desert Ecoregion.

BOX 11.1—The GAP Analysis Process

Species Richness Map

1. Determine those species that occur in the region that are of concern or interest.
2. Collect and compile habitat relationship and occurrence data for those species.
3. Create a map of where the habitats occur in the region based on existing vegetation.
4. Overlay the wildlife habitat data with the habitat map to determine areas of rich species diversity.

GAP Map (see Figure 11.7)

1. Prepare a general land ownership map that classifies lands into public and private ownership.
2. Assign a management status of 1 to areas that are managed for wildlife, such as wildlife refuges and Nature Conservancy lands.

3. Assign a management status of 2 to areas that are managed for natural conditions, such as U.S. Fish and Wildlife Service (USFWS) refuges managed for recreational uses and Bureau of Land Management (BLM) areas of critical environmental concern.
4. Assign a management status of 3 to areas that are prevented from being permanently developed, including most BLM and USFWS lands.
5. Assign a management status of 4 to private and public lands not managed for natural conditions.
6. Overlay this map with the habitat relationship data to determine habitats that are offered the least protection in the region, with status 1 lands providing the highest protection.

Source: USDA, NRCS 1999.

Habitat evaluation procedures generally use an indicator species or a habitat or diversity index

Focal (Multi-) Species

An **indicator** or **umbrella species** is an organism whose presence or absence, population density or dispersion, or reproductive success can indicate habitat conditions that are too difficult to measure for other species (FISRWG 1998). Indicator species are used to signal the effects of contamination, population trends, and habitat quality. The assumption is that if the habitat is suitable for the indicator species, it is suitable for others.

However, each species is different in its habitat needs and habitat niche, so the effectiveness of indicator species to fully represent a wide range of species and habitats is limited. If an indicator species is used, care should be taken so that:

- It is sensitive to and responds directly to changes in environmental attributes of concern, such as water quality or habitat fragmentation. For example, high-profile game species (e.g., bear or elk) are usually not good indicators of habitat quality, because their populations are affected by hunting mortality, which can mask environmental effects.
- It has a larger home range and population density than other species to ease measurement. For example, rare and endangered species have special importance, but they are not good indicators because they are difficult and expensive to measure.

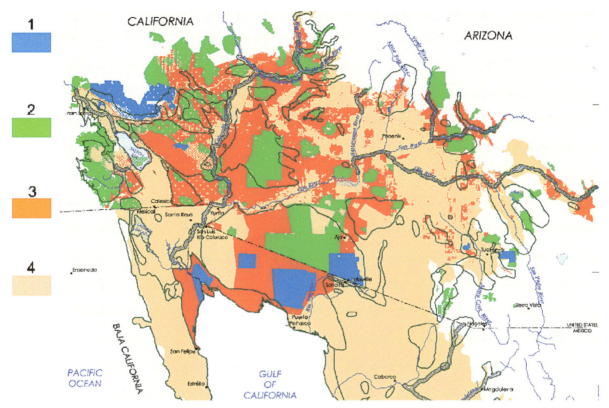

Figure 11.7 GAP Analysis, Sonoran Desert Ecoregion. Conservation sites and GAP status codes (1–4) are shown (1=highly protected, 4=not protected). (*Source:* Rob Marshall, The Nature Conservancy, 1999. Used with permission.)

Because of the limitations of a single indicator species approach, conservation biologists have argued for using a multi-, **focal species** approach, which uses a suite of species, each of which can indicate different landscape attributes necessary for ecosystem health. Providing for the needs of these focal species can therefore provide for the needs of the ecosystem (Lambeck, 1997).

Diversity Indices

Biological diversity measures species abundance and variety in an area. It is measured at different levels of complexity depending on the objectives of the study: genetic, population/species, community/ecosystem, and landscape, the last three being most appropriate for environmental planning (Noss and Cooperrider 1994). In addition to overall diversity, studies often focus on subsets of habitats, such as native species, rare species, habitat guilds (species having common habitats, like cave dwellers), or taxonomic groups (e.g., amphibians, breeding birds) (FISRWG 1998).

Diversity is usually measured at a defined scale: a single community (*alpha diversity*), across community boundaries (*beta diversity*), or in large areas with many communities (*gamma diversity*). While planning for alpha diversity may increase localized diversity, Noss and Harris (1986) suggest that this may create a less diverse regional or gamma diversity. They recommend that diversity studies and wildlife habitat plans have a landscape context even when focusing on a specific community.

Richness indices are the most widely used diversity measures. They measure the number of species or the number of species divided by the overall population. **Abundance measures** account for the evenness of species distribution. Other measures are based on **proportional abundance** and combine richness and evenness. Applying diversity indices to species subsets can enhance their effectiveness. For example, Pielou (1975) suggests three indices for terrestrial ecosystems: plant diversity, habitat diversity, and local rarity.

The Habitat Suitability Index

The **habitat suitability index (HSI)** is a species-specific measure of suitability based on a habitat's vegetative, physical, and chemical characteristics, ranging from 0 (unsuitable) to 1 (optimum habitat). HSI models have been developed for different species by the USFWS. A basic unit is the habitat unit (HU), which integrates habitat quantity and quality. It is defined as

$$HU = Area \times HSI$$

where HU is the number of habitat units (in units of area) and area is the extent of the habitat.

Habitat evaluation can assess changes in HUs over time, or in response to some negative action, such as a land development proposal, or a positive action, like a habitat restoration project (FISRWG 1998).

Rural Habitat Inventories and Conservation Corridor Planning

The first edition of this book contained additional material on habitat inventories and a section on conservation corridor planning. Those materials are posted on the book website (www.envirolanduse.org).

State Wildlife Action Planning

In 2000, Congress enacted the State Wildlife Grants Program to encourage and support state programs that broadly benefit wildlife and habitats, and particularly species of greatest conservation need. To receive funding under this program, state wildlife agencies had to prepare and submit a comprehensive wildlife conservation plan or Wildlife Action Plan to the USFWS in 2005. For fiscal year 2011, federal funding for states to implement their plans increased significantly, to $76.5 million.

The Wildlife Action Plan includes eight elements:

1. *Wildlife:* Information on the distribution and abundance of wildlife, including low and declining populations, that describes the diversity and health of the state's wildlife.

2. *Habitats:* Descriptions of locations and relative conditions of habitats essential to species in need of conservation.
3. *Problems:* Descriptions of problems that may adversely affect species or their habitats, and priority research and survey efforts.
4. *Conservation actions:* Descriptions of conservation actions proposed to conserve the identified species and habitats.
5. *Monitoring:* Plans for monitoring species and habitats, as well as plans for monitoring the effectiveness of the conservation actions and for adapting them in response to new information.
6. *Review:* Descriptions of procedures to review the plan at intervals not to exceed 10 years.
7. *Coordination:* Coordination with federal, state, and local agencies and Indian tribes in developing and implementing the wildlife action plan.
8. *Public participation:* Broad public participation in developing and implementing the wildlife action plan.

(For information on each state plan, see the USFWS or the Association of Fish & Wildlife Agencies websites: http://wsfrprograms.fws.gov/subpages/grantprograms/SWG/SWG.htm and http://www.wildlifeactionplans.org/.)

The California Essential Habitat Connectivity Project

California has long been engaged in wildlife planning because of its diverse ecosystems and environmental awareness and high development growth pressures on habitats. The California Department of Fish & Game (CDFG) developed a state wildlife action plan in 2006 and a missing linkages study in 2001 recognizing the importance of wildlife corridors. In 2007, a new law (SB 85) called for new vegetation and wildlife habitat mapping standards; in 2008, another law (AB 2785) required a state map of essential wildlife corridors. In addition, a 2005 federal transportation bill mandated greater consideration of wildlife movement in transportation planning for both environmental and safety reasons.

Responding to these directives, the **California Essential Habitat Connectivity Project (CEHCP)** was completed in February 2010 (Spencer et al. 2010). It includes the statewide and regional wildlife connectivity map, an assessment of identified connectivity areas, and a strategic plan to supplement and interpret the map. Expanding on previous wildlife plans and studies, the project aimed to be transparent and scientifically defensible. Its goals include promoting the integration of wildlife needs in infrastructure and conservation planning at a statewide scale, and providing methodology for connectivity analysis at a finer scale.

The map and strategic plan are conservation and transportation planning tools, and are not intended for land use regulation. They are for broad-scale (e.g., 10,000-acre) assessment, but not for fine-scale identification of every habitat and small reserve. Essential "blobs" and "sticks" to connect them are indicated, but these are not the only lands of importance. Although basic connectivity is represented, the map and plan do not reveal solutions for providing linkages.

The CEHCP is a multidisciplinary, multiagency project involving the following steps:

1. *Define the analysis area*. This includes the state with an additional buffer.

2. *Define the areas to be connected*. These natural landscape blocks (NLB) or "blobs" are areas of high ecological integrity, initially 6,000-acre minimum. Using available datasets at 100-m resolution, GIS models used land conversion, residential housing, road effects, forest structure, and other factors to delineate 850 NLBs of 2,000–3.7 million acres.

3. *Define essential connectivity areas (ECAs)*. These are "sticks" to connect the blobs. GIS models used a least-cost corridor method of connecting the centroid of wildland blocks using rule sets based on nearest neighbor and network analysis. "Cost" or resistance to movement was determined by adding a 0–20 scale factor based on the land's ecological integrity (from 0 for natural areas to 10–15 for agricultural to 20 for high-density development and roads) and a 0–5 scale factor based on future protection (0 for GAP1 lands, such as protected wilderness areas, to 2 for conservation easements to 4 for no protection). Buffered river corridors were added if not already included. The analysis identified 193 linkage polygons and 31 potential "interstate sticks" to coordinate with neighboring states.

4. *Produce the CEHCP statewide and regional maps*. Figure 11.8 shows the statewide map and, as an inset, an example of a regional map, the Sonoran Desert Ecoregion in southeast California (compare to the GAP analysis of the ecoregion in Figure 11.7). Note the green NLBs, the yellow ECAs, the blue buffered river corridors, and the red lines depicting potential interstate connections.

5. *Compare the map to previous conservation studies*. Point out close correlations and contradictions.

6. *Develop a strategic plan*. The plan must provide a methodology and framework for using the map in statewide, regional, and local-scale analyses; road mitigation; and integration with conservation and infrastructure planning. These activities include statewide transportation and water and sewer planning, wildlife action, land acquisition, and climate change adaptation plans. (Connectivity is a primary strategy for accommodating shifts in species ranges in response to climate change.) Additional activities are regional and local habitat conservation planning and land use, growth management, and infrastructure planning.

The major barrier to terrestrial wildlife connectivity is, of course, roads and highways. Of the 850 NLBs, 744 neighboring NLBs need conserved or enhanced connectivity. Of those, 552 are separated by roads, with no sign of fragmentation by urban or intensive agricultural land use. Of the 192 ECAs, 66% are crossed by major roads and 92% by secondary roads. The study identified 552 "road mitigation sticks" to enhance connectivity. The best way to provide connectivity is for roads to avoid ECAs, but when this is not possible and for existing crossings, mitigation is needed. Mitigation is generally provided by wildlife road crossings using overpasses, underpasses, bridges, and culverts. Figure 11.9 shows a bridge design

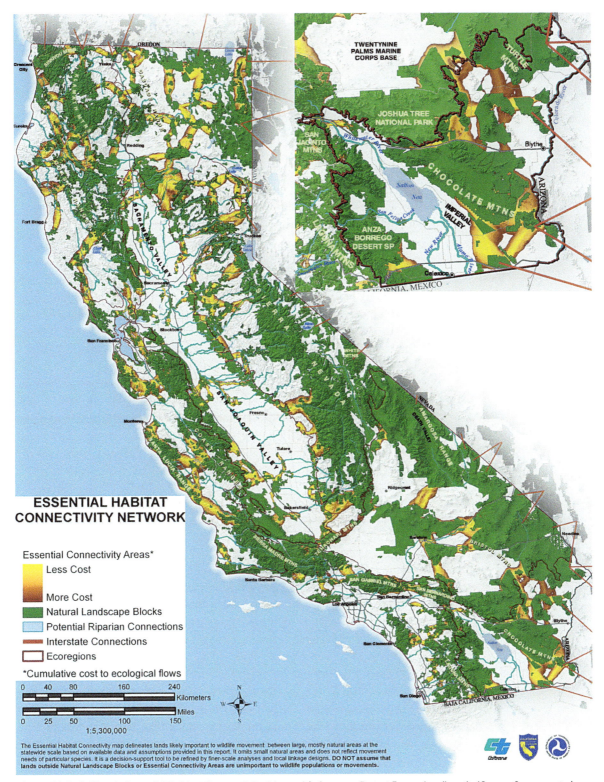

Figure 11.8 California Essential Habitat Connectivity Map, with Sonoran Desert Ecoregion (inset). (*Source:* Spencer et al. 2010.)

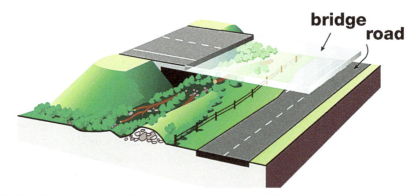

Figure 11.9 A Bridge Underpass. This design accommodates wildlife connectivity as well as vehicles. (*Source:* FISRWG 1998.)

with sufficient underpass for wildlife movement, but wildlife-specific underpasses and overpasses are sometimes used. Arizona is constructing five new wildlife overpasses for large mammals, especially bighorn sheep. For more information, see the *Wildlife Crossings Guidance Manual* (Meese et al. 2009) and the Wildlife and Roads website of the Transportation Research Board (http://www.wildlifeand roads.org/).

The vision provided by the CEHCP map is a statewide ecosystem, incorporating large core habitat reserves with effective connectivity. This outcome can be achieved only by a commitment to integrating the vision in statewide, regional, and local planning for conservation, land use, and infrastructure, especially roads. The project's strategic plan details opportunities for this integration, and we discuss its recommended process for local wildlife connectivity planning next.

Urban Biodiversity and Wildlife Management

Increasing interest in urban wildlife issues developed in the late 1970s and 1980s, as people began to appreciate the environment, and the presence of wildlife was a kind reminder of their connection to nature. In addition, it became increasingly apparent that certain synanthropic species adapted quite well to the urban environment, and there was a need to not only attract but also manage wildlife populations (Adams and Dove 1989; Leedy et al. 1978).

More recently this interest in urban wildlife has broadened to encompass **urban biodiversity**. This apparent oxymoron has come into vogue for two reasons. First, studies have shown urban areas often contain more biological diversity than their surrounding farmland; and second, remaining natural areas in cities provide not only habitat for many species but also treasures for a human populace that increasingly values natural surroundings. Although the context for urban biodiversity is different from wildland and rural biodiversity, many of the same principles and approaches apply. However, the successful protection and restoration of urban biodiversity, and the benefits they accrue for both people and wildlife, depend on the integration of biodiversity objectives with other compatible programs for environmental management, recreation, and natural hazard mitigation.

Urban and Regional Wildlife Planning

The main challenge of urban wildlife planning is satisfying habitat requirements, especially for species of wildlife not well adapted to urban environments. The basic needs of wildlife—food, water, cover, and space for breeding and group territories—are all constrained in urban areas. Although natural areas and habitats exist in urban locations—including parks and open spaces, fringe area woodlands and fields, and wetlands, lakes, and streams—they often lack the size of essential core reserves and are highly fragmented by urban roads and land development.

Urban wildlife habitat planning and management focus on providing core habitat as patches in the urban matrix, buffers between core habitat and urban uses, and connecting corridors. Edge habitats benefit only certain species (e.g., opossums, raccoons, skunks, cowbirds, red-tailed hawks, white-tailed deer, and northern cardinals), often at the expense of interior habitat species. Most wildlife species inhabiting edges are considered habitat generalists. Interior core habitat is generally unaffected by its edge and is necessary for certain interior species, like bobcats, wood thrushes, bobolinks, and ovenbirds (Barnes 1999).

Scale is an important factor in providing core habitat. Landscapes of less than 250 acres support only a limited set of species and may not be large enough to include a diversity of habitat patches. Smaller animals may thrive, but medium-sized animals are compromised, and large animals are usually rare or transient. A landscape of interconnected patches of 250–12,000 acres begins to be large enough to support populations of medium-size animals, such as coyotes, bobcats, and hawks. At this size, the region may encompass the variety of habitats these animals need to live and reproduce. Landscapes greater than 12,000 acres begin to protect ecosystem integrity and function. These large areas may be included in a large regional park or wildlife preserve that is part of a metropolitan wildlife plan.

Common Failings in Designing Connectivity Corridors

As discussed earlier, connectivity is critical for wildlife in fragmented landscapes like urban areas. Wildlife planners have learned to focus on corridors, but these efforts have a number of common failings:

- A homogenous corridor is assumed to provide connectivity for a heterogeneous array of species and ecosystem functions.
- A corridor transects a highly heterogeneous landscape in a manner that may restrict use, often because pathways are blocked by unsuitable habitats.
- The level of habitat degradation affects the capacity of a corridor to support species movement.
- The width or length of corridors fails to provide unimpeded pathways for movement.

- The degree of permeability across the landscape matrix approaches the permeability of a wildlife corridor.
- Limited funds and time demand that each land acquisition has the maximum functional significance to populations and ecosystems, and corridors are judged in isolation (USDA, NRCS 1999).

Reducing the Impacts of Urban Development on Wildlife

An urban wildlife conservation program begins by *minimizing negative habitat impacts* from development and continues by *providing permanent protection* of important habitat core patches, buffer areas, and corridors. Several methods of development practice designed to reduce or mitigate environmental and natural hazard impacts (e.g., stormwater, soil erosion, landslides, flooding, nonpoint source pollution, tree canopy) are very compatible with habitat mitigation. For example, cluster development groups structures on portions of the site most favorable to building, while leaving the remainder preserved as open space. This practice can both preserve habitat and reduce other environmental impacts. Here are some guidelines for urban development approaches that are sensitive to wildlife.

- Before development, maximize open space and protect the most valuable wildlife habitat by placing buildings on less important portions of the site.
- Design stormwater controls, such as bioretention and constructed wetlands, to benefit wildlife.
- Retain and plant native plants that have value for wildlife as well as aesthetic appeal.
- Provide habitat-enhancing elements like bird-feeding stations and nest boxes for cavity-nesting birds.
- Educate residents about wildlife conservation and provide opportunities for wildlife observation, such as a nature trail through open space (Barnes 1999).

Reducing impacts is not, by itself, sufficient because project-by-project development can incrementally consume and isolate core habitats. Fragmentation can only be arrested by more proactive wildlife planning on a landscape scale, requiring permanent habitat and corridor protection through land acquisition, conservation easements, habitat restoration, and other means.

Local and Regional Planning for Wildlife Connectivity: Local Linkage Design

The California Essential Habitat Connectivity Project discussed above outlines a process for local and regional wildlife planning. It focuses on designing local linkages for focal species between natural landscape blocks or core habitat reserves. The emphasis on focal species is intended to tailor the process to local wildlife needs. The process has the following steps:

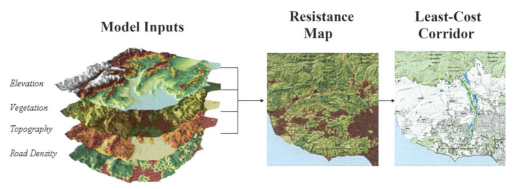

Figure 11.10 A GIS Connectivity Model. This model is used to identify and compute the cost (resistance) to species movement and the least-cost corridor. (*Source:* Spencer et al. 2010.)

1. *Delineate natural landscape blocks.* Connectivity is meaningful only with reference to the areas to be connected. Stakeholders and wildlife experts should help select NLBs that have high ecological integrity, are protected areas, and/or are designed on existing biodiversity maps.

2. *Engage stakeholders.* The implementers (e.g., land management and infrastructure agencies, conservation groups) and local wildlife experts need to be involved from the start. Workshops are a good mechanism to engage them (see Chapter 4).

3. *Select focal species.* Focal species should be selected by stakeholders and represent a diversity of habitat requirements and movement needs.
    a. Selected species may be area-sensitive (requiring a large home range), barrier-sensitive, less mobile, habitat specialists, or ecological indicators.
    b. For each focal species, calculate habitat suitability as a function of GIS pixel attributes (e.g., distance to road, topography, vegetation).
    c. Map patches of breeding habitats.
    d. Develop a resistance map based on the inverse of habitat suitability if wildlife movement data are not available.
    e. Select patches within NLBs as end points and calculate cost-weighted distance from each terminus (Figure 11.10).

4. *Map corridors for focal species.* Conduct least-cost corridor analysis for each focal species to identify one or several swaths of habitat that support movement and gene flow of all species.

5. *Consider climate change.* Add additional swaths of habitat to increase the utility of the linkage under unknown future climate, which is likely to cause range shifts by plants and animals and reassembly of biotic communities. Enhancing connectivity is an essential adaptation strategy.

6. *Evaluate and refine the preliminary linkage design.* The most permeable landscape identified in the previous two steps may not be very permeable for some species. Planners should analyze the spatial distribution of suitable habitat for each species, especially habitat patches large

enough to support breeding, so they can assess whether the preliminary linkage design is likely to serve the species. If not, they can propose additional habitat to ensure all selected focal species are accommodated. All major rivers and streams should also be added to the linkage design if not already included.

7. *Assess in the field.* Conduct fieldwork to ground-truth existing habitat conditions, document existing barriers and potential passageways, identify restoration opportunities, and consider management options.

8. *Develop the linkage design action plan.* Compile the results of analyses and fieldwork into a comprehensive report that considers existing plans and specifies what is required to conserve and improve linkage function, including priority lands for conservation, specific management recommendations, and prescriptions for mitigating roads and other barriers.

Managing Urban Biodiversity

Efforts to manage urban biodiversity aim to minimize and mitigate impacts, protect and connect remaining habitats, and restore damaged natural areas. Many communities across the United States have been engaged in urban biodiversity conservation, whether they call it that or not. Programs for watershed protection and restoration, urban forestry, green infrastructure, parks and recreation, conservation design, and stormwater management have their own objectives, but if done appropriately, they can also advance the core objectives of urban biodiversity.

A good example of an urban biodiversity program is the **Chicago Wilderness**, a partnership of 185 community and environmental organizations, private firms, and local, state, and federal agencies dedicated to enhancing the Chicago region's biodiversity. Its foundation is 200,000 acres of protected conservation land, some of the largest and best surviving woodlands, wetlands, and prairies in the Midwest (Figure 11.11). In addition to these lands and a larger matrix of public and private lands that support nature, the Chicago Wilderness purposely includes among its prominent species the region's people who protect and live compatibly with it. These lands are documented in the Chicago Wilderness *Atlas of Biodiversity*, and the program's 1999 Biodiversity Recovery Plan is "both a plan and a process" that sets out eight biodiversity and public involvement goals and strategies for achieving them.

The program's intent is that the plan be a living document to evolve during the long-term effort of biodiversity recovery. The plan's goals include the following:

- Preserve more land with existing or potential benefits for biodiversity.
- Manage more land to protect and restore biodiversity.
- Protect high-quality streams and lakes through watershed planning and mitigation of harmful activities to conserve aquatic biodiversity.
- Continue to expand research and monitoring.
- Apply both public and private resources more extensively and effectively to inform the region's citizens of their natural heritage and what must be done to protect it.

Figure 11.11 The Chicago Wilderness. This region of 200,000 acres touches four states and contains an extensive array of existing and recommended protection areas. (*Source:* Chicago Wilderness Consortium 2006.)

- Adopt local and regional development policies that reflect the need to restore and maintain biodiversity.

Since the plan's publication, members of the Chicago Wilderness Consortium have taken actions toward this goal, including restoration efforts and education, outreach, research, monitoring, and policy initiatives. In 2006, the Consortium conducted an evaluation of progress and produced a report card of its biodiversity resources on a four-letter-grade scale. All resources (prairies, wetlands, streams, lakes, birds, reptiles/amphibians, fish, insects, mammals) were evaluated as grade C to D, where C is fair with some biodiversity remaining but declining, and D is poor with rapidly losing biodiversity or little remaining. This poor assessment was not surprising given the legacy of a century or more of urban development, as well as industrial and agricultural impacts. The Consortium concedes that it will take decades of work to recover.

The Consortium uses the 2006 evaluation as a call to action and celebrates the good news that more than 20,000 acres of lands and waters were added to forest preserves and conservation districts; the region boasts a number of well-managed individual sites that are graded A with excellent, high-quality, stable biodiversity. Individuals volunteer $1 million worth of their time annually in efforts to restore natural areas and monitor wildlife. As more local governments adopt ordinances and development policies aimed at protecting habitats and natural areas, Chicago and its region are gaining notice as among the nation's leaders in sustainable development practices (Chicago Wilderness Consortium 2006).

Challenges and Opportunities for Urban Biodiversity

Randolph and Bryant (2002) explored issues of urban biodiversity in a study of the highly urbanized Holmes Run/Cameron Run watershed in Fairfax County, Falls Church, and Alexandria (Virginia), shown in Figure 11.12. The watershed is about 40% impervious surface, and no portion of the landscape has escaped significant alteration. The areas that appear "natural" are highly fragmented in most cases, affected by various pollutants and stormwater flows, and filled with invasive species. The study identified some important issues of urban biodiversity:

1. *Protecting what's left.* Despite high urban density and extensive assaults on biotic integrity, a significant portion of the riparian corridor in the watershed is in public ownership or protection, due in part to Resource Protection Area (RPA) designation under the Chesapeake Bay Preservation Act (see Chapter 18). Although highly urbanized settings lack the biodiversity of urban fringe and wildland settings, the ecological and sociological functions of remnant natural areas are still important, perhaps more valuable because there is so little left.

2. *Managing exotic and native species.* Efforts to protect and restore native species are important in urban areas, but eliminating invasive species is a financial and practical impossibility in most cases because they are rampant. Urban ecological niches are often subject to physical conditions that are harsher than those found outside the city, and invasive synanthropic species have a competitive advantage. Wildland biodiversity protection attempts to prevent and eradicate non-native invasive species, but in urban areas, a different approach is warranted, which is to restore natives and manage invasives.

3. *Balancing urban core versus suburbs, the value of near nature, and Smart Growth management.* Smart Growth management strategies aim

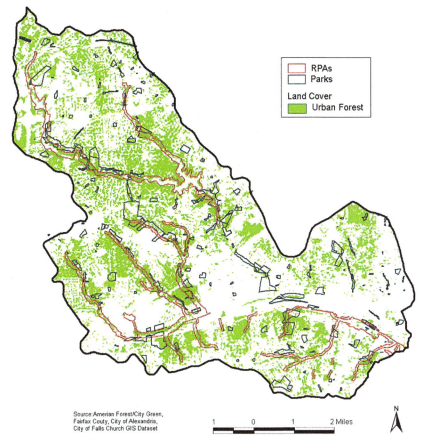

Figure 11.12 Urban Biodiversity Elements in the Holmes Run Watershed. Parks, urban forest, and riparian corridors, including regulated resource protection areas, are key elements for biodiversity in this highly urbanized watershed in Fairfax County and the cities of Falls Church and Alexandria, Virginia. (*Source:* Bryant et al. 2003.)

to contain urban development in areas of existing and planned infrastructure; to infill, redevelop, and revitalize existing communities; and to prevent sprawl that impacts outlying greenfields, habitats, and working landscapes. Does Smart Growth sacrifice urban core open space and biodiversity for the sake of enhanced ex-urban biodiversity? On a regional level, Smart Growth's urban containment may protect and enhance suburban or ex-urban biodiversity, but its infill development may put additional pressure on remaining urban patches and corridors, thereby reducing habitat potential in the urban core. Although biodiversity is limited in the core, such areas still need to provide parks and protect floodplains and riparian corridors that have habitat value. Urban redevelopment, also a part of Smart Growth, can offer opportunities to incorporate conservation designs to enhance biodiversity.

4. *Engaging stakeholders.* Enhancing urban biodiversity requires the involvement of researchers, property owners, citizen groups, educational organizations, and local agencies. To reach that goal, it needs to

engage a constituency to help set priorities, gather data through volunteer monitoring, educate the community, and ultimately act on the information through land conservation and stewardship. Enhancing urban biodiversity requires a commitment, and it is this constituency who can communicate the community value of biodiversity treasures in the political process. The Chicago Wilderness program is an excellent example.

5. *Integrating objectives, tools, and programs.* Few communities can dedicate large financial resources to biodiversity protection. However, significant resources are available for a variety of local, federal, and state programs, the objectives of which are very compatible with urban biodiversity protection. These include water quality protection, stormwater management, floodplain management, stream restoration, parks and recreation, urban forestry, and greenway creation. The regulatory and nonregulatory tools these programs use are also appropriate for urban biodiversity protection. They include overlay zoning, stormwater ordinances, land acquisition, conservation easements, and education. By partnering with these programs, urban biodiversity can be advanced with little or no additional financial investment.

Green Infrastructure: Integrating Wildlife Habitat and Open Space Planning

Green infrastructure planning is based on this last point. It can provide a comprehensive approach that integrates wildlife habitat requirements with the associated water quality, open space, and recreation opportunities for people. As such, it provides a mechanism for communities with limited financial or political support for wildlife protection to incorporate habitat needs in a larger context.

Green infrastructure (GI) is defined as an interconnected network of green space that conserves natural ecosystem values and functions, supports biodiversity and provides habitat for diverse communities of native flora and fauna, and provides associated benefits to human populations. The network consists of stream corridors, lakes, wetlands, woodlands, prairies, and other natural areas; greenways, parks, and other conservation lands; and working farms, ranches, and forests that provide habitat value. The following basic components of a GI network are a variation of landscape ecology and similar to the CEHCP terms (Table 11.1):

TABLE 11.1 **Different Terminology, Same Intent**

Landscape Ecology	Green Infrastructure	California's CEHCP
Patches	Hubs	Natural landscape blocks (NLBs): "globs"
Corridors	Links	Essential connectivity areas (ECAs): "sticks"

- **Hubs**, such as wildlife reserves, forest native landscapes, working lands, regional parks, and community parks.
- **Links**, such as landscape linkages, conservation corridors, greenways, greenbelts, and riparian floodplains.

Green infrastructure planning will be discussed in greater detail in Chapters 14 and 15.

Neighborhood and Backyard Wildlife Habitat Protection

While broader-scale regional and statewide approaches are critical for ecosystem management, the enhancement of wildlife habitat in cities can be strengthened by grassroots efforts at the neighborhood scale. The National Wildlife Federation, the Natural Resources Conservation Service, and many other national organizations and countless local groups sponsor backyard wildlife programs to educate residents and enhance habitat. Several groups have neighborhood or citywide programs, such as San Francisco's Nature in the City (Box 11.2).

BOX 11.2—San Francisco's Nature in the City Program

San Francisco has long had a unique combination of a stunning natural environment and an active ecologically minded population. These come together in the Nature in the City project, spearheaded by the Earth Island Institute and engaging a wide range of civic and government agencies. The goals of Nature in the City are to conserve and restore the nature and biodiversity of San Francisco, and connect people with nature where they live, through public education, community stewardship, conservation advocacy, ecological restoration, and collaboration. It sponsors and facilitates a number of neighborhood projects and volunteer activities. The Nature in the City map identifies natural areas in the city (Figure 11.13).

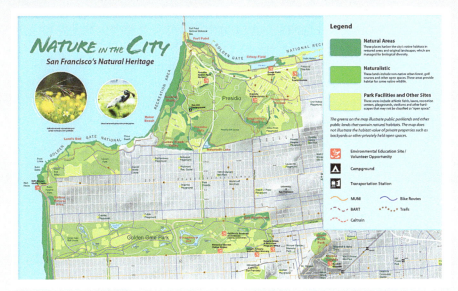

Figure 11.13 San Francisco's Nature in the City Map. (*Source:* Earth Island Institutes, www.natureinthecity.org.)

Endangered Species and Habitat Conservation Planning

The federal Endangered Species Act (ESA) of 1973 established legal requirements for the protection of threatened species, thereby setting in motion a complex program for identifying, listing, and preserving endangered species and their habitats. The USFWS and the National Marine Fisheries Service (NMFS) (for marine species) manage the variety of ESA programs. Most states also administer state laws protecting such species. In the 1980s, The Nature Conservancy (TNC) established the National Diversity Information Program, with operations in each state. The program's goal was to identify locations of the habitats of unique species so that their disturbance could be avoided. The classification of special species contains several categories, listed in Box 11.3. Included are the federal and state classifications, which have legal requirements, and state and global ranks, which do not.

Most states took over the operation of the National Diversity Information Program in the late 1980s. State Natural Heritage agencies maintain lists and locations of special species habitats by jurisdiction. In Virginia and other states, lists are available on the Internet (Table 11.2; also http://www.state.va.us/~dcr/dnh/coindex.htm). Mapped locations for individual species are not provided as part of the public record, mainly to protect the habitat. Generalized statewide distribution maps of rare plants, animals, and communities are available. Table 11.2 gives a partial list of the 74 specially classified species and communities in Montgomery County, Virginia. This long list, typical for most localities, underscores the need to be sensitive to the legal and conservation needs of threatened species in the process of land use and development.

Conservation Tools of the ESA and Habitat Conservation Planning

Box 11.4 and Figure 11.14 show the status of nearly 45,000 ranked species, and the variety of program tools that have developed under the ESA. Under the 1973 ESA (section 9), any "take" of a classified species or its habitat on public or private

TABLE 11.2 **Natural Heritage Resources of Montgomery County, Virginia: 6 of 74 Listed Species and Communities**

Species Type	Common Name	Global Rank	State Rank	Federal Status	State Status	Seen since 1980?
Amphibian	Hellbender	G4	S2S3	SOC	SC	N
Community	Appalachian cave Epikarstic community	G2	S2			N
Fish	Orangefin madtom	G2	S1S2	SOC	LT	Y
Invertebrate	Simmons stonefly	G2G4	S1			Y
Mammal	Indiana bat	G2	S1	LE	LE	N
Plant	Piratebush	G2	S2	SOC	LE	Y

Federal Status

The standard abbreviations for federal endangerment developed by the USFWS, Division of Endangered Species and Habitat Conservation:

LE: Listed Endangered

LT: Listed Threatened

PE: Proposed Endangered

PT: Proposed Threatened

C: Candidate (formerly C1, Candidate category 1)

SOC: Species of Concern (formerly C2, Candidate category 2)

State Status, Virginia Example

The Virginia Division of Natural Heritage uses similar abbreviations for state endangerment:

LE: Listed Endangered

PE: Proposed Endangered

SC: Special Concern

LT: Listed Threatened

PT: Proposed Threatened

C: Candidate State Rank

State and Global Ranks

The following ranks are used by state agencies to set protection priorities for natural heritage resources. These ranks should not be interpreted as legal designations.

S1: Extremely rare; usually 5 or fewer populations or occurrences in the state; or may be a few remaining individuals; often especially vulnerable to extirpation.

S2: Very rare; usually between 5 and 20 populations or occurrences; or with many individuals in fewer occurrences; often susceptible to becoming extirpated.

S3: Rare to uncommon; usually between 20 and 100 populations or occurrences; may have fewer occurrences, but with a large number of individuals; may be susceptible to large-scale disturbances.

S4: Common; usually >100 populations or occurrences, may be fewer with many large populations; may be restricted to only a portion of the state; usually not susceptible to immediate threats.

S5: Very common; demonstrably secure under present conditions.

SA: Accidental in the state.

SB: Breeding status of an organism within the state.

SH: Historically known from the state, but not verified for an extended period, usually >15 years; this rank is used primarily when inventory has been attempted recently.

SN: Nonbreeding status within the state; usually applied to winter resident species.

SU: Status uncertain, often because of a low search effort or cryptic nature of the element.

SX: Apparently extirpated from the state.

SZ: Long-distance migrant whose occurrences during migration are too irregular, transitory, and/or dispersed to be reliably identified, mapped, and protected.

Global ranks are similar, but they refer to a species' rarity throughout its total range. Global ranks are denoted with a G followed by a character. Note that GA and GN are not used, and GX means apparently extinct. A Q in a rank indicates that a taxonomic question concerning that species exists. Ranks for subspecies are denoted with a T. The global and state ranks combined (e.g., G2/S1) give an instant grasp of a species' known rarity.

BOX 11.4—Endangered Species Act Conservation Tools

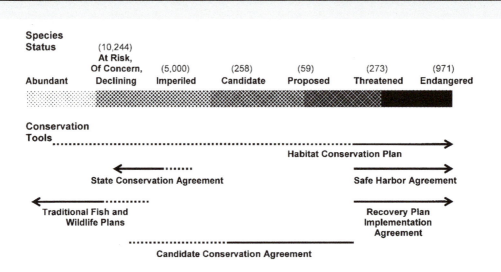

Figure 11.14 The Continuum of Conservation Tools under the Endangered Species Act. (*Source:* International Association of Fish and Wildlife Agencies 2001.)

Recovery plan (1973): A plan for species population and habitat improvement, leading to the delisting of endangered species.

Habitat conservation plan (HCP) (1984): A plan for species conservation, allowing for the "incidental take" of habitat to accommodate species needs, while letting some development continue.

"No surprises" assurances (1994): Under an HCP, landowners are assured that if "unforeseen" circumstances arise, the federal government will not require additional land, water, or other resources beyond the level agreed to in the HCP, as long as the permittee is implementing the terms of the HCP in good faith.

Safe harbor agreement (1999): A voluntary arrangement between the USFWS/NMFS and nonfederal landowners intending to benefit endangered species, while giving landowners assurances from additional restrictions. Agreements must assure "net conservation benefit" to the species and establish baseline conditions that may include population or habitat characteristics.

Candidate conservation agreement (CCA) (1999): An agreement between the USFWS/NMFS and landowners or other participants to provide actions to stabilize or restore candidate species so that listing the species is no longer necessary. A CCA "with assurances" provides landowners with assurances that their efforts to stabilize or restore candidate species will not result in future regulatory obligations in excess of those in the CCA.

State conservation agreement (emerging): A proactive, voluntary approach led by state wildlife or natural heritage agencies to develop partnerships among government agencies, NGOs and land trusts, and landowners, to develop agreements to protect precandidate species and ecological communities before they become imperiled.

Source: Adapted from IAFWA 2001.

land is illegal. Recovery plans and their implementation agreements are developed by the USFWS and NMFS for listed endangered species. As the number of species on the federal lists grew, many became concerned that this provision would preclude any development in certain urban areas or resource development in natural areas, especially since it was estimated that 90% of endangered species habitats are at least partially on private land (General Accounting Office 1994). In addition, the law focused on listed species and had few proactive elements for managing species and habitats, in order to prevent their being listed.

In response to these concerns and to make the ESA more flexible, new approaches for wildlife planning were developed during the 1980s and 1990s. They include **habitat conservation plans** (HCPs), safe harbor agreements, candidate conservation agreements (CCAs), and state conservation agreements. What has emerged is a complex conservation program that engages private landowners in the conservation process, provides incentives and assurances that actions taken will not lead to further requirements, and focuses on species and habitat conservation before they are listed.

Habitat conservation planning aims to produce plans for the conservation of classified species habitats, while accommodating some development in the vicinity of the habitats. Many wildlife advocates criticize this development as a serious diminution of endangered species protection. Others argue that habitat conservation planning is a proactive approach to species protection and that some accommodation of development is necessary to prevent repeal of the ESA at a time of increasing political interest for private property rights.

In the early 1980s, an experimental plan was developed for San Bruno Mountain, an economically valuable undeveloped area just south of San Francisco. The mountain was home to several classified species, including unique butterflies. The objectives of the experimental plan were to provide preservation of the species through conservation of their habitat and to identify areas that could be developed with minimal impact on the habitat. Based on the San Bruno experience, the ESA was amended in 1982, and a new provision, section 10(a)(1)(B), was added to achieve more flexibility.

The section provides that the USFWS can allow land or resource development in the vicinity of an endangered or classified species habitat by issuing an "incidental take permit" if the landowner or developer has prepared a satisfactory HCP. The basic objective of the HCP is to demonstrate how the endangered species habitat will be conserved, while allowing for land development in habitat area.

According to the regulations, an "incidental take permit" can be issued if the HCP identifies:

- Impacts on endangered species.
- Measures to minimize and mitigate impacts.
- Alternatives are considered and action is justified.

In addition, the HCP must show that:

- The taking, if any, is incidental.
- The taking will not appreciably reduce the likelihood of survival.

- The applicant will minimize/mitigate to the maximum extent possible.
- Adequate funding is assured for plan implementation.

HCPs are not required to contribute to the recovery of the listed species, but rather to ensure that its prospects for recovery are not reduced. Typical measures for minimizing and mitigating the impacts of development are land acquisition (sometimes at another site), conservation easements, translocation of species, habitat restoration, the removal of invasive species, and funding to support research on the species (James 1999).

The HCP Process

The habitat conservation planning process is presented in the USFWS's *HCP Handbook* (1996). Key elements include engaging all stakeholders early in the process, gathering and analyzing biological data, projecting "take" levels, developing mitigation measures, and developing funding and monitoring schemes. Here is an outline of the process:

I. Preplanning Process
   A. Determine the applicant
   B. Gather steering committee members; representative of all stakeholders involved
   C. Designate a neutral facilitator
   D. Consult with the FWS
II. Plan Development
   A. Define the land area to be included in the HCP
   B. Gather biological data
      1. Determine the species to be included in the HCP
      2. Gather and review existing data
      3. Develop new data through new biological studies as needed
   C. Identify activities to be included in the HCP land area
   D. Determine the anticipated lake levels resulting from proposed activities
   E. Develop mitigation measures (the following in descending priority, as given by the FWS)
      1. Avoid the impact
      2. Minimize the impact
      3. Rectify the impact
      4. Reduce or eliminate the impact over time
      5. Compensate for the impact
   F. Develop monitoring measures for determining success and/or problems with the HCP
   G. Plan for unforeseen circumstances and plan amendments
   H. Develop a funding scheme to pay for HCP and any mitigation measures
   I. Describe alternatives considered and reasons why alternative not chosen

III. Submit the Plan for Permitting to the FWS

IV. If Permitted, Implement the Plan

    A. Implement mitigation measures

    B. Monitor

    C. Amend plan as necessary

First-Generation HCPs

The results of one first-generation HCP, the well-studied 1992 Balcones Canyon Conservation Plan (BCCP) for an area near Austin, Texas, are shown in Table 11.3. The area is home to several classified species, including the black-capped vireo, the golden-cheeked warbler, and different karst species in the Edwards Aquifer region. The city, county, USFWS, other public agencies, TNC, developers, and landowners were participants in the process. The planning process resulted in a preserve implementation plan that included a federal wildlife refuge, acquisition of preserve lands, lands protected through a resolution trust corporation, and other public lands. Just over half of the occupied warbler habitat is protected, about one-third of the potential vireo habitat is protected, and one-fifth of the potential karst habitat is protected.

The BCCP also illustrated the costs associated with first-generation HCP preparation and implementation. Just preparing the plan cost $760,000, of which $200,000 was for biological study, $400,000 for plan preparation, and $160,000 for the environmental impact assessment. The many stakeholders contributed funds for the planning studies. Land acquisition costs associated with the plan were estimated at $56 million, not including management and administrative costs. Core funding came from a $22-million public bond referendum that was passed by city and county voters. Additional funding came from a $1,500 per acre mitigation fee on development in the area and a building fee surcharge on development activities throughout the city and county. Revenues were pooled into a Habitat Mitigation Trust Fund (Beatley 1994).

Box 11.5 lists key issues concerning the adequacy and implementation of HCPs, identified by studies of first-generation HCP experiences (Beatley 1994; Smith 1995). Beatley (1994) also provides a useful checklist for future HCPs that may improve their effectiveness and ease of preparation and implementation.

TABLE 11.3 Remaining Habitat to Be Protected in the BCCP Preserve System

Type of Habitat	Total Protected	Percentage Protected	Total Unprotected	Percentage Unprotected
Potential karst invertebrate	9,298 acres	21%	36,070 acres	80%
Occupied black-capped vireo	1,164	56%	904	44%
Potential black-capped vireo	10,503	39%	16,475	61%
Golden-cheeked warbler	13,969	37%	23,870	63%

Source: Smith 1995.

BOX 11.5—Issues from First-Generation HCPs

1. The extent to which habitat is protected. *How much protection is enough?*
2. The biological adequacy of conservation measures and the long-term viability of habitat, given limited knowledge. *Do we really know what will happen?*
3. The ability to promote constructive political compromise. *With a wide range of stakeholders, how can we make effective and acceptable decisions?*
4. The ability to implement compromise. *Can an agreement hold together over time?*

5. The costs of HCP efforts. *What are equitable, efficient, and acceptable means of generating the large revenues required?*
6. The time for plan preparation and approval; delays affect both development costs and opportunities and habitat impacts. *How long is this going to take?*
7. Landowner uncertainties that new habitats or constraints are discovered after HCP investments. *What surprises await?*

BOX 11.6—An HCP Checklist Based on First-Generation Plans

1. Incorporate a thorough biological and scientific information base.
2. Represent stakeholders.
3. Integrate the HCP into local and regional plans.
4. Develop long-term equitable funding.

5. Protect habitat simultaneously for multiple species.
6. Dovetail habitat conservation with other community goals: open space, recreation, water quality.

Points 3, 4, 5, and 6 in Box 11.6 propose that HCPs should not be stand-alone plans, but should be integrated into regional and other local plans, and should focus on multiple species when possible.

The "No-Surprises" Policy and Second-Generation HCPs

By 1992, 10 years after the 1982 ESA amendments, only fourteen HCPs had been prepared. Among the reasons for this low level of activity are the issues listed in Box 11.5, especially the last one. Land and resource developers believed that once they began the HCP process, they acknowledged the presence of endangered habitats and became committed to preservation at all costs. Future "surprise" information could constrain any development and require unanticipated costs for species protection. As a result, most declined to enter into the HCP process.

Recognizing these constraints, Bruce Babbitt, Secretary of the Interior, promulgated a new HCP policy in 1994, intended to remove the cloud of uncertainty from potential HCP activity. The "No-Surprises" policy indicated that if, in the course of development, a landowner invests money and land to protect species covered in an approved HCP, the government will not later require that the landowner pay more or provide additional land, even if the needs of species change over time (Fisher 1996).

Some ESA advocates criticized the policy, saying that nature is full of surprises, and therefore land and resource developers should be required to respond to them for the sake of endangered species. Others acknowledged that the policy was necessary to move the HCP process forward. It was better to engage the land and resource development community in proactive habitat protection planning than to have them sit on their hands and incrementally consume and impact habitats.

If the objective was to increase HCP activity, it worked:

- From 1982 to 1994, 14 HCPs were produced.
- From 1994 to 2009, 661 HCPs and 950 incidental take permits were approved.

The plans included collaborative HCPs, such as the BCCP, involving land developers; federal, state, and local governments; environmental groups; and land trusts. They also included HCPs by natural resources firms for company-owned lands. While there are HCPs in about half the states, the majority are in California, Texas, Florida, and Colorado.

After 1994, there continued to be a cry for greater scientific integrity of the plans and an ecological, multispecies approach rather than a single-species approach (Noss et al. 1997). A study sponsored by the National Center for Ecological Analysis and Synthesis and the American Institute of Biological Sciences (Kareiva et al. 1999) found that:

- 82% of the HCPs focused on a single species.
- Many had insufficient data to support recommendations.
- Only half of them estimated the species "take" quantitatively.
- Most provided no data that proposed mitigation measures would succeed.
- Only 7 of 43 plans studied in detail had a clear monitoring plan.

The study recommended that the following steps be taken:

- More explicit scientific standards should be developed.
- When information is lacking, greater mitigation should be applied to provide a margin for error.
- Adaptive management should be employed; that is, management and monitoring should provide new information.
- The scientific community should be engaged in reviewing plans.

Natural Community Conservation Planning in California: Regional Conservation for Multiple Species

In 1991, California established its own program for endangered species protetion. At the time, both conservation advocates and development interests were critical of habitat conservation planning under the federal ESA because it generally

BOX 11.7—HCP Issues Leading to California's Natural Community Conservation Planning (NCCP) Act

Criticisms of the Project-by-Project Approach

- Interfering with development projects impedes economic growth, causes conflicts with private property rights, and creates backlash against the endangered species laws.
- The project-by-project approach leads to patchy, ad hoc mitigation measures and does not prevent the fragmentation of habitat and ecosystems.
- Separate review of each development project creates costly delays, red tape, and uncertainty.
- An emphasis on individual projects is reactive and limits the ability to plan for species recovery or prevent species from declining.
- Enforcement of the project-by-project approach is contentious, often ending in costly court battles.

Criticisms of the Single-Species Approach

- Ecosystems require large areas of unfragmented landscapes, encompassing large-scale natural processes and multiple habitat types (not just the immediate areas where the listed species live).
- Functioning ecosystems depend on the interactions of a wide variety of plant and animal species, not just those that happen to be listed.
- The single-species approach is an "emergency room" model that did not enforce protections until a given species' habitat and populations are so badly eroded that recovery is difficult or impossible.
- Single-species conservation efforts can be undermined by new listings or new information (as occurred with the Stevens' kangaroo rat in Riverside County).

Source: Pollak 2001a.

focused on one project and one species at a time (Box 11.7). To property owners and developers, this was burdensome, costly, and unpredictable. To conservationists, it did not address the overall needs of species and populations at risk, did not prevent fragmentation of habitats and ecosystems, and did not provide the habitat enhancement often needed for ecosystem conservation.

The Natural Community Conservation Planning (NCCP) Act of 1991 aimed to be broader, more flexible, and more predictable than rules under the federal HCPs. The goal was to overcome the project-by-project and single-species approaches by focusing on regional ecosystems and multiple species (both listed and nonlisted). It shared the HCP goal to provide effective conservation of the state's wildlife heritage, while continuing to allow appropriate development and growth.

Although the legislative history was quite critical of the federal approach, the USFWS and the Department of the Interior encouraged the establishment of the California program, believing it to be a useful proving ground for new approaches to habitat conservation that could be incorporated into the HCP process. The NCCP Act established a pilot program in Southern California, where controversy raged over the HCP prepared for the kangaroo rat in Riverside County. The main habitat of concern was the coastal sage scrub, which is home to several endangered species and was being rapidly converted to development. At the time of the NCCP Act, it was estimated that about 343,000–444,000 acres of coastal sage scrub remained in California, only 14–18% of its historic extent. The coastal sage scrub is the habitat of a small bird, the California gnatcatcher, which was being considered for state and federal listing as an endangered species. It was feared this species could provoke a "birds vs. economy" conflict like the northern spotted owl in the Pacific Northwest. Its fate was also seen as an indicator of conflicts to come, as Southern California's many diverse habitats became imperiled.

This regional landscape seemed ideal for testing a regional multispecies approach. The pilot program has been ambitious and complex, with a goal of reconciling the needs of ecosystems with development pressure in a highly urbanized 6,000-square-mile area containing a human population of 17.5 million. This experience has proven to be an unprecedented effort that takes a broad-scale, ecosystem approach to planning for sustaining biological diversity, while allowing for economic land uses.

There are now 24 NCCP efforts around the state, including both completed and in-progress plans covering more than 9 million acres. The implementation cost of these efforts is enormous, but California voters have supported the NCCP process. In 2000, they passed Proposition 12, which included $100 million for the acquisition of land for NCCP plans and $50 million for the Department of Parks and Recreation to acquire lands with priority given to projects that protect habitat for rare, threatened, or endangered species pursuant to an NCCP plan. In 2003, the NCCP Act was amended, requiring every plan to establish linkages between reserves within NCCP areas and to adjacent habitats. Nearly every NCCP plan addresses habitat connectivity and wildlife movement corridors. (For more information, see http://www.dfg.ca.gov/habcon/nccp/.)

San Diego County Multiple Species Conservation Program

The Southern California Multiple Species NCCP program has become a grand experiment in wildlife habitat planning and ecosystem management in a major metropolitan region. It includes eleven separate plans, ranging from San Berdardino Valley west of Los Angeles, south to several plans in the San Diego region. San Diego County manages three planning areas, shown in Figure 11.15.

The overall San Diego Multiple Species Conservation Plan (MSCP) was approved in 1997, but implementation and refinements to the plan continue. Table 11.4 lists the primary metrics of this large-scale habitat conservation plan, which tries to address habitat needs for 85 species. In the half-million-acre planning area, there are more than 300,000 habitat acres, more than half of which are to be conserved. The land area to be conserved at the time of plan adoption was 90,000 acres, at an estimated cost of $300 million. Developer mitigation is responsible for two-thirds of the conserved acres.

Figure 11.16 represents the many maps and documents produced in implementing the San Diego County MSCP. The two maps show a portion of the North County section. The top map (Figure 11.16A) shows habitat evaluation for areas both within and outside preapproved mitigation areas. The bottom map (Figure 11.16B) also shows the preapproved mitigation areas and prenegotiated take authorized areas.

San Diego County has adopted a Biological Mitigation Ordinance to help implement the MSCP. It details the regulations for core reserves and mitigation areas in the context of development projects, and specifies mitigation ratios and other

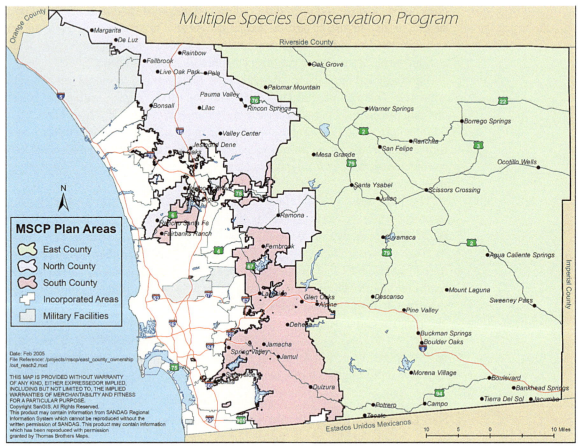

Figure 11.15 Planning Areas of the San Diego County Multiple Species Conservation Plan. (*Source:* San Diego County 2010.)

TABLE 11.4 Primary Metrics of the San Diego MSCP (approved Auguest 1998)

Planning Area	582,243 acres
Acres of Habitat in Planning Area	315,940 acres
Acres of Habitat to Be Conserved	171,920 acres
Percent of Habitat to Be Conserved	54%
Percent of Conserved Habitat Already Publicly Owned or Dedicated at Time of Plan Adoption	48%
Percentage of Coastal Sage Scrub to Be Protected	62%
Total Additional Land Needing Protection at Time of Plan Adoption	90,170 acres
Plan's Projection of Land Acquisition Costs	$262–$360 million
Local Government Share	13,500 acres
State and Federal Share	13,500 acres
Developer Mitigation/Exaction Share	63,170 acres
Number of Species Covered	85

Source: San Diego County 2010.

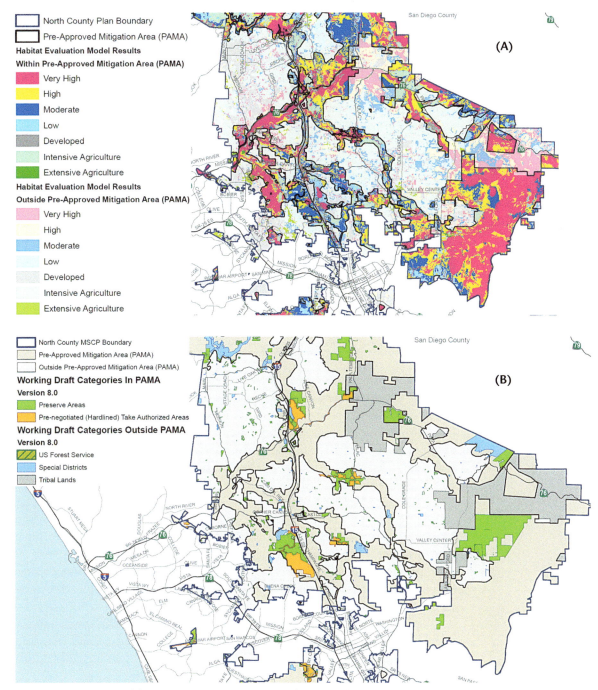

Figure 11.16 A Portion of the San Diego County MSCP North County Plan Area. A: Habitat evaluation. B: Preapproved mitigation, preserve, and prenegotiated take areas. (*Source:* San Diego County 2010.)

requirements. Although the program sets a high standard for habitat conservation, the county makes it clear that this program aims not only to conserve habitat, but also to facilitate the development process.

It will take some time and evaluation research to assess the effectiveness of the California NCCP program to determine whether it is achieving its ambitious objectives of conserving multiple species habitats at the regional scale, while accommodating development. At minimum, the program is creating significant land conservation parcels and their associated ecological, environmental, and social benefits for perpetuity. Only time will tell whether they will lead to the ultimate survival of endangered species.

To convince developers, the county argues that *without the MSCP*: developers/local agencies bear full conservation costs, permits are required from multiple agencies, project-by-project mitigation has to be negotiated, disruption is possible from future listing and from uncertainty and time delays. However, *with the MSCP*: cost is shared by developers/local/state/federal agencies, permits are granted by the county, mitigation is pre-established, and there is no disruption from future listing and a clear and streamlined approval process.

Summary

Land use planning for wildlife conservation and biodiversity has taken on new meaning in recent years, with increased attention in both urban and agricultural landscapes. Landscape ecology has contributed greatly to understanding the basic building blocks and management tools for habitat protection. Habitat core patches and functional corridors can help arrest the habitat fragmentation in converted landscapes, and retain and restore wildlife habitats. Since 2000, states have been able to received federal funds for statewide wildlife habitat planning, and the funding has increased for fiscal year 2011. Some states have taken full advantage of this support. California's recent Essential Habitat Connectivity Project has applied innovative conservation and geospatial methods to producing guidance for all land, resource, and infrastructure planning in the state.

Implementation of the federal Endangered Species Act through habitat conservation planning has led to collaborative efforts to analyze and protect threatened habitats. The Natural Community Conservation Planning program in California is developing multispecies and regional ecosystem approaches. Still, much improvement is needed in conservation planning to meet the complex and competing objectives of financial and implementation feasibility, scientific reliability, and stakeholder acceptability.

As interest in protecting natural areas in urban settings continues to increase, conflicts among habitat conservation advocates, development pressures, and property values will escalate. Lessons from habitat planning for listed species, especially as they are applied to multiple species in a regional context, will inform other communities wishing to enhance their urban biodiversity. Later chapters in Part III address methods for land conservation, development design, and growth management relevant to urban wildlife and habitat protection.

12 ■ Energy, Air Quality, and Climate Change

Climate change has become the defining environmental issue of the century. Despite much political rhetoric to the contrary, climate scientists are in near perfect agreement that "climate change is occurring, is caused largely by human activities, and poses significant risks for—and in many cases is already affecting—a broad range of human and natural systems" (National Research Council 2010d).

Planning efforts focus on climate protection or mitigation through the reduction of greenhouse gas (GHG) emissions by advancing energy efficiency and low-carbon energy sources, reforestation, and soil management. Lessening GHG emissions also benefits energy security by lowering oil consumption and imports, minimizes urban air pollution, and decreases coal-related environmental impacts. But do what we will to mitigate climate change, it is already upon us, and its impacts will increase in coming decades. We must adapt to extreme weather hazards, drought, sea-level rise, coastal flooding, water supply constraints, shifting ecosystems, and changes in agricultural productivity, as well as indirect economic, social, and political disruptions that climate change will bring.

In this chapter, we explore planning for the mitigation of climate change by reducing carbon emissions and planning for adaptation to the effects of climate change. Mitigation strategies are mostly about energy use, which is also the major cause of urban air pollution, so energy planning to reduce carbon and other pollutant emissions is a necessary approach. After reviewing the dilemma of energy use, air quality, and climate change, we focus on climate protection and pathways to a low-carbon, energy-efficient, healthy air community. The chapter concludes with a discussion of land use climate adaptation needs and strategies.

Energy, Urban Air Pollution, and Climate Change

Climate change is being caused by global atmospheric warming, forced primarily by human-caused emissions of carbon dioxide from the combustion of fossil fuels, which still account for more than 80% of the world's commercial energy. In 2009, annual emissions of CO_2 varied from about 18 metric tons per capita (mt/c) in the United States to 7 mt/c in Europe to 6 mt/c in China to 1 mt/c in Africa. During the 2008–2010 recession, U.S. and European emissions dropped by 6% and Chinese emissions increased by 9% per year.

Higher carbon emissions per capita in the U.S. relative to other countries result from greater consumption of fossil fuel energy for household, commercial, and transportation uses. Larger houses and commercial buildings, more electricity, greater automobile dependency, more vehicle miles traveled, and less-efficient vehicles all combine for greater carbon emissions. Sprawling land use patterns are a main cause of increased reliance on automobile transport, decreased transit use, and fewer nonmotorized forms of transportation. As a result of higher energy use, these patterns are also the major cause of urban air pollution. Over half the U.S. population still lives in cities that exceed the air quality health standard for ozone, which is caused mostly by vehicle emissions.

Our Energy Dilemma

Energy is the keystone of nature and society. All life on Earth is made possible by incident solar energy that is captured and stored by plants and passed through ecosystems. Human civilization was spawned by innovation in acquiring and using diverse sources of energy, first by cultivating plants and domesticating animals, and eventually by building machines that could use energy stored in fossil fuels. In fact, each phase of development of civilization was triggered by changes in energy use that provided opportunities for the growth of human populations and economic systems. Since 1850 and the dawn of the industrial revolution, the population, the economy, and energy use have surged, fueled by oil, natural gas, and coal.

This growth will soon be limited by diminished availability of inexpensive oil and gas and environmental constraints on fossil fuel use, probably sooner than most realize. Some envision catastrophe ahead, characterized by abrupt climate change resulting from increasing carbon emissions from fossil fuel consumption, or constraints on oil and natural gas supplies, or political and military upheaval over access to energy resources, or economic depression triggered by increasingly volatile and rising energy prices—or all of the above.

Others see the beginning of a period of transition to a stabilized population and sustainable energy. **Sustainable energy** refers to those patterns of energy production and use that can support society's present and future needs with the least economic, environmental, and social costs. A mix of energy sources will continue to be necessary, but our energy security and sustainability depend on significant improvements in the efficiency of use and increased development of renewable energy systems (Randolph and Masters 2008).

To characterize our energy dilemma and sustainable solutions, it is helpful to look at some sets of threes. Simply put, our energy problem has three components:

1. *Oil.* Petroleum is still the source of 35% of world energy (2008) and 37% of U.S. energy (2010, down from 40% in 2005). Oil reserves are

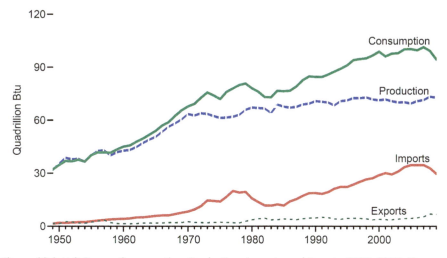

Figure 12.1 U.S. Energy Consumption, Production, Imports, and Exports: 1950–2009. (*Source:* U.S. Energy Information Administration 2010a.)

concentrated in the politically volatile Middle East, and the date when conventional oil production will peak looms closer. Figure 12.1 shows trends in the U.S. reliance on imports, a major concern for energy security.

2. *Carbon.* The global climate is already changing due to carbon emissions from fossil fuels, which still provide 87% of world energy (2008) and 83% of U.S. energy (2010, down from 86% in 2005). Global carbon emissions increased by 2.4% per year from 2004 to 2008.

3. *Expanding global demand.* The developing world needs more energy to satisfy basic needs. China's energy use is doubling every decade. Global energy usage grew by 2% per year from 1970 to 2002 and 3% per year from 2002 to 2008. Figure 12.1 shows U.S. energy demand, which has dropped from its all-time peak of 101.5 quadrillion Btus (quads) in 2007 to 94.6 quads in 2009. This is good news except for the reason: economic recession. Economic recovery will resume the growth of energy demand, which rebounded to 98 quads in 2010.

There are three complicating factors:

1. *Progress is slow* in developing alternatives to oil and carbon, and to the growth in energy demand. We are nearly as dependent on fossil fuels now as we were in the 1970s. Although energy demand growth in developed countries has slowed, it has been offset by the increasing demand for energy in the developing world. World energy usage more than doubled from 1975 to 2008, and we remain dependent on fossil fuels, especially oil.

2. *Change is hard* because of uncertainty, social norms, and vested interests. The transition to sustainable energy faces barriers to change,

including uncertainty about supply options and their impacts, economic and political interests that fight to protect their status quo, and people resistant to changing their behavior. Consumers continue to desire bigger cars and houses and more energy-consuming products.

3. *Time is short,* and the time to act was yesterday. Over the past three decades, the economy and environment have provided clear signals that our energy patterns are not sustainable. Despite these warnings, we have done little to alter our patterns of use.

In the U.S., our energy consumption is dominated by three sectors:

1. *Buildings* consume nearly half of our energy use, including the operation of heating and cooling equipment, electrical appliances, and the embodied energy of materials and construction. They contribute 40% of carbon dioxide (CO_2) emissions, the main cause of global climate change. We have made improvements in building energy efficiency, but significant opportunities remain.

2. *Electricity* used in buildings and industry requires 40% of our energy consumption, and it is growing. In 2010, 45% of electricity generation came from coal, 20% from nuclear power, 24% from natural gas, and 11% from renewable energy sources. From 2004 to 2010, natural gas electricity increased by 38% and wind and solar electricity increased by 92%. Electricity generation caused 40% of U.S. CO_2 emissions in 2009. Wind and solar photovoltaic power have the fastest percentage rates of growth of all sources of electricity, but they still account for just 2.3% of central station electricity and 1% of U.S. commercial energy use.

3. *Transportation* uses two-thirds of our oil consumption, is 96% dependent on oil, and is the source for 34% of U.S. carbon emissions. Its fuel combustion is the major cause of urban air pollution. Transportation energy and emissions depend on vehicle efficiency, vehicle miles traveled (VMT), modal (e.g., car, transit, walking) availability and choice, land use patterns, and the price of fuel. Sustainable transportation must address all of these factors, as well as alternative fuels, such as biofuels and electricity.

We can also characterize the solutions to our energy problem in three primary objectives or ends, and three means to those ends. We need to:

1. *Improve the efficiency of energy use to reduce demand growth.* We have made progress in improving the efficiency and economic effectiveness of our energy use, but we still have huge opportunities for improvement.

2. *Replace oil with other energy sources* to avoid economic and security consequences of oil dependence. Perhaps the best immediate opportunities are biofuels and electricity for transportation.

3. *Increase carbon-free energy sources,* reduce fossil fuel use, and sequester carbon emissions. Renewable energy sources, including solar, wind, and biomass, may offer the best opportunity for carbon-free energy. There is also strong interest in reviving the nuclear industry and in clean coal

technology with carbon sequestration, both of which require overcoming economic, technical, security, and environmental uncertainties. Carbon sequestration progress is slow, and the nuclear power revival was set back by the 2011 tsunami-induced Fukushima nuclear plant meltdown and contamination in Japan.

Finally, we can achieve these objectives through three diverse means, all of which are needed for rapid energy market transformation to improve efficiency, replace oil, and increase carbon-free sources:

1. *Advanced sustainable energy technologies*, including efficient production and use, renewable energy systems, and selected clean and safe fossil fuel and nuclear technologies.
2. *Consumer and community choice* for investment in efficiency and sustainable technologies, and conservation through modifying practices and behavior. Consumer and community choice for sustainable energy is driven by economic, environmental, social, health, security, and other factors, and can take the form of a social movement.
3. *Planning and public policies* to develop and deploy technologies and enhance consumer and community choice through investments, incentives, and regulations. Policies can originate in international agreements and federal, state, and local government market transformation programs.

Our Urban Air Quality Challenge

One of the significant environmental impacts of energy use is urban air pollution, caused by the combustion of fossil fuels. Fuel combustion produces 90% of all U.S. air pollutant emissions. Two primary pollutants cause nonattainment of air quality standards in urban areas: ozone and small particulate matter (PM 2.5). Fuel combustion emits more than 60% of fine particle pollution, and 90% of nitrogen oxides (NOx) and 55% of volatile organic compounds (VOCs); NOx and VOCs both cause photochemical smog that is measured in ozone concentration.

We have made steady progress in the U.S. in reducing air pollutant emissions, mostly by improved technology. The 1970 Clean Air Act (CAA) required that new car emissions be reduced by 90%, and this goal was achieved by the early 1980s. Figure 12.2 shows total emission trends from 1990 to 2008 for all criteria pollutants, which include sulfur dioxide (SO_2), carbon monoxide (CO), large particles (PM 10), and lead, in addition to the above mentioned PM 2.5, NOx, and VOCs. More than half the total emissions come from CO, so this pollutant dominates the total trend line, but all the criteria pollutants have declined since 1990. The real success shown in Figure 12.2 is the reduction of emissions juxtaposed with significant growth of gross domestic product (GDP), VMT, energy, and population in the past four decades.

Urban air pollution persists, however. The most prominent air quality problem is ground-level ozone. The map in Figure 12.3A highlights monitored counties' 2008 urban ozone concentrations. Although most sites met the 8-hour average

Figure 12.2 U.S. Air Emissions Trends Versus Other Indicators, 1990–2008. (*Source:* U.S. EPA 2010d.)

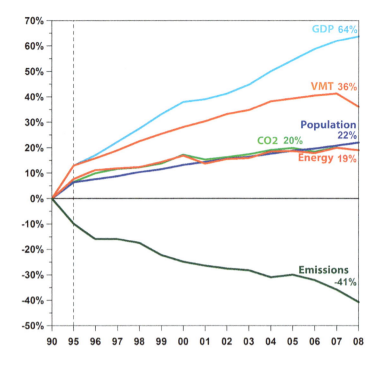

ozone air quality standard of 0.075 part per million (ppm), 377 sites representing 122 million people did not, and 41 sites, mostly in California, exceeded 0.096 ppm. In 2010, the EPA proposed more stringent ozone standards between 0.060 and 0.070 ppm. In September of 2011, President Obama withdrew the tougher standards for political reasons. The new standard would have significantly increased the number of violating counties from 345 to 515 at 0.070 ppm and 650 at 0.60 ppm (Figure 12.3B) (McCarthy 2010; U.S. EPA 2010d).

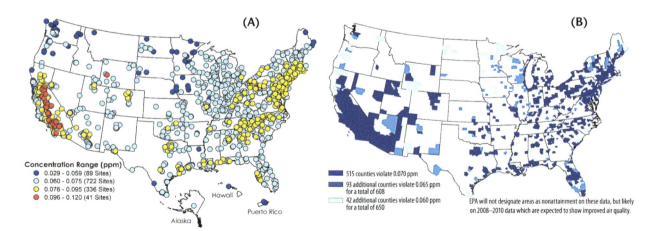

Figure 12.3 U.S. Urban Ozone Pollution Nonattainment. A: Ozone concentrations in ppm, 2008 (fourth highest daily maximum 8-hour concentration). Some 32% of all sites were above the 0.075 ppm standard. B: Counties that would violate the EPA proposed standard would have increased from 345 to 515–650. (*Source:* McCarthy 2010; U.S. EPA 2010d.)

Our Climate Change Imperative

Climate change will dramatically affect the future, in terms of energy sources and use, fresh water supply, extreme weather, biodiversity, agriculture, human settlement, the global economy, and related social disruptions, and some of these effects of climate change are being experienced worldwide. As shown in Figure 12.4, the global atmospheric temperature in 2010 was the warmest on record, and ten of the eleven warmest years on record were 2001–2010. Such a global problem requires international response, but also national policy and local action to protect the climate and adapt to the consequences of climate change. Protecting the climate or mitigating climate change requires reducing human emissions of greenhouse gases, especially CO_2. While total emissions are the problem, the equitable solution lies in accounting for the average emissions per person, or CO_2 per capita. Regardless of our efforts to reduce emissions, our past century of GHG emissions has already created atmospheric concentrations that will continue to increase temperatures and create impacts to which we must adapt.

Despite the need for international climate change agreements and national and state policies to implement them, where the rubber hits the road for these goals and policies is in cities and communities, where GHG emissions originate and where climate change adaptation must take place. Cities and communities must take their own actions for making the necessary changes in buildings, land use, transportation, and energy supply. Planners are in a critical position to lead this community climate action.

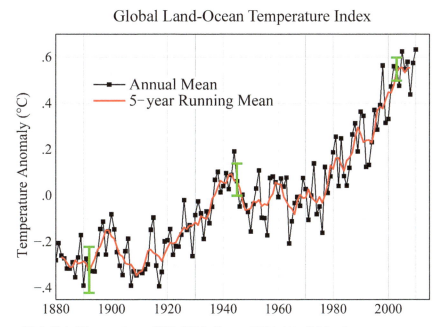

Figure 12.4 Global Temperatures, 1880–2010. (*Source:* NASA, http://data.giss.nasa.gov /gistemp/graphs/.)

Figure 12.5 Achieving the Emissions Budget. Top: CO_2 emissions necessary to limit atmospheric concentration to 400 ppm. Bottom: 75% chance of not exceeding 2°C temperature. (*Source:* Meinshausen et al. 2009.)

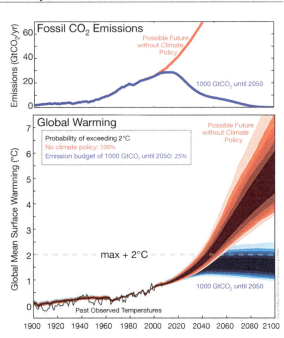

Less Than 2°C Global Temperature Increase or Bust!

The consensus of the Intergovernmental Panel on Climate Change (IPCC) is that if atmospheric global warming could be kept within a 2°C temperature increase above preindustrial conditions, impacts would be extensive but less catastrophic than higher temperatures (IPCC 2007a). These impacts include increased human deaths from heat waves, inland floods, hurricanes, droughts, malnutrition, and infectious diseases; water supply shortages; spatial shifts of ecosystems and agricultural systems; species extinction; and coastal sea-level rise and flooding. Most participants in this estimate agree that the maximum 2°C rise was a compromise between the desirable and the feasible, and not necessarily a safe level, but it has been adopted as a goal by the European Union and in 2009 by other G8 nations, including the U.S.

The IPCC estimates that atmospheric concentrations of CO_2 associated with such a 2°C temperature increase are 400–450 ppm (IPCC 2007b). In June 2011, the concentration was 393.7 ppm, increasing by 2 ppm per year. In research published in *Nature*, Meinshausen et al. (2009) estimate that a limit of 400 ppm would give a 75% probability that global temperature rise will not exceed 2°C by 2050. This would require an overall emissions budget from 1900 to 2050 of 1,000 gigatons (GT) of CO_2. Figure 12.5 shows their scenario for achieving that budget: The world would hold current emissions flat at about 30 million tons per year (Mt/yr) until 2020, then reduces them to about 10 Mt/yr by 2050 (about half of 1990 emissions) and to zero by 2080.

Emissions Trends: Way Up, Not Down

The world, however, is moving in the opposite direction. Figure 12.6 shows that 2009 global emissions of 30 Mt/yr are 27% higher than in 2001. About two-thirds

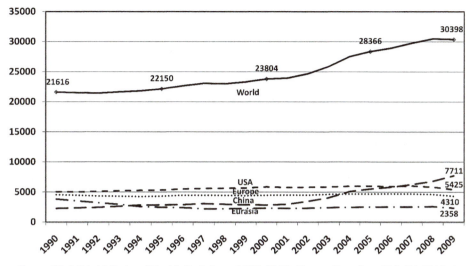

Figure 12.6 World Carbon Dioxide Emissions, 1990–2009. (*Source:* Data from U.S. EIA 2010a.)

of the growth is due to an increase in per capita emissions (+18%) and about one-third is because of population growth (+9%). The U.S., Europe, Eurasia, and China account for two-thirds of the world total. Since 1990, Western and Central Europe emissions rose only 3%, while those from Eurasia (Russia and eastern Europe) dropped 32%. U.S. emissions increased 1% to 2007, then fell 10% by 2009 due the economic recession. The biggest increase came in China with a 340% increase since 1990. Most of this emissions growth in China came from 2001 to 2009 when emissions rose 13% per year, a doubling rate of about 5 years. About 75% of the world's growth in emissions from 2001 to 2009 came from China. China (25%) and the U.S. (18%) emitted 43% of the world total in 2009. Global emissions have been flat or down slightly as a result of the 2008–2010 recession, but it is also expected that they will resume growth as the economy recovers; sure enough, emissions hit a record 33 Mt/yr in 2010.

Per Capita Emissions: The Best Indicator of Progress

Although it is total CO_2 emissions that contribute to global warming, total emissions do not tell the whole story, as we seek equitable means to mitigate climate change. The fair assessment of these emissions is measured better by CO_2 emissions per capita. In 2009, average global CO_2 emissions were 4.5 metric tons per capita (mt/c), but per capita emissions varied wildly for different countries, from 20 mt/c in Australia and 18 mt/c in the U.S. to 7 mt/c in Western Europe to 6 mt/c in China to 1.4 mt/c in India. While the developed world scolds the developing world, especially China, for its exploding growth of total emissions, China and India scold the developed world, especially the U.S., for its high per capita emissions.

Figure 12.7 shows that world per capita emissions increased 10% from 1990 to 2009, despite declining levels in the U.S., Europe, and Eurasia. World per capita

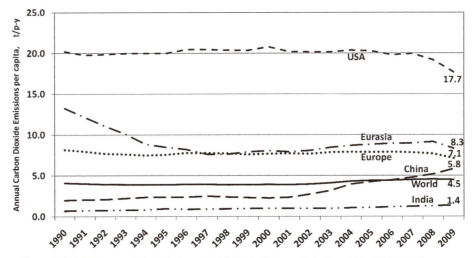

Figure 12.7 Per Person CO$_2$ Emissions, 1990 2009. (*Source:* Data from U.S. EIA 2010c.)

emissions actually decreased 5% from 1990 to 2001, but increased 16% (2% per year) from 2001 to 2009. This was largely driven by growth in China, where per capita emissions more than doubled from 2.3 to 5.8 mt/c from 2001 to 2009. India is poised for significant emissions growth, with its low 1.4 mt/c emissions in 2009 growing at 6% per year and a population expected to rise to 1.5 billion by 2030 (exceeding China's).

These total and per capita emissions growth trends run counter to reductions needed to keep global temperatures within a 2°C increase above preindustrial times. From 2001 to 2009, global emissions grew at 3.2% each year, a doubling rate of 22 years, even though the scientific community tells us we need to reduce our current 33 Mt/yr emissions to 10 Mt/yr within 40 years. If world population rises as expected to 9.3 billion by 2050, the average global CO$_2$ emissions per capita would have to drop from the 2007 level of 4.5 mt/c to 1.3 mt/c in 2050, about what the average Indian emits today, one-sixth the emissions of an average European, and one-fourteenth that of an average American. To reduce total U.S. emissions to 80% below 1990, per capita emissions must drop by 88% to account for population growth, calculating to what Peter Calthorpe calls the "12% solution" (Calthorpe 2011).

It's All About Energy (Mostly)

The climate change imperative requires this daunting task of reversing current trends and transforming the global economy to a post-carbon future within only a few decades. Despite new evidence that soil sequestration and methane and black carbon are key factors in controlling GHG emissions (Shindell et al. 2009) and afforestation is also a vital sink for carbon, this climate imperative is centered on energy. From 2001 to 2008, world energy consumption grew by 3% per year. In

2008, 87% of that energy came from fossil fuels, 35% from oil, 28% from coal, and 24% from natural gas. Most global energy projections expect these trends to continue.

The U.S. Energy Information Administration's (EIA) *International Energy Outlook 2009* and the International Energy Agency's (IEA) *World Energy Outlook 2009* offer similar projections for their reference case, which assumes no new climate change policies beyond those adopted by mid-2009. They project world energy to increase 44–45% between 2006 and 2030 (1.5% per year), with fossil fuels still contributing more than 80% to the mix in 2030. Carbon emissions are expected to increase by 1.4% per year to more than 40 Mt/yr in 2030 (IEA 2009; U.S. EIA 2010c). The IEA estimates that if these projections are extended out to 2050, they would result in an atmospheric GHG concentration of 1,000 ppm over the long term, more than twice the 400–450 ppm associated with a 2°C temperature increase (IEA 2009).

The 450 Scenario

In addition to the reference case, the IEA also provides what it calls the 450 Scenario, which is a set of emissions goals and policy options to stabilize the atmospheric concentration of GHG at 450 ppm. Reflecting current short-term barriers to emissions reductions, the scenario has an "overshoot" trajectory, increasing concentrations to 510 ppm in 2035 where they remain level until 2045 and then ultimately decline to 450 ppm.

As shown in Figure 12.8, under the 450 Scenario, global CO_2 emissions would increase slightly to 32 GT/yr in 2020 then decline to 26 GT/yr by 2030. The scenario's 35% reduction of CO_2 emissions from the reference case by 2030 comes from improved end-use efficiency of buildings, vehicles, and power generation (54%), new renewable energy and biofuels (23%), new nuclear power (9%), and carbon capture and storage (CCS) (14%). Per capita emissions for the 450 Scenario drop from 4.5 mt/c in 2009 to 3.2 mt/c in 2030.

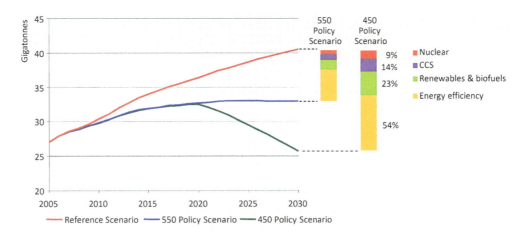

Figure 12.8 The IEA's 450 Scenario for World Energy to Achieve 450 ppm CO_2 Emissions by 2050. (*Source:* International Energy Agency 2009.)

U.S. per capita emissions for the IEA's 450 Scenario would drop to 8.6 in 2030. The European Union is assumed to reduce per capita emissions to 4.5 in 2030; Japan from 9.6 mt/c in 2007 to 5.4 mt/c; Russia from 11.1 to 10.4 mt/c; while China and India are assumed to have per capita emissions of 4.8 and 1.5 mt/c in 2030, respectively. China's were already at 5.8 mt/c in 2009.

The IEA's 450 Scenario is the first major energy forecast that tries to account for the climate imperative. While it is aggressive relative to current trends in its assumptions to reduce total and per capita emissions, it still may fall well short of those necessary to achieve a maximum 2°C increase for three reasons:

1. The 450 Scenario describes a pathway only to 2030; downward trends would have to continue through 2050. The 450 Scenario has global emissions at 26.4 GT in 2030, still 26% higher than 1990, when latest estimates require halving 1990 emissions (to 10.4 GT) by 2050.

2. It has an overshoot trajectory; concentrations would rise to 510 ppm in 2035, then must drop. But CO_2 has such a long detention time in the atmosphere, and it is uncertain how and when concentrations would fall to 450 ppm. Mathews and Caldiera (2008) conclude that in an overshoot scenario atmospheric CO_2 would only decrease at a rate determined by declining ocean uptake, and atmospheric temperatures would not decrease appreciably or quickly.

3. Whether 450 ppm is sufficiently low to keep global temperatures within a 2°C increase is controversial. Meinshausen et al. (2009) conclude that the probability that 2°C would not be exceeded is 75% for 400 ppm and it drops below 50% for 450 ppm. NASA climatologist James Hansen has long argued that a much lower concentration, 350 ppm, is necessary (Hansen et al. 2008).

Climate Protection: Mitigating Climate Change from Global to Local

What do we do about the climate change imperative? A few would say nothing, because they do not agree with the extremely well-accepted scientific assessment of the situation, or they think there is too much uncertainty, or they think there are matters of higher priority, or they do not want change because of their vested interests in the status quo. Most others, however, see the recent extreme weather, flooding, heat, drought, and wildfires of 2011 as merely a precursor of what is to come, and the serious need for acting quickly to mitigate future climate change by cutting GHG emissions. They also see cobenefits of such action by improving energy efficiency and saving billions of dollars in energy costs, reducing oil consumption and dependence on foreign sources, and enhancing air quality and human health.

Planning to mitigate climate change by reducing GHG emissions has been active at the international, national, state, and local levels. This section reviews some of those planning efforts and then characterizes the low-carbon community and possible pathways to its realization.

International Agreements: The U.N. Framework Convention on Climate Change

The IPCC's first assessment report prompted the formation of the United Nations Framework Convention on Climate Change (UNFCCC), and each year it holds a conference of parties (COP). The third COP held in Japan in 1997 produced the Kyoto Protocol, which required that by a first commitment period (2008–2012), developed countries would have to reduce combined emissions of GHG to at least 5% below 1990 levels. The Protocol came into force in 2005. The United States is the only major developed country not to ratify the Protocol.

The countries that have ratified and implemented the Kyoto Protocol have had mixed results. The European Union and Russia reduced their emissions by 4% and 22%, respectively, from 1990 to 2007. But Japan increased its emissions 20% and Canada 24%. Emissions went up 69% for late ratifier Australia, and 19% for nonratifier U.S. And the Kyoto Protocol set no emissions targets for developing countries. It has provisions for industrialized countries to assist developing countries with low-carbon technologies and to invest in them to claim some credits toward their own emissions reduction targets. But this approach has been ineffectual, as emissions rose between 1990 and 2007 for all developing countries, including China (173%), India (140%), Indonesia (104%), Brazil (67%), and Mexico (50%).

At COP15 in Copenhagen in December 2009, the UNFCCC and member states tried to forge an agreement for mitigation action beyond the Kyoto Protocol's first commitment period, one that would include developing countries and be embraced by the Kyoto hold-out, the United States. Amid great hype, the conference attracted every head of state of 190 major nations to reflect the seriousness of climate change, and the developed nations committed billions of dollars to help developing countries meet emissions reductions. But the fragile state of the global economy in late 2009, as well as continued differences between rich and poor countries, tempered progress, and when all was said and done, the parties could not achieve a meaningful agreement for new mandatory targets for emission reductions. The discussion continued at the U.N. Climate Change Conference in Bonn in August 2010 and at COP16 in Cancun, Mexico, in December 2010, but an effective international program to set us on a path toward emissions reduction sufficient to contain global warming at 2°C continues to be elusive

U.S. National Climate Action Policies

So where do we turn? Many countries have developed climate action plans and policies influenced by IPCC findings and UNFCCC targets. The European Union got an early start and set member nation targets following Kyoto Protocol goals. In 2005, the EU adopted an approach first used successfully in the United States during the 1990s to control sulfur emissions from power plants. This regulatory program, known as the cap-and-trade program, allocates and caps carbon emissions from large stationary emitters, but allows them to sell or trade their allocations to others. The EU reduced emissions by 4% from 1990 to 2007, led by Germany (–11%) and the United Kingdom (–7%).

For the past decade, the U.S. Congress has been debating a climate change policy, including a carbon cap-and-trade program. The House of Representatives narrowly passed its version of the program in the summer of 2009—the American Clean Energy and Security Act (ACESA)—but the Senate delayed action because of other political priorities, and like the international accord, strong federal climate change legislation remains politically formidable. ACESA would have set emission caps of 3% below 2005 levels in 2012, 17% below in 2020, 42% below in 2030, and 83% below 2005 in 2050.

Congress requested the National Research Council of the National Academy of Sciences to address the climate change issue, and the NRC responded with a suite of panels and reports on advancing the science of climate change (NRC 2010d), limiting the magnitude of future climate change (NRC 2010c), adapting to the impacts of climate change (NRC 2010a), and informing effective decisions and actions related to climate change (NRC 2010b). The reports recommend a strong role for national federal programs in all of these areas, including an economy-wide carbon pricing system and regulations and incentives for energy efficiency and low-carbon sources.

State and Regional Climate Action Plans and Programs

In the U.S., because of slow federal action, 35 states have developed state climate action plans, most of which set emissions reduction targets. California is the only state to set mandatory reductions: Its AB 32 law caps statewide GHG emissions at 1990 levels by 2020, and several other laws provide implementing programs (Box 12.1). A study by Drummond (2010) indicates that these state efforts may already be reducing per capita GHG emissions by 2–3%. The Pew Center on Global Climate Change tracks all state and regional climate change policies, plans, and programs (http://www.pewclimate.org/).

Several states have initiated regional cap-and-trade programs, including the 2005 Regional Greenhouse Gas Initiative (RGGI) involving ten northeastern states. RGGI caps emissions at 2009 levels and reduces them 10% by 2019 (Box 12.2). The Western Climate Initiative (WCI) was established in 2007 and includes six western states and four Canadian provinces. In July 2010, the WCI released its Program Design, which aims to cap emissions at 15% below 2005 levels by 2020 (WCI 2010). Both of these regional programs provide useful lessons and a model for a national cap-and-trade program.

Local Climate Action Plans and Policies

Recognizing the critical role of communities in climate action, cities across the globe have initiated local programs to reduce GHG emissions. In 2005, representatives from the world's largest cities met in London to join forces in addressing climate change, and in 2006 the group partnered with the Clinton Foundation to form the C40 program of the 40 of the largest world cities (including New York, Los Angeles, Chicago, Philadelphia, and Houston) and 20 affiliate cities

BOX 12.1—The California Climate Protection Plan

The California Global Warming Solutions Act of 2006 (AB 32) set in motion the nation's most comprehensive state climate protection plan. AB 32 required the state to reduce GHG emissions to 1990 levels by 2020. That target of 427 million metric tons CO_2 equivalent (MMTCO2E) is 30% below business-as-usual (BAU) projections (596) and 10% below the 2002–2004 average emissions (469). This requires a reduction of per capita emissions from 14 mt/c to 10 mt/c by 2020.

In December 2008, the California Air Resources Board completed the Climate Change Scoping Plan (CARB 2008), which detailed strategies to meet these targets, as shown in Figure 12.9. California has an impressive array of other statutes and programs for energy efficiency and GHG emission reduction, including the 2002 Pavley

Act, requiring vehicle GHG emission reduction of 30% by 2016, strict energy efficiency codes and utility programs, a 33% renewable portfolio standard for utilities, and a vehicle low-carbon fuel standard. These components constitute the backbone of the plan, but it also calls for an umbrella cap-and-trade program to ensure the AB 32 targets are reached. The program will be developed by 2011 and implemented in 2012. The first compliance period (2012) applies to large emitting electricity generators and industries (> 25,000 tons/year), and the second period (2015) applies to upstream fuel suppliers of smaller industrial, residential, and commercial energy and transportation fuels. The plan calls for transitioning to full auction of allowances with revenue going to climate protection programs. After litigation, the ARB approved a revised plan in August 2011.

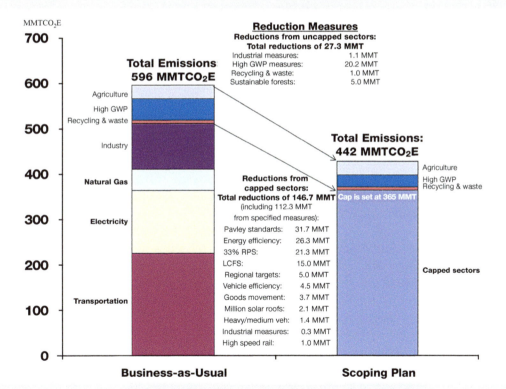

Figure 12.9 The California AB 32 Scoping Plan, 2008. The cap-and-trade program sets 2020 capped sector emissions at 365 MMT (million metric tons), requiring 147 MMT reduction from BAU (business-as-usual), of which 112 MMT can be met by existing programs. Noncapped sectors agriculture, high global warming non-CO_2 gases (refrigerants), and solid wastes are managed outside of the cap-and-trade program. (*Source:* California Air Resources Board 2008.)

Source: Adapted from California Air Resources Board 2008.

BOX 12.2—The RGGI CO_2 Cap-and-Trade Program

In 2005, ten northeastern states—Connecticut, Delaware, Massachusetts, Maryland, Maine, New Hampshire, New Jersey, New York, Rhode Island, and Vermont—formed the Regional Greenhouse Gas Initiative (RGGI), the first mandatory GHG emission cap-and-trade program in the nation. Its goal is to reduce CO_2 emissions at 2005 levels (188 MMT) from 2009 to 2014, and reduce them by 2.5% per year from 2015 to 2018 for a 10% reduction from 2005 by 2019. The program sets caps on emissions from the region's 209 large fossil fuel generating plants, which account for a quarter of total emissions. Utilities purchase emission allowances at auction. From its first auction in 2008 to its ninth auction in September 2010, allowances have sold at an average $2.70 per ton CO_2 ($1.86 in 2010), and proceeds have totaled $729 million. More than 80% of the proceeds are being invested in strategic energy programs to benefit consumers and build a clean energy economy.

A utility can purchase "offsets" from nonutility sources up to 3.3% of its compliance requirement if prices stay below $7/t and up to 10% if prices go above $10/t. Offsets can come from sources outside of the region (and in 2007, California agreed to participate) or from owners of forestland who engage in afforestation that is permanently protected by conservation easement. Daniels (2010) reviewed the prospects for forest carbon sequestration under such a cap-and-trade program to foster greater forestland conservation as a result of financial return to forestland owners. Utilities have yet to use forest offsets in the RGGI program, but it will be more likely as the price of allowances increases, and if RGGI and other such programs extend offsets to reforestation and forest management projects.

Source: Adapted from RGGI 2010.

(including Austin, New Orleans, Portland, Salt Lake City, San Francisco, and Seattle), pledging to improve energy efficiency, reduce GHG emissions, and coordinate and share their experiences.

In the U.S., many cities stepped forward with climate action planning activities as early as the late 1990s. By 2009, more than 1,000 U.S. cities signed the U.S. Conference of Mayors Climate Protection Agreement, committing to Kyoto Protocol goals for the U.S., that is, reducing GHG emissions to 7% below 1990 levels by 2012. Although few if any cities will meet this goal, the commitment set in motion community climate action planning efforts across the country. More than 500 of these cities have joined ICLEI—Local Governments for Sustainability to use ICLEI's Cities for Climate Protection tools to develop climate action plans. We review this experiment of community energy and climate action planning later in this chapter.

Despite this activity, American cities in general lag behind others around the world in climate action planning, especially energy planning to reduce fossil fuel use and CO_2 emissions. They are at a distinct disadvantage after decades of low energy prices that have fueled land use and transportation patterns, buildings, and infrastructure, which are energy-inefficient and heavily dependent on carbon-based fossil fuels. This legacy stands U.S. cities apart from lower-emitting European cities, and it serves as both a major impediment to achieving low emissions per capita and a major opportunity to increase efficiency and reduce total emissions. Box 12.3 explains the factors that contribute to differences in per capita emissions in cities, especially related to land use and transportation.

BOX 12.3—Factors Affecting Current CO₂ per Capita in Cities

Carbon emissions per capita vary wildly throughout the world, from 18–22 mt/c (2007) in the U.S., Canada, and Australia; to 8–12 mt/c in Europe, Russia, and Japan; to 4–5 mt/c for Mexico and China; to 1–2 for India, Indonesia, Egypt, and Brazil. Emissions per capita also vary considerably for different cities. Although it is difficult to compare different cities' data on emissions because of different methodologies used and different boundaries assumed, the literature provides some distinct differences that suggest some useful lessons on strategies to reduce emissions.

1. **Most carbon emissions come from cities, but per capita emissions are less in cities than their national averages.** David Dodman and David Satterthwaite (2008, 2009) compare per capita emissions data from cities to their national averages, and argue: "Don't blame cities for climate change!" Well, cities are still the biggest source, so their statement would be better as "Don't blame *people* in cities for climate change!" As Table 12.1 shows, the per capita emissions for selected cities are 36–65% less than their national average levels. Brown et al. (2008) calculated household and highway transportation carbon emissions per capita for the 100 largest U.S. metropolitan areas. They found that these metros house two-thirds of the nation's population and three-quarters of its economic activity, but emit just 56% of U.S. carbon emissions.

2. **U.S. cities have much higher CO₂ per capita than European and other international cities.** The Table 12.1 data illustrate the difference between U.S. and European cities due to three energy use factors in the U.S.:

- *Higher per capita transportation energy* because of greater travel distances, vehicle miles traveled (VMT), and less use of transit and nonmotorized modes, largely because of land development patterns. Compared to U.S. cities, European cities follow to a much greater extent the five D's of efficient land use (Cervero and Kockelman 1997; NCR 2009):
  ○ Density: population/employment per area.
  ○ Diversity: mixed-use residential/commercial, jobs-housing balance.
  ○ Design: neighborhood aesthetics, street connectivity, sidewalks, bicycle lanes.
  ○ Destination accessibility: ease of trip destination from point of origin.
  ○ Distance to transit: 0.25–0.5 mile from home or work.
- *Lower energy prices* have resulted in less investment in building and vehicle efficiency;
- On average, *more consumptive behavior*, such as larger household dwelling size, larger vehicles, single-occupancy VMT, more electrical appliances, and lower summer and higher winter thermostat settings,

TABLE 12.1 Large-City CO₂ Emissions, Compared to National Averages

	City CO₂ Emission per Capita	National CO₂ per Capita	City % of National
New York	7.1 mt/c (2005)	20.3 mt/c (2005)	35
San Francisco	11.2 mt/c (2005)		61
Los Angeles	12.4 mt/c (2005)		63
Chicago	12.7 mt/c (2005)		
Toronto	9.6 mt/c (2003)	17.5 mt/c (2003)	47
London	5.9 mt/c (2006)	9.7 mt/c (2006)	64
Barcelona	3.4 mt/c (1996)	6.1 mt/c (1996)	56
Tokyo	4.8 mt/c (1998)	8.9 mt/c (1998)	54

Source: Adapted from Dodman 2009; city data from city GHG inventories, national data from U.S. EIA 2009.

BOX 12.3—Factors Affecting Current CO₂ Per Capita in Cities (cont.)

resulting in greater energy use and emissions per capita.

3. **Urban density affects transportation energy use**. Lower-density metropolitan areas have greater vehicle miles traveled and car fuel use per capita than higher-density cities, and higher-density cities have greater use of transit and nonmotorized transport (e.g., Dodman and Satterthwaite 2009; Ewing et al. 2007; Kenworthy 2006; Newman 2006; NRC 2009).

   - *Car fuel use per capita is much higher in less dense cities*. Newman (2006) showed that the ten American cities in Kenworthy and Laube's (2001) 84 world city sample, led by Atlanta and Houston, had the highest car fuel use per capita. The ten American cities, again led by Atlanta and Houston, were among the 18 least dense cities of the 84.

   - *Automobile CO_2 emissions per capita are much higher in the urban core and inner suburbs than the outer suburbs*. The Center for Neighborhood Technology's Housing and Transportation Affordability Index program has developed an interactive web-based map that compares household auto GHG emissions per acre and per household for major metropolitan areas in the U.S. Figure 12.10 shows maps for the Boston area. While dense central cities have higher emissions per acre, surrounding less-dense suburbs have much higher emissions per household.

4. **Carbon emissions depend on energy efficiency, energy systems and sources, weather, and behavior**. In cities, energy use and carbon emissions come from residential and commercial buildings, personal and freight transportation, and industry.

   - Building, equipment, and vehicle efficiency dramatically lower emissions per capita. California's per capita electricity consumption is half of Texas', largely because of the former's aggressive electricity efficiency programs.

   - Low-carbon energy sources and efficient systems like combined heat and power and district heating/cooling dramatically lower emissions per capita. Hydro-powered Seattle is carbon neutral in electricity. As a result, Brown et al. (2008) found that in coal-powered Washington, DC, households had ten times the residential carbon emissions per household as Seattle households. European cities have lower emissions, due in part to their combined heat and power, as well as their district heating.

   - Places with milder climates, that is, lower heating degree-days, have much lower emissions per capita. Brown et al. (2008) found that relatively mild West Coast cities had lower residential carbon emissions per capita than the cold Midwest and Northeast and the hot South.

   - Personal and consumer behavior and community choice can dramatically reduce energy use and emissions per capita.

Figure 12.10 Boston Metro Auto CO₂ Emissions. Left: Auto emissions per acre are much higher in the central city. Right: Auto emissions per household are much higher in the suburbs. (*Source:* Center for Neighborhood Technology. www.cnt.org.)

Pathways to the Low-Carbon Community

The goal of these local climate initiatives, state plans, regional cap-and-trade programs, and national initiatives is to reduce GHG and carbon emissions, and to transform from a high-carbon to a low-carbon economy. This is manifest where people live. What does a low-carbon community look like? It is reflected in technologies and designs, community choice and behavior, and plans and policies that can lead to lower CO_2 emissions per capita. Let's explore these three pathways.

1. Low-Carbon Community Technologies and Designs

To characterize the low-carbon community, it is easiest to look at the physical components. These include green technologies and designs that reduce energy and fossil fuel use, and are applied at various scales, from building to site to neighborhood to community to region. In addition to climate change mitigation, they aim to provide energy, land, water, and material efficiency; renewable energy; air quality protection; and waste minimization. These technologies and designs are too expansive to describe in detail here, but some examples applied at different scales illustrate the extent of opportunities. They need to be key elements of climate action plans.

Building Scale. Almost half of our energy use is for buildings, and that use results in more than 40% of GHG emissions in the U.S. About 38% of building operating energy use is for space heating and cooling, and the rest for lighting, appliances, and equipment. The past few decades have seen significant advances in building technologies and designs to reduce energy, materials, water, and emissions. These advances have been part of the Green Building Movement, which has accelerated in the past few years. There were only 230 LEED-certified buildings in 2007; there were 13,500 in 2010 and another 56,000 registered and undergoing the certification process (see Chapters 14 and 16). Building efficiency improvements include the following:

- Thermal envelope improvements, such as advanced windows, super-insulation, cool roofs, infiltration control, and heat recovery.
- Heating, ventilating, and air conditioning (HVAC) system efficiency improvements for furnaces, boilers, air conditioners, and distribution ducts driven by federal standards and industry innovations. Figure 12.11 shows the cumulative influence of a cost-effective thermal envelope and HVAC improvements over a traditional code house in 5,000 heating degree-days/year. They can reduce heating energy, related emissions, and cost by more than two-thirds.
- Building energy codes still only address the thermal envelope of buildings, but most of the primary energy used is attributed to electricity for lighting, appliances, and equipment. Considering electricity use, along with thermal energy, is necessary to achieve efficient buildings and is referred to as the *whole building energy* approach. With the prodding of state and federal appliance efficiency standards, industry has made

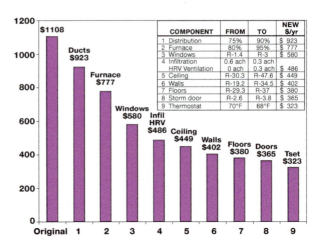

Figure 12.11 Energy-Efficient Improvements. This graph shows step-by-step savings in dollars (also energy and CO_2 emissions) from cost-effective efficiency measures in a code house in Blacksburg, Virginia. (*Source:* Randolph and Masters 2008.)

	COMPONENT	FROM	TO	NEW $/yr
1	Distribution	75%	90%	$ 923
2	Furnace	80%	95%	$ 777
3	Windows	R-1.4	R-3	$ 580
4	Infiltration	0.6 ach	0.3 ach	
	HRV Ventilation	0 ach	0.3 ach	$ 486
5	Ceiling	R-30.3	R-47.6	$ 449
6	Walls	R-19.2	R-34.5	$ 402
7	Floors	R-29.3	R-37	$ 380
8	Storm door	R-2.6	R-3.8	$ 365
9	Thermostat	70°F	68°F	$ 323

great advances in new equipment technologies that use often a fraction of the energy for the same functional use. For example, compared to 20 years ago, refrigerators sold in the U.S. today are on average 25% bigger, are half as expensive, and use only 25% of the energy. Compact fluorescent lamps (CFL) are a symbol of sustainability today, because they use one-fifth the energy of an incandescent lamp and last 8–10 times longer. However, they will soon be replaced by LED lamps that use half the energy and last 6 times longer than CFLs.

- Building size affects energy use directly. A 3,000 sq ft suburban house may use 25% more heating and electricity energy than a 2,500 sq ft urban house and 250% more than a 1,000 sq ft multifamily unit.

- Energy efficiency in new buildings will not be sufficient to achieve the low-carbon energy necessary in time to mitigate climate change, because of the legacy of existing inefficient buildings. It is imperative that we *retrofit existing buildings* by applying energy-efficient technologies to the thermal envelope and upgrades of HVAC, lighting, and equipment. This can be done at any scale, from weatherizing a single-family home to the Empire State Building, where a retrofit project will save 40% of its energy use and carbon emissions.

Site Scale. While a building's site design and associated technology can have a major impact on the environment, they can also provide opportunities. Buildings and sites have always been viewed as consumers of energy and sources of emissions. But with advanced technology, orientation, and design, both new and existing buildings and sites are now looked at as potential sources of energy. Orientation and design can provide passive energy gain, daylighting, and natural cooling. *Onsite electricity generation* turns buildings and sites from just energy consumers to energy producers. Rooftop photovoltaic (PV) systems and other onsite distributed generation, like microturbines and fuel cells, can produce a significant portion of a building's energy needs. Figure 12.12A represents a *net zero energy building* (NZEB), in which whole building energy efficiency achieves a 60–70% energy savings compared to a conventional code house, and a grid-connected rooftop PV system produces the rest (Figure 12.12B). The **net metering** system feeds excess

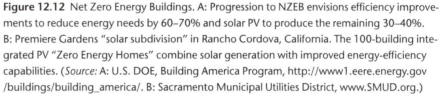

(A)   (B)

Figure 12.12 Net Zero Energy Buildings. A: Progression to NZEB envisions efficiency improvements to reduce energy needs by 60–70% and solar PV to produce the remaining 30–40%. B: Premiere Gardens "solar subdivision" in Rancho Cordova, California. The 100-building integrated PV "Zero Energy Homes" combine solar generation with improved energy-efficiency capabilities. (*Source:* A: U.S. DOE, Building America Program, http://www1.eere.energy.gov /buildings/building_america/. B: Sacramento Municipal Utilities District, www.SMUD.org.)

power to the grid during the day, balancing grid power used in the building at night and on cloudy days.

Neighborhood Scale. The assemblage of buildings and sites in a neighborhood or campus creates opportunities for distributed energy and efficiency. It also affects options for efficient modes of transportation and green infrastructure.

- *Neighborhood/community energy systems*. Onsite distributed energy is important, but further opportunities for efficiency and generation exist at the neighborhood scale. *Combined heat and power* (CHP) systems can increase the energy efficiency of electricity production from 30% to 80%, as normally wasted heat is used for productive purposes. If that heat is utilized in a district heating/absorption cooling system, it can provide much of the space heating and cooling energy for neighborhood buildings. European cities provide excellent examples. Mannheim, Germany, has a large 1,600-MW coal power plant, the waste heat from which feeds the city's *district heating system* 26 km away with only a 1°C temperature loss. The city is zoned for only district heating, so no other types of central heating systems can be installed. Complemented with wood- and waste-fueled power plants and an effective and efficient transit system, Mannheim, a coal-based industrial city of 350,000, has achieved CO_2 emissions per capita of 6 mt/c.
- *Efficient land use: Driving and the built environment*. Much has been written about the effect of land use on vehicle miles traveled (VMT), energy use and related GHG emissions, and climate change, and some of the literature argues that if we were to apply the five D's of efficient land use—density, diversity, design, destination accessibility, and distance to transit (see Box 12.3)—we would be on the road to carbon neutrality

(e.g., Ewing et al. 2007). The 2009 NRC study, *Driving and the Built Environment: The Effects of Compact Development on Motorized Travel, Energy Use and CO_2 Emissions*, shed considerable light on the issue. It concluded that doubling density may reduce VMT by 5%, to as much as 25% if accompanied by mixed uses, good walkable neighborhood designs, employment concentrations, and accessible transit. Its scenario of aggressive compact development patterns—75% of new and replacement housing at double current density, with its residents driving 25% less—would reduce total VMT and associated energy and carbon emissions of both new *and* existing households by 7–8% relative to a 2030 baseline projection and 8–11% by 2050. More conservatively, if only 25% of new housing were compact and its residents drove only 12% less, these numbers would be 1% relative to 2030 and 1.3–1.7% by 2050.

What does this mean? Compact, mixed-use development with access to transit can have a notable impact (up to 25% reduction) on the incremental increase in VMT carbon emissions, but because of the legacy of existing development patterns in the U.S., the absolute effect on emissions reduction is small. We must recognize, however, that there are other benefits of such development patterns, including land conservation, public health, and sense of place and community. Still, we must look to other means besides compact development, such as vehicle technology, low-carbon fuels, and transit improvements. (See Chapters 16–18 on Smart Growth.)

The NRC conclusions also suggest that we cannot depend on new development to "grow our way" to lower emissions. Just as existing buildings need to be retrofitted for energy efficiency, our inefficient suburban neighborhoods must also be redeveloped to convert old shopping centers into walkable town centers, to provide greater density and mixed use, and to provide better nonvehicle access to commerce and open space. There is a growing movement to retrofit and redevelop suburbia (Durham-Jones and Williamson 2008).

- *Housing size, location, and consumer choice and behavior.* Compact development also implies smaller residential unit size, which in turn affects thermal and electricity energy use. Figure 12.13 and Table 12.2 illustrate the impact of density, size, and location of residential development. Suburban houses are generally bigger and consume more thermal and electrical energy than smaller "urban single-family" and "urban multifamily" units. Travel distances are usually longer for members of suburban households than urban ones, and this translates into greater transportation energy usage. Figure 12.13 also shows that consumer choice for green, higher-efficiency buildings and vehicles, as well as conserving behavior, can affect energy use. Such a green suburban household can reduce energy use by 50%, compared to a conventional suburban household. The urban multifamily, green urban single-family, and green multifamily households have the lowest consumption and related emissions of all (Randolph 2008; Randolph and Masters 2008).

Figure 12.13 Typical Household Energy Use by Type, Location, and Choice. The lowest energy consumption is achieved by the urban multifamily, green urban single-family, and green multifamily (MF) households.

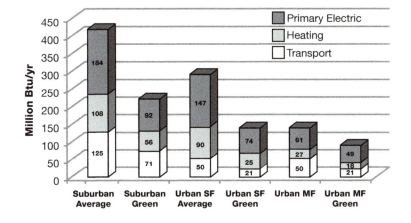

TABLE 12.2 **Assumptions for Figure 12.13: Residential Energy Use by Design Type**

	VMT/yr	MPG	Thermal Index*	House Size	Elect. kWh/mo
Suburban Average	25,000	25	8	3,000	1,500
Suburban Green	20,000	35	5	2,500	750
Urban SF Average	8,000	20	8	2,500	1,200
Urban SF Green	5,000	30	5	2,000	600
Urban MF	8,000	20	6	1,000	500
Urban MF Green	5,000	30	4	1,000	400

4,500 degree-days; primary electricity = 3 × end-use.
*TI = Btu/HDD-sq ft; 8 reflects standard code, 5 approaches green building standard.

Community and Metropolitan Scale. The green and sustainable community must also capture the economies of scale of community-wide and regional technologies and designs, in order to save energy, water, materials, and land, as well as create regional identity and economy.

- *Metropolitan land use and transportation.* Efficient land use does not stop at the neighborhood scale but extends community- and metro-wide. Transit-oriented development (TOD) creates density that is near transit stops, promoting walkable and bicycle-friendly places and less reliance on cars, thereby connecting places of residence to places of employment, education, and commerce. Research in California showed that members of households in TODs drive 5,000–7,500 miles less per year, use transit five times more, and emit 2–3.4 tCO_2/household less than non-TOD households (CalTrans 2002). Transit-oriented developments must be linked with different transport options, including light rail, commuter rail, and express buses. Transit is enabled by density, and metro-scale density is enhanced by arresting sprawl through urban growth boundaries, which aim to contain growth and conserve working landscapes beyond the boundary (see Chapter 16).

- *Smart grid.* At the community and metropolitan scale, the electrical grid needs to be upgraded to increase reliability and allow the seamless two-way flow of electricity required by onsite generation and net-metering and for vehicle-to-grid flow. Smart meters can give real-time feedback of energy use to consumers, provide time-of-day pricing, and lead to smart house controls.

- *Renewable energy.* While there are opportunities for onsite distributed energy within neighborhoods, the regional scale offers centralized possibilities to convert from carbon-based energy to renewable sources, including regional wind farms, hydroelectric, biofuels, and large-scale solar. The potential depends on local resources. Austin (TX) and Sacramento (CA) are two good examples of cities with municipal utilities that have invested heavily in wind and solar power to reduce carbon emissions. Other localities served by investor-owned utilities have negotiated with their providers (like Chicago), or used *community choice aggregator* options (like San Francisco) to increase the portfolio of renewable electricity serving their cities.

- *Electrification of vehicles and vehicles-to-grid.* The NRC 2009 study concludes that efficient land use can affect VMT, related petroleum energy use, and GHG emissions, but not enough to meet the dramatic reductions needed in our fast-approaching carbon-rich and oil-poor future. Biofuels, especially cellulosic ethanol and algae-based biodiesel, are likely to contribute, but most analysts believe that vehicle electrification provides the best opportunity to reduce GHG and urban air pollutant emissions and petroleum consumption, even without a dramatic reduction in VMT. These technologies include plug-in hybrid vehicles (e.g., the Chevrolet Volt) and all-electric vehicles (e.g., the Nissan Leaf). Both the Volt and the Leaf came on the market in 2011, and the Toyota Plug-in Prius, the all-electric Toyota RAV-4, and the Tesla Model S are scheduled to be launched in 2012.

Vehicle electrification may be a game-changing technology for reducing petroleum, carbon emissions, and urban air pollution. Here are the potential benefits of vehicle electrification:

- Reduced petroleum dependence for transportation.
- Lower fuel cost (at 12¢ per kWh, it is equivalent to about 90¢ per gallon of gasoline).
- Reduced carbon emissions (CO_2 emissions are half of gas-powered vehicles, assuming U.S. current 50% coal electricity generation).
- No additional electricity-generating capacity needed. With overnight charging of plug-in vehicles, 73% of the nation's passenger VMT could be fueled by overnight charge, without adding to the nation's generating capacity (Kintner-Meyer et. al 2008).

- Enhanced market for renewable electricity. Overnight charging would provide a market for intermittent wind power and complement onsite solar PV generation, which would feed the grid during the day when utilities need the power and charge vehicles at night when utilities have excess capacity (Randolph and Masters 2008).

A large fleet of plug-in electric drive and batteried vehicles could provide an additional benefit to the metro power infrastructure. Night-charge vehicles parked during the day in parking lots and garages could be plugged into the grid and provide a highly dispatchable electricity storage bank that utilities could draw from during peak demand. Such a *vehicles-to-grid* (V2G) system would also benefit vehicle owners who could buy cheap overnight power from the utilities and sell back the power during the day at higher rates. The city of Austin is already planning a V2G infrastructure.

There are some barriers to this vision, however, including the availability, expense, and market penetration of electric vehicles; the cost of lithium-ion batteries; a battery-charging infrastructure; and the improvements for creating the smart grid that is necessary for a seamless flow of power to and from the grid. Smart grid improvements are expected well before electric fleets grow, and advances in the energy density and cost reduction of batteries are expected. There are urban planning implications, especially with regard to charging infrastructure. Already there are more than 500 charging stations in the U.S. (400 of these in California), but the number is increasing quickly. ECOtolity is investing $115 million, matched by U.S. DOE funding, in 15,000 charging stations in 16 cities in 6 states (California, Arizona, Tennessee, Texas, Oregon, and Washington), plus Washington, DC. Coulomb Technologies is investing $37 million in hundreds of free charging stations in New York City, Michigan, and California (www.ecotality.com, www.coulombtech.com).

2. Low-Carbon Community Choice and Behavior

To be adopted widely, sustainable technologies and designs must be cost-effective, easily implemented, readily available, and part of mainstream design and practice. Accelerating the adoption requires consumer and investor choice, and that choice depends on the assurance that such designs and technologies work as promised and are cost-effective. However, choice is driven not only by the utilitarian values of cost-effectiveness, but also by the emerging social movement that is embracing sustainability values. Informed, responsible choice depends on the assurance that such designs and technologies will provide the environmental benefits they claim. Moreover, this social movement brings with it a desire for individuals and households to modify their behavior to conserve energy and materials and reduce their carbon emissions. Many believe that the awareness that accompanies this movement, along with the behavior, choice, and political action for climate action that it spawns, is critical to achieving the low-carbon community.

Mobilizing the Community. The process of community climate action planning is a vehicle for educating and motivating individuals, households, and community groups so they can become involved in the social movement of climate action. In fact, many of the local climate action planning efforts have resulted from citizens and groups through political action. The planning process should engage the public, to the greatest extent possible, to help educate, encourage, and motivate conservation behavior. Chicago's Climate Action Plan, calling on individual action, estimates that the city's 12.7 mt/c CO_2 emissions could be reduced by 20% through simple behavioral measures by the city's residents, including recycling, maintaining cars and furnaces, replacing lights with CFLs, adjusting thermostats, and planting trees (Chicago 2008a).

Good Information.   Those who are motivated to act need good information, in order to be assured that their actions are effective. For individuals and households, there are carbon footprint calculators and consumer information sources, like GoodGuide.com, that can help guide their choices. Household smart meters installed as part of smart grid technology upgrades have an added advantage of being able to provide households with real-time data on their consumption of energy, carbon emissions, and costs. Studies have shown that simply providing such information to consumers can result in a 5–15% reduction in energy use (e.g., Armel 2009; Mitchell-Jackson 2005; Mountain 2006; Parker et al. 2006, 2009.)

Green rating systems also provide good information for consumers and investors, ensuring that products meet desired benefits. Starting with automobile fuel efficiency and appliance energy-efficiency labels in the 1970s, green rating programs attempt to counter market failures caused by misinformation and consumer emphasis on first-cost rather than life-cycle costs and benefits. The EPA's ENERGY STAR rating system began in 1992 to promote appliances, equipment, and homes that exceed efficiency standards and codes. ENERGY STAR Homes are based on the Home Energy Rating System (HERS). The U.S. Green Building Council (USGBC) was established in 1993 to promote buildings that are environmentally responsible, profitable, and healthy through consensus-based green rating systems.

USGBC's suite of LEED green building protocols is not the only such rating system, but it has become the industry standard. LEED rating systems exist for new construction (NC), commercial interiors (CI), existing buildings (EB), homes (H), and neighborhood development (ND). Although most green building systems affect new construction, LEED-EB is used in the important retrofitting and renovation of existing buildings. The LEED-H protocol addresses the building envelope, "whole building" electricity, and building materials and indoor air quality.

USGBC partnered with the Congress for New Urbanism (CNU) and the Natural Resources Defense Council (NRDC) to develop the LEED Neighborhood Development protocol to assess neighborhood sustainability. After 5 years of development and an extensive pilot phase, LEED-ND was launched in early 2010. The protocol includes building and onsite criteria for energy and material efficiency, onsite electricity generation, and green infrastructure, but the majority of the points address location efficiency, compact development, and connectedness (see Chapters 14 and 16).

3. Community Plans and Policies

The low-carbon community of the future will include the range of sustainable technologies and designs, as well as a community social movement embracing consumer choice, behavior, and political action, described above. Randolph and Masters (2008) refer to the former as the "techno-economic solutions" and the latter as the "social solutions." They further propose that the "policy solutions" are necessary for accelerating and achieving both of the other two categories of solutions, through regulations, incentives, education, research, and demonstration. And it is planning that is needed to formulate the techno-economic, social, and policy solutions appropriate for a given community.

Community Climate Action and Energy Plans and Policies

Cities can incorporate climate action planning in their general or comprehensive plans, or they can provide a more focused climate action plan, community energy plan, or sustainability plan. Most cities have focused on a climate action plan (CAP). About 500 U.S. localities have joined the Climate Protection Program (CCP) of ICLEI–Local Governments for Sustainability and are using ICLEI's climate action planning process. This process includes five basic steps (ICLEI 2009):

1. Conduct a community energy and GHG emissions inventory.
2. Set a target for emissions reduction by a certain date.
3. Develop a local action plan of policies, programs, and measures to meet the target.
4. Implement the local plan.
5. Monitor energy use and emissions over time to evaluate the plan.

Box 12.4 illustrates some of these steps from Blacksburg, Virginia's climate action planning process. The Blacksburg process illustrates the first three steps: the GHG inventory, setting targets, and identifying specific strategies and quantifying their potential emissions reductions to meet the target. Blacksburg is one of many U.S. cities that have used federal economic stimulus funds through the Energy Efficiency and Conservation Block Grant (EECBG) program, which has distributed $3 billion to localities and states for community energy programs. This significant funding has prompted a grand experiment in energy and related climate action planning in the U.S.

Learning from Climate Action Plans and Their Implementation

In climate action planning, the "laboratory" is the community, and there is much to be learned from the growing body of experience in cities and states in the U.S. and abroad. A number of reviews and evaluation studies have been conducted (e.g., Bailey 2007; Bestill and Bulkeley 2007; Boswell et al. 2010, 2011; Pitt and Randolph 2009; Wheeler 2008). The most recent study could document only about 120 completed CAPs by February 2011 (Boswell et al. 2011). Their earlier content analysis of 30 plans focused on the link between GHG emission inventories and the CAP results (Boswell et al. 2010). They found that the inventories

BOX 12.4—Preparing a Climate Action Plan: A Snapshot from Blacksburg

The ICLEI five-step process provides a useful framework for climate action planning. ICLEI also provides some software tools for GHG emission inventories and assessing reductions strategies. In the Blacksburg CAP project, we conducted a GHG inventory for the Town and Virginia Tech, then separated nonuniversity community energy and emissions (35% of the total) to focus on the community plan (the university developed its own climate action plan). ICLEI tools were useful for the transportation component, but we relied mostly on our own spreadsheet analysis of utility and other local data. Figure 12.14 gives a breakdown of sector energy use and GHG emissions (ICLEI's step 1). Because of our coal-based electricity, 40% of energy use in residential and commercial buildings turned into almost 60% of GHG emissions. These and transportation were then the best opportunities for reductions.

The Town Council set a target for 80% emission reduction below 1990 levels by 2050 (step 2). This target is presented in Figure 12.15. The figure also shows "conservative" and "maximum" reduction scenarios for approaching the target, based on specific measures from different sectors compared to a business-as-usual projection (step 3). A third "aggressive" scenario identifies reductions that fall between conservative and maximum.

Blacksburg is beginning to implement the plan. The initial focus is on the residential sector through its EECBG funding and partnership in a regional Community Alliance for Energy Efficiency.

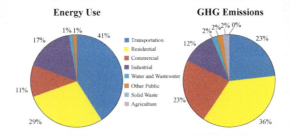

Figure 12.14 Blacksburg Energy Use and GHG Emissions. Emissions percentage in building sectors is greater than energy percentage because of the reliance on coal-generated electricity. (*Source:* Pitt et al. 2011.)

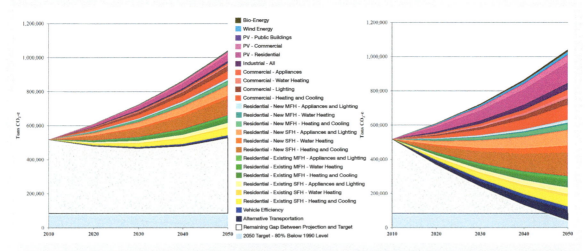

Figure 12.15 Blacksburg GHG Emission Reduction Scenarios and Target for 2050 (blue band at bottom). A: "Conservative" reduction scenario includes measures that would only maintain current emission levels. B: "Maximum" reduction scenario includes measures that would reduce emissions below target. (*Source:* Pitt et al. 2011.)

Source: Adapted from Pitt et al. 2011.

were technically accurate, but forecasts and targets did not account well for exogenous change factors (e.g., technology, state policies), and mitigation actions were poorly linked to targets. They suggested better documentation in GHG inventories and focusing on per capita emissions to account for population growth. Their *Local Climate Action Planning* book (Boswell et al. 2011) uses a compilation and synthesis of U.S. community experience to detail rationale, planning and participation process, and implementation strategies for climate change protection and adaptation.

Table 12.3 summarizes the climate action plans for eighteen cities, including ten American cities and eight in other countries. Ten of the plans are for large cities, and eight are under 1 million population, including four under 300,000. Box 12.5 provides a closer look at one plan, the 2009 Climate Action Plan for the City of Portland and Multnomah County, Oregon. Building on Portland's two decades of experience in energy and climate planning, this CAP provides a model for other communities.

The plans in Table 12.3 have similar emissions goals, including IPCC recommended levels of 80% below 1990 levels by 2050, but many have short-term targets to motivate immediate action. San Francisco and Los Angeles have the most aggressive short-term targets of the U.S. cities (20% below 1990 by 2012 and 2010, respectively), and London (60% below 1990 by 2020) and Stockholm (4% below 1990 by 2010) top the other cities studied. Berkeley was the first city to set its target by voter referendum, creating a political foundation for subsequent planning and implementation.

Of the cities studied, Portland, Berkeley, Seattle, Heidelberg, and Stockholm had early starts, with energy and climate plans developed in the 1990s. Heidelberg has been able to maintain 2006 emissions at 1987 levels, and Stockholm cut a half-million tons in emissions from 1990 to 2000 (half of its total goal to 2005) and achieved per capita emissions of 4 mt/c in 2005, among the lowest among large developed cities. Their history of CHP and district heating systems, transit systems, and compact mixed development have benefited these and other European cities. In the U.S., the 20 years of results from Seattle, Berkeley, and Portland prove that citywide energy planning and efficiency improvements, plus a community social movement, can have lasting benefits.

The following are innovative action measures and policies included in the CAPs that address opportunities for emissions reductions at the building, site, neighborhood, and community/ metropolitan scales:

- *New building energy codes*. Paris sets performance standards for new buildings at 50 kWh/m^2/yr. Boulder has a green building code requiring green points beyond the base energy code. Austin and Berkeley plan an NZEB code by 2015 and 2020, respectively.
- *Building efficiency retrofits*. This is a critical element of most plans. Berkeley and San Francisco have time-of-sale energy standards for existing buildings. Seattle's municipal utility has offered demand-side retrofits for 38 years, saving 1 million megawatt hours (MWh) per year by 2006. Philadelphia has focused on residential weatherization, increasing

TABLE 12.3 Climate Action Plans for Eighteen Cities

City	Population	Per Capita GHG	GHG Target	Actions
Austin	750,000	NA	Carbon neutral	• Municipal facilities carbon-neutral by 2020 • 700 MW of efficiency/conservation by 2020 • 30% renewable power by 2020: PV rebates • Smart grid development • Building codes: 75% more efficient • NZE-capable by 2015
Berkeley, CA	90,000	6.4 mt/c	80% < 1990 by 2050 public vote (−2%/yr) Actual: −9% 2000–2005	• Building energy −35% by 2020: time of sale code (1980); NZEB code by 2020; retrofit • Renewable power: FIRST PV financing • Transport: transit, TOD, parking pricing • Mobilization: Measure G movement; Green Neighborhood Challenge
Boulder, CO	293,000	17.7 mt/c	7% < 1990 by 2012	• Carbon tax on electricity: $860K/yr revenue • Green building code • 1st Smart Grid city in U.S. • ClimateSmart outreach programs
Chicago	2.8 million	12.7 mt/c	20% < 1990 by 2020	• Building efficiency (30% of reductions) • Clean/renewable energy (34%) • Transit/TOD/vehicle efficiency (23%) • Reduced waste, industrial emissions (13%)
Los Angeles	3.8 million	12.4 mt/c	20% < 1990 by 2010 35% <1990 by 2030	• 20% renewable power by 2010, 35% by 2030; replace coal power with natural gas • Smart Grid development • Energy efficiency rebates, giveaways • Transit alternative fuels, TOD land use
New York	8.2 million	7.1 mt/c	30% < 2005 by 2030	• Improved building efficiency (50%) • Clean and renewable power (34%) • Sustainable transportation (18%)
Philadelphia	1.5 million	NA	20% < 1990 by 2015	• Weatherize 15% of housing stock by 2015 • Reduce building energy by 10% by 2015 • 20% renewable power by 2015 • Increase tree canopy by 30% by 2015 • Reduce VMT by 10% by 2015
Portland	568,000	1990: 14.7 mt/c 2008: 11.9 mt/c Goals: 2030: 5.1 mt/c 2050: 1.3 mt/c	40% < 1990 by 2030 Actual: 1.2% < 1990 in 2008	• Early start 1993. 2008: 1.2% renewable power, 64% recycle rate; 40 green cert buildings, 750,000 trees planted since 1996 • Transit, walk/bike, TOD corridor zoning • Building energy efficiency services • Onsite power, district heating
San Francisco	765,000	11.2 mt/c	20% < 1990 by 2012	• Building efficiency (31%): time of sale code, commercial retrofit, new building code • Transportation (37%): expand transit use, vehicle efficiency, congestion pricing • Renewable energy (21%): wind, solar • Solid waste (11%)

(table continues)

City	Population	Per Capita GHG	GHG Target	Actions
Seattle	594,000	11.5 mt/c	7% < 1990 by 2012 80% < 1990 by 2050 Actual: –8% 1990-2005	• Seattle City Light: zero-net GHG in 2008; demand side rebates, giveaways • Expand transit, complete streets, drive smart, parking tax • Mobilization: green business partnership
Freiburg	216,000	8.5 mt/c	40% < 1992 by 2030; achieved 7.3% < 1992 by 2005	• 80% efficient Combined Heat & Power (3% of power 1993 to 52% in 2006) • Renewable power: 10% by 2010 • Public transit/alternative modes • Abandoning nuclear power (60% in 1993 to 30% in 2006)
Hamburg	1.7 million	9.0 mt/c	–2 Mt/yr 2007–2012 –25% mt/c 1990–2012	• Mobilization: Work & Climate Protection Initiative (1998) • Efficient buildings • Renewable power
Heidelberg	140,000	NA	20% < 2004 by 2015	• Early action: 1991 goal: 20% < 1987 by 2005 (actual 2% > 1987 in 2006) • CHP, district heating; renewable power • Mobilize: climate is looking for protection
London	7.5 million	5.9 mt/c	60% < 1990 by 2025	• 10 low-carbon zones/neighborhoods funded; emissions –20.12% by 2012, –60% by 2025 • 25% renewable power by 2025 • Congestion charge of £8/day to enter city to reduce congestion and increase transit use
Paris	2.2 million	10.9 mt/c	75% < 2004 by 2050; 25% < 2004 by 2020	• Building energy performance code (50 kWh/m^2/yr) plus density bonus for better • 25% reduction in energy use by 2020 • 25% renewable power by 2020
Stockholm	1.3 million	4 mt/c	4% < 1990 by 2010; 4 mt/c by 2005 –1 mill tons 1990–2005	• Early action: 1998 plan and reduction of ½ Mt from 1990–2000 • District heating • Green electricity • Transit, congestion charges
Sydney	4.3 million	NA	50% < 1990 by 2030 70% < 2005 by 2030	• Green Transformers: CHP and district heat • Renewable power: 25% by 2030 • Walkable places; increased transit
Toronto	5.5 million	9.6 mt/c	6% < 1990 by 2012 30%, 2020 80%, 2050	• Better Building Partnerships: retrofits • Sustainable transportation • Renewable power • Double tree canopy, 17 to 34%

Portland completed its latest CAP in October 2009. This plan represents a success story and therefore a future prescription for what may be the most sustainable city in the United States. It also serves as a model for other communities.

Here are several unique aspects of Portland's CAP:

- It emphasizes the cobenefits of the actions for protection: creating green jobs and a vibrant economy, known as climate prosperity; improving social equity; saving money by saving energy; enhancing air quality; promoting healthier residents; becoming energy self-sufficient; establishing livable neighborhoods; and enhancing quality of life.
- It looks anew at how carbon emissions are measured, in ways that can guide improved means of mitigation. Traditional GHG invento-

ries use a "sector method," which takes a supply-side view of energy distributed to different consuming sectors, but misses life cycle and embodied energy and emissions of consumer products and food. In addition, the plan applies a "systems method," which takes a demand-side look at consumption and attempts to measure the life cycle emissions of products and energy used.

- The citywide and countywide CAP zooms in on neighborhoods and their differences, so actions can be tailored to their needs. It provides maps with such data as average single-family house size and natural gas use per household by census tract. It contains a spatial representation of the "20-minute complete neighborhood concept" that maps throughout the city the range of accessibility by a quality 20-minute walk to daily destinations and transit (Figure 12.16).

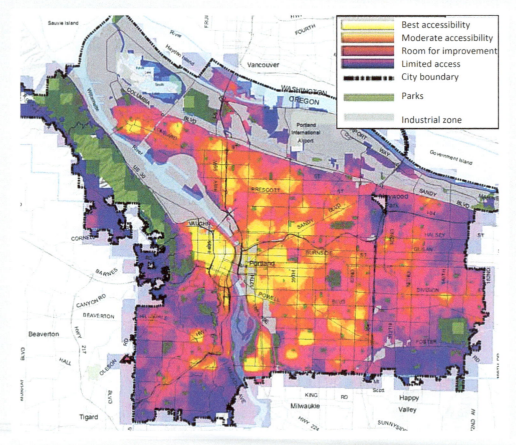

Figure 12.16 The 20-Minute Complete Neighborhood Concept, Portland, Oregon. This map shows the levels of accessability, based on destinations of daily life, distance, and quality of walking environment. (*Source:* City of Portland 2009. Portland Climate Action Plan, Bureau of Planning and Sustainability. Used with permission.)

The climate action plan of 2009 builds on Portland's notable previous success. After increasing CO_2 emissions by 15% from 1990 to 2000, Portland has reduced emissions to 1.2% below 1990 in 2008 (despite a population increase of 22%) and reduced per capita emissions by 24% from 14.7 mt/c in 1990 to 11.9 mt/c in 2008. This decline in emissions resulted from:

- Controlling landfill methane and diverting more waste to recycling.
- Lower total residential and industrial electricity (although offset by an increase in commercial use).
- Improved vehicle efficiency (although offset by a slight increase in VMT per capita).
- Lower carbon fuel mix for electricity, including wind (4%) and natural gas (24%) (although coal still contributed 44% in 2008).
- Improved transit, light rail, and trolley service.
- Improved land use efficiency through Smart Growth and transit-oriented development.
- Climate-conserving behavior, including bicycle commuting (highest in the country and eight times the national average), doubling transit use since 1990, a recycling rate at 64% (highest in the nation and twice the national average), and the most hybrid cars per capita in the nation.

The 2009 CAP intends to take this success much farther, with goals to reduce emissions to 40% below 1990 by 2030 and 80% below by 2050. Table 12.4 presents actual data and targets on emissions, VMT, and electricity, as well as the plan's goals for per capita emissions of 5.1 mt/c in 2030 and 1.3 mt/c in 2050.

To achieve these targets, the planners developed a broad range of 2030 community objectives and strategies in six categories:

1. Buildings and energy

- Reduce the total energy use of all buildings built before 2010 by 25%.
- Achieve zero net greenhouse gas emissions in all new buildings and homes.
- Produce 10% of the total energy from onsite renewable sources and clean district energy systems.
- Ensure that new buildings and major remodels can adapt to the changing climate.

2. Urban form and mobility

- Create vibrant neighborhoods, where 90% of Portland residents can easily walk or bicycle to meet all basic daily, nonwork needs and have safe pedestrian or bicycle access to transit.
- Reduce per capita daily VMT by 30% from 2008 levels.
- Improve the efficiency of freight movement within and through the Portland metropolitan area.
- Increase the average fuel efficiency of passenger vehicles to 40 miles per gallon.
- Reduce the life cycle GHG emissions of transportation fuels by 20% through cellulosic ethanol and electricity (10% electric vehicles by 2030, 25% by 2050).

3. Consumption and solid waste

- Reduce total solid waste generated by 25%.
- Recover 90% of all waste generated.
- Reduce the GHG impacts of the waste collection system by 40%.

TABLE 12.4 **Portland Energy and Emissions 1990–2008 and 2009 CAP Goals**

	Actual			Targets	
	1990	2000	2008	2030	2050
Emissions, million tons CO_2	8.60	9.19	8.46	5.13	1.70
% change from 1990	—	+15.2%	–1.2%	–40%	–80%
Population	584,000	660,000	715,000	999,000	1,355,000
Per capita emissions, tons/person	14.7	13.9	11.9	5.1	1.3
Passenger VMT/person/day	17.4	18.2	18.5	13.4	6.8
Electricity kWh/person/day	13,049	14,177	12,081	7,869	3,815

BOX 12.5—A Climate Action Plan for Portland and Multnomah County, Oregon (cont.)

4. Urban forestry and natural systems

- Expand the urban forest canopy to cover one-third of Portland, and at least 50% of total stream and river length in the city to meet urban water temperature goals as an indicator of watershed health.

5. Food and agriculture

- Reduce the consumption of carbon-intensive foods.
- Significantly increase the consumption of local food.

6. Community engagement

- Motivate all Multnomah County residents and businesses to change their behavior in ways that reduce GHG emissions.

Portland was an early entry into energy and climate protection planning. The latest climate action plan builds on this experience and on Portland's community culture both for sustainability and for developing an aggressive strategy to mitigate climate change and achieve significant benefits.

Source: Adapted from Portland 2009.

houses served to 800 per year. Toronto, New York, and Portland partner with the private sector to provide building energy services.

- *Increased city's renewable energy portfolio.* All the plans call for more renewable power, with targets depending on current sources. Seattle has already achieved zero net carbon emissions in electricity, with its large hydro base and offsets. Other cities aim to develop more onsite photovoltaic generation, region wind, and biomass power through their municipal utilities (Austin, Los Angeles, Seattle), negotiation with investor-owned utility (Chicago, New York), community choice agreement (San Francisco), green marketing (Austin), and incentives (Austin, Los Angeles).

- *Smart grid development.* To accommodate renewable and other distributed energy, Austin and Los Angeles, through their municipal utilities, and Boulder, through its investor-owned provider, are developing smart grid infrastructure, including smart meters that provide real-time consumption information to customers.

- *Combined heat and power and district heating.* European cities have long used the efficiency advantages of CHP and district heating, which is a main reason for their low emissions per capita (Stockholm, Freiberg, Heidelberg). Sydney's Green Transformers CHP program is its CAP's biggest saver of energy and emissions.

- *Financial incentives.* To accelerate the diffusion of low-carbon measures, many plans rely on financial rebates, tax credits, low-interest loans, and giveaways (audits, CFLs, water measures). Austin's solar PV rebate of $5.80/W installed is the highest in the nation. Berkeley's financing incentive for renewable solar technology (FIRST) program finances onsite residential solar, with repayment incorporated into property taxes paid over 20 years. This property assessment for clean energy (PACE) approach has promise but has met with some resistance after the 2009–2010 mortgage default crisis.

- *Financial disincentives.* London was the first city to adopt a "congestion charge" (of £8) for cars entering the central city; it has reduced congestion and increased transit use. Stockholm's and San Francisco's plans include a congestion charge. Boulder adopted the first carbon tax on electricity consumption; revenues of $850,000 are used to implement the climate action plan. Many plans rely on parking fee structures to discourage single-occupancy commuting and encourage ride sharing and transit (Seattle, Los Angeles, Berkeley).

- *Increased transit ridership, expanded transit.* Cities with significant vehicle emissions intend to get more transit ridership through expanded and improved services, along with the disincentives mentioned above (Chicago, Freiberg, New York, Philadelphia, Seattle, San Francisco, Stockholm).

- *Land use, transit- and pedestrian-oriented development, walkable neighborhoods.* Portland has a light rail transit station overlay zone that has led to dense walkable and mixed-use development around transit stops and increased transit ridership. Seattle, Freiberg, New York, Los Angeles, and Berkeley all have TOD objectives and sustainable transportation as part of their plans.

- *Increased tree canopy cover, increased recycling, waste diversion from landfills.* Several plans have goals to increase recycling rates (Portland has achieved a 64% rate and plans higher) to divert wastes from landfills and reduce methane GHG. Many have community programs to plant trees that sequester atmospheric CO_2 and provide other environmental benefits (Chicago, Philadelphia, Portland, Toronto, Atlanta, New York, Los Angeles).

- *Mobilization, education, and outreach.* To motivate volunteer action, behavior change, and political support, most plans include outreach and mobilization programs. London aims to achieve its targets one neighborhood at a time, in ten "low-carbon zones" that receive city funding to retrofit their neighborhood to achieve emission reductions of 12% by 2012 and 60% by 2025. Berkeley has a Green Neighborhood Challenge. Boulder has ClimateSmart programs, including the low-cost Residential Energy Audit Program (REAP) and Neighborhood Sweep. Seattle and Toronto have green business partnerships, and Heidelberg has a public campaign called "Climate Is Looking for Protection."

Protecting the Climate

Climate action and energy planning are sweeping the globe, with more and more cities joining the grand experiment of community response to the climate imperative. Those new entries have much to learn from the experience to date, especially from those cities that have had implementation success. European cities especially have much experience to offer, given their history of higher energy prices, efficient CHP and district heating systems, compact and mixed development, and effective transit systems. Stockholm, London, Mannheim, and Heidelberg are among those European cities that have achieved incredibly low CO_2 emissions per capita (4–6 mt/c).

Several American cities also have lessons for newcomers to climate action planning. Portland's 2009 Climate Action Plan builds on its two decades of experience, leading to a 24% drop in per capita emissions since 1990 and an 8% drop in total emissions since 2000. Seattle, Austin, Los Angeles, and other cities having a municipal electric utility offer distinct advantages for providing energy efficiency, renewable energy, and smart grid services to their residents and businesses. Chicago, New York, Portland, Berkeley, San Francisco, and Boulder have shown what communities without a municipal utility can do in partnership with their investor-owned utilities. Many U.S. cities have a growing body of experience with progressive building codes and ordinances; land use measures, such as TOD overlay zones and mixed-use and density bonuses; creative financing and other incentives; transit improvements; urban forestry; and community mobilization efforts for building energy retrofits, education, and friendly neighborhood competitions. These programs are among the repertoire of climate action measures that should be part of community efforts to reduce emissions per capita.

Planners must play a pivotal role in developing plans and implementing programs to protect the climate. Energy and climate planning is still foreign to most practicing planners (and unfortunately to planning education). But planners know the planning process, and they should lead climate planning efforts. The critical issues of land use and building ordinances, transportation and transit planning, and community engagement are squarely within the planners' domain.

Climate Adaptation Planning

Action planning has focused primarily on climate protection, or strategies to reduce GHG emissions to lessen future global warming and its consequences. It has just begun to address climate change adaptation, or strategies to adapt to the consequences of climate change, knowing that they will be severe even if we halted GHG emissions today. This challenge is complicated by the long-term nature of climate change, as well as the uncertainties about the timing, location, and extent of impact.

Adaptation, in the context of climate change, can be defined as a process, action, or outcome in a system in order for the system to better cope with, manage, or adjust to a changing condition, risk, or opportunity. A system's capacity for adaptation or resilience is its ability to absorb perturbations without being undermined or becoming unable to adapt, self-organize, and learn. Effective **climate change adaptation**, then, must be anticipatory, identify vulnerabilities, stress preparedness for change, and build the capacity for resilience among those likely affected by change (Randolph 2011; Smit and Wandel 2006; Tompkins and Adger 2004).

Planning for adaptation to climate change is still in its infancy, and much of the work is based on the past experience of natural hazard planning (see Chapter 13).

The few adaptation plans that are being developed employ traditional rational planning models. But there is an important role for collaborative planning and collective action to build up the capacity for resilience to change. Thus far, adaptation to climate change has focused on two objectives:

1. Lessening the impacts using technology and planning, such as seawalls to fend off sea-level rise and resulting storm surges, expanded irrigation to counter more frequent droughts, and more dams and reservoirs to contain flood flows and store water to compensate for reduced snowmelt.
2. Anticipating impacts, and changing the patterns of human settlement and agriculture now, so we can live with those impacts in the future, including relocating vulnerable populations and adopting climate-adapting development designs.

State Adaptation Plans

Several countries, regions, states, and communities are beginning to develop adaptation plans. The level of activity depends on the state's perceived vulnerability to climate change. Florida is a case in point: A 1-meter sea-level rise would place a large portion of coastal Florida under water. A July 2007 Executive Order charged the state's Action Team on Energy and Climate Change with the task of creating adaptation plans and strategies to lessen adverse impacts to Florida's society, public health, the economy, and natural communities. The Florida planning process is traditional top-down, rational planning, emphasizing the scientific study of possible impacts and the effectiveness of different response strategies, including (Deyle et al. 2007):

- *Protection:* Seawalls, levees, storm surge gates.
- *Retreat:* Rolling easements, buyout, abandonment of facilities.
- *Accommodation:* Elevations, flood proofing, setbacks, prohibiting building in hazard zones, alternative water supplies.

California released its *2009 California Climate Adaptation Strategy* in response to a 2008 Governor's Executive Order (California Natural Resources Agency 2009). The plan focused on seven critical impact areas, and a relevant state agency was charged with taking the lead in each, so all of state government was involved. Here are the impact areas:

1. *Public health:* Higher mortality and morbidity, increased air pollution, increased allergens, spread of disease vectors, decreased food security, reduced water availability.
2. *Biodiversity and habitat:* Barriers to species migration, temperature rise impacts on aquatic habitat, increased invasive species, threats to endangered species, loss of ecosystem services.
3. *Ocean and coastal resources:* Increased temperature and extreme events, higher runoff and flood risk, sea-level rise and risk of flooding, erosion, saltwater intrusion.

4. *Water management:* Reduced supply from Sierra snowpack, changes in water quality, increased evapotranspiration, soil moisture deficits, increased irrigation needs.
5. *Agriculture:* Crop yield changes; new weed, disease, and pest invasions; flooding, heat waves and heat stress, drought.
6. *Forestry:* Changes in forest productivity, tree mortality, invasive species, moisture deficits, increased wildfire risk.
7. *Transportation and energy infrastructure:* Increased cooling demands, less hydropower generation; impacts on seaside airports, roads, railroads, and docks.

The guiding principles for the strategy include the following:

- Use the best available science in identifying climate change risks and adaptation strategies. Understand that knowledge about climate change is still evolving. As such, an effective adaptation strategy is "living" and will itself be adapted.
- Involve all relevant stakeholders in identifying, reviewing, and refining the state's adaptation strategy. Establish and retain strong partnerships with federal, state, and local governments, tribes, private businesses, landowners, and NGOs to develop and implement adaptation strategy recommendations over time.
- Give priority to adaptation strategies that initiate, foster, and enhance existing efforts that improve economic and social well-being, public safety and security, public health, environmental justice, species and habitat protection, and ecological function.
- Understand the need for adaptation policies that are effective and flexible enough for circumstances that may not yet be fully predictable.
- Ensure that climate change adaptation strategies are coordinated with other local, state, national, and international efforts to reduce GHG emissions.

Among the recommendations are establishing a climate adaptation advisory panel; water conservation requirements to achieve a 20% reduction in per capita water use; avoiding development in vulnerable areas; ensuring communities are healthy in order to build resilient responses to the spread of disease and temperature increases; incorporating assessments of climate change impacts, vulnerability, and risk-reduction strategies in local general plans; and implementing a major public outreach effort, using a new CalAdapt website to synthesize climate impact research and statewide and local climate change scenarios.

Local Adaptation Plans

Several communities are developing adaptation plans at the local level. Two good examples are King County (Washington) and the San Francisco Bay Area (California). King County is a member of ICLEI–Local Governments for Sustainability's Climate Resilient Communities (CRC) program. ICLEI's CRC was launched in

2005 to help localities "develop their capacity to identify and reduce vulnerabilities, and thus improve resilience; learn to use tools and develop strategies that reduce hazards and manage risk related to regulations, planning, urban design, and investments; determine how to integrate climate preparedness strategies into existing hazard mitigation plans; reduce costs associated with disaster relief; and prioritize vulnerabilities" (ICLEI 2010).

King County formed an interdepartmental climate adaptation team in 2006 to enhance expertise in its county departments so that climate change would be considered in future planning, policy, and capital investments. With the help of the University of Washington's Climate Impact Group, the county's 2007 King County Climate Plan outlines several strategic focus areas for future adaptation efforts, including climate science, public health, safety and emergency preparedness, surface water management, freshwater quality and water supply, land use, buildings and transportation, financial and economic impacts (now called economic, agriculture, and forestry), and biodiversity and ecosystems.

The King County Global Warming Preparedness and Mitigation Plan was the result of an executive order of Ron Sims, the county executive. The 2007 plan was integrated into the comprehensive plan update in 2008. Table 12.5 highlights the impacts addressed in the plan. Actions taken include improved flood plain management, measures to protect wastewater facilities from coastal flooding exacerbated by sea-level rise, and modifications of transportation infrastructure.

ICLEI's *Climate Resilient Community Guidebook* uses the King County experience to suggest a process and checklist for local adaptation planning:

1. Initiate your climate resiliency effort.
   a. Scope the climate change impacts.
   b. Build and maintain support to prepare for climate change.
   c. Build your climate change preparedness team.
   d. Identify your planning areas relevant to climate change.
2. Conduct a climate resiliency study.
   a. Conduct a climate change vulnerability assessment.
   b. Conduct a climate change risk assessment.
   c. Prioritize planning areas.

TABLE 12.5 **Impacts of Climate Change in the Pacific Northwest**

Climate changes in...	*will impact ...*	*and affect ...*	*with consequences to ...*
Temperature	Snowpack	Agriculture	Public health
Precipitation	Stream flow	Stormwater	Economic livelihood
Storm intensity	Flooding	Wastewater treatment	Financial sector
Storm frequency	Water supply	Wildfire risk	Insurance industry
	Sea level	Hydropower	Individual comfort
	Soil water content	Forest health	Recreation
			Salmon and biodiversity

Source: Center for Science in the Earth System 2007.

3. Set preparedness goals and develop your preparedness plan.
   a. Establish a vision and guiding principles.
   b. Set preparedness goals.
   c. Develop, select, and prioritize preparedness actions.
4. Implement your preparedness plan.
5. Measure your progress and update your plan.
   a. Develop and track measures of resilience.
   b. Update your plan.

The San Francisco Bay Conservation and Development Commission (BCDC) developed a sea-level rise strategy for the Bay. While the region has other serious climate change impacts, including source water supply impacts of reduced Sierra snowpack, BCDC's jurisdiction is the Bay shoreline, and sea-level rise is the biggest threat. From its Sea-Level Rise Strategy:

> A bold, new plan for the Bay is needed to meet the challenges of sea-level rise head-on. The goal of the plan should not be to restore the Bay to historic conditions because climate-induced changes will not allow a return to past conditions. Instead, the plan should be a vision for resilient communities and adaptable natural areas around a dynamic and changing Bay that will have different sea level elevations, salinity levels, species and chemistry than the Bay has today. A new pattern of development will be needed to respond to these changing conditions. Because the rate of sea level rise and other impacts of climate change are still uncertain, the plan should embrace a pro-active adaptive management strategy that can respond to changes that will come about in the future as a result of climate change. (San Francisco BCDC 2008, 4)

The strategy calls for a complete sea-level rise adaptation plan within 4 years that looks forward over the next 50 years. The first step is socioeconomic and ecological assessment within 2 years that determines:

- The social and economic value of all existing and permitted built resources within the area expected to be impacted by sea-level rise.
- The cost of protecting these resources from inundation through the construction of seismically safe levees or seawalls, raising the elevation of infrastructure, or implementing ecologically sustainable shoreline protection strategies.
- The economic and ecological value of all natural resources expected to be impacted by sea-level rise.
- The cost of acquiring any upland areas needed to allow wetlands to migrate as sea levels rise or otherwise mitigating the impacts of sea-level rise on wetlands and other important habitats.
- The cost of removing or relocating resources in those areas projected to be inundated.

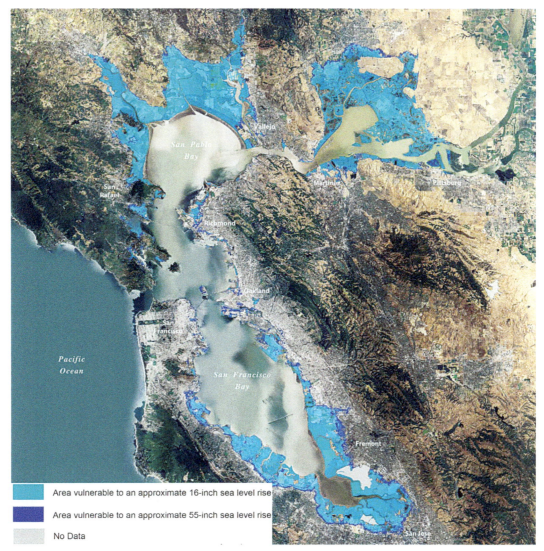

Figure 12.17 The Threat of Sea-Level Rise. This map shows the San Francisco Bay shoreline inundation estimates for climate-induced sea-level rises of 16 and 55 inches. (*Source:* San Francisco Bay Conservation and Development Commission 2008.)

To help its constituencies visualize the prospects of climate-induced sea-level rise, BCDC prepared maps of inundated sections of the Bay for 16-inch and 55-inch rises. Figure 12.17 shows the map for the entire San Francisco Bay.

Summary

Energy, air quality, and climate change mitigation are inextricably linked, and planning for one generally addresses the other. If we can use energy more efficiently and rely more on low-carbon sources, especially renewable energy, we can address our energy security and sustainability problem, our urban air quality challenge, and our climate change imperative.

But this is not easy. Our global economic system depends on oil and fossil fuels, and changing that dependency is hard. There have been frustrations at both the international and the U.S. national levels to tackle the problems with international agreements and effective federal policies. States have tried to fill the void, and their efforts serve as policy laboratories for national initiatives. California's energy and climate change planning and RGGI's cap-and-trade program offer valuable lessons for planning and policy.

Energy is consumed, and carbon emissions originate, mostly in cities, and this is where mitigation must occur. We identified some pathways to the low-carbon community that start at the building scale and move to the site, the neighborhood, and the community and metropolitan area. These pathways involve technologies and designs; consumer, investor, and community choice; and planning and policy from not only local, but also state and national governments.

Community energy and climate action planning is very active in U.S. and international cities, but it is still too early to tell what is the model approach. It appears that effective planning is context-specific, so there is no single, easy answer. Some localities, like Seattle which is carbon-neutral in electricity, must focus on transportation; others dependent on coal-fired electricity need to emphasize electricity efficiency in buildings and low-carbon electricity sources. Clearly, the world of energy, buildings, land use, and transportation that we know now in the U.S. must change dramatically—and soon—if we are to solve our energy use and climate problems.

We will not be able to avoid climate change and its impacts, so we must also develop plans to adapt to a changing world. Sea-level rise, extreme heat and weather events, and impacts on agriculture, water supplies, and ecosystems must be anticipated. "Anticipatory governance" must not only apply best science and technology to adapt to impacts, but must also engage people and organizations in developing plans to build the capacity for resilience in response to change, especially change we cannot foresee.

Even more than energy and climate protection planning, adaptation planning is in its infancy. We have much to learn from the first adopting innovators in adaptation, both in the U.S. and especially abroad.

The topics in environmental planning are interconnected. We can apply lessons from our previous discussions of collaborative planning, geospatial information, soil and water analysis, stormwater management, source water protection, and forest, wetland, and habitat analysis and protection to climate change mitigation and adaptation planning. Subsequent chapters provide even more tools and lessons, especially Chapter 13 on natural hazard mitigation planning, and also the chapters on land conservation, sustainable community design, growth management, and ecosystem and watershed management.

13 ■ Natural Hazard Mitigation for Community Resilience

Throughout human history, people have had to confront and combat the elements of nature, seeking security from the hazards of flooding, hurricanes, tornadoes, extreme heat and cold, earthquakes, tsunamis, volcanoes, landslides, avalanches, wildfire, pestilence, and environmentally transmitted diseases. These natural hazards continue to pose significant risk to human populations. The **Federal Emergency Management Agency (FEMA)** estimated in 2000 that 1 million people still die each decade from natural disasters (FEMA 2000b).

That's a gross underestimate for the first decade of the twenty-first century. Let's recall: The 2004 Indian Ocean tsunami killed 230,000 and the 2010 Haitian earthquake killed 222,000; they both rank in the top 10 death-toll disasters of all time. Extreme heat killed 30,000 in Europe in 2003 and 15,000 in Russia in 2010. The Chinese Sichuan earthquake killed 70,000 in 2008, and the 2010 Pakistan floods killed 1,600, displacing 10–20 million. In 2011, Australia and Brazil experienced unprecedented floods, the U.S. was hit by record tornadoes and floods in the Midwest, and Japan had a devastating earthquake and tsunami that killed more than 20,000 and caused the meltdown of the Fukushima nuclear power station. And the list goes on.

Death toll is the most dramatic indicator of disasters, but there are also countless people injured and displaced, and trillions of dollars in property damage. Hurricane Katrina killed 1,500, but it was also the mostly costly U.S. natural disaster, with $81 billion in damages. Nine of the U.S. top 12 costliest hurricanes of all time occurred between 2001 and 2005, including four that hit Florida in 2004. While the big disasters get most of the attention, it is smaller events that take the biggest cumulative toll on people's livelihoods. Of the 560 U.S. presidential declared disasters from 2000 through 2009, 11% were classified as hurricanes or typhoons, 4% floods, 3% fires, 1% earthquakes, 8% specific storm types (severe ice, snow, coastal, tornado), and the rest (71%) were simply "severe storms." And these events do not include the countless natural hazard episodes not declared disasters, the smaller floods and storms, the landslides and wildfires, the extreme summer heat—all of which severely affect the social and economic fabric of people and communities.

Natural hazards, and the damages and heartbreak they cause, will always be with us. But by being smart in land use planning, engineering, and design, we can mitigate hazards and lessen the risks they pose to life and livelihood. As discussed in the previous chapter, natural hazard mitigation is a critical component of adaptation to the impacts of climate change, especially extreme heat and weather events, flooding, and coastal storms. We defined adaptation as a process or action to better cope with or adjust to risk. And a community's capacity for adaptation or **resilience** is its ability to absorb perturbations without being undermined or becoming unable to adapt, self-organize, and learn. Resilience is a necessary ingredient of a sustainable community (Randolph 2011).

Effective natural hazard mitigation, then, is adaptation for resilient communities. It must be anticipatory, it must identify vulnerabilities, it has to focus on preparedness for change, and it must build the capacity for resilience among those who are likely to be affected by change. It has social as well as economic and technical dimensions.

This chapter first discusses some background and approaches to natural hazard mitigation planning. A decade ago, just a handful of U.S. communities were formally doing comprehensive natural hazard planning. Now, prompted by federal legislation and planning grants, there are some 19,000 FEMA-approved natural hazard mitigation plans. The chapter explores the process and describes lessons learned from prior experiences. Mitigation responses to specific hazards—flooding, coastal erosion and storms, geologic seismic and slope problems, and wildfire—constitute the balance of the chapter.

Natural Hazard Mitigation

Through the millennia, people and their institutions have tried to relieve the effects of natural hazards that threaten human health, safety, and welfare. Estimates of the worldwide death and damage tolls from natural disasters do not include the millions of daily incidents of natural hazard damage and injury not classified as "disasters." In the U.S., disaster relief grew from $2.8 billion in 1992 to $34.4 billion in 2005. Although a series of unusually large events affected this increase, the government recognized that continued increases in population and property values, as well as climate change–induced extreme weather events, are likely to drive these federal obligations upward (U.S. GAO 2007).

As a result of growing federal disaster assistance, Congress passed the Disaster Mitigation Act of 2000 (DMA 2000, or the Stafford Act), a national hazard mitigation program with these goals:

1. To reduce the loss of life and property, human suffering, economic disruption, and resulting disaster assistance costs from natural hazards.
2. To establish, within state and local governments with the help of federal grant funding, a natural hazard mitigation planning program to identify

risks and vulnerabilities, and develop long-term strategies for protecting people and property in future hazard events.

Before discussing the details of this FEMA-directed program and its outcome of natural hazard mitigation plans, we introduce some concepts of natural hazard risk and mitigation.

Hazard, Exposure, Vulnerability, and Risk

It is important to understand the differences between hazard, exposure, vulnerability, and risk.

- **Hazard** is the inherent danger associated with a potential problem, such as an earthquake or avalanche. It includes regional susceptibility, as well as the relative hazard of specific areas within that region. For example, the San Francisco Bay Area is an earthquake-prone region, yet within the region, areas underlain by soft materials have a ground-shaking hazard much greater than other areas.
- **Exposure** is the extent that the human population, ecological resource, or property is exposed to the hazard.
- **Vulnerability** is the unprotected nature of the exposure. Vulnerability can be reduced by engineering design (e.g., floodproofing, earthquake-resistant design, heating and air-conditioning systems to temper extreme heat and cold).
- **Risk** is the probable degree of injury and damage likely to occur from the exposure of people and property to the hazard over a specific time period. As shown in Figure 13.1, risk analysis involves combining the assessments of relative hazard, exposure, and vulnerability (or overlaying as maps), as well as analyzing the probability of occurrence. This statistical assessment relies on inventory, historical, and scientific data. For example, flood hazard probability relies on historical hydrologic data, and earthquake probability is based on subsurface geologic data.

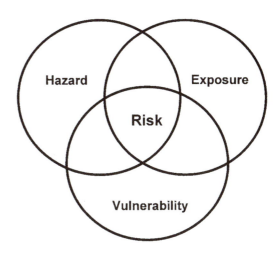

Figure 13.1 Hazard, Exposure, Vulnerability, and Risk. Risk is where a hazard, exposure to the hazard, and vulnerability to damage overlap, as well as the probability of occurrence.

People can sometimes increase the degree of hazard. For example, undercutting steep slopes increases landslide hazard, and paving parking lots and roads increases impervious surfaces, thereby exacerbating flooding downstream. More often, however, people increase their exposure and vulnerability by placing themselves in harm's way and doing so without necessary precautions or protection. For example, they build in a seismic or flood-prone area without proper design. Environmental risks to humans are increased by poor location and poor design of land developments.

Hazard Mitigation

In the United States, a number of agencies are charged with managing natural hazards. All have responsibility for specific hazards: The U.S. Geological Survey (USGS)—geologic hazards, the National Oceanic and Atmospheric Administration (NOAA)—weather-related hazards, the U.S. Army Corps of Engineers—flooding and disaster response, the Centers for Disease Control and Prevention (CDC)—environmental disease, the U.S. Forest Service (USFS)—wildfires, and the Environmental Protection Agency (EPA)—contaminants. FEMA has broad responsibilities for disasters and relief, and it also administers the National Flood Insurance Program (NFIP) and the Natural Hazard Mitigation Program. In reviewing the national program for natural hazard mitigation in 2007 after Hurricane Katrina and other major events, the Government Accountability Office (GAO) concluded this fragmented approach does not provide an effective national strategy for mitigation. The GAO recommended a better coordinated, comprehensive framework for defining national goals, establishing joint strategies, leveraging resources, and assigning responsibilities among stakeholders (U.S. GAO 2007).

Hazard mitigation is the collective actions taken to reduce long-term reduction risk and the effects from hazards on human life and property. The term *mitigation* is applied to many aspects of environmental planning and management. As discussed in Chapters 11 and 14, mitigation is an important issue in wetlands management and environmental impact assessment. In general, mitigation strategies aim to lessen impacts, and they follow a clear hierarchy:

1. Avoid the impact (move away altogether).
2. Lessen the impact by modifying the location (move away to lesser impact area).
3. Lessen the impact by modifying the design (apply engineering or design features).
4. Offset the impact (compensate via monetary relief, reconstruction, or re-creation).

The Federal Disaster Mitigation Act

The federal Natural Hazard Mitigation Program was initiated by the 1988 Robert T. Stafford Disaster Emergency Assistance Act, last amended in 2000, when it was renamed the Disaster Mitigation Act (DMA). The program was prompted by the growing perception that the nation was not dealing effectively with natural

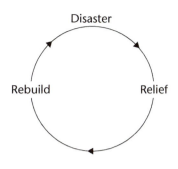

Figure 13.2 The Disaster-Relief-Rebuild-Disaster Cycle.

hazards. Indeed, despite ever-increasing federal funds for damage mitigation, emergency preparedness, forecasting, and disaster response, damage costs from natural hazards were continuing to rise. The nation seemed locked in a **disaster-relief-rebuild-disaster (DRRD) cycle** (Figure 13.2). Following a natural hazard damage or disaster, the government usually provided monetary and humanitarian relief, including funds to clean up and rebuild. Rebuilding often occurred in the same location, only to be followed by subsequent disasters, with potentially greater damage and more required relief. The fundamental hazard, exposure, vulnerability, and risk were not adequately addressed.

Some federal programs have tried to address this DRRD syndrome. The NFIP stipulates that for a community's residents to obtain subsidized federal flood insurance (the only flood insurance available), the community must implement floodplain zoning—restricting new development, or significant rebuilding after a flood—in the floodway. This applies to hurricane flooding as well. However, in the past, inadequate enforcement of these provisions limited their effectiveness (Godschalk et al. 1999).

The 1988 Stafford Act intended to break this cycle by creating further requirements for disaster relief applicable to all natural hazards. Under section 409, the provision of disaster relief requires a state to have a natural hazard mitigation plan certified by FEMA (the so-called 409 Plan). The Act also provided grants for "mitigation" projects under section 404. A study by Godschalk et al. (1999) traced the implementation of the Act in the 1990s and showed the program had limited effectiveness in addressing the syndrome, and in fact, in many respects, had exacerbated it. Their findings included the following:

- Mitigation plans were reactive rather than proactive. The 409 plans were often prepared in response to a disaster so that the state could receive relief funds. To become eligible as soon as possible, the plans were often hurried and inadequate, more a "hoop to jump through" than a carefully prepared, implementable plan.
- Section 404 grants were mostly directed to rebuilding projects, not mitigation programs, and there was little implementation connection between the 409 plans and the section 404 projects. The contribution of section 404 projects to long-term risk reduction was not evident.

Godschalk et al. (1999) recommended that plans become more proactive and preventive, that they be prepared with care before disasters occur, that they be revised and improved after each hazard event, and that they deal with multiple hazards rather than different plans for single hazards. Mitigation grants should focus on risk reduction programs rather than recovery projects. Programs can go beyond temporary relief of hardship to long-term avoidance of risk, such as buyout and relocation programs, and improved building and land use regulations to lessen exposure and vulnerability.

As mentioned above, the Stafford Act was amended as the Disaster Mitigation Act in 2000. Section 322 improved the section 409 planning process by requiring a state multihazard mitigation plan as a condition for receiving Hazard Mitigation Grants Program (HMGP) funds. The DMA did the following:

1. Provided additional funds for states that adopt "enhanced state mitigation plans."
2. Required local multihazard mitigation plans.
3. Authorized up to 7% of HMGP funds for mitigation planning.
4. Required state and local governments to develop and adopt hazard mitigation plans by November 2004 to qualify for HMGP funding after that date.

By July 2009, more than 19,000 local jurisdictions had FEMA-approved hazard mitigation plans, and this volume continues to grow as more localities seek eligibility for grant funding, since these plans are now a precondition for all FEMA mitigation project grants (Schwab 2010).

Natural Hazard Mitigation Planning

As promoted by the Natural Hazard Mitigation Program, **natural hazard mitigation planning (NHMP)** should follow specific planning principles. FEMA suggests the following process, which is embedded in the basic planning process introduced in Chapter 2 (see Box 2.1):

0. Scoping
- *Organize to prepare the plan.* Selecting the right person to lead the planning effort is important.
- *Involve the public.* Emphasize participation of key stakeholders, including at-risk homeowners, business owners, managers of critical facilities, and technical staff.
- *Coordinate with other agencies and organizations.* They can provide technical assistance and inform the community of relevant activities and programs that can support your efforts.

1. Identification of Issues, Opportunities, Concerns

2. Analysis of Planning Situation
- *Hazard and risk assessment.* Identify the particular hazards affecting your community and the risks they pose to your community's critical infrastructure.

- *Evaluate the problem.* Getting participants to agree on a problem statement is the first step in reaching consensus on solutions to the problem.
- *Set goals.* Establish goals as positive and achievable statements that people can work toward.

3. Formulation of Alternatives

- *Review possible strategies and measures.* Include a range of hazard mitigation measures for consideration. While some measures may be quickly eliminated, others should be evaluated carefully to determine how they work, as well as their costs and benefits.

4. Assessment of Impacts

5. Evaluation and Selection of Plan

- *Draft an action plan.* Keep it brief. Include sections on how the plan was prepared, recommended mitigation actions, and a budget and schedule.
- *Formally adopt the plan.* Gaining public acceptance is vital to reducing conflicts, building support for the recommendations, and getting the plan formally adopted. Keep the public informed and educated so they will readily accept the plan.

6. Implementation, Monitoring, Evaluation, Modification

- *Implement, evaluate, and revise the plan.* Develop procedures to measure progress, assess strengths and weaknesses, and decide on necessary changes.

Fundamental planning objectives are critical in order to avoid, prevent, and reduce the impacts from natural hazards. A key part of the process is **hazard and risk assessment**, which involves three steps:

1. *Hazard identification:* Provides descriptions and inventory maps of hazards, including history, generalized hazard boundaries, and critical facilities. It reviews not only existing development but future development.
2. *Hazard exposure and vulnerability assessment:* Combines the information from hazard identification with an inventory of the existing (or planned) property and population exposed to a hazard, and predicts how a hazard will affect different properties and population groups.
3. *Risk analysis:* Estimates the community-wide or site-specific damage, injuries, and costs likely to occur in an area over a period of time. Risk includes the magnitude of the harm that may result and the probability of the harm occurring (Oregon Department of Land Conservation and Development 2000).

There are many tools for hazard and risk assessment, and we review some of these under specific hazards later in this chapter.

Mitigation planning can be used iteratively to break the disaster-relief-rebuild-disaster cycle, thus minimizing impact and the cost of relief from subsequent natural hazard events. Preventive mitigation is a continual adaptive process that responds to successive disaster events. Mitigation planning should learn from each event so that mitigation investments can be targeted to progressively reduce the damages and relief costs of the next disaster. Plans should address multiple hazards, although specific assessments and alternatives depend on the hazards involved.

Implementing NHMP

Natural hazard mitigation plans should be integrated into a community's comprehensive plan and implementation mechanisms, including growth management and land use zoning, building codes, capital improvement plans, education programs, and emergency preparedness and evacuation procedures. Many of the objectives for natural hazard mitigation are compatible with other community sustainability objectives, such as open space, riparian buffer and habitat protection, and shoreline protection, and a multiple-objective approach can not only address multiple hazards but also integrate hazard mitigation into community sustainability planning.

The Institute for Business and Home Safety (IBHS) developed a Community Land Use Evaluation questionnaire, for assessing a community's comprehensive plan for natural hazards, and used it in a national survey (IBHS 2001). Results showed that communities in states that mandate hazards elements in local plans are preparing for safety. However, many fail to identify natural hazard issues in their comprehensive or general plans, and they also lack specific data, policies, or implementation strategies for natural hazard loss reduction (IBHS 2001). A more recent study of local hazard mitigation plans in California showed positive results on the quality of plans and the adoption of implementing measures; but again, deficiencies in integrating and linking to the general plan and other state and local plans were not sufficiently strategic, often listing unprioritized mitigation actions (Boswell et al. 2008).

Schwab (2010) describes effective means of integrating hazard mitigation planning into comprehensive or general plans, and into capital improvement and other plans. A stand-alone plan is better than no plan at all, but if it is not integrated into the comprehensive plan, it will not have the legal status of the comprehensive plan. It should be noted that only 23 states require local comprehensive plans, and of those, just ten have requirements for hazard mitigation. (See Chapters 3 and 17 for more on comprehensive planning.)

Natural hazard mitigation planning must also be reflected in implementing regulations, including building codes, land use zoning, and subdivision ordinances. Box 13.1 gives a list of implementation methods, all of which are discussed further in Chapter 17. Godschalk (2010) describes opportunities for land use controls to (1) regulate the location of future development to keep it out of known hazard areas and (2) strengthen existing development to resist hazards by community and onsite structural and nonstructural mitigation. Land use floodplain zoning and other overlay zoning, as well as infrastructure location specified in the capital improvement plan, are principal means of meeting the first objective. Community mitigation projects and retrofit building codes can address the second. For more information on Schwab's and Godschalk's work, and case stud-

BOX 13.1—Implementing the Natural Hazard Mitigation Plan

- **Building standards** include floodproofing requirements, seismic design standards, and wind-bracing and anchoring requirements for new construction and similar requirements for retrofitting existing buildings.
- **Development regulations** control the location, type, and intensity of new development, including flood zone regulations; setbacks from faults, steep slopes, and coastal erosion areas; overlay zoning districts that apply additional development standards for sensitive lands, such as wetlands, dunes, and hillsides; and the transfer of development rights from high-risk to low-risk areas.
- **Capital improvement programs** determine where schools and other public buildings, streets, storm sewers, and other utilities are built. Plans for roads and utilities will determine where new development is located; therefore, this infrastructure must avoid hazard areas.

- **Land and property acquisition** means purchasing properties in hazard-prone areas with public funds and restricting development to uses that are less vulnerable to disaster-related damages. This can be accomplished through the acquisition of undeveloped lands, development rights, and damaged buildings.
- **Taxation and fiscal policies** can distribute the public costs of private development in high-hazard areas more equitably, specifically shifting more of the cost burden directly onto the owners of such properties.
- **Public awareness** occurs through the dissemination of information on natural hazards, including educational materials and hazard disclosure requirements, to the construction industry, residents, and businesses.

Source: Adapted from FEMA 2002.

ies of hazard mitigation planning, see the Planning Advisory Service report 560 Natural Hazard Mitigation: Integrating Best Practice into Planning (Schwab 2010), available for download on the FEMA website.

Assessment Techniques for NHMP

To assist mitigation planning, a number of analytical techniques have been developed. Two are summarized below.

FEMA Mapping Software: HAZUS

FEMA provides free a ArcGIS extension for assessing the physical, social, and economic impacts from earthquakes, hurricane winds, and floods. The HAZUS-MD provides spatial assessment of hazards, assets, estimated losses, and mitigation options. Figure 13.3 shows two examples of HAZUS-MD products. Figure 13.3A overlays flooding potential and population density in Austin, Texas. Figure 13.3B is a retrospective map of wind exposure during Hurricane Katrina. HAZUS is intended to map and visualize hazard impacts and communicate not only their spatial extent but social and economic effects.

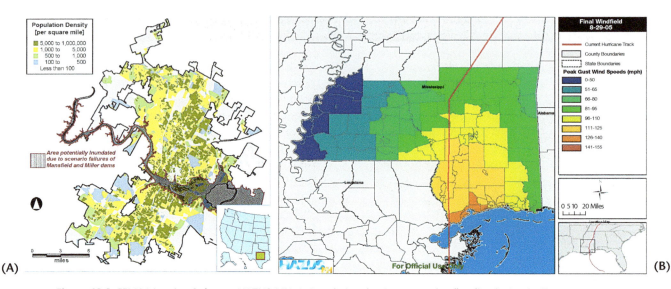

Figure 13.3 FEMA Mapping Software: HAZUS-MH. A: Population density exposed to flooding in Austin, Texas. B: Hurricane Katrina wind estimates. (*Source:* FEMA 2008.)

The Safe Growth Audit

One of the deficiencies of current NHMP identified by Boswell et al. (2008) and Schwab (2010) is its limited attention to the hazard impacts on future growth. Godschalk (2009) developed a method to assess how a community's range of policies and ordinances stack up in addressing hazard risks from growth. The Safe Growth Audit is a simple set of questions, the answers to which provide a concise evaluation of a growth-guidance framework, including the comprehensive plan, land use zoning ordinances, the capital improvement program, and the building code on future hazard vulnerability (Box 13.2). Like build-out analysis, the Safe Growth Audit helps the community and its elected officials understand to what extent their growth management system allows growth in hazard areas. Based on the results, they can revise the plans and ordinances before new development is put at risk.

Flooding and Flood Hazard Mitigation

When stormwater and/or snowmelt flows exceed channel capacity, water will overtop channel banks and spread out as floods. We discussed the analysis of stormwater flow, channel capacity, and floodplain mapping in Chapters 7 and 8. Flooding is also discussed here because of its importance in natural hazard mitigation. During the last century, U.S. flooding damage caused $1 billion per year in damages and an average 100 fatalities per year (FEMA 2000b). In the decade 2001–2010, damages from freshwater flooding (not including coastal storm surges, the cause of most hurricane damage) exceeded $10 billion per year,

BOX 13.2—The Safe Growth Audit: Selected Questions

Comprehensive Plan

Land Use

- Does the future land use map clearly identify natural hazard areas?
- Do the land use policies discourage development or redevelopment within natural hazard areas?
- Does the plan provide adequate space for expected future growth in areas located outside of natural hazard areas?

Transportation

- Does the transportation plan limit access to hazard areas?
- Is transportation policy used to guide growth to safe locations?
- Are movement systems designed to function under disaster conditions (e.g., evacuation)?

Environmental Management

- Are environmental systems that protect development from hazards identified and mapped?
- Do environmental policies maintain and restore protective ecosystems?
- Do environmental policies provide incentives to development that is located outside of protective ecosystems?

Public Safety

- Are the goals and policies of the comprehensive plan related to those of the FEMA Hazard Mitigation Plan?
- Is safety explicitly included in the plan's growth and development policies?
- Does the monitoring and implementation section of the plan cover safe growth objectives?

Zoning Ordinance

- Does the zoning ordinance conform to the comprehensive plan in discouraging development within hazard areas?
- Does the ordinance contain natural hazard overlay zones that set conditions for land use within such zones?
- Do rezoning procedures recognize natural hazard areas as limits on zoning changes for greater intensity of use?
- Does the ordinance prohibit development within, or filling of, wetlands, floodways, and floodplains?

Subdivision Regulations

- Do the subdivision regulations restrict the subdivision of land within or adjacent to natural hazard areas?
- Do the regulations provide for conservation or cluster subdivisions in order to conserve environmental resources?
- Do the regulations allow density transfers where hazard areas exist?

Capital Improvement Program (CIP) and Infrastructure Policies

- Does the CIP limit expenditures on projects that would encourage development in natural hazards areas?
- Does the CIP provide funding for hazard mitigation projects identified in the FEMA mitigation plan?

Other

- Does the building code contain provisions to strengthen or elevate construction to withstand hazard forces?
- Is there an adopted evacuation and shelter plan to deal with emergencies from natural hazards?

Source: Adapted from Godschalk 2009.

TABLE 13.1 **U.S. Weather-Related Annual Fatality Statistics**

Weather Event	10-Year Average (2000–2010)	30-Year Average (1981–2010)
Flood	71	92
Lightning	39	55
Tornado	56	56
Hurricane	116	47
Heat	115	NA
Cold	25	NA
Winter storm	42	NA
Wind	41	NA

Source: National Weather Service Natural Hazard Statistics. http://www.weather.gov /om/hazstats.shtml.

although there were fewer fatalities as a result of better flood warning systems (NWS 2011). Table 13.1 compares U.S. flooding annual average fatality statistics to other weather-related hazards during the past decade and past three decades. Figure 13.4 shows the distribution of flood disaster declarations from 1980 to 2005 and gives a visual indicator of where community flooding problems are most frequent.

Approaches to Flood Hazard Mitigation

Several approaches can be taken to mitigate flood hazards and reduce damages. Box 13.3 distinguishes between structural and nonstructural measures. In its

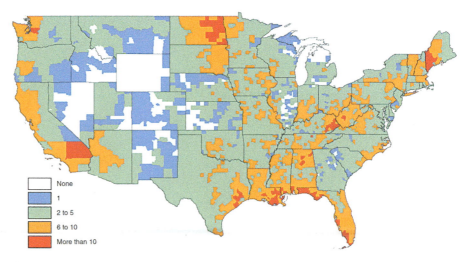

Figure 13.4 Major Flood Disaster Declarations by County, 1980–2005. (*Source:* U.S. GAO 2007.)

BOX 13.3—Approaches to Flood Hazard Mitigation

Structural Measures

- Guide floodwaters by building levees, floodwalls, channel enlargement (flood protection).
- Lessen floodwaters (peak discharge) through upland runoff control measures, including detention (dams and reservoirs) (flood abatement).
- Adjust site characteristics by elevating sites with fill material.
- Adjust building characteristics by elevating and floodproofing structures and related infrastructure.

Nonstructural Measures

- Provide emergency preparedness measures, such as flood warnings.
- Provide relief through private and federal disaster assistance.
- Provide affordable insurance for flood damages.
- Provide information, such as maps of floodplains and general information about flood risks and safe floodplain building practices.
- Adjust future land use by floodplain planning, vacant land acquisition, and regulatory zoning.
- Adjust existing land use by acquiring and relocating buildings.

efforts to mitigate flood damages, prior to 1973 the federal government focused on structural measures built by the U.S. Army Corps of Engineers and other agencies. These measures were euphemistically referred to as "flood control," but after an investment of more than $11 billion in such measures while flood damages continued to rise, it became clear that structures alone would not solve the problem. Increasingly, federal and local planners have turned to nonstructural measures, such as floodplain management, land acquisition, and relocation of structures, to avoid future damages. Other measures, such as insurance and disaster relief, aim to manage the financial risk and hardship associated with flood damages.

Table 13.2 summarizes the structural measures. More than 260 large flood control **dams** and **reservoirs** have been built on rivers in the United States. Essentially large detention basins, they can detain runoff to reduce peak flows downstream, but they also permanently flood large areas of riparian lands and free-flowing channels within the reservoir pool. Some 6,000 miles of **levees, dikes**, and **floodwalls** across the country protect specific areas by artificially raising the channel bank. This prevents floods from spilling to their accustomed floodplains, but the water must go somewhere, so it often rises higher, thereby flooding areas not normally prone to flooding.

Channelization is the modification of streams, often by straightening, widening, or deepening, to increase channel capacity and speed water drainage. Although such modifications can benefit those living near them, they can increase the volume and velocity of water carried by the stream and thus cause greater peak flows downstream. Channelization can also destroy natural channels, their aesthetic qualities, and their ability to support aquatic and riparian life. Recent designs, such as the bench channel shown in Figure 13.5, can preserve the natural channel and one side of the riparian lands, while increasing capacity.

TABLE 13.2 **Structural Flood Mitigation Measures**

Measure	Effects	Problems
Traditional Flood Control		
Dams and reservoirs	Retain stormwater	Transfer flooding; false sense of security
Channel modification (widening, straightening, lining)	Increases capacity, speed of drainage	Destroys natural channels; increases flood flow downstream
Levees, floodwalls	Protect one side	Water surge may flood other side and areas previously not flooded
Innovative Stormwater Management		
Upstream detention and infiltration onsite or after preliminary concentration		

These structural flood control measures have prevented considerable damages. The U.S. Army Corps of Engineers estimated in 1975 that the $10 billion spent by federal agencies on control measures since 1936 prevented $60 billion in flood damages. However, as noted, total damages and deaths due to flooding have continued to increase over time. The major reasons are higher property values and expanded development in floodplains. Encroachment of development on the floodplain has been due in some cases to ignorance of the flood hazard and in others to a false sense of security provided by the presence of flood "control" measures. Flood control structures never give absolute protection; they merely make a devastating event less frequent.

Table 13.2 also lists innovative structural measures, including onsite detention and infiltration, which help diminish increases in flood flows due to urbanization (see Chapter 8). However, these onsite measures will not reduce flooding in naturally occurring flood-prone areas. Such areas require special attention. Experi-

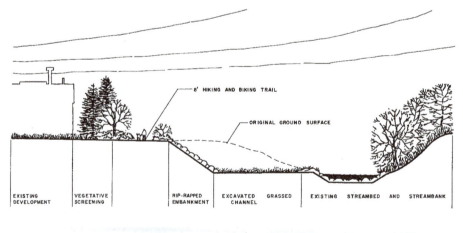

TYPICAL CHANNEL SECTION

Figure 13.5 The Bench Channel Method of Improving Stream Capacity. (*Source:* U.S. Army Corps of Engineers 1984.)

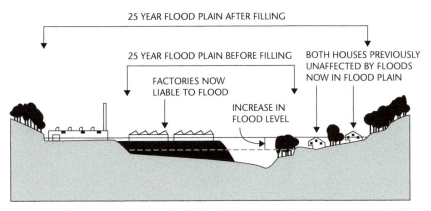

EFFECT OF FILLING APPROX 50% OF CROSS SECTIONAL AREA OF FLOOD PLAIN

Figure 13.6 The Effects of Floodplain Encroachment on Flood Elevation.

ence has shown that floodplain management is far more effective in reducing damages over time than localized structures, such as channel modification and floodwalls.

Floodplain Management

As the effectiveness of structural measures has been questioned, greater attention has been given to managing floodplain development as an alternative approach for mitigating flood damages. Floodplain management may involve a number of measures directed at new and existing development. Encroachment of new development onto the floodplain not only can expose new occupants to flood damage, but also can cause a surcharge in flood level due to cutting and filling. Figure 13.6 illustrates the effects of floodplain encroachment. As a result of land filling, the 25-year floodplain will be much wider than before.

The most straightforward way to control encroachment is by restricting land use in the floodplain to uses that are compatible with periodic flooding, such as recreation and agriculture. In response to certain requirements of the NFIP, nearly all of the estimated 60,000 flood-prone communities in the United States have implemented floodplain management, including **floodplain zoning** (see Chapter 17). Floodplain zoning prohibits development in the floodway and allows development with floodproofing in the 100-year floodway fringe. A 100-year event has a 1% chance of occurring in any year. Floodproofing usually involves elevating structures or portions of structures prone to damage above the 100-year flood elevation, plus the 1-ft surcharge. Here are definitions of the floodway and floodway fringe (see Figure 7.18):

- **Floodway:** A fairly narrow area close to the stream that must remain open so that flood waters can pass through.
- **Floodway fringe:** The area within the 100-year floodplain that can be subject to encroachment or filling without causing more than a 1-ft surcharge in the height of the 100-year flood carried by the floodway.

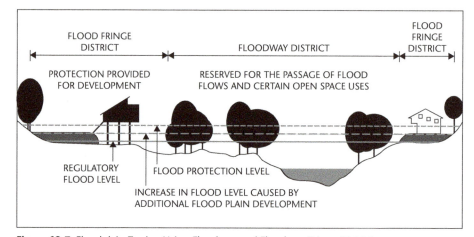

Figure 13.7 Floodplain Zoning Using Floodway and Floodway Fringe Districts.

Homeowners can only obtain flood insurance through the NFIP. Private insurers participating in the NFIP provide the policies under subsidized rates. However, homeowners can obtain this insurance only if their local government is implementing floodplain management and zoning. In addition, if localities do not have floodplain zoning in accord with the preceding conditions, they cannot receive any other federal financial aid, including disaster relief for flood damages or assistance for projects in the floodway fringe. FEMA provides enforcement of this provision.

Figure 13.7 shows how floodplain zoning can affect floodplain development. Appropriate uses of the floodplain include open space, recreation, and agriculture. The FEMA rules for floodplain management are limited. Although they may be effective in preventing development in the floodway (if enforced), they have been criticized for actually encouraging development of the floodway fringe. Such development may be safe from the 100-year flood, but a larger event will cause more damage than if this development did not occur. In addition, the floodway fringe may contain riparian vegetation that provides aesthetic benefits and wildlife habitat. By encouraging floodway fringe development, floodplain management impacts riparian and stream corridor values. Some communities prohibit development in the entire 100-year floodplain.

Planning Tools for Flood Hazard Mitigation

Flood damage mitigation planning requires analysis of the flood hazard, community preparedness, and implementation strategies. Three planning tools are described here.

FEMA Floodplain Mapping Service

FEMA manages the NFIP and provides Flood Hazard Boundary Maps and Flood Insurance Rate Maps to help communities develop and enforce floodplain management. Chapter 7 describes these maps and accessing them at the Map Service Center, http://www.msc.fema.gov/.

FEMA's Community Rating System

FEMA also provides a voluntary rating program within NFIP that allows local governments to go beyond the minimum NFIP requirements. As a reward, the localities earn credits toward reductions in flood insurance premiums. Points are assigned in the Community Rating System (CRS) for specific activities under four categories:

- Public Information: Elevation Certificates, Map Information, Outreach Projects, Hazard Disclosure, Flood Protection Information, Flood Protection Assistance.
- Mapping and Regulations: Additional Flood Data, Open Space Preservation, Higher Regulatory Standards, Flood Data Maintenance, Stormwater Management, Flood Damage Reduction Activities.
- Flood Damage Reduction: Floodplain Management Planning, Acquisition and Relocation, Flood Protection, Drainage System Maintenance.
- Flood Preparedness: Flood Warning Program: Levee Safety, Dam Safety.

For every 500 points, communities get a 5% discount on flood insurance for special flood hazard areas (SFHAs) shown on the flood hazard maps. Communites with no points have a Rate Class 10; each 500 points moves them up a class, until Class 1, in which SFHAs get a 45% discount and non-SFHAs get a 10% discount. The rather involved scoring system is described in FEMA CRS documents downloadable from http://training.fema.gov/EMIWeb/CRS/.

No Adverse Impact

The Association of State Floodplain Managers (ASFPM) developed No Adverse Impact (NAI) floodplain management, an approach that ensures that the action of any property owner, public or private, does not adversely impact the property and rights of others. This approach requires communities to look beyond business as usual, including relying simply on federal and state minimum standards. An adverse impact is measured by an increase in flood stages, flood velocity, flows, the potential for erosion and sedimentation, degradation of water quality, or increased cost of public services. NAI floodplain management extends beyond the floodplain to include managing development in the watersheds where floodwaters originate. ASFPM emphasizes that NAI does not mean "no development." It means that any adverse impact caused by a project must be mitigated, preferably as provided for in a community or watershed-based plan (ASFPM 2003).

The approach identifies three levels of floodplain management strategies:

1. *Basic:* Approaches typically used to meet minimum federal or state requirements for managing floodplains and coastal areas to minimize flood losses.
2. *Better:* Activities that are more effective than the basic level because they are tailored to specific situations, provide protection from larger

floods, allow for uncertainty in storm magnitude prediction, and serve multiple purposes.

3. *NAI:* Tools and techniques that go further than the measures defined as "better" by ensuring that private development, public infrastructure, and planning activities do not have direct or indirect negative consequences on the surrounding natural resource areas, private property, or other communities.

These tools are organized under seven building blocks, listed in the first column in Table 13.3.

TABLE 13.3 "No Adverse Impact" Building Blocks for Coastal Flood Mitigation

NAI Building Block	Basic	Better	No Adverse Impact
Hazard Identification and Mapping	Use FEMA Flood Insurance Rate Maps for land use decisions.	Gather and use detailed coastal hazard data (e.g., historic erosion rates, actual observed extents of floodwaters) for land use decisions.	Incorporate coastal hazard data (e.g., erosion rates, vulnerability of environmentally sensitive areas, and sea-level rise rates and impacts) into community-wide planning maps and regulations.
Planning	Use land use planning and zoning through a community master plan.	Develop floodplain management plans that include stormwater management and hazard mitigation measures. Promulgate detailed guidance focusing on reducing flood damage.	Design special area management plans to protect storm damage and flood control functions of natural resources, promote reasonable coastal-dependent economic growth, and improve protection of life and property in hazard-prone areas.
Regulations and Development Standards	Follow Federal Emergency Management Agency National Flood Insurance Program regulations.	Adopt conditions for siting new development. Regulate cumulative, substantial improvements. Revise regulatory tools for addressing erosion along shorelines, including relocation of threatened buildings, building setbacks, beach nourishment and bio-engineering, and stabilization of eroded areas.	Preserve sensitive areas through bylaws and regulations that may establish maximum densities for development, restrict structures between the shoreline and the setback line, mandate vegetative coastal buffers rather than human-made structures (bulkheads, seawalls, or groins), minimize impervious cover, and preserve stream corridor and wetland buffers. Regulate placement of fill.
Mitigation	Use common practices, such as flood proofing existing structures.	Elevate or relocate buildings. Acquire land. Encourage nonstructural methods for shoreline protection.	Stabilize shorelines with vegetation. Prohibit construction in especially damage-prone areas. Prevent filling of wetlands and other lowlands. Nourish beaches where appropriate. Protect watersheds. Monitor corrective efforts. Regulate construction of shore protection structures.

TABLE 13.3 "No Adverse Impact" Building Blocks for Coastal Flood Mitigation (cont.)

NAI Building Block	Basic	Better	No Adverse Impact
Infrastructure Siting and Design	Respond to storm events as they occur. After a storm, rebuild/repair to previous condition.	Upgrade damaged facilities to more hazard-resistant standards. Inventory hazard risks of all public buildings. Insure buildings for all hazards (as appropriate). Identify, and if possible, relocate or protect "critical facilities."	Prohibit major public infrastructure investments in special flood hazard areas. Ensure that roads, sewer lines, and utility upgrades don't encourage development in hazard-prone areas. Zone to prohibit construction in high-hazard areas. Locate new critical facilities above 500-year floodplain.
Emergency Services	Create and use generic hazard response plan.	Create and test community-wide hazard plans that involve all local boards and departments.	Create plans to ensure that all people who want or need to be evacuated can be moved to safe shelters and post-disaster plans that improve community flood resistance through willing land acquisition, determining which structures are "substantially damaged," and ensuring that appropriate reconstruction meets code requirements. Establish mutual aid agreements with neighboring communities.
Public Outreach and Education	Answer questions and provide information as requested by public.	Periodically inform residents of coastal hazards, vulnerability, and mitigation techniques through public workshops and in forums after storm recovery.	Create comprehensive education and outreach programs using expertise of state and federal agencies (when needed) to encourage community-wide proactive storm preparation. Establish coastal hazard disclosure requirements for property sales.

Source: Massachusetts OCZM 2008.

The table includes floodplain management strategy levels for coastal floodplains for Massachusetts coastal communities. The approach is compatible with the FEMA CRS program, and ASFPM and FEMA have developed pathways to NAI that achieve CRS points. The approach has been legally tested, and courts have shown deference to community efforts to reduce harm (Massachusetts Office of Coastal Zone Management 2008).

Coastal Zone Hazards

Coastal areas are subject to intense coastal storms and hurricanes and physical hazards of beach erosion, and the fact that people are attracted to the coast puts millions at risk of these natural hazards. Figure 13.8 illustrates a barrier island context and the dune development process, typical of the U.S. Atlantic and Gulf

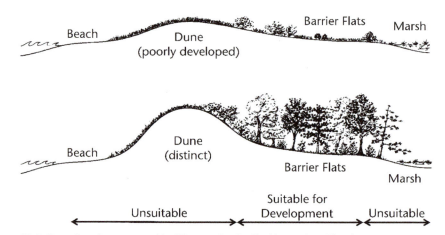

Figure 13.8 Dune Development and Its Effect on Barrier Flat Vegetation. The dune system creates suitability zones for development. (*Source:* Clark et al. 1980. Based on drawing by M. Mow in S. Leatherman, *Barrier Island Handbook,* National Park Coop. Research Unit, University of Massachusetts, Amherst.)

Coasts. Elements include the **beachfront**, the **dune systems**, the **barrier flats** (incorporating grassland and forest), **saltwater wetlands** and **marsh**, the **backbay** or coastal basin, and the landward **backbay shoreline**. The beach and dunelands are those areas most prone to the ocean's dynamic forces from normal wave action and violent storms, while the coastal basins, estuaries, and saltwater wetlands are ecologically productive. The barrier flats are most suitable for development because the barrier and dune systems are nature's protective mechanisms, but too often we damage these systems in our quest to get ever closer to the beach—and the hazards that brings.

Beach and bluff erosion processes are more typical of the West Coast. The constant action of waves on the beach is the prime force against the highly erodible sand. Wave action at an angle to the beach will produce a littoral current down the beach, causing a **littoral drift** of eroded sand. If a barrier such as a **groin** or breakwater is erected on the beach, it will slow the flow of water, causing the deposition of sand and a broadening of the beach; but the downflow side of the groin will experience continued erosion with no deposition, and there the beach will be narrowed. This littoral drift depends on the wave intensity and direction, which in turn depend on the shape of the underwater shelf and the season. Headlands not only experience waves first, but those waves have more energy. Wave direction often varies with the season, so the direction of the littoral drift and the shape of the beach may change throughout the year.

Beach erosion is a continuous process, and storm waves exacerbate the process. The higher water associated with storms takes higher, more eroding waves farther inland. This eroding force can undermine beach dunes, which provide the primary defense against the storms. These waves can also undermine seawalls designed to protect structures built too close to the beach. As mentioned above, Figure 13.8 shows the development of a dune system on a barrier beach. The primary force is the ocean wind that erodes beach sands and carries them inland until wind barriers (initially a poorly developed dune) reduce velocity and cause deposition. As the deposition grows a distinct dune, it provides increased protection from wind and storm waves. Vegetation can then proliferate behind the dune, adding more stability to highly erodible sandy soils. The vegetation on the dune itself is essential to its formation and stability. Dune grasses begin to halt the advance of sand, arresting erosion and contributing to deposition. If this dune vegetation is disturbed by construction or intensive recreation use, wind and storm waves are more likely to erode the dunes, reducing the storm protection they provide for the barrier flats. A cardinal rule of coastal management is to control development in storm-damage-prone beach areas, as well as on protective dunes.

Coastal Storm and Erosion Hazards

Natural hazards affecting coastal areas are caused by hurricanes and other coastal storms. Hazards include coastal flooding, high winds, wave and tidal surges, beach erosion, and bluff failure. The U.S. Pacific Coast and the Great Lakes are susceptible to storm wave erosion. Offshore earthquake-driven tsunamis are a threat on the Pacific Coast, Hawaii, and Alaska, and in other coastal regions of the world, as we know from the devastating 2004 Indian Ocean and 2011 Japanese tsunamis.

Tropical storms and hurricanes are the greatest coastal storm problem on the Atlantic and Gulf Coasts. South Florida, the stretch from southeast Texas to the Florida panhandle, and North Carolina have been the hardest hit and are the most susceptible to land-falling hurricanes (Figure 13.9A). Coastal storm hazards include severe wind, storm surge flooding, upland flooding, and tornadoes. Hurricanes are rated on the Saffir-Simpson 1–5 scale. Table 13.4 gives that scale and also some of the most destructive hurricanes of the past few decades in the U.S. We know too well the images of devastating hurricanes, such as Katrina in 2005 (Figure 13.9B, C).

Damages from coastal flooding result from hydrodynamic forces of wave action and tidal surge, hydrostatic forces of high water, sediment overwash, and beach and bluff erosion. In addition, heavy rains cause upland flooding well inland, including dangerous flash flooding in higher elevations. For example, Category 1 Hurricanes Agnes (1972) and Floyd (1999) caused little coastal damage, but their rains dumped 20–30 inches of rain inland and caused billions of dollars of flood damage.

Coastal damage also results from high winds. Minimum design loads and wind speeds for new buildings range from 85 mph on the West Coast to 120 mph in New England to 150 mph in south Florida. Because of storm surges, high winds, and highly mobile sandy soils, coastal areas are extremely vulnerable to erosion. The dynamic forces in the beach, dune, and bluff environment require careful consideration in siting and designing coastal development. Shoreline segments that lose more sediment than they gain are subject to *erosion,* segments that gain more than they lose are subject to *accretion,* and segments that balance gains and losses are said to be *stable.* Shoreline erosion is measured by linear retreat (e.g., feet of recession per year) or volumetric loss (e.g., cubic yards of eroded sediment per foot of shoreline per year).

Erosion rates are usually given as long-term average annual rates, but they are not uniform in time or location on the shoreline. Figure 13.10 illustrates the difference between medium-term and long-term shoreline dynamics. Storm induced

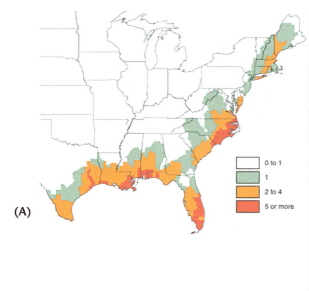

Figure 13.9 Hurricanes. A: Category 3 or higher hurricanes by county, 1980–2005. B, C: Aftermath of the 2005 Hurricane Katrina in Mississippi and New Orleans. (*Source:* A: U.S. GAO 2007. B, C: Marty Bahamonde/FEMA.)

TABLE 13.4 **The Saffir-Simpson Scale and Recent U.S. Hurricanes**

Category	Wind Speed	Surge Height	Coastal Damage	Examples
1	74–95 mph	4–5 ft	Minimal	Agnes (1972: Florida, Northeast U.S.)
2	96–110 mph	6–8 ft	Moderate	Frances (2004: Florida)
3	111–130 mph	9–12 ft	Extensive	Katrina (2005: Louisiana, Mississippi)
4	131–154 mph	13–18 ft	Extreme	Andrew (1992: Florida)
5	> 155 mph	> 18 ft	Catastrophic	Camille (1969: Mississippi)

erosion is rapid and dynamic, but longer-term erosion is caused by natural changes (e.g., littoral transport, tidal inlets) and human activities (e.g., dredging, damming rivers, alteration of vegetation or dunes). Storm-induced erosion can cause the equivalent shoreline change of several decades of long-term erosion. Large dunes can be eroded as much as 75 ft, and small dunes can be destroyed.

Mitigating Coastal Hazards Through Smart Land Development Practices

Coastal storms and hurricanes constitute some of the most damaging and dangerous natural hazards. Damages are exacerbated by poor locations of development

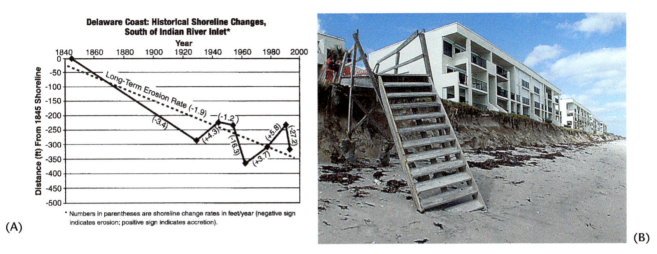

(A)

(B)

Figure 13.10 Erosion Rates. A: Long-term versus medium-term erosion rates and erosion vulnerability. B: Short-term erosion at Melbourne Beach, Florida, 1999. (*Source:* A: Douglas et al. 1998; FEMA 2000a. B: Photo by Ty Harrington/FEMA News Photo.)

and by substandard construction practices. In an effort to foster smarter development practices, the federal government has helped states improve planning and management through the Coastal Zone Management program (see Chapter 10). In addition, FEMA has developed land use regulations in conjunction with the NFIP, as well as technical guidelines for states and localities. As discussed earlier, the NFIP provides subsidized flood insurance only in those communities that implement zoning to restrict development in flood-prone areas. The following principles come from FEMA's *Coastal Construction Manual,* a comprehensive source for planning, siting, designing, constructing, and maintaining buildings in coastal areas (FEMA 2000a):

1. Hazard Identification
   - Flood damage results from both short-term and long-term increases in water levels, wave action, and erosion.
   - Long-term erosion increases flood hazards over time.
   - Flood hazards mapped as A zones on coastal flood insurance rate maps (FIRMs) can have greater hazard than riverine A zones because of wave height and changing site conditions (e.g., erosion, dune loss).
   - Slope stability hazards and landslides are exacerbated in coastal bluff areas due to the effects of drainage changes, removal of vegetation, and site development.
2. Siting
   - Building close to the shoreline is vulnerable and removes any margin of safety against hazards.
   - Because of erosion and shifting shoreline, even elevated buildings close to the shoreline may find themselves standing on active beach.
   - Building close to other structures and to protective structures can redirect and concentrate storm forces.

- Siting buildings on top of erodible dunes and bluffs renders them vulnerable to serious damage.
- Buildings near unstabilized tidal inlets are subject to large-scale shoreline fluctuations; even stabilized tidal inlets have high erosion rates.

3. Design
  - Shallow spread footing and slab foundations and continuous perimeter wall foundations may be subject to collapse in areas subject to wave action or erosion.
  - Designs should incorporate freeboard above required elevation of the lowest floor.
  - Corrosion-resistant materials are important in this salt-rich environment.

4. Construction
  - Special construction practices are required in harsh coastal environments: structural connections, pile or foundation embedment, properly installed utility system components, bracing and fastening roofs and wall, proper inspection.

5. Maintenance
  - Inspection, repair, and replacement of structural elements and connectors and maintenance of erosion and coastal flood protection measures are very important in the dynamic coastal environment.

Coastal Hazard Zones

Figure 13.11 shows the NFIP categories for FIRMs and coastal land use zoning. There are three hazard zones:

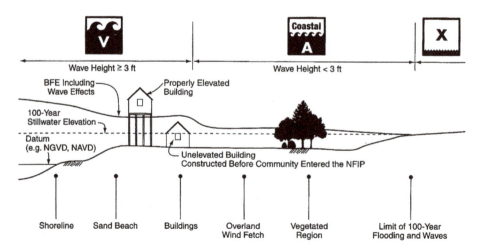

Figure 13.11 Elevation View of Coastal Flood Zones. (*Source:* FEMA 2000a.)

- *V zone:* Coastal high-hazard area (HHA) in the special flood hazard area (SFHA) extending from offshore to the inland limit of a primary frontal dune or any area subject to high-velocity wave action greater than 3 ft.
- *A zone:* Area of the SFHA within 100-year flood zone, subject to wave heights less than 3 ft, not within HHA.
- *X zone:* Shaded X (zone B) is in 500-year flood zone. Unshaded X (zone C) is above 500-year zone.

Site planning can reduce the coastal wind, erosion, and flooding hazards by placing buildings outside of the V zone. Figure 13.12 shows that a modified layout places homes on the landward portion of the lot. Better yet, a cluster layout can provide community open space and coordinated open space management. (Figure 10.21 also illustrates sensitive coastal development scenarios.) Further discussion of development design principles for environmental protection and sustainability is presented in Chapter 16.

Geologic Hazards

Geologic hazards include localized slope problems (e.g., landslides), support problems (e.g., subsidence), and wider-scale seismic hazards (e.g., earthquakes, volcanic activity). These geologic hazards create problems for building and development and must be considered in land use planning and management. Applying hazard mitigation planning to geologic hazards involves the key steps of *assessing and mapping the hazard*, as well as exposure and vulnerability; *formulating measures to reduce exposure and vulnerability*; and *implementing these measures*.

Most hazards pose relative risks, depending on location, and it is important to understand the relative risk spatially and apply mitigation measures accordingly. For example, an entire region may be susceptible to earthquake risk, but certain areas have a greater ground-shaking and damage risk due to the underlying geology. Some steep slope areas have a higher risk than others due to underlying materials. These relatively higher-risk areas must be identified, and measures to reduce exposure (restricting all development) and vulnerability (requiring strict building standards) must be applied.

Perhaps the best source of geologic information is the USGS geologic map. It provides a map of surficial geology at the scale of the USGS quadrangle series (1:24,000), as well as several cross sections. (Unfortunately, these maps are not available for the entire United States.) Where available, they identify bedrock formations, the degree of consolidation of materials, and the locations of areas of geologic interest, including mines and landfills, faults, sinkholes, and karst. The discussion accompanying the map provides geologic history and mineral resource potential of the area, as well as the geologic factors affecting land development.

This section discusses two major geologic hazards, slope stability and seismic hazards. The first edition of this book also presented information on **volcanic**

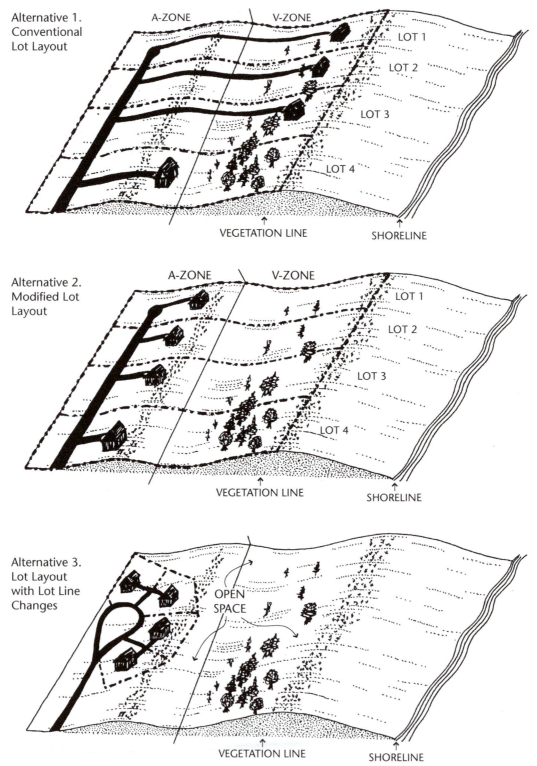

Figure 13.12 Residential Layout Options in the Coastal Zone. Alternatives 2 and 3 place homes outside the hazardous V zone and allow the dynamic forces of the beach and dune area to act without causing damage or danger to people and property. (*Source:* FEMA 2000a. Original graphic by Thomas Bartik, in Morris 1997.)

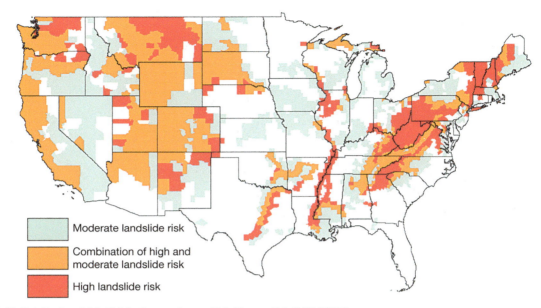

Figure 13.13 Relative Landslide Risk in the contiguous U.S. (*Source:* U.S. GAO 2007.)

hazards and **support problems**. The latter includes **soil settling** (see also Chapter 6); **karst or solution limestone weathering**, creating sinkholes and avenues for groundwater contamination (see Figure 9.6); and **subsidence**, in which the ground surface drops in response to the removal of underlying material, such as groundwater, oil and gas, or underground mining. Information on support problems and volcanic hazards is available on the book website (www.envirolanduse.org).

Slope Stability

Each year, landslides, debris flow, and avalanches in the United States cause about $1–2 billion in damages and 25 fatalities. Figure 13.13 shows a national map of landslide susceptibility, which is pretty much any location where there is sloped terrain. Figure 13.14 is a photograph of the 2005 La Conchita (California) landslide, which killed 10 and destroyed 36 homes.

Slope failure occurs when the gravitational force of slope materials exceeds the resisting forces of friction, strength, and cohesion of the supporting materials. Certain properties of sloped terrain (such as steepness, layering or fracturing of materials, and absence of vegetation) can make the terrain inherently susceptible to failure, and superimposing factors (such as additional moisture, overloading, and undercutting) can make matters worse (Box 13.4). These factors can occur naturally or can be induced by human activities. Box 13.5 describes various types of slope failure and some of the nomenclature used in the field.

Figure 13.14 The 2005 La Conchita Landslide. This landslide in Ventura County, California, killed 10 people. (*Source:* Photo by Mark Reid, U.S. Geological Survey.)

The hazards of slope failure or landsliding are obviously most prevalent in mountainous regions, although localized hazards may occur in other areas as well. The challenge to a local community concerned about landslide hazards involves first identifying and mapping potential landslide areas. Based on this information, the community can then assess the degree of hazard, and develop policies and controls to mitigate the hazard.

Inventorying and Mapping Landslide Hazards

In mapping landslide hazards, the USGS suggests a sequence of progressively more detailed steps so that a general distribution of hazardous areas emerges early and further study provides refinement. The first level of investigation, coincident with rapid assessment, involves preparing a **slope map** and a **landslide inventory**, both of which have become more routine with advances in GIS and remote sensing.

BOX 13.4—Factors Affecting Slope Failure: Gravity Versus Resistance

Inherent Factors

- Slope
- Properties of underlying materials
  Slippage potential
  Layering
  Fracturing
  Unconsolidated materials

- Vegetation
- Moisture

Superimposed Factors

- Deterioration of materials
- Increased moisture
- Overloading
- Undercutting
- Earthquakes or other shocks

BOX 13.5—Landslides and Types of Slope Failure

Figure 13.15 shows the nomenclature associated with a typical landslide, from crown to toe with head, body, and foot in between. Scarps and slump surfaces, traverse cracks, and ridges cross deposits horizontally, and radial cracks and ridges cross vertically. Landslides are composites of five different types of slope failure: falls, slides, slumps, flows, and lateral spreads. The last can may occur on flat or gently sloping land due to liquefaction of underlying materials.

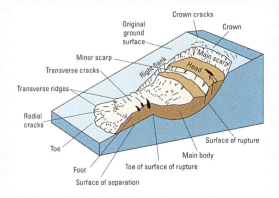
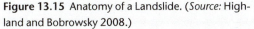

Figure 13.15 Anatomy of a Landslide. (*Source:* Highland and Bobrowsky 2008.)

Fall: Masses of rock and/or other material that moves downslope by falling or bouncing.
Slide: Incoherent or broken masses of rock and/or other material that has moved downslope by sliding on a surface.

Slump: Coherent or intact mass or rock and/or other material that moves downslope by rotational slip on surfaces that underlie and penetrate the landslide.
Flow: Masses of soil and other colluvial material that have moved downslope in a manner similar to the movement of a viscous fluid.

Flows can be characterized by the speed of movement and by the materials involved. In flows, materials actually take on the characteristics of a fluid. Air and water generally accompany the material, making it more fluid by reducing friction. Slow flows are generally laminar where materials move without pulling apart, and rapid flows generally become turbulent where materials are churned. Exceptionally rapid flows of soil, rock and water, snow, and/or ice on very steep slopes are called **debris avalanches**. These are triggered by heavy rain or snow, melting snow, added weight, or shocks from earthquakes or other causes. Slower flows of solid materials, air, and water are called **debris flows**. If more than half of the solid material is smaller than sand, it is referred to as a **mudflow**. Soils subject to liquefaction may be subject to spontaneous flows. Very slow downslope flow of soils is called **creep**. The average flow rate of materials can range from a fraction of an inch per year to 4–5 inches per week. Most slope failures occur not as strictly falls, slides, slumps, or flows, but as combinations called slide-flow combinations or **landslides**.

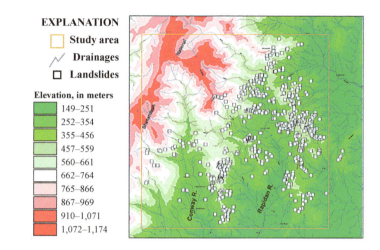

EXPLANATION

☐ **Study area**

⟋ **Drainages**

☐ **Landslides**

Elevation, in meters

	149–251
	252–354
	355–456
	457–559
	560–661
	662–764
	765–866
	867–969
	910–1,071
	1,072–1,174

Figure 13.16 A Landslide Inventory Map. This map shows the area east of Shenandoah National Park, Virginia. (*Source:* Highland and Bobrowsky 2008.)

Slope mapping can be conducted using a topographic map or digital elevation model (DEM) data in GIS. (See the book website for the manual method described in the first edition.) The inventory identifies areas where landslides have occurred. Simple inventories can be done by carefully reviewing high-resolution aerial photographs or satellite imagery for landslide deposits and scars. More detailed inventories involve some field investigation in addition to remote sensing analysis and may distinguish active from old slides, the type and depth of the slide, and the kind of geologic materials involved. Figure 13.16 gives an example of a landslide inventory map for a portion of Virginia east of Shenandoah National Park.

Slope stability maps distinguish the relative potential of different areas for landslides. As presented in Box 13.4, many factors influence an area's susceptibility to slope failure, and including all of these factors in an analysis of slope stability is impractical. The USGS has employed a fairly simple procedure that is reasonably well accepted. It is based on three parameters: the underlying bedrock material, steepness, and the presence or absence of earlier landslide deposits. The most important of these, landslide deposits, is used to pinpoint hazard areas. Figure 13.17 is a landslide hazard map for the Magnolia area of Seattle. Black dots represent landslide locations from the city's database, and relative hazard is based on their concentration.

Information on the two other factors is also useful. Steepness is represented in slope maps. Underlying geologic materials that are poorly consolidated contribute to landslide susceptibility. These include bedrock units with extensive shearing or jointing, or with structurally weak components (e.g., breccia), surficial deposits (e.g., alluvial, colluvial, terrace, and talus deposits), and artificial fill. The location of such materials can be interpreted from geologic maps. A simple method of identifying geologic units that may be susceptible to sliding is to overlay a landslide inventory map onto the geologic map. The types of geologic units where landslides have occurred are probably those most likely to fail.

Often locational information on the three variables—landslide deposits, slope, and geologic materials—is used to produce a composite map to rate areas for slope stability. In the slope stability mapping of the San Francisco Bay region, the following five categories were developed based on the three parameters (Nilsen et al. 1976):

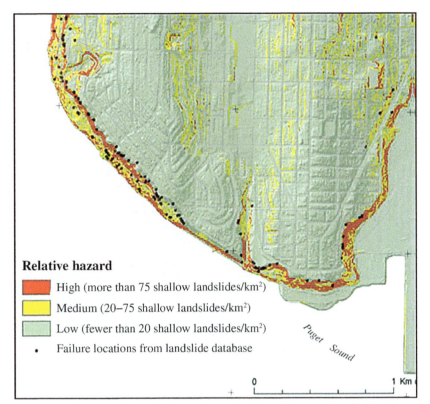

Figure 13.17 A Landslide Hazard Map. This map shows the Magnolia area of Seattle, Washington. (*Source:* Highland and Bobrowsky 2008.)

1. **Stable**: Areas of 0–5% slope that are not underlain by landslide deposits.
2. **Generally stable**: Areas of 5–15% slope that are not underlain by landslide deposits.
3. **Generally stable to marginally stable**: Areas of greater than 15% slope that are not underlain by landslide deposits or bedrock units susceptible to landsliding.
4. **Moderately unstable**: Areas of greater than 15% slope that are underlain by bedrock units susceptible to landsliding but not underlain by landslide deposits.
5. **Unstable**: Areas of any slope that are underlain by or immediately adjacent to landslide deposits.

Figure 13.18 shows a landslide susceptibility map for the Congress Springs area of Santa Clara County, California. To produce the map, several factors were considered: steepness of slope, type of rock or surficial deposit, and locations of bedrock faults, springs, and former marshes. Note the "Yes-No-Maybe" approach (green light, red light, yellow light) for recommended land use. "Maybe" areas are those shown as Yes* and No* in Figure 13.18. This type of overlay environmental zoning recognizes that some areas clearly are not hazardous and should be appropriate for construction and some areas are very hazardous and inappropriate for development. However, there are areas on the margin where moderate problems can be addressed with engineering design or construction practices, or where there is uncertainty. For these areas, a caution flag is raised by requiring an engineering site assessment before a building permit will be granted. (For more information on landslide hazards, including structural mitigation measures, see Highland and Bobrowsky 2008).

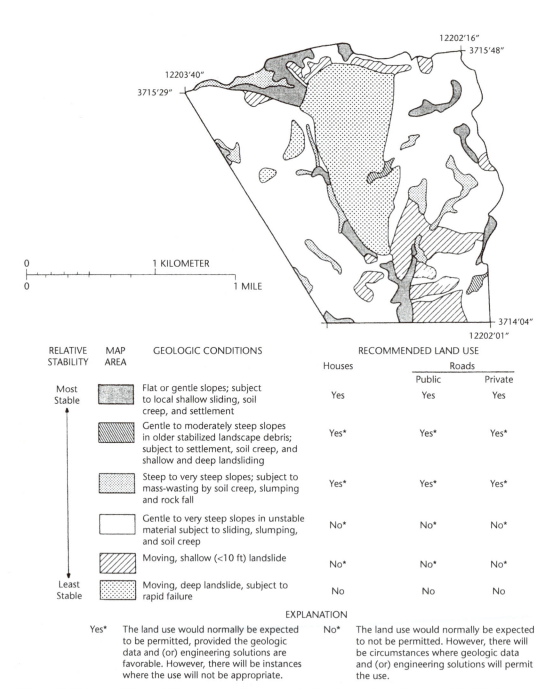

Figure 13.18 Potential Ground Movement and Recommended Land Use Policies. (*Source:* USGS 1982.)

Seismic Hazards

Earthquakes pose a severe risk throughout the world and in active areas of the United States, mostly in the Pacific states. The 2010 Haitian earthquake killed 222,000, and the 2008 Chinese Sichuan earthquake killed 70,000. Earthquakes triggered the 2004 Indian Ocean tsunami that killed 230,000 mostly in Indonesia, and the 2011 Japanese tsunami that killed more than 20,000. In the U.S., the 1994 Northridge, California, quake caused $30 billion in damage, and the 1989 Loma Prieta quake in northern California caused $6 billion (FEMA 2000b). Although there was some loss of life in those U.S. quakes, the relatively low number of fatalities is a testament to effective earthquake hazard mitigation planning, compared with major quakes in less prepared parts of the world.

Most earthquakes are caused by the tectonic movement of Earth's major crustal plates that float on more fluid interior materials. Stress is generated on these plates by convection currents in the fluid materials and is released by slippage along weaknesses or faults in the crust. Over time, plate movement builds up pressure that must be relieved periodically. If fault surfaces are smooth, plates may move *aseismically* without building pressure. However, if movement along faults sticks, compresses, or bends, pressure will build up, ultimately to be relieved *seismically* by a sudden dramatic movement—an **earthquake**. More than 95% of earthquake epicenters worldwide are located along the plate boundaries.

Nearly all of the earthquake history of the United States is at the intersection of the North Amercian Plate and the Pacific Plate on the Pacific Coast, as shown in the earthquake hazard map, Figure 13.19. But faults occur throughout the tectonic plates, and major intraplate fissures can result in significant quakes. The famous New Madrid, Missouri, quakes of 1811–1812 and the 1886 Charleston, South Carolina, quake were caused by major intraplate rifts near the middle of the North American Plate. As a result, both of these areas show on Figure 13.19.

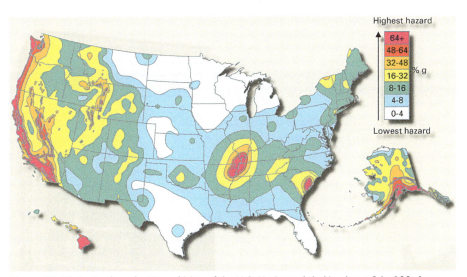

Figure 13.19 An Earthquake Hazard Map of the U.S. Horizontal shaking has a 2-in-100 chance of being exceeded in a 50-year period. Shaking is expressed as a percentage of gravitational force (g). (*Source:* USGS 2008.)

Earthquake Hazards

Earthquake magnitude and intensity are defined in Box 13.6. Earthquakes pose a number of hazards for human developments as a result of fault displacement, groundshaking, ground failure, flooding, and indirect effects such as fire, fuel or water line rupture, and damage to critical facilities. Seismic or aseismic **fault displacement** can cause significant damage to structures built on or near the fault line.

Most seismic damages, however, result from **groundshaking**, which extends far beyond the earthquake epicenter and can trigger landslides and liquefaction (the spontaneous flow of unconsolidated materials). Groundshaking is measured by peak ground acceleration (PGA) frequency and magnitude as a function of gravitational force (g). One way to assess risk is the probable PGA that will occur over a future time period based on geophysical models and seismic monitoring. The USGS maps probable PGA as a percentage of g for earthquake-prone areas, as shown in Figure 13.19, which shows 2% probability over 50 years for the U.S.

The USGS produces these maps for other probabilities at a finer scale for earthquake-prone areas and continues to update them based on new monitoring and research. The agency works with states and local governments to assess and map earthquake hazards in specific locations. See http://earthquake.usgs.gov /hazards/.

Although groundshaking in the vicinity of an earthquake will obviously depend on the magnitude of the quake and the distance from the epicenter, it also depends on the underlying soils and geology. As shock waves travel from dense rock to less dense rock to unconsolidated material such as alluvium and finally to saturated materials like muds, they tend to increase in amplitude and decrease in velocity. Ground motion thus lasts longer and is more severe in unconsolidated and water-saturated soils, and structures located on these materials will encounter greater damage.

Figure 13.20 shows groundshaking from the 1989 Loma Prieta earthquake in the San Francisco Bay Area, which caused the collapse of the Oakland I-880 free-

---

BOX 13.6—Measuring Earthquake Magnitude and Intensity

- **Earthquake magnitude** is the amplitude of the shock waves of a quake. It is a measure of the strain energy released by an earthquake, calculated from the record made by the event on a seismograph. In 1935, Charles Richter defined local magnitude, or Richter magnitude, as the logarithm (base 10) of the amplitude in micrometers of the maximum amplitude of seismic waves that would be observed on a standard torsion seismograph of a distance of about 60 miles from the epicenter.

- **Earthquake intensity** indicates the potential observed effects of an earthquake of an expected magnitude at a particular place. A 12-grade Modified Mercalli Intensity Scale is used today, ranging from I ("Not felt except by a very few") to V ("Felt by nearly everyone; some dishes broken; pendulum clocks may stop") to XII ("Damage total; waves seen on ground; objects thrown upward into the air").

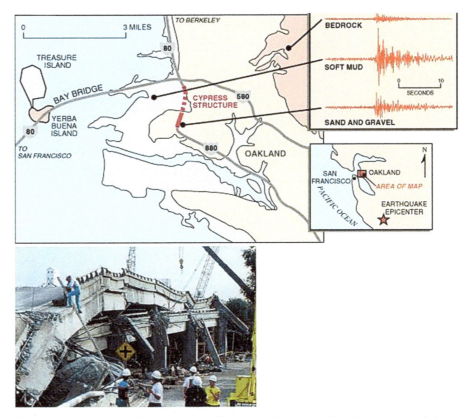

Figure 13.20 Earthquake Groundshaking. The extent of groundshaking depends on underlying materials. The Cypress freeway structure in Oakland, California, that stood on soft mud (dashed red line) collapsed in the 1989 magnitude 6.9 Loma Prieta earthquake, whose epicenter was 55 miles south. Adjacent parts of the freeway (solid red) that were built on firmer ground remained standing. Seismograms show that the shaking was especially severe in the soft mud. (*Source:* USGS 2001. Photo by Lloyd S. Cluff.)

way. Groundshaking grew in magnitude as the shock waves encountered the soft bay muds on which the freeway was built. Both the USGS (http://earthquake.usgs .gov/regional/nca/soiltype/) and the Association of Bay Area Governments (ABAG) have interactive mapping websites for mapping susceptible soils and ground-shaking potential based on underlying materials in the Bay Area (http://gis.abag .ca.gov/Website/Shaking_Prob/viewer.htm). Figure 13.21 shows a product of the ABAG website.

Potential damage due to groundshaking also depends on the structures them-selves. Wood-frame houses tend to be the safest, while old, unreinforced masonry structures are the most dangerous. Newer reinforced concrete buildings may allow some deformation without fracturing and thus can absorb some ground-shaking; modern steel-frame buildings generally are flexible enough to absorb shock, although the movement will likely damage glass and other rigid compo-nents (Jaffe et al. 1981). As the relationship between damage, groundshaking, and underlying geologic materials has become increasingly clarified, land use and

Figure 13.21 Interactive Earthquake Mapping. This image is from the ABAG Interactive WebMapper for the San Francisco Bay Area. (*Source:* Association of Bay Area Governments 2011.)

building codes have reflected this understanding. Figure 13.22 shows that building strength codes not only have become more strict in California but also have distinguished underlying materials, with higher standards required for construction on soft soil, compared to hard rock.

Ground failure by landslides, liquefaction, subsidence, and settlement can be triggered by earthquakes. In assessing earthquake hazards, it is important to locate areas susceptible to these slope and support problems. Flooding of low-lying areas can also be a potential hazard, as a result of earthquake-induced dam failure or tsunamis (the "tidal waves" caused by earthquakes in the bottom of the sea or

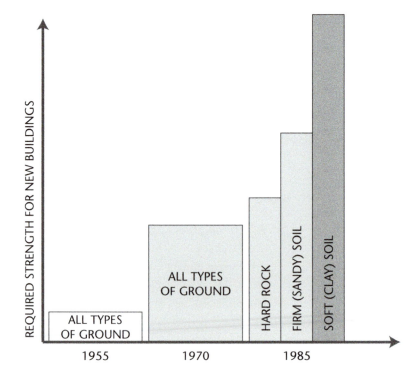

Figure 13.22 California Earthquake Building Codes for New Construction. (*Source:* USGS 2001.)

bay). In the 1906 San Francisco earthquake, most of the damage came not from the groundshaking and ground failure, but from the fires caused by them; further-more, ruptured water lines impeded the effort to control the fires. These and other **indirect earthquake hazards** should be considered in a comprehensive earth-quake risk assessment and mitigating effort. Of particular importance are poten-tial damages to "critical facilities." These may include facilities required to main-tain health and safety, such as hospitals and fire stations; large population centers, such as sports arenas; and facilities that could pose special dangers if damaged, such as nuclear power plants, chemical plants, and hazardous waste storage sites.

Seismic Hazard Mitigation

A first step in mitigation planning is assessing seismic-related hazards. USGS national and regional assessments (see Figure 13.19) and its finer-scale versions are a good place to start. If hazard mitigation is warranted, an inventory and map-ping of earthquake hazards should be conducted. Here are some examples:

- A map showing unconsolidated and water-saturated soils can indicate where groundshaking is likely to be most severe, as for the San Francisco Bay Area (see Figure 13.21).
- Maps showing unstable slopes, liquefaction hazard zones, and dam fail-ure and tsunami inundation areas can indicate areas susceptible to earthquake-induced landsliding and flooding. The differentiation of risk zones is the first step in land use planning for seismic hazard mitigation.
- A map showing critical facilities can locate important and hazardous facilities. Figure 13.23 is a portion of a map for the Puget Sound region, showing the location of earthquake groundshaking, ground rupture, and liquefaction zones, as well as critical lifelines that could be disrupted by an earthquake, such as transmission lines, pipelines, major roads, and railroads.

California's Seismic Hazard Mapping Act of 1990 mandated the California Department of Conservation (CDC) to identify and map the state's most promi-nent earthquake hazards. The department's Seismic Hazard Zone Mapping Pro-gram maps California's areas prone to liquefaction and earthquake-induced land-slides as overlays on quadrangle maps. Figure 13.24 shows a portion of the San Francisco map. Cities and counties use the maps to regulate development. They can withhold development permits until geologic or soils investigations are con-ducted for specific sites and mitigation measures are incorporated into devel-opment plans. Sellers of property use the maps to determine if their sites are in a hazard area; if so, they must disclose this to the buyer. The CDC produced the first maps in 1996 and continues to prepare them in 2010 (see http://www .conservation.ca.gov/cgs/shzp/Pages/Index.aspx).

All of these maps can provide the spatial or locational basis for developing safety policies and controls to mitigate seismic hazards, such as land use zoning and

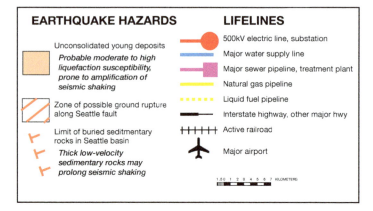

Figure 13.23 A Portion of the Puget Sound Region Lifelines and Earthquake Hazards Map. (*Source:* USGS 2010.)

building codes. States and localities must reflect these spatial hazard assessments in their zoning ordinances as overlay zones or performances standards (see Chapter 17). Figure 13.22 illustrates how California building codes became increasingly more stringent in seismic safety between the 1950s and the 1980s. Nelson and French's (2002) study of the 1994 Northridge earthquake argued that effective earthquake hazard mitigation must go beyond building codes to include retrofitting older buildings to current standards, quality comprehensive plans, and effective implementation of land use controls and codes.

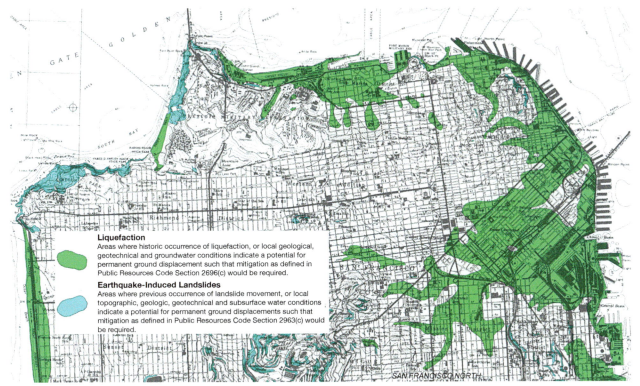

Figure 13.24 A Portion of the California Seismic Hazard Quad Map for San Francisco. (*Source:* California Department of Conservation 2011.)

Wildfire Hazards

Wildfires have always been a hazard to forestland, ecosystems, and watersheds, but suburban and ex-urban residential development has brought that danger to America's backyard. Figure 13.25 is a national wildfire map showing the number of wildfires by county that occurred between 1980 and 2005. Figure 13.26 shows the significant growth of California's annual wildfire acres burned from 1990 to 2008. Not only has burned acreage increased, but more people and property have been exposed as a result of outward urban development into wildland areas. And the threat of wildfires is expected to increase as a result of climate change.

Like most natural hazards, **wildfire** is plagued by the disaster-relief-rebuild-disaster cycle discussed earlier. People tend to ignore a hazard until a disaster occurs, then reach out for help, only to rebuild in the hazardous area and subject themselves (and others) to future disasters. After Oakland (California) lost 3,500 homes to wildfire in 1991, many rebuilt in the same area without vegetative cleanup or improved construction practices. Though they thought such a wildfire would never return, history showed that disastrous fires had struck in 1923 and 1970. Certain memories can be short.

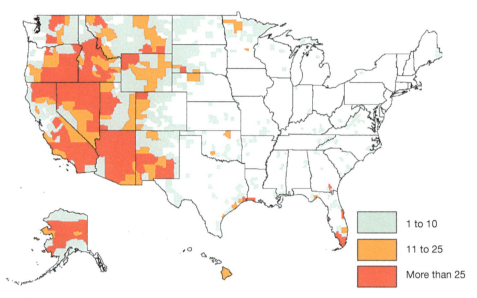

Figure 13.25 Number of Wildfires of more than 1,000 Acres by County, 1980–2005. (*Source:* U.S. GAO 2007.)

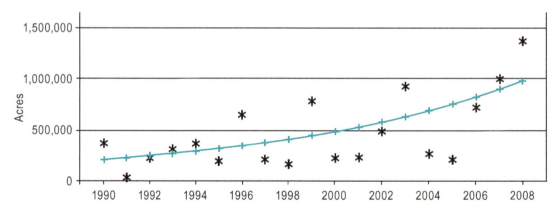

Figure 13.26 Annual Acres Burned as a Function of Time, 1990–2008. (*Source:* California Department of Forest Management and Fire Protection, CalFire 2010.)

Recognizing this growing threat, Congress passed the 2003 Healthy Forests Restoration Act (HFRA). It charged the Forest Service (USFS) and the Bureau of Land Management (BLM) to consider local communities when developing and implementing forest, hazardous fuel, and fire management. In partnership with the National Fire Protection Association and other organizations, the USFS had already established the National Wildland/Urban Interface Fire Program, which initiated the **FireWise Communities** program to mitigate wildfire hazards by education and technical assistance to community firefighters, urban planners, landscape architects, building designers, and contractors (FireWise Communities

2001). The **wildland-urban interface (WUI)** zone is where human development structures meet and intermingle with undeveloped wildland with vegetative fuels.

Community Wildfire Protection Plans (CWPP) under HFRA were intended for communities near USFS and BLM lands so that they could influence federal agency plans and projects for fuel reduction and federal and proximate nonfederal land. The CWPP is not necessarily a comprehensive approach to wildland fire mitigation, but it is a start. CWPP minimum requirements include (Communities Committee et al. 2004):

1. *Collaboration:* A CWPP must be developed collaboratively by local and state government representatives, in consultation with federal agencies and other interested parties.
2. *Prioritized Fuel Reduction:* A CWPP must identify and prioritize areas for hazardous fuel reduction treatments and recommend the types and methods of treatment that will protect one or more at-risk communities and essential infrastructure.
3. *Treatment of Structural Ignitability:* A CWPP must recommend measures that homeowners and communities can take to reduce the ignitability of structures throughout the area addressed by the plan.

Many states and communities have gone further to mitigate fire hazard in WUI areas. Following the basic natural hazard mitigation planning process, they have engaged stakeholders, identified and mapped the hazard areas, and developed plans and programs to mitigate the hazard. The FireWise Communities program developed a useful wildfire risk assessment form to determine relative risk. It includes a number of factors that are combined in a sum-of-weighted-factors method to produce a wildfire hazard score:

- Means of access, both exit for residents and entry for firefighters.
- Vegetation based on fuel models: light (grasses), medium (brush, small trees), heavy (dense brush, timber, hardwoods), slash fuels (logs, stumps, broken understory).
- Topography within 300 ft of structure; steeper slopes produce thermal currents that spread fire.
- Building construction: materials and setbacks.
- Roofing assembly: rated for fire hazard.
- Available fire protection: water sources, distance to fire station.
- Placement of electric and gas utilities: underground or aboveground.

The California Department of Forestry and Fire Protection (CalFire) has done much to advance wildfire mitigation in response to state law. The agency provides a detailed statewide forest assessment (CalFire 2010). It also assesses and maps very high fire hazard zones and designates state, federal, or local responsibility for managing those areas. Figure 13.27 shows a portion of the fire hazard severity zone map for San Diego.

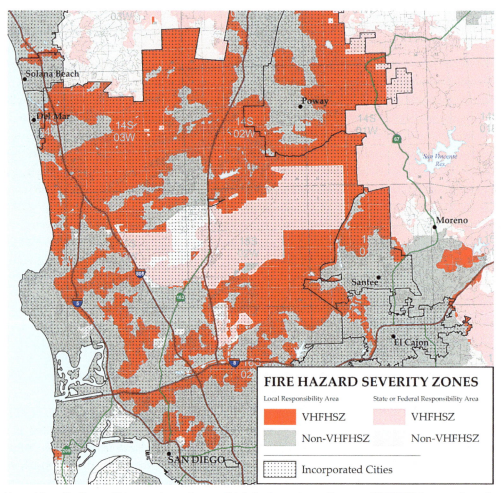

Figure 13.27 Fire Hazard Severity Zones. This map shows the very high fire hazard severity zones (VHFHSZ) for a portion of the San Diego Local Responsibility Area. The Resource Assessment Program of CalFire (California Department of Forestry and Fire Protection) maps hazard zones and designates state, federal, and local responsibilities for hazard mitigation. (*Source:* CalFire 2007.)

Mitigating the wildfire hazard in WUI areas requires action. Specific measures for reducing wildfire hazard include fire-resistant landscaping and construction materials, maintenance of wild vegetation that serves as fuel, and improved fire protection and response. Protecting a building from wildfire takes a two-pronged approach: (1) removing flammable materials from around the building and (2) constructing the building of fire-resistant material.

Building codes, subdivision and zoning regulations, and maintenance ordinances are necessary to achieve these objectives. A mitigation siting and landscaping concept used in landscaping and maintenance ordinances is the **defensible space**. Figure 13.28 depicts the California legal requirements for vegetative management around occupied dwellings, showing 100 ft of defensible space.

The FireWise Community program, and especially the Community Wildfire Protection Planning process, has gotten more people involved in what previously

Figure 13.28 Defensible Space. California law requires landowners to create and maintain a wildfire defensible space around buildings. 1: Lean, Clean, Green Zone: 30 ft around the home: short herbaceous plants, deciduous trees. 2: Reduced Fuel Zone: 70 ft or to property line, remove surface litter; guidelines for (a) grasses, horizontal and vertical clearance for shrubs and trees; (b) continuous canopy pruning. (*Source:* CalFire 2007.)

was a technical process of fire suppression management. The Forest Service, The Nature Conservancy, and other organizations have established and maintained the Fire Learning Network involving 70 landscape collaboratives, with a common goal of mitigating the hazard but also restoring ecosystems that depend on fire. Wildfire mitigation does raise issues about conflicting objectives in environmental planning and management. We could mitigate the wildfire hazard by removing the fuel or reducing our forest canopy, or we could arrest the decline in urban and suburban canopy cover and to plant trees for their economic, ecological, environmental, and social benefits (see Chapter 10). The Fire Learning Network is grappling with these conflicts, and the approach has lessons for other areas of environmental planning.

Summary

This chapter explored natural hazard mitigation planning and its application to flooding, coastal hazards, geologic hazards, and wildfire. There are many other natural hazards, including weather-related tornadoes, winter storms, extreme heat, and drought, as well as geologic support problems and volcanic hazards. Some of these were included in the first edition, and that material is on the book website (www.envirolanduse.org).

Effective natural hazard mitigation is adaptation for resilient communities. It must be anticipatory, identify vulnerabilities, stress preparedness for change, and build capacity for resilience among those likely affected by change. It has social as well as economic and technical dimensions.

Effective hazard mitigation requires understanding the hazard, mapping relative hazard based on that understanding, and formulating and implementing enforceable measures to mitigate exposure and vulnerability. The basic objectives are to keep future development from being exposed to known hazard areas, keep hazards from affecting existing developed areas, and strengthen existing development to reduce vulnerability. Measures include land use and building regulations that preclude development in high hazard areas and require stringent standards in moderate hazard areas, property acquisition and relocation in high hazard areas; education, and emergency preparedness. Natural hazard mitigation plans should address multiple hazards, be prepared in anticipation rather than after a natural disaster, and be reevaluated and modified as necessary after each hazard event.

Like many other topics presented in previous chapters, the quality of information, especially geospatial information related to natural hazards, has improved significantly since this book's first edition. These improvements have aided both technical assessment and community education and involvement.

Inland flooding hazard mitigation requires quality mapping and land use controls. Through FEMA, the U.S. NFIP has made flood hazard boundary maps available to all flood-prone communities. In addition, the availability of flood insurance is conditional on local floodplain management, including restrictive zoning in the 100-year floodplain. These standards provide a baseline of protection for new development, but many communities have gone beyond these requirements to protect more flood-prone and riparian areas, and have addressed existing exposed developments through relocation.

Coastal hazards result from the dynamic nature of beach, dune, and bluff processes and exposure to coastal storms, including hurricanes. Restricting development in hazard areas and preserving natural protection mechanisms like dune systems are important elements of coastal hazard mitigation. Slope stability hazards are a function of slope steepness and underlying materials. Mapping these features and especially past landslides can give a good spatial representation of slope stability and provide information on which to base land use regulation to reduce exposure and vulnerability.

Unlike slope problems, earthquake hazards affect entire regions. More pervasive hazards from earthquake groundshaking require more widespread controls, like building standards for all new development. Still, there are areas within earthquake regions that are more susceptible to groundshaking hazards than others due to underlying materials, such an unconsolidated materials, clays, and muds. Effective mitigation requires identifying and mapping these areas of higher relative hazard and applying more stringent mitigation measures.

Effective mitigation requires selective relocation and retrofit of existing buildings and developments that are exposed or vulnerable to natural hazards. Like energy and stormwater, we cannot develop our way out of the problem. In addition to being smart about future development, we need to correct what we have.

14 ■ Integration Methods and Synthesis Metrics

The preceding chapters addressed principles of soils, geology, hydrology, ecology, energy, and climate change and how they affect, and are affected by, human use of the land. Yet everything is connected, and it is important to synthesize this information and integrate it into land use planning and management, for the protection of productive and valued natural systems, and to avoid construction and damage costs. This chapter reviews some useful methods of integrating these considerations for use in decision making. It also presents emerging metrics that synthesize green and sustainability objectives for buildings, neighborhoods, and communities.

The **environmental land inventory** involves gathering and usually mapping a number of natural and often socioeconomic factors that have a bearing on land use. Inventories first used hand-drawn maps but now are almost universally part of a GIS dataset. The inventory itself can help guide development, but with the ease of GIS spatial analysis, it is used for further analysis. **Rapid assessment** is a term given to initial data gathering, usually at a general or coarse scale, from readily available information and secondary sources. Like environmental inventories, there is little analysis but some interpretation, and products take the form of hand-drawn or rudimentary maps and preliminary reports. See the book website (www .envirolanduse.org) for material from the first edition on rapid assessment.

Land suitability analysis combines inventory information to produce composite maps that display the relative suitability for a specific use (in siting studies) or a number of uses (in comprehensive planning). Both hand-drawn maps (using transparent overlays) and GIS maps can be used for land suitability analysis. These techniques are closely related; in fact, one builds on the other. Inventories can stand alone or serve as the database for GIS and land suitability studies.

Human carrying capacity studies aim to determine the level or impact of human population that an area can support based on natural (e.g., land area, soils) and/or socioeconomic factors (e.g., water or sewer capacity). Variations of the carrying capacity model are used in "ecological footprint" studies and Limits of Acceptable Change studies for wilderness area management.

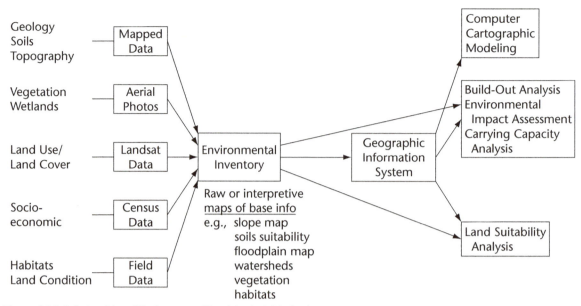

Figure 14.1 Relationships of Environmental Land Analysis Methods.

Environmental impact assessment is a well-used technique for forecasting impacts associated with project development; it has many practical applications in the assessment of land use and development. Finally, **build-out analysis** is a form of impact assessment that is useful to portray visually the implications of full implementation of community land use plans and zoning ordinances. Figure 14.1 shows the relationships among these land analysis methods.

Green infrastructure planning is a method of synthesizing the objectives for open space, wildlife and riparian habitat, working and visual landscapes, and watershed protection into the land conservation and development process. This chapter concludes with a discussion of **sustainability indicators** and indices that synthesize a range of environmental, economic, and social factors to assess and rate green buildings, neighborhoods, and communities.

The Environmental Inventory

The environmental land inventory has become a routine task in land use planning. There are four objectives of the inventory:

1. To provide a useful display of land information in maps.
2. To "red flag" areas of concern for planners, citizens, landowners, and developers.
3. To provide base data for siting and environmental impact studies.
4. To provide input for GISs and land suitability analysis.

Typically, an inventory simply maps spatial information; there is little or no evaluation of the information. The components of the inventory will vary with the area being studied, its conditions, and the planning objectives. Generally, maps are included on soils and geologic conditions or limitations, slope and elevation, watersheds and flooding potential, vegetation and habitats, and other natural factors. In addition, the inventory often includes information on the built environment, such as land use, transportation systems, land ownership, storm and sanitary sewerage, and cultural information, like historic and archaeological sites.

The data displayed in an environmental inventory come primarily from available sources, sometimes with interpretation and analysis. The previous chapters outlined a number of procedures for interpreting specific sources to produce inventory maps. Those sources include aerial photographs, satellite imagery, topographic maps, soil surveys, geologic maps, floodplain maps, vegetation and habitat maps, and other locally produced maps and studies. Sometimes field studies may be necessary to validate the map information.

The usefulness of the inventory depends not only on the completeness and accuracy of the information but on the quality of the graphic presentation. Useful maps should do more than simply display data; information should jump out at the map user. Line weights, textures, colors, symbols, and text should be carefully chosen to provide emphasis, order, and readability. Major factors should be shown in the strongest colors or tones.

Let's look at a couple of examples of inventories—one old, one new—to see how they have changed in quality and utility in the past 30 years. The 1981 Blacksburg study is described below. The 2009 Portland Natural Resource Inventory is presented after the introductory section on land suitability analysis, because it, like most current environmental inventories, is brought to life with the analytical capabilities of GIS.

The Blacksburg Environmental Inventory (1981)

I conducted my first environmental inventory in 1981 for the town of Blacksburg, Virginia, a rural college town with a population of 30,000 at that time. The purpose of the inventory was to identify **environmentally sensitive areas** and integrate that information into the town's growth management program. These were defined as (1) areas having environmental value (e.g., important habitats, prime agricultural soils, scenic areas) and (2) areas posing a natural hazard to development (e.g., floodplains, steep slopes). In addition, the inventory included certain socioeconomic factors that reflected or created development pressures so that **environmentally critical areas**—those environmentally sensitive areas subject to development pressure—could be identified. The inventory was also used to determine how well the town could accommodate future growth while protecting environmentally sensitive areas (Anderson et al. 1981).

Table 14.1 lists the maps produced as part of the inventory and the sources of information. Figure 14.2 illustrates a recent update of four of the original maps on agriculture, geology, and open space. All the original hand-drawn maps were put into Blacksburg's GIS system in the mid-1990s. One of the Blacksburg maps was an inventory composite, which combined information from several maps. The

TABLE 14.1 **Factors and Data Sources for Blacksburg's Environmental Inventory**

I. Environmental Inventory

Base Map	USGS 7½ minute quadrangle Map
Elevation	Derived from USGS Quad
Slope	Derived from USGS Quad
Geologic Hazards	USGS 7½ Geologic Map
Watersheds, Floodplains, Stormwater Drainage	FEMA Floodplain Maps, Blacksburg P.W. Dept.
Erosion Potential	SCS Soil Survey
Suitability of Soils for Septic Tanks	SCS Soil Survey
Suitability of Soils for Agriculture	SCS Soil Survey
Vegetation	1" = 200' Aerial Photos
Habitats of Specially Classified Species	TNCVirginia Natural Diversity Program
Historic Sites	Town Historic Inventory
Visual Resources: Corridors, Viewsheds	Field Study

II. Land Use and Growth Potential

Generalized Land Use	Town data
Zoning	Zoning ordinance
Blacksburg Land Use Plan	Comprehensive Plan
Agricultural Districts; Use-Value Assessment	County, town data
Sewer Availability	Public Works Dept.
Land Development Potential	Interpreted

Source: Anderson et al. 1981.

map indicates areas of steep slopes and floodplains, areas with severe limitations to septic systems, and areas sewered or within easy sewer access. The acreage of currently sewered areas not subject to slope or flooding hazards was computed from the map and was found to well exceed the acreage required to accommodate even high projections of population growth.

The study recommended a number of options the town could use to manage growth to protect environmentally sensitive areas, including encouraging infill development in existing sewered areas. In particular, the consultants suggested that developers conduct a predesign environmental assessment to alert themselves and town planners to potential problems. The town incorporated much of the study's information into its subsequent comprehensive planning.

Land Capability and Suitability Analysis

Although environmental land inventories and rapid assessments can aid land planning without extensive analysis, the ability to combine information on different variables enhances their usefulness. For example, maps displaying locations of

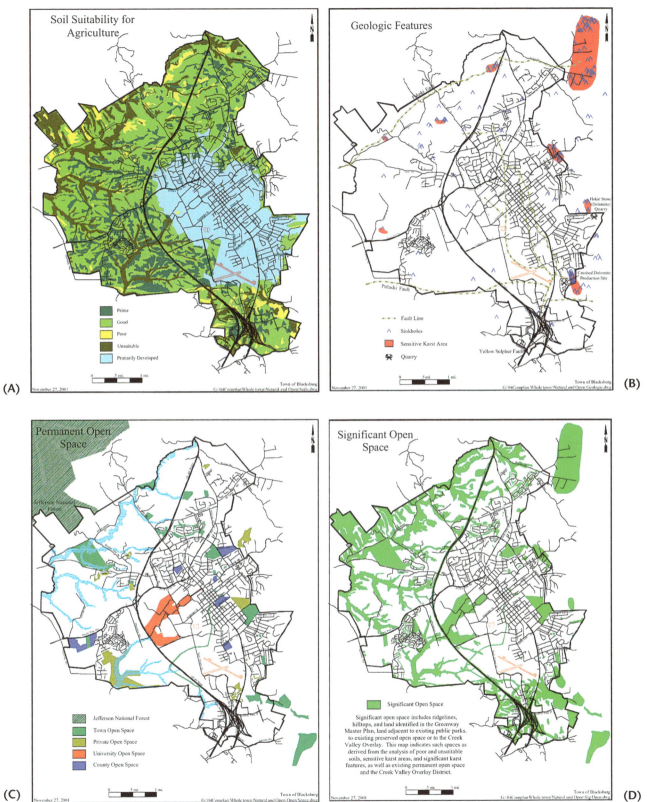

Figure 14.2 Maps from Blacksburg's Environmental Inventory. A: Agricultural Soil Suitability. B: Geologic Features. C: Permanent Open Space. D: Significant Open Space. (*Source:* Anderson et al. 1981; Blacksburg 2006.)

different natural hazards such as flooding, shrink/swell soils, steep slopes, and karst areas can be combined to show a composite of all natural hazards. Areas can be rated as poor, fair, or good for development based on the combination of hazards present. This composite or combination approach is the basis of land suitability studies.

A basic assumption of such studies is that land has an intrinsic suitability for particular uses that can be determined by combining information on individual factors. The objective of land suitability analysis is to determine the appropriate locations for certain uses based on those intrinsic characteristics (McHarg 1969). The appropriate location is determined by identifying the land's natural features that indicate the *vulnerability* of certain areas to impact or damage as a result of development (e.g., habitats, resources, aesthetic values, erosion, slope stability), and those features that indicate the *attractiveness* of certain areas for development (e.g., absence of natural hazards, good soils for foundations, permeable soils for septic systems, road access). The analysis may involve information on natural features and information on the built environment, such as proximity to highways and railroads, areas served by sewers and water, and existing land use.

Strictly speaking, a distinction can be made between land capability and land suitability. *Capability* refers to the physical capacity of the land to support development, whereas *suitability* refers to the physical capacity plus the social acceptability and economic feasibility of development. It is often difficult to distinguish between capacity and acceptability, however, so related studies, whether they go beyond natural factors or not, are often called **suitability studies**.

Land suitability studies incorporate different approaches, but they all share some general characteristics. All of them involve the display of land information in individual maps and combine the information by overlaying the maps either by hand or in a GIS to form a composite. That composite map can present several possible results, depending on the objectives of the study. Usually, it will identify the areas most attractive for a particular use.

Land suitability procedures can be applied to siting studies and comprehensive planning. The objective of **siting studies** is to identify the best location for a *specific use*, such as a park, a landfill, a shopping center, a powerline, or a power plant. By combining in some fashion the maps containing information deemed important to that use, a composite can be produced to show the most suitable alternative locations. The composite for a park might combine maps on vegetation, unique habitats, slope, existing roads, and so on (see Figure 5.16); for a landfill, it might combine maps on soils, slope, floodplains, existing land use, and other factors.

Alternatively, the goal may be to develop a **comprehensive plan** identifying the most suitable locations for a variety of land uses, such as housing, commercial and industrial development, and open space. A composite map is made for each use, again combining the factors perceived as important to each, perhaps based on public or agency criteria. These resulting composite maps can likewise be overlaid to identify areas suitable for more than one use, thus identifying potential land use conflicts. The final land use plan may be based on the composite as modified by certain social, economic, or environmental issues that were not part of the mapping procedure.

Methods of Combination

The basic procedure used in most land suitability studies is the same: Determine the objectives and data needs, develop inventory and data maps, and combine them to form a composite. However, several variations are worthy of description and comparison. The discussion below, drawn heavily from Hopkins (1977), outlines these variations and some concerns and gives examples of their use.

- **Gestalt method**. The Gestalt method of land suitability determination is different from the other methods in that it does not rely on the combination of specific factors to form a composite. Instead, using aerial photographs or site surveys, it divides the area under study into homogeneous units and implicitly specifies their relative suitability for a particular use. The method assumes that the nature of the land can be described by its *gestalt*, or total appearance. Way's terrain analysis using aerial photo interpretation is an example of the Gestalt method. A big disadvantage is that the results depend on the person performing the study, so it is hard to replicate.

- **Ordinal combination method**. This method, which is classic McHarg, began with hand-drawn transparent map overlays representing factors (e.g., soils, slope, vegetation), colored with lighter shades if suitable for the prospective land use and darker shades if not, and by laying them on top of one another; the lighter areas that shine through are more suitable. With GIS, numbers replace the shading, and the resulting overlap maps are easy to produce. In its pure form, ordinal combination assumes all factors are equally important to the prospective use, and that may not be true. It also assumes all factors combine linearly, that is, the combination of certain factor values does not have an unexpected effect. For example, the right combination of slope and underlying geology has a greater effect on slope stability than a linear combination might show.

- **Linear combination method**. This method attempts to solve one of the problems of the ordinal combination method by weighting factors by their relative importance. It uses numbers to denote the relative suitability of factor classes and also to denote the relative importance of factors to the land use under question. By multiplying factor value numbers by the factor weights, commensurate scores can be assigned to each factor value. By "overlaying" factor map overlays in GIS, a composite number can be determined by simply adding the weighted factor scores for cell.

- **Intermediate factor combination method**. The linear combination method, though very useful, does not solve the factor interdependence problem. The intermediate factor combination method does this by initially combining interactive factors (e.g., slope, soils, and geology) into intermediate interpretive maps (e.g., slope stability). These interpretive maps are then used the same way as factor maps in the linear combination method.

California Housing Development Projections and Constraints (2000)

Generally, land suitability analysis and environmental inventories are used in combination so that the factors limiting prospective land use are apparent. This is the approach taken in the California Department of Housing and Community Development (CDHCD) Raising the Roof study of environmental and land use constraints to future housing development through 2020. The study assessed housing needs and mapped physical and environmental constraints, including flood-prone areas, steep slopes, water features, wetlands, and prime farmlands. Developable lands were those undeveloped lands that were free of those constraints. This analysis was done for each county, and Figure 14.3 shows the suitability map for Santa Clara County. This map is a constraint map in which limiting factors for development are shown directly on the map, rather than being combined to show a development rating. This is often preferred in suitability studies so that the reviewer can see where specific constraints are located (CDHCD 2000).

The Portland Natural Resources Inventory and Land Suitability Modeling (2009)

Portland, Oregon, has a long history of environmental planning based on environmental inventories. The city conducted inventories of eight subareas of the city from 1989 to 1994 and used them to inform land use and zoning tools, including the Environmental Zoning and Willamette Greenway overlay zoning. Two major plans, the River Renaissance Vision (2001) and the Portland Watershed Management Plan (2005), both called for updating the natural resource inventories. The Portland Metro Council conducted an extensive inventory of habitat and other landscape features and modeled the criteria to rate habitat: 80,000 of the region's 280,000 acres were rated significant habitat. The City of Portland used Metro's inventory as the scientific and methodological basis for its inventory update, and it now has perhaps the most extensive environmental inventory of any U.S. urban area and is applying it to subarea planning.

Improvements in data quality from 2007 aerial photos and targeted site visits greatly enhanced the inventory of streams, floodplains, and vegetation. Figure 14.4 compares the level of detail of the original and revised mapped streams and vegetation, showing much finer grain detail.

The improved resources inventory has many uses. One of the primary applications of the inventory was its use in a GIS model for ranking composite riparian/wildlife habitat value. Figure 14.5 illustrates the model. Inventory data layers on streams and water bodies, wetlands, vegetation, flood areas, and steep slopes were combined to produce a layer on relative riparian resource value. Streams, wetlands, and vegetation were combined to produce a layer on relative wildlife habitat value. Riparian and wildlife habitat value layers, as well as a layer on special habitat location, were combined to give the composite riparian/wildlife habitat values as follows:

- High value: High riparian or high wildlife habitat value or special habitat area.

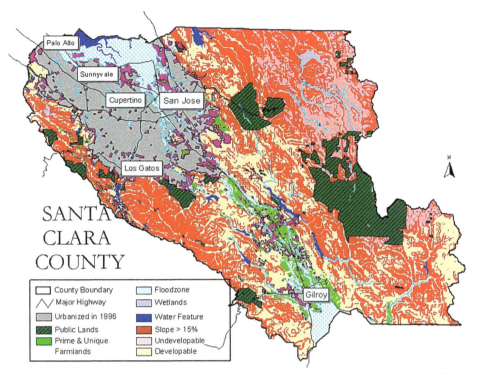

Figure 14.3 Development Suitability Map for Santa Clara County, California. (*Source:* CDHCD 2000.)

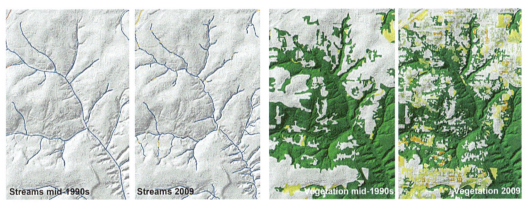

Figure 14.4 The Portland Natural Resources Inventory: 2009 Update. The recent inventory map has much finer resolution than the 1990s inventory on streams (left pair) and vegetation (right pair). (*Source:* Portland Bureau of Planning and Sustainability 2009b, 2009c.)

- Medium value: Medium riparian or medium wildlife habitat value.
- Low value: Low riparian or low wildlife habitat value.

The inventory provides the foundation for environmental planning at both fine and broad scales, from neighborhood to watershed to metro. The Internet

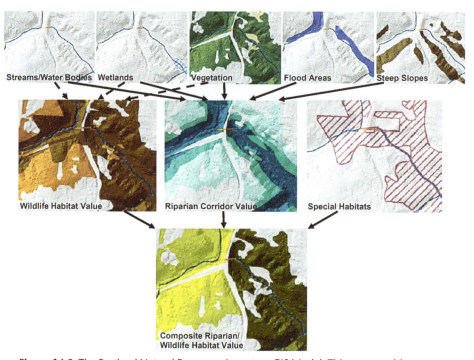

Figure 14.5 The Portland Natural Resources Inventory GIS Model. This map combines stream, wetland, vegetation, flood area, and steep slope layers to produce wildlife habitat and riparian value layers, then combines those value layers with special habitat layer to produce composite riparian/habitat value map. (*Source:* Portland BPS 2009d.)

webmapper prompts users for an address so they can zero in on locations. Figure 14.6 shows a neighborhood application in the Southwest Hills/Ross Island section of Portland. The land suitability analysis combines water features, vegetation, riparian value, and wildlife habitat value to produce a combined ranking of natural resources value. This information can be used to inform neighborhood plans and the Metro's Nature in the Neighborhood grant program for habitat restoration.

At the city and metro scales, the inventory is used to guide land use controls, land acquisition priorities, habitat conservation compliance, and watershed management. Figure 14.7 gives the inventory and composite value map for the city. Figure 14.8A compares the inventory to existing environmental overlay zones to identify outside of these zones. Using the inventory will help the city adopt stream and wetland setbacks to assist in compliance with its CWA TMDL plan for temperature and Metro's and USFWS habitat conservation requirements. The maps helped prioritize the city's Natural Area Acquisition Strategy. And for comprehensive planning, Figure 14.8B compares the inventory to The Portland Plan 2040 development centers and transportation stations and corridors so that the natural environment can help guide regional development (Portland 2009a, 2009b, 2009c, 2009d).

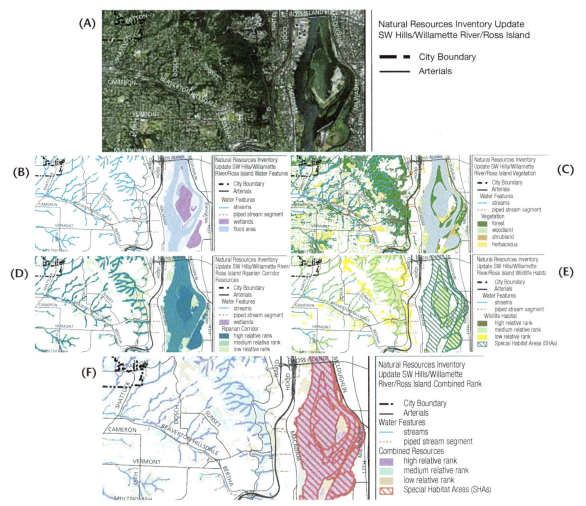

Figure 14.6 Neighborhood Application of the Portland Natural Resources Inventory. A: Aerial image of a portion of the Southwest Hills/Willamette/Ross Island area. B–E: These four inventory maps—water features (B), vegetation (C), habitat value (D), and wildlife value (E)—are combined to produce the natural resources combined rank shown in F. (*Source:* Portland BPS 2009a.)

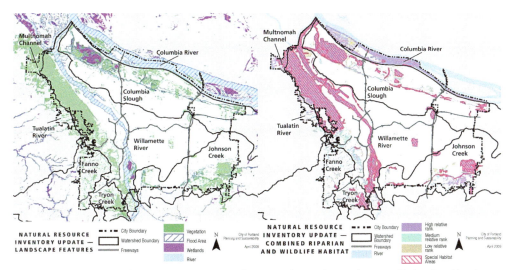

Figure 14.7 The Portland Citywide Natural Resources Inventory. Left: Vegetation and water features. Right: Combined riparian and wildlife habitat relative ranks. (*Source:* Portland BPS 2009a.)

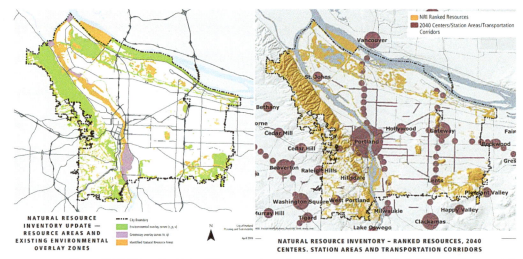

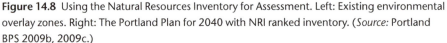

Figure 14.8 Using the Natural Resources Inventory for Assessment. Left: Existing environmental overlay zones. Right: The Portland Plan for 2040 with NRI ranked inventory. (*Source:* Portland BPS 2009b, 2009c.)

Human Carrying Capacity Studies

Assessment of an area's carrying capacity is a land analysis approach related to land suitability. Carrying capacity was first applied to wildlife and range management; *capacity* was defined as the maximum population of a particular species that a habitat can accommodate (Dasmann 1964). As introduced in Chapter 10, *carrying capacity* involves the level of population or development that can be sustained in an area without adversely affecting that area beyond an acceptable level. It is characterized by the asymptote of the S-shaped growth curve shown in Figure 14.9A.

The shape of the growth curve is based on environmental resistances the population confronts during its growth. For natural populations, the resistances relate to losses due to factors like predation, disease, and competition for food. For human populations, they relate to costs of development, costs to offset the adverse effects of development, costs of adding infrastructure (e.g., water supply), public opposition, and controls on development. Theoretically, the resistances are initially small, and there is increasing growth early; but as population grows, environmental resistances increase and greater resources are required to overcome them. Growth slows as resources required for the next increment of growth increase, until growth stops when the cost of obtaining the next increment is greater than the benefits of growth it allows. In natural systems, uncertainty and innovation resulting from adaptation and succession act to modify carrying capacity (Figure 14.9B). In human systems, technological innovation can change the capacity for growth (Figure 14.9D).

In natural systems, the resources expended to overcome resistances for the sake of growth are generated internally, and thus growth rates are usually self-regulated. However, in human systems, the costs can also come from external sources (e.g., subsidies for water and sewage systems), and these do not act to

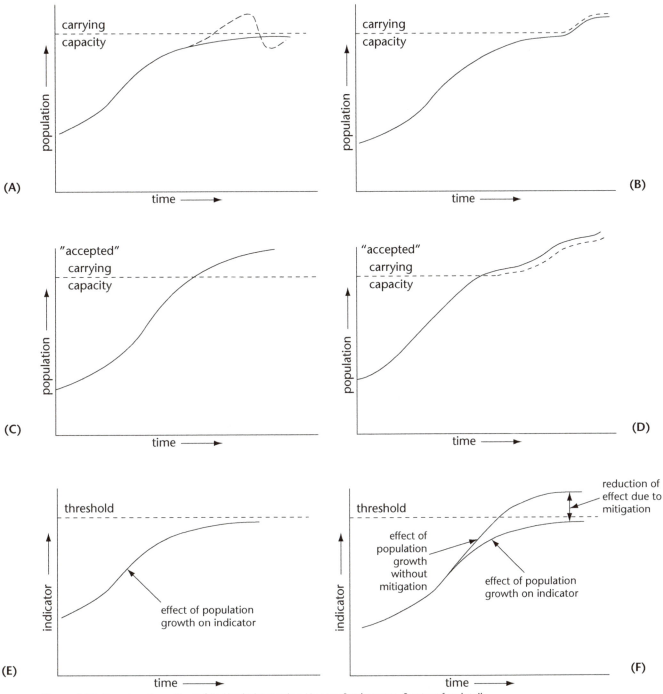

Figure 14.9 Carrying Capacity and Its Use in Managing Human Settlements. See text for details.

regulate growth. In addition, the human system does not depend on the natural system for survival. As a result, human population often grows beyond the carrying capacity without incurring the costs of growth and causes deterioration of the environment. Thus, human carrying capacity must be socially determined, and growth must be socially controlled if deterioration beyond an acceptable level is to be avoided (Figure 14.9C).

A variety of limiting factors can be investigated in carrying capacity studies, depending on local conditions. Factors that can determine an area's carrying capacity or ability to support growth include total land area, soil limitations for septic systems, sewer capacity, stormwater drainage capacity, water supply capacity, air quality and meteorological conditions, water quality, visual quality, even school or hospital capacity.

The application of the carrying capacity concept in managing human systems hinges on initially deciding the level of adverse effect that is "unacceptable" and then determining the threshold of population or development at which that level is reached. The approach is complicated by two considerations. The first is that deciding what is unacceptable—that is, what a community is willing to put up with in terms of the effects of population growth—is largely based on the values of the community. Thus, determining the human carrying capacity, although it is based on certain scientific information, is ultimately a judgmental act, requiring community involvement through the planning and political process. (See the Sanibel Island carrying capacity case study on the book website, www.envirolanduse.org.)

A second complicating consideration is that human intervention can increase the population limit for a given level of acceptable quality. The population carrying capacity can be increased by expanding the capacity of some important or limiting factor, such as by importing water or annexing land. In addition, population capacity can be expanded by reducing the effect each additional person has on the factors of interest by technological improvements (e.g., water conservation devices or land use designs that reduce runoff) or by changing behavior to a more conserving lifestyle (e.g., use of bicycles rather than automobiles creates less air pollution.

From Population Levels to the Attribute-Indicator-Threshold Approach

The ability to reduce individual impact raises questions about defining human carrying capacity in terms of a population limit. What is important is not necessarily the overall population, but the *effect* that population has on the environment or on one or more factors of interest. In Figure 14.9E and F, the carrying capacity curve is shown not in terms of population but in terms of a specific environmental attribute of interest (e.g., air quality, water supply, visual quality) measured by a specific indicator (e.g., pollutant concentration, gallons per day capacity, visibility in miles). The carrying capacity is given by the acceptable threshold for that factor measured by that indicator. As Figure 14.9E shows, innovation resulting from behavioral changes (affecting what each person does) and technological mitigation (affecting the impact of what each person does) can reduce the effect of a given growth of population on that indicator.

Whereas some applications of human carrying capacity have been based on an acceptable population threshold, more recent attempts have recognized that the overall objective is to control not population numbers per se, but rather the effect of that population on specific environmental factors or resources of interest. This offers a good illustration of the well-known environmental impact equation popularized by Barry Commoner:

$$I = PAT \rightarrow Impact = Population \times Affluence \times Technology$$

This means that the impact on the environment is not just a matter of population levels. It also depends on the level of affluence of that population (as measured by the impact per person associated with lifestyle and consumption) and on the mitigation of impact that technology provides. For example, the impact on water supply depends not only on the number of people (population) but also on the average use per person (water-consuming lifestyle) and on technology used to mitigate the impact (water conservation devices like low-flow showerheads and toilets).

Using impact thresholds instead of population has become the basis for carrying capacity studies. This **threshold approach** is the basis for the Limits of Acceptable Change method for wilderness area management and for environmental management in the Lake Tahoe Basin (discussed below).

The threshold approach first identifies a number of important environmental components, resources, or variables. The variables may involve the **natural environment** (air quality, water quality, fish and wildlife habitat, noise, etc.), **human-built infrastructure** (water supply, sewage capacity, road capacity, etc.), or **community perceptions** (visual quality, congestion, etc.). For each component, one or more **indicators** are identified that measure the quality of the component. For example, for the variable water quality, the indicator may be the concentration of a specific pollutant, water clarity measured by Secchi disk test, dissolved oxygen content, or all three.

Specific **thresholds** for these variables are determined from scientific study (e.g., for healthful air quality) and/or community involvement (e.g., for visual quality). Specific programs and/or regulations are then developed to ensure achievement or compliance with the thresholds.

This **variable-indicator-threshold approach** has certain advantages over applying a population threshold. It better matches the objectives of the human carrying capacity concept to control the effect of population rather than the population per se. It provides for human and technological innovation to reduce the impacts per person. And it is far more systematic and far less arbitrary, which supports its use and protects it from legal challenge.

Environmental Thresholds in the Lake Tahoe Basin

The Lake Tahoe area of California and Nevada exhibits exceptional environmental amenities, and, perhaps for that reason, it has experienced extreme development pressures. A long history of attempts to manage growth and the environment culminated in the 1986 Tahoe Regional Plan from the Tahoe Regional Planning Agency (TRPA). TRPA has been preparing a major update to that plan, and a set of draft plan documents was released in July 2011. A brief history of the planning effort and the plan itself are described in Chapter 18. The carrying capacity concept and the use of environmental thresholds played an important part in the environmental management of the basin.

TRPA defined environmental threshold carrying capacity as an environmental standard needed to maintain the significant scenic, recreational, educational, scientific, or natural value or to maintain public health and safety within the region (TRPA 1982). The process for developing the thresholds involved considerable public participation. It consisted of the following six steps:

1. Identify the environmental components or variables for which thresholds would be established.
2. Identify variables affecting the components.
3. Determine which measures would be appropriate as threshold indicators.
4. Determine the acceptable threshold level for each appropriate indicator.
5. Evaluate mechanisms to achieve each threshold to see if it is meaningful and possible.
6. Adopt the thresholds.

The 1982 environmental variables for which indicators and thresholds were established are given in Figure 14.10, along with selected thresholds. The thresholds take three different forms: a *numerical standard*, or quantifiable level that can be monitored; a *management standard*, or nonquantifiable level of quality for which certain actions are prescribed; and a *policy statement*, or decision to carry out a chosen course of action. Threshold statements could thus be made about variables that do not lend themselves to quantitative measurement. In addition, by including policy statements and management standards, the thresholds, once adopted, offered considerable guidance to the development of the regional plan.

A major challenge of the plan was that many of the adopted numerical threshold standards were already exceeded. The plan had to provide actions to improve quality while still accommodating some additional development. Monitoring the thresholds in 2006 showed that some are being met and some are not, some are improving and some are not. They are still in effect as of this writing (2011), but TRPA is in the process of revising the thresholds for the first time since 1982 because of improved scientific understanding, the need to better manage redevelopment in the nearly built-out basin, making environmental improvements, and improving biological functions in undeveloped areas (TRPA 2007a, 2007b, 2011). (See also Chapter 18.)

Limits of Acceptable Change

For decades, federal resource agencies have struggled with the challenges of providing for mandated multiple uses of public lands, while managing the natural

Environmental Components/Variables for which Thresholds Established	Selected Thresholds

Water Quality →
- Pelagic Lake Tahoe
- Littoral Lake Tahoe
- Tributaries
- Surface Runoff
- Groundwater
- Other Lakes

* Reduce dissolved inorganic nitrogen loading from all sources by 25 percent of the 1973-81 annual average to reverse the trends of water quality degradation in the pelagic zone and, over an extended period of time, achieve the following water quality standards:

- Annual mean phytoplankton primary productivity: 52 gmC/m2/yr.
- Annual mean Secchi disk transparency: 29.7 m.

Soil Conservation
- Natural Pervious Surface →
- Allowable Soil Loss
- Stream Environment

* Natural pervious surface shall meet the following limits for specified land capability districts:

Land Capability District	Max. Land Cover	% Acreage in Basin
1,2	1%	76%
3	5%	6%
4	20%	4%
5	25%	8%
6,7	30%	6%

Air Quality
- Carbon Monoxide
- Ozone
- Regional Visibility →
- Subregional Visibility
- Nitrate Deposition
- Odor

* Achieve 171 kilometers (103 miles) visibility at least 50% of the year.

Vegetation Preservation
- Common Vegetation →
- Uncommon Plant
- Sensitive Plants

Increase plant and structural diversity of forest communities through appropriate management practices, as measured by diversity indices of species richness, relative abundance, and pattern.

Wildlife →
- Special Int/Endangered Species
- Habitats of Special Significance

** A non-degradation standard shall apply to significant wildlife habitat consisting of deciduous trees, wetlands and meadows while providing for opportunities to increase the acreage of such riparian associations.

Fisheries
- Stream Habitat
- Instream Flows
- Lahontan Cutthroat Trout
- Lake Habitat

Noise
- Single Noise Events
- Cumulative Noise Events

Recreation
- Undeveloped Areas →
- Shore Zone
- Access
- Existing Developed

*** It shall be the policy . . . to preserve high quality, semi-primitive, non-motorized, undeveloped areas in their natural state and preserve them for low density use.

Scenic Resources
- Roadway and Shoreline →

* Restore scenic quality in roadway units rated 15 or below and shoreline units rated at 7 or below.

*   numerical standard
**   management standard
*** policy statement
Source: TRPA, 1982

Figure 14.10 Environmental Thresholds for the Lake Tahoe Basin. (*Source:* TRPA 1982.)

conditions of those lands. For example, recreational overuse of the national parks, national forests, and other lands often damages the resource and diminishes the natural experience of users, especially in wilderness areas. The U.S. National Park Service (NPS) has tried to use the carrying capacity concept to determine appropriate levels of recreation use to achieve their mandate of serving the greatest number of people, while still protecting the natural ecosystems. The 1978 National Parks and Recreation Act required the NPS to determine each park's "visitor capacity," the amount of use that allows for quality experiences without unacceptable impacts to the park's significant resources (National Park Service 2001).

After many attempts to quantify visitor carrying capacity and manage visitor population, the agencies have turned to the threshold approach. Stanley et al. (1985) developed the *Limits of Acceptable Change (LAC)* process for wilderness area planning in the national forests. A variation of this method, the Visitor Experience and Resource Protection (VERP) framework, was developed for the national parks (National Park Service 1997). Both rely on determining acceptable thresholds or desirable future conditions, and formulating planning and management actions to achieve them.

For wilderness areas, the LAC process aims not to prevent any human-induced change to the wilderness, but rather to decide how much change will be allowed to occur, as well as where and what actions are needed to control that change. LAC requires deciding what kinds of natural resource conditions and social experience conditions are acceptable, then prescribing actions to protect or achieve them. The LAC process consists of nine steps within four major components (Box 14.1). Implementing the process requires considerable resource inventory, as well as public (user) participation to determine desirable conditions and thresholds. By emphasizing conditions, impacts, and thresholds rather than numbers of users, LAC and VERP apply the carrying capacity concept in an objective and systematic way that can achieve desirable resource and social results through management actions.

The Ecological Footprint

The concept of the ecological footprint is like the inverse of carrying capacity. Whereas carrying capacity tries to measure the capability of an area to support and sustain a population within acceptable limits, the **ecological footprint** tries to measure the corresponding area of productive land and aquatic ecosystems required to produce the resources used, and to assimilate the wastes produced, by a defined population wherever on Earth that land area might be located (Rees 1996; Wackernagel and Rees 1995). The **carbon footprint** is variation of the ecological footprint with emphasis on one's carbon dioxide emissions and impact on climate change.

The ecological footprint accounts for the fact that unlike most natural habitats, human settlements are not contained ecosystems. Our communities import energy, food, water, and material resources from around the world, and export wastes far beyond their borders. For example, Rees (1996) calculated the ecological footprint of an average citizen in his hometown of Vancouver, British Columbia.

BOX 14.1—The Limits of Acceptable Change Process for Wilderness Area Management

- Identify Issues, Concerns, Opportunities
  1. Identify area issues and concerns.
  2. Define and describe recreational opportunity classes (based on recreational opportunity spectrum from pristine to primitive to semiprimitive nonmotorized to roaded natural), including resource, social, and management descriptions for each.

- Determine Present Condition of Wilderness Area
  3. Select indicators of resource conditions (e.g., trail erosion, campsite scars) and social conditions (e.g., solitude, noise).
  4. Inventory existing resource and social conditions.
  5. Specify measurable thresholds or standards for the resource and social indicators selected for each recreational opportunity class.

- Determine Action Plan
  6. Compile information from components I and II and identify alternative opportunity class allocations.
  7. Identify what management actions would be needed to meet thresholds for each alternative allocation from 6.
  8. Evaluate and select a preferred alternative. This will be the action plan.

- Implement and Monitor the Action Plan
  9. Implement actions for the preferred alternative and monitor conditions.

Source: Stankey et al. 1985.

Based on the average Canadian food diet, wood and paper consumption, fossil energy consumption, and corresponding carbon emissions, each Vancouverite requires 4.2 hectares (ha) of land to support these needs. With a population of 472,000, Vancouver has an ecological footprint of 2 million ha, 174 times its city area of 11,400 ha. Based on these per capita needs of 4.2 ha, the population carrying capacity of Vancouver's area would be just 2,500 people.

The ecological footprint concept is useful for recognizing the impact of our patterns of consumption in a world of limited resources. Rees (1996) advances the measure as an indicator of community sustainability, but poor community-specific data often limit its effectiveness.

Environmental Impact Assessment in Land Use and Development

An **environmental impact assessment (EIA)** is one of the most mandated and useful tools in environmental planning. Created initially by the National Environmental Policy Act of 1969, the method has been adopted by half of the states in the United States and by foreign governments around the world. Its major applications are in large planning and resource development projects conducted, funded, or approved by a government agency. Still, the method has useful applications in land use and development, and is used by several localities and states to assess the environmental impacts of development projects.

The objective of an EIA is simply to identify and predict the impacts of prospective actions or projects so that that information can be used in the development

BOX 14.2—Possible Effects of an Environmental Impact Assessment

Possible Effects of EIA on Projects
- Withdrawal of unsound project
- Legitimization of sound project
- Selection of improved project location
- Reformulation of plans
- Redefinition of goals
- Mitigation of project impacts
  ○ Dropping damaging elements of proposed project
  ○ Minimizing adverse effects by scaling down or redesigning project
  ○ Repairing or restoring environment adversely affected
  ○ Creating or acquiring environments similar to those adversely affected

EIA as an Impetus for Administrative Change
- Often increases access of citizens, NGOs, and other agencies to information on project
- Enhances interagency coordination
- Affects power relations between ministries, increases power of environmental agencies

Source: Ortolano and Shepherd 1995.

design and ultimately the approval of the project. Usually, mitigation measures are identified to offset or reduce the impacts, and these are incorporated into the final design. In its evolution over 25 years, two uses have emerged. First, the EIA is a planning tool—a rational means of gathering and analyzing information intended to influence management and development decisions. Second, the EIA is a political tool—a means of influencing the attitudes of top officials, a mechanism that has increased the status and strategies of project opponents. After all, the EIA intends to "hang out dirty laundry," to clearly identify the impacts, including the negative aspects, of a proposal. The real purpose of the EIA is not just to assess impacts, but to improve the quality of decisions. This is done through both planning and political negotiation.

Therefore, as shown in Box 14.2, the potential effects of EIA on project development include effects on both projects and administrative actions. One desirable project effect is that information on environmental impacts be considered from the very beginning in planning and design (Ortolano and Shepherd 1995).

"With-Without" Analysis: Impact Variables, Indicators, and Thresholds

In conducting an EIA, it is important to assess the environment systematically. Generally, the assessment focuses on indicators of change. The following list defines impact variables, impact indicators, and thresholds or standards for those indicators. This framework is the same one used in the threshold (or impact) approach to carrying capacity discussed earlier.

- *Impact variables:* Components of the environment that are important (e.g., water quality).
- *Impact indicators:* Measures that indicate change in an impact variable (e.g., dissolved oxygen).

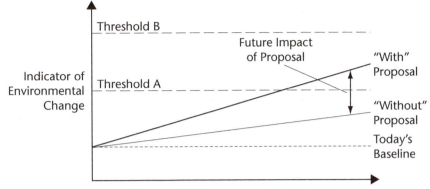

Figure 14.11 An Environmental Impact Assessment "With-Without" Analysis.

- *Impact thresholds or standards:* Values of impact indicators above or below which there is a problem; used to evaluate the impact (e.g., 5 ppm minimum of dissolved oxygen).

An EIA aims to predict future change in impact indicators that are likely to result from the proposed action. "With-without" (W-W/O) analysis is used to do this (Figure 14.11). The future change of a selected indicator is predicted with the proposed action and plotted on the graph. It is important to know the change that actually results from the action, so it is necessary to also plot the change in the indicator that would result if the action were not undertaken. The "without" line plots this change. The "impact" of the proposed action is the difference between the "with" and "without" lines, not the difference between the "with" line and today's value or baseline.

The figure also illustrates the use of thresholds or standards in the evaluation of impacts. If the accepted threshold or standard for the indicator is Threshold B, neither the "with" nor the "without" would approach it, and the impact may be deemed of minor importance. However, if the standard is Threshold A, the "without" case would not exceed the threshold, while the "with" case would. Therefore, the impact of the proposal is far more significant.

The EIA Process

Below is an outline of a generalized EIA process. It begins with an early scoping exercise intended to gather key parties and stakeholders to design the process and identify key issues, impact variables, and impact indicators. The process is designed to be flexible so that it can be adapted to the individual case at hand. Scoping, data studies, and impact identification come early in the process. Prediction of impacts is really the heart of the process and generally the most important. Many of the techniques discussed in previous chapters can be used for data studies, impact identification, and impact prediction. For example, peak discharge analysis, channel erosion and capacity analysis, soils suitability mapping, DRAS-TIC, wellhead protection, vegetation, wetland and habitat inventories, and other methods are especially useful. In addition to prediction, however, evaluation and presentation of impacts are also critical because interpretation, discussion, and negotiation about impacts will determine how decisions are affected by the EIA.

1. *Scoping:* Design the process; draft work program; identify issues, impact variables, parties to be involved and methods to be used.
2. *Baseline Data Studies:* Collect initial information on baseline conditions and important impact variables, which may include socioeconomic as well as environmental parameters.
3. *Identification of Impacts:* Concurrent with baseline studies, identify and screen impacts of alternative actions: variables, indicators, and thresholds.
4. *Prediction of Impacts:* Estimate the magnitude of change in important impact variables and indicators that would result from each alternative using W-W/O analysis. Employ project outputs, simple algorithms, simulation models as needed.
5. *Evaluation of Impacts and Impact Mitigation:* Compare indicator impacts to thresholds; determine relative importance of impacts to help guide decisions; evaluate plans for mitigation of impacts.
6. *Presentation of Impacts:* Present impacts of alternatives in concise and understandable format.

Using EIA in Land Development

As mentioned, in the United States, EIA is required of major federal government actions affecting the environment. It is also required of government agency actions in about half the states. Five of those states require EIA for all "public" actions, so EIA extends to the actions of local governments. In Washington state, those local actions specifically include permitting decisions of private land development. In other states, some localities have incorporated EIA into their development review process. Washington's State Environmental Policy Act (SEPA) process illustrates how EIA can be used effectively in assessing and mitigating environmental impacts of development (State of Washington 1998).

The SEPA process begins with a threshold determination. If the proposed project is not exempt (e.g., building a single house is exempt), the threshold determination depends on whether the expected impact is significant or not. This is a critical decision, because if the proposal's impact is declared significant, the applicant must prepare a costly and time-consuming **environmental impact statement (EIS)**. The applicant must prepare an assessment form to provide information for this determination. The checklist asks for responses on the project's description and its impact on a list of environmental variables or elements. The lead agency evaluates the checklist responses and often asks for more information or negotiates with the applicant before making the threshold determination.

If the agency declares that the proposal will likely pose a significant environmental impact, the applicant must prepare an EIS. A draft is prepared for 30-day public review, followed by a final EIS that responds to comments received. Based on the EIS, the lead agency must decide whether the proposal, including impact mitigation, should be permitted under SEPA. Even if the proposal meets existing zoning and other local ordinances, it can still be ruled in violation of SEPA because of excess environmental impact. Therefore, project approval becomes a "discretionary" decision based on environmental impacts rather than simply a "ministerial" decision based on meeting local codes. Local officials have two points of leverage on local development proposals. First, early in the process in the threshold determination, they can offer a nonsignificant impact determination in exchange for project design changes or mitigation measures that lessen the environmental impact. Second, and more obvious, they can grant a permit only if certain measures or changes are included in the proposal.

Common Problems in EIA Implementation

There are a number of perennial problems that limit the effectiveness of EIA to achieve its objectives. The list below is based on a wide range of experience, primarily in U.S. federal implementation as well as that in other countries (Ortolano and Shepherd 1995). The major concerns are that EIA comes *too late* in the planning process, EIA information is *not integrated* into decisions, and *cumulative impacts* that extend beyond an individual project are not assessed. Efforts should be made to generate information early so that it can be integrated into planning decisions and to consider impacts beyond the project's primary effects (Randolph and Ortolano 1976). Here are the typical, recurring problems in EIA implementation:

- EIA requirements are often avoided.
- EIA is often not carefully integrated into planning.
- EIA doesn't ensure environmentally sound projects.
- EIA is done primarily for projects, not programs or policies.
- Cumulative impacts are not assessed frequently.
- Public participation in EIA is often inadequate.
- Proposed mitigations may not be implemented.
- Post-project monitoring is rarely conducted.
- Assessments of risk and social impacts are often omitted from EIAs.

Despite these limitations, EIA has emerged as one of the most useful tools for environmental planning and project assessment. Phillips and Randolph (2000) found that effective EIA and NEPA compliance and ecosystem management can go hand in hand for federal agencies.

Build-Out Analysis

Developed at the Center for Rural Massachusetts, build-out analysis is a method for assessing the impacts of community plans and zoning ordinances. As shown in Figure 14.12 from Jeffrey Lacy's classic *Manual of Built-Out Analysis* (1990), communities will build out over time. **Build-out analysis** applies existing rights

Figure 14.12 Build-Out Analysis. These maps show the incremental build-out of Longmeadow, Massachusetts: 1942 (left), 1957 (middle), and 1987 (right). (*Source:* Lacy 1990. Courtesy: Center for Rural Massachusetts, University of Massachusetts–Amherst.)

provided by the zoning ordinance, builds it out, shows it visually in maps, then assesses the environmental and social impacts.

Build-out analysis is essentially EIA—not of a project, but of a large-scale community vision. Conceptually the analysis is quite simple. After preparing a base map of environmental features and existing development, the analysis takes the zoning ordinance and shows on the map the virtual implementation of the densities and uses allowed. The use of GIS can greatly facilitate this step. The resulting build-out map can show dramatically, both visually and through impact assessment, what the existing ordinance will mean in terms of future development. The analysis can be very useful in prompting public discussion about current plans and ordinances. Here are the basic steps of a build-out analysis:

1. Develop base map, including environmental inventory; identify existing developments and unbuildable areas (extremely steep slopes, floodplains, etc).
2. Create an overlay zoning map indicating development types and densities.
3. For each zone, build out development according to the allowed density following the existing patterns of development for those densities.
4. Produce a build-out map showing this development.
5. Determine the impacts associated with the build-out, including water demand, sewage flows, school population, road traffic, and environmental impacts (e.g., habitats, open space, agricultural lands, stream corridors, aquifer recharge, wellheads, impervious surface and peak discharge and baseflow).
6. Conduct a public workshop to solicit comment on the build-out analysis and potential need for revision of the comprehensive plan and zoning ordinance.

Build-Out Analysis in Massachusetts' Community Development and Preservation Planning

In December 2002, Massachusetts was the first state to be awarded an EPA Smart Growth Award for its Community Preservation Initiative and build-out analysis program. In 1999, the state launched its Community Preservation Initiative, for the purpose of empowering communities to develop a vision and plan for their future. The initiative was followed a year later with Executive Order 418 that provided state assistance for community development plans. The Community Preservation Act was enacted in September 2000. It allowed localities to establish a local fund for open space, historic preservation, and affordable housing and provided state matching funds.

Build-out analysis was one of the analytical centerpieces of the community preservation programs. The Department of Environmental Affairs, working with the 13 regional planning agencies and private planning firms, provided a full build-out analysis for each of Massachusetts 351 cities and towns, GIS data layers and orthophotomaps for each community's own study, and tools for alternative futures planning and fiscal impact assessment.

Each build-out analysis used local zoning and land use maps, zoning and subdivision ordinances, and other data to produce three GIS maps and an impact report. Specifically, the products included the following:

1. *Orthophotomap:* Base map image and GIS DOQQ data "clipped" for each locality at the same scale as build-out maps, providing a zoomable aerial view to check other map accuracy and locate community features.
2. *Map 1: Zoning and Absolute Development Constraints:* Includes lands already developed, permanently protected (e.g., conservation easements), and other absolute constraints to development (e.g., 100-ft buffers under the Massachusetts Rivers Protection Act [MRPA]). Land available for development appears in white (Figure 14.13).
3. *Map 2: Developable Lands and Partial Constraints:* Includes lands available for future development (white areas in Map 1 of Figure 14.13). In color, the map distinguishes each zoning district. Partial constraints are those included in the zoning district ordinances (e.g., minimum lot sizes) and other partial constraints (e.g., second 100-ft buffer under MRPA) (Figure 14.14).
4. *Build-Out Tables:* Data provided in Map 2 for each zoning district including acres available for development and calculations on buildable area, commercial space, dwelling units, water demand, solid waste, new roads, and number of students (Table 14.2).
5. *Map 3: Composite Development Map:* Simplifies the information on the first two maps by showing in purple all areas available for development, in yellow all areas unavailable for development, and in a shaded pattern all of the partial constraints that limit growth (Figure 14.15).
6. *Summary Build-Out Statistics:* Aggregates the build-out tables to reveal the total impacts of build-out (Table 14.3).

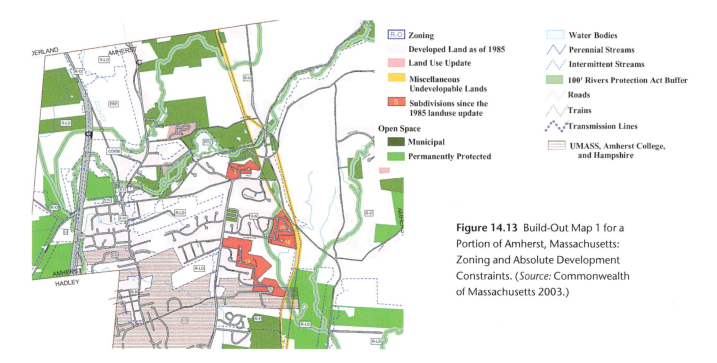

R-O Zoning

Developed Land as of 1985

Land Use Update

Miscellaneous Undevelopable Lands

5 Subdivisions since the 1985 landuse update

Open Space

Municipal

Permanently Protected

Water Bodies

Perennial Streams

Intermittent Streams

100' Rivers Protection Act Buffer

Roads

Trains

Transmission Lines

UMASS, Amherst College, and Hampshire

Figure 14.13 Build-Out Map 1 for a Portion of Amherst, Massachusetts: Zoning and Absolute Development Constraints. (*Source:* Commonwealth of Massachusetts 2003.)

TABLE 14.2 **Build-Out Table Showing Zoning District Build-Out Area from Map 2 and Impacts**

	Land Area (Acres)	Lots	Comm./Ind. Floor Area (Square Feet)	Res. Water Use (GPD)	Comm/Ind Water Use (GPD)	Municipal Solid Waste (Tons)	New Students	New Roads (Miles)
District B-G Developable Area:								
Total Area:								
including wetlands	2.9	9	87,164				3	
not including wetlands	2.9	9	87,164	1,769	6,537	12	3	0.02
District B-L Developable Area:								
Total Area:								
including wetlands	20.3	14	495,190				5	
not including wetlands	18.7	11	455,575	2,162	34,168	15	4	0.03
Wetlands Area:	1.6	0	0				0	
District B-VC Developable Area:								
Total Area:								
including wetlands	13.7	11	304,354				4	
not including wetlands	13.6	11	301,310	2,162	22,598	15	4	0.03
100 Year Flood Plain:	1.2	2	23,993				1	
Rivers Protection Area 100'-200':	1.8	3	0				1	
Wetland Area:	0.1	0	0				0	

TABLE 14.3 **Summary Build-Out Statistics for Amherst, Massachusetts** (Additional Development and Impacts)

Developable land area (sq ft)	331,648,523
Total residential lots	4,632
Dwelling units	4,632
Future residents	12,599
Students	2,779
Residential water use (Gal/day)	944,950
Commercial/industrial buildable floor area (sq ft)	4,846,298
Commercial/industrial water use (Gal/day)	363,472
Municipal solid waste (tons)	6,463
Nonrecycled solid waste (tons)	4,596
New roads (miles)	93

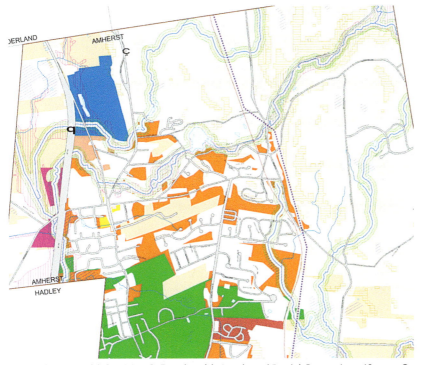

Zoning Districts

R-LD	Low Density Residence
R-O	Outlying Residence
R-N	Neighborhood Residence
R-G	General Residence
R-F	Fraternity Residence
R-VC	Village Center Residence
B-VC	Village Center Business
B-L	Limited Business
B-G	General Business
COMM	Commercial
OP	Office Park
PRP	Professional Research Park
LI	Light Industrial
ED	Educational
FPC	Flood Prone Conservancy

Figure 14.14 Build-Out Map 2: Developable Lands and Partial Constraints. (*Source:* Commonwealth of Massachusetts 2003.)

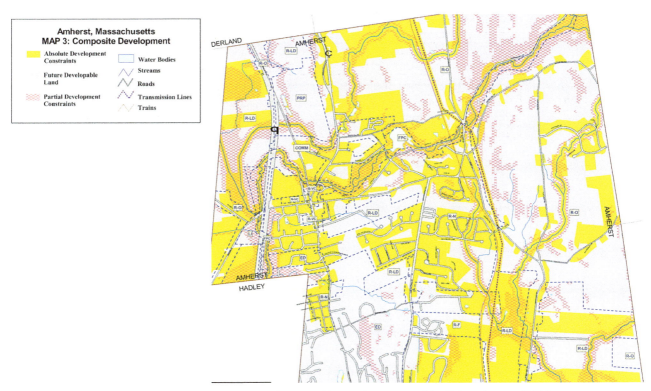

Amherst, Massachusetts
MAP 3: Composite Development

Absolute Development Constraints	Water Bodies
Future Developable Land	Streams
	Roads
Partial Development Constraints	Transmission Lines
	Trains

Figure 14.15 Build-Out Map 3: Composite Development. (*Source:* Commonwealth of Massachusetts 2003.)

Table 14.3 gives summary statistics. For Amherst, build-out according to existing plans and zoning would add about 12,500 residents in 4,652 units, 2,779 new students, 1.3 million gpd of water use, 93 miles of new roads, and 6,500 tons of solid waste. The program is described in detail in *The Buildout Book* (Commonwealth of Massachusetts 2002). The build-out methodology is described, and the build-out maps and analyses and GIS data layers for each city and town are available at http://commpres.env.state.ma.us/content/buildout.asp.

Green Infrastructure to Integrate Environmental Land Objectives

Chapter 11 introduced planning for **green infrastructure (GI)**, and we saw examples from the Chicago Wilderness and California Essential Habitat Connectivity study. Since GI has emerged as a useful integration method, we elaborate here and will also touch on it again in the next chapter on land conservation.

The Conservation Fund has been instrumental in promoting green infrastructure and defines it as a "strategically planned and managed network of natural lands, working landscapes and other open spaces that conserve ecosystem values and functions and provide associated benefits to human populations" (Conservation Fund 2011). The network consists of waterways, wetlands, woodlands, wildlife habitats, and other natural areas; greenways, parks, and other conservation lands; and working farms, ranches, and forests. GI differs from conventional approaches to open space planning because, rather than looking at land conservation in isolation or in opposition to development, it aims to work in concert with land development, growth management, and built infrastructure planning. GI is "smart conservation." It is proactive not reactive, systematic not haphazard, holistic not piecemeal, multijurisdictional not single jurisdictional, multifunctional not single purpose, and multiscale not single scale (Benedict and McMahon 2002). Figure 14.16 illustrates the basic components of a GI network:

- **Cores,** such as habitat reserves, native landscapes, working lands, and regional and community parks. Cores are also called hubs.
- **Corridors,** such as riparian floodplains, landscape linkages, conservation corridors, greenways, and greenbelts. Corridors are also called links.

Benedict and McMahon (2002, 2006) discuss several potential benefits of the GI approach to land conservation: It recognizes the needs of people and nature, it is a mechanism to balance environmental and economic factors, it is a framework for integrating natural resources and growth management, it ensures that green space and development go where they are needed and appropriate, it identifies opportunities for restoration, and it provides predictability and certainty for both conservation and development interests.

There are several principles of GI. Localities and states should do the following:

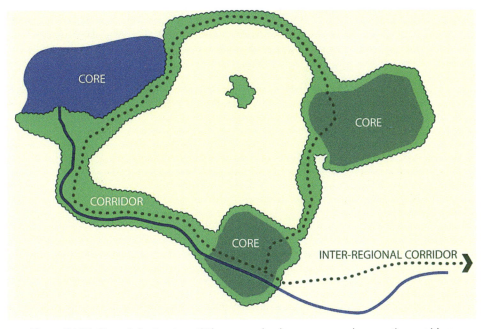

Figure 14.16 Green Infrastructure. GI focuses on landscape cores and connecting corridors. (*Source:* Green Infrastructure Center, www.greeninfrastructure.net/. Used with permission.)

1. Use GI as the framework for both conservation and development. Just as transportation infrastructure needs be linked to land use and development, so should green infrastructure.
2. Design and plan GI before development.
3. Provide a network of conservation rather than just islands of parks; linkage is the key.
4. Plan GI functions across multiple jurisdictions and at different scales, from the neighborhood to the region.
5. Ground GI in sound science and land use planning theories and practices.
6. Consider GI as a critical public investment, as it contributes to quality of life for people and ecosystems.
7. Involve diverse stakeholders in GI planning and design.

Green Infrastructure Planning in Virginia

There is a growing body of experience in Green Infrastructure planning, and we've seen some examples already in Chapter 11. The first edition of this book described Maryland's GreenPrint program initiated in 2001. That material is posted on the book website (www.envirolanduse.org). The Conservation Fund's green infrastructure website has many other GI case studies (see www.green infrastructure.net/).

Virginia has been active in GI planning. The Virginia Department of Conservation and Recreation conducted the Virginia Natural Landscape Assessment (VNLA), which serves as an excellent year 2000 database for GI initiatives throughout the state. The Green Infrastructure Center (GIC) in Charlottesville has helped advance many of these initiatives. Box 14.3 describes the GIC's approach and one recent GI project for New Kent County.

Synthesis Metrics, Indicators, and Indices

To achieve environmental sustainability, we need to make sense out of complex information and relationships to instruct and inspire action. The analytical methods discussed in this chapter are intended to integrate and organize land use data and objectives, to produce results that inform citizens and decision makers. What is also needed is a synthesis of information that can provide a bottom line assessment of a given product or action to inform consumers and communities about the many options before them. In economics and finance, for example, such bottom line indicators are net benefits over costs and return on investment.

There are no such easy measures in the sustainability movement, so there has been a strong need for synthesis indicators that reflect green environmental and broader sustainability criteria. As consumers, investors, and communities increasingly prefer that their actions are green and foster sustainability, these guiding measures have become important. This section reviews some of these synthesis metrics for green and sustainable products, buildings, neighborhoods, and communities.

Indicators, Indices, Weights, Thresholds

We discussed the use of attributes, indicators, and thresholds in relation to carrying capacity and environmental impact assessment. They are also the foundation of green and sustainability metrics. It is helpful to distinguish again indicators, indices, weights, and thresholds:

- An **indicator** is a single measure of a condition of an environmental element that represents the status or quality of that element. For example, fecal coliform content and dissolved oxygen in water and ozone concentration in the air are useful indicators of water and air quality. Carbon emissions are the best indicator of climate change impact.
- An **index** is a synthesis of several indicators that are combined into an overall measure of status or quality of an environmental element. It is usually derived by a sum-of-weighted-factors analysis. Indicator **weights** are used to assign relative importance to different indicators. For example, the Air Quality Index (AQI) and the Index of Biological Integrity (IBI) are often used as measures of air quality and biodiversity. LEED score is an index of green building.

The Green Infrastructure Center (GIC) has conducted several GI studies for regional and local communities in Virginia. GIC uses best available geospatial data, GIS models and analysis, and extensive public involvement, in a model approach involving the following steps:

1. Map the county's natural assets with the best data, GIS analysis, and public involvement: ecological integrity, existing protected core/riparian lands, water resources, heritage and natural resource-based recreation, working landscape farms and forests, land use change.
2. Map large, intact, and connected natural lands, and assess by level of protection. GIC used innovative techniques to assess:
   - Recent land use change impact on VNLA year 2000 database by mapping 100 ft buffers around new developments to determine impact of ecological cores.
   - Future level of protection by assessing parcel-size data and possible future impact on contiguous forest blocks.
3. Map Natural Asset Network and highlight protected areas, working lands, cultural heritage and recreation lands.
4. Map high-value-asset connected intact landscapes.
5. Compare high-value GI assets with County Comprehensive Plan and zoning ordinance.
6. Engage the community in identifying protection priorities and conservation opportunities.

Figure 14.17 is one of the product maps, showing the priority connected intact landscapes, areas with some protection (also connected intact), contributing intact landscapes, and other forest cover (either fragmented, unconnected, or likely to be changed).

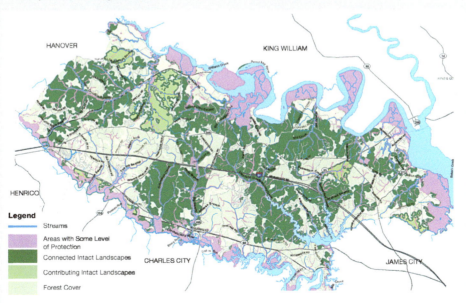

Figure 14.17 Green Infrastructure Network, New Kent County, Virginia. This map shows connected intact landscapes (CIL) and those CIL that are protected areas. (*Source:* GIC 2009. Used with permission.)

Source: GIC 2009; http://www.gicinc.org/index.htm.

- A **threshold** is the value of an indicator or index that represents a desirable outcome or a problem condition. A threshold is often defined by a goal that a community wants to achieve or by an established standard, such as an air or water quality standard. LEED certification colors (silver, gold, platinum) are thresholds of achievement. Thresholds should be attainable, meaningful, and manageable in the planning or design process.

Indicators and indices help identify problems, represent important factors and relationships, understand current conditions, establish community goals, and measure change, trends, and progress. Indicators must be measurable with available information, verifiable, reproducible, and meaningful and understandable to a range of users. An indicator or index can be used to monitor change and progress toward a desirable (or problem) threshold.

What Is "Green"?

These measures have many applications in the world of sustainability. First, there is the "what is green?" question. Consumers who want to live more lightly on Earth desire low-impact "green" products, and green, organic, and low-carbon product labeling has become a growth industry. "Green-washing," or the deceptive use of green marketing for public relations, is a potential problem, so third-party programs have emerged to "certify" products. For example, the marketing of "green" or clean electricity has been successful, but since consumers are just getting electrons, they need assurance that their extra fees are paying for renewable electricity. The third-party "Green-e" certification program was established to provide that verification.

Governments have been involved. The green labeling system in the European Union has had EU guidance. The U.S. EPA and DOE manage the very successful ENERGY STAR rating system for appliances. There are now ENERGY STAR Homes based on the Home Energy Rating System (HERS). The DOE announced a new energy rating system for existing buildings in October 2010.

LEED Green Building and Neighborhood Indices

ENERGY STAR appliances are easy to certify because efficiency is a simple indicator to measure. Energy use, weighted by energy source, can indicate carbon emissions, so it can address climate change objectives. But as we try to address broader definitions of "green" or sustainability, the indicators and indices become more complicated. Such is the case with green buildings, and even more so as we scale up to measure the sustainability of neighborhoods and communities.

For example, the index for LEED (Leadership in Energy and Environmental Design) Green Building certification includes indicators and weights for such factors as location, site remediation, water, materials, waste management, energy, health and indoor air quality, and livability. It is no easy task to come up with an acceptable index for such wide-ranging criteria, so the U.S. Green Building Council (USGBC) relies on consensus review by its 80,000 members of periodic revisions of its protocols. There are actually some eighty Green Building programs in the United States, mostly on the state and local level, including notable programs in Colorado, California, Austin (Texas), and Boulder (Colorado), and many more operate abroad. But the USGBC LEED program is the best-known emerging standard in Green Building certification. The USGBC has developed a number of Green Building protocols that define "green" and are used to evaluate, score, and certify buildings. The building rating systems have been developed for new construction, shell buildings, existing buildings, commercial interiors, schools, retail, homes, residential remodels, and neighborhood developments. In early 2007, there were only 230 LEED-certified buildings in North America; but by August 2010, there were more than 13,500 certified and another 56,000 registered and undergoing the certification process.

The LEED process requires registration of the building, then a LEED accredited professional assesses the building against established criteria, which are grouped in 8–10 categories. Maximum points are assigned to each category, and credits within the categories indicate their weight. If required prerequisite measures are met, points are then accumulated for building credits to a total score. A certified rating is awarded if about 40% of maximum points are achieved, silver if 50%, gold if 60%, and platinum if 80%. These are thresholds in our metric vernacular.

LEED New Construction and Major Renovation Criteria

Table 14.4 presents the checklist for new construction and renovation. It includes categories (attributes), credits (indicators), and assigned maximum points (weights). The categories are typical for all LEED building protocols:

- **Sustainable Sites**: 26 of total 110 points or 24% weight. Construction pollution prevention, site selection, brownfield redevelopment, habitat/open space protection, green roof.
- **Water Efficiency**: 9% weight. Water use reduction in building and landscaping.
- **Energy and Atmosphere**: 32% weight. Optimize energy performance, onsite renewable, green power.
- **Materials and Resources**: 13% weight. Building reuse, construction waste management, recycled materials.
- **Indoor Environmental Quality**: 14% weight. Indoor air quality, low emitting materials, ventilation, controllable systems, daylighting.
- **Innovative Design and Regional Priority Credits**: 9% weight.

The score for certified status is 40–49 points; for silver, 50–59 points; for gold, 60–79 points; and for platinum, 80–110 points.

LEED Neighborhood Development Criteria

The USGBC has developed protocols for a wide range of building types, but realized that buildings alone do not make sustainable communities. In collaboration

TABLE 14.4 Checklist for LEED New Construction and Major Renovations Possible

Sustainable Sites	26 points
Prereq 1 Construction Activity Pollution Prevention	Required
Credit 1 Site Selection	1
Credit 2 Development Density and Community Connectivity	5
Credit 3 Brownfield Redevelopment	1
Credit 4 Alternative Transportation: transit access, bicycle storage, parking cap	12
Credit 5 Site Development: protect habitat, maximize open space	2
Credit 6 Stormwater Design: quantity, quality	2
Credit 7 Heat Island Effect: roof, nonroof	2
Credit 8 Light Pollution Reduction	1

Water Efficiency	10 points
Prereq 1 Water Use Reduction	Required
Credit 1 Water-Efficient Landscaping	2–4
Credit 2 Innovative Wastewater Technologies	2
Credit 3 Water Use Reduction	2–4

Energy and Atmosphere	35 points
Prereq 1 Fundamental Commissioning	Required
Prereq 2 Minimum Energy Performance	Required
Prereq 3 Fundamental Refrigerant Management	Required
Credit 1 Optimize Energy Performance	1–19
Credit 2 Onsite Renewable Energy	1–7
Credit 3 Enhanced Commissioning	2
Credit 4 Enhanced Refrigerant Management	2
Credit 5 Measurement and Verification	3
Credit 6 Green Power	2

Materials and Resources	14 points
Prereq 1 Storage and Collection of Recyclables	Required
Credit 1 Building Reuse	1–4
Credit 2 Construction Waste Management	1–2
Credit 3 Materials Reuse	1–2
Credit 4 Recycled Content	1–2
Credit 5 Regional Materials	1–2
Credit 6 Rapidly Renewable Materials	1
Credit 7 Certified Wood	1

Indoor Environmental Quality	15 points
Prereq 1 Minimum Indoor Air Quality Performance	Required
Prereq 2 Environmental Tobacco Smoke (ETS) Control	Required
Credit 1 Outdoor Air Delivery Monitoring	1
Credit 2 Increased Ventilation	1
Credit 3 Construction Indoor Air Quality Plan	2
Credit 4 Low-Emitting Materials	1–4
Credit 5 Indoor Chemical and Pollutant	1
Credit 6 Controllability of Systems	1–2
Credit 7 Thermal Comfort	1–2
Credit 8 Daylight and Views	1–2

Innovation in Design	6 points
Credit 1 Innovation in Design	1–5
Credit 2 LEED® Accredited Professional	1

Regional Priority	4 Points
Credit 1 Regional Priority Credit: Region Defined	1–4

Project Totals 100 + 10 Innovation/Regional Points

Certified: 40–49 points, *Silver:* 50–59 points, *Gold:* 60–79 points, *Platinum:* 80+ points

Source: USGBC 2010a.

with the Congress for New Urbanism (CNU) and the Natural Resources Defense Council (NRDC), the USGBC developed a protocol for green neighborhoods. Because of the complexity of the project, it took an especially long period of piloting and consensus review. Piloting began in 2006, and the protocol was not launched until April 2010. Table 14.5 presents the LEED-ND checklist. The categories include:

TABLE 14.5 Checklist for LEED Neighborhood Development

Smart Location and Linkage	27 points
Prereq 1 Smart Location	Required
Prereq 2 Imperiled Species and Ecological Communities	Required
Prereq 3 Wetland and Water Body Conservation	Required
Prereq 4 Agricultural Land Conservation	Required
Prereq 5 Floodplain Avoidance	Required
Credit 1 Preferred Locations	10
Credit 2 Brownfield Redevelopment	2
Credit 3 Locations with Reduced Automobile Dependence	7
Credit 4 Bicycle Network and Storage	1
Credit 5 Housing and Jobs Proximity	3
Credit 6 Steep Slope Protection	1
Credit 7 Site Design for Habitat/Wetland/Water Body Conservation	1
Credit 8 Restoration of Habitat or Wetlands and Water Bodies	1
Credit 9 Long-Term Conservation Habitat/Wetlands/ Water Bodies	1

Neighborhood Pattern and Design	44 points
Prereq 1 Walkable Streets	Required
Prereq 2 Compact Development	Required
Prereq 3 Connected and Open Community	Required
Credit 1 Walkable Streets	12
Credit 2 Compact Development	6
Credit 3 Mixed-Use Neighborhood Centers	4
Credit 4 Mixed-Income Diverse Communities	7
Credit 5 Reduced Parking Footprint	1
Credit 6 Street Network	2
Credit 7 Transit Facilities	1
Credit 8 Transportation Demand Management	2
Credit 9 Access to Civic and Public Spaces	1
Credit 10 Access to Recreation Facilities	1
Credit 11 Visitability and Universal Design	1
Credit 12 Community Outreach and Involvement	2
Credit 13 Local Food Production	1
Credit 14 Tree-Lined and Shaded Streets	2
Credit 15 Neighborhood Schools	1

Green Infrastructure and Buildings	29 points
Prereq 1 Certified Green Building	Required
Prereq 2 Minimum Building Energy Efficiency	Required
Prereq 3 Minimum Building Water Efficiency	Required
Prereq 4 Construction Activity Pollution Prevention	Required
Credit 1 Certified Green Buildings	5
Credit 2 Building Energy Efficiency	2
Credit 3 Building Water Efficiency	1
Credit 4 Water-Efficient Landscaping	1
Credit 5 Existing Building Use	1
Credit 6 Historic Resource Preservation and Adaptive Reuse	1
Credit 7 Minimized Site Disturbance in Design and Construction	1
Credit 8 Stormwater Management	4
Credit 9 Heat Island Reduction	1
Credit 10 Solar Orientation	1
Credit 11 On Site Renewable Energy Sources	3
Credit 12 District Heating and Cooling	2
Credit 13 Infrastructure Energy Efficiency	1
Credit 14 Wastewater Management	2
Credit 15 Recycled Content in Infrastructure	1
Credit 16 Solid Waste Management Infrastructure	1
Credit 17 Light Pollution Reduction	1

Innovation and Design Process	6 points
Credit 1 Innovation and Exemplary Performance:	1–5
Credit 2 LEED® Accredited Professional	1

Regional Priority Credit	4 Points
Credit 1 Regional Priority Credit: Region Defined	1–4

Project Totals (Certification estimates) 110 Points

Certified: 40–49 points, *Silver:* 50–59 points, *Gold:* 60–79 points, *Platinum:* 80+ points

Source: USGBC 2010a.

- **Smart Location and Linkages**: 27 of 110 total points (25% weight). Conservation of habitat, wetland, farmland, floodplains, steep slope, brownfield redevelopment, reduced auto dependence.
- **Neighborhood Pattern and Design**: 40% weight. Walkability, compact development, connected community, mixed use, mixed income,

street network, transit, access to civic and recreation, tree canopy, neighborhood schools, local food production.
- **Green Infrastructure and Buildings**: 26% weight. Certified green building, energy and water efficiency, existing building use, historic preservation, stormwater management, onsite renewable energy, district heating/cooling, solid waste management.
- **Innovation and Design Process and Regional Priority**: 9% weight.

The score for certified is 40–49 points; for silver, 50–59 points; for gold, 60–79 points; for platinum, 80+ points.

From its April 2010 launch to August 2010, 74 projects had been LEED-ND certified and 188 had been registered. Many of these were part of the pilot program. Green buildings and green neighborhoods are both discussed further in Chapter 16.

Green and Sustainable Community Indicators

Many cities have adopted measures of sustainability to see how they are doing relative to indicators of community importance, and to monitor their progress toward improvement. Like Lake Tahoe, these indicators are not usually collected into a total score or index of sustainability, but rather are monitored individually. Sustainable Seattle and Chattanooga (Tennessee) were two of the first communities to try to develop sustainability indicators, and they and others got help from various sources (The Center for Livable Communities, http://www.lgc.org /center/about/center.html; EPA's Green Communities program, http://www.epa .gov/region03/greenkit/index.html; Hart 1999).

These **community sustainability indicators** include not only environmental factors but also economic and social conditions to reflect the objectives of sustainability. The use of community indicators and thresholds should be viewed as a process that begins with engaging citizens, groups, firms, and other stakeholders in a dialogue about community issues, concerns, and goals. The choice of indicators and thresholds must be based on this process, and monitoring indicators should become a community activity. It should be clear what each indicator is measuring or is linked to, and what community purposes it represents. Table 14.6 gives a hypothetical list of community environmental, economic, and social indicators, their measurement, related outcomes and purposes, and goals and thresholds. The table illustrates the considerations needed in selecting indicators; they need to be meaningful, measurable, and manageable.

Sustainable Community Rating Systems

Although communities do not need to aggregate their indicator measures into an index to compare progress among cities toward sustainability, this does not keep others from doing so. SustainLane, an online green advocacy community, developed a methodology for community sustainability using 16 criteria; every 2 years, they rank the 50 largest cities in the U.S. The criteria and weights are shown in Table 14.7.

TABLE 14.6 **Hypothetical Community Indicators, Relationships, Purposes, and Thresholds**

Indicator/Index (units)	Related to What Outcome?	Community Purpose	Current Level	Goal or Threshold
Environmental				
Impervious surface (acres or % of total area)	Biodiversity in stream corridors (–)	Improve stream health	15% of total area	15% (maintain current levels)
	Stream impairment (+) Economic loss from flooding (+)	Reduce flooding		
Vehicle miles traveled (miles)	Air quality (–)	Encourage efficient development patterns	25,000 miles/day	Reduce by 5%
	Energy consumption (+) Congestion (+) Social stress (+)	Reduce congestion Improve air quality		
Days AQI in good range (no.of days/year)	Human health (+) Impact on tourism (+)	Improve air quality Improve human health	10 da/yr	5 da/yr
Stream miles "impaired" (not meeting WQS) (miles)	Aquatic habitat degradation (+) Aesthetic/recreation capacity (–)	Improve water quality Enhance recreation opportunities	25 miles	10 miles
Solid waste recycled (% of generated)	Material resource conservation (+) Landfill soil/GW pollution (–)	Minimize landfilling Reclaim materials	10%	25%
Land in open space (acres)	Aesthetic greenness (+) Urban wildlife habitat (+)	Enhance wildlife	10,000 acres	10,000 acres (maintain current)
Economic				
Unemployment (%)	Families on govt support(+) Personal income (–) Poverty/homelessness (+)	Increase no. of jobs Ensure family income Reduce poverty	8%	4%
Income per capita ($/cap)	Economic vitality Tax revenues	Enhance family income Enhance local revenues	$25,000/cap/yr	$30,000/cap/yr
Employed in locally owned businesses (%)	Local reinvestment self-reliance	Enhance local economic	40%	50%
Social				
Below poverty level (%)	Poverty, personal income	Reduce poverty	10%	8%
Homeless (no. of people)	Poverty, community character	Reduce homelessness	1,000	500
Access to adequate healthcare (% of pop)	Community health	Improve community health	75%	85%
Voting rate (% of eligible)	Community engagement	Improve democracy	50%	75%

TABLE 14.7 **SustainLane Community Sustainability Criteria and Relative Weights**

Air quality	1.0	Local food/agriculture	1.0
City innovation	1.0	Metro congestion	0.5
Commute to work	1.5	Metro transportation	1.0
Energy and climate policy	1.0	Natural disaster risk	0.5
Green (LEED) building	1.0	Planning/land use	1.0
Green economy	1.0	Source water supply	1.5
Housing affordability	0.5	Tap water quality	1.0
Knowledge base/ communications	1.0	Waste management	1.0

Source: SustainLane, http://www.sustainlane.com/us-city-rankings/.

The process uses a variety of public and nongovernmental data sources and its own analysis for a few indicators. The index is normalized to 100 for the highest score. Who won? Portland, San Francisco, Seattle, and Chicago were 1-2-3-4 in both 2006 and 2008. Are these indicators the best ones to measure sustainability? For example, do they adequately represent urban ecosystems and green infrastructure? Or social equity?

Another sustainable or green city ranking system was developed by Siemens AG using the eight categories shown in Figure 14.18: CO_2 emissions, energy, buildings, transport, water, waste and land use, air quality, and environmental governance. All categories were given equal weight, but each was a composite of 3–5 indicators that varied in weight. The Green City Index protocol was applied to 30 European cities, each the major city in its country.

Who were the winners? Copenhagen, Stockholm, Oslo, Vienna, and Amsterdam were the top five cities overall. Are these the best criteria for Green Cities? The index lacks economic and social categories so it could not be called a sustainability index, but even as a green index, it lacks ecological and green infrastructure criteria. Siemens is developing modified indices for cities in Asia and Africa (Siemens 2009).

The STAR Community Index

The USGBC, ICLEI—Local Governments for Sustainability, and the Center for American Progress have embarked on a project to develop a defensible system for measuring community sustainability. They are developing the STAR Community Index, a national index of community sustainability that will provide (ICLEI 2010):

- Consistency in comparing efforts across jurisdictions.
- Consistency for communities in collecting common data and enabling them to learn better from each other's best practices.
- Verification of claims.
- Flexibility in advancing local sustainability through many paths to success.

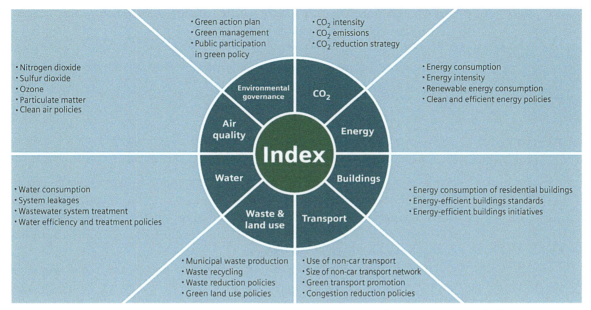

- Green action plan
- Green management
- Public participation in green policy

- CO_2 intensity
- CO_2 emissions
- CO_2 reduction strategy

- Nitrogen dioxide
- Sulfur dioxide
- Ozone
- Particulate matter
- Clean air policies

- Energy consumption
- Energy intensity
- Renewable energy consumption
- Clean and efficient energy policies

Environmental governance

CO_2

Air quality

Energy

Index

Water

Buildings

- Water consumption
- System leakages
- Wastewater system treatment
- Water efficiency and treatment policies

Waste & land use

Transport

- Energy consumption of residential buildings
- Energy-efficient buildings standards
- Energy-efficient buildings initiatives

- Municipal waste production
- Waste recycling
- Waste reduction policies
- Green land use policies

- Use of non-car transport
- Size of non-car transport network
- Green transport promotion
- Congestion reduction policies

Figure 14.18 Siemens AG Attributes and Indicators for European Green Cities Index. (*Source:* Siemens 2009.)

- Enhanced local investment and political support for sustainability efforts.

Given the breadth of sustainability, this is a difficult task, and, like LEED-ND, it will probably take much longer to develop, pilot, achieve consensus, and launch than anticipated. As of 2011, the partners had developed goals and guiding principles and a draft protocol, and selected ten communities to beta-test the process. The STAR Community Index framework has the following criteria:

Environment
- *Natural Systems*, including indicators for ecosystems and habitat, water and stormwater, air quality, waste, and resource conservation.
- *Planning and Design*, including land use, transportation and mobility, and parks, open space, and recreation.
- *Energy and Climate*, including energy, emissions, renewable energy, and green building.

Economy
- *Economic Development*, including clean technologies and green jobs, local commerce, tourism, and local food system.
- *Employment and Workforce Training*, including green job training, employment and workforce wages, and youth skills.

Society
- *Education, Arts and Community*, including education excellence, arts and culture, and civic engagement and vitality.
- *Children, Health and Safety*, community health and wellness, access to health care, and public safety.

- *Affordability and Social Equity*, affordable and workforce housing, poverty, human services and race and social equity.

You can access documents and monitor progress toward this national STAR Community Index at http://www.icleiusa.org/star.

Summary

Previous chapters presented a wide range of techniques used to gather and analyze environmental information for use in planning and management. Rarely are these methods used alone. More often, planners, publics, and decision makers need to make sense of the results of these analyses and to integrate them into more comprehensive or holistic assessments.

The methods presented in this chapter aim to provide this integration. The environmental inventory simply assembles spatial data in an understandable form, without analysis, so the user can make his or her own conclusions. Land suitability analysis takes baseline information further, combining sometimes diverse spatial data to assess the land's intrinsic capability for different purposes. It can screen sites for a particular use, gauge vulnerability of sensitive areas for certain uses, evaluate development pressure, and develop comprehensive plans. With better quality data and GIS techniques, both the inventory and suitability analysis have advanced greatly in recent years, as demonstrated by Portland's experience.

Carrying capacity is an ecological concept originally used for wildlife and range management. It has had considerable appeal for managing human settlements but proved ineffective when used to estimate appropriate population levels. When applied to the impacts of population growth, however, the concept became more effective. Instead of an optimal level of population, this approach sets acceptable levels of thresholds of impact measured by indicators of change or condition in selected environmental and socioeconomic attributes. The "impact threshold" approach to carrying capacity has been used effectively in managing development in the Lake Tahoe Basin and in managing visitor use in wilderness areas.

Environmental impact assessment is one of the most used environmental analysis methods in the world. Despite its limitations, EIA has been a consistent source of environmental information for federal decision making. Its use in community land use and development is limited, but states like Washington and California, which use EIA routinely in local land use and development planning and decisions, have proven its potential benefits. EIA needs to occur early in the development process to be effective.

Green infrastructure planning is an integration technique that can combine multiple objectives for habitat protection and connectivity, water resource protection, preservation of working farmland and forestland, and recreation and open space. Better geospatial data and GIS techniques have advanced GI planning applications, as demonstrated by the work of the Green Infrastructure Center in Virginia.

Finally, the chapter reviewed synthesis metrics for measuring green benefits and costs and sustainability values. These use the attribute-indicator-index-threshold approach used in some of the integration methods. The success of green building protocols under the USGBC's LEED program has prompted the development of more expansive indices for sustainable communities.

Planning, Design, and Policy Tools for Environmental Land Management

15 ■ Land Conservation for Sustainability

Part III of the book turns from the technical analysis of Part II to the policy approaches for taking action to protect the environment and achieve sustainable communities. We have addressed many policy issues and programs already, because in many cases they are closely tied to technical assessment. This was true for onsite wastewater control, flood and natural hazard mitigation, nonpoint source pollution and stormwater management, urban forestry, and habitat conservation. Part III focuses on remaining design and policy approaches in environmental land management. This chapter presents one such approach.

Land conservation is the permanent protection of land areas by withdrawing them from development. It is conducted by diverse public, private, and nonprofit participants, employing a number of tools for a variety of purposes. These objectives include the following:

- Protection of the natural-resource-based "working landscapes" such as agriculture, forestry, fisheries, and ecotourism.
- Preservation of open space and natural character.
- Provision of outdoor recreation opportunities.
- Protection and restoration of ecological functions and wildlife habitat.
- Mitigation of natural hazards and protection of water supplies.

These purposes are not mutually exclusive but can work in concert to enhance overall benefits and justify financial investment in conservation. For example, working landscapes can be managed to minimize environmental impact and provide visual open space, rural character, and wildlife habitat. Open space and greenways provide recreation as well as habitat and ecological functions. Urban forests provide carbon sequestration, mitigation of urban heat islands, and benefits to people and wildlife. Ecological protection provides not only wildlife habitat but also human water supply protection, high-value natural areas, scenic beauty, passive recreation, and scientific education. Mitigation of natural hazards by restricting land use in floodplains, steep slopes, and coastal dunes also provides open space, recreation, and wildlife habitat.

As a result of this broad range of objectives, a diverse set of participants is engaged in land conservation. They include all of the actors given in Figure 1.1: government; land trusts, citizens, and community groups; and private landowners. There has been a continuing growth of interest in and resources for land conservation, and participants are realizing the opportunities for partnerships and collaborative programs and projects meeting multiple objectives of mutual interest.

A number of tools are used for land conservation, including land acquisition, conservation easements, collaborative design for conservation and development, green infrastructure management, private land stewardship, and enhancing the economic viability of farm and forest use of the working landscape. In most cases, a combination of tools is most effective to meet conservation objectives. Land conservation through regulation is constrained by constitutional limits protecting private property rights, but it can be used to protect human health and welfare (e.g., mitigate natural hazards, protect water supplies) and implement specific policies (e.g., wetlands protection, endangered species habitat protection). Government regulation for protection of environmentally sensitive lands is discussed in Chapters 17 and 18.

This chapter introduces the participants in land conservation, describes government land conservation acquisition programs, and focuses on the roles of land trusts and private landowners. It describes various tools for land conservation, including acquisition, conservation easements, green infrastructure implementation, collaborative conservation and development designs, and land stewardship. Finally, it discusses the role of land conservation in growth management.

Dimensions of Land Conservation: The Conservation Machine!

Land conservation has become a big deal. According to the Land Trust Alliance's (LTA) 5-year National Land Trust Census, the conservation of private land from 2000 to 2005 averaged 2.6 million acres per year (about half the size of New Jersey). This exceeds the 2.2 million acres developed each year as estimated by the National Resources Inventory (NRI). Conservationists began alluding to the "Conservation Machine" in deference to the "Growth Machine" label long attached to the land development industry.

Who does land conservation? Federal, state, regional, and local governments; national and local land trusts; community groups and citizens; farmers, rangers, land developers, and other property owners—all are involved in land conservation in the United States. Table 15.1 provides a measure of land conservation by these groups. It estimates land protected in the U.S. by land ownership and other means. For government, land protected is given by government-owned land. The federal government holds more than 460 million acres, or 24% of the lower-48 state land area. State governments own about 90 million acres, or 5% of total area. Land owned by regional and local governments is not well documented and is

TABLE 15.1 **Land Conservation by Various Parties in the United States**

Land Protected by	Total Acres, Contiguous States	% Total Contiguous States	Total Acres Alaska (5)	% Total Contiguous + Alaska
Federal government	463 million (1)	24.4%	220 million	36.0%
State government	91 million	4.8%	105 million	8.7%
Local/regional government	25–50 million (2)	1.3–2.6%	little	1.1–2.2%
Land trusts	37 million (3)	2.0%	little	1.6%
Private land conservation	35 million (4)	1.8%	0	1.4%

(1) Federal land administered by BLM, USFS, NPS, and USFWS.
(2) From estimates of publicly owned forested land in metropolitan areas.
(3) Includes lands owned, protected by easement, and transferred to public ownership/management, 2005.
(4) Includes only farmland/rangelands enrolled in Conservation Reserve Program and Wetlands Reserve Program, 2010.
(5) Federal and state governments own 89% of Alaska's 365 million acres.

Source: Hollis and Fulton 2002; LTA 2006; BLM, USFS, NPS, USFWS websites for federal land holdings.

given by estimates of publicly owned urban and metropolitan forested lands, including parks and open space.

Land protected by land trusts includes land owned, protected by conservation easements, and purchased and transferred to public ownership. This 37-million-acre total is dominated by The Nature Conservancy (12.3 million acres), The Conservation Fund (3 million), and the Trust for Public Land (TPL; 1.3 million). More than 1,660 local and regional land trusts have protected 11.9 million acres, as of 2005. Private land protection in Table 15.1 includes only those lands on farmland and rangeland enrolled in the federal Conservation Reserve Program and the Wetland Reserve Program. This 35-million-acre figure grossly underestimates private land conservation, since it does not include considerable undeveloped natural acreage in private ownership that is de facto open space and habitat.

Table 15.1 indicates the relative importance of different participants in land conservation, but the numbers should be put in perspective. The federal land listed is managed by public land agencies, the U.S. Forest Service (193 million acres [Ma]), the National Park Service (84 Ma), the Fish and Wildlife Service (150 Ma), and the Bureau of Land Management (256 Ma). In addition, other lands are managed by the Departments of Defense and Energy. These federal lands are concentrated in the western states. Federal lands make up 50% of western states and less than 6% of midwestern and eastern states. They are managed for multiple uses, including resource production, as well as recreation, wildlife habitat, and wilderness.

State land ownership is more evenly distributed. Leading states with more than 10% ownership are New York (35%), Pennsylvania, New Jersey, Michigan, Minnesota, Arizona, New Mexico, and Alaska. Most of the states' lands are managed for similar purposes as national forests and parks. Local/regional land ownership varies considerably across the country; most lands are used for human use in parks and open space. There are a total of about 1.4 Ma of parks in our 77 largest cities (TPL 2009). Land enrolled in federal conservation and wetland reserves is concentrated in the Midwest's farm states.

Government Land Conservation

Government land conservation includes the extensive lands owned by federal, state, and local governments, as well as land conserved through government regulatory and incentive programs.

Federal Land Conservation

Federal land conservation includes management of the public lands, funding for conservation, land acquisition, and programs that affect private land conservation.

Public Lands

Federal public lands serve as the core of the national land conservation effort. However, as already mentioned and shown in Figure 15.1, most federal lands are in the western United States, with more modest holdings in the rest of the country. Also, the land management objectives vary for these lands. The national forests include prime forestlands and grasslands, which are managed for multiple uses of timber and mineral production, recreation, wildlife, and wilderness. Bureau of Land Management (BLM) lands are those federal lands not placed in national forests, parks, or refuges, and they are managed for similar multiple uses. National parks contain the nation's "natural jewels" and are managed for passive recreation and wildlife. The national wildlife refuges are managed for recreation and fish and wildlife.

There is a constant tension about the often-competing uses of these lands, as agencies are confronted with diverse stakeholders representing commodity production, recreation, and preservation interests. Each agency follows planning procedures to determine the most appropriate management program within these competing uses. In recent years, agencies have worked to apply ecosystem management principles in these plans to protect the health of the resource, while providing for production and recreation use (see Chapter 19).

National Parks, Wilderness Areas, Wildlife Refuges, Forest Roadless Areas.

The core conservation areas of the federal public lands are the parks, wilderness, refuges, and roadless areas that are not open to most resource development. The National Parks and their 84 million acres are now referred to as "America's Best Idea." The National Wildlife Refuge System has expanded to 150 million acres. The National Wilderness Preservation System was established by Congress in 1964 and designated areas within the parks, forests, refuges, and rangelands that are managed for wilderness and restrict other uses. In 2009, the Omnibus Public

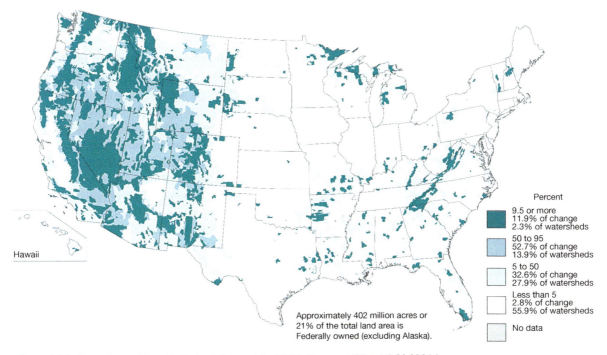

Figure 15.1 Percentage of Land in Federal Ownership, 1997. (Source: USDA, NRCS 2001.)

Lands Act added 2 million acres to the Wilderness System, the most in 15 years, and it now totals 756 areas and 110 million acres. In addition, the parks, refuges, and wilderness areas have restricted resource development but they are all open to people, and recreation impacts the ecological resources. The U.S. National Park Service (NPS) and other agencies have developed planning tools to help manage recreation use and impacts to acceptable levels, such as the Limits of Acceptable Change approach (see Chapter 14).

In addition to these designated areas, the public lands contain millions of road-less acres in the national forests; without road access they are de facto wilderness. In its final days in 2001, the Clinton administration issued a rule curtailing most road building and timber cutting in these areas. Then in 2005, the Bush administration replaced this rule with one allowing state governors time to petition the U.S. Forest Service (USFS). After a complicated series of court rulings, the Clinton rule now applies in Arkansas, Arizona, California, Idaho, Hawaii, Nevada, New Mexico, Oregon, and Washington, and the Bush rule applies in the rest of the country (Gorte et al. 2009).

The National Landscape Conservation System. BLM recognized that certain of its 250 million acres had unique ecological significance, and in 2000 it designated 26 million acres as the National Landscape Conservation System. The 2009 Omnibus Act made the system permanent. For a map of the system, see http://ironwoodforest.net/documents/ConservationMap.jpg.

TABLE 15.4 **Growth of Local and State Land Trusts in the United States**

Year	Number of Trusts	Acres Protected
1950	53	NA
1965	130	NA
1985	479	NA
1990	887	1.9 million
2000	1,263	6.2 million
2005	1,667	11.9 million

Source: Land Trust Alliance 2006.

California leads the nation with 198, followed by Massachusetts (161), and Connecticut (128). California also has the most land trust protected acres with 1.7 million, followed by Maine (with its 762,000-acre easement on the Pingree forest), Colorado, and Virginia, the last two states boosted by their land conservation tax credit. As of 2005, local and state trusts have protected 11.9 million acres of conservation lands, more than six times the 1.9 million acres protected in 1990 (LTA 2006).

These land trusts provide protection in three ways:

1. They own about 14% of the land they protect that was conveyed to them in fee simple.
2. They accept conservation easements on about 53% of their protected land.
3. They acquire and reconvey to public agencies or conserve by other means about 33%.

The LTA conducted the 2010 census and released the results in October 2011, too late for this edition. It continues to be the best source of information on this growing local movement, and its website provides the most comprehensive listing and links to land trusts across the country. The LTA also chronicles land trust success stories to share lessons and network among its 1,200 member trusts. Some recent success stories, related in Box 15.3, demonstrate the land deals that land trusts broker to conserve open space, habitats, and working landscapes. Box 15.4 highlights Virginia's Piedmont Environmental Council, which has facilitated a rush of land conservation in the northern Piedmont west of Washington, DC, from Leesburg south to Charlottesville.

National/International Land Trusts

About a dozen national land trusts operate in the United States, led by The Nature Conservancy (more than 12 million acres protected in the U.S., 119 million acres globally), The Conservation Fund (6.5 million acres), and the TPL (2.8 million acres). These organizations protect land in all 50 states. Six states have more than 1 million acres protected by all land trusts. States with the largest protected areas

example, Georgia's Greenspace Program was created in 2000 and establishes a framework for high-growth counties to protect lands and receive formula grants to do so. The program is voluntary and noncompetitive. To qualify, a county must prepare and implement a greenspace plan to permanently protect at least 20% of the county's geographic area that meets one or more of nine conservation goals. After a county's plan and program fully comply with the program rules, grant funds for implementation are transferred from the Georgia Greenspace Trust Fund. The fund is made up of state-appropriated, federal, and donated funds.

Local Government Land Conservation

Local governments have also established land acquisition and protection programs. They include acquisition for parks and open space and purchase of conservation easements. In addition, many localities use innovative regulatory programs, such as agricultural zoning, overlay zoning, open space zoning, and the transfer of development rights, to protect conservation lands. These regulatory programs for land protection are discussed in Chapter 17.

There are 88 localities in 20 states that have PACEs. In total, these programs have expended $1.5 billion local appropriations, bonds, real estate transfer tax, and some state and federal funding to protect several hundred thousand acres of farmland. The largest programs include Howard and Harford Counties (Maryland), Suffolk County (New York), Marin and Sonoma Counties (California), and King County (Washington). For details on these programs, including expenditures, acres, and funding sources, see Farmland Information Center 2010 (http://www.farmlandinfo.org/).

Land Trusts

A **land trust** is a nonprofit conservation organization that accepts land donations; buys conservation easements; negotiates with landowners, developers, and local governments; and manages natural areas—all in an effort to conserve natural and cultural resources and working landscapes in perpetuity. These land trusts, including national groups like The Nature Conservancy and hundreds of local land trusts, have played an increasingly important role in land preservation. They have acquired lands strategically to meet conservation objectives and worked with landowners and developers; federal, state, and local agencies; and citizens groups to bring about creative and negotiated land development that has served the interests of both land conservation and development.

The Growing Role of State and Local Land Trusts

The first land trust in the United States was established in Massachusetts in 1891, but the growth of land trusts has been recent. According to the latest LTA National Land Trust Census (LTA Census), as of 2005, there were 1,667 state and local land trusts in the United States, an increase of 32% since 2000 (Table 15.4).

TABLE 15.4 **Growth of Local and State Land Trusts in the United States**

Year	Number of Trusts	Acres Protected
1950	53	NA
1965	130	NA
1985	479	NA
1990	887	1.9 million
2000	1,263	6.2 million
2005	1,667	11.9 million

Source: Land Trust Alliance 2006.

California leads the nation with 198, followed by Massachusetts (161), and Connecticut (128). California also has the most land trust protected acres with 1.7 million, followed by Maine (with its 762,000-acre easement on the Pingree forest), Colorado, and Virginia, the last two states boosted by their land conservation tax credit. As of 2005, local and state trusts have protected 11.9 million acres of conservation lands, more than six times the 1.9 million acres protected in 1990 (LTA 2006).

These land trusts provide protection in three ways:

1. They own about 14% of the land they protect that was conveyed to them in fee simple.
2. They accept conservation easements on about 53% of their protected land.
3. They acquire and reconvey to public agencies or conserve by other means about 33%.

The LTA conducted the 2010 census and released the results in October 2011, too late for this edition. It continues to be the best source of information on this growing local movement, and its website provides the most comprehensive listing and links to land trusts across the country. The LTA also chronicles land trust success stories to share lessons and network among its 1,200 member trusts. Some recent success stories, related in Box 15.3, demonstrate the land deals that land trusts broker to conserve open space, habitats, and working landscapes. Box 15.4 highlights Virginia's Piedmont Environmental Council, which has facilitated a rush of land conservation in the northern Piedmont west of Washington, DC, from Leesburg south to Charlottesville.

National/International Land Trusts

About a dozen national land trusts operate in the United States, led by The Nature Conservancy (more than 12 million acres protected in the U.S., 119 million acres globally), The Conservation Fund (6.5 million acres), and the TPL (2.8 million acres). These organizations protect land in all 50 states. Six states have more than 1 million acres protected by all land trusts. States with the largest protected areas

TABLE 15.3 **State Purchase of Conservation Easements Programs, 2000–2010**

State	Acres Preserved	Dollars Spent	$/acre
Pennsylvania	428,708	$710 million	$1,660
Colorado	431,479	$138 million	$320
Maryland	347,637	$599 million	$1,720
New Jersey	182,953	$826 million	$4,500
Vermont	130,748	$57 million	$435
Delaware	93,935	$124 million	$1,320
Massachusetts	64,018	$182 million	$2,840
Utah	78,907	$13 million	$165
Ohio	37,908	$24 million	$630
Connecticut	35,518	$116 million	$3,270
16 other states	191,419	$269 million	$1,400
Total	2,023,230	$3,058 million	$1,500

Source: American Farmland Trust 2010.

acreage; New Jersey, Connecticut, and Massachusetts have spent the most per acre for development rights, and Utah, Colorado, and Vermont, the least per acre. The Farmland Information Center (FIC), a partnership between the American Farmland Trust and the NRCS, monitors these programs (http://www.farmland info.org/). Conservation easements and purchase of development rights are described in detail in later sections of this chapter.

State Tax Incentives for Land Conservation

Some states rely on tax incentives to promote land conservation. As of 2007, eleven states offered tax credits (California, Colorado, Connecticut, Delaware, Georgia, Maryland, New Mexico, New York, North Carolina, South Carolina, and Virginia) and six others were considering adopting them (Idaho, Kentucky, Massachusetts, Minnesota, Nebraska, and West Virginia). Landowners who wish to donate fee title or conservation easement on their land can claim a state tax credit on a portion of the value of the land or easement. This is in addition to a federal tax deduction they can claim on the donation. Lots of rules apply, but it has created a significant incentive especially in the four states that allow landowners to transfer the credits to other taxpayers. These are Colorado, New Mexico, South Carolina, and Virginia. In Virginia, the land preservation tax credit has promoted a rush to conservation and allowed the last two governors of very opposite political views to each set attainable goals of 400,000 new acres of conserved land during their 4-year terms. We review the specific rules under these tax credits for the transferability states, as well as a hypothetical application, later in the chapter.

State Green Infrastructure Programs

Green infrastructure (GI) planning was discussed in Chapters 11 and 14. Many states have used this approach to identify and prioritize land for conservation. For

TABLE 15.2 **State and Local Land Conservation Ballot Initiatives, 2000–2010**

Date	Number of Measures	Pass? (total)	Conservation Funds Approved (total)
2000	209	171	$4,993,222,298
2001	198	138	$1,369,510,437
2002	183	135	$5,486,074,357
2003	126	95	$1,255,696,985
2004	216	162	$3,972,214,265
2005	141	111	$1,598,003,889
2006	183	136	$6,705,777,535
2007	99	65	$1,951,415,707
2008	128	91	$8,047,714,140
2009	40	25	$607,668,083
Total	1,523	1,129	$35,987,297,696

Source: TPL 2009.

LWCF grants, most states and local governments provide funds for conservation land acquisition and protection. Some of these funds are used to match LWCF grants, but most are used to purchase park and recreation lands, and in some cases, to protect working landscapes and habitat lands. Most open space protection is by acquisition, while most working landscape protection is by conservation easement or purchase of development rights.

State Land Acquisition

Public interest in land conservation remains strong despite significant budget problems in many states. As shown in Table 15.2, from 2000 to 2009, ballot initiatives approved $36 billion for land conservation. Among the funding sources are state bonds, taxes on property transfer, general funds, lottery revenues, and sales taxes. The Trust for Public Land's LandVote database monitors and maps these ballot initiatives (http://tplgis.org/LandVoteLaunch/).

State Farmland Protection

Protection of working lands is a major issue in many states. The 2007 NRI showed that more than 4 million acres of agricultural land and 1.4 million acres of prime land were converted to development from 2002 to 2007. The only good news is that the rate of conversion (816,000 acres/yr) was down 20% from the 1997–2002 period. In part, this drop was due to state farmland preservation programs.

Twenty-six states have purchase of agricultural easements (PACE) programs, in which public funds are used to purchase development rights from farmers to promote local agriculture and prevent conversion to development. In these programs, landowners voluntarily sell development rights to the government agency. Table 15.3 shows the top ten state programs and totals for the 26 states. The programs have permanently protected 2 million acres of farmland at an average cost of $1,500 per acre. Pennsylvania, Colorado, and Maryland are the leading states by

BOX 15.2—Federal Agricultural Conservation Programs

Land Retirement Programs

- **Conservation Reserve Program (CRP).** Established in 1985, CRP provides annual rental payments, cost sharing for land practices, and technical assistance to farmers who retire highly erodible lands from production for at least 10 years. The 2008 Farm Bill lowered the CRP acreage cap from 36 to 32 million acres, and 31.3 million acres were enrolled in 2010. CRP expenditures of $1.9 billion per year ($53 per acre) amount to more than half of the agriculture conservation budget.
- **Conservation Reserve Enhancement Program (CREP).** Established in 1996, CREP targets high-priority areas for higher CRP retirement rents in states that enroll and pay additional costs; 1.2 million acres in 2010.
- **Wetland Reserve Program (WRP).** Established in 1990, WRP provides annual rental payments, cost sharing for land practices, and technical assistance to farmers who retire wetlands from farm production. In 2010, 2.2 million acres were enrolled, 35% in Louisiana, Mississippi, and Arkansas. More than 90% of the acreage is under permanent easement, and 5% is under 10-year retirement. The 2008 Farm Bill increased the cap to 3 million acres.

Disincentives to Cultivate Highly Erodible Lands and Wetlands

- **Sodbuster** (1985) disqualifies from most farm program benefits farmers who cultivate highly erodible land not cultivated between 1981 and 1985.

- **Swampbuster** (1990) similarly disqualifies farmers who convert wetlands to produce crops.
- **Conservation compliance** (1985) requires all farmers to obtain an approved conservation plan to obtain farm program benefits.

Other Conservation Funding Programs

- **Environmental Quality Improvement Program (EQIP).** Established in 1996, the $200 million EQIP provides cost-sharing assistance to support structural, vegetative, and land management practices for water quality and conservation improvements.
- **Farmland Protection Program (FPP).** Established in 1996, FPP provides grants to assist states and localities for agricultural conservation easements to protect farmland. The program is capped at $35 million per year.
- **Wildlife Habitat Incentives Program (WHIP).** Established in 1996, WHIP provides cost sharing for habitat enhancements. The $50 million program is funded from CRP allocations.

Technical Assistance Programs

- **Natural Resources Conservation Service.** NRCS provides a range of technical assistance on a voluntary basis to farmers to conserve and improve natural resources and to support funding programs. Program expenditures are about $1 billion per year. Other programs include local soil and water conservation districts and cooperative extension.

at about $60 million annually since 2001, the program has put 2 million forest acres in conservation easements.

State and Local Land Conservation

State land conservation programs have expanded considerably in the past decade through funding for land acquisition, farmland protection programs, green infrastructure programs, and tax credits for land preservation. In addition to federal

BOX 15.1—Federal Programs Affecting Conservation on Private Lands

Incentives

- **Tax laws.** Governing charitable contributions provide perhaps the largest incentive for private land conservation. Landowners, corporations, philanthropic organizations, and citizens can deduct the value of land donations, bargain sales, conservation easements, and financial contributions for land conservation by nonprofit land trusts.
- **Agriculture conservation programs.** The Conservation Reserve Program (CRP) and Wetlands Reserve Program (WRP) provide payments to farmers to take highly erodible lands and wetlands out of farm production and to manage them for conservation (see Box 15.2).
- **National Flood Insurance Program (NFIP).** This program provides subsidized insurance for flood-prone properties, but only in localities engaging in floodplain management. This requires floodplain zoning restricting development in floodplains, thereby providing conservation benefits. Many communities have combined this flood damage mitigation with riparian greenways for recreation and wildlife habitat (see Chapters 7 and 13).

Regulations

- **Endangered Species Act.** The ESA bans "taking" habitat of listed species. An "incidental take" is allowed with an approved habitat conservation plan (HCP) showing that permanent conservation lands can provide for needs of species, while accommodating some development. More than 408 HCPs have been approved, 75% of which have been in the southwestern and Pacific states (see Chapter 11).
- **Wetlands permits.** These are required under the Clean Water Act for dredging or filling wetlands. The U.S. Army Corps of Engineers and the EPA jointly administer the program, which has been credited with slowing the conversion of wetlands to agricultural and urban uses (see Chapter 10).

descriptions are taken from Congressional Research Service reports that are frequently updated (Stubbs 2009).

Forest conservation programs are not as extensive as the farm programs, but the USFS, in addition to managing the national forests (NF), has several cooperative programs for non-NF forests:

- *Urban and Community Forestry* provides financial, research, and educational assistance.
- The *Forest Stewardship Program* has produced 270,000 multipurpose plans for 31 million acres of nonindustrial private forests.
- The *Forests on the Edge Project* and *Cooperating Across Boundaries* promote rural land conservation partnerships among local and state agencies, landowners, and land trusts to advance private forest conservation in the planning and land development process.
- The *Forest Legacy Program* partners with the states to protect environmentally sensitive forest lands. The program has provided matching funds for acquiring conservation easements that restrict development, require sustainable forestry practices, and protect other values. Funded

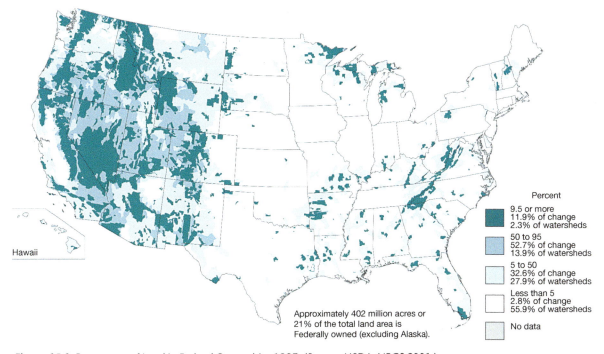

Hawaii

Approximately 402 million acres or
21% of the total land area is
Federally owned (excluding Alaska).

Percent

9.5 or more
11.9% of change
2.3% of watersheds

50 to 95
52.7% of change
13.9% of watersheds

5 to 50
32.6% of change
27.9% of watersheds

Less than 5
2.8% of change
55.9% of watersheds

No data

Figure 15.1 Percentage of Land in Federal Ownership, 1997. (Source: USDA, NRCS 2001.)

Lands Act added 2 million acres to the Wilderness System, the most in 15 years, and it now totals 756 areas and 110 million acres. In addition, the parks, refuges, and wilderness areas have restricted resource development but they are all open to people, and recreation impacts the ecological resources. The U.S. National Park Service (NPS) and other agencies have developed planning tools to help manage recreation use and impacts to acceptable levels, such as the Limits of Acceptable Change approach (see Chapter 14).

In addition to these designated areas, the public lands contain millions of roadless acres in the national forests; without road access they are de facto wilderness. In its final days in 2001, the Clinton administration issued a rule curtailing most road building and timber cutting in these areas. Then in 2005, the Bush administration replaced this rule with one allowing state governors time to petition the U.S. Forest Service (USFS). After a complicated series of court rulings, the Clinton rule now applies in Arkansas, Arizona, California, Idaho, Hawaii, Nevada, New Mexico, Oregon, and Washington, and the Bush rule applies in the rest of the country (Gorte et al. 2009).

The National Landscape Conservation System. BLM recognized that certain of its 250 million acres had unique ecological significance, and in 2000 it designated 26 million acres as the National Landscape Conservation System. The 2009 Omnibus Act made the system permanent. For a map of the system, see http://ironwoodforest.net/documents/ConservationMap.jpg.

Funding for Conservation Land Acquisition: The Land and Water Conservation Fund

One of the principal funding sources for federal public land acquisition is the Land and Water Conservation Fund (LWCF). Established in 1965 and supported by about 10% of federal revenue from offshore oil and gas drilling, LWCF has provided about $15 billion for land acquisition. This should be a dedicated fund of $900 million per year, but appropriations peaked at $800 million in 1978 and have averaged about $300 million per year since except for a onetime boost of $700 million in 1997. The Obama administration has restored the full fund, which is expected to continue through 2014 (U.S. NPS, LWCF 2010).

About 70% of these funds have been used for the purchase of more than 5 million acres of federal public lands, mostly national parks, such as Cape Cod and Padre Island national seashores, Voyageurs and Redwoods national parks, and Santa Monica Mountains National Recreation Area. About 20% of these federal land funds have purchased land in California, 10% in Florida, and a combined 20% in Washington, Texas, Oregon, Nevada, and Georgia.

About 30% of the LWCF ($3.5 billion) has been used for grants to match state and local money in support of state and local conservation projects. The grants have supported the purchase of 2.3 million acres of recreation land and development of 27,000 recreation facilities. However, most of these grants were made in the 1970s. In 2009, $27 million was granted to state and local projects. This will not come close to meeting the state-estimated needs of $12 billion for state and local parks (U.S. NPS, LWCF 2010).

Federal Influence on Private Land Conservation

Federal government programs affect conservation on private lands through regulations and incentives given in Box 15.1. The federal government has steered away from land regulation, a domain vested in state and local government. However, certain issues of national importance such as endangered species habitats, wetlands, and mine land reclamation have prompted federal regulatory programs. The habitat and wetlands programs were discussed in Chapters 10 and 11.

Federal tax laws for charitable contributions have created a huge incentive for land conservation. Not only can people deduct donations of monetary contributions to nonprofit land trusts, but the law allows an income tax deduction for owners of property for dontaing the value of conservation easements that give up certain rights of ownership to preserve their land for future generations. We discuss these and state tax incentives later in the chapter.

Agriculture conservation programs provide the largest federal budget outlay for private land conservation, about $3 billion a year, about 10–20% of the $14–$28 billion agricultural support payments under the Farm Bill (Box 15.2). The Natural Resources Conservation Service (NRCS) and the Farm Service Agency (FSA) administer these programs. Program objectives include land retirement and use disincentives on environmentally sensitive areas, farmland protection, wildlife habitat enhancement, and water quality improvement. Program

BOX 15.3—Local Land Trust Success Stories

Montana Land Reliance: Conservation Easements, Protection of Habitat, and Working Landscape

After a year of negotiations, in 2000 the Montana Land Reliance (MLR) brokered a deal to allow four neighbors to purchase 1,637 acres along 7 miles of the North Fork of the Blackfoot River. The Blackfoot is recognized as one of the nation's best trout rivers, providing habitat for the endangered bull trout. As part of the deal, the neighbors donated conservation easements on the land, permanently protecting the rich fish and wildlife habitat and scenic open space, yet allowing compatible timber and agricultural management. The land had been owned by Plum Creek Timber Company. The MLR, The Nature Conservancy, and the U.S. Fish and Wildlife Service hold 27 easements in the area, covering more than 50 miles of the river. MLR, a statewide land trust with conservation easements on more than 360,000 acres, is protecting a number of contiguous properties.

Source: Adapted from Land Trust Alliance, Land Trust Success Stories: http://www.lta.org.

Maryland Environmental Trust, Lower Shore Land Trust: Conservation Easement, Habitat

The Maryland Environmental Trust and the Lower Shore Land Trust worked for about 2 years to place a conservation easement on 987 acres on the Chesapeake Bay in Somerset County. The land trusts, approached by a person who owned only a 5% interest in the property, had to locate the 15 other co-owners to consummate the deal. The natural resources value of the property—which includes 8 miles bordering the Chesapeake Bay and its tributaries, and an abundance of wildlife as well as a great blue heron rookery—spurred the land trusts to pursue the deal. Eventually, the land trusts found a conservation buyer for the land, an individual willing to purchase the property with its conservation easement restrictions. In this case, the easement prohibits subdivision and limits construction to a single residence. The land trusts also found the property's owners, some of whom lived as far away as Miami, Florida. The landowner who had originally offered to donate the land continued to decline payment for his share of the property.

by both national and state/local land trusts are Nevada and California, each with 2.5 million acres. Vermont has by far the largest percentage of the state protected by land trusts (15%), followed by New Hampshire, Massachusetts, Connecticut, Delaware, New Jersey, and Maryland. In all, about 10% of New England acreage is protected by land trusts.

Perhaps the best-known national land conservation nongovernmental organization (NGO) is **The Nature Conservancy (TNC)**. Since 1951, TNC has protected more than 12 million acres of natural areas throughout the country, and 92 million acres around the world, using outright purchases, land trades, conservation easements, and land donations. To provide revolving cash funds for additional acquisitions, the group has transferred about one-third of the land it acquires to federal, state, and local governments and to other owners, usually with deed restrictions. Still, TNC manages 1,400 preserves. With more than a million members, it is the world's largest environmental organization.

In 2002, it began a $1 billion campaign to save 200 of the world's Last Great Places, and its tally of protected areas is 119 million acres. As TNC has grown, its

BOX 15.4—Virginia's Piedmont Environmental Council

The Piedmont Environmental Council (PEC) in Virginia has operated for nearly 40 years to safeguard the landscapes, communities, and heritage of the Piedmont by involving citizens in public policy and land conservation. The Virginia Piedmont, which stretches from Charlottesville and Albemarle County north to Leesburg and Loudoun Counties, bordering Shenandoah National Park, is a treasure of natural rolling landscapes and historic significance. Growth pressures from Washington, DC, have threatened the landscape, and PEC has been instrumental in conserving land in the region.

PEC has had an advocacy role, as well as being a land trust and facilitator of land conservation. In the mid-1990s, PEC led the opposition to the proposed Disney America theme park in Haymarket. During the late 1999s, it lobbied hard for the Land Preservation Tax Credit and has helped preserve it through legislative amendments. In addition, PEC has been active in advocating battlefield preservation and promoting smart growth. But PEC's most lasting legacy is the way it has facilitated land conservation. Figure 15.2 shows the northern portion of its service area, which has the highest concentration of conservation easements in the commonwealth. As of 2009, there were 325,000 acres conserved in the region, 17,000 acres added in 2009.

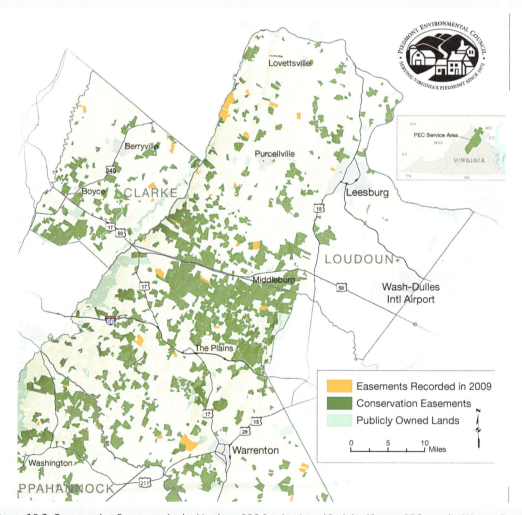

Figure 15.2 Conservation Easements in the Northern PEC Service Area, Virginia. (*Source:* PEC map by Watsun Randolph, used with permission.)

mission has become more ambitious. Once focused on the protection of unique places, the Conservancy now sees a larger potential in piecing those places together to preserve the diversity of life on Earth by protecting the lands and waters that natural communities require in order survive. Under its policy of conservation by design, TNC's goal is to conserve what it calls "portfolios of functional conservation areas" within and across ecoregions. It plans to take direct action to conserve 500 functional landscapes in the United States and 100 more in 35 other countries, and to leverage action to protect 2,000 more functional conservation areas in the U.S. and 500 abroad. TNC's ecoregional planning is discussed further in Chapter 19.

Tools for Land Conservation

Land trusts and government land conservation programs employ a number of conservation tools to protect lands. Some of these are dependent on conservation objectives; others are generic to a range of programs. They include program design, tools for acquiring land and development rights, collaborative conservation and development, green infrastructure planning, tools for protecting the working landscape, and private land stewardship.

Designing a Land Conservation Program

Land conservation programs vary according to their purpose, size, and the organization running them. Some aim to preserve ecological resources, others provide recreation, still others intend to maintain working landscapes. Some are administered by government agencies, others by nonprofit land trusts. Despite these differences, certain dimensions and procedures are common to most land conservation programs. The TPL provides technical assistance for public land conservation mostly by local government, and the LTA advises nonprofit land trusts. They have developed principles and procedures of designing and managing land conservation programs.

The TPL's key elements for local government land conservation programs are organization, community involvement, partnership building, program design and planning, financing, land acquisition, and land management. The LTA's principles for land trusts stress structure, rational decision making, and accountability (see LTA 2003; TPL 2002).

Acquiring Land and Development Rights

The key step in land conservation is protecting land for intended purposes. There are many means of controlling land use and development, including government land use zoning and districting, use-value tax assessment, and infrastructure planning (see Chapter 17). However, these methods are only available to government agencies, and even when available, they do not provide effective permanent protection. Permanent protection requires acquisition of the land or at least the land's development rights.

Associated with each parcel of land is a bundle of rights. Like a bundle of sticks, these rights can be separated and held by different parties. For example, I may own a piece of property, but a mining company may own the subsurface mineral rights; that separation of ownership is reflected in the deed or title to the property. As a result of this bundle of rights, there are various ways of acquiring land or the rights associated with it (Table 15.5).

A **fee-simple purchase** provides all rights and guarantees protection, but it is costly because the land is bought at market value. **Conservation easements** or **selling development rights** restrict the owner from specified development uses. This method provides permanent protection, as the easement or development right restrictions become part of the property deed and remain intact as the property is bought and sold. **Purchase with leaseback**, **leasing**, and **undivided interest** are also included in the table, but they have more limited use in land conservation.

Most organizations do not have the financial capability to protect large tracts of land through a fee-simple purchase. They can stretch their financial resources by acquiring easements and development rights rather than full title. The manner in which the land or rights are acquired also has financial consequences. Table 15.6 describes ways in which land or rights can be acquired by land trusts or public agencies for land conservation. A **fair market value sale** is the most costly means of acquisition.

Bargain sales and donations save considerable expense for the trust or agency, and they can provide large tax benefits to the seller to offset the lower compensation from the sale or gift. In a land or conservation easement **donation**, to either a government agency or an IRS-registered land trust, landowners can claim the market value of the land as a charitable contribution and income tax deduction. A **bargain sale** is selling the land (or its development rights) at less than market value; the landowner benefits by being able to claim the difference between the purchase price and the market value as a tax deduction. The benefit depends on the owner's tax bracket, and whether he or she can claim the contribution as a state as well as a federal income tax deduction.

Bequest and **donation with reserved life estate** are similar in that the trust or agency does not gain use of the property until the death of the landowner. A donation with reserved life estate provides immediate tax benefits to the landowner, whereas a bequest does not. **Land exchanges** can be used by both land trusts and agencies to acquire conservation lands in exchange for developable lands they may have received by donation or bequest. Finally, **eminent domain** and **tax foreclosure** acquisition are restricted to government agencies.

Conservation Easements

As discussed, the conservation easement does not involve a transfer of property ownership. A normal easement is an acquired use of someone else's land for such purposes as road access, placement of a septic drain field, or crossing the land with a transmission line. A conservation easement is a "reverse" easement in that it does not acquire a use of the land but instead restricts the use of the land by the landowner. Here is a complete definition:

TABLE 15.5 **Rights and Interests in Property That Can Be Acquired**

Method	Definition	Advantages	Disadvantages
Fee-Simple Ownership	Obtaining full ownership of the land. (Wherever possible, this should be used for larger tracts of land with a lower cost per acre.)	Gives trust or agency full control. Provides full access to the property. Guarantees permanent protection.	Expensive. Usually removes land from tax base. Ownership responsibility includes liability and maintenance.
Conservation Easement/ Development Rights	Legal agreement a property owner makes to restrict the type and amount of development that may take place on his or her property. A partial interest in the property is transferred to an appropriate nonprofit or governmental entity either by gift or purchase. As ownership changes, the land remains subject to the easement restrictions. (Well suited for preserving agricultural land and scenic areas.)	Less expensive than fee simple. Tailored to the protection requirements of the landowner and the property, and the desire of the landowner. Landowner retains ownership and property remains on the tax rolls, often at a lower rate because of restricted use. Potential income and estate tax benefits from donation. More permanent and often more restrictive than land use regulations, which often change with the political climate.	Public access may not be provided. Easement must be enforced. Restricted use may lower resale value.
Purchase of Land with Leaseback	As part of purchase contract, trust or agency agrees to lease land back to the seller, subject to restrictions.	Income through lease-back. Liability and management responsibilities assigned to lessee.	Public access may not be available. Land must be appropriate for leaseback (e.g., agricultural).
Lease	Short- or long-term rental of land.	Low cost for use of land. Landowner receives income and retains control of property.	Does not provide equity and affords only limited control of property. Temporary.
Undivided Interest	Ownership is split between different owners, each with fractional interest extending over the whole parcel.	Prevents one owner from acting without the consent of the others.	Several landowners can complicate property management issues, including payment of taxes. Each owner has equal rights to entire property.

Source: Trust for Public Land 2002.

Table 15.6 Techniques for Acquiring Land Title or Rights by a Land Trust or Public Agency

Technique	Explanation	Advantages	Disadvantages
Fair Market Value Sale	Land is sold at its value at highest and best use.	Highest sales income (cash inflow) to seller.	Can be expensive.
Bargain Sale	Part donation/part sale— property is sold at less than fair market value.	Often the landowner is eligible for a tax deduction for the difference between the sale price and the fair market value because the sale is treated like a charitable contribution.	Seller must be willing to sell at less than fair market value. Can be expensive.
Outright Donation	A donation by landowner of all interest in property.	Allows for permanent protection without direct public expenditure. Tax benefits to seller since property's market value is considered a charitable contribution.	Ownership responsibility includes liability and maintenance.
Bequest	Landowner retains ownership until death.	Management responsibility usually deferred until donor's death.	Date of acquisition is uncertain. Donor does not benefit from income tax deductions. Landowner can change will.
Donation with Reserved Life Estate	Landowner donates during lifetime but has lifetime use.	Landowner retains use but receives tax benefits from donation.	Date of acquisition is uncertain.
Land Exchange	Exchange of developable land for land with high conservation value.	Low-cost technique if trade parcel is donated. Reduces capital gains tax for original owner of protected land.	Properties must be of comparable value. Complicated and time-consuming.
Eminent Domain	The right of the government to take private property for public purposes upon payment of just compensation.	Provides government with a tool to acquire desired properties if other acquisition techniques are not workable.	High acquisition costs. Can result in speculation on targeted properties. Potentially expensive and time-consuming litigation.
Tax Foreclosure	Government acquires land by tax payment default.	Limited expenditure. Land might not be appropriate for public open space but can be sold to provide funds for open space acquisition.	Cumbersome process.

Conservation easement: A less-than-fee-simple interest in land that is voluntarily donated or sold by a landowner to a unit of government or an IRS-recognized, nonprofit conservation organization to protect open space or recreation, ecological, agricultural, or historic resources. Most easements are granted in perpetuity. Land use restrictions are clearly defined in the deed and are negotiated between the property owner and the easement receiver, based on the landowner's needs and an analysis of the property. The conveyed easement serves as a jointly held and legally binding plan for how the land will be used.

Conservation easements have several advantages over other means of land protection, and we will later compare them to other government mechanisms, like purchase and transfer of development rights and zoning. Among the advantages are the following:

- They are permanent protection.
- They are less costly than outright acquisition.
- They offer compensation to landowners by payment or tax benefit.
- They stay in private ownership, which reduces liability exposure and management costs, and land stays on tax rolls.
- They generally come about as a result of interest in stewardship and preservation.

The steps in developing a conservation easement include initial meetings, title search, site assessment, negotiation of easement restrictions, easement appraisal, tax benefit estimation, notification of local government, finalization of agreement, deed filing, and, finally, site stewardship. Appraisal is an important step because it will determine the payment or donation value of the easement. The property is appraised for its "highest and best use" given existing zoning and market conditions. It is then appraised with use restrictions of the conservation easement. The difference between the two appraised values is the value of the easement.

Tax Incentives for Land Conservation

The use of conservation easements has grown exponentially as more landowners recognize the financial benefits. Tax incentives were introduced earlier and include federal income tax deductions (enhanced by 2006 changes in the tax code) and several states' tax credits for donation of conservation easements. This is especially true in certain states, such as Virginia, Colorado, South Carolina, and New Mexico, where land preservation tax credits are transferable. Table 15.7 gives some details on the tax credits in those states. Box 15.5 explains how the land conservation tax credit works in Virginia.

Purchase of Development Rights

Purchase of development rights (PDR) is very similar to purchased conservation easements in that the development rights are separated from the property title,

TABLE 15.7 **Land Conservation Tax Credit Rules in States Allowing Credit Transfers**

	Virginia	*Colorado*	*New Mexico*	*South Carolina*
Legislation	Virginia Land Conservation Incentives Act, 1999	Credit Against Tax Conservation Easements 1999	Land Conservation Incentive Act, 2004	South Carolina Conservation Incentives Act, 2001
Lands Eligible to Earn Credits	• Fee Title & Conservation Easement • IRC § 170(h)	• Conservation Easement only • IRC § 170(h)	• Fee Title & Conservation Easement • IRC § 170(h)	• Fee Title & Conservation Easement • IRC § 170(h)
Credit Value and Limitations	• 40% FMV • Unlimited credit. • $100,000 cap on credit applied to taxes/yr. (Note unlimited amount may be transferred and used by 3rd parties.) • Statewide cap of $100,000,000/year.	• 50% FMV • $375,000 max credit. • $375,000 cap on credit applied to taxes/yr. • Individual/entity limited to one credit /yr.	• 50% FMV • $250,000 max credit. • $250,000 cap on credit applied to taxes/yr. • Individual/entity limited to one credit/yr.	• Lesser of $250/Acre or 25% of Federal Conservation Easement deduction • Unlimited credit. • $52,500 cap on credit applied to taxes/yr.
Entities Eligible to Earn Credits	Individual/Corporate Pass-Through Entities	Resident Individual Corporate/Pass-Through Entities	Individual/Corporate Pass-Through Entities	Individual/Corporate Pass-Through Entities
Entities Eligible to Hold a Donation	• IRC § 170(h) • Governmental entities limited to State or its subdivisions; nonprofits must have office in state for 5 yrs.	• IRC § 170(h) • Nonprofits must have operated for 2 years.	• IRC § 170(h)	• IRC § 170(h)
Carry Forward?	10 yrs.	20 yrs.	20 yrs.	Unlimited
Transferable?	Yes	Yes	Yes	Yes
Refundable?	No	Conditional on state Surplus and limited to $50,000/yr.	No	No
Certification?	Yes, but only credits > $1 million	No	Yes—by NM agency. Scope of review: conservation values.	No, unless credits are being transferred. If transfer, certified by SC Dept of Revenue.

Source: Pentz et al. 2007.

BOX 15.5—The Land Conservation Tax Credit in Virginia

The Virginia Land Preservation Tax Credit was enacted in 1999 and amended in 2002 and 2006. A state tax credit can be claimed for the part of the value of a donation of land fee title or conservation easement to an IRS-qualified organization, such as a land trust or the Virginia Outdoors Foundation.

- *Calculate easement value.* The donation is equal to the value of the land or easement determined by a real estate appraisal. For an easement, the land is appraised at full market value then again with the conditions of the easement. The fair market value (FMV) of the easement is the difference between the two appraisals.
  - For example, let's say you have a large natural parcel that is appraised at full market for $1,000,000 and appraised with the easement restrictions for $400,000. The FMV of the donated easement is the difference, or $600,000.

- *Apply state rules.* The state's rules are then applied to see what tax credit can be claimed (see Table 15.7). In Virginia, 40% of the FMV can be claimed as a tax credit.
  - In our example, your potential tax credit would be 0.40 x $600,000 or $240,000. But the rules also say there is a limit of $100,000 tax credit claimed each year. Does that mean you can only claim $100,000? And who pays $100,000 on his or her state taxes, anyway? At a Virginia tax rate of about 6%, you'd have to earn $1.5 million to pay $100,000 in taxes, $3.6 million to claim $240,000.
  - Maybe this isn't such a good deal after all?

- *Carryover credit.* Carryover helps solve this dilemma. Carryover allows taxpayers to carry any unused tax credit for 10 additional years.
  - If you have a $10,000 state tax liability each year, you can take that credit for a total of 11 years or $110,000; but that is still less than half the value of a $240,000 easement credit. And if you are an income-poor, land-rich farmer, you probably have very little tax liability against which to claim the credit. Or if you are an absentee landowner who has no state tax liability, this state credit will not

entice you to donate a conservation easement.
  - Maybe this isn't such a good deal after all?

- *Transfer credit.* Transferability solves this problem. In Virginia, you are allowed to sell or transfer your tax credit to other taxpayers. And the $100,000 credit cap applied to one year's tax does not apply to transfers.
  - Therefore, you can sell your $240,000 tax credit for the best price you can get and pocket the money all in the first year. In Virginia, there is now a large market for these tax credits, which have been going for about 80¢ on the dollar. At that rate you can get $0.80 x $240,000, or $192,000, right away. And the buyers of your tax credits are buying dollars for 80¢—not a bad deal for them either.

- *Federal tax benefit.* You can still claim a federal tax deduction on the full $600,000 donation. The federal tax rules limit the deduction to 50% of your adjusted gross income (AGI) in year one (100% if you are a farmer), but you can carry over the residual for 15 years.
  - In our example, if your AGI is $100,000, you can deduct $50,000 this year and $50,000 for 11 more years until your reach $600,000. But unlike the state tax credit, you don't get a reduction of your taxes by that amount; you get a deduction of your income on which your tax is based. So, if you are in the 25% tax bracket, your potential tax dollar savings in the first year is 0.25 x $50,000 or $12,500, and over the 12 years you take the deduction, the dollar benefit is 0.25 x $600,000 or $150,000.

Total Financial Benefit

In our example, you can apply a conservation easement on your property and still own and use the property subject to the restricted uses of the easement. The market value of the property is diminished by $600,000, but you get a return of $192,000 right away from the transfer of your state tax credits, and $150,000 over the next 12 years on your federal tax savings, for a total of $342,000. The public benefit is that this land will remain in conservation in perpetuity.

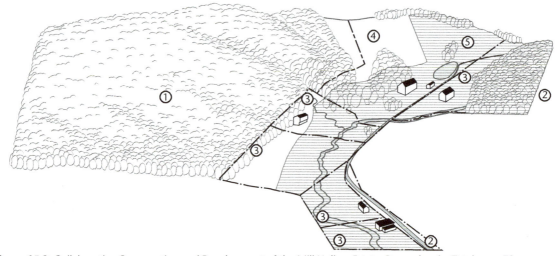

Figure 15.3 Collaborative Conservation and Development of the Mill Hollow Estate, Pennsylvania. Total area: 70 acres. (1) 40 acres convey to trust. (2) One acre traded to town for road. (3) Five parcels subdivided, sold at market. (4) Owner retains residence and 15 acres. (5) Stream Valley Conservation Easement (hatched line area). (*Source:* Metzger 1983.)

sold, and reflected in a new deed with development restrictions. Only government agencies use PDR programs, whereas both agencies and land trusts use conservation easements. Most PDR programs are used for protection of farmland and open space. Programs for purchase of agricultural conservation easement are a form of PDR for working landscapes (see Table 15.3). They require a funding source, usually a state or local bond. Yet they are popular with 26 state and 88 local programs in 20 states, and they have applied about $4.5 billion to conserve 2.5 million acres of farmland and other conservation land (American Farmland Trust 2001).

Collaborative Conservation and Development

Collaborative conservation and development is a negotiated compromise development plan involving the landowner, developer, designer, local government, and land trust in which conservation of natural and/or cultural resources and development are accommodated, generally using cluster development, conservation easements, agricultural and natural reserves, and land management and stewardship.

The 70-acre Mill Hollow Estate in Delaware County, Pennsylvania, shown in Figure 15.3, is a good example of the use of a conservation easement and land donation to a land trust as part of a comprehensive plan for site development and environmental protection. The Natural Land Trust prepared a master plan of the parcel for the landowner who wished to remain on the land but needed to realize a financial gain through subdivision and development.

The plan called for five uses shown on the map, with the owner retaining a portion, five parcels subdivided, and most of the rest conserved by the trust or by conservation easement. The trust was also given a percentage of the sale price of each parcel to be used to manage the property. Although the direct financial return to

Figure 15.4 Rural Cluster and Conservation Subdivision Design. Collaborative development leads to residential use and land conservation for active and passive recreation, wildlife habitat, and working farmland. (*Source:* Arendt 1999. Used by permission of Island Press.)

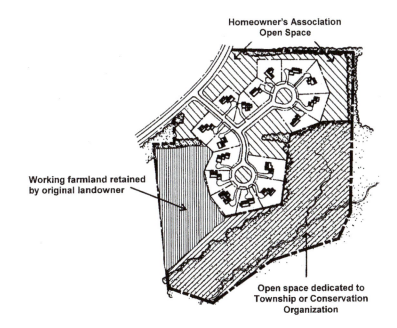

the landowner for this transaction was less than if the entire estate were subdivided and sold, such a sale would have exposed the family to high capital gains taxes. The owner chose the master plan because it enabled the family to remain on the property and was sufficiently attractive financially since it included the tax-deductible charitable contribution of land to the trust (Metzger 1983).

Collaborative conservation and development is the principle behind rural cluster and conservation subdivision design popularized by Randall Arendt (see Chapter 16). Open space, working landscapes, historic sites, and wildlife habitats set aside in such development designs can have easements or property rights deeded to a land trust for permanent protection and stewardship. This is illustrated in Figure 15.4, which shows a hypothetical rural cluster subdivision with common recreation open space held by all of the residents through the homeowner's association, noncommon working landscape open space retained by the original landowner/farmer, and wildlife and passive recreation open space dedicated to a land trust or the local government. This collaborative development provides for new housing, a financial return to the original owner, a diverse mix of open space, and potential tax benefits to the developer (and reduced costs to new residents) for the land donation (Arendt 1999).

Tools to Conserve the Working Landscape

Because of the significant conversion of agricultural land to urban development in the past several decades, states, communities, and land trusts have developed programs to protect the working landscape. These programs have a number of objectives: to provide for local food production, to conserve the open space and rural character agricultural land provides, and to keep viable an agricultural economy sector (Stokes et al. 1997).

More recently, certain communities have expanded these objectives to include other natural resource–based land uses, such as forestry and fisheries, and included them all under the label "working landscapes." Tools used to conserve these lands and land uses are similar to other conservation methods discussed previously in this chapter and to growth management tools discussed in Chapters 17 and 18. However, it is useful to summarize them here, along with their advantages and disadvantages for conservation of the working landscape.

Of the tools listed in Table 15.8, conservation easements and development rights purchase and transfer are the only methods that provide permanent protection. Zoning, even exclusive agricultural zoning, is subject to rezoning decisions. Agricultural districting, right-to-farm, and differential taxation help to provide a better climate for working lands, but landowners can still choose to convert their lands to other permitted uses.

Obtaining development rights keeps land out of development, but it still does not guarantee that working uses of the land will remain economically viable. A combination of measures in addition to development rights acquisition is needed. These include districting and right-to-farm, but also farming economy programs like development of farmers markets and cooperatives.

Design and Planning Tools for Open Space, Greenways, and Green Infrastructure

Local land conservation planning and design have evolved in the past few decades (Table 15.9). Although environmental designers from Olmsted and Howard to McHarg and Corbett have long relied on undeveloped natural open space, often called *greenspace*, to provide a range of social and environmental purposes, local land conservation in the United States prior to 1980 was dominated by "parks and rec" planning. This involved identifying and acquiring properties for recreation and scenic amenity, developing them according to active recreation standards, and maintaining the parks. After 1980, open space in many communities broadened planning objectives to passive recreation and protection of urban forests and outlying farmland, and tools expanded to include conservation easements. By the 1990s, there was a growing awareness of the benefits of linear greenways along stream and other corridors for passive recreation, wildlife habitat and movement, and flood damage mitigation. As a result, more communities engaged in greenway planning, design, and development.

And as we have seen in Chapters 10, 11, and 14, land conservation programs have recently expanded in scope to integrate protected lands on a regional and state scale, not only for people's recreation and enjoyment and local wildlife habitats, but also for broader-scale ecological functions. Many communities and states have begun to see open space less as an afterthought of development and more as an integral part of the land development process and growth management strategies. And this takes us once again to green infrastructure planning. Although emerging trends in government land conservation are toward green infrastructure, it is also useful to discuss more conventional planning and design tools for open space and greenways.

Table 15.8 Tools to Conserve Agricultural Land and the Working Landscape

Tool	Description	Advantages	Disadvantages	Number of States/ Number of Localities
Exclusive Agricultural Zoning	Regulatory zoning prohibiting nonagricultural building.	Provides strict control as long as zoning is in place.	Property rights and legal takings issues; subject to rezoning.	Localities in Oregon
Nonexclusive Agricultural Zoning	Regulatory zoning designating farming as primary use and limiting nonfarm land use by large-lot residential density.	Sets farming as primary use.	Large-lot zoning does not provide contiguous working land; may consume productive farmland at a faster rate.	Localities in 23 states
Cluster Zoning	Allows onsite density transfers or requires clustering of development to set aside open space or working land under permanent protection.	Accommodates development while permanently protecting some working land.	May not leave a critical mass of contiguous working land; may create conflicts between farms and residences.	Numerous localities
Agricultural Conservation Easements/ PDR	Landowners sell or donate their right to develop their property.	Provides permanent protection of working land.	Purchasing easements or development rights is costly to government or land trusts.	26 states; 88 localities in 20 states
Transfer of Development Rights	Allow landowners to transfer right to develop on one parcel (designated "preservation") to another (designated "development").	Provides permanent protection of working land at minor public cost compared with PDR.	Requires complex administration to designate preservation and development areas, and broker development rights.	Localities in 15 states
Agricultural Districting	Farmers form special districts in which agriculture is encouraged and protected by right-to-farm, differential taxation, PDR eligibility, etc.	Can provide a critical mass of contiguous working land and benefits to farmers.	Does not provide permanent protection; farmers sign on for time period and may opt out with minor penalty.	16 states; localities in 3 states
Differential Property Taxation	Working land is taxed at use value rather than development value; "circuit breaker" programs give tax credits.	Prevents property taxes from forcing farmers to sell or develop.	Does not provide permanent protection; farmers sign on for time period and may opt out with minor penalty.	49 states
Circuit Breaker Tax Relief	Working land is taxed at market value, but landowners are eligible for tax credit to offset property taxes based on income.	Prevents property taxes from forcing farmers to sell or develop.	Does not provide permanent protection; farmers sign on for time period and may opt out with minor penalty.	4 states
Right to Farm	Farmers are protected from nuisance suits; generally applied to agricultural zones or districts.	Supports farm activities.	Does not protect working land, only farming activities, from lawsuits.	50 states

Source: Implementation data from American Farmland Trust 2002, 2010.

TABLE 15.9 **The Evolving Nature of Local Government Land Conservation in the United States**

Period	Type	Conservation Tools	Primary Objectives
< 1980	Parks and recreation planning	Land acquisition; park planning and management	Active recreation, scenic amenity
1980s	Open space planning	Land acquisition and easement; park planning and management	Active recreation, scenic amenity, farmland protection, urban forestry
1990s	Greenways and open space planning	Land acquisition, easement, floodplain zoning; park and greenway planning and management	Active and passive recreation, scenic amenity, farmland protection, urban forestry, urban wildlife
2000s	Green infrastructure	Land acquisition, easement, floodplain management, Smart Growth management tools, conservation land development, partnerships with landowners, land trusts	Core hubs and linking corridors for active and passive recreation, scenic amenity, farmland protection, urban forestry, urban wildlife, regional and state ecological systems, integration of conservation and growth management

Open Space and Greenway Planning and Design

The greenbelt concept was born in the English Garden City movement of the nineteenth century. Frederick Law Olmsted designed Boston's Emerald Necklace, a series of parks and greenways from Franklin Park to the Charles River that were part of Boston's original design produced between 1878 and 1890. Greenways are open natural areas that have a linear form (Smith and Hellmund 1993). The most successful greenspace and greenway designs are those that provide multiple objectives and are integrated into developed land uses. These objectives include recreation, transportation (bike/pedestrian), open space, conservation of wildlife corridors and riparian habitats, stream channel protection and restoration, water quality improvement, flood damage mitigation, neighborhood linkages, and education. Open space and greenway planning is a useful mechanism to integrate a broad range of environmental planning objectives, including parks and recreation, farmland preservation, natural hazard mitigation, floodplain management, stream restoration, urban forestry, habitat conservation, and wetland protection. As a result, many communities include a chapter on open space and greenways in their comprehensive plan to address a wide range of environmental land issues and to serve as the policy basis for land conservation.

Boulder, Colorado, was one of the earliest communities to develop a comprehensive open space and greenway system to serve multiple objectives. The city purchased considerable land, made possible by revenue from a 1967 sales tax increase of 0.4% dedicated to open space acquisition. Figure 15.5A shows the greater Boulder greenbelt/greenway system including its Open Space and Mountain Parks. Figure 15.5B zooms in on a central portion of the city greenways. (See

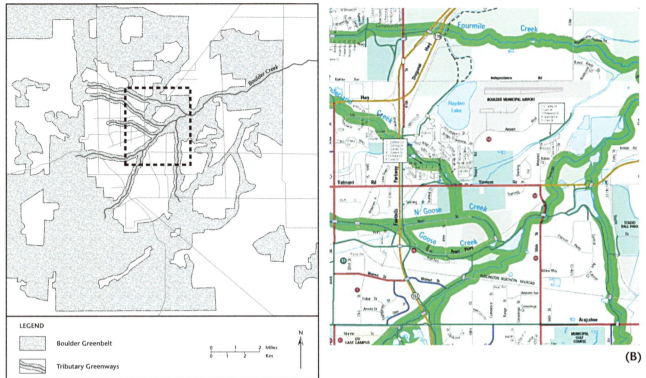

Figure 15.5 Open Space and Greenway Planning. A: Boulder, Colorado's greenbelt and greenway system. B: A closer view of some of the city's greenways. (*Source:* A: Smith and Hellmund 1993, used with permission of Paul Hellmund. B: City of Boulder 2001.)

Boulder 2010 for a high-resolution map of the system.) Boulder increased its open space sales tax to 0.73% in 1989 and continues to plan and upgrade its system. The system includes 375 separate properties comprising 45,000 acres purchased at cost of $150 million. In an indication that the recession may have an effect of citizens willing to pay for conservation, in 2009, Boulder County residents voted down an extension of its 0.25% sales tax for land acquisition scheduled to expire in 2019, a measure the county required in order to take on long-term debt for current acquisitions (see Chapter 17).

Green Infrastructure for Open Space, Greenways, Working Landscapes, and Habitat

The emergence of **green infrastructure (GI)** as an approach to statewide and local land conservation planning is a major improvement over haphazard practices of the past, which often conserved "leftover" land not developed or farmland whose owners simply stepped forward in voluntary programs. The GI process, introduced in Chapters 11 and 14, brings several benefits (Benedict and McMahon 2002):

- *GI is science-based.* It analyzes the land, soils, habitat, ownership, and development trends to identify critical core hubs (that may be habitat reserves, large farms, or regional parks) and connecting corridor links (that may be riparian streamways or forests tracts) to define an interconnected network of green space that can work for people and wildlife.
- *GI is integrative.* It both prioritizes land for conservation and informs land development planning, so it is not planned in isolation but at the same time as gray infrastructure.
- *GI builds on existing land conservation.* Through gap analysis, it starts with existing protected lands and identifies gaps in protection and priorities for critical cores and corridors.
- GI is *proactive* not reactive, *systematic* not haphazard, *holistic* not piecemeal, *multijurisdictional* not single jurisdictional, *multifunctional* not single purpose, and *multiscale* not single scale.

Although green infrastructure planning is a key to effective land conservation, it does not conserve land by itself. It will design potential interconnecting networks and prioritize areas for conservation, but actually protecting the priority cores and corridors depends on the tools presented above and in Chapters 16–18: acquisition, conservation easements, land regulation, and consideration in planning roads, water and sewer, and land development design.

There are a growing number of great examples of GI planning. In Chapter 11, we reviewed California's Essential Connectivity study, which contributed to the 2010 assessment of forests and rangelands that produced the priority landscape GI map, a portion of which is shown in Figure 15.6. It shows protected areas and high- and medium-priority areas.

One of the best examples of statewide GI planning is Maryland's GreenPrint program. The $35 million program was established in May 2001 with the lofty objective of preserving an extensive, interconnected network of land vital to the long-term survival of native plants and wildlife, as well as industries dependent on a clean environment and abundant natural resources (State of Maryland 2001). The purpose of the program is threefold:

1. Identify, using state-of-the-art computer mapping techniques, the most important unprotected natural lands in the state.
2. Identify linkages to connect these lands through a system of corridors.
3. Save those lands through targeted acquisitions and conservation easements.

The state used satellite imaging and GIS technology to inventory the state and local green infrastructure. Hubs and links were ranked according to a GI assessment method that evaluates sites based on ecological value and vulnerability, on both local and regional scales. Figure 15.7 shows the statewide basemap. The system is now mapped on a web-based interactive map so that users can zoom into their area of interest (http://www.greenprint.maryland.gov/greenprint_map.asp).

Maryland uses the program as a guide for its many conservation programs, including the Maryland Agricultural Land Preservation Foundation (the source of

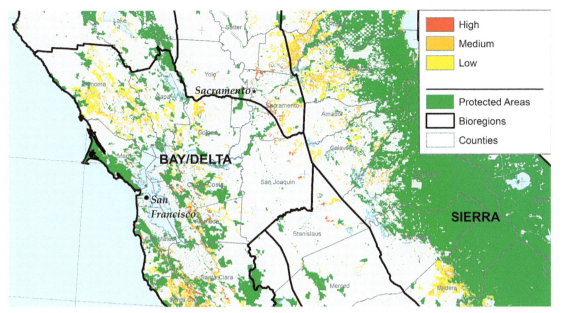

Figure 15.6 California's Green Infrastructure Priority Landscape. This map shows a portion of protected areas and priority core and corridors. (*Source:* CalFire 2010.)

PACE funding; see Table 15.3), the Maryland Environmental Trust (MET), the Rural Legacy Program, and its Chesapeake Bay program. Figure 15.8 shows the detailed GI map for Montgomery County. It shows developed lands (roaded areas), state and federally protected lands, county parks, private conservation lands, MET and state and local PACE lands, and existing and proposed greenways and unprotected hubs and links.

Private Land Stewardship

Despite the wide range of land conservation programs of government and land trusts, about 1.4 billion acres, or almost 75% of the total land in the contiguous 48 states, are in private ownership. This can be categorized as farmland (33%), rangeland (27%), forestland (26%), and developed land (10%) (USDA, NRCS 2009). Most of the first three categories are managed for food, fiber, and timber production, but some is in large idle blocks of private roadless land not currently in forestry or agricultural use. These idle lands provide conservation benefits, even though they are unprotected. Likewise, the developed metropolitan areas contain private open space lands in individual or common ownership. Because of the large proportion of these private lands, environmental quality depends on appropriate stewardship to reduce environmental impact and enhance ecological integrity.

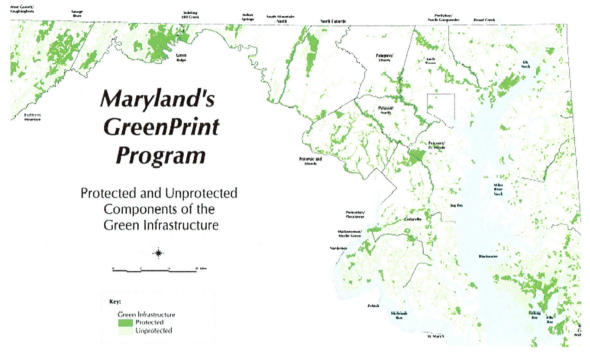

Figure 15.7 Maryland's GreenPrint Program. Protected and unprotected components of the green infrastructure. (*Source:* Maryland 2001.)

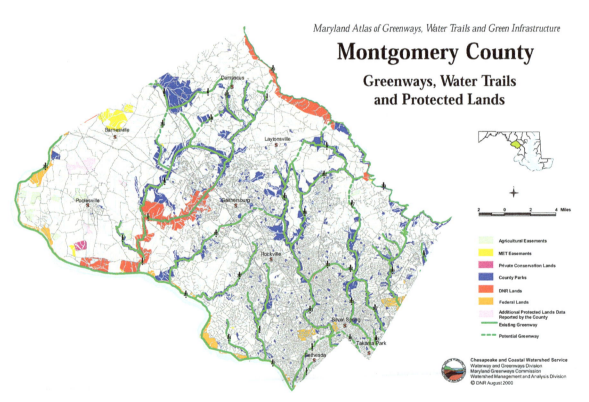

Figure 15.8 Montgomery County, Maryland, Green Infrastructure. This map shows greenways, water trails, and protected lands. (*Source:* Maryland 2001.)

Figure 15.9 Conservation Stewardship. Users of nature—be they farmers, foresters, fishermen, or other producers and recreaters—are important conservation stewards and advocates of the working landscape. They are the best promoters of its economic, social, and environmental benefits. (Photo by Peter Beck, www.peterbeck.com, used with permission.)

And this depends on the owners and users of these lands, those depicted in Figure 15.9.

The working landscape consisting of productive farmland, ranchland, and harvested forestland provides important scenic and open space benefits, but it also can create environmental impacts. These impacts include soil erosion and sedimentation, polluted runoff, riparian habitat and streambank damage, and groundwater contamination, among others. Stewardship of these lands cannot only reduce these impacts but also enhance their open space and ecological value.

Stewardship involves using best-management practices (BMPs) for water quality and land protection. These practices include conservation tillage, vegetative buffers, nutrient management, integrated pest management, low-impact selective timber harvesting, reforestation, and set-aside of highly erodible lands, wetlands, and riparian buffers. Private lands in metropolitan areas are important because of their proximity to population and the roles they play in urban open space, environmental quality, and urban biodiversity. These include private parks, golf courses, utility rights-of-way, common areas in subdivisions, and individual land parcels. These private properties contribute to environmental degradation through impervious surfaces, polluted runoff, introduction of invasive species, removal of natural vegetation, and overuse of fertilizers and pesticides. Efforts to minimize impacts, restore environmental resources, and enhance wildlife habitats have increased in communities throughout the country. Community environmental organizations, master gardeners, neighborhood "ecoteams," and other efforts have improved scenic resources, environmental quality, and urban wildlife habitat.

All of the national, state, and local resource protection agencies realize the importance of private land stewardship, and most have outreach and education programs. For example, the USFS's Forest Legacy Program funds private forest conservation, and the NRCS Backyard Conservation series provides information for a range of homeowner and neighborhood activities to enhance land stewardship. Guidance fact sheets are available for backyard ponds and wetlands, composting, mulching, tree planting, water conservation, and wildlife management. See http://www.nrcs.usda.gov/feature/backyard/.

Smart Conservation and Growth Management

For decades, land conservation has been addressed by public and nonprofit programs in isolation from—and often in conflict with, or reacting to—land development. More recently, government programs and land trust activities have recognized that land conservation should be used in conjunction with development, either as part of growth management or as an integral component of economic development. In a 2002 Brookings study, Hollis and Fulton (2002) reviewed the status of land conservation programs by government and land trusts and their role in growth management. They concluded the following:

- There has been a surge of interest in open space programs in the last decade, especially in rapidly urbanizing areas.
- Open space is still protected through a complex and decentralized system that tends to be reactive and hard to assess.
- Local land trusts tend to focus on lands that are locally significant but may not fit a larger strategic objective for metropolitan growth, while government and national land trusts may be strategic but tend to focus on significant resources and not on metropolitan growth.
- Growth management programs that establish urban growth boundaries have a significant effect on land conservation, especially protection of the working landscape outside the boundary. Still, there are few metropolitan areas with strong urban growth boundaries and their effects vary.
- The connection between open space programs and urban and metropolitan growth policy is rarely made. Federal programs focus on rural landscapes, except for Habitat Conservation Planning under the Endangered Species Act, which has affected urban growth in California and the Southwest. However, even these programs tend not to be coordinated with urban growth policies. States with strong growth management usually have strong land conservation programs, but they are rarely connected by policy. Two exceptions are Maryland (discussed earlier) and

Florida, where communities seeking conservation funds must show that their proposals conform to their comprehensive growth management plans that are also subject to state review.

- Understanding of the impact of land conservation programs on metropolitan growth patterns is sketchy at best. More research is needed to see how the different strategies for land conservation in different parts of the country affect urban growth.

This 2002 assessment was accurate, but we are seeing new emphasis on land conservation at all levels of government. Interest appears to be growing in connecting land conservation and urban growth management. Science-based green infrastructure programs aim to coordinate conservation and development. This approach is being advocated by the Trust for Public Land, The Conservation Fund, and the Sprawl Watch Clearinghouse, among others. We explore issues of sprawl, land development design with nature in mind, and Smart Growth management in the next three chapters.

Summary

Land conservation of open space, recreation lands, ecological habitats, and working landscapes has become a huge multi-billion-dollar enterprise that engages all levels of government, nonprofit land trusts, local citizens groups, and major philanthropic foundations. Voters continue to support three-quarters of bond referenda and other initiatives for land acquisition and easements for open space, recreation, and protection of the working landscape.

Land trusts have grown in number, in land holdings, and in influence. There were 1,667 in 2005, twice as many in 1990, and they protect well more than 37 million acres in the United States. Government agencies, at all levels, and land trusts are applying stronger ecological science to land evaluation, they are better integrating conservation interests with development through landscape preservation and green infrastructure frameworks, and there continue to be significant resources invested in conservation that can follow this integrated scientific guidance. They are using cost-effective tools for acquiring conservation, including conservation easements, purchase and transfer of development rights, and other means of protection without an outright purchase of the land. New financing tools, like conservation easement tax credits, have gotten more landowners and investors involved in conservation. The past decade has seen a growing interest in environment and sustainability, and this social movement also has impacted the investment in land conservation.

Effective land protection for ecological function, wildlife, and people requires all of these actors and activities, including private land stewardship. Land conservation is emerging as an integral part of growth management. Greenways and greenbelts can effectively define growth areas, and green infrastructure can best be planned along with gray infrastructure in the development process.

16 ■ Design with Nature for People: Sustainable, Livable, and Smart Growth Communities

The last half-century has seen unprecedented growth in both global population and land development. The world population was 3 billion in 1960 and is expected to exceed 7 billion in 2012. In the United States, the population doubled from 1950 to 310 million in 2010 and is expected to increase by another 100 million by 2050. This level of population growth is not sustainable with current patterns of development. The increase in the number of humans is enough to overtax environmental resources, but the impact per person in terms of consumption of land, energy, water, food, and resources has also been increasing. For example, the massive highway construction that began in the 1950s and the rise of the automobile as the primary mode of personal transportation in the U.S. have encouraged a sprawling, haphazard development pattern that requires more land and results in greater pollution and fossil fuel consumption. Unfortunately, these automobile-dependent, land-consumptive, energy-intensive, carbon-emitting, and environment-impacting development patterns have caught on in other parts of the world.

Decades later, many of the suburban residents have moved closer to the city or farther out to the ex-urbs, leaving fractured communities, vacant properties, and contaminated brownfields in their wake. Recall from Chapter 3 that **sprawl** is land-consumptive, dispersed, and automobile-dependent land development patterns made up of homogeneous, segregated land uses highly dependent on collector roads (Figure 16.1; see also Box 3.1). Some residents appear satisfied with suburban living. However, many are increasingly unhappy with the dysfunctional social, environmental, and transportation problems of these land use patterns, and yet they resign themselves to dealing with the problems as necessary evils of modern America. Fast-growing suburban development also lacks resilience to changing economic times, as evidenced by the recent economic recession and mortgage foreclosure crisis.

Others believe there is a better way—not only for choice of lifestyle, but also for economic resilience and environmental protection. The past decade has seen

Figure 16.1 Suburban Sprawl. A: Sprawling homesites outside Las Vegas. B: New homes replace farmland in Dallas County, Iowa, as the suburbs of Clive and Waukee grow on the west side of Des Moines. (*Source:* Photos by Lynn Betts, USDA, NRCS.)

forward-thinking planners, developers, designers, and government officials formulate new principles of land use development that originated in traditional neighborhoods in the U.S. and in European cities. These concepts are characterized by several related movements, including "sustainable communities," "new urbanism," "green urbanism," "livable places," "pedestrian- and transit-oriented development," "healthy communities," "retrofitting suburbia," "brownfields redevelopment," "community revitalization," and "smart growth." Libraries and websites are filling with information on sustainable community design. And increasingly these design approaches have caught the interest of the consumer market in the U.S. and have merged with objectives for public health, social justice, affordability, and green infrastructure. This chapter discusses the basic principles and practices applied under these labels for what we will simply call **sustainable communities** and how they can advance resource efficiency and the protection and restoration of the natural environment.

Urban Sprawl and Its Impacts

The amount of development land required for each individual grew by four times from the 1950s to the 1980s (Benfield et al. 1999); and from 1982 to 2003, developed land grew 20% more than the population (USDA, NRCS 2009). In most sprawling developments, everyone is forced to drive everywhere. Collector road designs and long commuting distances increase vehicle miles traveled, congestion, petroleum consumption, and air pollution. Sprawl consumes agricultural land, open space, and natural wildlife habitats and creates vast water-impacting impervious surfaces for subdivisions, shopping centers, roads, and parking lots. Local governments struggle financially to provide urban infrastructure, services, and schools in response to rapidly growing dispersed developments.

The *Emerging Trends in Real Estate* 2007 report from the Urban Land Institute (ULI) also suggested a transforming market: "Energy costs add fuel to the fire—people want greater convenience in their time-constrained lives. Far-flung greenfield homes may cost less, but filling the gas tank burns holes in wallets. Both empty nesters and their young adult offspring gravitate to live in more exciting and sophisticated 24-hour places—whether urban or suburban—with pedestrian-accessible retail, restaurants, parks, supermarkets, and offices. Transit-oriented development at subway or light-rail stations almost cannot miss" (ULI 2006, 14).

The Government: How Can Local Government Facilitate Sustainable Communities?

Leinberger (2007) also documents this shift in market and estimates a 30–40% consumer preference, but suggests that only 5–10% of the need is being met in most markets. In some cases, this is the fault of developers who are not keeping up with consumer preference, but in many localities, developers are constrained by antiquated local government regulations and must endure the often arduous variance and rezoning process. This, too, is changing as more and more localities are adopting Smart Growth principles and working to modify their ordinances to allow (remove barriers), encourage (incentivize through tax credit and density bonuses), and increasingly mandate these development patterns. These mandates include performance-based ordinances, form-based codes (FBC), and "smart" codes. These measures and other government growth management programs are the subject of Chapter 17.

The Principles and Practice of Sustainable Community Design

This section introduces the basic principles and some historical background. Then we'll describe the evolving practice of sustainable community design. Many of these concepts have long been alive and well in Europe (Beatley 2000), and in traditional city neighborhoods in the U.S. The basic principles merge compatible objectives for protecting and restoring the natural environment, conserving resources, and providing more livable communities for people.

Natural Systems as the Foundation for Community Design (1900–1970)

The concepts associated with designing land development in accord with natural systems have evolved for well over a century. In the mid- to late nineteenth century, Frederick Law Olmsted, the "father of landscape architecture," developed plans as diverse as California's Yosemite Valley, New York's Central Park, the self-contained Riverside community near Chicago, and the Fens and the Riverway park plan for Boston, based on the natural drainage system. He influenced H.W. S. Cleveland's plan for the distributive park system in the lake-rich Twin Cities of St. Paul and Minneapolis (Minnesota) in 1888. In the late nineteenth century, Ebenezer Howard popularized the British Garden City, a form of new town devel-

Figure 16.1 Suburban Sprawl. A: Sprawling homesites outside Las Vegas. B: New homes replace farmland in Dallas County, Iowa, as the suburbs of Clive and Waukee grow on the west side of Des Moines. (*Source:* Photos by Lynn Betts, USDA, NRCS.)

forward-thinking planners, developers, designers, and government officials formulate new principles of land use development that originated in traditional neighborhoods in the U.S. and in European cities. These concepts are characterized by several related movements, including "sustainable communities," "new urbanism," "green urbanism," "livable places," "pedestrian- and transit-oriented development," "healthy communities," "retrofitting suburbia," "brownfields redevelopment," "community revitalization," and "smart growth." Libraries and websites are filling with information on sustainable community design. And increasingly these design approaches have caught the interest of the consumer market in the U.S. and have merged with objectives for public health, social justice, affordability, and green infrastructure. This chapter discusses the basic principles and practices applied under these labels for what we will simply call **sustainable communities** and how they can advance resource efficiency and the protection and restoration of the natural environment.

Urban Sprawl and Its Impacts

The amount of development land required for each individual grew by four times from the 1950s to the 1980s (Benfield et al. 1999); and from 1982 to 2003, developed land grew 20% more than the population (USDA, NRCS 2009). In most sprawling developments, everyone is forced to drive everywhere. Collector road designs and long commuting distances increase vehicle miles traveled, congestion, petroleum consumption, and air pollution. Sprawl consumes agricultural land, open space, and natural wildlife habitats and creates vast water-impacting impervious surfaces for subdivisions, shopping centers, roads, and parking lots. Local governments struggle financially to provide urban infrastructure, services, and schools in response to rapidly growing dispersed developments.

Sprawl's greatest triumph has been creation of the personal and family "private realm," be it home, yard, or car. But along with this private triumph has come an environmental, social, and civic failure. Land uses have separated, and as people have become more segregated, they have retreated from a more public life to a more controlled life, from experiential communities of place to communities of interest (Calthorpe and Fulton 2001; Duany et al. 2000).

Sprawling development has spoiled the visual and cultural diversity of communities, as suburban areas in all parts of the country now look the same, dominated by activity centers of superstores, office parks, and homogeneous residential subdivisions.

Participants in Creating Sustainable Communities

The parties who can create new patterns of development to arrest sprawl are the same parties who created sprawl: land developers and their investors, urban planners and designers, architects, local governments, and consumers. In addition, community groups and land trusts can play the advocate and partner in creative development plans. Sustainable patterns of growth will be:

- More **dense and compact**, consuming less land per household and freeing land for **common open space**, green infrastructure, and habitat and water protection.
- Less homogeneous in land use, with a **mixed use** of land for residential, commercial, employment, and education purposes.
- Less homogeneous in types of housing available, with **mixed residential** single-family detached houses, townhomes, and multifamily apartments that can accommodate **mixed-income households** and greater resident diversity.
- More **walkable**, enabled by compact and mixed-use development, leading to more resident interaction and a greater sense of community.
- **Transit-oriented**, with denser development around transit stops, again facilitated by compact land use and walkability.
- Focused on **infill redevelopment** when possible, including retrofitting older suburbs to revitalize existing communities and preserve outlying greenspace.

The Consumer: Do Consumers Want This Pattern of Development?

The consuming public states its preferences for the location, type, and amenities of residential living through its choices and purchasing power. Consumer preference has long characterized the "American dream" primarily by the ownership of a large-lot residence, usually in the suburbs. Some evidence indicates that this preference is still alive and well (Audirac 1999; Talen 1999, 2001). But there is also evidence from consumer surveys that support for more compact and mixed-use forms of housing is strong and growing (Handy et al. 2008). Lewis and Baldassare

(2010) found in two surveys, one in California in 2002, the other in four other southwestern states in 2007, that support for compact form was "significant," although only half the respondents indicated so. But perceptions vary with people's life cycle—young professionals and empty nesters like compact community life, young families with children still prefer suburban form; sociodemographic characteristics—gender, race/ethnicity, education; attitudes toward land use and environment issues; and political ideology (Lewis and Balassare 2010).

The Developer: What Does the Real Estate Market Tell Us?

The more important indicator of consumer preference is what they are buying. Of course, they can only choose from what is on the market, and in many markets, there may not be a range of choice beyond traditional development. However, evidence indicates that the demand for central urban residential development is on the rise, as opposed to suburban development.

The EPA's analysis of residential building permits in the 50 largest metropolitan areas from 1990 to 2008 found that half of the regions had a dramatic increase in the share of new construction built in the central city and inner suburbs versus the outlying suburbs. As shown in Figure 16.2, in the early 1990s, 7% of the building permits granted in the Chicago region were in the city of Chicago, during 2002–2008 the city had 27%. New York City's share increased from 15% to 47%; Portland, Oregon's share went from 9% to 26%; Atlanta's from 4% to 14%. These trends held true even as the construction industry began to decline in 2008. The EPA report concluded that "this acceleration of residential construction in urban neighborhoods reflects a fundamental shift in the real estate market" (U.S. EPA 2010b, 1).

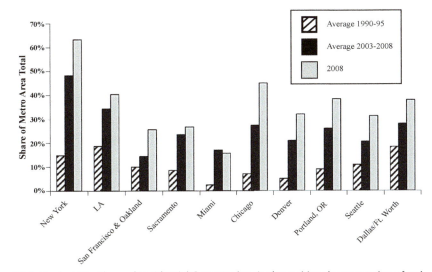

Figure 16.2 Central City Share of Residential Construction. In these cities, the proportion of residential units issued building permits has increased during the past two decades. (*Source:* U.S. EPA 2010b.)

The *Emerging Trends in Real Estate 2007* report from the Urban Land Institute (ULI) also suggested a transforming market: "Energy costs add fuel to the fire—people want greater convenience in their time-constrained lives. Far-flung greenfield homes may cost less, but filling the gas tank burns holes in wallets. Both empty nesters and their young adult offspring gravitate to live in more exciting and sophisticated 24-hour places—whether urban or suburban—with pedestrian-accessible retail, restaurants, parks, supermarkets, and offices. Transit-oriented development at subway or light-rail stations almost cannot miss" (ULI 2006, 14).

The Government: How Can Local Government Facilitate Sustainable Communities?

Leinberger (2007) also documents this shift in market and estimates a 30–40% consumer preference, but suggests that only 5–10% of the need is being met in most markets. In some cases, this is the fault of developers who are not keeping up with consumer preference, but in many localities, developers are constrained by antiquated local government regulations and must endure the often arduous variance and rezoning process. This, too, is changing as more and more localities are adopting Smart Growth principles and working to modify their ordinances to allow (remove barriers), encourage (incentivize through tax credit and density bonuses), and increasingly mandate these development patterns. These mandates include performance-based ordinances, form-based codes (FBC), and "smart" codes. These measures and other government growth management programs are the subject of Chapter 17.

The Principles and Practice of Sustainable Community Design

This section introduces the basic principles and some historical background. Then we'll describe the evolving practice of sustainable community design. Many of these concepts have long been alive and well in Europe (Beatley 2000), and in traditional city neighborhoods in the U.S. The basic principles merge compatible objectives for protecting and restoring the natural environment, conserving resources, and providing more livable communities for people.

Natural Systems as the Foundation for Community Design (1900–1970)

The concepts associated with designing land development in accord with natural systems have evolved for well over a century. In the mid- to late nineteenth century, Frederick Law Olmsted, the "father of landscape architecture," developed plans as diverse as California's Yosemite Valley, New York's Central Park, the self-contained Riverside community near Chicago, and the Fens and the Riverway park plan for Boston, based on the natural drainage system. He influenced H.W. S. Cleveland's plan for the distributive park system in the lake-rich Twin Cities of St. Paul and Minneapolis (Minnesota) in 1888. In the late nineteenth century, Ebenezer Howard popularized the British Garden City, a form of new town devel-

opment that emphasized greenways and open space, especially as a ring around the central city. Garden cities are intended to be self-contained, having their own industry and surrounded by agricultural fields.

Clarence Perry was instrumental in developing the organizing design concept of the neighborhood. He advocated the separation of through-transportation roads from local streets and independent pedestrian paths and vehicular roads. Some of these concepts were manifest in Clarence Stein's and Henry Wright's plan for the city of Radburn, New Jersey, in the 1920s. This plan introduced the cul-de-sac, houses were reversed so that living rooms faced the rear gardens, and pedestrian paths led to continuous park space. In the 1920s, Benton MacKaye was one of the first to recognize the significant influence of the automobile and highway development on urban form. The strip development occurring along highways even at that early date gave rise to his notion of the "Townless Highway." His alternative was the "Highwayless Town," which separated communities from the highway and kept major traffic corridors uncluttered by commerce and development.

In the mid-twentieth century, a new breed of designers and scientists argued for land development compatible with natural systems. Aldo Leopold's *Sand County Almanac* (1949) did not specifically address community or development design, but it had a tremendous influence on designers who followed. It suggested a "land ethic," that the land itself and its intrinsic values should serve as the basis for how it is used. By the 1960s, Ian McHarg popularized the concept of conforming development design to the opportunities and constraints provided by the land. Heavily influenced by Leopold's land ethic, McHarg's *Design with Nature* (1969) had a significant effect on subsequent environmental design and planning. As a first stage in his design process applied to scales from a site to a region, McHarg called for an environmental inventory. His 1968 inventory for the Twin Cities (Minnesota) metropolitan region served as a basis for subsequent regional planning, especially development of the regional park system. The process builds on basic environmental information to reveal areas suitable for human activities. McHarg's method of overlaying environmental data is the basis for GIS land suitability analysis. His firm, Wallace, McHarg, Roberts, and Todd (now WRT), also produced the 1963 Plan for Greenspring and Worthington Valleys in Baltimore County (Figure 16.3). The Plan for the Valleys is recognized as an early model for sustainable growth management. A Plan Supplement was prepared in 1989, and the Plan continues to influence the sweeping valley landscape today. The Plan received the 2010 American Planning Association Landmark Award (WRT 2010).

The Sustainable Neighborhood Subdivision: Village Homes (1970s)

The emphasis on natural systems was not explicit in the design of compact European and traditional U.S. neighborhoods. They were compact by necessity because of transportation limitations, but they worked (and still do). However, with the growth of automobile ownership in the U.S. and the post–World War II highway and housing boom, development patterns changed rapidly as people fled the hectic, polluted, cramped, and dangerous inner city for the calm, clean, spacious, and safe suburbs.

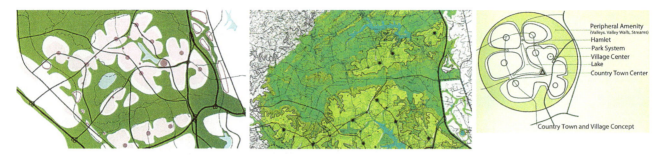

Figure 16.3 The Plan for the Valleys: Greenspring and Worthington Valleys, Baltimore, Maryland. Left: Original plan. Center: Revised plan. Right: The Country Town and Village Concept. (*Source:* WMRT 1963; WRT 2010. Used with permission.)

These patterns took hold, but there were a few exceptions. In 1972, a young builder named Michael Corbett began implementing a development concept for an intentional cooperative community that he, his wife, Judy Corbett, and some friends had been developing for several years. Corbett and his friends were heavily influenced by Howard's Garden City and McHarg's village concept in the Plan for the Valleys; "new town" developments in Reston (Virginia), Columbia (Maryland), and Woodlands (Texas) (a McHarg design); and the environmental movement and emerging energy concerns. What Corbett called at the time "wholistic community design" and "design with nature for people" he applied to a 70-acre neighborhood community development, Village Homes, in Davis, California. The development became one of the first recognized examples of "sustainable community" design. Corbett collected his design concepts in a 1981 book, *A Better Place to Live* (Corbett 1981), and he and Judy describe their 20-year experience of designing (and living) in Village Homes in a 2000 book, *Designing Sustainable Communities: Learning from Village Homes* (Corbett and Corbett 2000).

Figure 16.4 shows the layout of Village Homes. The 68-acre community contains 220 single-family homes and 20 apartments, commercial and community buildings, 25% open space, including common recreational areas, community gardens, orchards, and vineyards (24% of the community's produce is grown onsite). The layout is designed around the natural drainage of the site. There is vehicle access to each house on narrow 20- to 24-ft-wide streets. However, fences and shrubs face the street, forming courtyards, while the main focus of the house is from the opposite side toward the common open space, bicycle paths and footpaths, and creekside natural drainage (Figure 16.5). All buildings have south-facing solar access and incorporate passive solar heating and cooling principles. Corbett showed that incorporating solar and efficient design principles could be done with little or no added investment, because of cost savings from downsized furnaces and air conditioners.

The experience with Village Homes led the city of Davis to change its energy building code, and that code later became the basis for California's building code—still one of the most progressive energy building codes in the country. Studies of Village Homes compared with control neighborhoods in Davis have shown that Village Homes residents use 36% less energy for vehicular driving, 47% less electricity, and 31% less natural gas. Initially, houses in Village Homes sold for the

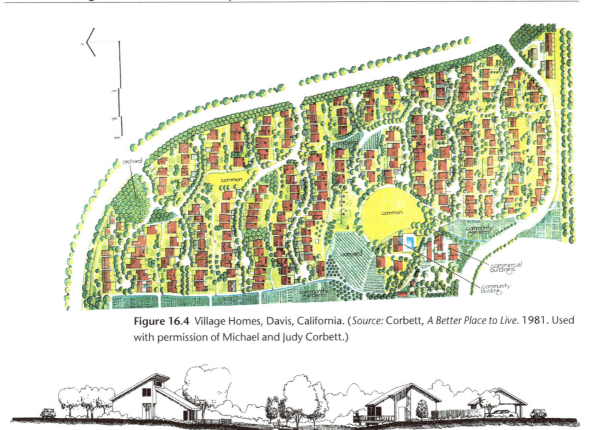

Figure 16.4 Village Homes, Davis, California. (*Source:* Corbett, *A Better Place to Live*. 1981. Used with permission of Michael and Judy Corbett.)

Figure 16.5 A Typical Village Homes Section, Davis, California. Streets are more like alleys, and houses face the common area and natural drainage channels. (*Source:* Corbett, *A Better Place to Live*. 1981; Corbett and Corbett 2000. Used with permission of Michael and Judy Corbett.)

same price as other houses in Davis, but by the mid-1990s, they sold for $11 per square foot more. Village Homes showed that it is possible to design very compact and attractive neighborhoods by using natural areas to provide a sense of space.

The Ahwahnee Principles (1991) and Charter for the New Urbanism (1993)

In 1991, California's Local Government Commission (LGC), founded by Judy Corbett, brought together six prominent designers to develop a set of community planning principles. These principles, which were presented to a group of 100 local elected officials at a conference at the Ahwahnee Hotel in Yosemite National Park, came to be known as the Ahwahnee Principles for Resource-Efficient Communities; they are summarized in Box 16.1. The Ahwahnee Preamble states:

Existing patterns of urban and suburban development seriously impair our quality of life. The symptoms are: more congestion and air pollution resulting from our increased dependence on automobiles, the loss of precious open

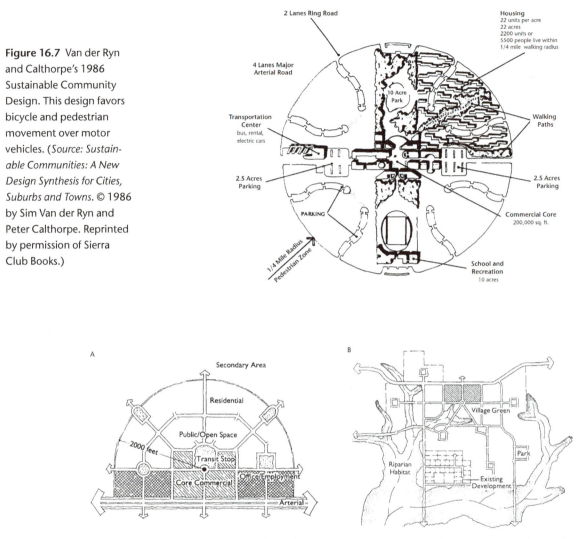

Figure 16.7 Van der Ryn and Calthorpe's 1986 Sustainable Community Design. This design favors bicycle and pedestrian movement over motor vehicles. (*Source: Sustainable Communities: A New Design Synthesis for Cities, Suburbs and Towns.* © 1986 by Sim Van der Ryn and Peter Calthorpe. Reprinted by permission of Sierra Club Books.)

Figure 16.8 Transit-Oriented Development. A: Calthorpe's original TOD concept. B: Conserving natural drainage in a TOD neighborhood. (*Source:* Peter Calthorpe, *The Next Metropolis: Ecology and the American Dream.* © 1993 Princeton Architectural Press. Used with permission.)

centers. Calthorpe envisions regional development that ties a central city to its surrounding bounded urban growth area made up of TODs linked by rail and bus transit.

There are many contemporary examples of TODs (see California TOD database, http://transitorienteddevelopment.dot.ca.gov/, and Reconnecting America's Center for TOD, www.cnt.org/tcd/ctod). Figure 16.9 illustrates TOD in Arlington County (Virginia). When the Washington Metro rail system was being developed, Arlington County lobbied to run the system underground along its existing commercial corridor rather than aboveground along the freeway corridor. This brilliant

Figure 16.6 The Spatial Impact of Automobile Dependency. A: 40 Tampa Bay residents in their cars. B: The same people sitting where their cars were. C: Their locations if they were on a bus. D: The same 40 people walking and riding their bicycles. (*Source:* Beamguard 1999. Used with permission of the *Tampa Tribune.*)

Cities, McHarg's Plan for the Valleys (see Figure 16.3C), and Corbett's Village Homes. Walkability has become a consistent design feature for community and neighborhood revitalization.

Peter Calthorpe championed the transportation aspects of sustainable design, first through the "pedestrian pockets," then transit connection, finally through regional integration (Calthorpe 1993; Calthorpe and Fulton 2001). Figure 16.7 shows a sustainable community design from Van der Ryn and Calthorpe (1986), which includes mixed use, a discrete town center, and neighborhoods within a short walking radius. This town design could accommodate 5,500 people within 0.25 mi of the town center, while still providing about 20% open space.

Calthorpe's well-known **transit-oriented development (TOD)** concept is illustrated in Figure 16.8A. TOD is a mixed-use community within walking distance of a transit stop and core commercial area. Each TOD is a pedestrian pocket, with residential and public spaces within 2,000 ft of the transit stop. Although the 2,000-ft-radius TOD is intended to be densely developed, the design aims to conserve riparian lands and other environmentally sensitive areas, as shown in Figure 16.8B. Secondary areas, those outside the central area, have lower densities and accommodate agricultural uses. TODs are linked together and to urban centers by bus or rail transit to form a network of dense, walkable, mixed-use community

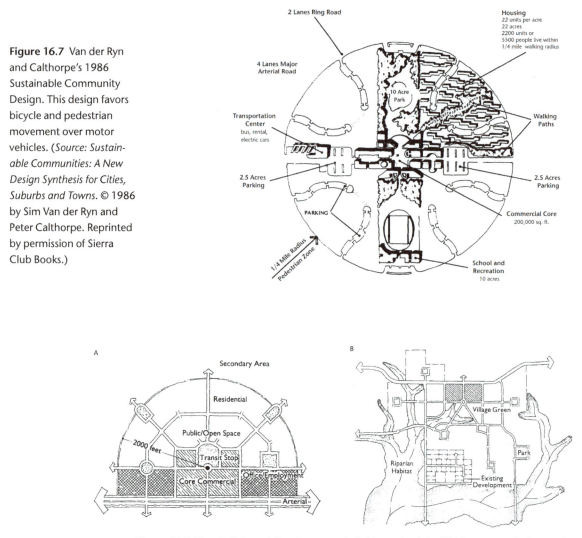

Figure 16.7 Van der Ryn and Calthorpe's 1986 Sustainable Community Design. This design favors bicycle and pedestrian movement over motor vehicles. (*Source: Sustainable Communities: A New Design Synthesis for Cities, Suburbs and Towns.* © 1986 by Sim Van der Ryn and Peter Calthorpe. Reprinted by permission of Sierra Club Books.)

Figure 16.8 Transit-Oriented Development. A: Calthorpe's original TOD concept. B: Conserving natural drainage in a TOD neighborhood. (*Source:* Peter Calthorpe, *The Next Metropolis: Ecology and the American Dream.* © 1993 Princeton Architectural Press. Used with permission.)

centers. Calthorpe envisions regional development that ties a central city to its surrounding bounded urban growth area made up of TODs linked by rail and bus transit.

There are many contemporary examples of TODs (see California TOD database, http://transitorienteddevelopment.dot.ca.gov/, and Reconnecting America's Center for TOD, www.cnt.org/tcd/ctod). Figure 16.9 illustrates TOD in Arlington County (Virginia). When the Washington Metro rail system was being developed, Arlington County lobbied to run the system underground along its existing commercial corridor rather than aboveground along the freeway corridor. This brilliant

spaces, the need for costly improvements to roads and public services, the inequitable distribution of economic resources, and the loss of a sense of community. By drawing upon the best from the past and present, we can plan communities that will more successfully serve the needs of those who live and work within them. Such planning should adhere to certain fundamental principles. (Ahwahnee Principles 1991, 1)

These principles spawned subsequent LGC Ahwahnee Principles for economic development (1997), water (2005), and climate change (2008) (see http://www .lgc.org/ahwahnee/principles.html). They also were the basis for the Congress for the New Urbanism (CNU), founded in 1993, and its Charter of the New Urbanism ratified by CNU in 1996 (http://www.cnu.org/charter). Among the Charter's proclamations:

We stand for the restoration of existing urban centers and towns within coherent metropolitan regions, the reconfiguration of sprawling suburbs into communities of real neighborhoods and diverse districts, the conservation of natural environments, and the preservation of our built legacy. We advocate the restructuring of public policy and development practices to support the following principles: neighborhoods should be diverse in use and population; communities should be designed for the pedestrian and transit as well as the car; cities and towns should be shaped by physically defined and universally accessible public spaces and community institutions; urban places should be framed by architecture and landscape design that celebrate local history, climate, ecology, and building practice. (CNU Charter 1993, 1)

New Urbanist communities emphasize compact form, walkability, and public space. In 1999, *Newsweek* called the "New Urbanism" movement the great vision for community development in the new century. The issue featured Peter Calthorpe, a California architect and planner known for his work in sustainable communities (Van der Ryn and Calthorpe 1986), and Andres Duany, a Florida architect known for new community designs in Seaside, Florida, and Kentlands, Maryland.

New Urbanism (NU) and Smart Growth have become the defining movements for sustainable community design and development. Initially, there were three basic critiques of New Urbanism:

1. Some advocates of design freedom criticized the restrictive nature of many NU community covenants that they thought inhibited new ideas and innovation.
2. Social justice advocates criticized the "upscale" and expensive nature of many early NU developments that worked against goals of mixed-income housing and social diversity; few NU projects have successfully accommodated affordable housing, and this continues to be one of the biggest challenges for the NU movement.
3. Environmentalists criticized some early eastern U.S. NU developments for limited integration of environmental factors. Indeed, the charter

emphasizes social, economic, and community-identity issues and includes only the following environmental planning and design principles:

- *For the region:* The metropolitan area should gain definition from its natural boundaries, and it has a necessary and fragile relationship with its agrarian hinterland and natural landscapes.
- *For the neighborhood:* Conservation areas and open lands should be used to define and connect different neighborhoods and districts; walkable neighborhoods conserve energy and reduce air pollution.
- *For the block and building:* Natural methods of heating and cooling can be more resource-efficient than mechanical systems.

Smart Mobility to Reduce Automobile Dependency: Pedestrian- and Transit-Oriented Development

The automobile enabled sprawl, and sprawl is dependent on the automobile. As a result, our collective dependence on cars is one of the main causes of environmental damage done by communities, with its direct links to urban air pollution, carbon emissions, impervious surfaces for roads and parking, and traffic congestion. Figure 16.6 illustrates the spatial impact of auto dependency in Tampa Bay (Florida).

Reducing the amount of reliance on motor vehicles is a major step toward a sustainable community. In Chapter 12, we introduced the notion of the five D's of efficient land use in the built environment that influence a decrease in driving, suggested by Cervero and Kockelman (1997) and expanded by others (Ewing and Cervero 2010; NRC 2009):

- *Density:* Population and employment per developed acre.
- *Diversity:* Mix of residential and commercial land uses, schools, public spaces, jobs-housing balance.
- *Design:* Neighborhood layout, sidewalks, street connectivity, shade, scenery, aesthetics.
- *Destination accessibility:* Ease and convenience of trip from point of origin.
- *Distance to transit:* Bus or rail stop within 0.25–0.5 mi from home or work.

Ewing and Cervano (2010) add two more D's to the list that influence travel choice: demand management of parking supply and cost, and demographics (e.g., age, income).

Getting people out of their cars requires giving them convenient, timely, safe, and cost-effective alternatives, which are primarily walking, bicycling, and using public transit. These options are not viable in suburban segregated land use patterns, where density is too low to support public transit and distances to destinations are too long for walking and biking. But the five D's of community design can reduce walking distances for daily activities. Walkable scale is a feature of traditional neighborhoods and planned communities, including Howard's Garden

Figure 16.4 Village Homes, Davis, California. (*Source:* Corbett, *A Better Place to Live.* 1981. Used with permission of Michael and Judy Corbett.)

Figure 16.5 A Typical Village Homes Section, Davis, California. Streets are more like alleys, and houses face the common area and natural drainage channels. (*Source:* Corbett, *A Better Place to Live.* 1981; Corbett and Corbett 2000. Used with permission of Michael and Judy Corbett.)

same price as other houses in Davis, but by the mid-1990s, they sold for $11 per square foot more. Village Homes showed that it is possible to design very compact and attractive neighborhoods by using natural areas to provide a sense of space.

The Ahwahnee Principles (1991) and Charter for the New Urbanism (1993)

In 1991, California's Local Government Commission (LGC), founded by Judy Corbett, brought together six prominent designers to develop a set of community planning principles. These principles, which were presented to a group of 100 local elected officials at a conference at the Ahwahnee Hotel in Yosemite National Park, came to be known as the Ahwahnee Principles for Resource-Efficient Communities; they are summarized in Box 16.1. The Ahwahnee Preamble states:

Existing patterns of urban and suburban development seriously impair our quality of life. The symptoms are: more congestion and air pollution resulting from our increased dependence on automobiles, the loss of precious open

1. All planning should be in the form of complete and integrated communities containing housing, shops, work places, schools, parks and civic facilities essential to the daily life of the residents.
2. Community size should be designed so that housing, jobs, daily needs and other activities are within easy walking distance of each other.
3. As many activities as possible should be located within easy walking distance of transit stops.
4. A community should contain a diversity of housing types to enable citizens from a wide range of economic levels and age groups to live within its boundaries.
5. Businesses within the community should provide a range of job types for the community's residents.
6. The location and character of the community should be consistent with a larger transit network.
7. The community should have a center focus that combines commercial, civic, cultural and recreational uses.
8. The community should contain an ample supply of specialized open space in the form of squares, greens and parks whose frequent use is encouraged through placement and design.
9. Public spaces should be designed to encourage the attention and presence of people at all hours of the day and night.
10. **Each community or cluster of communities should have a well-defined edge, such as agricultural greenbelts or wildlife corridors, permanently protected from development.**
11. Streets, pedestrian paths, and bike paths should contribute to a system of fully connected, interesting routes to all destinations. Their design should encourage pedestrian and bicycle use by being small and spatially defined by buildings, trees, and lighting; and by discouraging high-speed traffic.
12. **Wherever possible, the natural terrain, drainage and vegetation of the community should be preserved with superior examples contained within parks or greenbelts.**
13. **The community design should help conserve resources and minimize waste.**
14. **Communities should provide for the efficient use of water through the use of natu-** ral drainage, drought tolerant landscaping and recycling.
15. **The street orientation, the placement of buildings and the use of shading should contribute to the energy efficiency of the community.**

Regional Principles

16. The regional land-use planning structure should be integrated within a larger transportation network built around transit rather than freeways.
17. **Regions should be bounded by and provide a continuous system of greenbelt/wildlife corridors to be determined by natural conditions.**
18. Regional institutions and services (government, stadiums, museums, etc.) should be located in the urban core.
19. Materials and methods of construction should be specific to the region, exhibiting a continuity of history and culture and compatibility with the climate to encourage the development of local character and community identity.

Implementation Principles

20. The general plan should be updated to incorporate the above principles.
21. Rather than allowing developer-initiated, piecemeal development, local governments should take charge of the planning process. General plans should designate where new growth, infill, or redevelopment will be allowed to occur.
22. Prior to any development, a specific plan should be prepared based on these planning principles.
23. Plans should be developed through an open process and participants in the process should be provided visual models of all planning proposals.

Natural environment and resource efficiency features are in boldface type.

Source: Adapted from Ahwahnee Principles (1991). Authors/Editors: Peter Calthorpe, Peter Katz, Michael Corbett, Judy Corbett, Andres Duany, Steve Weissman, Elizabeth Moule, Elizabeth Plater-Zyberk, Stefanos Polyzoides.

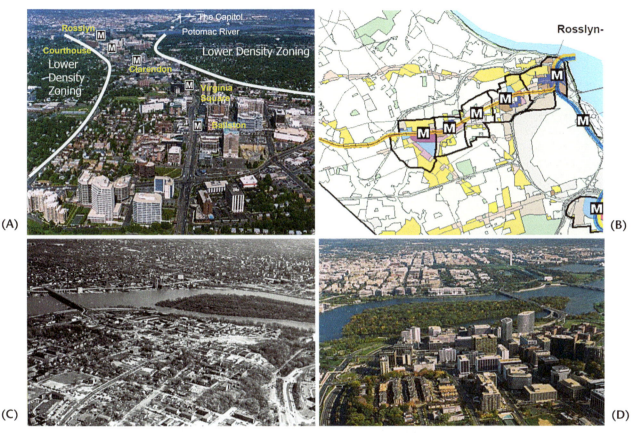

Figure 16.9 TOD in Arlington County, Virginia. A: The Arlington TOD corridor along the Washington Metro line. B: Map showing the Metro stations along the corridor. C: Roslyn before the Metro stations were built. C: Roslyn today. (*Source:* Arlington County 2009; Brosnan 2010.)

move enabled the development of several TODs along the Metro route, with Rosslyn and Ballston being principal nodes. Figure 16.9 shows the Metro stations along this corridor, the zoning approach to encourage dense development within the corridor, and aerial photos of Rosslyn before the Metro stations were built and the dense mixed-use transit-oriented community it is today (Arlington 2009).

Portland's growth management (see Chapter 18) has produced urban densities that support a diverse transit system, including the MAX rail transit system. Tri-Met operates the bus transit system and Portland has a downtown trolley system, both of which are coordinated with MAX. That system has facilitated the development of dense TOD community centers at the transit stations. Figure 16.10 shows the seventeen TODs that have been developed on the rail and trolley lines, and others on bus lines. It highlights four notable TODs: the well-celebrated Orenco Station, the Pearl District, Collins Circle, and the new Gateway/Oregon Clinic. Figure 16.11 is a photograph of Portland's light rail train at a TOD stop.

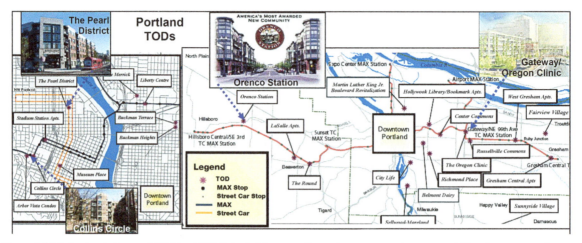

Figure 16.10 Portland, Oregon's Tri-Met MAX Light Rail System. Shown here are two downtown TODs: Gateway on the east side and Orenco on the west side. (*Source:* Randolph and Masters 2008.)

Figure 16.11 A Light Rail Stop in Portland at a Mixed-Use Neighborhood Center. (*Source:* www.pedbikeimage.org. Photo by Dan Burden.)

Not all locations can be rail transit TODs, but express bus nodes may also be appropriate for denser development. Still, not all developments can eliminate automobile dependency. Calthorpe Associates (2000) distinguishes three categories of communities based on transportation orientation:

1. *Walkable and/or transit-oriented areas* include villages, towns, traditional neighborhoods, TODs, and urban downtowns (e.g, Arlington and Portland TODs).

2. *Auto-oriented non-land-conserving developments* include large-lot sub-divisions, other residential subdivisions, and large activity centers like shopping malls or industrial parks (e.g. conventional suburban sprawl).

3. *Auto-oriented, land-conserving developments* include rural or residential clusters (e.g., Village Homes, conservation subdivisions). Residents of these developments, like suburban subdivisions, rely on motor vehicles for travel to work, school, and commerce, but their communities are compact, provide significant community open space, and can be dense enough to provide local walking-distance shops and services that reduce automobile use.

The Urban Transect and the Density Gradient

A standard design is not going to work everywhere, and we must plan, design, and develop to the specific location and environment. That is the point of Andres Duany's Urban Transect, which was introduced in Chapter 3 and is illustrated in Figure 16.12. First published as a note in *Scientific American* in 2000 (Duany 2000), the Transect was devised as a way of looking at a region's diversity in a way that might guide designers, planners, and developers in formulating sustainable designs, plans, and codes appropriate to the place. The **Urban Transect** is a geographic cross section or gradient of a region that reveals a sequence of environments; it identifies a set of human and natural environments that vary by their level and intensity of urban character, a continuum that ranges from natural zone and rural to urban core. Transect planning uses this range of environments as the

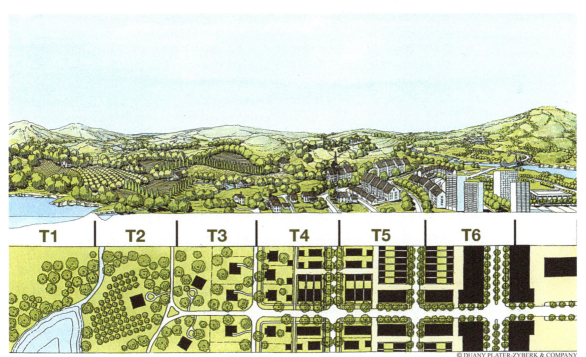

© DUANY PLATER-ZYBERK & COMPANY

Figure 16.12 Duany's Urban Transect. (*Source:* Duany Plater-Zyberk and Company 2011. Used with permission.)

basis for organizing the components of the land development: building, lot, land use, street, infrastructure, and other physical elements (Duany and Talen 2002).

The Transect shows six zones (plus an assigned district zone), which are unique in density and character and define an "immersive" or dominant environment that should determine its development form. As a tool for Smart Growth, this approach tries to eliminate "urbanizing the rural," or sprawl development, because it doesn't fit the dominant environment of the rural zone. Likewise, "ruralizing the urban" with undefined, vacant open space does not fit the model. The assigned district zone can provide some flexibility in what may appear to be an overly rigid approach. The six zones can be described in many ways. Here's a start:

- **T1, T2: Natural and Rural Zones** have strong ecological and agrarian elements with protected legacy farmlands, woodlands, viewsheds, water resources, natural drainage, and habitats, but have their own transects from small towns, hamlets, and villages.
- **T3, T4: Suburban and General Urban Zones** transition to urban and are primarily residential and some mixed-use, open swales and low-impact development, parks, and greens.
- **T5, T6: Urban Center and Core Zones** have the most density, greatest mixed use, largest buildings, more impervious surface, stormwater pipes and treatment, and plazas and squares.

The Transect has been applied to many different types of plans, including regional, new community, infill development, and comprehensive (Hall 2010). We discussed in Chapter 8 how Tom Low's light-imprint design approach for stormwater and green infrastructure is guided by the Transect (see Figure 8.4). Others use the Transect to discuss how to increase density and still fit dominant environments in various zones using small-footprint densities, including duplexes, fourplexes, and bungalow courts and cottages (Parolek et al. 2010).

The most significant application of the Urban Transect is its use in developing the **SmartCode**, which was released by Duany Plater-Zyberk and Company (DPZ) in 2003 and has taken the planning world by storm. It is a form-based code (FBC) that folds together zoning, subdivision regulations, urban design, public works standards, and basic architectural controls into an integrated land development ordinance. It is a unified ordinance that can move across the Transect and span scales from the region to the community to the building. (FBC and the SmartCode are discussed in Chapter 17.)

Traditional Neighborhood Design: Walkable Places, Complete Streets, Mixed Use, Mixed Income

Appropriate density along the Transect is but one of the key elements of sustainable community design. To become walkable and diverse, neighborhoods need to mix land uses and building types, and a proportion of residential housing units must be affordable enough to accommodate a diverse range of household incomes. This can be achieved with a mix of housing and building types, including apartments above first-floor mixed-use shops, multifamily apartment buildings,

Figure 16.13 Traditional Urban Neighborhoods. Left: A walkable street in Columbus, Ohio. Right: A vibrant mixed-use neighborhood center in Madison, Wisconsin. (*Source:* www.pedbikeimage.org. Eric Lowry, Dan Burden.)

and small-footprint density options, such as multiplexes and cottages. Walkability is enhanced by "complete" streets, which are designed and retrofitted to provide safe, convenient, and pleasing pedestrian access and (ideally) bicycle travel, while accommodating the automobile (Seskin 2010). Complete pedestrian streets are enhanced by "green street" retrofits that use vegetation, swales, bioretention, and other stormwater controls (see Chapter 8 and Portland EcoDistricts, below).

Traditional urban neighborhoods that were developed in the first half of the twentieth century in most U.S. cities have a greater diversity of housing types and residential, retail, and other services within walking distance, as well as access to transit (Figure 16.13).

During the past decade, there have been several hundred new developments and redevelopments that are labeled either traditional neighborhood design (TND) or New Urbanism developments, or they include the features of compact, mixed-use, and mixed-building type, and walkable design. Many have incorporated affordable housing units that add income diversity. King Farm is an example.

King Farm, Rockville, Maryland

This development, outside of Washington, DC, is close to both the Shady Grove Metro heavy rail transit station and Interstate 270. The 430-acre development includes single-family and multifamily residential units in two neighborhoods around a town center, parks and open space, and a commercial office activity center providing considerable local employment (Figure 16.14).

Green Neighborhoods, Green Buildings

Sustainable communities are, first and foremost, green communities. After hundreds of pages of this book, we should know the basic elements of an environmentally sustainable green community:

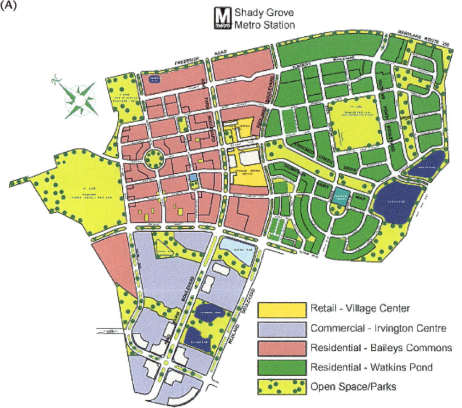

Shady Grove
Metro Station

Retail - Village Center

Commercial - Irvington Centre

Residential - Baileys Commons

Residential - Watkins Pond

Open Space/Parks

Interstate 270 - Exit 8

(A)

(B)

(C)

Figure 16.14 King Farm New Urbanism Development, Rockville, Maryland. A: Overall plan map. B: The village center. C: Single-family homes and open space. (*Source:* King Farm Associates, L.L.C. www.kingfarm.com. Used with permission.)

1. **Preservation and Restoration of Natural Systems**
   - Water resource protection (natural drainage, riparian lands, shore-lines, stormwater, groundwater, watershed management).
   - Environmental resource land protection (agricultural lands, recreation lands, open space).
   - Ecologically sensitive land preservation (natural heritage, wildlife habitats, wetlands).
   - Protection and resilience against natural hazards (floodplains, slopes, seismic hazard, coastal storms, impacts of climate change).

2. **Efficient Use of Resources**
   - Conservation of land (compact development).
   - Conservation of material resources (efficient use of indigenous materials, recycling).
   - Green energy (energy-efficient buildings, transportation, land use; distributed renewable energy).

3. **Environmental Health Protection**
   - Remediation of toxic and hazardous sites.
   - Air quality management, air pollutant and GHG emission reduction.
   - Water quality management, source water protection.
   - Waste management and recycling.
   - Secure, safe, healthy local food system, including community gardens and urban farms.
   - Opportunities for active living.

We also know many of the planning and design measures for achieving these elements: stormwater management, source water protection, natural hazard mitigation, climate change energy mitigation and adaptation, forest and habitat protection, green infrastructure planning, and land conservation.

The building blocks of green and sustainable communities are their buildings, sites, and neighborhoods. And it is important to fit those building blocks together with efficient land use and green transportation. Figure 12.13 showed the relative house and transportation energy use for conventional and green single-family and multifamily households in suburban and urban settings. Based on reasonable hypothetical assumptions, green households with efficient structures, vehicles, and conserving lifestyles consume about half the energy of their nongreen counterparts. But urban households with shorter travel distances, access to transit, and typically smaller dwelling units than their suburban counterparts consume about one-third less. The urban multifamily green household consumes just 21% of the suburban average and 40% of the suburban green household.

Green Building design and construction have begun to influence the real estate markets in many regions of the country. California and Colorado have statewide Green Building requirements, and many local Green Building programs, like those in Boulder (Colorado) and Austin (Texas), have captured the residential real estate market.

In Chapter 14, we discussed Green Building rating systems, and Table 14.4 is a checklist for the U.S. Green Building Council (USGBC) LEED protocol for new

Figure 16.15 USGBC LEED-Certified Projects in California. Left: Vista Dunes, La Quinta: Platinum for LEED-Homes. Right: Emeryville Marketplace: Platinum for LEED-ND. (*Source:* USGBC 2010.)

building construction. The criteria include measures for *sustainable sites* (e.g., brownfield redevelopment, habitat protection), *water efficiency* (indoors, land-scaping), *energy and atmosphere* (energy performance, onsite renewable generation), *materials* (regional sources, recycled content), *indoor environmental quality* (ventilation, low-emitting materials), and *design innovation*. In 2007, there were only 230 LEED-certified buildings in North America; by August 2010, there were 13,500 and more than 50,000 were registered and being reviewed for certification. Figure 16.15A shows a USGBC LEED Platinum profile of the La Quinta (California) City Redevelopment Agency's project, which turned 9 acres in a blighted neighborhood into 80 affordable rental units for those earning 30–50% of the area median income. A key feature is onsite solar generation of 70% of anticipated electricity demand.

Individual green buildings and sites are great, but we know that buildings alone will not make green neighborhoods. LEED-Neighborhood Development (ND) rates green neighborhoods and has quickly become an accepted measure for assessing neighborhood sustainability. Table 14.5, the checklist for LEED-ND, has three main categories: *smart location and linkage* (reduced auto dependence, housing and jobs proximity, habitat protection); *neighborhood pattern and design* (walkable streets, compact development, mixed use), and *green infrastructure and buildings* (certified green building, energy efficiency, stormwater management). Figure 16.16B is a profile of the Emeryville (California) Marketplace project, one of the program's pilots and the first project to get LEED-ND Platinum certification. The project is redeveloping a brownfield site into 1.2 million sq ft of rehabilitated and new office, retail, residential, and open space. It will provide 136 dwelling units per acre and generate more than 400 transit trips daily.

High Point, West Seattle

One of the best-known green neighborhood development projects is Seattle's High Point neighborhood. Originally the site of government housing during World War II, it served low-income residents through the 1990s. In 2003, the Seattle Housing Authority began a redevelopment of the 120-acre property into a mixed-income community, and with the design assistance of Mithun Architects and SvR Design Company, it has become a model for a green and affordable community. Its principal sustainable neighborhood features are its diverse socioeconomic population, its livable community design, its energy efficiency, and its superior natural drainage system (Phillips and Staeheli 2010).

Of the 1,700 housing units, 50% serve market rate owners and renters, 29% serve renters with less than 30% of median income, 16% renters with less than 60% median income, and 5% owners with less than 80% median income. Housing units feature BuiltGreen certification and Energy Star and Breath Easy ratings. With mixed use, narrow streets, and community open space, it is a quality pedestrian environment.

Figure 16.16 shows High Point's green features, of which its natural drainage system is the most unique. It has a drainage waterflow and open space system, community stormwater pond park, and sidewalks and narrow streets lined with 15,000 linear feet of swales. (The swale system and pond park are shown in Figures 8.17 and 8.23.)

Portland EcoDistricts

Portland EcoDistricts was launched in 2009 as a joint project of the Portland Sustainability Institute, the City of Portland, Portland Metro, and other partners to retrofit and redevelop specific neighborhoods to serve as models of sustainability. The project was inspired by neighborhood-based projects in Malmo, Sweden; the Vancouver Olympic Village; London's Low-Carbon Zones; and EcoCity Cleveland, among others. The EcoDistricts project is described as a "whole systems" green neighborhood investment strategy that integrates resource efficiency, ecological diversity, mobility, and community well-being, bringing together people and institutions in new governance structures to set goals, assemble capital, manage assets, and monitor results. It is an experiment using the community as the laboratory (Bennett 2010).

Figure 16.17A shows the location of the five EcoDistricts. The primary performance areas are GHG emissions, energy, mobility, water, habitat and ecosystem

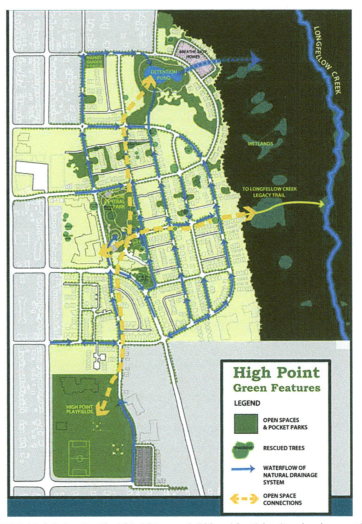

Figure 16.16 High Point, Seattle. This 120-acre, 1,700 residential unit redevelopment's green features include natural drainage and open space, with a stormwater pond park. (*Source:* Phillips and Staeheli 2010. SvR Design, Seattle. Used with permission.)

function, materials management, and community vitality. The EcoDistricts are likely to use a range of neighborhood-scale sustainable technologies (Figure 16.17B): green streets for natural drainage and other benefits, district heating and cooling, water reuse, and smart grid. The whole community approach will apply energy and carbon balance methods to determine a baseline and a basis for monitoring. Figure 16.17C shows initial opportunities for the South Waterfront EcoDistrict, including green street and mobility options, LEED development projects, and natural areas and natural drainage. The Ecodistricts will also pilot Portland's aggressive residential energy retrofit program, which aims to retrofit 32,000 homes over 3 years (Bennett 2010).

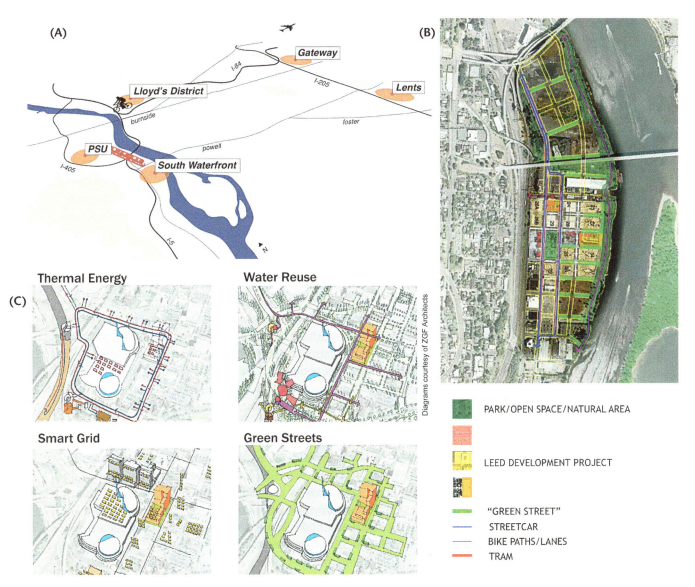

Figure 16.17 Portland EcoDistricts. A: The five EcoDistricts. B: Neighborhood-scale technologies. C: Systems integration options. (*Source:* Bennett 2010; PSI 2010. Used with permission.)

Green Redevelopment: Restoring Brownfields, Regenerating Shrinking Cities, and Retrofitting Suburbs

Many of the project examples presented above fit into this category of sustainable design and planning because they are redevelopment projects. In fact, most major projects in U.S. cities are redevelopments. And that is good, because redevelopment improves existing properties, infills where there is existing infrastructure, revitalizes rundown neighborhoods, and relieves development pressures on outlying green farmland and habitat. In other words, it is Smart Growth.

Highland Garden Village, Denver. Figure 16.18 illustrates this compact, mixed-use neighborhood built on 27 acres 10 minutes from downtown Denver. It was previously the site of Elitch Gardens Amusement Park, which was abandoned in 1994. The project transformed the site into a mixed-use neighborhood with diverse community amenities, new open spaces, and a variety of housing opportunities. The community's pedestrian-friendly design, developed by Jonathan Rose Company partnering with Calthorpe Associates, provides safe and

Figure 16.18 Highland Garden Village, Denver. A: The site plan shows this mixed-use redevelopment, built on a former amusement park site. B: A single-family residential area. C: The commercial center. (*Source:* Jonathan Rose Companies, 2010. Used with permission. U.S. EPA 2010b.)

The first edition of this book contained additional information on the federal Brownfields Program, and that material is posted on the book website (www .envirolanduse.org). Also, see the EPA website for more information, especially success stories, which you can identify by location (http://epa.gov/brownfields/ success/index.htm).

Regenerating Shrinking Cities

As Figure 16.2 indicates, several U.S. cities are enjoying an "urban rebound," with a large and growing share of regional development occurring in the central city. Others are not as lucky. Detroit, Cleveland, St. Louis, Rochester, Buffalo, and others have less than 10% of their region's development, and a declining share of it is in the central city. These are shrinking cities, which are characterized as older industrial cities with significant and sustained population loss and increasing levels of vacant and abandoned properties, including blighted buildings and brownfields. Revitalizing these shrinking cities is a major planning challenge.

As discussed in Chapter 3, Schilling and Logan (2009) describe a number of planning responses to "right-size" these shrinking cities, including building community consensus through collaborative neighborhood planning; limiting services; and stabilizing dysfunctional markets and distressed neighborhoods by replacing vacant and abandoned properties with green infrastructure and land banks, thus converting blighted land into community green space.

Several cities are taking this latter approach, and their plans reflect their intent:

- Reimagining a More Sustainable Cleveland
- Leaner, Greener Detroit
- Rochester's Project Green
- Philadelphia's Greenworks Plan
- Cincinnati Green Infrastructure
- Youngstown Vacant Property Initiative

Some of the initiatives include stabilizing vacant properties with vegetative planting, converting them to community gardens and pocket parks, and integrating low-impact development (LID) stormwater management measures, such as bioretention and swales (Schilling 2010). In 2007, Cincinnati developed an agreement with the EPA to use GI on vacant and other properties as one of its strategies in the municipal separate stormwater system (MS4) compliance.

Retrofitting Suburbs

Older suburban shopping centers and other ineffectively used suburban properties have become ripe for redevelopment. These so-called grayfields have been converted into greener, mixed-use, walkable, and livable neighborhoods. Retrofitting suburbs has become an emerging area of redevelopment (Slone 2010). Highland Garden Village in Denver is a good example.

Highland Garden Village, Denver. Figure 16.18 illustrates this compact, mixed-use neighborhood built on 27 acres 10 minutes from downtown Denver. It was previously the site of Elitch Gardens Amusement Park, which was abandoned in 1994. The project transformed the site into a mixed-use neighborhood with diverse community amenities, new open spaces, and a variety of housing opportunities. The community's pedestrian-friendly design, developed by Jonathan Rose Company partnering with Calthorpe Associates, provides safe and

Figure 16.18 Highland Garden Village, Denver. A: The site plan shows this mixed-use redevelopment, built on a former amusement park site. B: A single-family residential area. C: The commercial center. (*Source:* Jonathan Rose Companies, 2010. Used with permission. U.S. EPA 2010b.)

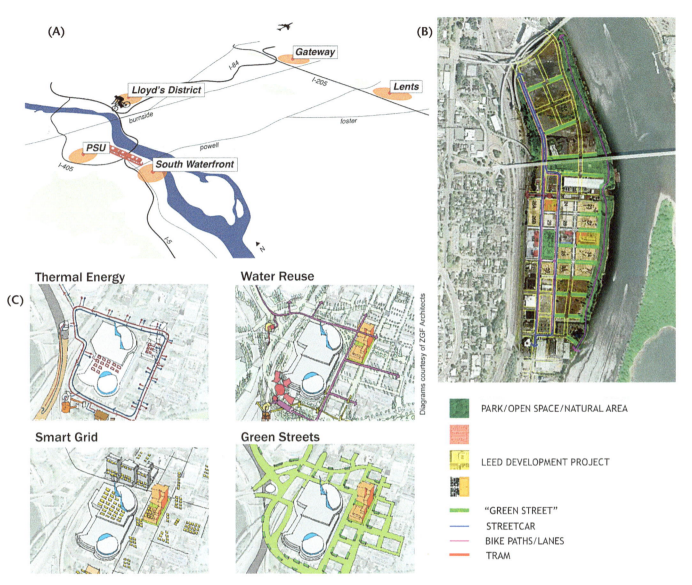

Figure 16.17 Portland EcoDistricts. A: The five EcoDistricts. B: Neighborhood-scale technologies. C: Systems integration options. (*Source:* Bennett 2010; PSI 2010. Used with permission.)

Green Redevelopment: Restoring Brownfields, Regenerating Shrinking Cities, and Retrofitting Suburbs

Many of the project examples presented above fit into this category of sustainable design and planning because they are redevelopment projects. In fact, most major projects in U.S. cities are redevelopments. And that is good, because redevelopment improves existing properties, infills where there is existing infrastructure, revitalizes rundown neighborhoods, and relieves development pressures on outlying green farmland and habitat. In other words, it is Smart Growth.

However, one problem with redevelopment for developers—especially large, innovative, and green development—is that creative designs rarely fit the existing land use zoning and building ordinances, so just about every significant project requires a rezoning or even a comprehensive plan revision. This causes considerable time, expense, and political and financial uncertainty, all of which constrain the redevelopment process (Nelson et al. 2009). The SmartCode was developed to relieve this problem. Federal, state, and local programs can also help by offering incentives for redevelopment projects and/or restricting development on outlying greenspace to make infill projects more desirable.

Three areas of interest for redevelopment are brownfields, regeneration of vacant land in cities with declining populations, and retrofitting suburbs from segregated automobile-oriented uses to more walkable, mixed-use, and livable places.

Restoring Brownfields

As defined by the EPA, **brownfields** are abandoned, idled, or underused industrial and commercial facilities where expansion or redevelopment is complicated by real or perceived environmental contamination. Obstacles to redevelopment are created by two uncertainties: the possible level of existing contamination on the site and the responsibility for that contamination should ties to the property be established. Federal cleanup laws, such as the Resource Conservation and Recovery Act (RCRA) and the Superfund Act, established strict standards for those responsible for contaminated property, thus discouraging many potential investors from redevelopment projects, even though most brownfield sites are not classified as Superfund sites.

Brownfields are a major environmental, real estate, community, and aesthetic problem in U.S. cities. In 2004, the U.S. GAO (2004) estimated there were 450,000–1,000,000 brownfield sites in communities across the United States. Brownfield redevelopment can provide the benefits of urban infill given above and can also help remove environmental hazards from the community. As a result, cleanup and redevelopment efforts have received wide-ranging community, state, and federal support. It appears that this money has been well spent. In 2001, the EPA estimated that for every brownfield acre redeveloped into residential and commercial uses, an estimated 21 acres of greenfields are protected (U.S. EPA 2001a). As of 2009, the EPA (2010a) estimated that federal funds for brownfield redevelopment have:

- Leveraged almost $18 for redevelopment for every federal dollar expended.
- Created 7.5 jobs per $100,000 from the EPA and 65,000 jobs since the inception of the Brownfields Program.
- Created greater locational efficiency than alternative greenfield development, thus reducing subsequent vehicle miles traveled and associated air pollution and GHG emissions by 32–57%, and decreasing stormwater runoff by 43–60%.
- Improved values of surrounding property.

convenient walking paths, with connectivity to primary areas of interest. The planning team developed the design and engaged surrounding neighbors in the process. There is a density gradient with highest densities near the commercial area and lowest densities near the existing neighborhoods of single-family homes. Important cultural amenities at Highland Garden Village include a school, a walkable retail village, and a historic theater from the former amusement park renovated by a local nonprofit organization. A network of gardens, plazas, and open spaces creates a vibrant, friendly neighborhood with ample public meeting space. The project won the EPA's 2005 National Award for Smart Growth Achievement (Calthorpe Associates 2010; Jonathan Rose 2010; U.S. EPA 2010b).

Rural Community Development

The focus of Smart Growth is concentrating growth in existing development areas, where infrastructure exists and it is more likely that densities to support mass transit can be achieved. This applies at the dense end of the Urban Transect, but it also applies at the less-dense rural end, where small cities and villages can also benefit from the same design principles.

Prairie Crossing, Grayslake, Illinois

There are not many transit-oriented rural community developments, but Prairie Crossing is one. Located 40 miles north of Chicago, the development is at the crossing of two major commuter rail lines (Figure 16.19). The 678-acre mixed-use development has 362 housing units on 135 acres, or 20% of the site; 69% is protected farmland (included a 100-acre organic farm) and amenity open space; and 11% is for commercial and industrial space, a community center, and three schools. Prairie Crossing has both single-family homes and condominium units. The community has ten principles: environmental protection and enhancement, a healthy lifestyle, a sense of place, a sense of community, economic and racial diversity, convenient and efficient transportation, energy conservation, lifelong learning and education, aesthetic design and high-quality construction, and economic viability. See Ranney et al. (2010) for more examples of mixed-use communities with farms.

The Working Landscape, Rural Clusters, and Conservation Subdivision Design

While at the University of Massachusetts, Randall Arendt and Robert Yaro developed rural cluster design principles for preserving rural character, the working landscape of farms and forests, and natural resources. In their design manual, *Dealing with Change in the Connecticut River Valley* (Yaro et al. 1988), they give several examples of hypothetical developments on real sites to make their point that rural, working landscapes and views, sensitive areas, and agriculture can be preserved while accommodating development. The approach uses clustered development, generally tucked into the forest fringe, and preservation of open lands and agriculture through conservation easements or similar means.

creative vision for the community. Today, designing involves making sense collaboratively. It is a collective process. The planner helps the community discover its vision of the future and explore ways to achieve it. Still, planners and designers are more than just facilitators. By providing good technical information, by offering creative and visual alternatives, and by clarifying opportunities, planners play a principal role in "organizing attention to possibilities" (Forester 1989, 17).

Pragmatic developers have long recognized the need to know what consumers want in order to market their products. Increasingly, they are realizing that successful developments also depend on community acceptability to generate support and relieve potential conflict. This is important for both new developments and especially for revitalization and redevelopment projects.

Chapter 4 described some tools for participation in the design process, including participatory mapping, photo simulations, visual surveys, and scenario development. The power of visualization cannot be underestimated. Indeed, ours has become such a visual culture that spatial plans and visual scenarios are essential for communicating opportunities. The success of New Urbanism ultimately is measured by residents' satisfaction, but its promotion has been advanced by the ability of architects and planners to create visual representations of community design. With the development of increasing numbers of sustainable neighborhoods, we now have a body of photographic images to communicate the possibilities, and this chapter has used them for this purpose.

To appreciate the power of visualization, you must browse the websites of the successful architecture and planning firms who are leading this sustainable community design movement. Their project descriptions and visual representations are the best measure of how far we have come in just the past decade. Here's a partial list to check out:

- Duany, Plater-Zyberk & Company: www.dpz.com
- Calthorpe Associates: www.calthorpe.com
- Dover, Kohl & Partners: www.doverkohl.com
- Mithûn: http://mithun.com
- SvR Design: www.svrdesign.com
- Wallace Roberts & Todd: www.wrtdesign.com
- Jonathan Rose Companies: http://www.rose-network.com/
- Congress for New Urbanism project database: www.cnu.org/search/projects
- U.S. Green Building Council LEED-ND project profiles: http://www.usgbc.org/
- Urban Advantage: www.urban-advantage.com

The Urban Advantage website takes you into the photo simulation world by Steve Price. This powerful visualization tool has been used in hundreds of applications to communicate the development possibilities to stakeholders, planners, and local officials. Figure 16.22 shows the simulation used by Calthorpe Associates in the Twin Cities Metro's St. Croix Valley study. The two photographs illustrate the downtown revitalization plan for Stillwater, a historic riverfront community, that

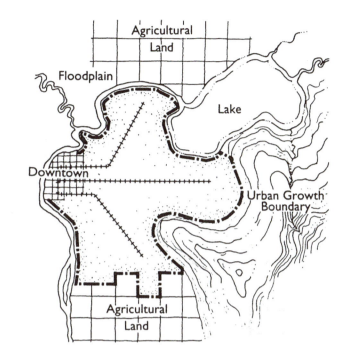

Figure 16.21 The Urban Growth Boundary. (*Source:* Peter Calthorpe, *The Next Metropolis: Ecology and the American Dream.* © 1993 Princeton Architectural Press. Used with permission.)

develop preferred 20-year growth scenarios. The process for all of these planning projects is participatory and uses visioning and scenario development (Calthorpe 2011).

The Process for Sustainable Community Design

The process for developing sustainable and livable community designs is technical, creative, participatory, and visual. It combines:

- Technical assessment and spatial land analysis to understand the land's natural features, development opportunities, and constraints, and to evaluate scientific and engineering considerations for water, energy, ecology, and mobility.
- Creative design that incorporates these opportunities, constraints, and considerations with land protection, community aesthetics, and livability.
- Stakeholder involvement, including community groups, local government, land conservation organizations, existing residents, and potential consumers, to provide local knowledge, perceptions, and cultural context.
- Visualization that brings to life the technical land analysis, creative design, and community vision.

Chapter 2 introduced the renewed need for design in planning today. It should not replicate the utopian planning of the past, where the designer created his own creative vision for the community. Today, designing involves making sense collaboratively. It is a collective process. The planner helps the community discover its vision of the future and explore ways to achieve it. Still, planners and designers are more than just facilitators. By providing good technical information, by offering creative and visual alternatives, and by clarifying opportunities, planners play a principal role in "organizing attention to possibilities" (Forester 1989, 17).

Pragmatic developers have long recognized the need to know what consumers want in order to market their products. Increasingly, they are realizing that successful developments also depend on community acceptability to generate support and relieve potential conflict. This is important for both new developments and especially for revitalization and redevelopment projects.

Chapter 4 described some tools for participation in the design process, including participatory mapping, photo simulations, visual surveys, and scenario development. The power of visualization cannot be underestimated. Indeed, ours has become such a visual culture that spatial plans and visual scenarios are essential for communicating opportunities. The success of New Urbanism ultimately is measured by residents' satisfaction, but its promotion has been advanced by the ability of architects and planners to create visual representations of community design. With the development of increasing numbers of sustainable neighborhoods, we now have a body of photographic images to communicate the possibilities, and this chapter has used them for this purpose.

To appreciate the power of visualization, you must browse the websites of the successful architecture and planning firms who are leading this sustainable community design movement. Their project descriptions and visual representations are the best measure of how far we have come in just the past decade. Here's a partial list to check out:

- Duany, Plater-Zyberk & Company: www.dpz.com
- Calthorpe Associates: www.calthorpe.com
- Dover, Kohl & Partners: www.doverkohl.com
- Mithûn: http://mithun.com
- SvR Design: www.svrdesign.com
- Wallace Roberts & Todd: www.wrtdesign.com
- Jonathan Rose Companies: http://www.rose-network.com/
- Congress for New Urbanism project database: www.cnu.org/search/projects
- U.S. Green Building Council LEED-ND project profiles: http://www.usgbc.org/
- Urban Advantage: www.urban-advantage.com

The Urban Advantage website takes you into the photo simulation world by Steve Price. This powerful visualization tool has been used in hundreds of applications to communicate the development possibilities to stakeholders, planners, and local officials. Figure 16.22 shows the simulation used by Calthorpe Associates in the Twin Cities Metro's St. Croix Valley study. The two photographs illustrate the downtown revitalization plan for Stillwater, a historic riverfront community, that

The Regional Context

The previous sections emphasized the importance of development strategies in neighborhoods and communities. However, local strategies alone are not sufficient to create land use patterns for arresting sprawl, protecting green infrastructure, reducing vehicle miles traveled to mitigate climate change and urban air pollution, and developing dense and interconnected sustainable communities—in other words, achieving Smart Growth. Local neighborhood and community plans and projects must be complemented with a metropolitan and regional approach to managing sprawl.

The Urban Transect has become an important framework for perceiving the spatial change across the region and the appropriate form of the built environment. It is a useful communication tool for raising awareness of both the region and the place local neighborhoods and communities hold in that region. With the development of the SmartCode, it has become even more than a communication tool (see Chapter 17).

This regional approach is not new, and metropolitan areas across the country have grappled with the best approach that fits their context. All of them have the seed of regional planning, as they have metropolitan transportation organizations (MTOs) and regional councils of government (COGs) for the mandated coordination of federally funded projects. But most metro areas have little authority. Some regional agencies, notably the Twin Cities Metro Council, the Portland Metro Commission, and the Tahoe Regional Planning Agency, are exceptions; they have acquired special authority by their states to manage regional growth (see Chapter 18).

The Twin Cities and especially Portland have come close to realizing Calthorpe and Fulton's (2001) vision for the "regional city," in which neighborhood, town, and urban design principles as the basic building blocks, but are overseen by regional policies for urban growth boundaries, transit and transportation, green infrastructure, watershed management, education balancing, and revenue sharing. The **urban growth boundary (UGB)**, illustrated in Figure 16.21, is an effective means of enclosing a development, promoting infill, and protecting greenfields and agricultural lands. Development is accommodated and encouraged within the boundary, and discouraged outside through regulation or reduced urban services and infrastructure.

Portland Metro is an exemplary model for urban growth boundaries (see Figure 18.6). Other metropolitan areas, including the Twin Cities, have also adopted them. The use of UGBs as a Smart Growth management tool is discussed in Chapters 17 and 18.

Several metropolitan areas have conducted regional planning workshops and charrettes to engage communities and residents in formulating a regional vision and the means to achieve it. Calthorpe Associates and partner firm Fregonese Associates have been engaged in many of these exercises, including Portland 2040, Smart Growth Twin Cities, Envision Utah (Salt Lake City region), Envision Central Texas (Austin region), Chicago 2020, and Vision California (statewide high-speed rail). California, based on successful regional planning in Sacramento, established the regional Blueprint planning program to fund regional efforts to

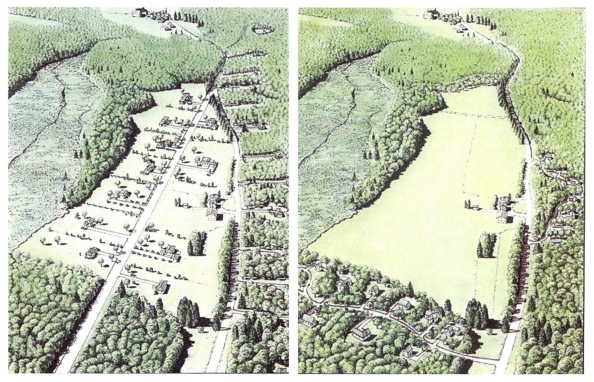

Figure 16.20 Conventional versus Conservation Development. Left: Conventional plan, with a new road and 26 large lots. Right: Conservation development plan, with 28 clustered lots tucked in the forest fringe and conservation easements on the common property. (*Source:* R. Yaro, R. Arendt, H. Dodson, and E. Brabec. 1988. *Dealing with Change in the Connecticut River Valley.* Courtesy, Center for Rural Massachusetts, University of Massachusetts–Amherst.)

1. The *background stage* investigates contextual issues, conducts an environmental inventory of the site, and prioritizes objectives and site features into primary and secondary conservation areas. The results take the form of overlay maps of the site.
2. The *design stage* begins with a conventional design to determine the development legally possible on the site. Putting that design aside, the alternative design begins with the overlay maps of primary and secondary conservation areas. Buildable areas are identified by avoiding these conservation areas and are used to locate house sites. Street and trail alignments are drawn to access house sites, but also are positioned to use foreground meadows to enhance views from the houses and to buffer views from main roads.

The first edition of this book listed Arendt's nine design steps for conservation subdivisions, which are now posted on the book website (www.envirolanduse.org). See Arendt (1996, 1999) for examples of this approach.

convenient walking paths, with connectivity to primary areas of interest. The planning team developed the design and engaged surrounding neighbors in the process. There is a density gradient with highest densities near the commercial area and lowest densities near the existing neighborhoods of single-family homes. Important cultural amenities at Highland Garden Village include a school, a walkable retail village, and a historic theater from the former amusement park renovated by a local nonprofit organization. A network of gardens, plazas, and open spaces creates a vibrant, friendly neighborhood with ample public meeting space. The project won the EPA's 2005 National Award for Smart Growth Achievement (Calthorpe Associates 2010; Jonathan Rose 2010; U.S. EPA 2010b).

Rural Community Development

The focus of Smart Growth is concentrating growth in existing development areas, where infrastructure exists and it is more likely that densities to support mass transit can be achieved. This applies at the dense end of the Urban Transect, but it also applies at the less-dense rural end, where small cities and villages can also benefit from the same design principles.

Prairie Crossing, Grayslake, Illinois

There are not many transit-oriented rural community developments, but Prairie Crossing is one. Located 40 miles north of Chicago, the development is at the crossing of two major commuter rail lines (Figure 16.19). The 678-acre mixed-use development has 362 housing units on 135 acres, or 20% of the site; 69% is protected farmland (included a 100-acre organic farm) and amenity open space; and 11% is for commercial and industrial space, a community center, and three schools. Prairie Crossing has both single-family homes and condominium units. The community has ten principles: environmental protection and enhancement, a healthy lifestyle, a sense of place, a sense of community, economic and racial diversity, convenient and efficient transportation, energy conservation, lifelong learning and education, aesthetic design and high-quality construction, and economic viability. See Ranney et al. (2010) for more examples of mixed-use communities with farms.

The Working Landscape, Rural Clusters, and Conservation Subdivision Design

While at the University of Massachusetts, Randall Arendt and Robert Yaro developed rural cluster design principles for preserving rural character, the working landscape of farms and forests, and natural resources. In their design manual, *Dealing with Change in the Connecticut River Valley* (Yaro et al. 1988), they give several examples of hypothetical developments on real sites to make their point that rural, working landscapes and views, sensitive areas, and agriculture can be preserved while accommodating development. The approach uses clustered development, generally tucked into the forest fringe, and preservation of open lands and agriculture through conservation easements or similar means.

Figure 16.19 Prairie Crossing, Illinois. A: This mixed-use rural development is located at the crossing of two commuter rail lines, 40 miles north of Chicago. B: Single-family homes. C: Condominiums in the denser community center. (*Source:* Ranney et al. 2010, www.prairiecrossing.com. Used with permission.)

Figure 16.20 shows an example. The 130-acre rural site contains farmland, wetlands, habitat, old-growth forest, and scenery. A proposal to subdivide the entire site into 26 large lots with a new road met with opposition (Figure 16.20A). An alternative creative design was developed, and the new plan called for 28 lots on 24 acres, preserving more than 100 acres of farmland, forest, and wetlands (Figure 16.20B). Most of the lots are clustered on three locations at the forest line to preserve farmland and views. The open space area was deeded in perpetuity to a homeowner's association that was established to manage the common property.

Randall Arendt continued this conservation design approach in his books *Rural by Design* (1994), *Conservation Design for Subdivisions* (1996), and *Growing Greener* (1999). The design concept is simple. Instead of simply dividing up a parcel into streets and house lots, first look at the land, see what it portrays in environmental and cultural opportunities and constraints, and then use them to design a compact community.

Arendt provides numerous side-by-side examples of development plans to illustrate the benefits of compact development combined with sensitive land protection and community open space. He provides a useful procedure for "conservation design of subdivisions" that has two stages (Arendt 1996):

Figure 16.22 A Simulated Photo Pair of Redevelopment and Revitalization in Stillwater, Minnesota. Left: Existing conditions. Right: The simulation shows that the strategic placement of vegetation and a few buildings can enhance the community. (*Source:* Steve Price, Urban Advantage. Used with permission.)

included construction of two mixed-use buildings, street trees, and special paving on some streets.

Synthesis and Summary

This chapter has presented a wide range of considerations in sustainable community design and how they have been manifested in real projects, neighborhoods, and cities. These considerations include walkability, mobility including pedestrian and transit orientation, mixed use, mixed building type, mixed-income households, natural drainage, habitat and open space, cultural context, and spatial context along the Urban Transect. Several designers, academics, agencies, and groups have tried to synthesize these considerations into a set of principles for sustainable community design. Let's look at two.

Box 16.2 lists ten principles for livable communities from the American Institute of Architects (AIA). Adopted with objectives to envision, create, and sustain, these principles only miss the regional context for sustainable communities. Box 16.3 is a summary of the useful *Smart Growth Manual* by Duany and Speck (2010), which puts together, concisely and visually, considerations in sustainable community design from the region down to the building. The manual defines Smart Growth by its outcomes: neighborhood livability, better access and less traffic, thriving cities, suburbs, and towns; shared benefits; lower costs and lower taxes; and keeping open space open. (Smart Growth from the public policy point of view is the focus of the next two chapters.)

Since 1950, land development patterns in the United States have been dominated by urban flight, suburban consumption of agricultural and natural areas,

BOX 16.2—The American Institute of Architects' Ten Principles for Livable Communities

1. **Design on a Human Scale**: Compact, pedestrian-friendly communities allow residents to walk to shops, services, cultural resources, and jobs and can reduce traffic congestion and benefit people's health.

2. **Provide Choices**: People want variety in housing, shopping, recreation, transportation, and employment. Variety creates lively neighborhoods and accommodates residents in different stages of their lives.

3. **Encourage Mixed-Use Development**: Integrating different land uses and varied building types creates vibrant, pedestrian-friendly, and diverse communities.

4. **Preserve Urban Centers**: Restoring, revitalizing, and infilling urban centers takes advantage of existing streets, services, and buildings and avoids the need for new infrastructure. This helps to curb sprawl and promote stability for city neighborhoods.

5. **Vary Transportation Options**: Giving people the option of walking, biking, and using public transit, in addition to driving, reduces traffic congestion, protects the environment, and encourages physical activity.

6. **Build Vibrant Public Spaces**: Citizens need welcoming, well-defined public places to stimulate face-to-face interaction, collectively celebrate and mourn, encourage civic participation, admire public art, and gather for public events.

7. **Create a Neighborhood Identity**: A "sense of place" gives neighborhoods a unique character, enhances the walking environment, and creates pride in the community.

8. **Protect Environmental Resources**: A well-designed balance of nature and development preserves natural systems, protects waterways from pollution, reduces air pollution, and protects property values.

9. **Conserve Landscapes**: Open space, farms, and wildlife habitat are essential for environmental, recreational, and cultural reasons.

10. **Design Matters**: Design excellence is the foundation of successful and healthy communities.

Source: American Institute of Architects 2010.

dependence on motor vehicles, and growing transportation gridlock from congestion. Over the last couple decades, architects and planners have responded with new, more sustainable models of development, for the purpose of protecting natural areas, relieving automobile dependency, and at the same time creating more livable neighborhoods and communities. These models are land-conserving, compact, walkable, and often transit-oriented; they have mixed-income residential and commercial uses, and they set aside greenspace for recreation and environmental protection. They also focus on revitalization of existing communities through infill, brownfield, suburban, and downtown redevelopment to create more livable neighborhoods, as well as town and city centers, and relieve development pressures on greenfield working landscapes and natural areas.

These sustainable models have grabbed the attention of government officials, builders, and consumers alike. Government officials call it Smart Growth. Builders and realtors call it Green Building and development. Designers call it New Urbanism. Consumers call it livable communities.

The sustainable communities movement has taken off. Projects carrying all these various labels are increasing exponentially—green, livable, sustainable, and so on. People are returning to live in center cities and towns. Studies show a grow-

In the Region:

- Growth is inevitable and should be guided by the Urban Transect from urban core to suburban zone to rural and natural zones, and by
- a *regional plan*, which directs regional transportation, green infrastructure, including water security and farmland for food security, gray infrastructure, urban growth boundaries, and which sets
- *growth priorities* that distribute undesirable land uses fairly within the region and steer growth to areas of existing infrastructure to infill and revitalize communities and
- *neighborhoods*, which are a community's social fabric and identity and become more livable by compactness, walkability, connectedness to the community and region, and diversity of mixed land uses, of housing types, of income levels and affordability, and which enjoy
- *scaled governance* from neighborhood associations to city government to regional authorities, all of which embrace community involvement and coordinate policies for shared benefits and costs of growth.

The Regional Plan must map the green infrastructure, development priorities, neighborhoods, districts, corridors, and regional centers. It should control and incentivize Smart Growth through such means as urban growth boundaries, transfer of development rights, tax incentives, and the SmartCode.

Regional Transportation must be planned along with land use and provide multi-modal balance and transportation choices, including pedestrian and bicycle networks, as well as transit that works and is accessible.

2. The Neighborhood:

- is founded on its natural context and must preserve and celebrate natural features including trees, soils, streams, wetlands,

managed stormwater, and urban parks and corridors;
- has many components, including mixed use, housing diversity and density, retail and workplace distribution, civic sites, neighborhood schools, local open space, gardens, and farms; and
- has structure, scaled to the pedestrian, organized around a center and within its edge, connected to the outside by being transit oriented, and guided by such tools as form-based codes and LEED-ND rating.

The Streets:

- are part of a network of connected thoroughfares that embrace sidewalks and walkable scales including small block size and pleasing design;
- are planned as "complete" streets accommodating cars, pedestrians, bicycles, public spaces, and tree cover; have appropriate speed control, flows, and parking; and incorporate rear alleys, passages and paths; and
- are designed as a community amenity rather than an eyesore, with vegetative treatment for stormwater management, street trees, pavement materials, buried utilities, relation to buildings, and parking management.

The Buildings:

- should include a variety of types directed by form-based codes rather than conventional prescriptions; and
- incorporate green design and construction, including energy and water efficiency, sustainable materials, occupant health lighting and ventilation, and onsite energy and landscape features; and embrace design elements to preserve cultural heritage and regional building vernacular.

Source: Adapted from Duany and Speck 2010.

Community Planning and the Comprehensive/General Plan

Comprehensive planning was introduced in Chapter 3. The **comprehensive plan**, or general plan, presents a broad vision for the community and aims to guide physical development and community services. The vision, strategies, and policies are based on detailed analysis and public participation, so the comprehensive plan provides both the technical and the political basis for local government programs, including growth management, land use regulations, infrastructure investments, and other services. For a short history of comprehensive planning presented in the first edition of this book, see the book website (www.envirolanduse.org).

The comprehensive plan sets the stage for Smart Growth management by providing:

- A future vision developed by the community through a participatory process.
- The technical and analytical basis for local government programs.
- The political and legal foundation for growth management formally adopted by elected officials.

It has a long-term time horizon of about 50 years and is updated every 4–10 years. Comprehensive planning is part of a community planning process made up of the four elements listed in Box 17.2. Planning "intelligence" includes the background inventories, analyses, and public participation that serve as the foundation of the planning effort. The main products are the "network of plans," which

---

BOX 17.2—Community Planning Framework

1. Intelligence: Background Data and Planning Analysis

Land use intelligence involves environmental inventorying and mapping, suitability and carrying capacity analysis, and assessment of land use perceptions. Planning intelligence is used in the process of general, functional, and district planning.

2. The Network of Plans and Plan Making

a. Regional or areawide plan.
b. Long-range comprehensive community-wide plan.
c. Community-wide land use plan is the visual and spatial manifestation of the long-range plan.
d. Community-wide functional plans address single topics including transportation, infrastructure, natural environment, green infrastructure, housing, and economic development.

e. District and small-area plans focus on a neighborhood, central business district, TOD redevelopment area, or environmental preservation area. The land use plan for a community comes to life in these district or neighborhood plans.

3. Implementation Plans and Programs

Implementation plans and programs address the actions necessary to realize the vision, objectives, and strategies of the comprehensive, district, and functional plans. Actions include zoning and development regulations, capital improvement plans and budgets, tax policies, and other programs.

4. Building Community Consensus

Although listed separately here, building community consensus through stakeholder involvement and collaborative planning is necessary throughout the planning process.

Planning Tools for Smart Growth Management

The tools for Smart Growth management have also evolved. And change they must, because the basic approach to land development control, the conventional zoning used in U.S. cities for 100 years, has been one of the causes of the sprawling segregated development patterns we are now trying to reverse. The following sections review these conventional and emerging tools for Smart Growth management, categorized as planning tools, regulatory tools, and nonregulatory tools. They are listed in Box 17.1.

Planning tools provide the technical, political, and policy framework for growth management implementation programs that are regulatory or nonregulatory in nature. **Regulatory tools** include mandatory controls on the type, location, and timing of development. We discuss the legal context for land use regulation, then describe conventional zoning and subdivision ordinances and more innovative regulatory mechanisms, including flexible and performance zoning, form-based codes, and the SmartCode. **Nonregulatory tools** include land acquisition, tax policies, and using infrastructure development to guide the timing and location of development. Most effective growth management programs use a combination of tools.

BOX 17.1—Smart Growth Management Tools

Planning Tools

Political and technical (including environmental) basis for land use management

- The comprehensive or general plan
- Functional plans, such as capital improvement plan, stormwater management plan, green infrastructure plan, climate action plan

Regulatory Tools

1. Conventional land use regulations
   - Zoning ordinance: use and density restrictions
   - Subdivision regulations: rules for land division
2. Innovative land use regulations
   - Development standards, environmental ordinances (green building, stormwater, tree protection), and plan review (environmental impact review, Smart Growth scorecard)
   - Variations on use and density restrictions (e.g., agricultural zoning, cluster/conservation zoning)
   - Overlay districts: environmental zoning
   - Performance/flexible zoning: performance criteria
   - Transfer of development rights (TDR)
   - Phased development: timing of development
3. Comprehensive development codes
   - Unified codes
   - Sustainability codes
   - Form-based codes, SmartCode

Nonregulatory Tools

1. Land acquisition, conservation easements, purchase of development rights
2. Infrastructure development: Roads and sewers determine location of development
3. Differential development impact fees
4. Tax policies: use-value taxation, level-of-service areas

Community Planning and the Comprehensive/General Plan

Comprehensive planning was introduced in Chapter 3. The **comprehensive plan**, or general plan, presents a broad vision for the community and aims to guide physical development and community services. The vision, strategies, and policies are based on detailed analysis and public participation, so the comprehensive plan provides both the technical and the political basis for local government programs, including growth management, land use regulations, infrastructure investments, and other services. For a short history of comprehensive planning presented in the first edition of this book, see the book website (www.envirolanduse.org).

The comprehensive plan sets the stage for Smart Growth management by providing:

- A future vision developed by the community through a participatory process.
- The technical and analytical basis for local government programs.
- The political and legal foundation for growth management formally adopted by elected officials.

It has a long-term time horizon of about 50 years and is updated every 4–10 years. Comprehensive planning is part of a community planning process made up of the four elements listed in Box 17.2. Planning "intelligence" includes the background inventories, analyses, and public participation that serve as the foundation of the planning effort. The main products are the "network of plans," which

---

BOX 17.2—Community Planning Framework

1. Intelligence: Background Data and Planning Analysis

Land use intelligence involves environmental inventorying and mapping, suitability and carrying capacity analysis, and assessment of land use perceptions. Planning intelligence is used in the process of general, functional, and district planning.

2. The Network of Plans and Plan Making

a. Regional or areawide plan.
b. Long-range comprehensive community-wide plan.
c. Community-wide land use plan is the visual and spatial manifestation of the long-range plan.
d. Community-wide functional plans address single topics including transportation, infrastructure, natural environment, green infrastructure, housing, and economic development.

e. District and small-area plans focus on a neighborhood, central business district, TOD redevelopment area, or environmental preservation area. The land use plan for a community comes to life in these district or neighborhood plans.

3. Implementation Plans and Programs

Implementation plans and programs address the actions necessary to realize the vision, objectives, and strategies of the comprehensive, district, and functional plans. Actions include zoning and development regulations, capital improvement plans and budgets, tax policies, and other programs.

4. Building Community Consensus

Although listed separately here, building community consensus through stakeholder involvement and collaborative planning is necessary throughout the planning process.

less suitable for development, to achieve livable and affordable neighborhoods, thriving communities, protected ecosystems and open space, better mobility, and lower costs.

Growth management is not new. For the past three or four decades, many rapidly growing localities have tried to control the pace and location of development, using an array of management tools, including innovative zoning regulations, urban growth boundaries, infrastructure investments, community planning procedures, tax policies, land acquisitions, and others (Benfield et al. 2001; Nelson and Duncan 1995). During that period, however, growth management was not without critics or controversy. In some places, there is a general opposition to land use regulation, or any government "tampering" with how landowners wish to use their property. In some slow-growth or economically disadvantaged communities, the desire for more development overshadows that need to control it. Some have argued that growth controls can constrain development, cause escalating housing costs, and reduce affordability.

But growth management has evolved during this time. In the mid-1990s, Governor Glendenning started Maryland's Smart Growth program to emphasize development in areas of existing infrastructure, revitalize existing communities, and deemphasize development in surrounding farmlands and natural areas. Growth management had long sought this basic objective, but the label "smart growth" gained attention, especially considering the contrary label. Smart Growth has evolved as well, incorporating the objectives of sustainability and New Urbanism, including ecosystem, water, and habitat protection; community design; livability; walkability, smart mobility and transit orientation; active living and healthy communities; revitalization of shrinking cities; environmental justice and affordability; and climate change mitigation and adaptation. A good source for exploring the evolving nature of Smart Growth is the collective conference themes and presentations of the New Partners for Smart Growth annual conferences held since 2002. These are posted on its website (www.newpartners.org/2010/past_conferences .html).

The Ten Principles for Smart Growth from the U.S. EPA are now well established and accepted. Here they are:

1. Preserve open space, farmland, natural beauty, and critical environmental areas.
2. Strengthen and direct development toward existing communities.
3. Take advantage of compact building design.
4. Mix land uses.
5. Create a range of housing opportunities and choices.
6. Provide a variety of transportation choices.
7. Create walkable neighborhoods.
8. Foster distinctive, attractive communities with a strong sense of place.
9. Encourage community and stakeholder collaboration.
10. Make development decisions predictable, fair, and cost-effective.

17 ◾ Community Smart Growth Management

Local governments are in a strategic position to plan and manage land use, development, and conservation. Although a few states and regional areas have retained some authority for land use management, local governments have the bulk of the responsibility for guiding and regulating land use development. They are the closest governmental unit to community life, the primary planning agent for the community's future, and the first "line of defense" for solving community problems. Therefore, we start here with a presentation of basic and emerging local Smart Growth management tools. Effective Smart Growth must have regional oversight and state guidance, and those programs are the focus of Chapter 18.

The previous chapter established design principles for livable and sustainable communities. While designers and developers are a key driving force for the built environment, government policies for growth can inhibit, allow, encourage, or mandate these sustainable design practices. This chapter discusses the role of local government in managing land use development in the United States. We begin by defining Smart Growth management and then explore a number of planning, regulatory, and nonregulatory tools for controlling development, using several innovative local programs to illustrate them.

Smart Growth is the *end*—the result of effective growth management. Growth management is the *means*—the set of governmental tools needed to achieve Smart Growth. Here are some useful definitions:

- **Growth management** consists of the governmental policies, plans, investments, incentives, and regulations used to guide the type, amount, location, timing, and cost of development, for the purpose of achieving a responsible balance between protecting the natural environment and development to support growth, a responsible fit between development and necessary infrastructure, and enhanced quality of community life.
- **Smart Growth** emphasizes compact and mixed-use development in areas of existing infrastructure and discourages development in areas

BOX 16.3—Sustainable Community Design Principles from *The Smart Growth Manual*

In the Region:

- Growth is inevitable and should be guided by the Urban Transect from urban core to suburban zone to rural and natural zones, and by
- a *regional plan*, which directs regional transportation, green infrastructure, including water security and farmland for food security, gray infrastructure, urban growth boundaries, and which sets
- *growth priorities* that distribute undesirable land uses fairly within the region and steer growth to areas of existing infrastructure to infill and revitalize communities and
- *neighborhoods*, which are a community's social fabric and identity and become more livable by compactness, walkability, connectedness to the community and region, and diversity of mixed land uses, of housing types, of income levels and affordability, and which enjoy
- *scaled governance* from neighborhood associations to city government to regional authorities, all of which embrace community involvement and coordinate policies for shared benefits and costs of growth.

The Regional Plan must map the green infrastructure, development priorities, neighborhoods, districts, corridors, and regional centers. It should control and incentivize Smart Growth through such means as urban growth boundaries, transfer of development rights, tax incentives, and the SmartCode.

Regional Transportation must be planned along with land use and provide multimodal balance and transportation choices, including pedestrian and bicycle networks, as well as transit that works and is accessible.

2. The Neighborhood:

- is founded on its natural context and must preserve and celebrate natural features including trees, soils, streams, wetlands, managed stormwater, and urban parks and corridors;
- has many components, including mixed use, housing diversity and density, retail and workplace distribution, civic sites, neighborhood schools, local open space, gardens, and farms; and
- has structure, scaled to the pedestrian, organized around a center and within its edge, connected to the outside by being transit oriented, and guided by such tools as form-based codes and LEED-ND rating.

The Streets:

- are part of a network of connected thoroughfares that embrace sidewalks and walkable scales including small block size and pleasing design;
- are planned as "complete" streets accommodating cars, pedestrians, bicycles, public spaces, and tree cover; have appropriate speed control, flows, and parking; and incorporate rear alleys, passages and paths; and
- are designed as a community amenity rather than an eyesore, with vegetative treatment for stormwater management, street trees, pavement materials, buried utilities, relation to buildings, and parking management.

The Buildings:

- should include a variety of types directed by form-based codes rather than conventional prescriptions; and
- incorporate green design and construction, including energy and water efficiency, sustainable materials, occupant health lighting and ventilation, and onsite energy and landscape features; and embrace design elements to preserve cultural heritage and regional building vernacular.

Source: Adapted from Duany and Speck 2010.

ing preference for compact and walkable neighborhoods, as many empty nesters and young families are choosing the walkable community and cultural life of cities and towns over the car-dependent private isolation of the suburbs.

The key elements of this movement include regional integration, urban infill and redevelopment, suburban revitalization, conservation design of rural and greenfield development, and village and small town development. Duany's Urban Transect has helped put all of these elements together.

includes the comprehensive plan, the long-range land use plan, and district small area plans. Functional plans address specific topics and may or may not be part of the comprehensive plan. They can address sustainability topics, such as climate action plans, watershed management plans, and green infrastructure plans.

Blacksburg, Virginia's 2010 comprehensive plan was presented in Box 3.4, and the land use plan for 2046 is in Figure 3.4. The plan has four parts: the natural environment, the built environment, the human environment, and the planned environment. The first three parts contain functional planning sections, and the last part has community-wide land use and district plans. The Figure 3.4 map shows land uses by district, including rural very low-density residential; low-, medium-, and high-density residential; light- and heavy-impact commercial; research/light industrial; industrial; university; and parkland/open space. The plan shows seven mixed-use overlay areas, which were added with the 2010 update.

Figure 17.1 shows a portion of the comprehensive land use map for King County, Washington. About the size of Delaware (2,130 sq mi), King County contains some of the most beautiful scenery, diverse ecosystems, productive farmland, and vibrant economies in the nation. Its 1.7 million people are concentrated in 39 cities, including Seattle. The 2008 comprehensive plan focuses on the county's unincorporated (noncity) land, which is 82% of its area and holds 21% of its population (360,000). The plan is heavily influenced by the 1990 Washington State Growth Management Act, which required 13 planning goals of all local comprehensive plans, including the establishment of urban growth boundaries. Among its nine chapters are Regional Planning, Rural Legacy and Natural Resource Lands, Environment, and Preserving and Enriching Our Communities. Figure 17.1 shows land use for most of the county and delineates the urban growth areas and rural areas (separated by an urban growth boundary), as well as protected open space and agricultural and forest production districts (King County 2008).

Figure 17.2 shows the northern portion of Seattle's comprehensive plan future land use map, including prominent uses, urban centers, urban villages, and mixed-use commercial areas. The Seattle Plan, Toward a Sustainable Seattle, has been updated almost every year.

Functional and Small-Area Plans

Functional and small-area plans provide an opportunity to focus on specific areas and issues. For example, Seattle's comprehensive plan includes an Urban Villages Element that focuses on services and infrastructure in specified urban centers, and hub and residential urban villages (see Figure 17.2). Seattle references climate change in the Environment Element of the plan, but it has a stand-alone Climate Protection Initiative, as well as other stand-alone sustainability initiatives.

Regulatory Tools for Growth Management

As discussed previously in Chapter 2, the Tenth Amendment to the U.S. Constitution grants states the police power to regulate private activities to protect public

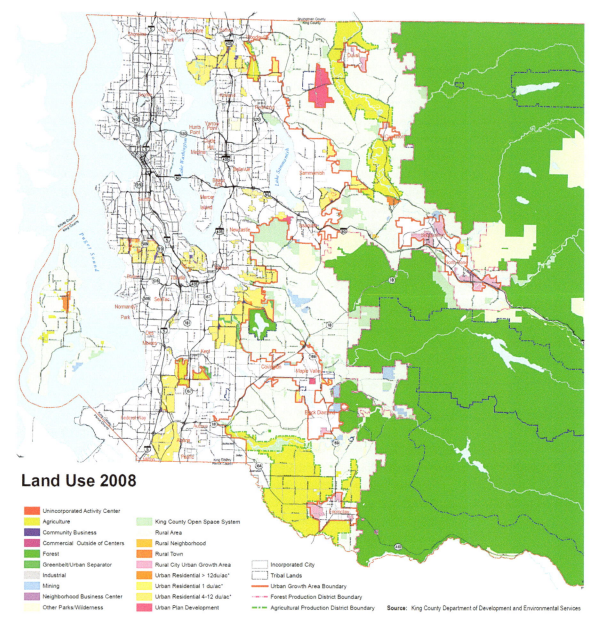

Figure 17.1 The Comprehensive Plan Land Use Map for Nonincorporated King County, Washington. Notice the urban growth boundaries, agriculture and forest reserve, greenbelt, and various development uses. (*Source:* King County 2008.)

health, safety, and welfare. These private activities include land development, and since the U.S. Supreme Court affirmed the use of land use zoning in the 1926 case *Village of Euclid, Ohio v. Ambler Realty Co.*, local governments have used land use regulations to create orderly development and protect public welfare. This authority is constrained by the private property rights protection and the due process clause of the Fifth and Fourteenth Amendments.

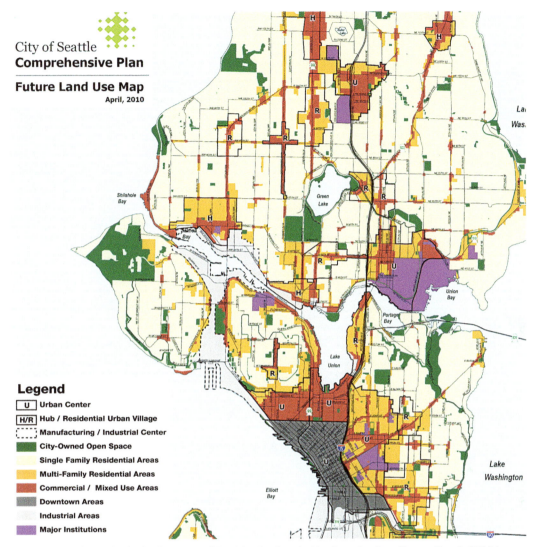

City of Seattle
Comprehensive Plan

Future Land Use Map
April, 2010

Legend

- U — Urban Center
- H/R — Hub / Residential Urban Village
- Manufacturing / Industrial Center
- City-Owned Open Space
- Single Family Residential Areas
- Multi-Family Residential Areas
- Commercial / Mixed Use Areas
- Downtown Areas
- Industrial Areas
- Major Institutions

Figure 17.2 The Future Land Use Map for Seattle, Northern Section. (*Source:* Seattle 2010.)

In addition, local authority is constrained in the majority of the states, so-called Dillon Rule[1] states, in which localities only have those powers explicitly granted by the state. In Home Rule states, localities are free to exercise regulatory authority, *unless* specifically prohibited by the state. This constitutional variation among the states affects the constraints and opportunities available to both state and local governments in their efforts to control land use. What works for one state may not be available to another; what has been successful in one community may not be legal for a locality with similar problems in another state (Richardson 2002).

---

1. The Dillon Rule is named for Judge John Foster Dillon, who in 1868 (*City of Clinton v. Cedar Rapids and Missouri Railroad Co.*, 24 Iowa 455) formulated the doctrine that municipalities only have those powers "expressly granted" to them by the state.

Property Rights and Legal Constraints on Environmental Land Use Regulation

In all communities, the police or regulatory powers that local governments can employ to control land use are constrained by the rights of personal property provided by the U.S. Constitution, which bar government from "taking" private property for public use without just compensation. Land use regulation for orderly development or environmental protection may diminish the value of private property and could be considered a taking, even though it does not physically take title to the property. The legal question is: When do the regulations go too far in restricting private property use and become taking without just compensation? If a regulation is ruled a taking, the courts can enjoin the regulation and/or order compensation. However, the definition of "too far" is not always clear, and local governments must consider potential takings litigation when designing regulatory programs to manage growth and protect the environment.

In the 1970s, courts tended to view the public welfare quite broadly and ruled in favor of a broad range of community regulatory devices, especially when they addressed health and safety issues and were based on technical analysis and a publicly adopted comprehensive plan. In the 1980s and 1990s, legal advocates for property rights argued successfully for their interests in several cases, and even though takings law continues to evolve, some legal clarity has emerged. The U.S. Supreme Court decided three major takings-issue cases in 1987,[2] two more in the early 1990s,[3] and one in 2002,[4] which all helped establish a judicial "taking equation" consisting of a three-level inquiry. Some of the key issues are discussed in Box 17.3.

The first inquiry involves whether the purpose of the regulatory action is a legitimate state interest and whether the means used to achieve the objective substantially advances that purpose. The legitimacy of the state interest is clear for the protection of public safety, such as for floodplain zoning, but is less clear for protecting environmental resources, such as agricultural lands or nonendangered wildlife habitat.

The second inquiry concerns whether a reasonable use of the property by the landowner remains after the regulation. If the government acquires title to the property or physically invades the land, the regulation will generally be a taking. If the landowner retains the land but is left with no reasonable use, the burden is on the government to demonstrate that any use of the land would significantly impact the interest of the state.

If some use of the property remains after the regulation, the third inquiry involves a balancing test of economic impact. The court would decide whether the

---

2. *Keystone Bituminous Coal Association v. DeBenedictis*, 107 S. Ct. 1232 (1987); *First English Evangelical Lutheran Church v. County of Los Angeles*, 107 S. Ct., 2378 (1987); *Nollan v. California Coastal Commission*, 107 S. Ct. 3141 (1987).

3. *Lucas v. South Carolina Coastal Council* (1992), *Dolan v. City of Tigard* (1994).

4. *Tahoe Sierra Preservation Council, Inc. v. Tahoe Regional Planning Agency* (2002). Called the "most definitive win for good planning in over a decade," the decision validated development moratoria, emphasizing the value of a community's taking time to "develop a citizen-based plan for conserving its treasured resources" (Lucero and Soule 2002). Planning for Lake Tahoe is discussed in Chapters 14 and 18.

BOX 17.3—Property Law and the "Taking" Issue

- The Tenth Amendment to the U.S. Constitution grants government *police power* to protect public health and welfare. The Fourteenth Amendment extends this power to state and local government.
- The Fifth Amendment protects *private property*; the *takings clause* requires "just compensation when government affects a taking of property." This does not prohibit condemning private property for the public good through eminent domain so long as just compensation is provided.

Key issues in determining if regulations are an appropriate use of the police power:

- The regulation must *substantially advance legitimate state interests*. The legitimate state interests must be based on the prevention of public harm rather than the provision of public benefit.
- The regulation involves a *connection (nexus)* between the potential private action and achieving the state interest. The regulation cannot impose a requirement that is not closely related to the state interest or the public impact.
- The regulation does not deny an owner *reasonable use* of his or her property. Reasonable use often involves a balancing test of state interests versus economic impact on the owner.

public interest is outweighed by the economic or other burden on the landowner. The inquiry will look at the reasonableness of remaining use and the diminution in value caused by the regulation.

On a related property rights issue, the courts have established the government's power of **eminent domain** to take property for public purpose *with* just compensation. In its 2005 decision in *Kelo v. City of New London* (545 U.S. 469 [2005]), the Supreme Court affirmed the use of eminent domain for economic development, or using eminent domain condemnations that transfer property from one private owner to another solely on the grounds to improve the local economy. This may have a bearing on environmental regulations that can diminish the value of private property on the grounds to improve the environment. Some feared that if courts banned economic development (ED) takings, they might also inhibit environmental regulations. But Somin and Adler (2006) suggest there is no such evidence from the several states that have banned or constrained ED takings. They do argue, however, that widespread use of ED takings could threaten environmental protection by making more vulnerable conserved land owned or under easement by land trusts. Such lands could be condemned for economic development. However, this threat is diminished by the narrow margin of the Kelo decision (5–4) and the level of controversy it has generated.

Conventional Land Use Regulations

Box 17.4 summarizes the land use regulations that are used to control growth and protect the environment. They range from conventional zoning to the SmartCode. The following discussion elaborates on these regulatory tools.

Zoning has long been the principal land use regulation used by localities. Conventional Euclidean zoning specifies the location of different types of land use (e.g., residential, commercial, industrial, agricultural, conservation) by dividing

A. Conventional Land Use Regulations

1. **Conventional Zoning**: Use and density restrictions, often some design standards, such as setbacks. For environmental objectives, large-lot zoning is sometimes used.
2. **Subdivision Ordinance**: Requirements for the layout of streets, drainage, water, sewer, etc., to achieve orderly development at the land subdivision stage.

B. Variations and Innovations in Conventional Regulations

1. **Development Standards and Plan Review**: In addition to zoning and subdivision standards, projects must meet specific requirements: e.g., stormwater management, floodplain management, green buildings, tree protection, landscaping, wetland protection, hazard mitigation, and parking. Plans may be subject to review for environmental impact, design, Smart Growth scorecard, or other measures.
2. **Agricultural Zoning**
   a. Exclusive: Prohibits the construction of nonfarm buildings. Possible "takings" conflicts, but often supported in courts when part of comprehensive planning and when development areas are specified.
   b. Nonexclusive: Allows a limited amount of nonfarm development.
      i.   Large-lot zoning: May actually convert farmland to development at a faster rate.
      ii. Sliding-scale zoning: Number of units per acre decreases as parcel size increases; also,
3. **Overlay Zoning**: Protects environmental resources or safeguards natural hazard areas. An overlay district is determined by boundaries of environmental resource or hazard and is placed on top of existing zoning. In an overlay district, special additional land use restrictions apply, such as restricted development, extra standards, or extra documentation. Used for floodplain zones, seismic hazards, wellhead protection areas, watersheds, habitat zones, riparian zones.
      i.   maximum acreage per development unit (e.g., 2 acres).
4. **Incentive Zoning**: Provides density bonuses, reduction of impact and processing fees, and other incentives for development proposals that meet desirable criteria, such as additional open space, affordable housing, and energy efficiency.
5. **Conditional Zoning**: Although zoned for a specific use (e.g., high-density residential, large-scale commercial, industrial), this zone requires a special-use permit before approval. This permit may require conditions and/or fees and gives local officials negotiating leverage. Proffers (voluntary design features) are often used with conditional zoning.
6. **Conservation, Open Space, or Cluster Zoning**: Provides density transfers onsite to enable clustering or concentrating development on buildable areas, while leaving permanently undisturbed open space on sensitive areas.
7. **Performance Zoning**: Requires meeting certain performance criteria rather than prescriptive standards.
8. **Flexible Zoning**: Provides for planned developments or negotiated development based on performance criteria or negotiation. Less prescriptive and allows for innovative development design.
9. **Urban Growth Boundaries**: Contains development within a set boundary separating urban and rural uses.
10. **Transfer of Development Rights**: Enables transfer of development rights from a preservation zone to a development zone. Landowners in the preservation zone are compensated from payments made by landowners in the development zone.

BOX 17.4—Land Use Regulations for Growth Management and Environmental Protection (cont.)

11. **Phased Development**: Controls not the location but the rate of development or the number of units per year to keep pace with the provision of public services.

12. **Concurrency**: Development plans can be approved only if they are "concurrent" with plans for infrastructure and/or other public services.

C. Comprehensive Development Codes

1. **Unified code:** Combines zoning and subdivision ordinances and development stan-

dards in one document to better coordinate project design and development.

2. **Sustainability code**: Unified code focused on sustainability measures: environmental protection, affordability, etc.

3. **Form-based code**: Controls building form and location, but not use or density.

4. **SmartCode**: Form-based code linked to the Urban Transect from urban core to rural preserve.

the community into specific land use zones. The first zoning ordinance was created in 1909, and by 1929 after the *Euclid* case, 800 cities had zoning ordinances. Planning and zoning aimed to remedy urban externalities and create orderly places by separating and decentralizing land uses. Zoning regulations contributed to sprawl. Our sprawling land development patterns were not haphazard at all; they were orderly, designed, and controlled by our zoning codes.

In conventional zoning, different residential, agricultural, and conservation zones are distinguished by development density, or the maximum number of dwelling units allowed per acre. In addition, zoning regulations define other development parameters, including maximum building height, lot size, maximum percent of lot covered, and minimum setbacks from property lines. Figure 17.3 gives a typical zoning map for the town of Blacksburg, Virginia.

Subdivision ordinances, which set requirements for the layout of streets, drainage, water and wastewater, and so on, are another traditional measure to achieve "orderly development" at the land subdivision stage. Although conventional zoning and subdivision ordinances have done much to separate incompatible land uses and standardize subdivision practices, they have not met all the land use control needs of many communities.

One critique of conventional zoning is that it assumes use and density restrictions can protect environmental and community values. These restrictions are not sufficient because they assume all land is the same (i.e., there are not environmentally sensitive lands). Large-lot zoning (e.g., 1 unit per 5 acres or 1 unit per 20 acres) can reduce some of the impacts associated with dense development but may cause others. For example, this practice consumes more land per dwelling unit, can be socially exclusionary (i.e., only the rich can afford such large lots), and can lead to greater sprawl. In many cases, when local governments have "downzoned" property (e.g., from 1 unit per acre to 1 unit per 5 acres) to protect open space or environmental resources, property owners have sued, arguing a "taking" of property without due compensation.

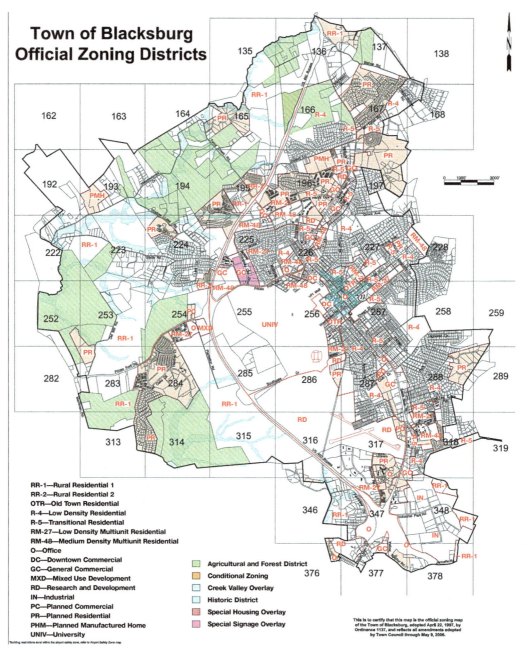

Figure 17.3 Blacksburg, Virginia, Zoning Map. (*Source:* Blacksburg 2010b.)

Variations of Conventional Zoning and Innovations to Protect the Environment

Several innovations in response to the critique of conventional zoning aim to protect environmental resources more effectively (see Box 17.3). **Development standards and plan review** are used by localities to establish design and review criteria to achieve community objectives and enhance the quality of development.

A few states and several localities require environmental impact assessments (EIAs) for development proposals. State-led programs, like Washington's SEPA (State Environmental Policy Act) requirements, are discussed in the next chapter, and EIA procedures were presented in Chapter 14.

More recently, localities have developed design criteria and review standards to address Smart Growth and green building objectives (see Chapter 16). Most of these are voluntary and marketing programs. Some localities, like Boulder, require a minimum number of "green points" for new development or renovation projects. These green points go beyond minimum building codes. For example, new construction must document a minimum number of points (e.g., 65 for a new 2,000-sq-ft house) drawn from a list of design enhancements, such as use of recycled materials, xeriscape landscaping, water conservation, lumber from sustainable forestry, energy efficiency, solar energy, and indoor air quality measures.

Agricultural zoning is for preserving agricultural land use, production, and rural character. Exclusive agricultural zoning prohibits the construction of non–farm-related buildings. Some communities have been successful with exclusive agricultural zoning (e.g., the Oregon state program; see Chapter 18). However, because of potential takings conflicts, most communities have opted for nonexclusive agricultural zoning, which allows a limited amount of nonfarm development. This has been done primarily with large-lot zoning, but as already discussed, it has often accelerated the conversion of productive agricultural lands to nonagricultural uses.

Sliding-scale zoning is similar to large-lot zoning, but it provides for different densities according to the property size. It can also limit the acreage of lots that are developed. One of the best-known examples of sliding-scale zoning is in Clarke County, Virginia. Table 17.1 shows the development right allocation system for 6 of the 14 parcel-size classes. The rights per acre decrease with increased parcel size. For example, a 10-acre parcel has 1 development right (1 per 10 acres), while a 120-acre site has 4 rights (1 per 30 acres), and a 480-acre property has 10 rights (1 per 48 acres). Subdivision of land is limited by the allocated development rights, and development parcels are limited to 2 acres each.

TABLE 17.1 **Sliding-Scale Zoning Development Right Allocation, Clarke County, Virginia**

Size Class (Acres)	Average Parcel	Number of Development Rights	Nonfarm Acres/Average Parcel*	Farm Acres Average Parcel*	Percentage of Site in Agriculture
0–14.9	4.2 acres	1	2	0	0
15–39.9	23.6 acres	2	4	20	83
40–79.9	51.6 acres	3	6	46	88
80–129.9	102.7 acres	4	8	95	92
400–499.9	418.7 acres	10	20	399	95
860–1,029.9	930.0 acres	14	38	902	97

* 2-acre minimum.

Source: Adapted from Coughlin 1991.

Figure 17.4 Overlay Zoning for Wellhead and Lake Watershed Protection. (*Source:* Jon Witten and Scott Horsley. 1995. *A Guide to Wellhead Protection.* Planning Advisory Service Report 457/458. Used with permission of the American Planning Association.)

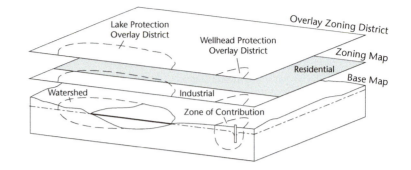

Table 17.1 shows how this system preserves farmland. Column 4 gives the acreage in development for an average size parcel under each size class. Columns 5 and 6 show what acreage and percentage of land would be left in agriculture for an average parcel. If the county were "built out" under the sliding-scale zoning program, 76,000 of the county's 83,000 acres of agricultural land would be left in agriculture (Coughlin 1991).

Perhaps the most useful innovation in zoning for environmental protection is **overlay zoning**, which acts to protect environmental resources or safeguard land use in natural hazard areas. What is referred to as an "overlay district" is applied on top of existing zoning requirements, so its conditions apply to different conventional zones, such as low-density residential, commercial, and so on. The overlay district boundaries are determined by an environmental inventory or land analysis that shows the location of a resource or hazard. Within the overlay district, special additional land use restrictions apply. These may include restricted development, extra standards, or extra documentation. Overlay zoning is used for floodplains, watersheds, wellhead protection areas, habitats, slope instability, seismic hazards, and fire hazards (Figure 17.4).

Figure 17.5 shows a portion of the Desired Development Zone map for Austin, Texas, which contains overlay zones for drinking water aquifer protection and creek buffers (Austin 2010). Austin also has a large overlay district for the Balcones Canyon habitat protection (see Chapter 11).

Environmental zoning can use overlays or simply establish special requirements for designated areas. A good example is the Environmental Quality Corridor (EQC) system adopted by Fairfax County, Virginia, in 1990. As shown in Figure 17.6, the EQC includes 100-year floodplains; areas of 15% or greater slope adjacent to floodplains or 50 ft from streams; all wetlands connected to stream valleys; and all land measured from the streambank 50 ft plus 4 ft per percent slope. To provide habitat, wildlife corridors, pollution reduction, and aesthetic benefits, the developing of EQC land is prohibited. The policy provides for onsite density transfers, allowing for sites containing EQC to be developed to their overall gross density, but with development concentrated on non-EQC land (Fairfax County 1991).

Based on the Fairfax EQC model, Blacksburg (Virginia) adopted its Creek Valley Overlay District in 1997. The district is shown in the zoning map in Figure 17.3, and it provides the core of the parks and open space component of the comprehensive plan (see Figure 3.4). Like the Fairfax EQC, the district provides an **onsite density transfer** to allow development to achieve development rights

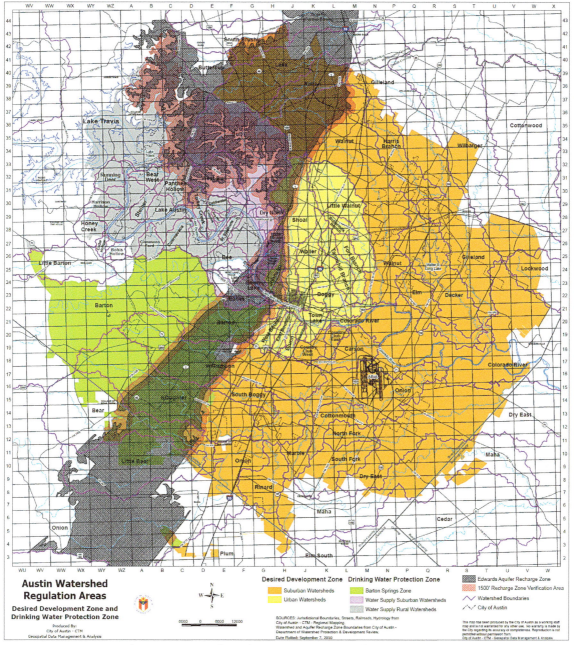

Figure 17.5 Desired Development Zones and Drinking Water Protection Zones, Austin, Texas. (*Source:* Austin 2010.)

and still protect the Creek District by clustered development on the site. The Transfer of Residential Development Potential document states that development density as measured in units per acre, otherwise allowed on land located within the Creek Valley District and outside the 100-year floodplain, may be transferred to those portions of the same lot or other lots within the same planned development, as long as those portions are located outside the Creek Valley District.

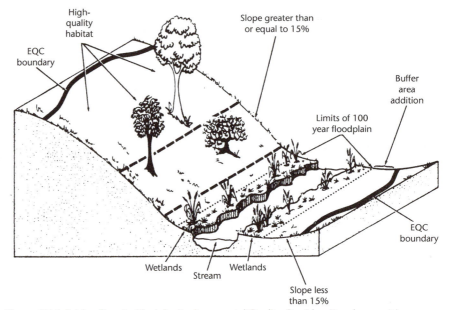

Figure 17.6 Fairfax County, Virginia: Environmental Quality Corridor. Development is prohibited in the EQC. (*Source:* Fairfax County 1991.)

Blacksburg's zoning ordinance also illustrates the use of **conservation or cluster zoning**, which basically applies Arendt's conservation subdivision concept (Arendt 1999). The Rural Residential (RR-1) zone is applied to most of the Tom's Creek Basin on the northwest section. Intended to preserve the rural character of the basin, the RR-1 zone calls for gross density of 1 unit per acre, but developments are required to cluster development onsite to provide a minimum 50% permanent open space. The text of the RR-1, given in this book's first edition, is now posted on the book website (www.envirolanduse.org).

The ordinance also includes an Open Space Design Overlay District (OSDOD) to encourage open space within most residential zoning districts of the town. The underlying district prescribes the gross density, but if a minimum of 30% of the site is designated as permanent open space protected by conservation easement, that density can be clustered on the remaining 70% of the site.

Blacksburg's RR-2 zone is an example of **incentive zoning**, which provides a **density bonus** of 1–2 units per acre if the landowner voluntarily incorporates one or more of 14 specified features that are in the town's interest. These include additional open space, recreational facilities, land dedication to town park or greenway, visual buffers and affordable housing. The Ashland, Oregon, 1980 zoning ordinance, for example, provides the following density bonuses (to a maximum 60%) for planned unit developments (PUDs) (Randolph 1981):

- Energy-efficient housing up to 40% bonus
- Solar hot water up to 5%
- Common open space up to 15%
- Recreational facilities up to 10%
- Low-cost housing up to 10%
- Good design features up to 10%

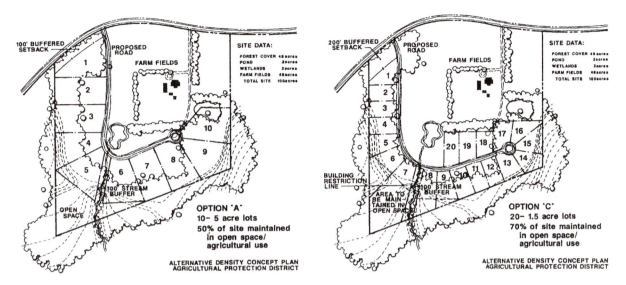

Figure 17.7 Density Bonus Options in Isle of Wight County, Virginia. Left: Base zoning provides 1 unit per 10 acres and requires 50% open space. Right: Increasing open space to 70% gives a 100% density bonus. (*Source:* Reprinted with permission from Randall Arendt, *Rural by Design*, copyright 1994 by the American Planning Association, Suite 1600, 122 South Michigan Ave., Chicago, IL 60603-6107.)

Figure 17.7 illustrates the incentive zoning concept. In Isle of Wight County, Virginia, developers have options for open space design in a zone with a permitted density of 1 unit per 10 acres and a requirement for 50% permanent open space. The first option (Figure 17.7A) is an onsite density transfer that provides the 50% open space and ten 5-acre lots. The second option provides 70% open space and gives a density bonus of 100%, allowing 20 lots of 1.5 acres each (Figure 17.7B).

Conditional zoning aims to manage impacts of specific developments, such as industrial plants or large subdivisions. While an area is zoned for a particular use, such as residential or industrial, the conditional zone requires a **special-use permit** that may require meeting certain conditions, such as impact fees to offset the environmental impacts of the development or cover the public services required by the project. Impact or development fees are described later under nonregulatory programs. The special-use permit gives local officials negotiating leverage about the design of the development. **Proffers** are voluntary modifications, design features, or fees added to the development proposal to enhance the prospects of obtaining a special-use permit. Conditional zoning is often applied to natural hazard overlay zones. For example, a conditional zone might be established for a steep slope; development will be allowed only if the development plan is approved by a licensed engineer for slope safety.

Performance zoning varies from conventional zoning by providing performance criteria or standards, rather than prescriptive requirements for developments. For example, instead of specifying a specific size for a detention basin to mitigate storm discharges, a performance approach might simply specify a zero net increase and let the developer decide and demonstrate how the requirement will be met. Generally, performance criteria allow for more creativity in development design but require more documentation in the development proposal to

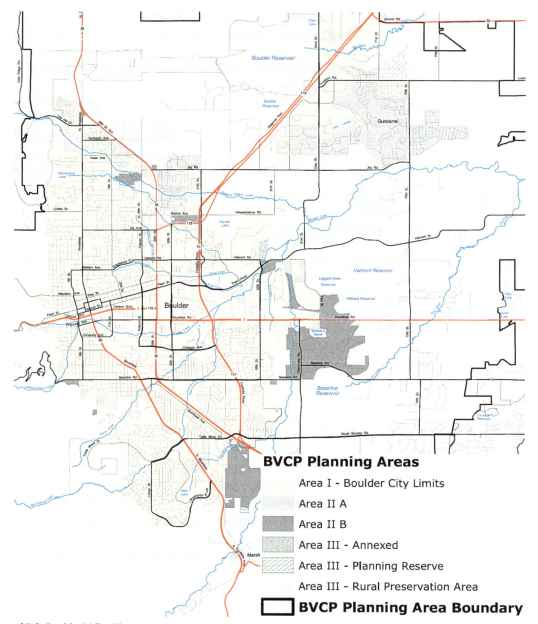

Figure 17.8 Boulder Valley Planning Areas. Areas I and II are available for development within the planning period (15 years). Area III includes preservation lands as well as a planning reserve for development beyond the planning period. (*Source:* Boulder 2010.)

advantage of TDR to the community is that the costs of development right purchase are borne by private landowners in the receiving area, not the local government. More importantly, it establishes areas of desired increased density, such as around a transit station, and provides a mechanism for developers to acquire development rights there, while at the same time compensating preservation landowners to permanently protect their land. TDR tends to be more complex than PDR; it requires a buyer of rights, not just a seller, and a mechanism to get these parties together to transfer the rights or to bank or broker the rights.

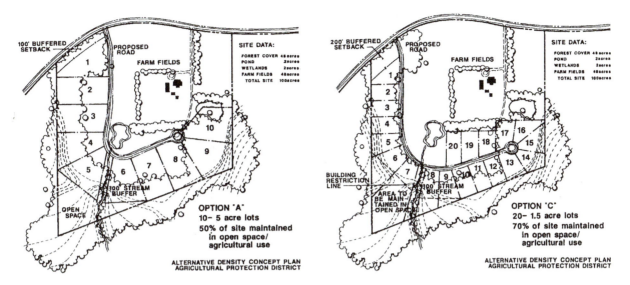

Figure 17.7 Density Bonus Options in Isle of Wight County, Virginia. Left: Base zoning provides 1 unit per 10 acres and requires 50% open space. Right: Increasing open space to 70% gives a 100% density bonus. (*Source:* Reprinted with permission from Randall Arendt, *Rural by Design,* copyright 1994 by the American Planning Association, Suite 1600, 122 South Michigan Ave., Chicago, IL 60603-6107.)

Figure 17.7 illustrates the incentive zoning concept. In Isle of Wight County, Virginia, developers have options for open space design in a zone with a permitted density of 1 unit per 10 acres and a requirement for 50% permanent open space. The first option (Figure 17.7A) is an onsite density transfer that provides the 50% open space and ten 5-acre lots. The second option provides 70% open space and gives a density bonus of 100%, allowing 20 lots of 1.5 acres each (Figure 17.7B).

Conditional zoning aims to manage impacts of specific developments, such as industrial plants or large subdivisions. While an area is zoned for a particular use, such as residential or industrial, the conditional zone requires a **special-use permit** that may require meeting certain conditions, such as impact fees to offset the environmental impacts of the development or cover the public services required by the project. Impact or development fees are described later under non-regulatory programs. The special-use permit gives local officials negotiating leverage about the design of the development. **Proffers** are voluntary modifications, design features, or fees added to the development proposal to enhance the prospects of obtaining a special-use permit. Conditional zoning is often applied to natural hazard overlay zones. For example, a conditional zone might be established for a steep slope; development will be allowed only if the development plan is approved by a licensed engineer for slope safety.

Performance zoning varies from conventional zoning by providing performance criteria or standards, rather than prescriptive requirements for developments. For example, instead of specifying a specific size for a detention basin to mitigate storm discharges, a performance approach might simply specify a zero net increase and let the developer decide and demonstrate how the requirement will be met. Generally, performance criteria allow for more creativity in development design but require more documentation in the development proposal to

TABLE 17.2 **Performance Zoning Criteria**

Burks County (PA) Protection Performance Zoning		Queen Anne County (MD) Resource Protection Standards			
		Open Space Ratios			
Resource	% Open	Resource	Coast	Upland	Agriculture
100-year floodplains	100	Wetlands			
Alluvial soils	100	Tidal	1.0	—	—
Wetlands	100	Nontidal	1.0	1.0	0.8
Natural retention areas	90	Drainageways	0.5	0.3	0.8
Lake and pond shores	70–80	Woodlands			
Forests	60–80	Mature hardwood	0.8	0.7	0.5
Steep slopes over 25%	85	Mature evergreen	0.8	0.6	0.5
Steep slopes 15–25%	70	Young	0.8	0.3	0.2
Steep slopes 8–15%	60	Old-field succession	0.3	0.0	0.85
Class I agricultural soils	95	Farm fields	0.0	0.0	0.85
Class II agricultural soils	85	Erosion hazard area	1.0	—	—
Class III agricultural soils	80	Beach	1.0	—	—
Class IV agricultural soils	60	Bluffs	1.0	—	—
		Shore buffer	1.0	—	—

show how the criteria will be met. Some performance-based zoning specifies land coverage or open space percentages or ratios that must be met for certain environmentally sensitive areas. Onsite density transfers are usually provided. Burks County, Pennsylvania, was one of the first localities to use this approach. Its criteria and those of Maryland's Queen Anne County are given in Table 17.2. Based on a site land cover inventory, the performance criteria require leaving open a certain percentage or ratio of the land in resource areas.

Flexible zoning includes planned unit developments, cluster zoning, and floating zones, which are all designed to reduce the rigid standards imposed by conventional zoning. **Planned unit developments (PUDs)** do not rely on specific regulations but rather on a process of administrative review of proposed development plans and negotiation between the developer and planning agency. They can also be applied to **floating zones**, which identify a zone and its requirements, but not its location. PUDs can incorporate creative designs not allowed by conventional zoning. However, if they are relied on too much, development becomes just a project-by-project negotiated exercise, with little consistency with, or guidance from, the comprehensive plan. One of the EPA's Smart Growth fixes to correct existing zoning is to rely less on PUDs and to provide more consistency through more specific guidance (U.S. EPA 2009). Still, flexible zoning can allow for creativity and innovation in development design but requires a fairly sophisticated planning staff; the process is enhanced by public involvement.

Communities have also enacted a long list of other codes and ordinances with specific requirements for developers. Los Angeles' grading ordinance has helped

limit land and landslide damages. Building codes are applied in nearly all communities. Erosion and sedimentation control ordinances and tree removal and planting ordinances are also examples of environmental controls.

Urban growth boundaries (UGBs) are a method of containing development within a set boundary separating urban and rural land uses (see Figure 16.21). UGBs were first used in Oregon's Land Conservation and Development program, established in 1973. They have become an important tool for achieving Smart Growth's objective to emphasize development in areas with existing infrastructure and discourage development in greenfields. UGBs are usually intended to accommodate growth for a specified period of time; 15–20 years is common.

Other states and localities have adopted UGBs. Washington's 1990 Growth Management Act requires a UGB for the state's cities and urban counties. Figure 17.1 shows King County's, Washington's UGB. The Twin Cities Metro Council established a UGB called the Metro Utility Service Area (MUSA). Maryland has attempted to establish UGBs without regulation. The state provides financial support for development infrastructure in Priority Funding Areas, essentially UGBs identified by localities (Chapter 18 discusses regional and statewide UGB programs.)

Boulder Valley's growth management program in Colorado depends significantly on a UGB that is divided into planning areas. Boulder has adjusted the UGB over time to accommodate development needs. Figure 17.8 shows the boundaries for the various growth areas:

- Area I is the area within the city of Boulder that has adequate urban facilities and services and is expected to continue to accommodate urban development.
- Area II is the area now under county jurisdiction, where annexation to the city can be considered consistent with comprehensive plan policies. New urban development may occur only with the availability of adequate facilities and services. Departmental master plans project the provision of services to this area within the planning period. Area IIA is the area of immediate focus within the first 3 years, and Area IIB is available to accommodate development within the balance of the 15-year planning period.
- Area III is the remaining area in the Boulder Valley, generally under county jurisdiction. Area III is divided into the Area III—Rural Preservation Area, where the city and county intend to preserve existing rural land use and character, and the Area III—Planning Reserve Area, where the city and county intend to maintain the option of expanded urban development in the city beyond the time frame of the 15-year planning period (Boulder 2001).

Transfer of development rights (TDR) transfers rights from areas the community wishes to protect to areas that are more appropriate for development (Figure 17.9). Such a program requires the designation of a "preservation" or sending area, from which rights are transferred, and a "development" or receiving area, where those development rights are applied. Compared to PDR, the

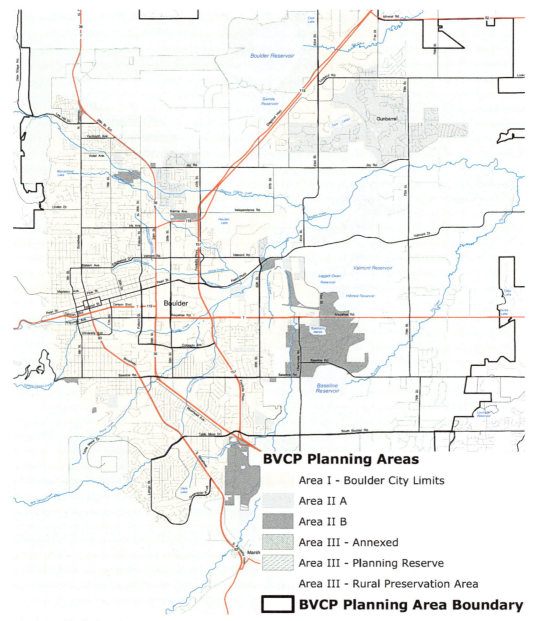

Figure 17.8 Boulder Valley Planning Areas. Areas I and II are available for development within the planning period (15 years). Area III includes preservation lands as well as a planning reserve for development beyond the planning period. (*Source:* Boulder 2010.)

advantage of TDR to the community is that the costs of development right purchase are borne by private landowners in the receiving area, not the local government. More importantly, it establishes areas of desired increased density, such as around a transit station, and provides a mechanism for developers to acquire development rights there, while at the same time compensating preservation landowners to permanently protect their land. TDR tends to be more complex than PDR; it requires a buyer of rights, not just a seller, and a mechanism to get these parties together to transfer the rights or to bank or broker the rights.

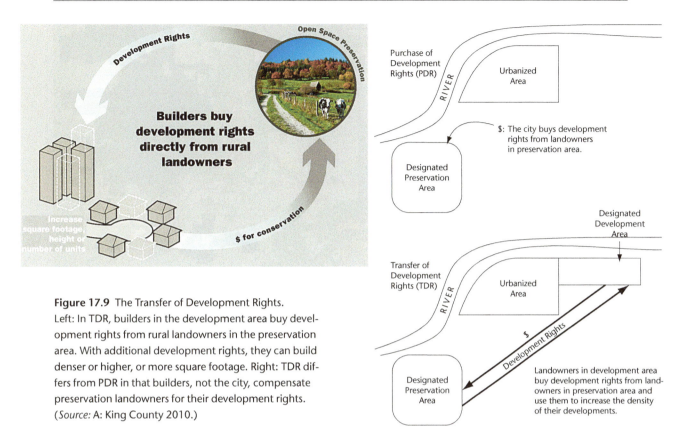

Figure 17.9 The Transfer of Development Rights. Left: In TDR, builders in the development area buy development rights from rural landowners in the preservation area. With additional development rights, they can build denser or higher, or more square footage. Right: TDR differs from PDR in that builders, not the city, compensate preservation landowners for their development rights. (*Source:* A: King County 2010.)

In 2002, Hollis and Fulton (2002) found that 24 states permit localities to use TDR programs. Pruetz (2003) identified 124 local and regional TDR programs designed to protect working landscapes, open space, resource lands, and historic districts. Regional growth management programs for the Lake Tahoe and the Pinelands (New Jersey) areas include a TDR component (see Chapter 18). Montgomery County, Maryland, has one of the most successful TDR programs, which has operated since 1980. The TDR program has protected more than 50,000 acres of farmland. Other local easement and trust programs protect another 12,000 acres. The programs have helped maintain an agricultural industry in the county, amounting to more than 875 farms and enterprises, 10,000 jobs, and a $350 million contribution to the local economy (Montgomery County 2002, 2003, 2006).

King County, Washington, adopted two TDR programs in the late 1990s. One provides up to 150% of baseline zoning in receiving areas in existing residential and commercial zones in the unincorporated parts of the county. The other provides transfers from rural parts of the county to incorporated cities through a partnership between the county and the cities. The county acts as facilitator and broker and maintains a TDR Exchange Bank, which buys, holds, and sells TDRs and thus stabilizes the market. Figure 17.10 illustrates the rural sending areas and the urban receiving areas. As of 2010, some 141,400 acres have been preserved via public (TDR Bank) and private transactions.

TABLE 17.3 Some of the EPA's Essential Smart Growth Fixes of Existing Codes and Ordinances

Fix Needed	Modest Adjustments	Major Modifications	Wholesale Changes
Allow or require mixed-use zones	Define mixed-use in land use plan. Permit residences in upper floors of comm. districts.	Remove obstacles to mixed use with mixed use by right. Develop mixed-use districts.	Synchronize zoning codes and area plans to coordinate mixed-use development.
Use urban dimensions in urban places	Tailor dimension standard to promote compact development. Allow residential development in commercial districts.	Incentives for multiple housing types through dimensional standards. Produce better connections and walkability by reducing block lengths/perimeters.	Coordinate new form-based dimensional standards with zoning map changes.
Rein in and reform the use of planned unit developments	Reform PUD process to ensure PUD fits site. Reduce PUD by fixing dimensional standards. Create PUD standards.	Prohibit PUD as alternative to comprehensive plan zoning codes.	Create distinctive area and sector plans that give clear guidance on intended built-out development. Public master-plan PUD site.
Fix parking requirements	Create parking overlay district and reduce minimum off-street parking supply requirements.	Revise parking ordinance Develop system of shared parking credits. Improve parking enforcement.	Develop commuter transit pass bundled with parking permit. Paid parking in parking districts.
Increase density and intensity in centers	Set minimum not maximum densities in plans and zoning districts. Designate high-density centers in comprehensive plan.	Tailor development standards to accommodate denser development. Rezone areas designated as activity centers.	Redevelopment agency to purchase critical parcels. Establish minimum densities in mixed-use centers and TOD.
Modernize street standards	Revise street design standards to add bike lanes and on-street parking. Update design standards for street trees. Test green street designs.	Embed street design in comprehensive plan. Create multimodal corridor designation. Set internal connectivity standards for new subdivisions.	Multimodal transport master plan. Reintroduce public alleys. Set minimum internal and external connectivity standards for new development.
Enact standards to foster walkable places	Develop standards for street crossing design, tree and shade structures. Safe route to schools program.	Designate one or more pedestrian districts with zoning ordinance changes for street crossing, building setbacks. Require in new large developments pedestrian level of service and connectivity.	Prepare pedestrian circulation element in comprehensive plan. Require pedestrian circulation plans in new development.
Designate and support preferred growth and development sites	Identify preferred growth areas in comprehensive plan. Create district/area plan. Vary fees for development based on location.	Enact concurrency adequate public facility ordinance (APFO).	Establish urban service area or urban growth boundary and support by zoning. Allow denser development around transit stops.
Use green infrastructure (GI) to manage stormwater (SW)	Add water elements to comprehensive plan to allow GI SW alternatives. Offer incentives for GI in development proposals.	Performance standard requiring infiltration. Update SW design manual with GI examples. Review and change codes to ensure GI is legal. Implement SW fee based on impervious surface.	Give fiscal credit to developers toward SW requirements for preservation of GI to decrease impervious surface.

Source: Adapted from U.S. EPA 2009.

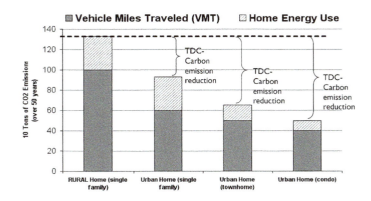

Figure 17.11 Estimated GHG Emission Mitigation Associated with King County Transfer of Development Credits (TDC). (*Source:* Greve et al. 2010.)

velopment permits per year. After Petaluma's program was upheld by the Supreme Court in 1972, other communities established similar programs, including Boulder and Fort Collins, Colorado, and the Lake Tahoe region (see Chapter 18).

Concurrency policies attempt to achieve the same objectives of phased development by requiring that development plans are concurrent with plans for infrastructure, such as water and sewer service, roads, and other public services. This approach became part of Florida's statewide growth management (see Chapter 18) and has been adopted by other localities across the country.

Emerging Smart Growth Land Use Regulations

Most localities rely on these variations and innovations to conventional land use regulations. However, many communities are beginning to implement some new emerging approaches that aim to foster Smart Growth development principles to a far greater extent than conventional zoning. These approaches include unified development codes, Smart Growth codes and audits, and form-based codes. The SmartCode, developed by New Urbanism master Andres Duany, is a form-based code that is getting significant attention.

Smart Growth Fixes

Most localities are not in a position to completely transform their codes. To help them, the EPA has developed some technical assistance materials. Table 17.3 lists some of the EPA's essential Smart Growth fixes for zoning codes. Knowing that many communities need an incremental approach, the EPA categorizes three level of correction (modest adjustments, major modifications, and wholesale changes) to move toward nine Smart Growth objectives from mixed-use zones to green infrastructure (Nelson 2010; U.S. EPA 2009).

Sustainability Codes

There are a number of assistance materials that fit under the general category of sustainability codes. They integrate useful features of innovative land use regula-

TABLE 17.3 Some of the EPA's Essential Smart Growth Fixes of Existing Codes and Ordinances

Fix Needed	Modest Adjustments	Major Modifications	Wholesale Changes
Allow or require mixed-use zones	Define mixed-use in land use plan. Permit residences in upper floors of comm. districts.	Remove obstacles to mixed use with mixed use by right. Develop mixed-use districts.	Synchronize zoning codes and area plans to coordinate mixed-use development.
Use urban dimensions in urban places	Tailor dimension standard to promote compact development. Allow residential development in commercial districts.	Incentives for multiple housing types through dimensional standards. Produce better connections and walkability by reducing block lengths/perimeters.	Coordinate new form-based dimensional standards with zoning map changes.
Rein in and reform the use of planned unit developments	Reform PUD process to ensure PUD fits site. Reduce PUD by fixing dimensional standards. Create PUD standards.	Prohibit PUD as alternative to comprehensive plan zoning codes.	Create distinctive area and sector plans that give clear guidance on intended built-out development. Public master-plan PUD site.
Fix parking requirements	Create parking overlay district and reduce minimum off-street parking supply requirements.	Revise parking ordinance Develop system of shared parking credits. Improve parking enforcement.	Develop commuter transit pass bundled with parking permit. Paid parking in parking districts.
Increase density and intensity in centers	Set minimum not maximum densities in plans and zoning districts. Designate high-density centers in comprehensive plan.	Tailor development standards to accommodate denser development. Rezone areas designated as activity centers.	Redevelopment agency to purchase critical parcels. Establish minimum densities in mixed-use centers and TOD.
Modernize street standards	Revise street design standards to add bike lanes and on-street parking. Update design standards for street trees. Test green street designs.	Embed street design in comprehensive plan. Create multimodal corridor designation. Set internal connectivity standards for new subdivisions.	Multimodal transport master plan. Reintroduce public alleys. Set minimum internal and external connectivity standards for new development.
Enact standards to foster walkable places	Develop standards for street crossing design, tree and shade structures. Safe route to schools program.	Designate one or more pedestrian districts with zoning ordinance changes for street crossing, building setbacks. Require in new large developments pedestrian level of service and connectivity.	Prepare pedestrian circulation element in comprehensive plan. Require pedestrian circulation plans in new development.
Designate and support preferred growth and development sites	Identify preferred growth areas in comprehensive plan. Create district/area plan. Vary fees for development based on location.	Enact concurrency adequate public facility ordinance (APFO).	Establish urban service area or urban growth boundary and support by zoning. Allow denser development around transit stops.
Use green infrastructure (GI) to manage stormwater (SW)	Add water elements to comprehensive plan to allow GI SW alternatives. Offer incentives for GI in development proposals.	Performance standard requiring infiltration. Update SW design manual with GI examples. Review and change codes to ensure GI is legal. Implement SW fee based on impervious surface.	Give fiscal credit to developers toward SW requirements for preservation of GI to decrease impervious surface.

Source: Adapted from U.S. EPA 2009.

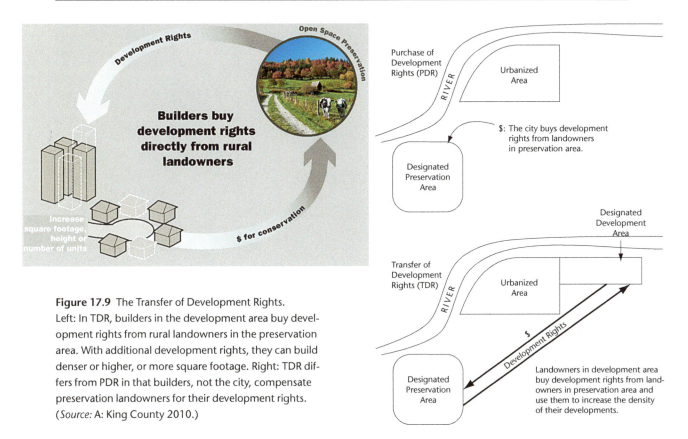

Figure 17.9 The Transfer of Development Rights. Left: In TDR, builders in the development area buy development rights from rural landowners in the preservation area. With additional development rights, they can build denser or higher, or more square footage. Right: TDR differs from PDR in that builders, not the city, compensate preservation landowners for their development rights. (*Source:* A: King County 2010.)

In 2002, Hollis and Fulton (2002) found that 24 states permit localities to use TDR programs. Pruetz (2003) identified 124 local and regional TDR programs designed to protect working landscapes, open space, resource lands, and historic districts. Regional growth management programs for the Lake Tahoe and the Pinelands (New Jersey) areas include a TDR component (see Chapter 18). Montgomery County, Maryland, has one of the most successful TDR programs, which has operated since 1980. The TDR program has protected more than 50,000 acres of farmland. Other local easement and trust programs protect another 12,000 acres. The programs have helped maintain an agricultural industry in the county, amounting to more than 875 farms and enterprises, 10,000 jobs, and a $350 million contribution to the local economy (Montgomery County 2002, 2003, 2006).

King County, Washington, adopted two TDR programs in the late 1990s. One provides up to 150% of baseline zoning in receiving areas in existing residential and commercial zones in the unincorporated parts of the county. The other provides transfers from rural parts of the county to incorporated cities through a partnership between the county and the cities. The county acts as facilitator and broker and maintains a TDR Exchange Bank, which buys, holds, and sells TDRs and thus stabilizes the market. Figure 17.10 illustrates the rural sending areas and the urban receiving areas. As of 2010, some 141,400 acres have been preserved via public (TDR Bank) and private transactions.

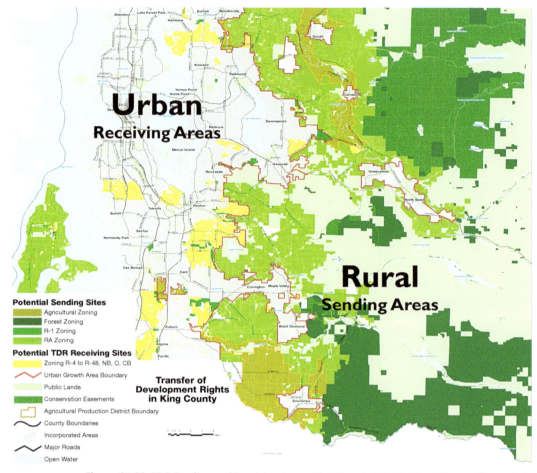

Figure 17.10 TDR Sending and Receiving Areas, King County, Washington. (*Source:* Greve et al. 2010.)

An interesting element of King County's program is that developers can claim GHG emissions mitigation credits associated with the TDRs they buy, each called a **transfer of development credit (TDC)**. GHG emissions and mitigation measures must be assessed for new developments under new State Environmental Policy Act (SEPA) guidelines. Because TDR transfers development from potential sprawl in rural areas to dense urban development, there will be fewer GHG emissions from vehicle travel and smaller housing units. Figure 17.11 estimates the carbon mitigation benefit of one TDC, ranging from 400 to 720 tons/TDC depending on the urban housing unit type.

Although regulations may specify the location and type of land use, many communities need to control the rate at which development takes place. Rapidly growing communities have been confronted by their infrastructure carrying capacity; they have had difficulty providing public services such as water, sewage treatment capacity, school facilities, and police and fire protection to meet the needs of an expanding population. In the 1970s, Petaluma, California, and Ramapo, New York, established **phased development** programs by capping the number of de-

tions, address natural and human-made systems, and are based on both the local comprehensive plan and public involvement. Here are some examples:

- **Comprehensive or unified codes** combine conventional and innovative regulations to provide better consistency among them and the comprehensive plan; they facilitate compliance for designers and developers (Morris 2009).
- **Sustainability code**, developed by the Rocky Mountain Land Use Institute, addresses critical sustainability concerns, including climate change, energy, food supply, water conservation, habitat protection, and human health and safety (RMLUI 2010).
- **State level guidance** assists with codes and code reform, such as New Hampshire's Innovative Land Use Planning Techniques (NHDE 2008).
- **Code assessment tools** help evaluate and upgrade ordinances to incorporate sustainability objectives, such as the EPA's Green Building code assessment tool, the Center for Watershed Protection's (CWP) Code and Ordinance Worksheet (COW), and the EPA's Water Quality Scorecard (CWP 2004; U.S. EPA 2009).
- **Project assessment tools**, such as Smart Growth scorecards or indices and green building and neighborhood ratings systems, evaluate projects against standardized criteria (e.g., LEED-NC, LEED-ND).

Project assessment tools are useful for evaluation, education, and project marketing, but they have sometimes found their way into codes. Boulder's building code requires green rating points; Austin uses a Smart Growth Matrix (Austin undated), not in regulatory review but as a basis to waive development fees. Some anticipate the advance of LEED-ND into codes (Nelson 2010).

Form-Based Codes

New Urbanism has affected new development designs and housing markets, but with the advance of **form-based codes (FBCs)**, its influence expanded to land use regulation. An objective of FBCs is to reverse the 100-year tradition of Euclidean zoning in the U.S. Table 17.4 compares elements, goals, and outcomes of Euclidean and FBC zoning. Instead of regulating land use types, density, and bulk dimensions, FBC rules emphasize building form and location and relationships: between streets and buildings, between pedestrians and vehicles, between public and private spaces, and between buildings, the block, and the neighborhood. They aim to create a predictable public realm by controlling the physical form of private developments. FBCs are complex, and their implementation generally requires considerable community participation and visioning.

Figure 17.12 is from a description of Palo Alto, California's Zoning Ordinance Update, prepared by Van Meter Williams Pollack, and it illustrates the FBC approach. Instead of regulating the land use and density, the FBC controls building forms and relationships with streets to enhance opportunities for mixed use and walkability. FBCs will vary for different locations in a city, from central city to neighborhood centers, and thus there may be different FBC zones within

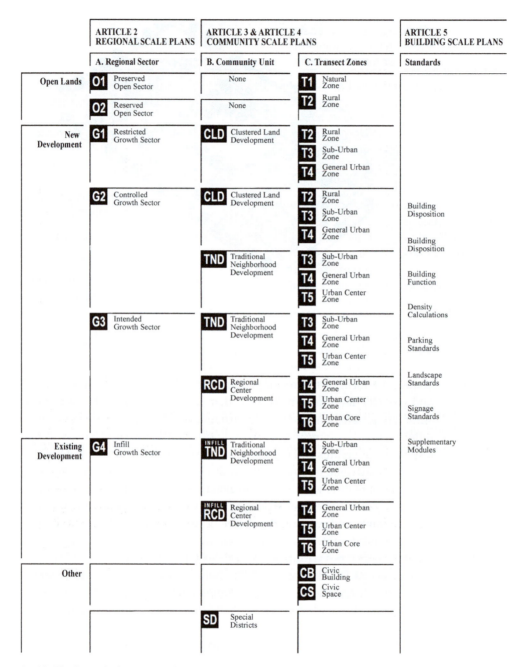

Figure 17.13 The SmartCode: Basic Outline. (*Source:* SmartCode 9.2, 2010.)

- Article 6 contains diagrams and tables supporting the other articles.
- Article 7 contains terms and definitions supporting the other articles.

Figure 17.14 shows the sector and community allocations in the SmartCode, and the relationship between planning and regulation. It defines the geography of both natural and infrastructure elements in the top section, identifies areas that

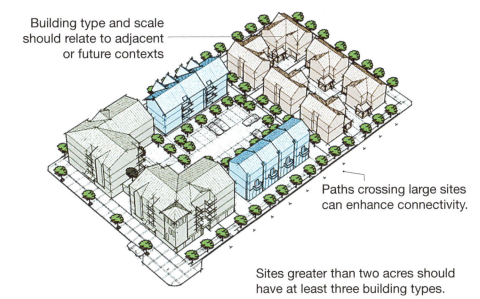

Building type and scale should relate to adjacent or future contexts

Paths crossing large sites can enhance connectivity.

Sites greater than two acres should have at least three building types.

Figure 17.12 The FBC Approach to Regulating Site Development. (*Source:* Palo Alto 2009.)

come—the form of the region, community, block, and building—which creates and protects development patterns that are compact, walkable, and mixed use; stimulating; safe; and ecologically sustainable. It recognizes that people thrive in different places—some in the urban center, some in the rural hamlet. People need a system that creates and preserves meaningful choices in their habitats.

The SmartCode outline is shown in Figure 17.13, including the nested relationships of planning scales: the Regional Sector, the Community Units, and the Transect Zones. The plan strategies involve the application of open lands, new development, and existing development areas where infill and redevelopment are prominent strategies. At the Community Unit scale, the following development strategy types are applied: Clustered Land Development (CLD), Traditional Neighborhood Development (TND), and Regional Center Development (RCD). The Transect Zone scale contains building standards appropriate to them.

The SmartCode is contained in about 30 pages in seven articles:

- Article 1 contains the general instructions pertaining to all other articles.
- Article 2 prescribes how Regional Plans designate the Open Sectors intended for open lands and the Growth Sectors intended for development and redevelopment. It also prescribes what Community Unit types belong in each sector.
- Article 3 prescribes the requirements for New Communities, including the Transect Zones that make up each type.
- Article 4 prescribes the infill requirements for areas already urbanized.
- Article 5 prescribes lot and building standards within each Transect Zone.

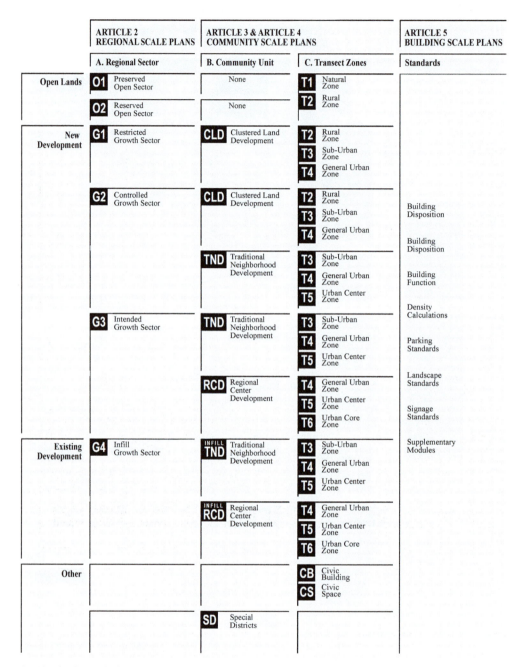

Figure 17.13 The SmartCode: Basic Outline. (*Source:* SmartCode 9.2, 2010.)

- Article 6 contains diagrams and tables supporting the other articles.
- Article 7 contains terms and definitions supporting the other articles.

Figure 17.14 shows the sector and community allocations in the SmartCode, and the relationship between planning and regulation. It defines the geography of both natural and infrastructure elements in the top section, identifies areas that

tions, address natural and human-made systems, and are based on both the local comprehensive plan and public involvement. Here are some examples:

- **Comprehensive or unified codes** combine conventional and innovative regulations to provide better consistency among them and the comprehensive plan; they facilitate compliance for designers and developers (Morris 2009).
- **Sustainability code**, developed by the Rocky Mountain Land Use Institute, addresses critical sustainability concerns, including climate change, energy, food supply, water conservation, habitat protection, and human health and safety (RMLUI 2010).
- **State level guidance** assists with codes and code reform, such as New Hampshire's Innovative Land Use Planning Techniques (NHDE 2008).
- **Code assessment tools** help evaluate and upgrade ordinances to incorporate sustainability objectives, such as the EPA's Green Building code assessment tool, the Center for Watershed Protection's (CWP) Code and Ordinance Worksheet (COW), and the EPA's Water Quality Scorecard (CWP 2004; U.S. EPA 2009).
- **Project assessment tools**, such as Smart Growth scorecards or indices and green building and neighborhood ratings systems, evaluate projects against standardized criteria (e.g., LEED-NC, LEED-ND).

Project assessment tools are useful for evaluation, education, and project marketing, but they have sometimes found their way into codes. Boulder's building code requires green rating points; Austin uses a Smart Growth Matrix (Austin undated), not in regulatory review but as a basis to waive development fees. Some anticipate the advance of LEED-ND into codes (Nelson 2010).

Form-Based Codes

New Urbanism has affected new development designs and housing markets, but with the advance of **form-based codes (FBCs)**, its influence expanded to land use regulation. An objective of FBCs is to reverse the 100-year tradition of Euclidean zoning in the U.S. Table 17.4 compares elements, goals, and outcomes of Euclidean and FBC zoning. Instead of regulating land use types, density, and bulk dimensions, FBC rules emphasize building form and location and relationships: between streets and buildings, between pedestrians and vehicles, between public and private spaces, and between buildings, the block, and the neighborhood. They aim to create a predictable public realm by controlling the physical form of private developments. FBCs are complex, and their implementation generally requires considerable community participation and visioning.

Figure 17.12 is from a description of Palo Alto, California's Zoning Ordinance Update, prepared by Van Meter Williams Pollack, and it illustrates the FBC approach. Instead of regulating the land use and density, the FBC controls building forms and relationships with streets to enhance opportunities for mixed use and walkability. FBCs will vary for different locations in a city, from central city to neighborhood centers, and thus there may be different FBC zones within

TABLE 17.4 **Comparing Euclidean Zoning and Form-Based Codes**

Euclidean Zoning	*Form-Based Zoning*
Elements of a Euclidean Code: • Regulations and map indicating allowed activities in regulated areas • Special district regulations; special exceptions; overlay districts • Administration	**Elements of a Form-Based Code**: • Regulations and map indicating allowed activities in regulated areas • Building form standards for configuration, features, functions of buildings with illustrations • Public space/street standards • Administration
Goals of Euclidean Zoning: • Prevention of illegal overcrowding • Separation of uses based on size, height, density, noise, pollution, parking requirements	**Goals of Form-Based Zoning**: • Mixed-use activities within buildings and blocks that are walkable distances to offices, residences • Promote walkability through a greater emphasis on the pedestrian spaces • Promote transit by establishing nodes of greater intensity concentrations
Outcomes of Euclidean Zoning: • Suburban sprawl with segrated land uses • Bedroom communities with long commutes • Automobile-dependent, unsustainable development patterns • Excess parking and streets built only for cars • Necessary special districts to areas which require mixed uses or others beyond standard uses	**Outcomes of Form-Based Zoning**: • Zoning areas with greater intensity • Mixed-use zones • More traditional zones created by emphasis on form rather than use • A more predictable physical result based on prescriptive standards (state what you want) rather than proscriptive standards (state what you don't want) • A zoning code that is proactive not reactive • Codes that are easier to read and more predictable

Source: Adapted from Miami 2009.

commercial corridors. A good example is Arlington County, Virginia's Columbia Pike Special Revitalization District Plan, which has applied FBC along the corridor through regulating plans, building envelope standards, and street and architectural standards. The plan was a product of intense planning and community participation, including a community design charrette (Arlington County 2011).

The SmartCode

The SmartCode was developed by Duany Plater-Zyberk and Company (DPZ) in 2003 as a means to integrate form-based codes and the Urban Transect. It is now an open source code and freely available from www.smartcodecentral.org.

According to its version 9.2, the **SmartCode** addresses the problemmatic way that existing codes have contributed to sprawl and isolated residential subdivisions. It operates at the intersection of law and design to solve this problem. As a form-based code, the SmartCode envisions and encourages a certain physical out-

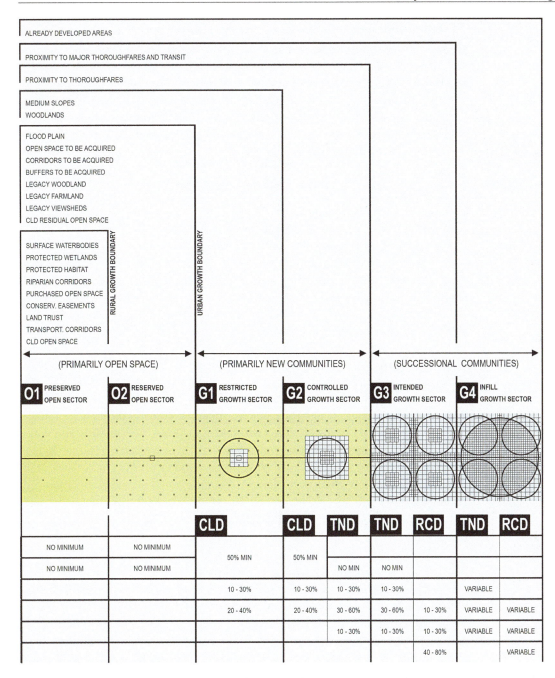

ALREADY DEVELOPED AREAS

PROXIMITY TO MAJOR THOROUGHFARES AND TRANSIT

PROXIMITY TO THOROUGHFARES

MEDIUM SLOPES
WOODLANDS

FLOOD PLAIN
OPEN SPACE TO BE ACQUIRED
CORRIDORS TO BE ACQUIRED
BUFFERS TO BE ACQUIRED
LEGACY WOODLAND
LEGACY FARMLAND
LEGACY VIEWSHEDS
CLD RESIDUAL OPEN SPACE

SURFACE WATERBODIES
PROTECTED WETLANDS
PROTECTED HABITAT
RIPARIAN CORRIDORS
PURCHASED OPEN SPACE
CONSERV. EASEMENTS
LAND TRUST
TRANSPORT. CORRIDORS
CLD OPEN SPACE

RURAL GROWTH BOUNDARY

URBAN GROWTH BOUNDARY

(PRIMARILY OPEN SPACE) | (PRIMARILY NEW COMMUNITIES) | (SUCCESSIONAL COMMUNITIES)

| **O1** PRESERVED OPEN SECTOR | **O2** RESERVED OPEN SECTOR | **G1** RESTRICTED GROWTH SECTOR | **G2** CONTROLLED GROWTH SECTOR | **G3** INTENDED GROWTH SECTOR | **G4** INFILL GROWTH SECTOR |

		CLD	**CLD**	**TND**	**TND**	**RCD**	**TND**	**RCD**
NO MINIMUM	NO MINIMUM	50% MIN	50% MIN					
NO MINIMUM	NO MINIMUM			NO MIN	NO MIN			
		10 - 30%	10 - 30%	10 - 30%	10 - 30%		VARIABLE	
		20 - 40%	20 - 40%	30 - 60%	30 - 60%	10 - 30%	VARIABLE	VARIABLE
				10 - 30%	10 - 30%	10 - 30%	VARIABLE	VARIABLE
						40 - 80%		VARIABLE

Figure 17.14 SmartCode Sector and Community Allocations. The top section shows the SmartCode geography of natural/infrastructure elements. Also shown are planning suitability for open space, new communities, and successional communities, and potential allocation of transect zones in community types. (*Source:* SmartCode 9.2, 2010.)

are primarily suitable for open space, new communities, and successional communities in the middle section; and allocates the proportion of Transect Zones (T1–T6) within each Community Type (CLD, TND, RCD).

Although the SmartCode appears rigid at first glance (and in many ways is), it is intended to be dynamic and undergoes continual review and revision. More than

30 plug-in supplementary modules have been developed to address a range of issues, including renewable energy, tree preservation, natural drainage, natural hazards, and habitat protection. More importantly, the SmartCode is intended to be locally "calibrated" through public charrettes and other forms of local involvement, to incorporate community character and metrics. Log on to SmartCode-Central, download the manual, and Google it to find the growing number of applications throughout the country, including California's statewide application.

Nonregulatory Tools for Smart Growth Management

Regulations alone are necessary but not sufficient for effective Smart Growth management. **Nonregulatory** tools can complement regulations and help to move growth management beyond the legal and political limits posed by regulations. Four basic nonregulatory tools are often used in growth management: acquisition of land or development rights, selective provision of urban services and infrastructure, financial incentives and disincentives (including development fees and exemptions), and tax policies.

Land Acquisition, Conservation Easements, Purchase of Development Rights

Permanent protection of environmentally sensitive lands is difficult to achieve through regulation. Parcels are often rezoned in response to economic and political pressure. Perhaps the best way to protect sensitive environmental lands is to buy them, and many state and local governments and local land trusts have established funds to do so. Boulder, Colorado, has an extensive land acquisition program for parks, open space, and greenbelts (see Figure 15.5). In 1967, city voters passed a measure to levy a 0.4% sales tax to fund land acquisition; this was increased to 0.73% in 1989. The program has acquired about 45,000 acres of protected lands.

However, limits on local finances constrain the land area that can be acquired for parks, open space, and natural area protection. **Purchase of development rights (PDR)** and **conservation easements** have become common methods for protecting agricultural lands and natural areas without fee-simple purchase of the property. As discussed in Chapter 15, associated with a parcel of land is a bundle of distinct rights, one of which is the right to develop the land. Without purchasing the land itself, the development rights can be acquired at a far lower cost than the land itself. This easement is reflected in the title to the land and remains there when the land is sold. Several local communities have passed bond measures for purchase of land and easements for parks, open space, and farmland protection.

Provision of Urban Services and Infrastructure

Where infrastructure goes, so goes development. "Build it, they will come." Conversely, "Don't build it, and they can't come." Public services and infrastructure necessary for development—roads, sewers, water lines—affect the location and amount of development that will occur. Thus, one way to guide development according to the community land use plan is to link that plan to the capital improvement plan for its infrastructure. Development densities in environmentally sensitive areas can be kept low simply by not planning or providing the services that large-scale or dense development requires.

Many have used their authority to decide where services will go and linked this to the development process through concurrency requirements. As Chapter 18 discusses, the Twin Cities Metropolitan Council has used effectively the provision of sewer extensions to guide metropolitan development. Maryland's Smart Growth program identifies growth areas as priority funding areas (PFAs) that are eligible for state funds for infrastructure; areas outside PFAs can be developed, but state funds will not be provided. Florida's growth management program aims to restrict development that does not have concurrent plans and financing for necessary infrastructure and services.

In the mid-1950s, Boulder witnessed considerable development pressure on higher elevations overlooking the city. The city planners did not favor sprawling development up the mountainside and also realized that the cost of extending city services, especially water supply, to higher elevations would be prohibitive. In 1958, the city established a "blue line" at 400-ft elevation above the city center, above which no city services would be made available. Since well water was nearly unattainable in the area, this policy essentially halted this development trend.

Development Impact Fees

Development impact fees, also called exactions, are fees charged to developers for the impacts of their projects. Some communities use these fees as an incentive or a disincentive to help steer development toward desirable and away from undesirable locations. Albuquerque, New Mexico's recent comprehensive plan and development policies use impact fees to establish a graduated urban development boundary. The fee schedule is based on the local government costs of services necessary to support development. Impact fees are zero for developments within the area of existing infrastructure, but they are considerable for development outside the boundary and increase quickly for development farther away. Thus, developers have a strong incentive to locate developments within a growth boundary and a disincentive to locate outside.

Austin uses its Smart Growth Matrix scoring system as a basis for waiving development and other fees. The matrix provides a quantitative measure of how well a development project accomplishes the city's Smart Growth goals. It incorporates scores on 10 factors that reflect the city's three Smart Growth goals: determining the appropriate location of development, enhancing quality of life, and increasing the tax base. The maximum score is 705. Incentives begin at 251 points and increase at different point thresholds. These include waiving of application and especially development fees, savings on infrastructure costs, and property tax incentives (Austin 2001).

The incentives have proven very attractive to the development community. Developers have contacted the city to score their projects on the matrix early in the process to increase their chances of achieving a certain threshold and fee reductions and other benefits. If they are close to the next threshold, they often make changes needed to increase their score (Fleissig and Jacobsen 2002).

Tax Policies and Voluntary Practices

As discussed earlier, 49 states provide for differential taxing of farmland and/or forestland by local governments (see Table 15.8). Landowners who participate in the program have their property assessed based on its use value as farmland, forestland, or open space, not on its development value. In exchange, landowners agree to keep their land in that use for a period of time.

Agricultural and forestal districting, used in 16 states, offers use-value taxation as well as right-to-farm protection to those landowners who voluntarily enroll in the program. Participating landowners can pay a penalty and back out of the program, so these measures do not provide permanent land protection. However, they can help farmers maintain their land in productive agricultural use.

Integrating Tools for Smart Growth Management, Sustainable Communities, and Environmental Protection

The most successful local government growth management and land conservation programs are those that integrate several regulatory and nonregulatory tools into a comprehensive program. For example, Austin uses a strong comprehensive plan, environmental overlays to protect water supplies and threatened habitat, Smart Growth development zones, rail infrastructure, a Green Building program, and incentives tied to a Smart Growth scorecard. All of these measures work together for a common objective—better development. Together they also send a message to citizens, developers, and landowners that Smart Growth is the city's policy.

Programs need to be integrated across jurisdictional boundaries. One locality may have very effective growth management, only to transfer haphazard development to a neighboring community. Boulder and Austin are good examples of cities that have partnered with their surrounding counties and neighboring jurisdictions. Portland, Oregon, and the Twin Cities in Minnesota also have developed excellent interjurisdictional programs with the assistance of state or regional guidance (see Chapter 18).

The success of emerging land use management programs, and tools like form-based codes and the SmartCode, will likely depend on the extent to which they can be integrated with other regulations and nonregulatory approaches, and how they can be applied to a variety of scales from building to regional. The SmartCode is geared for coordinating scales across the Urban Transect, but protection of the environmentally sensitive rural and natural end of the transect will depend more on land conservation acquisition and transfer of development rights than on regulations, even though urban growth boundaries will help.

Summary

This chapter presented local Smart Growth management as a means of conserving environmental lands and arresting sprawl, using several examples of successful communities. A wide range of regulatory and nonregulatory tools are available, and effective programs are those that are tailored to the needs, resources, and political climate of the community. The foundation of any local program is a comprehensive plan based on sound technical information, including an environmental inventory and other studies, as well as extensive public involvement.

Traditional, conventional zoning is flawed, and many argue that it is a major contributing factor to the unsustainable patterns of suburban development we now have in most metropolitan areas. Innovative regulatory tools, such as overlay environmental zones, flexible and performance zoning, conservation cluster zoning, transfer of development rights, and urban growth boundaries, can steer development toward appropriate areas and away from environmentally sensitive ones. New methods like form-based codes and the SmartCode show promise in reversing the nature of land use regulation to promote more livable and walkable communities, and produce appropriate urban densities to support transit, while protecting environmental resources of the rural landscape and people's choice of living habitat. In many cases, compensation is required to achieve environmental objectives, and land acquisition, conservation easements, or the purchase or transfer of development rights is appropriate. The location of development infrastructure is a useful tool for directing development to growth centers and for reducing sprawl.

In many cases, local government action is not enough to manage growth and development effectively. Some states have stepped in with regional or statewide programs to complement or guide local action. Several examples are discussed in the next chapter.

18 ■ Regional, State, and Federal Management of Growth and the Environment

Local governments are not alone in Smart Growth management and environmental land protection. Indeed, effective programs for environmental land use planning and management require coordination, guidance, resources, and sometimes mandates from higher levels of government. Regional, state, and federal agencies play important roles in conserving land and improving the management of land use and the environment.

Most of the growth and land use management in the United States still falls to local governments. However, regional, state, even federal agencies have stepped in to assist or take over when localities failed to adequately control land use, and they get involved when growth problems are beyond local management capabilities. Such initiatives, especially at the regional and state levels, have become models for effective environmental management, and they are being used to design other proactive environmental and land use programs.

This chapter discusses some of these model programs. It begins by describing some innovative substate regional efforts for environmental land protection and growth management. Although most regional approaches lack sufficient authority, agencies in the Lake Tahoe area, the Twin Cities in Minnesota, the Portland metropolitan area, the New Jersey Pinelands, and Adirondack Park in New York demonstrate the advantages of regional authority.

Several state approaches to Smart Growth management are presented next. About half the states have adopted statewide programs of varying types and authority to manage growth or protect critical environmental areas. Finally, the chapter discusses federal programs that affect private land use. Although the federal government has in most cases steered away from direct regulatory land use controls, it has provided a range of incentives and assistance for state and local land use planning and management, and for landowners to conserve environmental lands and working landscapes.

Regional Programs for Smart Growth Management and Environmental Land Protection

A regional approach to managing the environment has long been proposed in the United States, but there were few applications through the mid-1960s. The Tennessee Valley Authority, established in 1933, used water and power development in the Tennessee River Basin as a vehicle for economic development. The Delaware River Basin Commission, established in 1961, had broad responsibilities for water pollution control and water resources development. Most other river basin regional organizations had limited authority. The river basin approach appeared dead until the plethora of grassroots, cross-jurisdictional watershed management associations took hold in the 1990s. The broader-scale Chesapeake Bay Program and Great Lakes Joint Commission have also had some success. But even these programs have been limited to planning and technical and financial assistance of local governments and groups. We will look at the Chesapeake Bay Program as an example of ecosystem management in Chapter 19.

Most metropolitan areas engage in some sort of regional planning or coordination. Single-mission regional agencies dealing with transportation, sewage and water, air pollution control, or other activities are common. Regional planning districts, councils of governments (COGs), and metropolitan planning organizations (MPOs) have been established in nearly all rural and metropolitan areas in response to requirements for regional review of federal grant applications. These regional organizations are generally made up of representatives of local jurisdictions, but they have limited authority, especially over the control of land use activities. The need for regional approaches has never been more apparent. Metropolitan sprawl is clearly a regional problem that individual localities cannot manage alone.

As discussed in previous chapters, Calthorpe and Fulton (2001) argue that the end of sprawl requires a regional approach. They envision the "regional city" containing effective regional transit, affordable housing fairly distributed, environmental preserves, walkable communities, urban reinvestments, and infill development. They see the region providing social identity, economic interconnectedness, and the ecological fabric relating urban centers to bioregional habitats and protected farmlands. They also encourage regional growth boundaries, federal transportation and open space investments, and environmental policies consistent with regional goals. Urban center reinvestment is critical to focus development within urban areas and away from outlying natural areas.

Around the country, a few regional agencies established in the late 1960s to early 1970s have been effective in managing growth for large multijurisdictional areas. Despite their success, few comparable agencies have emerged elsewhere. Most of the now successful regional programs experienced environmental land use problems that were not being adequately addressed by local governments. In response, the states involved (and in two cases with federal legislation) established regional governing bodies to deal with the problems. The experiences of regional agencies in four areas—San Francisco Bay (California), Twin Cities (Minnesota), Lake Tahoe Basin (California and Nevada), and Portland (Oregon)—provide examples of the opportunities and problems of the regional approach to environmental land management. This book's first edition also presented case examples of the Adirondack Park Commission (New York) and the Pinelands Commission (New Jersey), and that material is now posted on the book website (www .envirolanduse.org).

San Francisco Bay Conservation and Development Commission

By the early 1960s, development along the shores of San Francisco Bay had resulted in the filling of one-third of the Bay's saltwater marshes. In 1961, the U.S. Army Corps of Engineers produced a long-term plan for the Bay, depicting it as the "San Francisco River" (Figure 18.1). At that time, local citizens' groups called for action to avert the alarming trend of filling in the Bay. (It is interesting to compare Figure 18.1 and Figure 12.17. The problem in the mid-twentieth century was filling until there was no bay; the problem in the twenty-first century is a growing and flooding bay from climate change induced sea-level rise.) Some look back on this early 1960s outcry as the beginning of the modern national environmental movement.

In 1965, the state legislature established the San Francisco Bay Conservation and Development Commission (BCDC) to develop a plan for the Bay. Upon the completion of the plan in 1969, the legislature made BCDC a permanent agency to implement its plan. The original Bay Plan is still active, but it has been amended occasionally, most recently in 2008 with new maps.

Figure 18.2 is the plan map for the Central Bay North. The numbers denote specific BCDC policies for specific locations that are described in the document. For example, here are three of the statements that indicate the range of BCDC policies for public access, ecological protection, and shorefront redevelopment:

4: *Point San Pablo Peninsula*. Create a regional open space and park facility. Limited commercial development at Point Molate should be compatible with proposed regional park.

8: *Castro Rocks*. Protect harbor seal haul-out and pupping site where harbor seals rest, give birth, and nurse their young.

15: *Berkeley Waterfront—Cesar Chavez Park*. Preserve marina, beach, small boat launch, windsurfing access, fishing pier, interpretive center, and multiuse trails. Possible ferry terminal. Allow if compatible with park and marina use; serve with bus public transit to reduce traffic and parking needs. Provide signage regarding fish consumption advisories for anglers.

The authority granted the BCDC in 1969 was straightforward: A permit from the BCDC is required for all development in the San Francisco Bay and in any shoreline area extending 100 ft inland from high tide. Permits are granted if the developments are consistent with the San Francisco Bay Plan or they are necessary for the health, safety, or welfare of the people in the area. Although the Com-

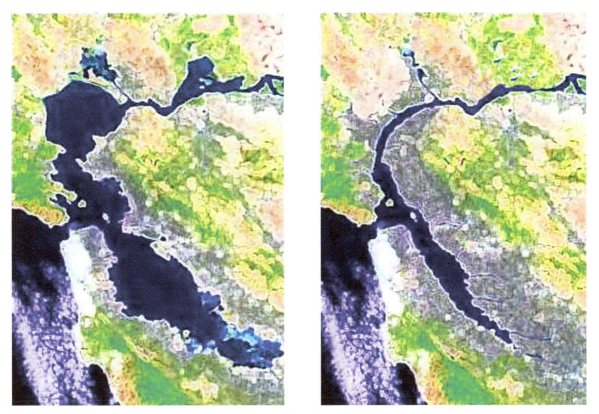

Figure 18.1 A Depiction of the Filling Rate of San Francisco Bay during the 1960s. A: Bay boundaries and shoreline in 1960s. B: Bay boundaries and shoreline projected with 1960s filling rate. (*Source:* San Francisco BCDC 1998.)

mission was initially criticized by some environmental groups as being too accommodating to developers, in its first 10 years it succeeded in essentially halting the filling of the Bay (NRDC 1977). The BCDC served as a model for the regional coastal commissions established by the California Coastal Zone program in 1972 (see Chapter 10).

Twin Cities Metropolitan Council

The postwar housing boom in the suburban areas of Minneapolis and St. Paul, Minnesota, led to a serious public health problem. In 1959, it was discovered that nearly half of the individual home wells of the area were being contaminated by effluent from septic tanks. As a result of investigations in response to this crisis, it became evident that the fragmented control of local jurisdictions was not leading to orderly growth of the area and that the regional Metropolitan Planning Commission did not have sufficient authority to rectify the situation. In response, the state legislature established the Twin Cities Metropolitan Council in 1967 to oversee development in the 3,000-sq-mi region, which included seven counties and several cities and towns.

The authority of the Council grew incrementally in the years that followed. Initially, it had the authority to prepare Development Guides for the region, to review

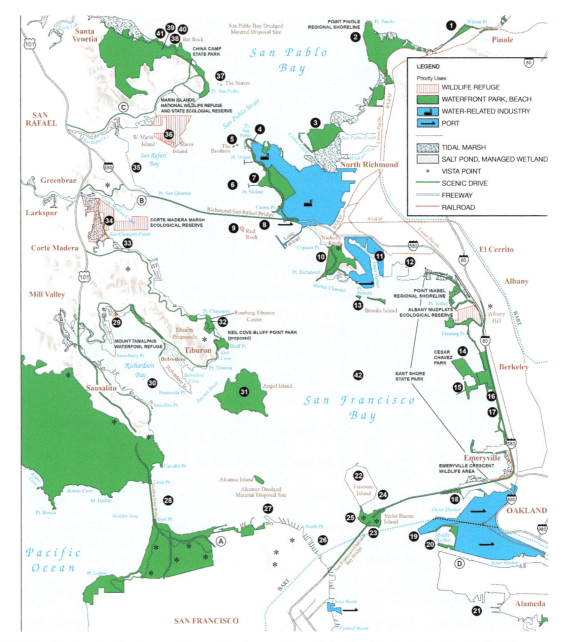

Figure 18.2 The San Francisco Bay Conservation and Development Commission Plan Map for Central Bay North. This map shows certain land uses and BCDC location policies. (*Source:* San Francisco BCDC 2008.)

and approve plans for a number of regional functional agencies, and to review plans of local jurisdictions. At first, the strongest authority of the Council was its "sewer power." One of the functional agencies under its control was the Metropolitan Sewer Board, later changed to the Metropolitan Waste Commission. Due to the water and sewer problems of the area, septic systems were severely restricted, and the location of sewer lines did much to regulate growth in the region. In its review and approval of the Waste Commission's sewerage plans, the Council was able to steer sewer lines, and thus development potential, according to its Development Guides.

In 1974, the Metropolitan Council was authorized by the state legislature to spend $40 million to acquire parkland and thus establish a true regional park system. The Council used the 1968 ecological study prepared by Wallace, McHarg, Roberts, and Todd (WMRT) to develop its protection and recreation open space plans. By 2000, the regional open space system included 50,000 acres in parks and trails, and the 2001 Regional Recreation Open Space Policy Plan called for additions of 5,000 acres (Twin Cities Metropolitan Council 2002).

In 1976, the Council was given added authority over local jurisdictions; local comprehensive plans were not only to be reviewed by the Council, but also to be approved to ensure compliance with the Development Guides. One of the keys to the success of this regional approach was a **tax-revenue-sharing** scheme, providing that all jurisdictions shared in tax-revenue benefits of the region's growth. This reduced typical jurisdictional competition and bred more cooperation.

By the 1990s, the Metropolitan Council had matured into an effective regional government with considerable authority over regional infrastructure and open space, and approval authority over local comprehensive plans. The Council developed a Smart Growth program and retained Calthorpe Associates to provide design and planning assistance (see Figure 16.22) (Calthorpe Associates 2000). The Smart Growth program established urban growth boundaries, called metropolitan urban service areas (MUSAs). The Smart Growth Blueprint 2030 plan, developed in 2002, anticipates 461,000 new households in the metro area by 2030. Figure 18.3 shows the current MUSA for 2020, the 2040 Urban Reserve for growth beyond 2020, rural residential area, and permanent agriculture and rural designated areas. Table 18.1 shows that 30% of growth by 2030 will be located in central cities, 45% in the established 2020 MUSA and rural growth centers, and 20% in expanded MUSA. At most, 5% of new housing units will be in rural areas.

TABLE 18.1 **Smart Growth in Twin Cities Metro**

New Housing Units, 2000–2030	Location	Development/Land Type
30%	In central cities, in developed and developing suburbs, and in rural and regional growth centers	On redeveloped land or infill
45%	Within 2020 MUSA and rural growth centers	On new land *inside* current 2020 MUSA
20%	In expanded MUSA (2030)	On new land *outside* current 2020 MUSA
< 5%	In rural areas	Using onsite systems outside MUSA cities and rural growth centers

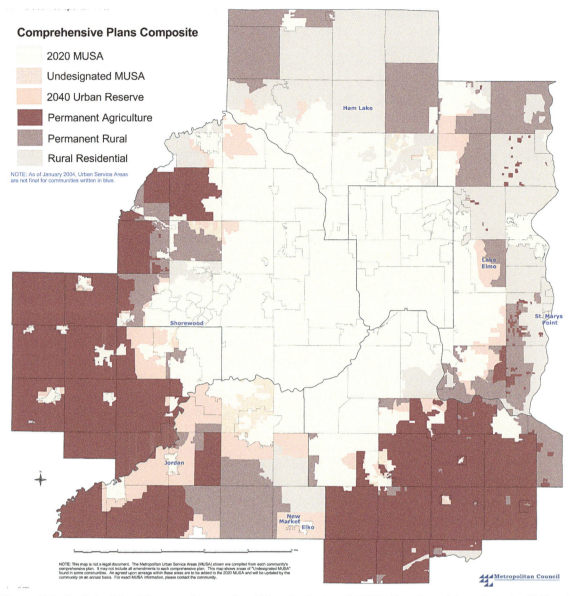

Figure 18.3 The Twin Cities, Minnesota, Metropolitan Urban Service Area (MUSA) Urban Growth Boundaries for 2020 and 2040 Urban Reserve, with Permanent Rural and Agriculture. (*Source:* Twin Cities Metropolitan Council 2010a.)

The Regional Development Framework adopted in 2004 includes strategies around four policies:

1. Accommodating growth in a flexible, connected, and efficient manner.
2. Slowing the growth in traffic congestion and improving mobility.
3. Encouraging expanded choices in housing locations and types.
4. Working to conserve, protect, and enhance the region's vital natural resources.

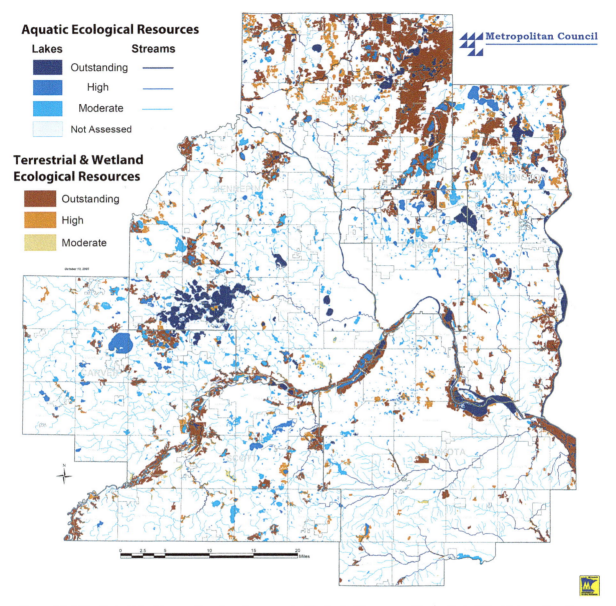

Figure 18.4 The Twin Cities Metropolitan Area Assessment of Ecological Resources. (*Source:* Twin Cities Metropolitan Council 2010b.)

The Metropolitan Council's planning has long been guided by the region's natural ecosystem ever since the WMRT ecological study in 1968. It served as the basis for the regional park system. Figure 18.4 shows the current assessment of the region's ecological resources. The aquatic systems rating is based on indicators of biological and habitat quality (including rare and endangered species), riparian vegetative cover, water clarity, and stream channel geometry. The terrestrial and wetland systems rating was derived from ecological modeling using GIS using criteria of size, shape, connectivity, and adjacent land use.

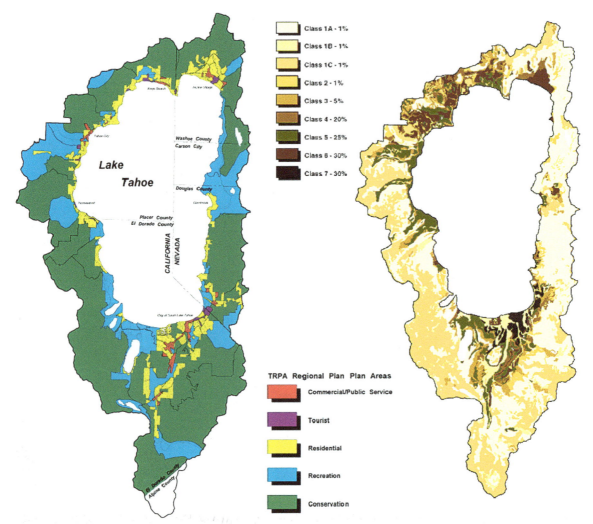

Figure 18.5 The Lake Tahoe Basin. A: The TRPA Regional Plan planning areas. B: Land capability classes, with maximum impervious surface percentages. (*Source:* TRPA 1986.)

Tahoe Regional Planning Agency

The Lake Tahoe Basin, shown in Figure 18.5, is one of the most naturally beautiful, as well as one of the most studied and planned, areas of the country. After 40 years of planning, the region has adopted an innovative and effective program to protect the basin's natural resources and accommodate additional development.

Lake Tahoe's problems began in the 1950s when the area of only 3,000 permanent residents was discovered for second-home and recreational development. The pristine lake, the second deepest in the world, surrounded by 10,000-ft peaks, offered outstanding potential for lake-related summer sports, skiing in the winter, and gambling in Nevada-side casinos. By 1978, the permanent population ballooned to 60,000, with 150,000 visitors on a peak summer day; there were 12 casinos, 22 improved public beaches, and numerous hotels.

The victim of this growth was the lake and the Basin's overall environmental quality. Planning to control land use began in 1958. However, due to the institutional complexity of the region— with two states, five counties, and several municipalities involved—little was achieved until the 1969 formation of a bi-state planning compact and the Tahoe Regional Planning Agency (TRPA) by the legislatures of both states and the U.S. Congress.

TRPA's first 10 years were controversial, as the agency's ten members (five from each state) repeatedly split over decisions on development proposals: California representatives took a pro-environmental stance, and Nevada representatives voted pro-development. The 1969 compact provided that tie votes would be considered approval. In response, California strengthened the California TRPA, which acted to slow development on the California side but had no effect in Nevada. California then withdrew funds from the bi-state TRPA in 1978 and 1979.

However, the state legislatures and Congress adopted a new compact in 1980 that changed the complexion of TRPA. The membership of the agency was increased to fourteen (seven from each state), and tie votes were no longer considered sufficient—development proposals required an affirmative vote for approval. The compact required TRPA to establish environmental thresholds characterizing the region's carrying capacity and to adopt a regional plan by August 1983 to achieve these thresholds.

The overall environmental management process is presented in Box 18.1. It involves three main components: threshold development, plan development, and implementation. (The development of threshold standards was discussed in Chapter 14.) Based on the thresholds, three alternative planning strategies were developed and labeled: maximum regulation, development with mitigation, and redirection of development. (Two other strategies, no action and maximum

---

BOX 18.1—The Environmental Management Process of the Tahoe Regional Planning Agency

Threshold Development

1. Identify issues and environmental components.
2. Identify the variables that affect the environmental components.
3. Evaluate relationships among the variables and select the best variables for use as thresholds.
4. Develop thresholds for selected variables.
5. Adopt the thresholds.

Plan Development

1. Develop goals and policies based on the thresholds.
2. Formulate five alternative planning strategies.
3. Prepare EIS on five alternative planning strategies.
4. Adopt regional plan and the plan area statements.

Implementation

1. Develop and adopt necessary ordinances.
2. Adopt a single-family residence evaluation system.
3. Implement a development management system for residential and commercial developments.
4. Coordinate capital improvements with local jurisdictions.

development, were eliminated.) After 9 months of public hearings, a final plan was developed and adopted in April 1984.

The plan includes a wide range of implementation programs designed to achieve the thresholds. These are summarized in Box 18.2. "Plan area statements" provided specific direction to 175 planning areas in the region. Each area was given one of five land use designations (conservation, recreation, residential, commercial and public service, tourist) and one of the three management strategies. "Redirection of development" was applied to most developed and partly developed areas to encourage infill and redevelopment. "Maximum regulation" was applied to four large wilderness areas.

"Development with mitigation" was the predominant designation; it allows development as long as all onsite and offsite impacts are mitigated. The development management system puts upper limits on the amount of new residential and commercial development. Residential permit applications are evaluated on a point system. All development must meet the requirements of the land capability system (designated maximum coverage of lots) and mitigation (e.g., offset 150% of water quality impacts). A TDR system allows development right transfer from environmentally sensitive areas to suitable development areas in an effort to "retire" some 70,000 acres in these sensitive areas. The Environmental Improvement Program (EIP) targets specific areas for ecological restoration and has grown to $58 million per year, but it has identified almost $1.5 billion in needed projects.

TRPA has monitored progress and revised its program accordingly. Table 18.2 summarizes the 2006 Threshold Evaluation, showing 15 of the 36 threshold indicators. Of the 36 threshold indicators, only 9 were in "attainment" in 2006 (compared with 8 in 2001), 23 were in "non-attainment" (25 in 2001), and 4 were unknown. However, 20 showed a positive trend, while only 2 showed a negative trend, and 14 showed no trend (TRPA 2007). The evaluation concluded that many elements of the 20-year-old standards require study for recalibration or amendment.

At this writing, TRPA is in the midst of the first major revision of the thresholds since 1982, as well as a major revision of the Regional Plan. The revision of threshold standards intends to change specific thresholds where scientific evidence and technical information indicate: two or more standards are mutually exclusive, evidence to provide a basis for a standard does not exist, a threshold standard cannot be achieved, or a standard is not sufficient to maintain a significant value of the region. A draft of the proposed changes are given in TRPA 2007 and TRPA 2011b.

The Regional Plan update is considering the following three alternative strategies (TRPA 2011a):

- *Alternative 4* contracts and condenses today's land use pattern through the transfer of development into five community centers.
- *Alternative 3* assumes continuation of the present land use pattern and build-out (with intensification) of the existing Community Plans.
- *Alternative 2* is a hybrid that allows for modest amounts of additional development concentrated in the already existing nine community centers. Further concentration of existing development out of sensitive environments will be achieved through transfer incentives.

BOX 18.2—Implementation Programs for the TRPA Regional Plan

Plan Area Statement for 175 Planning Areas

One of the following three general strategies is applied to each of 175 planning areas:

1. Development with mitigation (most common strategy)
2. Redirection of development (restoration, relocation)
3. Maximum regulation (applied to sensitive areas)

Development Management System: Phased Development

- Maximum of 1,800 residential permits allowed over 3 years.
- Maximum 10 major commercial permits per year (major > 1000 sq ft); maximum 65,000 sq ft major and minor commercial each year.

Residential Evaluation System

Point system based on environmental constraints, service access, site design, and mitigation measures.

Land Capability Classification

Maximum land coverage for different size capability districts. (See Figure 18.5B showing districts.)

measures, or by contributing to an implementation fund for such projects.
- All minor residential and commercial projects must pay an air pollution offset fee; all major projects must file an environmental impact and integration statement.

Transfer of Development Rights

Allows transfer of development rights from residential lots in environmentally sensitive areas, which cannot be developed, to areas able to support development.

Financing

Sources of funds: government jurisdictions, mitigation fund, property transfer tax, and various user fees and taxes.

Environmental Improvement Program

Target specific projects for restoration that will improve progress toward achievement of thresholds.

Monitoring and Evaluation

- Progress toward achieving thresholds monitored every 5 years.
- If necessary, adjustments will be made to thresholds and programs.

District	1A	1B	1C	2	3	4	5	6	7
Max. Impervious Cover	1%	1%	1%	1%	5%	20%	20%	30%	30%
Acreage, % of basin		76%			6%	4%	8%	6%	

Mitigation Requirements

- All residential, commercial, and public projects must offset 150% of water quality impacts, which can be accomplished by providing offsite erosion and runoff control

Source: Adapted from TRPA 1986, 2002.

TABLE 18.2 **Tahoe Basin Environmental Threshold Compliance Status for 15 of 36 Indicators**

Threshold		1991	1996	2001	2006	Trend
I.	**Air Quality**					
AQ-4	Visibility	**Attainment**	Nonattainment	Nonattainment	**Attainment**	▲
AQ-7	Vehicle Miles Traveled	Nonattainment	Nonattainment	Nonattainment	Nonattainment	▲
II.	**Water Quality**					
WQ-1	Turbidity (Shallow)	**Attainment**	**Attainment**	**Attainment**	**Attainment**	—
WQ-2	Clarity, Winter	Nonattainment	Nonattainment	Nonattainment	Nonattainment	▼
WQ-3	Phytoplankton Primary Production	Nonattainment	Nonattainment	Nonattainment	Nonattainment	▼
III.	**Soil Conservation**					
SC-1	Impervious Coverage	Nonattainment	Nonattainment	Nonattainment	Nonattainment	▲
IV.	**Vegetation**					
V-1	Relative Abundance and Pattern	Nonattainment	Nonattainment	Nonattainment	Nonattainment	▲
V-2	Uncommon Plant Communities	**Attainment**	**Attainment**	**Attainment**	**Attainment**	▲
V.	**Fisheries**					
F-1	Lake Habitat	Nonattainment	Nonattainment	Nonattainment	Nonattainment	▲
F-4	Lahontan Cutthroat Trout (New)			**Attainment**	**Attainment**	
VI.	**Wildlife**					
W-2	Habitats of Special Significance	**Attainment**	Nonattainment	Nonattainment	Nonattainment	▲
VII.	**Scenic Resources**					
SR-2	Scenic Quality Ratings	Nonattainment	Nonattainment	Nonattainment	Nonattainment	▲
SR-4	Community Design	Unknown	Nonattainment	Nonattainment	Nonattainment	▲
VIII.	**Noise**					
N-3	Community Noise	Nonattainment	Nonattainment	Nonattainment	Nonattainment	—
IX.	**Recreation**					
R-1	High Quality Recreational Exper.	Unknown	Unknown	Nonattainment	**Attainment**	▲

Source: TRPA 2007.

Alternative 2 reflects the extensive place-based visioning process that involved 2,500 residents. The TRPA staff recommendation for implementation relies on a combination of incentives, regulation, and collaboration to achieve the environmental thresholds. For more information on the Plan and Thresholds revision, see www.trpa.org.

Portland Metro Council

As we know from our many references throughout this book, Portland, Oregon, is a successful and livable community, often ranked among the most sustainable

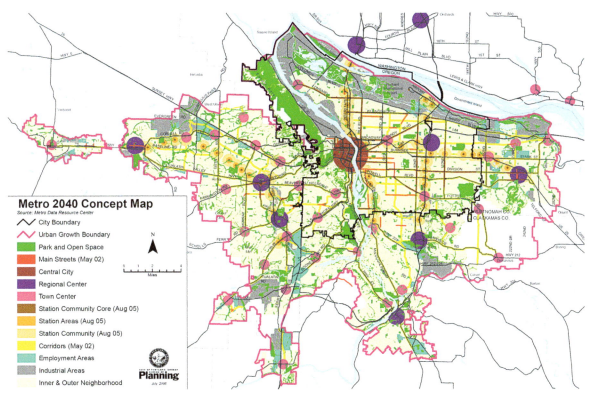

Figure 18.6 The Portland Metro 2040 Concept Map. The map shows urban growth boundary development centers and TODs. (*Source:* Portland Metro Council and City of Portland 2006.)

cities in the nation. It has done much to deserve this recognition, but much credit goes to its regional body, the Metro Council. The Oregon state legislature approved the creation of Metro in 1977, voters approved it, and Metro was established in 1979. It is the only regional government agency in the U.S. whose governing body is elected by district every 4 years in nonpartisan races. Its charter mandates the provision of planning, policy making, and services to preserve and enhance the region's quality of life. Its earliest responsibilities included urban growth boundary management, transportation planning, waste disposal planning and management, and operating the zoo.

Metro has a detailed charter and a range of authority under its Metro Code, but its primary responsibility is regional land use planning. One of its first tasks in 1979 was establishing the urban growth boundary (UGB). It has completed a number of related plans: Regional Urban Growth Goals and Objectives (1991), 2040 Growth Concept (1994), The Future Vision (1995), Regional Framework Plan (1997), and Regional Transportation Plan (2000). The last emphasizes transit-oriented development, and Metro won APA's 2008 National Planning Award for the TOD program.

Figure 18.6 shows the Metro 2040 Concept Map. You can see that the City of Portland makes up the north central area, but large areas of Multnomah, Clackamas, and Washington Counties are included in the Metro urban growth boundary. The map also shows parks and open space and industrial and employment areas

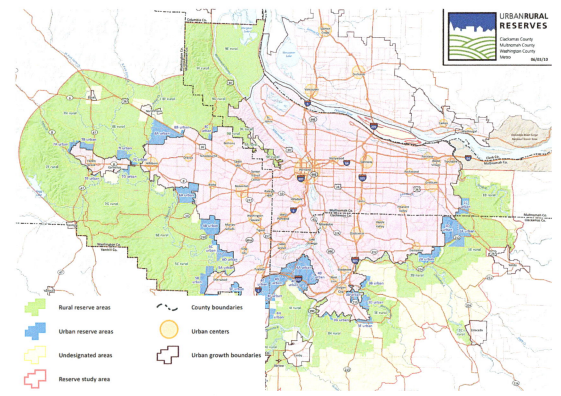

Figure 18.7 Portland Metro Urban Reserve and Rural Reserve Areas Beyond the UGB. (*Source:* Portland Metro Council 2010b.)

within the UGB. Metro manages the UGB. Prior to 2007 and Senate Bill 1011, Metro and its citizens worked to identify areas for urban expansion. Using this process, Metro added 25,000 acres of land to the urban growth area between 1998 and 2005, the largest addition being 19,000 acres added in 2002 to provide nearly 40,000 housing units and area for jobs development.

The map shows regional and town growth centers, and designated transit station TOD areas. In 1998, Metro's TOD program was the first in the country to get authorization to use federal transportation funding to acquire land for redevelopment next to light rail stations. This was a policy shift that opened the door for TOD throughout the U.S. From 2000 to 2010, Metro's TOD program completed 20 TOD projects, including more than 500,000 transit trips, creating 2,100 housing units walkable to transit (more than half of which are targeted as affordable housing), and developing 250,000 sq ft of well-designed mixed-use retail and office space; and leveraged more than $300 million in development investment (Portland Metro Council 2010a).

While much attention is given to the area within the UGB, the natural and working landscapes outside the boundary are also important. Figure 18.7 shows the green rural reserve area and the blue urban reserve areas that are likely next additions to the UGB. Metro uses a unique collaborative process to identify these designations. Metro and the three counties decided that the reserve designation would last for 50 years (Portland Metro Council 2010b). For more on Metro's planning programs, see www.oregonmetro.gov.

These regional agencies—in San Francisco, Lake Tahoe, the Twin Cities, and Portland—have much to teach other metropolitan areas of the country. BCDC's regional permitting authority, Tahoe's environmental thresholds, the Twin Cities Metro Council's revenue sharing, and Portland Metro's urban growth boundary are the measures that set them apart. The critical ingredient shared by all is regional authority over land use and development, but it does not stop there. They all blend human and ecological needs, and use collaborative processes not only of member jurisdictions, but also of citizens of the region, to help formulate regional policies.

State Growth Management Programs: Toward Smart Growth

Localities obtain their authority and requirements for planning from the states. As discussed in Chapter 17, about three-fourths of the states have adopted some version of the Dillon Rule, meaning localities have only those powers vested to them by the state. The remainder are primarily Home Rule states, in which localities are free to implement programs that the state does not explicitly restrict.

In the last two decades, several states have recognized that local control of growth and development has been insufficient to arrest sprawl and create livable communities. They have developed statewide programs to foster better local planning or to create state planning. State planning legislation varies considerably from state to state. In reviews of state land use planning programs, the American Planning Association (1999, 2002) concluded the following:

- About one-quarter of the states have moderate to substantial statewide planning reforms.
- About half of the states are using dated planning, enabling legislation dating back to the Standard City Planning Enabling Act from the 1920s.
- The vast majority of states make local comprehensive planning optional.
- In 2002, about one-third of the states were pursuing their first land use planning reforms.
- The most modernized state planning laws are in states on the East and West Coasts where urbanization and growth are significant (Figure 18.8).
- Six states have taken major initiatives in reforming planning legislation: Maryland, New Jersey, Oregon, Rhode Island, Tennessee, and Washington.
- As many as 12 other states (not in Figure 18.8) are studying or proposing planning legislation updates.
- There are different approaches to state land use planning programs.

These APA studies are 10 years old. Although there have been much talk and many studies in various states (Pennsylvania, Michigan, Virginia, Arizona, Con-

Figure 18.8 State Planning Reform Activity. (*Source:* Reprinted with permission from *Planning for Smart Growth, 2002 State of the States*, published by the American Planning Association, February 2002.)

necticut, Massachusetts, to name a few), political and economic issues have inhibited major state growth management policy development in the past decade (Schneider 2007).

A Lincoln Land Institute evaluation study of state Smart Growth policies compared various performance outcomes for four "Smart Growth policy" states (Florida, Maryland, New Jersey, Oregon) and four others (Colorado, Indiana, Texas, Virginia). Table 18.3 shows that the results are mixed for the states known for their Smart Growth policies. Although a "Smart Growth state" ranked first in each of the six categories, some of the other states outperformed Smart Growth states in some categories. Of course, the study's results depend on the methods used, and you can check out the full study if you are interested (Ingram et al. 2009).

Most states have simply left land use regulation to localities. States that have developed a state growth management program have taken different approaches, outlined below. Some states have formulated comprehensive statewide land use programs (referred to here as Type 1). Others have focused their programs on certain "critical areas," such as coastal areas, wetlands, or farmlands, or large development projects (Type 2). Those with statewide programs have taken one of four basic approaches: 1A, statewide planning and guidelines, with state approval of local plans and implementation; 1B, statewide economic incentives for Smart Growth; 1C, environmental impact assessment; and 1D, statewide planning and permitting. Here is the outline of the state approaches to growth management:

Type 1. Statewide Approaches
  1A. *Statewide planning, state criteria and guidelines with local plans and implementation; state approval of local plans and implementing programs.*

TABLE 18.3 **State Performance Rankings and Smart Growth Objectives**

	Spatial Structure	Environmental Protection	Transportation	Housing Affordability	Fiscal Dimensions
Smart Growth States					
Florida	8	6	5	5	3
Maryland	6	1	6	7	4
New Jersey	3	2	4	1	1
Oregon	1	6	1	8	8
Other States					
Colorado	2	2	3	6	2
Indiana	7	8	7	4	6
Texas	5	4	7	2	5
Virginia	4	4	2	3	5

Source: Ingram et al. 2009.

Initiated by Oregon in 1973, this approach has become the model for state growth management. Florida adopted it in 1985; New Jersey in 1987; Vermont, Maine, and Rhode Island in 1988; Georgia in 1989; Washington in 1991.

1B. *Economic incentives for development within designated urban growth boundaries and for resource conservation outside of such boundaries.* Maryland's Smart Growth program includes Priority Funding Areas and Rural Legacy program (1996–1997) and GreenPrint Program (2000). Tennessee adopted a similar program in 1999.

1C. *Environmental Impact Assessment (EIA) for new development.* Washington (since 1971) requires an EIA for discretionary approval of private projects. A few other states (e.g., New York, California) require EIAs for local government plans and decisions.

1D. *Statewide plan and state permitting for selected types of development.* Initiated by Hawaii in 1960 and adopted by Vermont and Maine in 1970, Colorado in 1973, and Rhode Island in 1978, this approach has essentially been abandoned by all except Hawaii.

Type 2. State Critical Area Approach

State programs focus on critical resources (e.g., coastal areas, wetlands, agricultural land) or geographic area; certain restrictions or permit requirements are applied to these critical areas with state agency or local implementation. Many states apply this approach to coastal development (e.g., Washington [1971], California [1972], Maryland [1986], Virginia [1988]), wetlands (Massachusetts [1972], Michigan [1979], Minnesota [1979]), and agricultural lands (nonregulatory programs in Maryland, Massachusetts, New Jersey).

Table 18.4 summarizes the features of six innovative state growth management programs highlighted by the American Planning Association (1999). The table compares the state laws or programs on their requirements for local planning, coordination with environmental programs, farmland and open space protection, historic and cultural preservation, economic development, transit planning, and affordable housing.

Statewide Land Use Programs (Type 1)

There are many variations in state growth management programs, and other sources provide a comprehensive comparison of their approaches and effectiveness (APA 1999, 2002; NGA 2001). It is useful here to profile a few examples to demonstrate the role of the states and the effectiveness of their programs. This section describes some Type 1 statewide programs, and the subsequent section highlights some Type 2 critical area programs.

TABLE 18.4 **Innovative State Growth Management Programs Profiled by the American Planning Association**

State	Year Enacted	Local Planning	Environment Protection	Farmland Open Space	Historic Cultural	Economic Development	Transit Planning	Affordable Housing
Maryland	1992/ 1997	Smart Growth optional	Chesapeake Bay	200,000 acre goal by 2011	Optional under local plan	Incentives for Smart development	Emphasis on multi-modal	Optional under local plan
New Jersey	1992	Grants for multijuris-diction	Pinelands, Meadow lands	$1 billion, 10-year bond	State bond support	Compact development encouraged	Transport/ economic linked	State over-sight of local efforts
Oregon	1973	UGB required	Salmon, other species	16 million acres protected	Must be ad-dressed in local plan	Strong emphasis on Smart development	Coordinate with land use plan	Addressed in local plan
Rhode Island	1988	21 of 39 have plan approved	Narragansett Bay, others	$15 million bond program	In two ele-ments of state plan	Incentives for Smart development	Emphasis on multi-modal	Mandatory element of local plan
Tennessee	1998	Consistent w/ county plan	Consistent w/ Natural Areas Act	Must identify rural areas for protection	Required under local plan	Incentive for growth management	May be addressed in county plans	Must be addressed in growth plans
Washington	1990–1991	Comp Plan requires growth measures	Salmon	Local plans must identify agricultural lands	Addressed in Growth Mgmt Act	For land use transportation, capital improvements	Consistent with regional transport goals	Locals laws must identify land for affordable housing

Source: American Planning Association 1999.

Oregon's Land Conservation and Development Act (Type 1A)

Many consider Oregon to have the most advanced state-administered, land use planning system in the country (APA 1999). With an approach to land use control that uses a structured relationship between state and local governments, Oregon established the 1A model, which has become the standard for state growth management programs. The planning framework was initiated by the Land Conservation and Development Act of 1973, which established the Land Conservation and Development Commission (LCDC) to promulgate state land use goals and guidelines.

Local governments then had to develop comprehensive land use plans in compliance with the 19 LCDC goals, which range from farmland and forestland protection to energy conservation and low-income housing (Box 18.3). Not only are the comprehensive plans reviewed and approved by the LCDC, but the Commission also reviews the implementing mechanisms, such as zoning ordinances, to ensure compliance with the plans. Other states mandate local governments to produce comprehensive plans, but this regulation for implementation and enforcement placed Oregon apart.

The main concern that prompted passage of the 1973 Act was agricultural land conversion, particularly in the fertile Willamette Valley. Thus, the program's strongest requirements relate to farmland protection. In their plans, communities must delineate urban growth boundaries (UGBs). Figure 18.9 shows the Oregon statewide UGBs. (For the Portland UGB, see Figure 18.6.) The UGBs are defined as areas adequate to provide 20 years of growth. Exception areas are lands outside UGBs determined to be committed by past development patterns or policies to rural residential uses. Areas outside of these boundaries having soil capabilities qualifying as farmland (classes I–IV soils in western Oregon, classes I–VI in eastern Oregon) must be placed in Exclusive Farm Use (EFU). (For soil capability classifications, see Box 6.2.) Fifteen million acres have been placed in these agricultural zones. An early 1980s case study of Salem showed that once the boundary was set, it was treated as a given; land speculation slowed, and farmers proceeded to invest in their land with reduced fear of suburban encroachment (Leonard 1982).

The Oregon program has a strong emphasis on land conservation, but its success has depended on how it accommodates urban development, and how well its balance of conservation and development matches the political winds. In the 1970s, state voters twice defeated efforts to repeal the law. Measure 65 (1998) and Measure 2 (2000) aimed to weaken the law, but both failed. However, in 2000, the voters passed Measure 7 by a 53% to 47% margin. The measure would require compensation when government regulation reduces the value of property. In February 2001, an Oregon district court, and in October 2002, the Oregon Supreme Court, ruled the measure unconstitutional. Opponents of the regulatory program came back in 2004, and voters passed Measure 37 by a 61% to 39% margin.

The law enacted by Measure 37 allows property owners whose property value is reduced by environmental or other land use regulations to claim compensation from state or local government. If the government fails to award compensation

BOX 18.3—Oregon's 19 Statewide Planning Goals

1. **Citizen Involvement**: To develop a citizen involvement program that ensures the opportunity for citizens to be involved in all phases of the planning process.

2. **Land Use Planning**: To establish a land use planning process and policy framework as a basis for all decisions and actions related to use of land and to ensure an adequate factual base for such decisions and actions.

3. **Agricultural Lands**. To preserve and maintain agricultural lands.

4. **Forestlands**. To conserve forestlands by maintaining the forestland base and to protect the state's forest economy by making possible economically efficient forest practices that ensure the continuous growing and harvesting of forest tree species as the leading use on forestland consistent with sound management of soil, air, water, and fish and wildlife resources, and to provide for recreational opportunities and agriculture.

5. **Open Spaces, Scenic and Historic Areas, and Natural Resources**. To protect natural resources and conserve scenic and historic areas and open spaces.

6. **Air, Water, and Land Resources Quality**. To maintain and improve the quality of the air, water, and land resources of the state.

7. **Areas Subject to Natural Disasters and Hazards**. To protect life and property from natural disasters and hazards.

8. **Recreational Needs**. To satisfy the recreational needs of the citizens of the state and visitors and, where appropriate, to provide for the siting of necessary recreational facilities including destination resorts.

9. **Economic Development**. To provide adequate opportunities throughout the state for a variety of economic activities vital to the health, welfare, and prosperity of Oregon's citizens.

10. **Housing**. To provide for the housing needs of citizens of the state.

11. **Public Facilities and Services**. To plan and develop a timely, orderly, and efficient arrangement of public facilities and services to serve as a framework for urban and rural development.

12. **Transportation**. To provide and encourage a safe, convenient, and economic transportation system.

13. **Energy Conservation**. To conserve energy.

14. **Urbanization**. To provide for an orderly and efficient transition from rural to urban land use.

15. **Willamette River Greenway**. To protect, conserve, enhance, and maintain the natural, scenic, historical, agricultural, economic, and recreational qualities of lands along the Willamette River as the Willamette River Greenway.

16. **Estuarine Resources**. To recognize and protect the unique environmental, economic, and social values of each estuary and associated wetlands; and to protect, maintain, where appropriate develop, and where appropriate restore the long-term environmental, economic, and social values, diversity, and benefits of Oregon's estuaries.

17. **Coastal Shorelands**. To conserve, protect, where appropriate develop, and where appropriate restore the resources and benefits of all coastal shorelands, recognizing their value for protection and maintenance of water quality, wildlife habitat, water-dependent uses, economic resources, and recreation and aesthetics.

18. **Beaches and Dunes**. To conserve, protect, where appropriate develop, and where appropriate restore the resources and benefits of coastal beach and dune areas; and to reduce the hazard to human life and property from natural or human-induced actions associated with these areas.

19. **Ocean Resources**. To conserve marine resources and ecological functions for the purpose of providing long-term ecological, economic, and social value and benefits to future generations.

Source: Adapted from http://www.oregon.gov/LCD/goals.shtml.

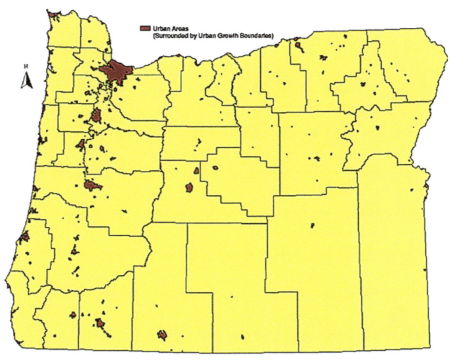

Figure 18.9 State of Oregon Urban Growth Boundaries. (*Source:* Oregon Department Land Conservation and Development 1997.)

within 2 years of the claim, the law lets the claimant use the property under only the regulations in place at the time the property was purchased. In 2005, a state circuit court declared the measure unconstitutional and directed the department (and all other defendants) to stop accepting claims and issuing reports and orders on claims; however, that trial court decision was reversed by the Oregon Supreme Court in 2006, and the measure was reinstated. By 2007, 7,500 claims, representing 750,000 total acres, had been filed. Some of the claims were for inappropriate land uses, but because municipalities cannot afford the billions in compensation, the laws were waived in every case.

In 2007, the Oregon legislature placed Measure 49 on the November special election ballot, and it passed with 62% in favor. The measure overturned and modified many Measure 37 provisions; it protects farmlands, forestlands, and lands with groundwater shortages in two ways. (1) Subdivisions are not allowed on high-value farmlands, forestlands, and groundwater-restricted lands; claimants may not build more than three homes on such lands. (2) Claimants may not use the measure to override current zoning laws that prohibit commercial and industrial developments, such as strip malls and mines, on land reserved for homes, farms, forests, and other uses. This compromise measure saved the basic framework of the Oregon program and its core objective to conserve high-value resource lands.

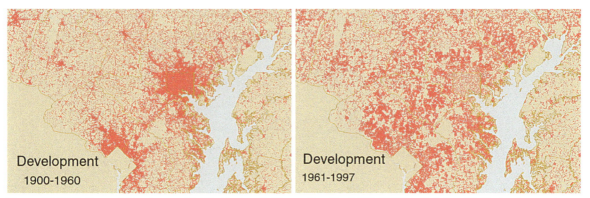

Figure 18.10 Patterns of Development in Washington-Baltimore Corridor 1900–1997. Left: Before 1960, development was concentrated in the cities and suburban fringe. Right: After 1960, almost all development was outside the cities in previously rural areas. (*Source:* Frece 2000.)

Maryland's Smart Growth and Neighborhood Conservation Initiative (Type 1B)

Maryland's Governor Glendening popularized the term "smart growth" in the mid-1990s and developed the Type 1B multifaceted, incentive-based approach to growth management, resource conservation, and economic development. The program was a response to the realization that Maryland's growth pattern was consuming rural land at an alarming rate. Figure 18.10 shows the dramatic change in growth patterns before 1960 and after. Before 1960, development was concentrated in urban centers; after 1960, the flight from the city began in earnest and consumed rural land in its wake.

Maryland's Smart Growth Program includes five component programs that focus on directing growth to areas where infrastructure is already in place (or is planned). In so doing, Smart Growth aims to revitalize existing communities and reuse older industrial sites, and to conserve agricultural and open space resources critical to the state's economy and its quality of life. Whereas many other state programs are regulatory, Maryland's is based on economic incentives, not regulations. However, to gain access to state financial resources for infrastructure (especially roads, water, and sewer), for rural land protection, and for redevelopment, localities must abide by the state rules for location of these projects. Here are the six components (Frece 1997):

1. **Smart Growth Areas or Priority Funding Areas**. One of the most powerful elements in the initiative steers the resources of the state's $15 billion budget to older towns and cities, or to other areas specifically designated by local governments for growth. Baltimore and all other municipalities in Maryland, as well as the heavily developed areas inside the Baltimore and Washington beltways, are automatically designated as Smart Growth areas or priority funding areas (PFAs), both of which are eligible for state assistance. PFAs are defined as those areas with approved water and sewer plans and other features. Figure 18.11 shows the PFAs, as of 2000.

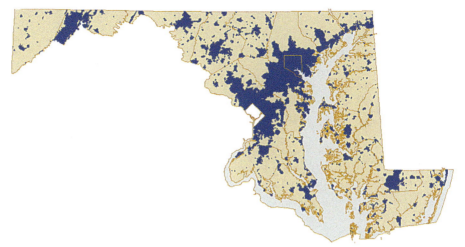

Figure 18.11 Maryland's Priority Funding Areas and Rural Legacy Areas, 2000. PFAs are blue; RLAs are green. (*Source:* Frece 2000.)

2. **Rural Legacy Areas**. Maryland earmarked up to $140 million over 5 years to protect its rural legacy areas (RLAs)—farmland, forests, and open spaces threatened by development. Under this program, local governments and private land trusts may apply for funds to buy the land outright or to acquire easements to preserve it from development. Figure 18.11 shows the RLAs, as of 2000.

3. **Brownfields Cleanup and Redevelopment Program**. Industrial redevelopment incentives are made available through the Brownfields Cleanup and Redevelopment Program, which provides for cleanup of previously developed and contaminated industrial sites. Fear of liability has driven potential developers to build elsewhere, too often on farmland or other open spaces where expensive new infrastructure is required. The program helps revitalize older urban areas, increase local government revenues, create jobs, and clean up contaminated land.

4. **Job Creation Tax Credit**. This tax credit encourages the development and expansion of small businesses within locally designated Smart Growth areas. It lowers from 60 to 25 the number of new jobs a business must create to qualify for a one-time income tax credit.

5. **Live Near Your Work**. Under this matching grant program, the state, local jurisdictions, and individual employers form a partnership that can provide at least $1,000 each to individual home buyers who agree to purchase homes near their work. This program strengthens neighborhoods by increasing homeownership; promotes linkages between employers and nearby communities; increases land values and revenue to local government; reduces commuting costs; reduces air pollution; reduces employee turnover, training, and recruitment costs; and makes Maryland a more attractive place for business to locate and expand.

6. **GreenPrint Program**. GreenPrint, the newest component of Maryland's Smart Growth Program, was adopted in 2001 (see Chapter 5). It

identifies and conserves a statewide green infrastructure made up of hubs and links. Maryland identified 2 million acres of ecologically significant land not yet consumed by sprawl; 1.5 million of these acres remain unprotected (see Figure 15.7). Through this program, planners hope to boost protected land conservation capacity by 10,000 acres per year, using state plans and funds to leverage resources from the federal government and foundations.

Since it relies on incentives rather than regulations, Maryland's program does not preclude sprawling development, it just makes it more costly to achieve compared with development within PFAs. In an evaluation study of the Maryland program, Lewis et al. (2009) found that after 10 years the PFAs have fallen short of expectations. They are not well integrated into land use decision making at the local level. State agencies have not altered budgetary systems to guide the allocation of funds effectively. Lewis et al. conclude that for Type 1B state programs to work, states must adopt consistent budgeting processes to match the program.

Florida's Growth Management Program

In 1972, Florida enacted the Environmental Land and Water Management Act. During the next decade, this approach proved to be inadequate for managing growth and protecting the environment under Florida's intense development pressures. The State and Regional Planning Act, passed in 1985, substantially changed the program.

Under the 1972 Act, the Division of State Planning recommended to the governor, and he designated, "critical areas of state concern." These areas could involve environmental or cultural resources of regional or state importance, sites of existing or proposed major public facilities, or sites with major development potential. The Act limited the areas so designated to only 5% of the land in the state. Within 6 months of the designation of the areas, local governments were to prepare development regulations following state guidelines to protect the areas. In addition, the Act established a procedure for regional and state review of proposals for developments of regional impact (DRI), such as an airport, stadium, power plant, transmission line, large industrial facility, or large shopping center. Although a state permit was not required for such projects, state and regional officials could influence the approval process.

The 1985 Act repealed the earlier program and established a Type 1A program with the dual aim of preventing urban and suburban sprawl, protecting the environment, and coordinating infrastructure construction and land development. The Act defined sprawl as "scattered, untimely, poorly planned urban development that occurs in urban fringe and rural areas and frequently invades lands important for environmental and natural resource protection" (Florida Department of Transportation 2009, 22).

The program established the concept of **concurrency**, requiring public services and facilities for supporting development to be available concurrent with development. These services included transportation, schools, water, sewer, solid

waste collection and disposal, parks and recreation, and stormwater management. This "pay-as-you-grow" approach meant that before permits could be issued to developments, plans and funding for these services had to be in place. The program also had an objective of fostering compact development and fostering urban growth boundaries. However, the approach gave localities more flexibility than Oregon's program and appears to have been less effective at containing growth within boundaries.

Virginia's Urban Development Areas

In 2010, Virginia's General Assembly passed, without fanfare, HB 3202, which required all localities with a decennial (10-year) growth rate of 15% or a growth rate of 5% and a population of at least 20,000 to designate at least one Urban Development Area (UDA) in their comprehensive plans by 2011. The area or areas must accommodate between 10 and 20 years of projected growth, and planners must consider proximity to urbanized areas and transportation, and the availability of water and sewer systems. Within these UDAs, the comprehensive plans must incorporate the principles of New Urbanism design, including mixed use, connectivity of road and pedestrian networks, and effective stormwater management. The Act specified minimum residential and commercial densities for the UDAs: four residential units per gross acre and 0.4 floor-area ratio (FAR) for commercial development (a one-story store has a FAR of 1; a two-story store has a FAR of 0.5).

By design, this growth management requirement applies to all urbanizing counties in Virginia. It is too early to tell the extent to which this program will be implemented and what effect it will have on the growth and development patterns in the state.

State Environmental Impact Requirements (Type 1C): Washington and California

More than half the states have passed legislation based on the National Environmental Policy Act, establishing a state environmental policy and some type of environmental impact statement (EIS) requirement. Most of the states simply target state agencies to prepare an environmental assessment of major actions. Only four states—California, Massachusetts, New York, and Washington—and Puerto Rico impose certain stipulations on both state and local public agencies. Massachusetts provides a form of impact assessment, build-out analysis, for all of its localities. (See Chapter 14 for EIS and build-out analysis procedures.)

All five jurisdictions apply EIS requirements to public projects, but only California and Washington apply them to local planning and permitting decisions. In New York, permitting decisions have been interpreted to be "ministerial," meaning that if codes and regulations are met, agencies have little or no discretion in granting approval. However, in California and Washington, permitting has been viewed as a discretionary act; that is, even though codes are met, public agencies are to examine the impacts of the proposal and decide whether the policies of the state environmental act are being met.

This interpretation has given local jurisdictions added responsibility and discretionary power in permit approvals. The guidelines for implementing Washington's State Environmental Policy Act (SEPA) establish the procedures agencies and developers must follow, as well as the types of projects that are exempt (State of Washington 1998). The procedure has increased the quality of developments, mostly through the negotiation process. The SEPA procedure includes the following decision points, when local planners have an opportunity to negotiate with the developer:

1. The "threshold determination" of whether or not an EIS is required ("Gee, if you made these changes to your proposal, you probably would not have to prepare a costly EIS").
2. When the draft EIS is circulated for review ("You know, we will have to decide on your project, and we'd really like to see these changes.")
3. At the approval decision.

Both California and Washington are using their environmental impact provisions to advance climate change mitigation. In Washington, SEPA rules will require developers to demonstrate what carbon emissions impacts they may have and how to mitigate (see Figure 17.11). In California, climate change impacts and mitigation must be considered in local general plans through the CEQA EIR process (California Attorney General's Office 2009).

State Critical Area Protection Programs (Type 2)

Several states have taken action to control specific developments, or development in specific critical areas, such as coastal areas, wetlands, and farmlands. Several of these state programs are discussed in other chapters, including state farmland protection programs (see Table 15.3) and coastal zone management and wetland protection (see Chapter 10).

Virginia, Maryland, and Pennsylvania were signatories to the 1983 interstate Chesapeake Bay Agreement. Virginia's most notable early compliance effort came in the Chesapeake Bay Preservation Act of 1988. In passing the Act, the General Assembly realized that only through effective and widespread land use controls to reduce nonpoint source pollution could the goals and objectives of the Agreement be achieved; it also realized that local governments must play the leading role in implementing those controls.

The Chesapeake Bay Preservation Act Regulations became effective in 1989. Tidewater localities (basically east of Interstate 95) were given a year from that date to adopt the criteria and 2 years to fully integrate them into their local governments' plans and ordinances. The regulations have three basic elements:

1. Specific local requirements and adoption deadlines for water-sensitive plans and zoning ordinances.
2. Criteria for designating local Chesapeake Bay Preservation Areas (CBPAs).
3. Performance criteria for land use and development in CBPAs.

The CBPAs are divided into resource protection areas (RPAs), which have special water quality value (e.g., tidal wetlands, tidal shores), and resource management areas (RMAs), which are less sensitive than RPAs but still may impact water quality. Areas outside of designated RPAs and RMAs are not subject to the regulations. Areas within RPAs and RMAs having existing development are designated as intensively developed areas (IDAs); these may be redeveloped, as long as the applicable performance criteria are met. Other non-IDAs that have existing development may also be redeveloped. Several localities are using RPA extensions (RMAs) to create riparian buffers and help manage stormwater and meet not only Chesapeake Bay regulations, but also MS4 requirements. We looked at Fairfax County's approach in Chapters 7 and 8.

Federal Programs for Environmental Land Use Planning and Management

Historically in the United States, the federal government's activities in land use have focused on the management of federally owned public lands. The control of private land use has been left to state and local governments. However, many activities of federal agencies—from highway funding to issuing flood insurance—have a significant influence on environmentally sensitive lands, and many private land use decisions impact federally managed resources, such as air and water quality. As a result, several federal programs have been enacted that influence private land use.

Federal Programs Affecting Private Land Use

Several federal government programs influence private land use on environmental grounds. Since the federal government is still reluctant to directly regulate private land use, the controls used are often subtle. The programs involve six different approaches:

1. **Financial assistance for land acquisition, land conservation**. For example:
   - The Land and Waters Conservation Fund, providing grants to states and localities for land acquisition (see Chapter 15).
   - The Conservation Reserve Program, Wetlands Reserve Program, and related programs, providing funding for farmer stewardship of highly erodible lands and wetlands (see Chapter 15).
   - The Agricultural Conservation Program, providing cost-share funds for soil and water conservation.
   - Other federal grants for community-based environmental programs.
2. **Technical assistance to private landowners**. For example:
   - The Natural Resources Conservation Service, providing technical assistance programs to farmers.
   - Other agencies' educational programs for private land stewardship.

3. **Funding for state or local environmental planning**. For example:
   - The Coastal Zone Management program, providing grants for state and local planning (see Chapter 10).
   - Clean Water Act funds (sec. 319), for nonpoint source pollution control grants (see Chapter 8).
4. **Withdrawal of federal funds from development or use in certain areas**. This approach is similar to Maryland's Smart Growth Program approach 1B. For example:
   - Sodbuster and swampbuster programs, cutting farm subsidies to farmers cultivating highly erodible land or wetlands (see Chapter 15).
   - The Coastal Barriers Resources Act of 1982, which withdraws all federal assistance for development in specified Barrier Resources Protection areas.
5. **Threatened withdrawal of federal funding**. For example:
   - The National Flood Insurance Program: Communities must implement floodplain management or residents cannot get subsidized flood insurance and communities cannot get federal assistance, including disaster relief, for any project in flood-prone areas. As a result, all 30,000 flood-prone communities have enacted floodplain management and zoning (see Chapter 13).
6. **Direct regulation**. Although rare, federal regulation of private land use occurs in special cases, including:
   - Wetlands permitting under the Clean Water Act (see Chapter 10).
   - Habitat Conservation Planning under the Endangered Species Act (see Chapter 11).
   - Surface mine reclamation under the Surface Mining Control and Reclamation Act. All surface mine operations must be permitted, and must develop and implement a post-mining reclamation plan.

Policies Guiding the Activities of Federal Agencies

In the 1970s, a number of laws and executive orders provided specific guidance to federal agencies concerning environmentally sensitive lands. The most universal directive came in the **National Environmental Policy Act (NEPA)** of 1969. Since NEPA, a number of more specific policies have been established concerning federal agency impacts on floodplains, wetlands, habitats of endangered species, and agricultural lands. Federal agencies involved in planning and managing the nation's public lands and water resources have had to respond to yet another set of statutory directives.

NEPA (PL 91–190) was signed into law on January 1, 1970, at the height of the environmental movement in the United States. It established an environmental policy for the federal government and aimed to implement that policy through an action forcing provision, the environmental impact statement. The EIS was to address potential impacts on not only environmentally sensitive lands, but also pollution discharges and other aspects of the human environment. NEPA's policy statement establishes an environmental priority, yet balances it with other national objectives: "It is the continuing policy of the Federal government . . . to create and maintain conditions under which man and nature can exist in productive harmony, and fulfill the social, economic, and other requirements of present and future generations of Americans" (quoted from NEPA, sec. 101[a]).

Section 102 contains several provisions that aim to implement the policy. Section 102(2)(a) directs federal agencies to utilize a systematic, interdisciplinary approach to ensure the use of scientific information and environmental design techniques in planning and decision making. NEPA's most specific and forceful provision, contained in section 102(2)(c), requires agencies to prepare a detailed statement on the environmental impacts of, and alternatives to, "major Federal actions significantly affecting the quality of the human environment." The EIS must be made available for review by all interested parties, including the public.

Public Land Management

The public lands contain nearly one-third of the U.S. land area and are administered primarily by the U.S. Forest Service (USFS), the Bureau of Land Management (BLM), the National Park Service, and the Fish and Wildlife Service (see Figure 15.1). In addition, the federal government has primary responsibility over the nation's navigable waters, and several agencies—including the U.S. Army Corps of Engineers, the Soil Conservation Service, the Bureau of Reclamation, and the Tennessee Valley Authority—actively plan, design, and construct water development projects for navigation, flood control, irrigation, water supply, power generation, and other purposes. For all of these agencies administering federal natural resources, a number of planning and management principles and procedures have been developed to ensure environmental considerations in management and development decisions. The public land agencies all operate under directives requiring management planning. Policies concerning the environmental resources of public lands involve two principles: the withdrawal of certain lands from development and multiple use.

The national parks, refuges, and wilderness areas are examples of **withdrawal programs**; however, even these programs are managed to balance recreation and resource protection. The BLM (330 million acres) and the USFS (190 million acres) manage the majority of the public lands. The Multiple Use and Sustained Yield Act of 1960 established for the Forest Service a set of appropriate uses for Forest Service lands, including timber production, grazing, recreation, watershed protection, fish and wildlife management, and mineral development. The Resources Planning Act of 1974 and the National Forest Management Act of 1976 required the USFS to develop management plans for each national forest. **Multiple-use areas** designated for timber production must be managed to protect water quality and fish and wildlife.

The BLM is guided by the Classification and Multiple Use Act of 1964, which established grazing, recreation, mineral development, and fish and wildlife as BLM's multiple uses. Like the Forest Service, BLM was charged with specific planning and management responsibilities by the Federal Lands Policy and Management Act (FLPMA) of 1976 and the Public Rangelands Improvement Act (PRIA) of 1978. In their current planning, BLM, the USFS, and the Park Service are applying more holistic "ecosystem management," which is discussed in the next chapter (Phillips and Randolph 1998; Randolph 1987).

Summary

In the 1970s, the Council on Environmental Quality wrote about the "quiet revolution" in land use control (U.S. Council on Environmental Quality 1974). That revolution fell silent in the early 1980s but resounded in the mid-1990s with an increasing number of state programs to promote Smart Growth in response to the problems of sprawl development. Oregon and Maryland are two states that have led the way with different programs: Oregon's regulatory program relies heavily on local implementation; Maryland's, too, relies on locals but uses incentives rather than regulations.

Both use the concept of defined development areas or urban growth boundaries and defined conservation areas. Some other states have followed suit. Regional authorities for land use control established in the 1960s and 1970s continue to be very active and show signs of effectiveness 40 years later, creatively using the full array of growth management tools available. Still, few regional metropolitan areas have developed the degree of cooperation and, especially, authority required for taking a regional approach to Smart Growth management. The federal government has some influence on the private use of specific environmental lands, but almost all authority remains with state and local governments.

19 ■ Integrative Management of Ecosystems and Watersheds

This book has explored a broad range of planning processes, methods, analytical techniques, technologies, designs, and policies—all of which are directed at more effectively controlling human–environment interactions, in order to achieve greater sustainability. Ecosystem management (EM) and watershed management (WSM) have emerged as integrative approaches that use these elements in interdisciplinary frameworks to manage lands, waters, and ecological functions, and the human activities that affect and depend on them.

These two approaches vary somewhat in their objectives: EM aims to manage natural land and water systems, ecological functions and resilience, and biodiversity, while WSM aims to manage lands and waters to restore and maintain water quality, aquatic ecology, and hydrologic functions. But the objectives often overlap, and they both attempt to balance coupled human–ecological systems. Their frameworks share common elements of best science (including what is now referred to as sustainability science), variable spatial scales, a long-term horizon, social learning through collaborative planning, and scientific learning through adaptive management.

Although EM and WSM have been applied at a variety of scales for two decades, they are still not yet fully integrated into environmental resource management programs. However, they offer great promise in our quest to achieve sustainable ecosystems and watersheds. In addition, they provide useful planning and management lessons for sustainable, livable, and green communities.

This final chapter starts by introducing the basic principles of, and frameworks for, ecosystem and watershed management. We then explore a few case examples that illustrate the opportunities and barriers to implementation. While doing so, we should keep in mind some of the concepts, analytical techniques, and public policies from previous chapters that serve as building blocks for EM and WSM. They include:

- The environmental movement, especially the Ecosystem Movement (Chapter 1).

- The environmental and land use planning process (Chapters 2 and 3).
- Collaborative learning and collaborative management (Chapter 4).
- Geospatial data and analysis (Chapter 5).
- The science of and analytical techniques for soils, hydrology, and ecology (Chapters 6–11).
- Stormwater management and stream restoration (Chapters 7 and 8).
- Landscape and urban ecology (Chapters 10 and 11).
- Planning for resilience through natural hazard mitigation and climate change adaptation (Chapters 12 and 13).
- Land suitability, carrying capacity, and environmental impact assessment (Chapter 14).
- Land conservation methods, policies, and programs (Chapter 15).
- Design with nature for people (Chapter 16).
- Land development growth management methods, policies, and programs Chapters 17 and 18).

Principles of Ecosystem Management

Historically, we have managed environmental resources with a singular, reductionist approach. In nature, however, these resources are inextricably linked not only to one another but also to human activities. It makes sense to look at them as a whole, to manage them as ecosystems. Ecosystems can be studied at a variety of scales, from an isolated tidal pool to a continent. Human society is an important component and must be viewed as part of the ecosystem to be managed. The current movement toward EM was prompted in the late 1980s by a number of converging factors, including the following:

- Heightened recognition of the "biodiversity crisis" of habitat destruction and species extinction.
- Limited success of piecemeal environmental laws and programs in meeting the expectations of a range of stakeholders, including both development and preservation interests.
- Theoretical and empirical developments in environmental management that called for more holistic and adaptive approaches.
- Changing societal values and attitudes about natural systems, requiring new ways of incorporating those values in management.

Since the early 1990s, managing ecosystem integrity and health has become the operating policy of federal land management agencies, such as the U.S. Forest Service and the U.S. Fish and Wildlife Service (Phillips and Randolph 1998). This emphasis developed in response to concerns over biodiversity loss and the limitations of species-specific wildlife management and commodity-based resource management to ensure resource sustainability. During the past two decades, the ecosystem approach has been adopted by many local and regional organizations for environmental management (Yaffee et al. 1996). This practice of ecosystem management has been enhanced by recent attention and advances in sustainability science and adaptive management.

As it evolved during the 1990s, EM can be defined as follows:

> **Ecosystem management (EM)** is an integrative, interdisciplinary, adaptive, and collaborative approach to policy making, planning, and management, grounded in the best scientific information available, recognizing uncertainties and the understanding that human activity and ecosystems are inextricably linked. The goal of EM is to sustain and/or restore ecosystem integrity, biological diversity, and coupled human–environment systems at all spatial and temporal scales through scientific understanding and collaborative decision making.

Box 19.1 outlines five EM criteria. Two of the primary ones are worthy of elaboration: sustainability science and adaptive management.

As introduced in Chapters 2 and 10, **sustainability science** is the integration of ecological and social sciences to advance basic understanding of coupled

---

BOX 19.1—Ecosystem Management Criteria

1. Ecological Orientation

- The ecosystem dictates use and management strategies.
- The integrity of the ecosystem is to be preserved in ways to seek sustainability.
- Natural biodiversity is to be maintained, focusing on how the biological community functions as a whole within the ecosystem.

2. Time and Spatial Scales

- Long-term time horizon, looking at future generations of species, including people.
- Boundaries are set by the ecosystem, not by jurisdictional borders.
- Hierarchy of ecosystem scales allows addressing larger landscape interconnections through site-scale actions.

3. Sustainability Science of Coupled Human–Natural Systems

- Acquire as complete a knowledge base as possible, including integrated ecological and social sciences.
- Use adaptive approaches to experiment and acquire new information to fill gaps in knowledge.

4. Humans and Society as Integral Components of Ecosystems

- Social, cultural, and economic values of humans must be considered in the management of land and ecosystems.
- Humans have damaged the environment: Practice restoration.
- Humans will change the environment: Minimize and mitigate impact.
- Collaborative planning and decision making requires stakeholder involvement.

5. Integrative Adaptive Management Actions

- Integrate management within and between agencies and organizations.
- Integrate interdisciplinary practices into management strategies.
- Monitor management practices for effectiveness.
- Practice adaptive management: Learn from monitoring and modify practices as necessary.

human–ecological systems; to facilitate the design, implementation, and evaluation of practical interventions that promote sustainability; and to improve linkages between research/ innovation and policy/ management (Liu et al. 2007; Reitan 2005; Turner et al. 2003). This emerging interdisciplinary field has become a focus of scientific literature, such as *Sustainbility Science* (2006) and *Sustainability: Science, Practice, & Policy* (2005), and an academic study, such as Harvard's Sustainability Science Program (2001) and the University of Washington's Urban Ecology Program.

In a synthesis of six major studies of coupled human–natural systems on five continents, Liu et al. (2007) demonstrated the value of integrated ecological–social science analysis by showing the variability of these coupled systems across space, time, and organizational frameworks. The studies showed nonlinear dynamics, thresholds of change, heterogeneity, recriprocal feedback loops, resilience, time lags, surprising outcomes, and legacy effects on future opportunities. They discovered relationships that singular ecological or social science analysis could not.

As introduced in Chapter 2, **adaptive management (AM)** is a systematic approach for improving resource management by learning from the outcomes of management actions—essentially, learning while doing. It promotes flexible decision making that can be adjusted in the face of uncertainties as these outcomes become better understood. Monitoring these outcomes both advances scientific understanding and helps adjust policies and operations as part of an iterative learning process (NRC 2004; U.S. DOI 2009).

In *passive adaptivc management*, managers use historical or comparative analysis to determine a "best guess" hypothesis of outcomes from a preferred action and then monitor real outcomes. The results are then used to revise the hypothesis and management action. This approach is appropriate where there is high level of confidence in predicted ecosystem responses and where regulatory or other constraints limit outcome variability.

In *active adaptive management*, managers generally define competing hypotheses of outcomes and then design experiments to test them. With multiple experiments, active AM can provide more meaningful data on outcomes in a shorter time frame than passive AM, but it is generally more costly to implement. Box 19.2 describes some criteria that affect the application of active and passive AM to environmental management, developed by Gregory et al. (2006). Four case examples illustrate the effect of the criteria on active and passive AM applicability.

The U.S. Department of the Interior's *Technical Guide to Adaptive Management* (2009) identifies some preconditions for adaptive management (Box 19.3). Adaptive management works best when stakeholders are engaged, there are explicit objectives, there are uncertainties, modeling and monitoring progress are possible, and/or management actions can be adjusted within existing legal frameworks. Figure 19.1 shows the importance of uncertainty and controllability. In an ideal situation of high controllability and low uncertainty, optimal control is possible. Low controllability and uncertainty often result in hedging strategies, and with low controllability and high uncertainty, scenario planning is most applicable. Adaptive management is best suited to high uncertainty situations where systems are controllable.

BOX 19.2—Applicability Criteria of Active and Passive Adaptive Management (AM)

Passive AM simply adds monitoring and evaluation to conventional plan implementation, in order to learn from outcomes. Active AM goes further, by explicitly developing research hypotheses and designing experiments to test them through monitored outcomes of plan implementation. Active AM can provide more effective and timely learning, but it is not applicable in all cases. The following criteria can help determine the applicability and appropriateness of active and passive AM:

- Spatial and temporal scales: project duration and timeline, spatial extent and complexity.
- Dimensions of uncertainty: parameter, structural, and stochastic uncertainty; confidence.
- Evaluation of costs, benefits, and risks: measurement, communication, magnitude, clarity.
- Institutional and stakeholder support: leadership, flexibility, capacity.

Gregory, et al (2006) developed four hypothetical ecosystem management cases, including examples given in Table 19.1, that demonstrate the effects of the criteria:

1. A field test to assess the response of seedling growth to alternative fertilization regimes on a set of cutblock regeneration sites.
2. Assessing the choice of alternative river restoration plans to meet federally mandated minimums for resident populations of salmonids.
3. Assessing the efficacy of forest fuels management treatments to reduce wildfire risk in a wildland urban interface community.
4. Assessing the effect of climate change on land use designations as part of a major regional land use plan.

Active AM is very appropriate for case 1, less so for cases 2 and 3, and inappropriate for case 4.

TABLE 19.1 **Application of AM Criteria to Four Hypothetical Ecosystem Management Problems**

Adaptive Management Criteria	1. Tree Fertilization Trials	2. ESA-Induced River Restoration	3. Forest Wildfire Risk Management	4. Land Use Plan/ Climate Change
Temporal and spatial scales	1.0	1.6	1.6	3.0
Dimensions of uncertainty	1.0	1.8	2.2	2.5
Costs, benefits, risks	1.2	2.2	2.5	2.2
Institutional support	1.2	2.2	2.2	2.0

1 = Not a major barrier to proceeding with an active experimental AM approach.

2 = Challenge that must be addressed in order to successfully proceed with an active AM approach.

3 = Significant challenge; active experimental AM infeasible unless resolved. Likewise, passive approach must resolve in order to be feasible.

Source: Adapted from Gregory et al. 2006.

Ecosystem Management Experience

Many government resources agencies, land trusts, and community organizations have experimented with EM during the last two decades. Although the concepts are well accepted, putting them into practice has proven difficult. Early experiments, such as the Greater Yellowstone Ecosystem Program, were too complex to overcome political and interagency conflicts (Goldstein 1992). The federal

BOX 19.3—Preconditions for Adaptive Management

The U.S. Department of the Interior's *Technical Guide to Adaptive Management* discusses important preconditions for effective adaptive management. These preconditions are identified in a series of questions about the resource problem, the planning and decision-making process, and the participants, all of which require positive answers for the effective application of adaptive management.

1. Is some kind of management decision to be made? YES
   Decision analysis and monitoring are unnecessary when no decision options exist.
2. Can stakeholders be engaged? YES
   Without active stakeholder involvement, an adaptive management process is unlikely to be effective.
3. Can management objective(s) be stated explicitly? YES
   Adaptive management is not possible if objectives are not identified.
4. Is decision making confounded by uncertainty about potential management impacts? YES
   In the absence of uncertainty, adaptive management is not needed.

5. Can resource relationships and management impacts be represented in models? YES
   Adaptive management cannot proceed without the predictions generated by models.
6. Can monitoring be designed to inform decision making? YES
   In the absence of targeted monitoring, it is not possible to reduce uncertainty and improve management.
7. Can progress be measured in achieving management objectives? YES
   Adaptive management is not feasible if progress in understanding and improving management is unrecognizable.
8. Can management actions be adjusted in response to what has been learned? YES
   Adaptive management is not possible without the flexibility to adjust management strategies.
9. Does the whole process fit within the appropriate legal framework? YES

Source: U. S. Department of the Interior 2009.

agencies have had problems institutionalizing the concepts of EM in their planning and management (Fitzsimmons 1999). In addition, the principles have been applied in literally thousands of ecological and watershed restoration projects, on private and public lands, with mixed success.

Ecosystem Management on Public Lands

Ecosystem management did not enter the federal government vernacular until the early 1990s, but its roots go back much further to the organic acts of the National Forest system (1891) and the National Park system (1916), which originated some of the criteria in Box 19.1. The multiple-use and sustained yield concepts of the 1950s and 1960s related to time and spatial scales and scientific analysis, but these issues were largely interpreted by the agencies to be a basis of commodity production, rather than ecosystem integrity. However, with the passage of the National Environmental Policy Act (NEPA) in 1970 and public lands planning legislation in the late 1970s, agencies began to incorporate broader issues into their planning. Still, it took some time before EM principles began to

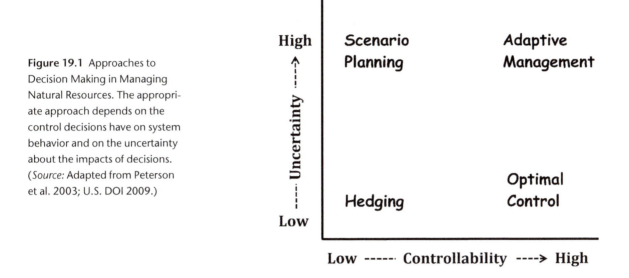

Figure 19.1 Approaches to Decision Making in Managing Natural Resources. The appropriate approach depends on the control decisions have on system behavior and on the uncertainty about the impacts of decisions. (*Source:* Adapted from Peterson et al. 2003; U.S. DOI 2009.)

replace commodity production objectives in the U.S. Forest Service and the Bureau of Land Management, and recreation interests in the National Park Service. Agencies have slowly moved away from expert-driven, commodity/recreation-based, rational-comprehensive planning and decision making to more participatory, ecosystem/integrity-based, adaptive planning, although most analysts agree that the transformation is not complete.

In the late 1980s in professional forestry associations and in the U.S. Forest Service, a movement called New Perspectives, then New Forestry, to reinvent forest management in response to diminishing public support, declining biodiversity, and long-term ecosystem health and sustainability began. By the early 1990s, this movement evolved to EM, which Forest Service Chief Dale Robertson declared in 1992 would be the policy for the National Forest system. However, it took until 2000 until revised Forest Service planning rules were adopted that reflected EM principles (USDA, USFS 2000).

Ecosystem management is not easy. In a recent study of agency ecosystem management, Koontz and Bodine (2008) found that agencies are challenged by adaptive management, the integration of social and economic information, and how to preserve ecological processes, while their biggest implementation barriers are political, cultural, and legal. Not surprisingly, agency personnel think they are implementing ecosystem management at a much higher level than nonagency stakeholders think they are.

These challenges are also demonstrated in case studies of adaptive ecosystem management posted by the U.S. Department of the Interior on its adaptive management website (www.doi.gov/initiatives/AdaptiveManagement). The Five Rivers Landscape Management Project in Oregon, for example, showed that adaptive management on a landscape scale provided opportunities for diverse strategies that accommodated both timber and habitat objectives, and for positive rather than polarizing involvement of more stakeholders. However, the process still encountered some stakeholder intolerance, legal ramifications that caused a 2-year delay, and difficulties integrating research and management.

Ecosystem Management on Private Lands

Many skeptics thought that EM would be limited to public land management because of the complexities involved. They assumed that single ownership of large blocks of natural landscapes was necessary to achieve ecosystem functions and objectives. However, in April 1993 Secretary of Interior Bruce Babbitt described three habitat conservation plans (HCPs) on private land under the Endangered Species Act (ESA) as examples of ecosystem management (see Chapter 11). Responding studies of HCP projects conducted at that time showed that they fell short of the EM criteria (Smith 1995). Still, his statement begged the question of whether or not EM could be practiced on private lands.

Land conservation efforts across the country during the 1990s indicated that EM principles could be used in managing ecosystem integrity and biodiversity at a variety of scales and ownerships by federal, state, and local agencies; property owners; and nonprofit groups. Inventories from Yaffee et al. (1996) and others list hundreds of examples of mostly community-based activities in ecological restoration, landowner stewardship, land trusts for habitats and biodiversity, and other programs and projects. Although these projects are labeled "ecosystem management," many of them used watersheds as the defining boundaries for planning and management.

The Nature Conservancy and Ecosystem Management.   Among the groups and agencies throughout the world engaged in some version of EM, The Nature Conservancy (TNC) is a good example. As a land trust, the Conservancy reports it has helped protect hundreds of millions of acres around the world. As TNC has grown, its mission has become more ambitious. Once focused on protecting unique sites ("the Last Great Places"), it now sees a larger potential to piece those places together to preserve the diversity of life on Earth by protecting the lands and waters natural communities need to be resilient in the face of change. As introduced in Chapter 15, under its "conservation by design" policy, TNC aims to conserve "portfolios of functional conservation areas" within and across ecoregions. Its ecoregional planning and management are comprehensive, scientific, collaborative, and community-based. Here are the four steps:

1. Set priorities at various scales: The ecoregion (of which there are 63 in the U.S.), portfolios (a suite of conservation areas within an ecoregion), and conservation targets (components of portfolios where conservation strategies are focused).
2. Develop conservation strategies: Analyze stresses, threats, and strategies for conservation targets, including platform sites that showcase effective ecosystem protection through analysis and collaboration.
3. Take direct conservation action: Conserve functional landscapes through actions to acquire or protect unroaded and other functional conservation areas and sites.

4. Measure conservation success by monitoring biodiversity and ecological health.

Virginia, for example, has six distinct ecoregions, and TNC has applied its conservation by design approach in six portfolio areas (Virginia Coast Reserve, Green Sea, Chesapeake Rivers, the Piedmont, Warm Springs Mountain, and Clinch Valley Reserve). In each area, TNC staff work with local communities on platform programs to conserve sites and ecological functions.

Ecological Restoration

Ecosystem management usually focuses on the protection and conservation of existing ecological resources. However, in many cases, human impacts have damaged resources and ecological functions to the extent that restoration is required. The growing field of ecological restoration has developed in response to challenges posed by overgrazing, surface-mined land, clear-cut forests, damaged wetlands, contaminated soils, and degraded surface and groundwater. Nature has amazing resiliency and restorative capacity. Left alone, damaged ecosystems have shown an inherent ability to recover. However, recovery takes considerable time and may not occur at all if the threats or causes of degradation are not removed. Active restoration practices can remove threats and accelerate recovery.

Some define ecological restoration as the return of an ecosystem to a close approximation of its condition prior to disturbance (NRC 1992). However, because of constraints on knowledge of preexisting conditions and costs, this ideal is often impractical. As a result, the Society for Ecological Restoration (SER) provides this definition: **Ecological restoration** is the process of assisting the recovery of an ecosystem that has been degraded, damaged, or destroyed. It involves restoring and managing ecological integrity, which includes a critical range of variability in biodiversity, ecological processes and structures, regional and historical context, and sustainable cultural practices (SER 2004). Several terms used in the restoration literature have subtle but important differences (SER 2004):

- **Restoration** aims to reestablish preexisting biotic integrity in terms of species composition and community structure.
- **Rehabilitation** emphasizes reparation of ecosystem processes and services (e.g., reforestation).
- **Reclamation** provides stabilization of terrain, public safety, aesthetic improvement, and return of the land to productive use (e.g., mined land reclamation).
- **Mitigation** lessens or compensates environmental damage (e.g., rehabilitating one wetland to compensate for filling another wetland).
- **Creation** is the establishment of a different kind of ecosystem from what occurred historically (e.g., created wetlands).
- **Ecological engineering**, or **bioengineering**, manipulates natural materials and living organisms to solve problems (e.g., streambank stabilization).

Restoration potential depends on the degree of disturbance of both the site and its surrounding landscape, but in most cases, restoration should focus on the site (NRC 1992). An important consideration in ecological restoration is the reference ecosystem, or conditions that serve as the model or goal for planning and evaluating a project. References are usually given as a composite description of conditions and processes taken from multiple sites.

The SER provides guidelines for developing and managing restoration projects (Clewell et al. 2000):

- *Conceptual planning* delineates the site, the type of restoration project, restoration goals, and interventions needed.
- *Preliminary tasks* include organizing and staffing, gathering baseline data, setting objectives, and engaging the public and other stakeholders.
- *Installation planning* provides more detailed plans, performance standards and monitoring procedures, and procurement of materials, prior to the actual *installation actions*.
- *Post-installation tasks* include site protection, maintenance, monitoring, and adaptive management as recommended by *evaluation*.

There are countless ecological restoration projects being conducted around the world varying in scale from small watersheds to major estuaries, from disturbed sites to extensive minelands, from wetlands to wildlife reserves. Many are community-based projects. The SER showcases restoration projects on its website. Many private consulting firms now specialize in ecological restoration services (e.g., Agrecol, Inc.; BioHabitats, Inc.; Bitterroot Restoration, Inc.; Ecological Restoration, Inc.).

Doyle and Drew (2008) provide a case study volume of five large-scale ecosystem restoration projects in the United States, including the Everglades, the Platte River Basin, the Sacramento Delta, Chesapeake Bay, and the Upper Mississippi River. All large-scale projects not only encounter scientific and technical uncertainties, but also must overcome political, jurisdictional, and economic challenges. This is apparent in the Everglades Restoration, described in Box 19.4.

Watershed Protection: Principles and Process

Water resources engineers have long recognized the need to manage watersheds to maintain yields and quality of water supply reservoirs. At a larger scale, U.S. river basin commissions were established in the 1960s to provide a broader approach to water management. Some of them, such as the Delaware River Basin Commission, were successful at improving water conditions, but others became mired in interjurisdictional conflicts across state boundaries.

In the 1990s, the U.S. EPA and other agencies recognized the limitations of point discharge controls and other conventional approaches to water quality and quantity management (see Chapter 7). It became clear that managing a water body requires managing the land that drains to it. The watershed or drainage

BOX 19.4—The Everglades Ecosystem Restoration Project

The Florida Everglades originally encompassed 3 million acres in its "river of grass" flowing southward from north of Lake Okeechobee to Florida Bay at the southern end of the Florida peninsula (Figure 19.2A). Plans to drain the wetlands and convert the wilderness to agriculture first emerged in the 1880s, but it was not until Governor Broward's ambitious investment and water control infrastructure plan in 1904 that modification of the Everglades began for agriculture and water supply for coastal cities. Over the years, the Everglades Agricultural Area to the north not only consumed precious water, but it also discharged phosphorus-laden runoff to the Everglades (Figure 19.2B). Despite preservation efforts by many groups and individuals, by the end of the twentieth century, more than half of the Everglades had disappeared and the remainder was in decline. In 1994, amid mediated negotiations and lawsuits, Florida passed the Everglades Forever Act (EFA), initiating the world's largest constructed wetlands project to treat runoff phosphorus pollution. In 1999, federal and state agencies initiated a combined effort in the Comprehensive Everglades Restoration Plan (CERP) to save the remaining Everglades by restoring flow and improving water quality (Figure 19.2C).

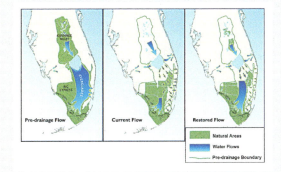

Figure 19.2 The Florida Everglades. Left: Historic predrainage. Center: Current. Right: CERP-planned restored flow in the drainage system. (*Source:* U.S. Army Corps of Engineers 2010.)

The multi-billion-dollar, multi-decade project is regarded as perhaps the grandest experiment in ecosystem restoration yet attempted. The CERP aims to:

- Increase water storage capacity with surface and in-ground reservoirs and aquifer storage.
- Apply stormwater treatment areas (STAs) to improve water quality.
- Reduce water loss through reuse and conservation.
- Reestablish predrainage hydrologic patterns to the extent possible.

Specific CERP projects are summarized in Figure 19.3. The CERP is complemented by other restoration projects, including the Kissimmee River Restoration, Lake Okeechobee Restoration, "Mod Waters" (Modified Water Deliveries to Everglades), and the EFA's Everglades Construction Project (ECP; 44,000 STA acres).

Figure 19.3 The Comprehensive Everglades Restoration Plan. (*Source:* U.S. Army Corps of Engineers 2010.)

The effort has been plagued by sheer scale; competing stakeholder interests for preservation, agriculture, and water supply; continuing population and development pressures; escalating costs; and changing politics. For example, after significant progress toward the ECP completion of STAs and the interim goal of 50 parts per billion (ppb) phosphorus concentrations, the state amended the EFA in 2003 under some pressure from the South Florida Water District and other

BOX 19.4—The Everglades Ecosystem Restoration Project (cont.)

development and sugar industry interests. The amendments creating some loopholes for water not meeting a final state standard expected to be 10 ppb. By 2008, there seemed to be a breakthrough in the announcement that the District was to purchase U.S. Sugar Corp. and its 300 sq mi in the Everglades Agricultural Area for $1.75 billion. Although the purchase has been supported by environmental groups, including the Audubon Society since it sets a precedent for the purchase of private agricultural land for public purposes, the primary motivation for the deal was not necessarily to reduce phosphorus pollution but to use the land to construct water supply reservoirs for new development in the Lower East Coast.

A National Research Council (NRC) committee was established to monitor CERP progress. Its 2008 biennial report stated: "The CERP is bogged down in budgeting, planning, and procedural matters and is making only scant progress toward achieving restoration goals. . . . It appears that planning rather than doing, reporting rather than constructing, and administering rather than restoring are consuming talents and time" (NRC 2008, 1–2).

Is the Everglades ecosystem restoration program successful? According to the NRC, not yet. There have been accomplishments, like STA con-

struction, state land acquisition, and water control modifications, but progress has been slow. Some fundamental projects, such as the two-decades-old Mod Waters, have not been realized. This will certainly be a multi-decades-long program.

Has the program applied the elements of ecosystem management? The CERP and related projects aim to apply science-based adaptive and collaborative planning and management. The NRC recommended an incremental adaptive restoration (IAR) approach in its 2006 report, and while it has been embraced by agencies and stakeholders, its 2008 report concluded that IAR has yet to be fully applied. In her Ph.D. dissertation on the process, Frank (2009) found that collaborative processes improved ecosystem management, but not to the extent expected by advocates of collaborative planning. Collaboration integrated values, information, activities, and political support, but it had limits and biases and focused on reaching agreements rather than exploring issues fully. Collaboration promoted adaptation and social learning in specific cases, but in the aggregate, it tended to maintain the status quo of dominant water agencies, technocratic paradigms, and capture by economic interests.

Source: U.S. Army Corps of Engineers 2010

catchment became a useful geographic boundary for managing land and water resources. Based on many experimental local programs, the EPA developed guidelines for what emerged as the watershed protection approach. Watershed management was not a new concept, but when coupled with new collaborative planning, it is recognized as an effective approach to environmental management. (See also Chapter 8.)

The EPA's Watershed Protection Approach

In 1996, the EPA promoted its watershed protection approach (WPA), which was based on the premise that water quality and ecosystem problems can best be addressed at the watershed level, not at the individual water body or discharge level (U.S. EPA 1996). By 2003, there were an estimated 3,500 active watershed groups in the United States implementing variations of this approach. Many states have adopted WSM as an organizing approach for their water quality management programs.

The WPA has four basic principles:

1. *Targeting priority problems and applying good science to understand them*. Assessment is a critical first step in identifying specific problems and priorities. CWA 305(b) assessments of impaired waters (described in Chapter 7) can be used, but more detailed analysis is required to determine causes and solutions.
2. *Promoting a high level of collaboration through stakeholder involvement*. Collaboration should occur at both a scientific level, through a technical advisory committee for example, and a community level, including local landowners and other stakeholders who have local knowledge and are likely to play a role in implementation.
3. *Integrating multiple solutions from multiple agencies and private parties*. Watershed management involves a wide range of interests (water quality, ecological integrity, recreation, stormwater management) and participants (land trusts; local, state, and federal agencies; landowners; environmental groups). Successful strategies should address multiple interests and engage diverse participants, using regulations, fiscal incentives, and voluntary action.
4. *Measuring progress through monitoring and adapting strategies accordingly*. Adaptive management assumes there is some uncertainty about the future effectiveness of WSM strategies. Therefore, participants need to evaluate the effects of these strategies on objectives for water quality, stormwater management, ecological integrity, and other factors, and modify them to improve WSM effectiveness.

The EPA embraced the watershed approach in its Clean Water Action Plan of 1998, but the approach is still not formally part of the Clean Water Act, which has not been reauthorized since 1987. In 2008, the EPA produced the useful *Handbook for Developing Watershed Plans to Restore and Protect Our Waters* to states, local governments, and watershed associations (U.S. EPA 2008). In 2009, the NRC's assessment of stormwater management in the U.S. stated that "the greatest improvement … most likely to check and reverse degradation of the nation's aquatic resources would be to convert the current piecemeal system into a watershed-based permitting system" (NRC 2009, 452).

The CWP's Concepts of Watershed Planning

In addition to its guidance on technical analysis and design techniques for stormwater, urban forests, wetlands, and streams that were featured in previous chapters, the Center for Watershed Protection (CWP) has also helped shape the planning, procedural, and institutional elements of watershed management. Among the basic concepts CWP promotes for watershed management are using a tiered approach that nests and classifies watersheds from catchment to basin, employing eight tools from land use planning to stewardship, applying good technical analysis, focusing on impervious surfaces in urban areas, and engaging stakeholders to achieve consensus.

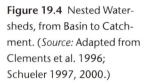

Figure 19.4 Nested Watersheds, from Basin to Catchment. (*Source:* Adapted from Clements et al. 1996; Schueler 1997, 2000.)

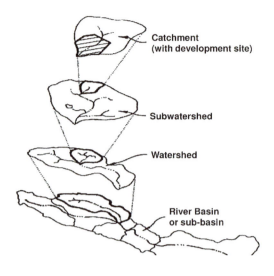

The **tiered approach**, or watershed nesting, relates to scale. Watersheds are defined by a point on a stream or river and include the land area draining to that point. (A method for delineating watersheds was described in Chapter 7.) Watershed size can range from very large basins to very small catchments (Figure 19.4):

- Basin: 1,000–10,000 sq mi
- Subbasin: 100–1,000 sq mi
- Watershed: 10–100 sq mi
- Subwatershed: 1–10 sq mi; second-order streams
- Catchment: Area that drains a development site to its first intersection with a stream

Table 19.2 summarizes the characteristics of each type of watershed unit. Going from larger basins to smaller catchments, the effect of impervious cover on watershed health increases, and management measures converge, moving from basinwide planning to onsite design and management practices.

Watershed units in the United States are defined by **hydrologic unit code (HUC)** using a system developed by the USGS. The hierarchy is related to the five watershed units in Table 19.2. HUCs are based on a classification system that divides the United States into progressively smaller hydrologic units. Each unit is identified by a unique HUC consisting of 2–8 digits based on the four classification levels, from Region (first) to Subregion (second) to Basin (third) to Subbasin (fourth). The Natural Resources Conservation Service (NRCS) and other agencies have further delineated fifth- and sixth-level watersheds in many states. HUCs for these additional watershed levels consist of 11 and 14 digits, respectively, and represent a scale from a few hundred down to tens of square miles. Fifth- and sixth-level HUCs and smaller catchments are generally a good scale for watershed projects.

Both larger-scale basin plans and smaller-scale subwatershed and catchment projects are important for effective watershed management. Basin plans should

TABLE 19.2 **Characteristics of Five Watershed Units**

Watershed Management Unit	Hydrologic Unit Level	Typical Area (sq mi)	Influence of Impervious Cover	Sample Management
Basin	3rd	1,000–10,000	Very weak	Basin planning
Subbasin	4th	100–1,000	Weak	Basin planning
Watershed	5th	10–100	Moderate	Watershed-based zoning
Subwatershed	6th	1–10	Strong	Stream classification and management
Catchment	—	0.05–0.50	Very strong	Practices and site design

provide guidance, policies, and financial and technical assistance. Subwatershed plans and projects should implement action strategies. If the subwatershed is small enough to be within one or a few jurisdictions, there is a strong influence of land use and impervious surface, there are fewer compounding pollutant sources than larger watersheds, it is small enough for monitoring and mapping at a workable yet detailed scale, and stakeholders have a close connection to the issues and are manageable in number.

The CWP's eight subwatershed management tools (Figure 19.5) are:

1. **Land use planning** to redirect development to suitable sites, preserve natural vegetation and sensitive areas, and reduce impervious cover within the subwatershed (see Chapter 17).
2. **Land conservation** of critical habitats, aquatic corridors, hydrologic reserve areas, water hazards, and historic areas, using land acquisition, conservation easements, and landowner stewardship (see Chapter 15).
3. **Aquatic buffers** must be protected or restored at the land-water interface through land conservation and riparian tree and vegetation planting (see Chapter 10).
4. **Better site design** of development projects reduces impervious cover they create and increases natural areas they conserve (see Chapter 16).
5. **Erosion and sediment control** reduces soil loss and sediment loadings during land clearing and construction, and also conserves buffers and forests on construction sites (see Chapter 6).
6. **Stormwater best-management practices** detain runoff, reduce pollutant loads, enhance infiltration to maintain groundwater recharge, and protect stream channels (see Chapter 8).
7. **Non-stormwater discharges** control onsite wastewater, land application of wastes, combined sewer overflows, and leaks and spills (see Chapters 6 and 7).
8. **Watershed and land stewardship**, programs that include watershed associations, education, and outreach, such as voluntary stream and watershed monitoring, watershed maintenance and restoration, and pollution prevention (see Chapters 4, 7, and 15).

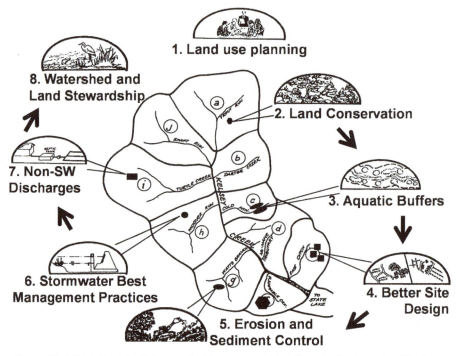

Figure 19.5 Eight Tools for Subwatershed Management in a Hypothetical Location. The letters represent catchments within the subwatershed. (*Source:* Adapted from Schueler 2000.)

The CWP's Smart Watershed Management

Beyond technical analysis, design, and planning, CWP's Smart Watershed model describes an array of 14 types of municipal programs to implement improved stormwater treatment, stream corridor restoration, and pollution reduction in urban watersheds. Together, the programs create a framework to integrate policies, regulations, and initiatives into a unified strategy for restoring urban watersheds that measurably improves water quality (Rowe and Schueler 2006). Here is an outline of the CWP program:

1. *Subwatershed Restoration Planning*
    To assess the characteristics of each subwatershed, evaluate restoration potential, and rank priority restoration practices for long-term implementation.
2. *Stream and Subwatershed Field Assessment*
    To conduct rapid assessments for critical information on current impacts and potential restoration opportunities, and to engage watershed stakeholders.
3. *Subwatershed Monitoring and Reporting*
    To determine major water quality, habitat, and biological impacts, and track progress over time to inform decisions.
4. *Watershed Restoration Financing*
    To identify current and alternative financing sources for programs.

5. *Management of Natural Area Remnants*
To protect remaining natural areas that provide opportunities for habitat, green space, and stormwater treatment. Those owned by the municipality can provide initial restoration action.
6. *Stormwater Retrofitting*
To treat and manage runoff from areas developed prior to stormwater management requirements, using reengineered ponds, wetlands, and bioretention.
7. *Urban Stream Repair/Restoration*
To enhance the appearance, structure, and function of urban stream networks to achieve restoration objectives.
8. *Illicit Discharge Detection and Elimination*
To target and eliminate combined and sanitary sewer overflows and illicit discharges.
9. *Maintenance, Inspection, and Enforcement*
To monitor and maintain existing stormwater and restoration practices.
10. *Smart Site Practices during Redevelopment*
To apply eleven site redevelopment design techniques to reduce the impacts of stormwater runoff.
11. *Watershed Education and Personal Stewardship*
To increase public awareness of behavior that can reduce stormwater pollution.
12. *Public Involvement and Neighborhood Consultation*
To engage citizens for long-term support of local watershed restoration efforts.
13. *Pollution Prevention at Stormwater Hotspots*
To reduce pollutant loading, spills, and leaks from hotspots that generate higher concentrations of pollutants.
14. *Pollution Prevention at Municipal Operation*
To lead by example with programs for street vacuuming, yard waste collection, household hazardous waste recycling, and so on.

Integrating Compatible Programs and Solutions

There is no "silver bullet" for protecting and restoring ecosystems and watersheds. A wide range of measures must be used to preserve existing values and improve degraded conditions. Watershed and ecosystem management measures include the development and enforcement of regulations, restoration projects, land acquisition, environmental monitoring, stewardship by land trusts and landowners, and education and research. Regulations take the form of permitting programs requiring compliance with rules or ordinances designed to protect lands, waters, and habitats. Although these regulations provide an important foundation for protective action, they are often inadequate for achieving effective management. While they may help prevent further degradation, the improvement and restoration of watersheds and ecosystems often require proactive measures to acquire, restore, steward, and monitor natural resources.

To accomplish this comprehensive array of goals, ecosystem and watershed planners and managers must be holistic and must collaborate with other program participants who have common and compatible objectives. Not surprisingly, a holistic approach to protecting and enhancing watersheds and ecosystems can also yield economic and social benefits. These include programs to mitigate natural hazards, arrest soil erosion, preserve farmland, treat polluted runoff, protect drinking water sources, restore impaired waters, manage forests, improve air quality, protect wetland benefits, manage fisheries, provide recreation and open space, and enhance the quality of life in our communities.

Watershed and ecosystem management adds ecological dimensions to human-related objectives, but in most cases they are compatible and mutually beneficial. Successful programs take advantage of the synergies provided by coordination and collaboration of diverse initiatives. Such programs enjoy a broader base of support, greater acceptability, improved cost-effectiveness, and smoother implementation.

Achieving this collaboration is easier said than done. Public interests, groups, and agencies are often fragmented in their objectives and programs. Competition for scarce resources (time, money, institutional capacity) often pits one against the other. Successful program managers have realized the advantages of building partnerships and pooling social, political, and financial capital into comprehensive efforts of common interest. Often this begins with appropriate institutional arrangements.

Institutional Arrangements for Ecosystem and Watershed Management

Ecosystem and watershed protection requires an integration of science, planning, policy, and politics. The tiered approach (or watershed nesting, see Figure 19.4) applies not only to scientific understanding, but also to institutional and political organization. Moving from catchment to watershed to basin and from landscape patch to matrix to ecosystem, the increasing geographic area captured crosses governmental jurisdictional boundaries. Increasing the number of jurisdictions complicates the institutional and political arrangements needed for effective management. Since watersheds and ecosystems rarely conform to government boundaries, WSM usually requires interjurisdictional collaboration. However, parochial interests, competition, and past conflicts often inhibit meaningful cooperation among neighboring localities and, at larger scale, states.

In addition, WSM must involve private landowners and the public, as well as governmental agencies in a collaborative partnership. Although some regulatory land use controls are important, effective watershed protection depends on a range of voluntary measures, including land stewardship and watershed monitoring. Watershed associations and groups are critical players in WSM.

These institutional issues are well recognized by researchers on the practice of ecosystem and watershed management. In 2001, an interagency federal watershed protection team, working with local and state partners and watershed practitioners, assessed the challenges to watershed health, recent successes of the watershed approach, and remaining obstacles. The process involved 1,000 participants at 20 regional roundtable discussions and culminated in the National Watershed Forum. The researchers concluded that the watershed approach offers the best hope for protecting and restoring the nation's waters and that much of the credit for success to date goes to *local leadership and engagement*: citizens are leading the effort to reverse impacts to watershed health (U.S. EPA 2001).

The Forum also cited the importance of federal and state agencies for coordinating and supporting local watershed protection with financial and technical support. The recommendations addressed mostly institutional issues of education, partnerships, planning, funding assistance, and implementation. Although scientific and technical factors are critically important in watershed and ecosystem management, these institutional issues continue to be the major challenges to effective protection and restoration (U.S. EPA 2001). As recently as 2009, the NRC recognized that we have yet to achieve a watershed approach and that it offers the best hope for improving U.S. waters (NRC 2009).

A good example of a local watershed management program with important federal and state involvement is the Anacostia River watershed, which includes much of Washington, DC, and the northern Maryland suburbs. Box 19.5 describes the development of the 2010 Anacostia Watershed Restoration Plan and its ambitious program for the "forgotten river" in our nation's capital.

Institutional Models for Watershed Management

Several organizational models for WSM and EM have emerged, and most involve a tiered approach and public-private-nonprofit partnerships. Although most management actions occur at the local level, larger-scale watershed and ecosystem institutional frameworks provide guidance and resources to smaller-scale planning and implementation efforts. Table 19.3 summarizes examples of WSM programs at various scales, from subnational regions to site-level catchments. Actions and measures are implemented at the subwatershed and catchment scales, but studies have shown that these programs often have limited effectiveness without technical and financial support from the regional subwatershed and state levels (Holst 1999).

Research on local environmental planning has shown that key ingredients for successful community initiatives are a *committed elected official* who can advance the cause politically, a *skillful planner* who can generate and manage technical information, and an *active constituency* that contributes political support and local knowledge (Corbett and Hayden 1981). This holds true for WSM as well. Support of elected officials is important for shepherding watershed protection regulations and funding. The planning role is often taken on by the watershed manager. The constituency can be represented by the watershed association or stakeholder group, which not only provides political support but also monitors watershed conditions and implements restoration measures through voluntary action.

The Watershed Group/Association

A local watershed association often plays an important role for subwatershed and catchment planning and implementation. The association is usually composed

BOX 19.5—The Anacostia Watershed Restoration Plan

Perhaps one of the best examples of watershed management planning that combines the key ingredients of intergovernmental cooperation, stakeholder involvement, and dedicated financial resources is the Anacostia River Watershed Restoration Plan (AWRP). The watershed drains 176 sq mi of now highly urbanized land through Washington, DC, to the Potomac River (Figure 19.6). Two centuries of deforestation, wetland loss, habitat fragmentation, sedimentation, and urbanization have resulted in a loss of 70% of forest cover and 6,500 acres of wetlands, the expansion of impervious surface to 25% of the entire watershed, streambank erosion, and discharges of toxic industrial waste and raw sewage from an antiquated combined sewer system—all at the front door of the capital of the wealthiest country in the world.

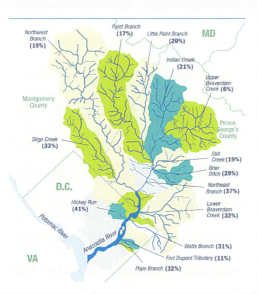

Figure 19.6 The Anacostia River Watershed and Sub-watersheds. This watershed occupies a large part of Washington, DC, and the northern suburbs of Maryland. Percentages represent impervious surfaces. (*Source:* AWRP 2010.)

Early efforts to manage the watershed were unsuccessful until 1987 when the Anacostia Watershed Restoration Agreement was signed by the District of Columbia, the State of Maryland and its Montgomery and Prince George's Coun-ties, the U.S. Army Corps of Engineers, the U.S. EPA, and the National Park Service.

The agreement led to a two-decade planning effort and the 2007 federal Water Resources Development Act, authorizing federal funding of $2.8 million for the AWRP that was released in 2010. The plan has unprecedented regional cooperation, federal investment, regulatory accountability, and stakeholder involvement in implementation.

The AWRP has six goals for restoration, including reducing pollution discharges, restoring ecological integrity (e.g., water quality and habitat), improving fish passage, increasing wetland acreage, expanding forest cover, and increasing public and private participation.

To achieve them, the plan lists eight restoration strategies involving more than 3,000 specific projects:

1. **Stormwater management control (SMC) retrofits**: SMCs have been required for new development since the 1970s, but 64% of the impervious area of the watershed has no stormwater controls. Proposed SMCs rely primarily on onsite LID and design measures to control 10,600 acres of impervious surface.
2. **Stream restoration**: SMCs will reduce future stormwater flows and enhance the effectiveness of 72 miles of streambank erosion restoration.
3. **Wetland creation and restoration**: Given the history of wetland degradation and conversion, recreating 134 acres of wetlands is a difficult but critical strategy necessary to restore ecological functions for water filtration, storage, and habitat.
4. **Fish blockage removal**: 125 barriers, such as road culverts and channelization, will be removed to reopen 42 stream miles to fish passage.
5. **Riparian reforestation and other watershed revegetation**: Forested riparian buffers are a key strategy, but other revegetation of watershed forests and meadows is needed to achieve watershed goals of 347 restored acres.
6. **Trash reduction**: 800 tons of trash enter the river annually. Each April, about 3,000 volunteers in boats and along shorelines collect tons of trash from the river.

BOX 19.5—The Anacostia Watershed Restoration Plan (cont.)

7. Toxic remediation: The legacy of toxic pollution locked in river sediments makes this difficult, but adaptive management projects to cap toxic sediment hot spots can evaluate this approach.

8. Parkland acquisition: The connectivity of existing public lands and parks along the river corridor by acquiring 2,500 acres will be increased.

Two other important projects will reduce sewage pollution of the Anacostia. The DC Long-Term Control Plan is a $3 billion program funded by an impervious surface fee to reduce combined sewer overflows by constructing increased storm-water storage capacity. The Washington Suburban Sanitary Commission Program is implementing a $350 million effort to reduce sanitary sewer overflows into the watershed from aging, leaking, and undersized sewer lines.

The estimated implementation cost of the eight strategies of the AWRP is $2.7 billion, not including the costs of the two other associated projects. Implementation will thus require a long-term commitment of federal, state, local, and private funds, as well as continuing political support from a wide range of stakeholders.

Source: Adapted from AWRP 2010.

principally of landowners in the subwatershed, but may also include government officials and interest groups. With landowner participation, the association can be instrumental in developing stewardship, monitoring, and other voluntary measures. In some cases, the group has legal authority.

For example, Virginia law allows the establishment of a watershed improvement district (WID) if voters and landowners approve such a district by large majorities. The WID is made up of landowners and has the authority to tax its members to fund watershed improvements. The Barcroft Reservoir WID in urban Fairfax County was established under this law in the 1970s. The district has developed a tax-supported fund to pay for monitoring and stormwater BMP retrofits. While the district has maintained the lake, its capacity to improve the watershed has been limited to lakeshore and tributary activities, rather than upstream measures in the heavily urbanized watershed.

Most associations are voluntary groups. The East Fork (Little River) Watershed Association in Floyd County, Virginia, was established by local landowners with the help of the National Committee for the New River (NCNR) in the early 1990s. The agricultural watershed is made up of fiercely independent landowners—some long-term natives known for their taste for moonshine, along with some "urban refugees" who migrated from the Northeast U.S. to enjoy a more communal life. While these groups are culturally very different, both of them are distrustful of government, guard their property rights, and take pride in the fact that all water flows out of Floyd County. The perceived threat of government action on their impaired watershed drew these diverse landowners together in a common cause. NCNR helped educate this group about the watershed's problems and convinced them that they should take action themselves before state agencies came in and told them what to do. This argument struck a chord, and the group succeeded in developing a plan, acquiring grant funds, monitoring watershed quality, and implementing livestock fencing and other measures to reduce runoff pollution.

TABLE 19.3 Institutional Participants and Issues for Watershed Management

Scale	Participants	Roles and Actions	Issues of Effectiveness	Examples
Region (*subnational*)	• Lead federal agency • Multiagency committee	• Federal commitment to watershed approach • Interagency agreements • Funding, technical support	• Scale • Complexity of multijurisdictions • Federal leadership	• Federal unified policy • Regional teams
Basin (*multistate*)	• Lead federal agency • Multistate advisory group • Committees, task forces, stakeholders groups	• Multistate commitment • Basin plan • State/federal financial support	• Scale • Complexity of multijurisdictions • Consistency in states' policies	• River basin commissions • Great Lakes Joint Commission • Chesapeake Bay program
Subbasin (*state*)	• Lead state agency • Statewide advisory committee • Committees, task forces, stakeholder groups	• State statutory/administrative directive for WSM • Statewide watershed protection plan • Requires regulatory "teeth"	• State leadership • State funding and regulations	• Oregon Plan for Salmon and Watersheds • Chesapeake Bay acts in Maryland and Virginia
Watershed (*substate*)	• Committees, task forces, stakeholder groups • Regional agency • WS advisory committee of local governments, regional groups, other stakeholders	• Technical and financial assistance to watershed/subwatershed programs • Interjurisdictional plans and agreements • Guidance, technical and financial support	• Critical planning scale • Stakeholder engagement • Multijurisdictional cooperation	• Cuyahoga River, OH • San Miguel River, CO • Anacostia Watershed, DC
Subwatershed (*local*)	• Watershed association (local government, landowners, interest groups) • Local watershed manager/coordinator	• Where the action is! • Land use controls • Stream/riparian restoration • Action limited without direction, financial, technical support from above	• Critical action scale • Landowner and volunteer engagement	• East Fork of Little River, VA • Bronx River, NY
Catchment (*site scale*)	• Watershed association, watershed coordinator • Landowners, developers, neighborhood groups	• Site development measures • Land stewardship • Stream/riparian restoration • Stream monitoring	• Project scale • Monitoring scale • Landowner and volunteer implementation	• Haskell Slough, WA

Whether the association has legal authority or not, it is well positioned to understand local problems and issues, to develop options to address them, and to implement these measures. At the subwatershed scale, associations provide a mechanism for local governments and interest groups to gather watershed stakeholders to plan and implement protection and restoration.

The Watershed Manager

The watershed manager is usually a paid staffer of local government or a large watershed association who plays a lead role in planning and coordinating watershed information, process, decisions, and implementation. The manager is usually the keeper of information, such as watershed data and analysis, as well as potential protection and restoration measures and costs. The manager will often coordinate the collaborative process, identifying stakeholders, setting up advisory committees, and organizing meetings.

Stakeholder Involvement and Advisory Committees

Stakeholder involvement is a critical part of watershed and ecosystem management. As discussed in Chapter 4, stakeholders are those who affect change in the watershed and those who are affected by it. Agencies, local governments, landowners and developers, and environmental, agricultural, and other interest groups are all stakeholders. Stakeholder groups are involved at all levels of watershed management, from basin to watershed to catchment scale.

Stakeholder groups are organized as information task forces, working groups, or advisory committees. Representation on stakeholder groups varies with scale. At the basin scale, committees are made up of representatives of federal and state agencies and national interest groups. At the watershed scale, stakeholder groups include state agency officials, local governments, and state or regional interest groups. At the subwatershed scale, groups may be the same as watershed associations, including landowners and community groups.

Bauer (2001) and Keuhl (2001) each studied the collaborative process of stakeholder groups in watershed planning. Bauer showed that community-level watershed groups are potentially more effective in learning and reaching consensus than basin-scale groups because they are closer to the problems and potential solutions. Keuhl (2001) investigated advisory committees in the Great Lakes Remedial Action Planning and found that the collaborative process led not only to consensus building, but also to increased knowledge of water and watershed systems and improved understanding of problems and solutions. The continuing evolution of collaborative processes to adaptive and social learning and collaborative management, as described as the fourth generation of participation in Chapter 4, holds great promise for watershed and ecosystem management.

Integrating Statewide and Local Watershed Programs

The plethora of case studies of the practice of WSM and EM has demonstrated the importance of local action (U.S. EPA 2010c). However, successful local programs rarely act alone. They often depend on administrative or statutory direction from above, guidance from basin and watershed plans produced at the state or regional level, technical assistance, and especially financial support from state and federal agencies. Likewise, statewide, basin, and watershed-scale programs require not only local action but also consistent reporting and monitoring of local restoration and protection projects.

A good example of integrating statewide and local programs is found in Oregon's regulatory framework. The state-level *Oregon Plan for Salmon and Watersheds*, funding from the Oregon Watershed Enhancement Board, watershed-scale programs like the Willamette Restoration Initiative, and the 90 subwatershed councils around the state provide the institutional structure. The Watershed Restoration Reporting system provides consistent and timely feedback on local activities to the state so that progress can be effectively monitored.

Other states, such as Wisconsin, Minnesota, North Carolina, and Maryland, have integrated the watershed management approach into their water quality programs. All these states provide technical and funding support for local subwatershed planning and implementation. These programs often build on established state programs and agencies, such as soil and water conservation districts in rural areas. However, local watershed groups are critical, especially in urban and suburban areas.

The first edition of this book described the Oregon watershed planning framework, as well as several other case examples and success stories of watershed and ecosystem management, including applications in the USFS and local subwatersheds, including the Bronx River in New York, the Cousauga River in Georgia and Tennessee, the Cuyahoga River in Ohio, and Haskell Slough in Washington state. These stories are posted on the book website (www.envirolanduse.org). See the U.S. EPA website for other success stories (U.S. EPA 2010c).

The Chesapeake Bay Program is perhaps the best example of a multiscale, multijurisdictional watershed management and ecosystem restoration project in the U.S. It illustrates the challenges of trying to restore a large-scale ecosystem in the face of population growth and competing economic and social objectives. This sustainability challenge is described in Box 19.6.

Integrative Management Lessons for Sustainable Communities

The principles of ecosystem and watershed management offer a desirable framework for most environmental and sustainability planning. These guiding principles include the following:

- **Best science**: Use best science and technical analysis to guide fact-based and evidence-based understanding and decisions.
- **Ecological integrity**: Long-term sustainability ultimately rests on the health of natural systems, and this requires maintaining ecological integrity.
- **Multiple scales**: In both planning and action, involve many scales—from catchment to watershed to basin; from site to neighborhood to

BOX 19.6—The Chesapeake Bay Program

The 200-mile-long Chesapeake Bay is the nation's largest estuary, encompassing 4,480 sq mi and more than 11,600 mi of shoreline. It is a national ecological and economic treasure. But by 1980, the Bay aquatic ecosystem was severely degraded by excessive nitrogen and phosphorus pollution, reduced underwater bay grasses, toxic chemical pollution, and overharvested fish and shellfish. While attention was initially directed at the Bay itself, it became increasingly apparent that the causes of degradation originated in the huge watershed of more than 64,000 sq mi, including parts of six states and the District of Columbia (DC), and home to 17 million people.

In the 1970s, the U.S. EPA conducted a 7-year study on the decline of Chesapeake Bay. As a result, the tri-state (Maryland, Pennsylvania, Virginia) Chesapeake Bay Commission was formed in 1980 to develop policy initiatives for restoration of the Bay. The first Chesapeake Bay Agreement was signed in 1983 by the commission representatives, the U.S. EPA, and representatives of Maryland, Virginia, Pennsylvania, and DC, thus establishing the voluntary partnership Chesapeake Bay Program (CBP). Maryland was first to act with its 1984 Chesapeake Bay Critical Areas Protection Act to control development along the shores of the Bay and its tidal rivers. Virginia passed a similar law in 1988 (see Chapter 18). In 1985, Maryland adopted a phosphate detergent ban, and DC, Virginia, and Pennsylvania followed suit by 1990. The 1983 agreement had no specific goals, but the 1987 Chesapeake Bay Agreement did. It called for a 40% reduction of nitrogen and phosphorus entering the Bay by the year 2000. Amended in 1992, it established a tributary strategy to focus on upstream sources. New amendments in 2000 set goals to further reduce nutrient and sediment pollution, and to remove the Bay and its tidal rivers from the EPA's impaired waters by 2010, along with more than 100 other commitments and actions. The CBP continues to monitor progress toward those goals.

The CBP can be viewed as a half-empty, half-full glass metaphor, depending on your point of view. Groups like the Chesapeake Bay Foundation (CBF) remind us that the Bay remains severely degraded. CBP members argue the Bay is far more stable than it would have been without the program. There has been a large measure of success through CBP partners: More than a million acres of farmland in the watershed are under nutrient management plans, industrial toxic releases decreased 67% from 1988 to 1996, significant upgrades were made to municipal wastewater treatment plants, Maryland and Virginia Bay protection laws severely restricted new development along Bay and tidal stream shorelines, and by 2001 grasses increased to 85,000 acres, the highest level since monitoring began in 1978.

Other indicators, however, are not as positive. A summer "dead zone" of depleted dissolved oxygen (hypoxia) developed in the middle reaches of the Bay (Figure 19.7), native oyster abundance remains at less than 10% of program goals, and the Bay and tributaries are still impaired (Figure 19.8).

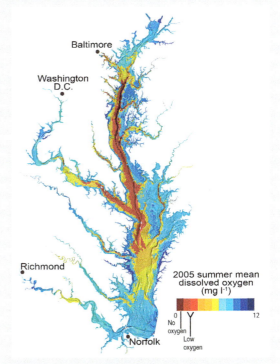

Figure 19.7 The Chesapeake Bay "Dead Zone" of Depleted Oxygen, 2005. Although the dead zone has shrunk through 2010 as a result of less nitrogen pollution due to lower stream flows, climate change is likely to expand and intensify these dead zones, thereby threatening oxygen-dependent aquatic organisms. (*Source:* USGCRP 2009; Wicks et al. 2007.)

BOX 19.6—The Chesapeake Bay Program (cont.)

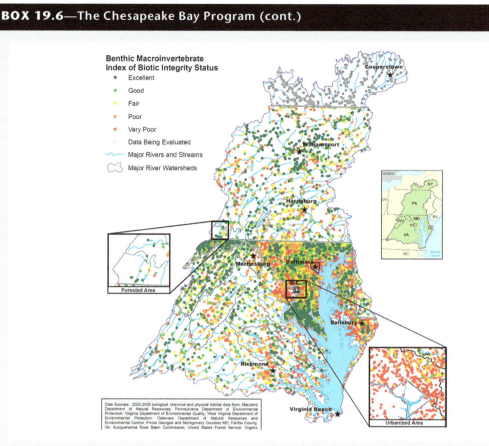

Figure 19.8 The Biotic Integrity of Chesapeake Bay Tributaries, 2008. (*Source:* U.S. EPA, CBP 2010a.)

The CBP has a significant monitoring program and publishes the annual Bay Barometer of progress toward goals established in the Chesapeake 2000 agreement. The CBF issues its own report card on progress. Table 19.4 summarizes recent CBP and CBF indicators of the state of Chesapeake Bay.

In May 2009, President Obama issued Executive Order 13508, the Chesapeake Bay Protection and Restoration. It established a Federal Leadership Committee and required an annual Chesapeake Bay Action Plan. The fiscal year (FY) 2011 Action Plan includes four goals (restore water quality, recover habitat, sustain fish and wildlife, and conserve land and increase public access) and five supporting strategies (expand citizen stewardship, develop environmental markets, respond to climate change, strengthen science, and implementation and accountability). The responsibility is spread across eleven federal agencies with a total $0.5 billion FY2011 budget, half of which is directed to the EPA for water quality.

The main water quality planning project is completion of the Chesapeake Bay TMDL Plan. (TMDL is total maximum daily load.) Since the Bay and its tributaries remain impaired and do not meet water quality standards, a TMDL plan is required by the Clean Water Act. Chapter 8 introduced TMDL planning and the CBP TMDL approach. The CBP released the multipollutant TMDL plan in late 2010, which established a "pollution diet" for the Bay. For nitrogen, the diet or maximum load is 187.7 million pounds per year (mpy) compared to 2009 levels of 243.3 mpy. A major task of the TMDL and the Watershed Implementation Plans (WIPs) is to allocate that load to effluent sources, including natural forest sources. The approach then builds the allocations into wastewater and urban stormwater permit requirements and controls on agricultural runoff, where the biggest reduction is needed. Implementation of the TMDL plan is required through state WIPs, to establish the means of achieving the allocations. The process is long. Phase II state WIPs with

BOX 19.6—The Chesapeake Bay Program (cont.)

TABLE 19.4 **Chesapeake Bay Resotration Progress**

Indicator	Percent Progress Toward 2010 Goals (Change from 2008)	CBF Grade 2008 Index: Grade
Bay Health	45% of 2010 goals (+6%)	28% of historic potential
Dissolved oxygen	12% of bay/tributaries (–5%)	14%: F
Water clarity	26% (+12%)	14%: F
Nitrogen	51%	17%: F
Phosphorus	67%	23%: D–
Underwater bay grasses	46% (+12%)	20%: D–
Bottom-dwelling species	56% (+15%)	
Adult blue crab	100% (223 million, most since 1993)	35%: C
Oysters	9%	4%: F
Restoration and protection	64%	
Pollution reduction	62% (+3% wastewater treat)	
Forest buffers	69% (+7%, 90% in PA)	56%: B+
WSM plans	61%	
Land preservation	100%	
Fostering stewardship	67%	

Source: Chesapeake Bay Foundation 2009; Chesapeake Bay Program 2010a.

local allocations are due by 2011 to meet 60% of the required TMDL allocations by 2017. Phase III WIPS are due in 2017 to identify remaining or modified allocations by 2025.

Some see this move to greater regulation that may come from the TMDL approach as a necessary component for Chesapeake Bay restoration. For example, a group of 57 scientists and policy makers believe the 30-year largely voluntary and collaborative restoration approach is failing, and they have developed their own 25-step Chesapeake Bay Action Plan. It emphasizes regulatory and enforcement programs to significantly reduce farm runoff, control development, protect forests and plant trees, upgrade septic systems, clean air, and improve wastewater treatment plants. (See http://www.bayactionplan.com/.)

The Chesapeake Bay watershed restoration and management experience illustrates the complexities of large-scale, multijurisdictional, and multiobjective ecosystem restoration. Progress has been real, but it has fallen short of established goals and targets, despite decades of attention and billions of dollars of investment. Complicating factors include a growing population and related land development, a complex ecosystem, competing political and economic interests, and reliance on standard regulations, supplemented by voluntary action. Impacts on the Bay are likely to be exacerbated by climate change. The TMDL process and EO 13508 start a new chapter in Bay watershed planning and restoration. Better scientific understanding, more watershed-wide public support, targeted regulations, and continued investment all bring hope for accelerated progress.

Source: U.S. EPA, Chesapeake Bay Program 2010a, 2010b; http://www.epa.gov/chesapeakebaytmdl/.

community to region—recognizing that higher-level guidance, policies, and resources can facilitate local action, and small-scale local actions can change the world.

- **Balanced values**: Integrate and balance the ecological, economic, and social values to meet sustainability goals.
- **Stakeholder participation**: Involve a wide range of interests and stakeholders, including citizens and groups, who together can share local knowledge and values, learn, and develop creative solutions.
- **Conservation and restoration**: Avoid and protect sensitive environments. Mitigate and compensate damage that cannot be avoided. Restore, enhance, and retrofit degraded environments. Adapt and build resilience to changing environments.
- **Diversity of actions**: Consider and integrate a wide range of actions to achieve objectives, including design, technology, education, voluntary participation, and policy regulations and incentives.
- **Transdisciplinary approaches**: Integrate scientific evidence, social values, economic constraints, and policy options to formulate solutions.
- **Mutually beneficial solutions**: Seek various solutions (e.g., forested urban riparian buffers) to multiple objectives for sustainability (e.g. recreation, walkability, health, livability) and environmental improvement (e.g., water quality, habitat, air quality, carbon sequestration).
- **Adaptive management**: Consider plans and actions as experiments with outcomes, monitor those outcomes, and use adaptive management to learn from the experience and modify the plans and actions as needed.

It is not surprising that these principles fit many planning contexts, including creating sustainable and livable communities. Indeed, this entire textbook details many approaches to implementing these principles—from environmental values and movements in Chapter 1; to the planning processes and collaboration in Chapters 2–4; to the science, engineering, and technical analysis in Chapters 5–14; to the water and ecological parameters in Chapters 7–11; to design concepts in Chapter 16; and to land conservation and development policies in Chapters 15–18.

While these principles and action measures make enormous sense, they are easier to talk and write about than they are to implement—easier said than done. The Everglades and Chesapeake Bay examples illustrate the challenges of ecosystem and watershed management on a large scale. Competing vested interests and resulting political conflicts, scientific complexity and uncertainty, limited resources, and resistance to change—all stand in the way of progress toward sustainable environments and communities.

But against many odds posed by tradition, parochialism, and self-interest, we continue to get better at understanding natural systems, designing systems and communities that protect them, providing for livable places, working together, and connecting our personal interests with those of other peoples and species. Effective environmental land use planning and management to create sustainable watersheds, ecosystems, and communities depend on our continuing capacity to grow and learn and improve.

References

Preface

Brand, S. 2009. *Whole Earth Discipline: An Ecopragmatist Manifesto*. New York: Viking.

Chapter 1

Alberti, M. 2008. *Advances in Urban Ecology. Integrating Humans and Ecological Processes in Urban Ecosystems*. New York: Springer.

Beatley, T. 1994. *Ethical Land Use: Principles of Policy and Planning*. Baltimore: Johns Hopkins University Press.

Birch, E. L., and S. M. Wachter, eds. 2008. *Growing Greener Cities: Urban Sustainability in the Twenty-First Century*. Philadelphia: University of Pennsylvania Press.

Brand, S. 2009. *Whole Earth Discipline: An Ecopragmatist Manifesto*. New York: Viking.

Brown, L. 1963. *Man, Land and Food*. Washington, DC: U.S. Department of Agriculture, Economic Research Service.

Brown, L. 2009. *Plan B 4.0. Mobilizing to Save Civilization*. New York: Norton.

Brundtland Commission. 1987. *Our Common Future*. Final Report of the World Commission on Environment and Development. Oxford, England: Oxford University Press.

Bullard, R. 2000. *Dumping in Dixie*, 3rd ed. Boulder, CO: Westview Press.

Bullard, R. 2005. *The Quest for Environmental Justice: Human Rights and the Politics of Pollution*. San Francisco: Sierra Club Books.

Calthorpe, P. 1993. *The Next Metropolis: Ecology and the American Dream*. Princeton, NJ: Princeton Architectural Press.

Calthorpe, P. 2011. *Urbanism in the Age of Climate Change*. Washington, DC: Island Press.

Carson, R. 1962. *Silent Spring*. Boston: Houghton Mifflin.

Colby, M. 1991. "Environmental Management in Development: The Evolution of Paradigms." *Ecological Economics* 3(3):193–213.

Commoner, B. 1971. *The Closing Circle*. New York: Knopf.

Corbett, M. 1981. *A Better Place to Live*. Emmaus, PA: Rodale.

Duany, A., E. Plater-Zyberk, and J. Speck. 2001. Tenth Anniversary Edition 2010. *Suburban Nation: The Rise of Sprawl and the Decline of the American Dream*. New York: North Point Press.

Duany, A., and J. Speck, with M. Lydon, 2010. *The Smart Growth Manual*. New York: McGraw-Hill.

Ehrlich. P. 1970. *The Population Bomb*. San Francisco: Sierra Club Ballantine.

Gell-Mann, M. 2010. "Transformations of the Twenty-First Century: Transitions to Greater Sustainability." In *Global Sustainability—A Nobel Cause*, edited by H. Schellnhuber et al., pp. 1–7. Cambridge, England: Cambridge University Press.

Gore, A. 2006. *An Inconvenient Truth*. Emmaus, PA: Rodale.

Gore, A. 2009. *Our Choice: A Plan to Solve the Climate Crisis*. Emmaus, PA: Rodale.

Hardin, G. 1968. "The Tragedy of the Commons." *Science* 162:1243–1248.

Hawken, P. 2007. *Blessed Unrest: How the Largest Movement in the World Came into Being and Why No One Saw It Coming*. New York: Penguin.

Hawken, P., A. Lovins, and L. H. Lovins. 1999. *Natural Capitalism: Creating the Next Industrial Revolution*. Boston: Little, Brown.

Hester, R. 2006. *Design for Ecological Democracy*. Cambridge, MA: MIT Press.

Leopold, A. 1949. *The Sand County Almanac*. New York: Oxford University Press.

Lovins, A, K. Datta, O-E Bustnes, J. Koomey, N. Glasgow. 2004. *Winning the Oil End Game*. Snowmass, CO: Rocky Mountain Institute.

Lucht, W. 2010. "Earth System Analysis and Taking a Crude Look at the Whole." In *Global Sustainability—A Nobel Cause*, edited by H. Schellnhuber et al., pp. 19–31. Cambridge, England: Cambridge University Press.

Meadows, D. 1994. "Seeing the Population Issues Whole." In *Beyond the Numbers*, edited by L. Mazur, pp. 23–33.Washington, DC: Island Press.

McGraw-Hill Construction (MHC). 2010. *Green Outlook 2011: Green Trends Driving Growth*. New York: McGraw-Hill.

Raskin, P., T. Banuri, G. Gallopin, P. Gutman, A. Hammond. 2002. *Great Transition: The Promise and Lure of the Times Ahead*. Stockholm: Stockholm Environmental Institute.

Schellnhuber, H., M. Molina, N. Stern, V. Huber, and S. Kadner, eds. 2010. *Global Sustainability—A Nobel Cause*. Cambridge, England: Cambridge University Press.

Schellnhuber, H. J. 1999. "Earth System Analysis and the Second Copernican Revolution." *Nature* 402, Suppl., C19–23.

Speth, J. G. 2008. *The Bridge at the Edge of the World: Capitalism, the Environment, and Crossing from Crisis to Sustainability*. New Haven, CT: Yale University Press.

Steiner, F. 2004. "Urban Human Ecology." *Urban Ecosystems* 7:179–197.

Stockholm Memorandum. 2011. Global Sustainability Symposium. Retrieved June 30, 2011, from http://globalsymposium2011.org/.

Stone, C. 1974. *Should Trees Have Standing? Toward Legal Rights for Natural Objects*. Los Altos, CA: Kaufmann.

Van der Ryn, S., and P. Calthorpe. 1986. *Sustainable Communities*. San Francisco: Sierra Club Books.

West, G. 2010. "Integrated Sustainability and the Underlying Threat of Urbanization." In *Global Sustainability—A Nobel Cause*, edited by H. Schellnhuber et al., pp. 9–18. Cambridge, England: Cambridge University Press.

Chapter 2

Arnstein, S. 1969. "The Ladder of Citizen Participation." *Journal of American Institute of Planners* 35:216–224.

Barber, B. 1984. *Strong Democracy: Participatory Politics for a New Age*. Berkeley: University of California Press.

Berke, P. 2008. "The Evolution of Green Community Planning, Scholarship, and Practice: An Introduction to the Special Issue." *Journal of the American Planning Association* 74:(4):393–407.

Birch, E., and C. Silver. 2009. "One Hundred Years of City Planning's Enduring and Evolving Connections." *Journal of the American Planning Association.* 75:(2): 113–122.

Bosselman, F., and D. Callies. 1971. *The Quiet Revolution in Land Use Control.* U.S. Council on Environmental Quality. Washington, DC: U.S. Government Printing Office.

Braisoulis, H. 1989. "Theoretical Orientations in Environmental Planning: An Inquiry into Alternative Styles." *Environmental Management* 13(4):381–393.

Brand, S. 2009. *Whole Earth Discipline: An Ecopragmatist Manifesto.* New York: Viking.

Campbell, S. 1996. "Green Cities, Growing Cities, Just Cities." *Journal of the American Planning Association* 62(3):296–312.

Corbett, J., and T. Hayden. 1981. "Local Action for a Solar Future." *Solar Law Reporter* 2(5):957.

Daniels, T. 2008. "Review Essay: Works on Green Cities: From Potential to Imperative." *Journal of the American Planning Association* 74(4):521–522.

Daniels, T. L. 2009. "A Trail Across Time: American Environmental Planning from City Beautiful to Sustainability." *Journal of the American Planning Association* 75(2): 178–192.

Forester, J. 1989. *Planning in the Face of Power.* Berkeley: University of California Press.

Forester, J. 1999. *The Deliberative Practitioner: Encouraging Public Participatory Planning Processes.* Cambridge, MA: MIT Press.

Friedmann, J. 1987. *Planning in the Public Domain: From Knowledge to Action.* Princeton, NJ: Princeton University Press.

Godschalk, D. 2004. "Land Use Planning Challenges: Coping with Conflicts in Visions of Sustainable Development and Livable Communities." *Journal of the American Planning Association* 70(1):5–13.

Hart, J. 1996. *Storm Over Mono: The Mono Lake Battle and the California Water Future.* Berkeley: University of California Press.

King, C., K. Feltey, and B. O'Neill. 1998. "The Question of Participation: Toward Authentic Participation in Public Administration." *Public Administration Review* 58(4):317–326.

Land Trust Alliance. 2005. Census of Land Trusts. Retieved from http://www.lta.org/.

Lindblom, C. 1959. "The Science of Muddling Through." *Public Administration Review* 19:79–88.

Loomis, J. 1993. *Integrated Public Land Management.* New York: Columbia University Press.

McAllister, D. 1980. *Evaluation in Environmental Planning: Assessing Environmental, Social, Economic, and Political Trade-offs.* Cambridge, MA: MIT Press.

McHarg, I. 1969. *Design with Nature.* Garden City, NY: American Museum of Natural History.

Mumford, L. 1961. *The City in History.* New York: Houghton Mifflin.

Newman, P. and I. Jennings. 2008. *Cities as Sustainable Ecosystems: Principles and Practice.* Washington, DC: Island Press.

Nolon, J. 1996. "National Land Use Policy Act." Seminar on the Law of Sustainable Development—United States. *Pace Environmental Law Review* 13:519.

Nolon, J. 2002. "In Praise of Parochialism: The Advent of Local Environmental Law." *Harvard Environmental Law Review* 26:365.

Nolon, J. 2005. "Comparative Land Use Law: Patterns of Sustainability." *The Urban Lawyer* 37(4):808.

Nolon, J., and P. Salkin. 2011. Land Use and Sustainable Development: Cases and Materials, 8th ed. Eagan, MN: Thomson-West.

Register, R. 2006. *Eco-Cities: Rebuilding Cities in Balance with Nature.* Gabriola Island, British Columbia, Canada: New Society Publishers.

Riddell, R. 2004. *Sustainable Urban Planning.* Malden, MA: Blackwell.

Salzman, J., and B. Thompson. 2006. *Environmental Law and Policy.* Eagan, MN: Foundation Press, Thomson-West.

Sayre, R., E. Roca, G. Sedaghatkish, B. Youg, S. Keel, R. Roca, and S. Sheppard. 2000. *Nature in Focus: Rapid Ecological Assessment.* The Nature Conservancy. Washington, DC: Island Press.

Somin, I. and J. Adler. "The Green Costs of Kelo: Economic Development Takings and Environmental Protection." *Washington University Law Review* 84:623–666.

Stone, C. 1974. *Should Trees Have Standing? Toward Legal Rights for Natural Objects.* Los Altos, CA: Kaufmann.

Susskind, L., and C. Ozawa. 1984. "Mediated Negotiation in the Public Sector: The Planners as Mediator." *Journal of Planning Education and Research* 3(3):5–15.

United Nations Human Settlements Programme (UNHSP). 2009. *Planning Sustainable Communities.* London: Earthscan.

Westman, W. 1985. *Ecology, Impact Assessment, and Environmental Planning.* New York: Wiley.

Chapter 3

Anderson, L. 1995. *Guidelines for Preparing Urban Plans.* Chicago: Planners Press.

Arendt, R. 1996. *Conservation Design for Subdivisions.* Washington, DC: Island Press.

Arendt, R. 1999. *Growing Greener, Putting Conservation into Local Plans and Ordinances.* Washington, DC: Island Press.

Benfield, F. K., M. D. Raimi, and D. T. Chen. 1999. *Once There Were Greenfields: How Urban Sprawl Is Undermining America's Environment, Economy, and Social Fabric.* Washington, DC: National Resources Defense Council.

Berke, P., D. Godshalk, and E. Kaiser. 2006. *Urban Land Use Planning*, 5th ed. Urbana: University of Illinois Press.

Blacksburg, Town of. 2007. Comprehensive Plan. Retrieved July 15, 2011, from http://www.blacksburg.va.us/Index.aspx?page=1152.

Calthorpe, P., and W. Fulton. 2001. *The Regional City.* Washington, DC: Island Press.

Cambridge Systematics. 2009. *Moving Cooler: Surface Transportation and Climate Change.* Washington, DC: Urban Land Institute.

Dalton, L. C., C. J. Hoch, and F. S. So. 2000. "Introduction: Planning for People and Places." In *The Practice of Local Government Planning*, 3rd ed., edited by C. J. Hoch, L. C. Dalton, and F. So, pp. 3–17. Washington, DC: International City/County Management Association.

Duany, A., E. Plater-Zyberk, and J. Speck. 2000. *Suburban Nation: The Rise of Sprawl and the Decline of the American Dream.* New York: North Point Press.

Duany, A., and J. Speck. 2009. *The Smart Growth Manual.* New York: McGraw-Hill.

Duany, A., and E. Talen. 2002. "Transect Planning." *Journal of the American Planning Association* 68(3):245–266.

Ewing, R., K. Bartholomew, S. Winkelman, J. Walters, and D. Chen. 2007. *Growing Cooler: The Evidence on Urban Development and Climate Change.* Washington, DC: Urban Land Institute.

Farr, D. 2008. *Sustainable Urbanism: Urban Design with Nature.* New York: Wiley.

Federal Emergency Management Agency (FEMA). 2003. *Disaster Factsheets and Backgrounders.* Retrieved from http://www.fema.gov/library/factshts.shtm.

Hester, R. 2006. *Design for Ecological Democracy.* Cambridge, MA: MIT Press.

Hoch, C. J., L. C. Dalton, and F. S. So. 2000. *The Practice of Local Government Planning,* 3rd ed. Washington, DC: International City/County Management Association.

Kenworthy, J. R. 2003. "Transport Energy Use and Greenhouse Gases in Urban Passenger Transport Systems: A Study of 84 Global Cities." Third Conference of the Regional Government Network for Sustainable Development. September 17–19.

Knox, P., and H. Mayer. 2009. *Small Town Sustainability.* Basel, Switzerland: Burkhauser.

Kunstler, J. H. 1994. *The Geography of Nowhere: The Rise and Decline of America's Man-Made Landscape.* New York: Free Press.

Lang, R. E., and J. Lefurgy. 2007. *Boomburgs: The Rise of America's Accidental Cities.* Washington, DC: Urban Land Institute.

Lynch, K. 1981. *Good City Form.* Cambridge, MA: MIT Press.

Newman, P. 2009. "Bridging the Green and Brown Agendas." In *Planning Sustainable Communities,* United Nations Human Settlement Programme (UNHSP), Chap. 9. London: Earthscan.

Newman, P. and I. Jennings. 2008. *Cities as Sustainable Ecosystems: Principles and Practice.* Washington, DC: Island Press.

Randolph, J., and G. M. Masters. 2008. *Energy for Sustainability: Technology, Planning, Policy.* Washington, DC: Island Press.

Riddell, R. 2004. *Sustainable Urban Planning.* Malden, MA: Blackwell.

Ritchie, A., and R. Thomas, eds. 2009. *Sustainable Urban Design: an Environmental Approach,* 2nd ed. London: Taylor & Francis.

Sargent, F .O., P. Lusk, J. A. Rivera, and M. Varela. 1991. *Rural Environmental Planning for Sustainable Communities.* Washington, DC: Island Press.

Schilling, J., and J. Logan. 2008. "Greening the Rust Belt: A Green Infrastructure Model for Right Sizing America's Shrinking Cities." *Journal of the American Planning Association* 74(4):451–466.

United Nations Human Settlement Programme (UNHSP). 2009. *Planning Sustainable Communities.* London: Earthscan.

U.S. Council on Environmental Quality (USCEQ). 1974. *The Costs of Sprawl.* Washington, DC: U.S. Government Printing Office.

U.S. Department of Agriculture (USDA), NRCS. 2009. *National Resources Inventory.* Washington, DC: U.S. GPO. http://www.nrcs.usda.gov/technical/NRI/.

Yaro, R., R. Arendt, H. Dodson, and E. Brabec. 1988. *Dealing with Change in the Connecticut River Valley.* Center for Rural Massachusetts, Environmental Law Foundation, Lincoln Institute for Land Policy (LILP). Cambridge, MA: LILP.

Chapter 4

Adger, W. N. 2001. "Social Capital and Climate Change." Working Paper 8. Norwich, England: Tyndall Centre for Climate Change Research.

Arnstein, S. 1969. "The Ladder of Citizen Participation." *Journal of American Institute of Planners* 35:216–224.

Barber, B. 1984. *Strong Democracy: Participatory Politics for a New Age*. Berkeley: University of California Press.

Bauer, M., and J. Randolph. 2000. "Characteristics of Collaborative Environmental Planning and Decision-Making Processes." *Environmental Practice* 2(2): 156–165.

Booher, D., and J. Innes. 2002. "Network Power in Collaborative Planning." *Journal of Planning Education and Research* 21:221–236.

Brabham, D. 2009. "Crowdsourcing the Public Participation Process for Planning Projects." *Planning Theory* 8(3):242–262.

Castells, M. 1996. *The Rise of the Network Society*. Oxford, England: Blackwell.

Castells, M. 2007. "Communication, Power and Counterpower in the Network Society." *International Journal of Communication* 1:238–266.

Chambers, R. 1994. "Participatory Rural Appraisal (PRA): Analysis of Experience." *World Development* 22(9):1253–1268.

Daniels, S., and G. Walker. 1996. "Collaborative Learning: Improving Public Deliberation in Ecosystem-Based Management." *Environmental Impact Review* 16: 71–102.

Dryzek, J. 1990. *Discursive Democracy: Politics, Policy, and Political Science*. New York: Cambridge University Press.

Fisher, R., W. Ury, and B. Patton, eds. 1991. *Getting to Yes: Negotiating Agreement Without Giving In*, 2nd ed. New York: Penguin.

Forester, J. 1999. *The Deliberative Practitioner: Encouraging Public Participatory Planning Processes*. Cambridge, MA: MIT Press.

Gil de Zúñiga, H., A. Veenstra, E. Vraga, and D. Shah. 2010. "Digital Democracy: Reimagining Pathways to Political Participation." *Journal of Information Technology and Politics* 7(1):36–51.

Goldstein, B., ed. 2011. *Collaborative Resilience: Moving Through Crisis to Opportunity*. Cambridge, MA: MIT Press.

Goldstein, B., and W. Butler. 2009. "The Network Imaginary: Coherence and Creativity Within a Multiscalar Collaborative Effort to Reform U.S. Fire Management." *Journal of Environmental Planning and Management* 52(8):1013–1033.

Goldstein, B., and W. Butler. 2010. "Expanding the Scope and Impact of Collaborative Planning." *Journal of the American Planning Association* 76(2):238–249.

Gray, B. 1989. *Collaborating: Finding Common Ground for Multi-Party Problems*. San Francisco: Jossey-Bass.

Hawken, P. 2007. *Blessed Unrest: How the Largest Movement in the World Came into Being and Why No One Saw It Coming*. New York: Penguin.

Healey, P. 1997. *Collaborative Planning*. Hampshire, England: Macmillan.

Hester, R. 2006. *Design for Ecological Democracy*. Cambridge, MA: MIT Press.

Innes, J. 1996. "Planning Through Consensus Building: A New Perspective on the Comprehensive Planning Ideal." *Journal of the American Planning Association* 62:460–472.

Innes, J., S. Connick, and D. E Booher. 2007. "Informality as a Planning Strategy: Collaborative Water Management in the CALFED Bay-Delta Program." *Journal of the American Planning Association* 7(2):195–210.

Innes, J., J. Gruber, M. Neuman, and R. Thompson. 1994. *Coordinating Growth and Environmental Management Through Consensus Building*. Berkeley: California Policy Seminar.

International Telecommunication Union. 2010. *Measuring the Information Society*. Geneva, Switzerland. Retrieved July 15, 2011, from http://www.itu.int/ITU-D /ict/publications/idi/2010/index.html July 15.

John, D. 1994. *Civic Environmentalism*. Washington, DC: Congressional Quarterly Press.

Kapucu, N. 2008. "Collaborative Emergency Management: Better Community Organizing, Better Public Preparedness and Response." *Disasters* 32:239–262.

Karl, H., L. Susskind, and K. Wallace. 2007. "A Dialogue, Not a Diatribe: Effective Integration of Science and Policy Through Joint Fact-Finding." *Environment* 49(1): 20–34.

Keuhl, D. 2001. "From Collaboration to Knowledge: Planning for Remedial Action in the Great Lakes." Ph.D. dissertation, Environmental Design and Planning, Virginia Tech, Blacksburg, Virginia.

London, S. 1995. "Collaboration in Action: A Survey of Community Collaboratives." Paper prepared for Pew Partnership for Civic Change. Retrieved from http://www .scottlondon.com/reports/ppcc-survey.html.

Margerum, R. 1999. "Getting Past Yes: From Capital Creation to Action." *Journal of the American Planning Association* 65(2):181–192.

Margerum, R. 2008. A Typology of Collaboration Efforts in Environmental Management." *Environmental Management* 41(3):487–500.

Ostrom, E. 1990. *Governing the Commons: The Evolution of Institutions for Collective Action*. Cambridge, England: Cambridge University Press.

Pew Research Center. 2010. *Internet and American Life* project.

Phillips, C., and J. Randolph. 1998. "Does the Forest Service Do Ecosystem Management?" *Journal of Forestry* 96(5):40–45.

Phillips, C., and J. Randolph. 2000. "Ecosystem Management and Implementation of NEPA." *Environmental Management* 26(1):1–12.

Porter, D., and D. Salvesen. 1995. *Collaborative Planning for Wetlands and Wildlife*. Washington, DC: Island Press.

Putnam, R. D. 1996. "The Strange Disappearance of Civic America." *The American Prospect* 7(24). Retrieved June 13, 2003, from http://www.prospect.org/print/V7/24 /putnam-r.html.

Putnam, R. D. 2000. *Bowling Alone: The Collapse and Revival of American Community*. New York: Simon & Schuster.

Randolph, J. 2011. "Creating the Climate Change Resilient Community." In *Collaborative Resilience: Moving Through Crisis to Opportunity*, edited by G. Goldstein. Cambridge, MA: MIT Press.

Randolph, J., and M. Bauer. 1999. "Improving Environmental Decision-Making Through Collaborative Methods." *Policy Studies Review* 16(3/4):168–191.

Shandas, V., and W. B. Messer. 2008. "Fostering Green Communities Through Civic Engagement: Community-Based Environmental Stewardship in the Portland Area." *Journal of the American Planning Association* 74(4):408–418.

Smit, B., and J. Wandel. 2006. "Adaptation, Adaptive Capacity and Vulnerability." *Global Environmental Change* 16:282–292.

Tompkins, E., and W. N. Adger. 2004. "Does Adaptive Management of Natural Resources Enhance Resilience to Climate Change?" *Ecology and Society* 9(2):10.

United Nations Human Settlement Programme (UNHSP). 2009. *Planning Sustainable Communities*. London: Earthscan.

Ury, W. 1993. *Getting Past No: Negotiating Your Way from Confrontation to Coopera-tion*, rev. ed. New York: Bantam Doubleday.

U.S. Department of Agriculture (USDA), Forest Service. 1996. *Collaborative Planning and Stewardship*. Retrieved June 30, 2003, from http://www.fs.fed.us/forum/nepa/colweb.htm.

U.S. Environmental Protection Agency (EPA). 1999. *Community-Based Environmen-tal Protection: A Resource Book for Ecosystems and Communities*. Washington, DC: Office of Policy, Planning, and Evaluation.

Weber, E. P. 1998. *Pluralism by the Rules: Conflict and Cooperation in Environmental Regulation*. Washington, DC: Georgetown University Press.

Wenger, E. C. 1998. *Communities of Practice: Learning, Meaning, and Identity*. Cam-bridge, England: Cambridge University Press.

Wenger, E. C. 2000. "Communities of Practice and Social Learning Systems." *Organi-zation* 7(2):225–246.

Wondolleck, J., and S. Yaffee. 2000. *Making Collaboration Work: Lessons from Innova-tion in Natural Resource Management.* Washington, DC: Island Press.

Zahm, D., and J. Randolph. 1999. "Participation and Partnerships in Planning." On-line tutorial prepared for the American Planning Association (APA) and American Institute for Certified Planners (AICP).

Chapter 5

Anderson, J. 2001. "Developing Digital Monitoring Protocols for Use in Volunteer Stream Assessment." Major paper for Master of Urban and Regional Planning. Vir-ginia Tech, Blacksburg, Virginia.

Anderson, J., E. Hardy, J. Roach, and R. Witmer. 1976. *A Land Use and Land Cover Classification System for Use with Remote Sensor Data*. Geological Survey Profes-sional Paper 964. Washington, DC: U.S. Government Printing Office.

Bagley, A., M. Roberts, A. Tovey, R. Walton, and H. Wolfe. 2007. Map: Changing Urban Edge, Maricopa County, Arizona. Maripoca Association of Governments. Esri Map Book 23.

Barbato, L., K. Mulligan, K. Rainwater, A. Warren, K. Masapari, P. Braden, S. Dorbala, and C. Van Nice. 2007. Ogallala Aquifer Saturated Thickness Change, 1990–2004. Esri Map Book 23. Texas Tech, Lubbock, Texas.

Brown, N. 2007. Map: Visualizing Pedestrian Access in Greater Portland (OR). Port-land, OR. Esri Map Book 23.

Butler, D., 2006. "Virtual Globes: The Web-Wide World." *Nature* 439:776–778.

Campbell, J. B. 1983. *Mapping the Land: Aerial Imagery for Land Use Information*. Washington, DC: Association of American Geographers.

Chandler, G., C. Huang, L.Yang, C. Homer, and C. Larson. 2009. "Developing Consis-tent Landsat Data Sets for Large Area Applications: The MRLC 2001 Protocol." *IEEE Geoscience and Remote Sensing Letters* 6(4):777–781.

Craglia, M., M. Goodchild, A. Annoni, G. Camara, M.Gould, W. Kuhn, D. Mark, I. Masser, D. Maguire, S. Liang, and E. Parsons. 2008. "Next-Generation Digital Earth." Position paper from the Vespucci Initiative for the Advancement of Geo-graphic Information Science International Journal of Spatial Data Infrastructures Research, Vol. 3, 146–167.

Craig, K., K. Forkner, K. Poste, and L. Wu. 2007. Map: Impact of Climate Change Sea Level Rise on Broward County, Florida. Esri Map Book 23. Cal Poly Pomona, California.

Drummond, W. J., and S. P. French. 2008. "The Future of GIS in Planning: Converging Technologies and Diverging Interests." *Journal of the American Planning Association* 74(2):161–174.

Earth Science Research Institute (Esri). Esri Map Book. Various volumes. http://www.esri.com/mapmuseum/index.html.

Earth Science Research Institute (Esri). 2002. "What Is GIS?" Retrieved from Esri website at http://www.gis.com/whatisgis/index.html.

Fry, J. A., M. J. Coan, C. G. Homer, D. K. Meyer, and J. D. Wickham. 2008. *Completion of the National Land Cover Database (NLCD) 1992–2001 Land Cover Change Retrofit Product. Open-File Report 2008–1379*. Washington, DC: U.S. Department of the Interior, U.S. Geological Survey.

Göçmen, Z. A., and S. J. Ventura. 2010. "Barriers to GIS Use in Planning,." *Journal of the American Planning Association* 76(2):172–183.

Goodchild, M. F. 2008. "The Use Cases of Digital Earth." *International Journal of Digital Earth* 1(1):31–42.

Gore, A. 1998. "The Digital Earth: Understanding Our Planet in the 21st Century." Speech at the California Science Center, Los Angeles, January 31, 1998. http://www.isde5.org/al_gore_speech.htm

Hirschman, D., J. Randolph, and J. Flynn. 1992. "The Can-Do Book of Local Water Resources Management." In *Sourcebook for Local Water Resources Management* (ten volumes), edited by J. Randolph, vol. C. Blacksburg: Virginia Water Resources Research Center.

Homer, C., J. Dewitz, J. Fry, M. Coan, N. Hossain, C. Larson, N. Herold, A. McKerrow, J. N. Van Driel, and J. Wickham. 2007. Completion of the 2001 National Land Cover Database for the Conterminous United States. *Photogrammetric Engineering & Remote Sensing*. April.

Kent, R., and R. Klosterman. 2000. "GIS and Mapping: Pitfalls for Planners." *Journal of the American Planning Association* 66(2):189–198.

Lillesand, T., and R. Kiefer. 2004. *Remote Sensing and Image Interpretation*. New York: Wiley.

Martin, K. 2008. Map: 3-D Land Use Inventory of Portland (OR) Central City. Portland Bureau of Planning. Esri Map Book 24.

McHarg, I. L. 1969. *Design with Nature*. New York: Wiley.

Muehrcke, P., and J. Muehrcke. 1998. *Map Use: Reading, Analysis and Interpretation*. Madison, WI: JP Publications.

National Research Council. 2005. *Earth Science and Applications from Space: Urgent Needs and Opportunities to Serve the Nation Committee on Earth Science and Applications from Space: A Community Assessment and Strategy for the Future*. Washington, DC: National Academy of Sciences Press.

Peters-Guarin, G., and M. McCall. 2010. Community Carbon Forestry (CCF) for REDD: Using CyberTracker for Mapping and Visualising of Community Forest Management in the Context of REDD. K:TGAL (Kyoto: Think Global, Act Local) Report. ITC, University of Twente, Enschede and CIGA UNAM, Morelia.

Rambaldi, G., P. Kwaku Kyem, M. McCall, and D. Weiner. 2006. Participatory Spatial Information Management and Communication in Developing Countries. *The*

Electronic Journal on Information Systems in Developing Countries. http://www.ejisdc.org.25(1):1-9.

Sayre, R., E. Roca, G. Sedaghatkish, B. Youg, S. Keel, R. Roca, and S. Sheppard. 2000. *Nature in Focus: Rapid Ecological Assessment.* The Nature Conservancy. Washington, DC: Island Press.

Tomlin, C. 1983. "Digital Cartographic Modelling Techniques in Environmental Planning." Unpublished doctoral dissertation, Yale University, New Haven, Connecticut.

Tomlinson, R. F., 2003. *Thinking About GIS: Geographic Information Systems Planning for Managers.* Redlands, CA: Esri Press.

Woodsong, G. 2006. Map: 3-D Visualization of Population Density, San Francisco Bay Area. Metropolitan Transportation Commission. Esri Map Book 22.

Zwick, P. 2010. The World Beyond GIS: GeoDesign. *Planning.* July.

Chapter 6

Angoli, T. 2001. "Summary of the Status of On-Site Wastewater Treatment Systems in the United States During 1998." In *On-site Wastewater Treatment: Proceedings of the 9th Symposium on Individual and Small Community Sewage Systems,* pp. 316–322. St. Josephs, MI: American Society of Agricultural Engineers.

Barker, A., E. Z. Harrison, A. Hay, U. Krogmann, M. McBride, W. McDowell, B. Richards, T. Steenhuis, and R. Stehouwer. 2007. Guidelines for Application of Sewage Biosolids to Agricultural Lands in the Northeastern U.S. E317. Rutgers, NJ: AES Cooperative Extension.

Brown, K. 2002. "Urban Agriculture and Community Food Security in the United States: Farming from the City Center to the Urban Fringe." Prepared by the Urban Agriculture Committee of the CFSC. Retrieved from http://www.foodsecurity.org/urbanag.html#III.

Coughlin, R., J. Pease, F. Steiner, J. Leach, A. Sussman, and J. A. Pressley. 1994. "Agricultural Land Evaluation and Site Assessment: Status of State and Local Programs." *Journal of Soil and Water Conservation* 49(1):6–13.

Craul, P. 1999. *Urban Soils: Applications and Practices.* New York: Wiley.

English, C., and T. Yeager. 2002. "Responsible Management Entities as a Method to Ensure Decentralized System Viability." *Small Flows Quarterly* 3(2):25–29.

Feiden, W., and E. Winkler. 2006. *Planning Issues for On-Site and Decentralized Wastewater Treatment.* PAS Report 542. Chicago: American Planning Association.

Gordon, S., and G. Gordon. 1981. "The Accuracy of Soil Survey Information for Urban Land Use Planning." *Journal of the American Planning Association* 47(3):301–312.

Home Depot Foundation. 2008. Troy Gardens, Madison Area Community Land Trust. 2008 Awards of Excellence. Case Study.

Marin, County of. 2007. 2007 Marin Countywide Plan. Retrieved from http://www.co.marin.ca.us/depts/cd/main/fm/index.cfm.

Mattingly, K., and M. Tremel. 2002. "A Unique Public Management Entity in the Town of Blacksburg, Virginia (STEP/STEG System)." Town of Blacksburg, Virginia.

Montgomery County (VA) Planning Department. 1984. *Land Evaluation and Site Assessment in Montgomery County, Virginia.* Christiansburg, VA: Author.

National Research Council, 2002. *Biosolids Applied to Land: Advancing Standards and Practices.* Washington, DC: National Academies Press.

Raja, S., B. Born, and J. K. Russell. 2008. *A Planners Guide to Community and Regional Food Planning.* PAS Report 554. Chicago: American Planning Association.

Rock County Planning, Economic & Community Development Agency. 2010. Town of Fulton Land Evaluation and Site Assessment (LESA) Program Manual. Rock County, Wisconsin.

U.S. Department of Agriculture (USDA), Agricultural Marketing Service. 2010. Farmers Market Services. Marketing Services Division. http://www.ams.usda.gov /WholesaleFarmersMarkets.

USDA, NRCS. 2000. "Erosion and Sedimentation on Construction Sites." Soil Quality—Urban Technical Note No. 1. Washington, DC: U.S. GPO.

USDA, NRCS. 2009. *National Resources Inventory.* Washington, DC: U.S. GPO. http://www.nrcs.usda.gov/technical/NRI/.

USDA, NRCS. 2010. *Application of Soil Survey to Assess the Effects of Land Management Practices on Soil and Water Quality.* Soil Survey Investigations Report No. 52.

USDA, Soil Conservation Service (SCS). 1983. *National Agricultural Land Evaluation and Site Assessment Handbook.* Washington, DC: U.S. GPO.

USDA, SCS. 1985. *Soil Survey of Montgomery County, Virginia.* Christiansburg, VA: Author.

U.S. Environmental Progection Agency (EPA). 1993a. *Safer Disposal for Solid Waste: The Federal Regulations for Landfills.* EPA 530-SW-91–092. Solid Waste and Emergency Response. Washington, DC: Author.

U.S. EPA. 1993b. *Solid Waste Disposal Facility Criteria: Technical Manual.* EPA 530-R-93–017. Washington, DC: Author.

U.S. EPA. 1998. *A Citizen's Guide to Phytoremediation.* Retrieved from http://www .clu-in.org/products/citguide/phyto2.htm.

U.S. EPA. 2000. EPA Guidelines for Management of Onsite/Decentralized Wastewater Systems. EPA 832-F-00–012. Washington, DC: Author.

U.S. EPA. 2002. *Onsite Wastewater Treatment Systems Manual.* EPA 625-R-00 –008. Office of Water. Retrieved from http://www.epa.gov/ORD/NRMRL/Pubs/ 625R00008/625R00008.htm.

U.S. EPA. 2005. Handbook for Managing Onsite and Clustered (Decentralized) Wastewater Treatment Systems. An Introduction to Management Tools and Information for Implementing EPA's Management Guidelines. Washington, DC: Office of Water.

U.S. EPA. 2008. Septic Systems Fact Sheet. Decentralized Wastewater Program, Washginton, DC: Office of Water.

U.S. EPA. 2010. Municipal Solid Waste Generation, Recycling, and Disposal in the United States: Facts and Figures for 2008. Retrieved from http://www.epa.gov/osw /nonhaz/municipal/msw99.htm.

Vasilas, L., G. Hurt, and C. Noble. 2010. Hydric Soils in the United States: A Guide for Identifying and Delineating Hydric Soils, Ver. 7.0. Washington, DC: USDA, NRCS.

Virginia Department of Conservation and Recreation. 2005. Division of Soil and Water Conservation. Richmond, VA: Virginia Nutrient Management Standards and Criteria.

Wischmeier, W. H., and D. D. Smith. 1960. "A Universal Soil Loss Estimating Equation to Guide Conservation Farm Planning." *Proceedings of the 7th International Congress Soil Science Society* 1:418–425.

Chapter 7

California Department of Fish and Game. 1996. *California Stream Bioassessment Procedures.* Aquatic Bioassessment Lab. Sacramento: Author.

Caraco, D. 2010. *Watershed Treatment Model (WTM) 2010 User's Guide – Draft.* Center for Watershed Protection. Retrieved from http://www.cwp.org/documents /cat_view/83-watershed-treatment-model.html.

Center for Watershed Protection. 2003. "Impacts of Impervious Cover on Aquatic Systems." Watershed Protection Research monograph No. 1. Ellicott City, MD: Author.

Chang, G., J. Parrish, and C. Souer. 1990. *The First Flush of Runoff and Its Effect on Control Structure Design.* Austin, TX: Environmental Resource Management Division.

Dunne, T., and L. Leopold. 1978. *Water in Environmental Planning.* San Francisco: Freeman.

Federal Emergency Management Agency (FEMA). 2009. Flood Insurance Study. Montgomergy County, Virginia. Retrieved from FEMA Map Service Center, www .msc.fema.gov.

Federal Emergency Management Agency (FEMA). 2010. Map Service Center. www .msc.fema.gov/.

Federal Interagency Stream Restoration Working Group (FISRWG). 1998. *Stream Corridor Restoration: Principles, Processes, and Practices.* 15 Federal agencies. U.S. GPO 0120-A; Docs No. A 57.6/2:EN 3/PT.653. Retrieved from http://www.usda.gov /stream_restoration/.

Gironás, J., L. Roesner, J. Davis. 2009. Storm Water Management Model Applications manual. EPA/600/R-09/077. Cincinnati, OH: EPA National Risk Management Research Center.

Izaak Walton League of America. 1994. *Save Our Streams Stream Quality Survey.* Gaithersburg, MD: Author.

Moglen, G. E., and S. Kim. 2007. "Limiting Imperviousness: Are Threshold-Based Policies a Good Idea?" *Journal of the American Planning Association* 73(2):161–171.

National Weather Service (NWS). 2002. Hydrologic Design Service Center. Retrieved from http://www.nws.noaa.gov/oh/hdsc/studies/prcpfreq.html.

Ohrel, R. 1996. "Simple and Complex Stormwater Pollutant Load Models Compared." Article 13 in *The Practice of Watershed Protection.* Ellicott City, MD: Center for Watershed Protection. Retrieved June 27, 2003, from http://www.stormwater center.net/Database_Files/Publications_Database_1Page470.html.

Prince George's County. 1999a. *Low-Impact Development: An Integrated Design Approach.* Largo, MD: Prince George's County, Maryland, Department of Environmental Resources.

Prince George's County. 1999b. *Low-Impact Development Hydrologic Analysis.* Largo, MD: Prince George's County, Maryland, Department of Environmental Resources.

Riley, A. 1998. *Restoring Streams in Cities: A Guide for Planners, Policy Makers and Citizens.* Washington, DC: Island Press.

Rose, F. 2010. Stormwater Management Program, Fairfax County, Virginia. Chesapeake Bay Program, Science and Technical Advisory Committee Workshop on Stormwater Management. May 13, Washington, DC.

Rosgen, D. 1994. "A Classification of Natural Rivers." *Catena* 22:169–199.

Schueler, T. 1987. *Controlling Urban Runoff: A Practical Manual for Planning and Designing Urban BMPs.* Washington, DC: Metropolitan Washington Council of Governments.

Schueler, T. 1994. "The Importance of Imperviousness." *Watershed Protection Techniques* 1(3):100–111.

Schueler, T. 2000. "Basic Concepts of Watershed Planning." In *The Practice of Watershed Protection*, edited by T. Schueler and H. Holland, pp. 145–161. Ellicott City, MD: Center for Watershed Protection.

Schueler, T. 2008. Implications of the Impervious Cover Model: Stream Classification, Urban Subwatershed Management and Permitting. Chesapeake Stormwater Network Technical Bulletin No. 3.

Schueler, T., L. Fraley-McNeal, and K. Cappiella. 2009. "Is Impervious Cover Still Important? Review of Recent Research." *Journal of Hydrologic Engineering*. 14(4): 309–315.

Sheng, J., and J. Wilson. 2009. "Watershed Urbanization and Changing Flood Behavior Across the Los Angeles Metropolitan Region." *Natural Hazards* 48:41–57.

Shoemaker, L., J. Riverson, K. Alvi, J. Zhen, S. Paul, and T. Rafi. 2009. "SUSTAIN— A Framework for Placement of Best Management Practices in Urban Watersheds to Protect Water Quality." Tetra Tech, Inc., EPA/600/R-09/095. Cincinnati, OH: U.S. EPA National Risk Management Research Center.

State of New York. 2001. *New York State Stormwater Management Design Manual*. Prepared by Center for Watershed Protection. Albany: New York Department of Environmental Conservation.

U.S. Army Corps of Engineers. 2010. Hydrology Engineering Center Models. http://www.hec.usace.army.mil/.

U.S. Department of Agriculture (USDA), National Resources Conservation Service (NRCS). 1998. *Stream Visual Assessment Protocol*. Technical Note 99-1. Washington, DC: Author. Retrieved June 27, 2003, from http://www.nrcs.usda.gov/technical/ECS/aquatic/svapfnl.pdf.

USDA, NRCS. 2008. Win TR-55, Small Watershed Hydrology. Tutorial powerpoint. http://www.wsi.nrcs.usda.gov/products/w2q/h&h/docs/WinTR55/WinTR55_tutorial.ppt.

USDA, Soil Conservation Service. 1986. *Urban Hydrology for Small Watersheds*. Conservation Engineering Division. Technical Release 55. Retrieved June 27, 2003, from ftp://ftp.wcc.nrcs.usda.gov/downloads/hydrology_hydraulics/tr55/tr55.pdf.

U.S. Environmental Protection Agency (EPA). 1993. *Guidance Specifying Management Measures for Sources of Nonpoint Pollution in Coastal Waters*. EPA-840-B-93-001c. Washington, DC: Office of Water.

U.S. EPA. 1997. *Volunteer Stream Monitoring: A Methods Manual*. EPA-841-B-97-003. Office of Water (4503F). Washington, DC: Author. Retrieved June 27, 2003, from http://www.epa.gov/owow/monitoring/volunteer/stream/.

U.S. EPA. 1999. *Rapid Bioassessment Protocols for Use in Stream and Wadeable Rivers: Periphyton, Benthic Macroinvertebrates, and Fish*, 2nd ed. EPA 841-B-99-002. Washington, DC: Office of Water. Retrieved September 11, 2003, from http://www.epa.gov/owow/monitoring.rbp/download.html.

U.S. EPA. 2000a. *Liquid Assets 2000: America's Water Resources at a Turning Point*. EPA-840-B-00–001. Office of Water (4101). Washington, DC: U.S. EPA.

U.S. EPA. 2000b. *The Quality of Our Nation's Waters: A Summary of the National Water Quality Inventory: 1998 Report to Congress*. EPA-841-S-00–001. Office of Water (4503F). Washington, DC: U.S. EPA.

U.S. EPA. 2000. Watershed Academy Web: Online Training in Watershed Management. Retrieved from http://cfpub.epa.gov/watertrain/index.cfm.

U.S. EPA. 2002. *Water Quality Conditions in the United States: A Profile from the 2000 National Water Quality Inventory.* EPA-841-F-02–003. Office of Water (4303F). Washington, DC: U.S. EPA.

U.S. EPA. 2009. *A Summary of the National Water Quality Inventory: 2004.* http://water.epa.gov/lawsregs/guidance/cwa/305b/2004report_index.cfm.

U.S. EPA. 2010a. BASINS model. Retrieved from http://www.epa.gov/waterscience/BASINS/.

U.S. EPA. 2010b. EnviroMapper for Water. http://www.epa.gov/waters/enviromapper/.

U.S. EPA. 2010c. STORET (STOrage and RETrieval) Data Warehouse. http://www.epa.gov/storet/.

U.S. EPA. 2010d. Storm Water Management Model (SWMM). http://www.epa.gov/ednnrmrl/models/swmm/.

U.S. EPA. 2010e. WQX Web: A Tool for Sharing Your Water Quality Data. Retrieved from http://www.epa.gov/storet/wqx/index.html.

U.S. Geological Survey (USGS). 2004. NHD Watershed Tool: Instructions for Preprocessing Supporting Data Layers. http://nhd.usgs.gov/watershed/watershed_tool_inst_TOC.html.

U.S. Geological Survey (USGS). 2010. National Stream Flow Information. http://water.usgs.gov/nsip/. Real-time data. http://waterwatch.usgs.gov/.

U.S. Weather Bureau (USWB). 1961. *Rainfall Frequency Atlas of the United States.* Technical Paper No. 40. Washington, DC: Author. Retrieved June 23, 2003, from http://www.erh.noaa.gov/er/hq/Tp40s.htm.

Virginia Department of Conservation and Recreation. 1992. *Virginia Erosion and Sediment Control Handbook.* Richmond: Author.

Virginia Department of Environmental Quality (DEQ). 2010. Final 2010 305(b)/303(d) Water Quality Assessment Integrated Report. http://www.deq.state.va.us/wqa/ir2010.html.

Washington Department of Ecology (WDOE). 2006. Water Quality Standards for Surface Waters of the State of Washington. Chapter 173-201A WAC. Olympia, Washington.

Chapter 8

California Stormwater Quality Association. 2009. *California Stormwater BMP Handbook.* Sacramento: Author. http://www.casqa.org/.

Cappiella, K., L. Fraley-McNeal, M. Novotney, and T. Schueler. 2008. Article 5: "Next Generation of Stormwater Wetland." Center for Watershed Protection. Wetlands and Watersheds Articles Prepared for Office of Wetlands, Oceans and Watersheds, U.S. Environmental Protection Agency.

Cappiella, K., and T. Schueler. 2001. "Crafting a Lake Protection Ordinance." *Watershed Protection Techniques* 3(4):750–762.

Caraco, D. 2010. *Watershed Treatment Model (WTM) 2010 User's Guide – Draft.* Center for Watershed Protection. Retrieved from http://www.cwp.org/documents/cat_view/83-watershed-treatment-model.html.

Center for Watershed Protection (CWP). 2000. Comparative Pollutant Removal Capability of Stormwater Treatment Practices. Article 64. The Practice of Watershed Protection.

Fairfax County, Virginia. 2005. Case Study One: Residential Single Family Redevelopment. Public Facilities Manual. Fairfax, VA: Author.

Fairfax County, Virginia. 2010. Watershed Management Program. http://www.fairfax county.gov/dpwes/watersheds/.

Federal Interagency Stream Restoration Working Group (FISRWG). 1998. *Stream Corridor Restoration: Principles, Processes, and Practices.* 15 Federal agencies. U.S. GPO 0120-A; Docs No. A 57.6/2:EN 3/PT.653. Retrieved from http://www.usda .gov/stream_restoration/.

Hinman, C. 2007. *Rain Garden Handbook for Western Washington Homeowners.* Graphics: Garry Anderson, AnderDesigns. Washington State University Pierce County Extension.

King County. 2008. *Surface Water Design Manual.* Department of Natural Resources and Parks.

Low, T. 2008. *Light Imprint Handbook.* Integrating Sustainability and Community Design. Version 1.3. Charlotte, NC: DPZ Architects and Town Planners. New Urban Press.

Maryland Department of the Environment (MDE). 2009. Maryland Stormwater Design Manual, rev. ed. Annapolis, MD: Author.

National Academy of Sciences. 2001. *Assessing the TMDL Approach to Water Quality Management. Commission on Geosciences, Environment and Resources.* Washington, DC: National Academies Press.

National Research Council (NRC). 1992. *Restoration of Aquatic Ecosystems: Science, Technology, and Public Policy.* Washington, DC: National Academies Press.

NRC. 2009. *Urban Stormwater Management in the United States.* Washington, DC: National Academies Press.

Nevue Ngan Associates, Eisen/Letunic, Van Meter Williams Pollack LLP, ICF International. 2009. *Stormwater Management Handbook: Implementing Green Infrastructure in Northern Kentucky Communities.* Washington, DC: U.S. EPA.

Nevue Ngan Associates, Sherwood Design Engineers. 2009. *San Mateo County Sustainable Green Streets and Parking Lots Design Guidebook.* San Mateo Countywide (California) Water Pollution Prevention Program. San Mateo: SMCW-PPP.

New York, State of. 2001. *New York State Stormwater Management Design Manual.* Prepared by Center for Watershed Protection. Albany: NY Department of Environmental Conservation.

Phillips, T. 2010. "High Point: A Case Study: Getting It Right: Connecting Housing, Community, Development, Water, and Sustainable Neighborhoods." New Partners for Smart Growth Conference, Seattle, WA.

Pierce County. 2008. *Pierce County 2008 Stormwater Management and Site Development Manual.* Tacoma, WA: Author.

Portland, City of. 2006. Stormwater Solutions Handbook. Environmental Services. Portland, OR: Author. Retrieved from http://www.portlandonline.com/bes/index .cfm?c=43110.

Portland, City of. 2008. Stormwater Management Manual. Environmental Services. Portland, OR: Author.

Prince George's County. 1999. *Low-Impact Development: An Integrated Design Approach.* Largo, MD: Prince George's County, Maryland, Department of Environmental Resources.

Prince George's County. 2002. *Low-Impact Development (LID): Integrated Management Practices Guidebook.* Largo, MD: Prince George's County, Maryland, Department of Environmental Resources.

PS Partnership (formerly Puget Sound Action Team) and WSU Extension. 2005. *LID Technical Guidance Manual for Puget Sound*. Lead author: C. Hinman. Graphics by AHBL, Inc.

Riley, A. 1998. *Restoring Streams in Cities: A Guide for Planners, Policy Makers and Citizens*. Washington, DC: Island Press.

River Network. 2009. "Watershed-Based Approach to Stormwater Permits." www.rivernetwork.org.

Rose, F. 2010. "Stormwater Management Program, Fairfax County, Virginia." Presentation to Chesapeake Bay Program Science and Technical Advisory Committee Workshop on Urban Stormwater Management, May 13, 2010, Washington, DC.

Schueler, T. 2000. "Basic Concepts of Watershed Planning." In *The Practice of Watershed Protection*, edited by T. Schueler and H. Holland, pp. 145–161. Ellicott City, MD: Center for Watershed Protection.

Seattle, City of. 2009. Best Available Science Review Stormwater Code Revisions. Seattle: Author.

U.S. Department of Agriculture (USDA). NRCS. Undated. National Conservation Practices Standards website. Retrieved from http://www.ftw.nrcs.usda.gov/nhcp_2.html.

U.S. Environmental Protection Agency (EPA). 2000. *Liquid Assets 2000: America's Water Resources at a Turning Point*. EPA-840-B-00–001. Office of Water (4101). Washington, DC: U.S. EPA.

U.S. EPA. 2004. *Water Quality Trading Assessment Handbook: Can Water Quality Trading Advance Your Watershed's Goals?* EPA 841-B-04-001. Washington, DC: U.S. EPA.

U.S. EPA. 2005. Using Smart Growth Techniques as Stormwater Best Management Practices. Retrieved from http://www.epa.gov/dced/pdf/sg_stormwater_BMP.pdf.

U.S. EPA. 2010a. Green Infrastructure Case Studies: Municipal Policies for Managing Stormwater with Green Infrastructure. Retrieved from http://www.epa.gov/owow/NPS/lid/gi_case_studies_2010.pdf.

U.S. EPA. 2010b. National Summary of Impaired Waters and Total Maximum Daily Load Information. Retrieved from http://iaspub.epa.gov/waters10/attains_nation_cy.control?p_report_type=T.

U.S. EPA Chesapeake Bay Program. 2010. Chesapeake Bay TMDL. http://www.epa.gov/chesapeakebaytmdl/.

U.S. EPA Chesapeake Bay Program. 2011. Guide for Chesapeake Bay Jurisdictions for the Development of Phase II Watershed Implementation Plans (WIPs). http://www.epa.gov/chesapeakebaytmdl/.

Virginia Department of Conservation and Recreation. 1999. *Virginia Stormwater Management Handbook*. Richmond: Author.

Vizzini, D. 2010. "Restoring Watershed Health: Integrating TMDLs, Stormwater Management and Watershed Restoration in Portland, Oregon." Bureau of Environmental Services. City of Portland, Oregon. Presentation to Chesapeake Bay Program Science and Technical Advisory Committee Workshop on Urban Stormwater Management, May 13, 2010, Washington, DC.

Walsh, C. J., A. H. Roy, J. W. Feminella, P. D. Cottingham, P. M. Groffman, and R. P. Morgan. 2005. "The Urban Stream Syndrome: Current Knowledge and the Search for a Cure." *Journal of the North American Benthological Society* 24(3):706–723.

Washington Department of Ecology (DOE). 2005. *Stormwater Management Manual for Western Washington*. Olympia: Author.

Winer, R. 2000. *National Pollutant Removal Database for Stormwater Treatment Practices,* 2nd ed. Ellicott City, MD: Center for Watershed Protection.

Chapter 9

Aller, L., T. Bennett, J. Lehr, R. Petty, and G. Hackett. 1987. *DRASTIC: A Standardized System for Evaluating Groundwater Pollution Potential Using Hydrogeologic Settings.* EPA-600/2–87–035. Washington, DC: U.S EPA.

Breeder, N., and J. Dawson. 1976. *Roanoke County Groundwater: Present Conditions and Prospects.* Commonwealth of Virginia, State Water Control Board (SWCB). Bureau of Water Control Management. Planning Bulletin 301. Richmond, VA: SWCB.

Crowley, J., and C. Tulloch. 2002. *Protocol Used to Identify High Risk UST Facilities inSanta Clara County (California).* Santa Clara, CA: Santa Clara Valley Water District.

Dunne, T., and L. Leopold. 1978. *Water in Environmental Planning.* San Francisco: Freeman.

Federal Interagency Stream Restoration Working Group (FISRWG). 1998. *Stream Corridor Restoration: Principles, Processes, and Practices.* GPO Item No. 0120-A; SuDocs No. A 57.6/2:EN 3/PT.653. ISBN-0–934213–59–3. Retrieved June 27, 2003, from http://www.usda.gov/stream_restoration/.

Fritch, T., C. McKnight, J. Yelderman, and J. Arnold. 2000. "An Aquifer Vulnerability Assessment of Paluxy Aquifer, Central Texas, USA, Using GIS and a Modified DRASTIC Approach." *Environmental Management* 25(3):337–345.

Hamilton to New Baltimore Groundwater Consortium (HNBGC). 2003. Description of Programs. Retrieved June 28, 2003, from http://www.govconsortium.org.

Hayman, J. 1972. "The Significance of Some Geologic Factors in the Karst Development of the Mt. Tabor Area, Montgomery County, Virginia." Master's thesis, Virginia Tech, Blacksburg, Virginia.

Hirschman, D., J. Randolph, and J. Flynn. 1992. "The Can-Do Book of Local Water Resources Management." Vol. C in *Sourcebook for Local Water Resources Management* (ten volumes), edited by J. Randolph. Blacksburg: Virginia Water Resources Research Center and College of Architecture and Urban Studies, Virginia Tech.

Massachusetts Department of Environmental Protection (DEP). 2001. "Developing a Local Wellhead Protection Plan: A Guidance Document for Communities and Public Water Suppliers." Boston: Bureau of Resource Protection.

Massachusetts Department of Environmental Protection (DEP). 2002. *Source Water Assessment and Protection (SWAP) Report for Worcester DPW.* Boston: Water Supply Division.

Massachusetts Department of Environmental Protection (DEP). 2010. Water Source Protection Area Map Viewer. http://maps.massgis.state.ma.us/WSPA/viewer.htm.

New Jersey Department of Environmental Protection. 2004a. Source Water Assessment Reports. http://www.state.nj.us/dep/swap/creport.htm.

New Jersey Department of Environmental Protection. 2004b. Statewide Summary of Source Water Assessments. http://www.state.nj.us/dep/swap/reports/swap_sum 200412.pdf.

Osborn, N., E. Eckenstein, and K. Koon. 1998. *Vulnerability Assessment of Twelve Major Aquifers in Oklahoma.* Oklahoma Water Resources Board (OWRB). Technical Report 98–5. Oklahoma City: OWRB.

Santa Clara Valley Water District, California. 2001. *Santa Clara Valley Water District Groundwater Management Plan*. Santa Clara, CA: Author.

Texas Commission on Environmental Quality (CEQ). 2010. Interpreting Source Water Map Colors. http://www.tceq.state.tx.us/permitting/water_supply/pdw/SWAP/map/sw_capture_colors.html/view.

U.S. Environmental Protection Agency (EPA). 1988. *Model Assessment for Developing Wellhead Protection Areas*. Washington, DC: Office of Groundwater Programs.

U.S. EPA. 2000. *Introduction to EPA's Drinking Water Source Protection Programs*. Washington, DC: Office of Water.

U.S. EPA. 2001. *Source Water Protection: Best Management Practices and Other Measures for Protecting Drinking Water Supplies*. Washington, DC: Office of Water.

U.S. EPA. 2010. "Public Drinking Water Systems: Facts and Figures." http://water.epa.gov/infrastructure/drinkingwater/pws/factoids.cfm.

U.S. Geological Survey. 1972. *Definitions of Selected Groundwater Terms*. USGS Water Supply Paper #1988. Washington, DC: Author.

U.S. Geological Survey. 1999. "Improvements to the DRASTIC Ground-Water Vulnerability Mapping Method." USGS Fact Sheet FS-066–99. Washington, DC.

Wilcox, J., M. Gotkowitz, K. Bradbury, and J. Bahr. 2010. "Using Groundwater Models to Evaluate Strategies for Drinking-Water Protection in Rural Subdivisions." *Journal of the American Planning Association* 76(3):295–304.

Virginia Cave Board. 1988. Poster: Karst Hydrologic System. Richmond: Author.

Witten, J., and S. Horsley. 1995. *A Guide to Wellhead Protection*. Planning Advisory Service. U.S. EPA. PAS Report 457/458. Chicago: American Planning Association.

Chapter 10

Alberti, M. 2008. *Advances in Urban Ecology. Integrating Humans and Ecological Processes in Urban Ecosystems*. New York: Springer.

Alberti, M., and J. Marzluff. 2004. "Ecological Resilience in Urban Ecosystems: Linking Urban Patterns to Human and Ecological Functions." *Urban Ecosystems* 7: 241–265.

American Forests. 2001a. "Gray to Green: Reversing the National Urban Tree Deficit." Retrieved June 27, 2003, from http://www.americanforests.org.

American Forests. 2001b. "Urban Ecosystem Analysis, Atlanta Metro Area: Calculating the Value of Nature." Washington, DC: Author. Retrieved June 28, 2003, from http://www.americanforests.org/resources/rea/.

American Forests. 2001c. "Urban Ecosystem Analysis, Willamette, Lower Columbia Region of Northwestern Oregon and Southwestern Washington State: Calculating the Value of Nature." Washington, DC: Author. Retrieved June 28, 2003, from http://www.americanforests.org/resources/rea/.

American Forests. 2002. *CITYgreen 5.0*. Washington, DC: Author.

American Forests. 2010. *Urban Ecosystem Analysis, Mecklenburg County and the City of Charlotte, North Carolina. Calculating the Value of Nature*. Washington, DC: Author.

Bernd-Cohen, T., and M. Gordon. 1998. *State Coastal Management Effectiveness in Protecting Beaches, Dunes, Bluffs, Rocky Shores: A National Overview* (Part of the Sea Grant National CZM Effectiveness Study for the Office of Ocean and Coastal Resource Management), National Ocean Service, NOAA, DOC. Washington, DC: NOAA.

California State Coastal Conservancy. 2011. Information retrieved July 10, 2011 from http://scc.ca.gov/.

Cappiella, K., and L. Fraley-McNeal. 2007. Article 6: "The Importance of Protecting Vulnerable Streams and Wetlands at the Local Level." Center for Watershed Protection. Wetlands and Watersheds Articles Prepared for Office of Wetlands, Oceans and Watersheds. Washington, DC: U.S. Environmental Protection Agency.

Cappiella, K., L. Fraley-McNeal, M. Novotney, and T. Schueler. 2008. Article 5: "Next Generation of Stormwater Wetland." Center for Watershed Protection. Wetlands and Watersheds Articles Prepared for Office of Wetlands, Oceans and Watersheds. Washington, DC: U.S. Environmental Protection Agency.

Cappiella, K., A. Kitchell, and T. Schueler. 2006. "Article 2: Using Local Watershed Plans to Protect Wetlands." Center for Watershed Protection. Wetlands and Watersheds Articles Prepared for Office of Wetlands, Oceans and Watersheds. Washington, DC: U.S. Environmental Protection Agency.

Cappiella, K., T. Schueler, J. Tasillo, and T. Wright. 2005. Article 3: "Adapting Watershed Tools to Protect Wetlands." Center for Watershed Protection. Wetlands and Watersheds Articles Prepared for Office of Wetlands, Oceans and Watersheds. Washington, DC: U.S. Environmental Protection Agency.

Cappiella, K., T. Schueler, J. Tomlinson, and T. Wright. 2006. *Urban Watershed Forestry Manual*. Part 3: Urban Tree Planting Guide. Center for Watershed Protection. Wetlands and Watersheds Articles. Prepared for and published by United States Department of Agriculture, Forest Service, Northeastern Area, State and Private Forestry.

Cappiella, K., T. Schueler, and T. Wright. 2005. *Urban Watershed Forestry Manual*. "Part 1: Methods for Increasing Forest Cover in a Watershed." Center for Watershed Protection. Wetlands and Watersheds Articles. Prepared for and published by U.S. Department of Agriculture, U. S. Forest Service, Northeastern Area, State and Private Forestry.

Cappiella, K., T. Schueler, and T. Wright. 2006. *Urban Watershed Forestry Manual*. Part 2: Conserving and Planting Trees at Development Sites. Center for Watershed Protection. Wetlands and Watersheds Articles. Prepared for and published by: United States Department of Agriculture, Forest Service, Northeastern Area, State and Private Forestry.

Commission for Environmental Cooperation. 1997. "Ecological Regions of North America Toward a Common Perspective." http://www.cec.org. Quebec, Ontario. Canada: Author. Retrieved June 28, 2003, from ftp://ftp.epa.gov/wed/ecoregions /na/CEC_NAeco.pdf.

Cowardin, L., V. Carter, and E. La Roe. 1979. *Classification of Wetlands and Deepwater Habitats of the United States*. FWS/OBS-79/31. Washington, DC: U.S. Department of the Interior, U.S. Fish and Wildlife Service.

Dahl, T. E. 2006. *Status and Trends of Wetlands in the Conterminous United States 1998 to 2004*. Washington, DC: U.S. Department of the Interior, U.S. Fish and Wildlife Service.

Environmental Law Institute (ELI). 2008. *State Wetland Protection: Status, Trends & Model Approaches. A 50-State Study by the Environmental Law Institute*. Washington, DC: Author.

Federal Interagency Stream Restoration Working Group (FISRWG). 1998. *Stream Corridor Restoration: Principles, Processes, and Practices*. Washington, DC: U.S. Government Printing Office. http://www.usda.gov/stream_restoration/.

Good, J., J. Weber, J. Charland, J. Olson, and K. Chapin. 1998. *Protecting Estuaries and Coastal Wetlands* (Part of the Sea Grant National Coastal Zone Management Effectiveness Study). Oregon Sea Grant Special Report PI-98–001. Corvallis: Oregon State University.

Goodwin, R., S. Hastings, and L. Ferguson. 1997. *Evaluation of Coastal Zone Management National Coastal Zone Management Effectiveness Study Programs in Redeveloping Deteriorating Urban Ports and Waterfronts*. Seattle: University of Washington.

Interagency Workgroup on Wetland Restoration (IWWR). 2002. "An Introduction and User's Guide to Wetland Restoration, Creation, and Enhancement." NOAA, EPA, U.S. Army Corps of Engineers, FWS, NRCS. Retrieved June 28, 2003, from http://www.epa.gov/owow/wetlands/finalinfo.html.

International Society of Arboriculture (ISA). 2001. "Guidelines for Developing and Evaluating Tree Ordinances." Retrieved June 23, 2003, from http://www.isaarbor.com/tree-ord/index.htm.

Landauer, R. 2001. "Exploring Cities' Leafy Frontier." Retrieved June 28, 2003, from http://www.sactree.com.

Lewis, R. 1990. "Wetlands Restoration/Creation/Enhancement Terminology: Suggestions for Standardization." In *Wetland Creation and Restoration: The Status of the Science*, edited by J. A. Kusler and M. E. Kentula, pp. 417–422. Washington, DC: Island Press.

Marsh, W. 1978. *Environmental Analysis: For Land Use and Site Planning*. New York: McGraw-Hill.

Maryland Department of the Environment. 2008. *Shore Erosion Control Guidelines for Waterfront Property Owners*, 2nd ed. Annapolis: Author.

Marzluff, J., E. Shulenberger, G. Bradley, M. Alberti, C. Ryan, C. ZumBrunnen, W. Endlicher, and U. Simon, eds. 2008. *Urban Ecology: An International Perspective on the Interaction of Humans and Nature*. New York: Springer.

McPherson, E. 2003. "Urban Forestry, The Final Frontier?" *Journal of Forestry* 101(3):20–25.

National Oceanic and Atmospheric Administration. 2010. "Alternatives for Coastal Development: One Site, Three Scenarios. How-to Guides." http://www.csc.noaa.gov/alternatives/.

National Research Council (NRC). 1995. *Wetlands: Characteristics and Boundaries*. Washington, DC: National Academies Press.

National Research Council (NRC). 2001. *Compensating for Wetland Losses Under the Clean Water Act*. Washington, DC: National Academies Press.

Odum, E., and G. Barrett. 2004. *Fundamentals of Ecology*, 5th ed. Florence, KY: Brooks/Cole.

Oleyar, M.D., A. Greve, J. Withey, and A. Bjorn. 2008. "An Integrated Approach to Evaluating Urban Forest Functionality." *Urban Ecosystems* 11:289–308.

Pincetl, S. 2009. "Implementing Municipal Tree Planting: Los Angeles Million-Tree Initiative." *Environmental Management* 45(2): 227–238.

Salveson, D. 1994. *Wetlands: Mitigating and Regulating Development Impacts*, 2nd ed. Washington, DC: Urban Land Institute.

Sayre, R., E. Roca, G. Sedaghatkish, B. Youg, S. Keel, R. Roca, and S. Sheppard. 2000. *Nature in Focus: Rapid Ecological Assessment*. The Nature Conservancy. Washington, DC: Island Press.

Schwab, J. C., ed. 2009. *Planning the Urban Forest: Ecology, Economy, and Community Development*. Planning Advisory Service Report 555. Chicago: American Planning Association.

Shandas, V., and M. Alberti. 2009. "Exploring the Role of Vegetation Fragmentation on Aquatic Conditions: Linking Upland with Riparian Areas in Puget Sound Lowland Streams." *Landscape and Urban Planning* 90:66–75.

Somers, A., K. Bridle, D. Herman, and A. B. Nelson. 2000. "The Restoration and Management of Small Wetlands of the Mountains and Piedmont in the Southeast: A Manual Emphasizing Endangered and Threatened Species Habitat with a Focus on Bog Turtles." Washington, DC: USDA. Retrieved June 28, 2003, from http://www.wcc.nrcs.usda.gov/watershed/piedmont/piedmont.html.

Strommen, B., K. Cappiella, D. Hirschman, and J. Tasillo. 2007. Article 4: "A Local Ordinance to Protect Wetland Functions." Center for Watershed Protection. Wetlands and Watersheds Articles Prepared for Office of Wetlands, Oceans and Watersheds. Washington, DC: U.S. Environmental Protection Agency.

U.S. Army Corps of Engineers. 1976. Water Resources Development Plan, Charles River Watershed, Massachusetts. Waltham, MA: U.S. Army Corps of Engineers, New England Division.

U.S. Department of Agriculture (USDA), Forest Service. 2003. Forest Health Protection website. Retrieved June 28, 2003, from http://www.fs.fed.us/foresthealth/.

USDA, Forest Service, Southern Region. 2001. *Urban Forestry: A Manual for the State Forestry Agencies in the Southern Region*. Retrieved June 27, 2003, from http://www.urbanforestrysouth.usda.gov.

USDA, NRCS. 1998. *Riparian Forest Buffer*. Conservation Practice Job Sheet 391. Reprinted in USDA, NRCS. 1999. CORE4 Conservation Practices Training Guide. Washington, DC: Author. Retrieved June 28, 2003, from http://www.ctic.purdue.edu/Core4/Core4TechnicalManual.pdf.

USDA, NRCS. 1999. *Conservation Corridor Planning at the Landscape Level*. C. Johnson, Principal Investigator. Washington, DC: Watershed Science Institute, Wildlife Habitat Management Institute. Retrieved June 27, 2003, from http://www.wcc.nrcs.usda.gov/watershed/wssi-products.html.

Washington State Department of Transportation. 2006. Springbrook Creek Wetland and Habitat Mitigation Bank Mitigation Bank Instrument. Olympia, WA: Author.

Wilson, E., ed. 1988. *Biodiversity*. Washington, DC: National Academies Press.

Wilson, E. 2002. *The Future of Life*. New York: Knopf.

Wright, T., J. Tomlinson, T. Schueler, K. Cappiella, A. Kitchell, and D. Hirschman. 2006. Article 1: "Direct and Indirect Impacts of Urbanization on Wetland Quality." Center for Watershed Protection. Wetlands and Watersheds Articles Prepared for Office of Wetlands, Oceans and Watersheds. Washington, DC: U.S. Environmental Protection Agency.

Zinn, J. 1997. *Wetlands Mitigation Banking: Status and Prospects*. Congressional Research Service. Library of Congress. Issue Brief for Congress. Order Code IB16991. Retrieved June 28, 2003, from http://www.ncseonline.org/NLE/CRS/abstract.cfm?NLEid=16298.

Zinn, J., and C. Copeland. 2003. *Wetland Issues*. Congressional Research Service. Library of Congress. Issue Brief for Congress. Order Code IB16991. Retrieved June 28, 2003, from http://www.ncseonline.org/NLE/CRS/abstract.cfm?NLEid=16991.

Chapter 11

Adams, L., and L. E. Dove. 1989. *Wildlife Reserves and Corridors in the Urban Environment: A Guide to Ecological Landscape Planning and Resource Conservation.* Columbia, MD: National Institute for Urban Wildlife.

Barnes, T. G. 1999. *A Guide to Urban Habitat Conservation Planning,* Pub. 74. Lexington: University of Kentucky Extension Service.

Beatley, T. 1994. *Habitat Conservation Planning: Endangered Species and Urban Growth.* Austin: University of Texas Press.

Bryant, M., B. Smith, J. Randolph, M. Jeong, and M. Lipscomb. 2003. "Urban Biodiversity in the Holmes Run/Cameron Run Watershed." Urban Biodiversity Information Node (UrBIN) Pilot. National Biological Information Infrastructure (NBII), U.S. Geological Survey.

Chicago Region Biodiversity Council. Undated. *Chicago Wilderness: An Atlas of Biodiversity.* Retrieved June 13, 2003, from http://www.epa.gov/glnpo/chiwild/. Chicago: Author.

Chicago Wilderness. 1999. *Biodiversity Recovery Plan.* Chicago: Chicago Wilderness.

Chicago Wilderness Consortium. 2006. *The State of Our Chicago Wilderness: A Report Card on the Ecological Health of the Region.* Chicago: Chicago Wilderness Consortium.

Diamond, J. 1975. "The Island Dilemma: Lessons of Modern Biogeographic Studies for the Design of Nature Preserves." *Biological Conservation* 7:129–146.

Federal Interagency Stream Restoration Working Group (FISRWG). 1998. *Stream Corridor Restoration: Principles, Processes, and Practices.* Washington, DC: Government Printing Office. Retrieved June 28, 2003, from http://www.usda.gov/stream_restoration/.

Fisher, E. 1996. "Habitat Conservation Planning under the Endangered Species Act: 'No Surprises' and the Quest for Certainty." *Colorado Law Review* 67:371.

Forman, R., and M. Godron. 1986. *Landscape Ecology.* New York: Wiley.

General Accounting Office (GAO). 1994. "Endangered Species Act: Information on Species Protection on Nonfederal Lands." GAO/RCED-95–16. Washington, DC: U.S. Government Printing Office.

Interagency Workgroup on Wetland Restoration (IWWR). 2002. *An Introduction to Wetland Restoration, Creation, and Enhancement.* Review draft.

International Association of Fish and Wildlife Agencies (IAFWA). 2001. *State Conservation Agreements: Creating Local and Regional Partnerships for Proactive Conservation.* Prepared by Mette Brogden. Washington, DC: IAFWA.

James, F. C. 1999. "Lessons Learned from a Study of Habitat Conservation Planning." *BioScience* 49(11):871–874.

Kareiva, P., S. Andelman, D. Doak, B. Elderd, M. Groom, J. Hoekstra, L. Hood, F. James, J. Lamoreux, G. LeBuhn, C. McCulloch, J. Regetz, L. Savage, M. Ruckelshaus, D. Skelly, H. Wilbur, and K. Zamudio. 1999. *Using Science in Habitat Conservation Plans.* Washington, DC: National Center for Ecological Analysis and Synthesis and American Institute for Biological Sciences.

Lambeck, R. 1997. Focal Species: A Multi-Species Umbrella for Nature Conservation. *Conservation Biology.* 11(4): 849-856.

Leedy, D., R. Maestro, and T. Franklin. 1978. *Planning for Wildlife in Cities and Suburbs.* Planning Advisory Service 331. Chicago: American Planning Association.

MacArthur, R. H., and E. O. Wilson. 1967. "The Theory of Island Biogeography." *Monographs in Population Biology* 1:1–203.

Meese, R. J., F. M. Shilling, and J. Quinn. 2009. *Wildlife Crossings Guidance Manual.* California Department of Transportation, Sacramento. http://www.dot.ca.gov/hq/env/bio/wildlife_crossings/.

Noss, R. F., and A. Y. Cooperrider. 1994. *Saving Nature's Legacy: Protecting and Restoring Biodiversity.* Washington, DC: Island Press.

Noss, R. F., and L. D. Harris. 1986. "Nodes, Networks, and MUMs: Preserving Diversity at All Scales." *Environmental Management* 10:299–309.

Noss, R. F., M. A. O'Connell, and D. D. Murphy. 1997. *The Science of Conservation Planning: Habitat Conservation under the Endangered Species Act.* Washington, DC: Island Press.

Pielou, E. C. 1975. *Ecological Diversity.* New York: Wiley.

Pollak, D. 2001a. *The Future of Habitat Conservation: The NCCP Experience in California.* Sacramento: California Research Bureau, California State Library.

Pollak, D. 2001b. *Natural Community Conservation Planning (NCCP): The Origins of an Ambitious Experiment to Protect Ecosystems.* Sacramento: California Research Bureau, California State Library.

Randolph, J., and M. Bryant. 2002. "Urban Biodiversity Enhancing Data and Decision Tools for Urban Ecological Conservation." Paper presented at annual conference of the Association of Collegiate Schools of Planning, Baltimore, Maryland.

San Diego, County of. 2010. NCCP MSCP Documents. http://www.sdcounty.ca.gov/dplu/mscp/index.html.

Scott, T. A., and M. Allen. Undated. "Functional Connectivity in Fragmented Landscapes." Working paper, Center for Conservation Biology, University of California, Riverside, California.

Scott, T. A., W. Wehtje, and M. Wehtje. 2001. "The Need for Strategic Planning in Passive Restoration of Wildlife Populations." *Restoration Ecology* 9(3):262–271.

Slingerland, G. 1999. *The Effect of the "No Surprises" Policy on Habitat Conservation Planning and the Endangered Species Act.* Master's thesis, Master of Urban and Regional Planning, Virginia Tech, Blacksburg, Virginia.

Smith, T. 1995. *Habitat Conservation Planning Under the Endangered Species Act: Is It Ecosystem Management?* Master's thesis, Urban and Regional Planning, Virginia Tech, Blacksburg, Virginia.

Spencer, W. D., P. Beier, K. Penrod, K. Winters, C. Paulman, H. Rustigian-Romsos, J. Strittholt, M. Parisi, and A. Pettler. 2010. California Essential Habitat Connectivity Project: A Strategy for Conserving a Connected California. Prepared for California Department of Transportation, California Department of Fish and Game, and Federal Highways Administration.

U.S. Department of Agriculture, NRCS. 1999. *Conservation Corridor Planning at the Landscape Level.* C. Johnson, Principal Investigator. Washington, DC: Watershed Science Institute, Wildlife Habitat Management Institute.

U.S. Department of the Interior, USFWS. 2011. Conservation Plans and Agreements Database. Retrieved July 2011, from https://ecos.fws.gov/conserv_plans/servlet/gov.doi.hcp.servlets.PlanReportSelect?region=9&type=HCP.

U.S. Fish and Wildlife Service, NMFS. 1996. *Habitat Conservation Planning Handbook.* Washington, DC: U.S. Department of the Interior.

Chapter 12

Adger, W. N. 2001. "Social Capital and Climate Change." Working Paper 8. Norwich, England: Tyndall Centre for Climate Change Research.

Adger, W. N., T. Hughes, C. Folke, S. Carpenter, and J. Rockstrom. 2005. "Social-Ecological Resilience to Coastal Disasters." *Science* 309:1036–1039.

Armel, K. C. 2009. "Behavior, Energy and Climate Change: A Solutions-Oriented Approach." http://www.stanford.edu/~kcarmel/carrie.html.

Austin, City of. 2008. Austin Climate Protection Plan and Action Items. Report to Austin City Council. http://www.coolaustin.org/acpp.htm.

Bailey, J. 2007. "Lessons from the Pioneers: Tackling Global Warming at the Local Level." Institute for Local Self-Reliance. http://www.newrules.org.

Berkeley, City of. 2009. Berkeley Climate Action Plan. http://www.berkeleyclimate action.org/.

Bestill, M., and H. Bulkeley. 2007. "Looking Back and Thinking Ahead: A Decade of Cities and Climate Change Research" *Local Environment* 12(5):447–456.

Binder, L. 2007. "Planning for Climate Change." Presentation to Washington City-County Management Association. Climate Impact Group, University of Washington, Seattle.

Boake, T. M. 2008. "The Leap to Zero Carbon and Zero Emissions: Understanding How to Go Beyond Existing Sustainable Design Protocols." *Journal of Green Building* 3:4.64–77.

Boswell, M., A. Greve, and T. Seale. 2010. "An Assessment of the Link Between Greenhouse Gas Emissions Inventories and Climate Action Plans." *Journal of the American Planning Association* 76(4):451–462.

Boswell, M., A. Greve, and T. Seale. 2011. *Local Climate Action Planning*. Washington, DC: Island Press.

Boulder, City of. 2009. "Climate Action Program Assessment." http://www.bouldercolorado.gov/index.php?option=com_content&task=view&id=1058&Itemid=396.

Brown, M., F. Southworth, and A. Sarzynski. 2008. "Shrinking the Carbon Footprint of Metropolitan America." Metropolitan Policy Program. Washington, DC: Brookings Institution.

California Air Resources Board. 2008. Climate Change Scoping Plan. Sacramento.

California Department of Transportation (CalTrans). 2002. "Statewide Transit-Oriented Development Study Technical Appendices."

California Natural Resources Agency. 2009. *2009 California Climate Adaptation Strategy. Report to the Governor in Response to Executive Order S-13-2008*. Retrieved from http://www.climatechange.ca.gov/adaptation/.

Calthorpe, P. 2011. *Urbanism in the Age of Climate Change*. Washington, DC: Island Press.

Center for Science in the Earth System (The Climate Impacts Group). 2007. *Preparing for Climate Change: A Guidebook for Local, Regional, and State Governments*. Joint Institute for the Study of the Atmosphere and Ocean, University of Washington; King County, Washington; ICLEI.

Cervero, R., and K. Kockelman. 1997. "Travel Demand and the 3Ds: Density, Diversity, and Design." *Transportation Research Part D* 2(3):199–219.

Chicago, City of. 2008a. "Chicago Climate Action Plan. Our City, Our Future." http://www.chicagoclimateaction.org/.

Chicago, City of. 2008b. *Chicago's Guide to Completing an Energy Efficiency & Conservation Strategy*. http://www.chicagoclimateaction.org/.

Clinton Climate Initiative. C40 Profile. Heidelberg, Climate Change. Heidelberg Climate Protection Campaign. http://www.heidelberg.de/servlet/PB/menu/1192649/index.html.

Cummings, J. 2008. *Pilot Evaluation of Energy Savings from Residential Energy Demand Feedback Devices*. FSEC-CR-1742-08. Florida Solar Energy Center.

Daniels, T. L. 2010. "Integrating Forest Carbon Sequestration into a Cap-and-Trade Program to Reduce Net CO_2 Emissions." *Journal of the American Planning Association* 76(4):463–475.

Deyle, R., K. Bailey, and A. Matheny. 2007. "Adaptive Response Planning to Sea Level Rise in Florida and Implications for Comprehensive and Public-Facilities Planning." 48th Annual Conference of the Association of Collegiate Schools of Planning, Milwaukee, Wisconsin.

Dodman, D. 2009. "Blaming Cities for Climate Change? An Analysis of Urban Greenhouse Gas Emissions Inventories." *Environment and Urbanization* 21(1):185.

Dodman, D., and D. Satterthwaite. 2009. "Climate Change: Are Cities Really to Blame?" *Urban World* 1(2):12–13.

Drummond, W. J. 2010. "Statehouse Versus Greenhouse. Have State-level Climate Action Planners and Policy Entrepreneurs Reduced Greenhouse Gas Emissions?" *Journal of the American Planning Association* 76(4):413–433.

Durham-Jones, E., and J. Williamson. 2008. *Retrofitting Suburbia: Urban Design Solutions for Redesigning Suburbs*. New York: Wiley.

Ewing, R., K. Bartholomew, S. Winkelman, J. Walters, and D. Chen. 2007. *Growing Cooler: The Evidence on Urban Development and Climate Change*. Washington, DC: Urban Land Institute.

Florida Climate and Energy Commission. 2007. Florida's Resilient Coasts: A State Policy Framework for Adaptation to Climate Change. Center for Urban and Environmental Solutions.

Hansen, J., M. Sato, P. Kharecha, D. Beerling, V. Masson-Delmotte, M. Pagani, M. Raymo, D. Royer, and J. Zachos. 2008. *Target Atmospheric CO_2: Where Should Humanity Aim?* http://arxiv.org/ftp/arxiv/papers/0804/0804.1126.pdf.

Heidelberg Climate Protection Progress Report. 2007. http://www.heidelberg.de/servlet/PB/menu/1126634_l2/index.html.

Hughes, K. 2009. "An Applied Local Sustainable Energy Model: The Case of Austin, Texas." *Bulletin of Science, Technology & Society* 29.2.108.

ICLEI—Local Governments for Sustainability, Climate Protection Communities. 2009. http://www.icleiusa.org/programs/climate/mitigation.

ICLEI—Local Governments for Sustainability, Climate Resilient Communities. 2010. http://www.icleiusa.org/programs/climate/Climate_Adaptation.

Intergovernmental Panel on Climate Change (IPCC). 2007a. 4th Assessment Report. Retrieved from http://www.ipcc.ch/.

Intergovernmental Panel on Climate Change (IPCC). 2007b. Climate Change 2007: Summary for Policy Makers. IPPC Fourth Assessment Report (AR4). Retrieved from http://www.ipcc.ch/.

International Energy Agency (IEA). 2009. *World Energy Outlook 2009*. http://www.iea.org/weo/.

Kenworthy, J. 2006. "The Eco-City: Ten Key Transport and Planning Dimensions for Sustainable City Development." *Environment and Urbanization* 18(1):67.

Kenworthy, J., and Laube, F. 2001. The Millennium Cities Database for Sustainable Transport, International Union of Public Transport (UITP), Brussels and Institute for Sustainability and Technology Policy (ISTP), Perth.

Kintner-Meyer, M., K. Schneider, and R. Pratt. 2008. "Impacts Assessment of Plug-In Hybrid Vehicles on Electric Utilities and Regional U.S. Power Grids, Part 1: Technical Analysis." Hanover, WA: Pacific Northwest National Laboratory.

London, Mayor of. 2009a. "London Low Carbon Zones." http://www.london.gov.uk /lowcarbonzones/.

London, Mayor of. 2009b. "Powering Ahead: Delivering Low Carbon Energy for London." http://www.london.gov.uk/mayor/publications/2009/10/powering-ahead.jsp.

Los Angeles, City of. 2008. "Climate LA: Municipal Program Implementing the GreenLA Climate Action Plan." http://www.environmentla.org/.

Matthews, H. D., and K. Caldeira. 2008. "Stabilizing Climate Requires Near-Zero Emissions." *Geophysics Research Letters* 35:1–5.

McCarthy, J. 2010. "Ozone Air Quality Standards: EPA's Proposed Janaury 2010 Revisions." Congressional Research Service. 7-5700. R41062. www.crs.gov.

Meinshausen, M., N. Meinshausen, W. Hare, S. C. B. Raper, K. Frieler, R. Knutti, D. J. Frame, and M. Allen. 2009. "Greenhouse Gas Emission Targets for Limiting Global Warming to 2°C." *Nature* 458:1158–1162.

Mitchell-Jackson, J. 2005. "The Behavioral Effects of Enhanced Energy Information: An Evaluation of the Statewide California Information Display Pilot." Proceedings of the 2005 International Energy Program Evaluation Conference, August 17–19, New York, New York.

Mountain, D., 2006. "The Impact of Real Time Energy Feedback on Residential Electricity Consumption: The Hydro One Pilot." Ontario, Canada: McMaster University.

National Research Council (NRC). 2009. *Driving and the Built Environment: The Effects of Compact Development on Motorized Travel, Energy Use, and CO₂ Emissions.* Committee for the Study on the Relationship Among Development Patterns, Vehicle Miles Traveled, and Energy Consumption. Washington, DC: Transportation Research Board.

National Research Council. 2010a. *America's Climate Choices: Adapting to the Impacts of Climate Change.* Washington, DC: National Academies Press.

National Research Council. 2010b. *America's Climate Choices: Informing Effective Decisions and Actions Related to Climate Change.* Washington, DC: National Academies Press.

National Research Council. 2010c. *America's Climate Choices: Limiting the Magnitude of Future Climate Change.* Washington, DC: National Academies Press.

National Research Council. 2010d. *America's Climate Choices: Panel on Advancing the Science of Climate Change.* Washington, DC: National Academies Press.

Newman, P. 2006. "The Environmental Impact of Cities." *Environment and Urbanization* 18(2):275.

New York City. 2007a. "Inventory of New York City Greenhouse Gas Emissions. PlaNYC." http://www.nyc.gov/html/planyc2030/html/plan/plan.shtml.

New York City. 2007b. "PlaNYC: Climate Change." http://www.nyc.gov/html/planyc 2030/html/plan/plan.shtml.

Paris, City of. 2007. "Paris Climate Protection Plan. Plan to Combat Global Warming." http://www.paris.fr/portail/Environnement/Portal.lut?page_id=8412.

Parker, D., and D. Hoak. Pew Center on Global Climate Change. 2009. "Climate Change 101: Local Action." www.pewclimate.org.

Parker, D., D. Hoak, A. Meier, and R. Brown. 2006. "How Much Energy Are We Using: The Potential for Energy Demand Feedback Devices." Proceedings of the American Council for an Energy-Efficient Economy 2006 Summer Study. Washington, DC: American Council for an Energy Efficient Economy.

Pew Center on Global Climate Change. 2010. "Adaptation Planning—What U.S. States and Localities are Doing." Retrieved from http://www.pewclimate.org.

Philadelphia, City of. "Greenworks Philadelphia." http://www.phila.gov/green/green works/.

Pitt, D., and J. Randolph. 2009. "Identifying Obstacles to Community Climate Protection Planning." *Environment and Planning B. Government and Policy* 27(5): 841–857.

Pitt, D., et al. 2011. Blacksburg Climate Action Plan. Town of Blacksburg, Virginia.

Portland, City of, Multnomah County. 2005. "Progress Report on Local Action Plan on Global Warming." http://www.portlandonline.com/bps/index.cfm?c=41896.

Portland, City of, Multnomah County. 2009. "Climate Action Plan 2009." http://www.portlandonline.com/bps/index.cfm?c=41896.

Randolph, J. 2008. "Comment on Ewing and Rong's 'The Impact of Urban Form on U.S. Residential Energy Use.'" *Housing Policy Debate* 19(1):45–52.

Randolph, J. 2011. "Creating the Climate Change Resilient Community." In B. Goldstein, *Collaborative Resilience: Moving from Crisis to Opportunity*. Cambridge, MA: MIT Press.

Randolph, J., and G. M. Masters. 2008. *Energy for Sustainability: Technologies, Planning, Policy*. Washington, DC: Island Press.

Regional Greenhouse Gas Initiative (RGGI). 2010. "Ten States Mark Second Anniversary of Regional Program to Reduce Greenhouse Gas Emissions." Press Release. New York, New York.

San Francisco, City of. 2008. SForward: Building a Bright Future. San Francisco's Environmental Plan 2008.

San Francisco Bay Conservation and Development Commission (BCDC). 2008. *Background Report on a San Francisco Bay Sea Level Rise Strategy*. Memo, Will Travis, Executive Director. San Francisco: Author. http://www.bcdc.ca.gov.

San Francisco Bay Conservation and Development Commission (BCDC). 2009. *Living with a Rising Bay: Vulnerability and Adaptation in San Francisco Bay and on Its Shoreline*. San Francisco: Author. http://www.bcdc.ca.gov.

San Francisco Department of Environment, Department of Public Utilities. 2004. "Climate Action Plan for San Francisco: Local Actions to Reduce Greenhouse Gas Emissions." www.sfgov.org/site/uploadedfiles/mayor/SForwardFinal.pdf.

Satterthwaite, D. 2008. "Cities' Contribution to Global Warming: Notes on the Allocation of Greenhouse Gas Emissions." *Environment and Urbanization* 20(2):539.

Schroepfer, T., and L. Hee. 2008. "Emerging Forms of Sustainable Urban Case Studies of Vauban Freiburg and Solarcity Linz." *Journal of Green Building* 3(2): 67–76.

Sentman, S. D., S. T. Del Percio, and P. Koerner. 2008? "A Climate for Change: Green Building Policies, Programs, and Incentives." *Journal of Green Building* 3(2): 46–63.

Shindell, D., G. Faluvegi, D. Koch, G. Schmidt, N. Unger, and S. Bauer. 2009. "Improved Attribution of Climate Forcing to Emissions." *Science* 326(5953):716–718.

Smit, B., and J. Wandel. 2006. "Adaptation, Adaptive Capacity and Vulnerability." *Global Environmental Change* 16:282–292.

Stockholm, City of. 2004. "Stockholm's Action Programme Against Greenhouse Gases." http://www.stockholm.se/KlimatMiljo/Klimat/Stockholms-Action-Programme-on-Climate-Change/.

Sydney, City of. "Sustainable Sydney 2030. Climate Change." http://www.cityofsydney.nsw.gov.au/2030/.

Tompkins, E., and W. Adger. 2004. "Does Adaptive Management of Natural Resources Enhance Resilience to Climate Change?" *Ecology and Society* 9(2).

Toronto, City of. 2007. "Change Is in the Air. Climate Change, Clean Air and Sustainable Energy Action Plan: Moving from Framework to Action." http://www.toronto.ca/changeisintheair/.

U.S. Energy Information Administration (EIA). 2010a. *Annual Energy Review.* http://www.eia.gov/aer/.

U.S. Energy Information Administration (EIA). 2010b. *International Energy Annual.* http://www.eia.gov/iea/.

U.S. Energy Information Administration (EIA). 2010c. *International Energy Outlook 2010.* http://www.eia.gov/oiaf/ieo/.

U.S. Environmental Protection Agency (EPA). 2010d. *Our Nation's Air. Status and Trends Through 2008.* http://www.epa.gov/airtrends/2010/index.html.

Western Climate Initiative (WCI). 2010. Draft Offset Protocol. http://www.westernclimateinitiative.org/.

Wheeler, S. 2008. "State and Municipal Climate Change Plans: The First Generation." *Journal of the American Planning Association* 74(4):481–496.

Wheeler, S., J. Randolph, and J. London. 2009. "Planning for Climate Change: An Emerging Research Agenda. Progress in Planning." Chapter 4 in H. Blanco et al. "Shaken, Shrinking, Hot, Impoverished and Informal: Emerging Research Agendas in Planning." Special issue of *Progress In Planning* 72(1):210–222.

Willson, R., and K. D. Brown. 2008. "Carbon Neutrality at the Local Level: Achievable Goal or Fantasy?" *Journal of the American Planning Association* 74(4):497–504.

Chapter 13

Association of Bay Area Governments (ABAG). 2011. Earthquake and Hazards Program. Retrieved from http://quake.abag.ca.gov/.

Association of State Floodplain Managers (ASFPM). 2003. *No Adverse Impact: A Toolkit for Common Sense Floodplain Management.* Madison: WI: Author.

Boswell, M., W. Siembieda, and K. Topping. 2008. *Local Hazard Mitigation Planning in California.* Report prepared for State of California Governor's Office of Emergency Services.

California Department of Conservation. 2011. "Seismic Hazard Mapping Program." Retrieved from http://www.conservation.ca.gov/cgs/shzp/Pages/Index.aspx.

California Department of Forest Management and Fire Protection (CalFire). 2007. "Why 100 Feet? . . . Because Defensible Space Is YOUR Responsibility." http://www.fire.ca.gov.

California Department of Forest Management and Fire Protection (CalFire). 2009. San Diego County. Fire Hazard Severity Zones, Local Responsibility Areas.

California Department of Forest Management and Fire Protection (CalFire). 2010. "Wildfire Threat to Ecosystem Health and Community Safety." Chapter 2.1 in *2010 Forest Assessment.* Retrieved from http://frap.fire.ca.gov/assessment2010.html.

Clark, J., J. Banta, and J. Zinn. 1980. *Coastal Environmental Management: Guidelines for Conservation of Resources and Protection against Storm Hazards.* The Conservation Foundation. Prepared for six federal agencies. Washington, DC: U.S. Government Printing Office.

Communities Committee, National Association of Counties, National Association of State Foresters Society of American Foresters, Western Governors' Association. 2004. *Preparing a Community Wildfire Protection Plan: A Handbook for Wildland-Urban Interface Communities.* Retrieved from http://www.communitiescommittee.org/pdfs/cwpphandbook.pdf.

Douglas, B., M. Crowell, and S. Leatherman. 1998. "Considerations for Shoreline Position Prediction." *Journal of Coastal Research* 14(3):1025–1033.

Federal Emergency Management Agency (FEMA). 2000a. *Coastal Construction Manual,* 3rd ed. Washington, DC: Mitigation Directorate, Project Impact.

Federal Emergency Management Agency (FEMA). 2000b. Hazards website for fact sheets and other information on natural hazards, http://www.fema.gov/hazards/.

Federal Emergency Management Agency (FEMA). 2000c. "Project Impact: Building Disaster Resistant Communities." Retrieved June 27, 2003, from http://www.fema.gov/impact/impact00.htm.

Federal Emergency Management Agency (FEMA). 2002. "Hazard Mitigation Planning and Hazard Mitigation Grant Program." *Federal Register* 67(190).

Federal Emergency Management Agency (FEMA). 2009. "HAZUS-MH. What Could Happen?" Retrieved from http://www.fema.gov/plan/prevent/hazus/hz_overview.shtm.

FireWise Communities. 2001. *FireWise Communities.* Quincy, MA: National Wildland/Urban Interface Fir Program. Retrieved June 29, 2002, from http://www.firewise.org/communities.

Godschalk, D. 2009. "Safe Growth Audits." *Zoning Practice.* American Planning Association, Issue 10.

Godschalk, D. 2010. "Integrating Hazards into the Implementation Tools of Planning." In *Hazard Mitigation: Integrating Best Practices into Planning,* edited by J. Schwab. Planning Advisory Service Report 560. Chicago: American Planning Association.

Godschalk, D., T. Beatley, P. Berke, D. Brower, and E. Kaiser. 1999. *Natural Hazard Mitigation: Recasting Disaster Policy and Planning.* Washington, DC: Island Press.

Goldstein, B., and W. Butler. 2009. "The Network Imaginary: Coherence and Creativity Within a Multiscalar Collaborative Effort to Reform US Fire Management." *Journal of Environmental Planning and Management* 52(8):1013–1033.

Griggs, G., and J. Gilchrist. 1983. *Geologic Hazards, Resources, and Environmental Planning.* Belmont, CA: Wadsworth.

Highland, L. M., and P. Bobrowsky. 2008. *The Landslide Handbook: A Guide to Understanding Landslides.* Reston, VA: U.S. Geological Survey, Circular 1325.

Institute for Business and Home Safety (IBHS). 2001. *Community Land Use Evaluation for Natural Hazards.* Tampa, FL: Author. Retrieved from http://www.ibhs.org/research_library/downloads/95.pdf.

Jaffe, M., J. Butler, and C. Thurow. 1981. *Reducing Earthquake Risks: A Planners Guide.* PAS Report 364. Chicago: American Planning Association.

Kemmerly, P. 1993. "Sinkhole Hazards and Risk Assessment in a Planning Context." *Journal of the American Planning Association* 58(2):222–233.

Larson, L., M. Klitzke, and D. Brown. 2003. "No Adverse Impact: A Toolkit for No-Nonsense Floodplain Management." Madison, WI: Association of State Floodplain Managers.

Massachusetts Office of Coastal Zone Management (OCZM). 2008. "Introduction to No Adverse Impact (NAI) Land Management in the Coastal Zone." Stormsmart Coasts Fact Sheet 1.

Morris, M. 1997. *Subdivision Design in Flood Hazard Areas*. FEMA and American Planning Association, Planning Advisory Service Report 473.

National Weather Service. 2011. Hydrologic Information Center, Flood Loss Data. Retrieved from http://www.weather.gov/hic/flood_stats/Flood_loss_time_series.shtml.

Nelson, A. C., and S. French. 2002. "Plan Quality and Mitigating Damage from Natural Disasters." *Journal of the American Planning Association* 8(2):194–207.

Nilsen, T., R. Wright, T. Vlasic, and W. Spangle. 1976. "Relative Slope Stability and Land-Use Planning in the San Francisco Bay Region, California." USGS Professional Paper 944. Menlo Park, CA: U.S. Geological Survey.

Oregon Department of Land Conservation and Development. 2000. *Planning for Natural Hazards*. Salem, OR: Author.

Schwab, J. 2009. "Making Hazards a Planning Priority." PAS Memo. Chicago: American Planning Association.

Schwab, J., ed. 2010. *Hazard Mitigation: Integrating Best Practices into Planning*. Planning Advisory Service Report 560. Chicago: American Planning Association.

U.S. Army Corps of Engineers. 1984. *Roanoke River Upper Basin*. Final Interim Feasibility Report and Environmental Impact Statement for Flood Damage Reduction. Wilmington, NC: Wilmington District.

U.S. Geological Survey (USGS). 1982. *Goals and Tasks of the Landslide Part of a Ground-Failure Hazards Reduction Program*. USGS Circular 880. Reston, VA: Author.

U.S. Geological Survey (USGS). 2001. Earthquake Shaking: Finding the Hotspots. Fact Sheet 001–01. Washington, DC: Author.

U.S. Geological Survey (USGS). 2008. National Seismic Hazard Maps. http://earthquake.usgs.gov/hazards/products/graphic2pct50.pdf.

U.S. Government Accountability Office (GAO). 2002. *Proposed Changes to FEMA's Multi-hazard Mitigation Program Presents Problems*. RPT Number GAO-02-1035. Washington, DC: Author.

U.S. Government Accoutability Office (GAO). 2007. *Natural Hazard Mitigation: Various Mitigation Efforts Exist, But Federal Efforts Do Not Provide a Comprehensive Strategic Framework*. GAO-07-403. Washington, DC: Author.

Chapter 14

Anderson, L., W. D. Conn, C. D. Loeks, and J. Randolph. 1981. *Growth Management for Blacksburg's Environmentally Critical Areas*. Blacksburg: Virginia Tech.

Benedict, M., and E. McMahon. 2002. *Green Infrasructure: Smart Conservation for the 21st Century*. The Conservation Fund. Washington, DC: Sprawl Watch Clearinghouse. Retrieved June 13, 2003, from http://www.sprawlwatch.org/greeninfrastructure.pdf.

Benedict, M. A., and E. T. McMahon. 2006. *Green Infrastructure: Linking Landscapes and Communities*. Washington, DC: Island Press.

Blacksburg, Town of. 2006. Comprehensive Plan. Retreived from http://www .blacksburg.gov/comp_plan/.

California Department of Housing and Community Development (CDHCD). 2000. *Raising the Roof: California Housing Development Projections and Constraints, 1997–2020*. Sacramento: Author. Retrieved June 28, 2003, from http://www.hcd .ca.gov/hpd/hrc/rtr/.

Commonwealth of Massachusetts. 2002. *Buildout Book. Where Do You Want to Be at Buildout?* Boston: Department of Environmental Affairs. Retrieved from http:// commpres.env.state.ma.us/content/publications.asp#.

Commonwealth of Massachusetts. 2003. *Buildout Analyses and Maps*. Executive Office of Environmental Affairs. Retrieved from http://commpres.env.state.ma.us /content/buildout.asp.

Conservation Fund, The. 2011. "What Is Green Infrastructure?" Retrieved from: http://www.greeninfrastructure.net/content/definition-green-infrastructure.

Dasmann, R. 1964. *Wildlife Biology*. New York: Wiley.

Firehock, K., S. Stewart, and M. Maupin. 2010. "Connecting Communities with Green infrastructure Planning." New Partners for Smart Growth Conference, Seattle, WA.

Green Infrastructure Center (GIC). 2009. *The Richmond Region Green Infrastructure Project*. Charlottesville, VA: Author.

Hart, M. 1999. *Guide to Sustainable Community Indicators*. Montreal: Quebec-Labrador Foundation, Atlantic Center for the Environment.

Hopkins, L. 1977. "Methods of Combination in Land Suitability." *Journal of the American Institute of Planners* 43(4):386–400.

ICLEI—Local Governments for Sustainability. 2010. STAR Sustainability Goals and Guiding Principles. Retrieved from http://www.icleiusa.org/programs/sustainability /star-community-index/star-goals-and-guiding-principles.

Lacy, J. 1990. *Manual of Build-Out Analysis*. Amherst, MA: Center for Rural Massachusetts.

McHarg, I. 1969. *Design with Nature*. Garden City, NY: American Museum of Natural History.

National Park Service. 1997. *VERP: A Summary of the Visitor Experience and Resource Protection (VERP) Framework*. Denver, CO: U.S. Department of the Interior, National Park Service.

National Park Service. 2001. National Park Service Management Policies. Washington, D.C.: U.S. Department of the Interior, National Park Service.

Ortolano, L., and A. Shepherd. 1995. "Environmental Impact Assessment: Challenges and Opportunities." *Impact Assessment* 3(1):3–30.

Phillips, C., and J. Randolph. 2000. "The Relationship of Ecosystem Management to NEPA and Its Goals." *Environmental Management* 26(1):1–12.

Portland, City of, Bureau of Planning and Sustainability (BPS). 2009a. Natural Resource Inventory Update: Natural Resource Inventory GIS Model. Portland: Author.

Portland, City of, Bureau of Planning and Sustainability (BPS). 2009b. Natural Resource Inventory Update: Stream and Drainageway Mapping Project. Portland: Author.

Portland, City of, Bureau of Planning and Sustainability (BPS). 2009c. Natural Resource Inventory Update: Vegetation Mapping Project. Portland: Author.

Portland, City of, Bureau of Planning and Sustainability (BPS). 2009d. Natural Resource Inventory Update: Portland Plan Background Report. Portland: Author.

Randolph, J., and L. Ortolano. 1976. "Effect of NEPA on Corps of Engineers Planning for the Carmel River." *Environmental Affairs* 5(2):213–253.

Rees, W. 1996. "Revisiting Carrying Capacity: Area-Based Indicators of Sustainability." *Population and Environment* 17(2):195–215.

Siemens A. G. 2009. European Green City Index. *Assessing the Environmental Impact of Europe's Major Cities, Conducted by the Economist Intelligence Unit.* Munich, Germany: Author.

Stankey, G., D. Cole, R. Luca, M. Peterson, S. Frissell, and R. Washburn. 1985. *Limits of Acceptable Change (LAC) for Wilderness Planning.* General Technical Report INT-176. Washington, DC: U.S.Department of Agriculture, Forest Service.

State of Washington. 1998. *SEPA Handbook.* Olympia: Department of Ecology.

Tahoe Regional Planning Agency (TRPA). 1982. *Environmental Threshold Study.* South Lake Tahoe, CA: Author.

Tahoe Regional Planning Agency (TRPA). 1986. *Regional Plan for the Lake Tahoe Basin.* Stateline, NV: Author. Retrieved June 2003 from http://www.trpa.org/Goals /preface.html.

Tahoe Regional Planning Agency (TRPA). 2007a. *Environmental Assessment for Threshold Updates for Regional Plan Update for the Lake Tahoe Region.* South Lake Tahoe, CA: Author.

Tahoe Regional Planning Agency (TRPA). 2007b. *2006 Threshold Evaluation Executive Summary.* South Lake Tahoe, CA: Author.

Tahoe Regional Planning Agency (TRPA). 2009. *Environmental Threshold Carrying Capacities (Thresholds) and Pathway Vision Statements.* South Lake Tahoe, CA: Author.

Tahoe Regional Planning Agency (TRPA). 2011. Regional Plan Update Re-Scope. Attachment D: Proposed Threshold Amendments. South Lake Tahoe, CA: Author.

The Nature Conservancy. 1999. *Pathways: Building a Local Initiative for Compatible Economic Development.* Arlington, VA: Author.

U.S. Green Building Council (USGBC). 2010a. "Checklist of LEED-NC. Checklist for LEED-ND." Washington, DC. Retrieved from http://www.usgbc.org/.

U.S. Green Building Council (USGBC). 2010b. "The LEED Green Building Program at a Glance." Washington, DC. Retrieved from http://www.usgbc.org/.

Virginia Department of Conservation and Recreation. 2000. *Virginia Natural Landscape Assessment.* Richmond, Virginia.

Wackernagel, M., and W. Rees. 1995. *Our Ecological Footprint: Reducing Human Impact on the Earth.* Philadelphia: New Society Publishers.

Way, D. 1978. *Terrain Analysis,* 2nd ed. New York: McGraw-Hill.

Chapter 15

Aldrich, R., and J. Wyerman. 2005. *The 2005 National Land Trust Census Report.* Washington, DC: Land Trust Alliance.

American Farmland Trust. 2002. "Fact Sheet: Farmland Protection Toolbox." Farmland Information Center. Retrieved from http://www.farmlandinfo.org/fic/tas/index .htm#fs.

American Farmland Trust. 2010. "Annual State-Level PACE Statistics." Farmland Information Center. Retrieved from http://www.farmlandinfo.org/.

Arendt, R. 1999. *Growing Greener, Pitting Conservation into Local Plans and Ordinances.* Washington, DC: Island Press.

Benedict, M., and E. McMahon. 2002. *Green Infrasructure: Smart Conservation for the 21st Century*. The Conservation Fund. Washington, DC: Sprawl Watch Clearinghouse. Retrieved June 13, 2003, from http://www.sprawlwatch.org/green infrastructure.pdf.

Boulder, City of. 2001. Greenways Master Plan. Boulder, CO: Author. Retrieved June 13, 2003, from http://www.ci.boulder.co.us/publicworks/depts/utilities /projects/greenways/index.htm.

Boulder, City of. 2010. Greenway and Open Space and Mountain Parks Map. http:// www.bouldercolorado.gov/files/Utilities/Greenways/greenways_map_2007.pdf.

California Department of Forestry and Fire Protection (CalFire). 2010. "California's Forests and Rangelands: The 2010 Assessment: Priority Landscape: Conserving Green Infrastructure." Sacramento: Author.

Chicago Region Biodiversity Council. Undated. *Chicago Wilderness: An Atlas of Biodiversity*. Retrieved June 13, 2003, from http://www.epa.gov/glnpo/chiwild/.

Farmland Information Center (FIC). "2007 NRI: Changes In Land Cover/Use—Agricultural Land." www.farmlandinfo.org.

Farmland Information Center (FIC). 2010. "Status of Local PACE Programs Farm and Ranch Lands Protection Program Fact Sheet 2010." www.farmlandinfo.org.

Gorte, R., C. Vincent, K. Alexander, and M. Humpries. 2009. Federal Lands Managed by the Bureau of Land Management and the Forest Service: Issues for the 111th Congress CRS 7-5700. www.crs.gov.

Greene, D., and T. Richmond. 2009. *Conservation Tools: An Evaluation and Comparison of the Use of Certain Land Preservation Mechanisms*. Final Report Prepared for Washington State Recreation and Conservation Office. Retrieved from http:// conservationtools.org/.

Hollis, L., and W. Fulton. 2002. "Open Space Protection: Conservation Meets Growth Management." Washington, DC: Brookings Institution Center on Urban and Metropolitan Policy.

Land Trust Alliance (LTA). 2003. "About LTA; Local Land Trust Success Stories." Retrieved June 30, 2003, from http://www.lta.org/.

Land Trust Alliance (LTA). 2006. *2005 National Land Trust Census*. Retrieved from http://www.landtrustalliance.org/land-trusts/land-trust-census/census.

Maryland, State of. 2001. "GreenPrint Project Assessment: Factors Considered to Establish Ecological Value." Retrieved from http://www.dnr.state.md.us/greenways /greenprint/.

Metzger, P. 1983. "Mill Hollow: One Land Trust Transaction by the National Lands Trust." *Letter. A Monthly Report on Environmental Issues*. Washington, DC: The Conservation Foundation.

Pentz, D., R. Ginsburg, and R. McMillen. 2007. "State Conservation Tax Credits Impact and Analysis." Conservation Resource Center. Retrieved from http://www.tax creditexchange.com/documents/StateConservationTaxCreditsImpactandAnalysis. pdf.

Piedmont Environmental Council. 2010. Annual Report. Warrenton, VA: Author.

Smith, D., and P. Hellmund, eds. 1993. *Ecology of Greenways: Design and Function of Linear Conservation Areas*. Minneapolis: University of Minnesota Press.

Stokes, S., A. E. Watson, and S. Mastran. 1997. *Saving America's Countryside: A Guide to Rural Conservation*. 2nd ed. Baltimore, MD: Johns Hopkins University Press.

Stubbs, M. 2009. Agricultural Conservation Issues in the 111th Congress. Congressional Research Service 7-5700. www.crs.gov.

Trust for Public Land (TPL). 2002. *Local Greenprinting for Growth, Volume I*. Retrieved from http://www.tpl.org/tier3_cd.cfm?content_item_id=10648&folder_id=175.

Trust for Public Land, Center for City Park Excellence. 2009. "2009 City Park Facts." Retrieved from http://www.tpl.org.

Trust for Public Land (TPL), Land Trust Alliance. 2009. "Americans Invest in Parks and Conservation." LandVote® 2009. http://www.landvote.org.

U.S. Department of Agriculture (USDA), NRCS. 2009. "National Resources Inventory." Washington, DC: U.S. Government Printing Office. Retrieved from www.nrcs.usda.gov/technical/NRI.

U.S. National Park Service (NPS). Land and Water Conservation Fund (LWCF). 2010. *LWCF Annual Report*. Retrieved from http://www.nps.gov/lwcf/.

Wright, J. 1993. "Conservation Easements: An Analysis of Donated Development Rights." *Journal of the American Planning Association* 59(4):487–93.

Chapter 16

Ahwahnee Principles. 1991. Retrieved from http://www.lgc.org/ahwahnee/principles.html.

American Institute of Architects (AIA). 2010. "Ten Principles for Livable Communities." Retrieved from http://www.aia.org/about/initiatives/AIAS075369.

Arendt, R. 1994. *Rural by Design*. Chicago: American Planning Association Press.

Arendt, R. 1996. *Conservation Design for Subdivisions*. Washington, DC: Island Press.

Arendt, R. 1999. *Growing Greener, Pitting Conservation into Local Plans and Ordinances*. Washington, DC: Island Press.

Arlington County. 2009. "The Arlington Experience: Congestion to Mobility—TOD and Community Sustainability." Joint Subcommittee to Study the Feasibility of Creating a Regional Rapid Transportation Network. Arlington County, VA: Author

Audirac I. 1999. "Stated Preference for Pedestrian Proximity to Community Facilities: An Assessment of New Urbanism 'Sense of Community.'" *Journal of Planning Education and Research* 19(1):53–66 and *JPER* Errata, 19(2):164.

Beamguard, J. 1999. "Packing Pavement." *Tampa Tribune* (July 18). Retrieved June 28, 2003, from http://www.silcom.com/~rdb/share/bguard.html.

Beatley, T. 2000. *Green Urbanism*. Washington, DC: Island Press.

Benfield, F. K., M. D. Raimi, and D. Chen. 1999. *Once There Were Greenfields*. Washington, DC: Natural Resources Defense Council.

Bennett, R. 2010. "Portland EcoDistricts Initiative." New Partners for Smart Growth Conference, Seattle, WA.

Birch, E. 2002. "Having a Longer View on Downtown Living." *Journal of the American Planning Association* 68(1):5–21.

Brosnan, R. 2010. "Arlington County. 40 Years of Transit-Oriented Development." Retrieved from http://www.fairfaxcounty.gov/dpz/projects/reston/presentations/40_years_of_transit_oriented_development.pdf.

Calthorpe, P. 1993. *The Next Metropolis: Ecology and the American Dream*. Princeton, NJ: Princeton Architectural Press.

Calthorpe, P. 2011. *Urbanism and Climate Change*. Washington, DC: Island Press.

Calthorpe, P., and W. Fulton. 2001. *The Regional City*. Washington, DC: Island Press.

Calthorpe Associates. 2010. Projects: Highland Garden Village. Retrieved from http://www.calthorpe.com/highlands-garden-village.

Cervero, R., and K. Kockelman. 1997. "Travel Demand and the 3Ds: Density, Diversity, and Design." *Transportation Research Part D* 2(3):199–219.

City of Austin. 2001. *Green by Design: 7 Steps to Green Building.* Retrieved from http://www.ci.austin.tx.us/greenbuilder/.

Congress for New Urbanism (CNU). 1993. Charter. Retrieved from http://www.cnu.org/charter.

Corbett, J., and M. Corbett. 2000. *Designing Sustainable Communities: Learning from Village Homes.* Washington, DC: Island Press.

Corbett, M. 1981. *A Better Place to Live.* Emmaus, PA: Rodale.

Duany, A., E. Plater-Zyberk, and J. Speck. 2000. *Suburban Nation: The Rise of Sprawl and the Decline of the American Dream.* New York: North Point Press.

Duany, A., and J. Speck, with M. Lyon. 2010. *The Smart Growth Manual.* New York: McGraw-Hill.

Duany, A., and E. Talen. 2002. "Transect Planning." *Journal of the American Planning Association* 68(3):245–266.

Duany Plater-Zyberk and Company. 2011. Center for Applied Transect Studies. Retrieved from http://transect.org/rural_img.html.

Ewing, R., and R. Cervero. 2010. "Travel and the Built Environment." *Journal of the American Planning Association* 76(3):265–294.

Ewing, R., R. Pendall, and D. Chen. "Measuring Sprawl and Its Impact." Smart Growth America 2002. Retrieved from http://www.smartgrowthamerica.org/.

Farr, D. 2008. *Sustainable Urbanism: Urban Design with Nature.* Hoboken, NJ: Wiley.

Forester, J. 1989. *Planning in the Face of Power.* Berkeley: University of California Press.

Hall, L. 2010. "SmartCode." New Partners for Smart Growth Conference, Seattle, WA.

Handy, S., J. F. Sallis, D. Weber, E. Maibach, and M. Hollander. 2008. "Is Support for Traditionally Designed Communities Growing? Evidence from Two National Surveys." *Journal of the American Planning Association* 74(2):209–221.

Jonathan Rose Companies. 2010. Projects: Highlands Garden Village. Retrieved from http://www.rose-network.com/all-projects/highlands-garden-village-mixed-use-and-mixed-income-community.

Knapp, G., Y. Song, R. Ewing, and K. Clifton. "Seeing the Elephant: Multidisciplinary Measures of Urban Sprawl." National Center for Smart Growth. Retrieved from http://www.smartgrowth.umd.edu/.

Leinberger, C. B. 2007. *The Option of Urbanism: Investing in a New American Dream.* Washington, DC: Island Press.

Leopold, A. 1949. *The Sand County Almanac.* New York: Oxford University Press.

Lewis, P., and M. Baldassare. 2010. "The Complexity of Public Attitudes Toward Compact Development." *Journal of the American Planning Association* 76(2):219–237.

Lund, H. 2006. "Reasons for Living in a Transit-Oriented Development, and Associated Transit Use." *Journal of the American Planning Association* 72(3):357–366.

McCullough, K. K. 2008. "Sustainable Residential Development: Planning and Design for Green Neighborhoods." *Journal of the American Planning Association* 74(4):526–527.

McHarg, I. 1969. *Design with Nature.* Garden City, NY: American Museum of Natural History.

Mohamed, R. 2006. "The Economics of Conservation Subdivisions Price Premiums, Improvement Costs, and Absorption Rates." *Urban Affairs Review* 41(3):376–390.

Mohamed, R. 2009. "Why Do Residential Developers Prefer Large Exurban Lots? Infrastructure Costs and Exurban Development." *Environment and Planning B: Planning and Design* 36:12–29.

Myers, D., and E. Gearin. 2001. "Current Preferences and Future Demand for Denser Residential Environments." *Housing Policy Debate* 12(4):633–659.

National Research Council (NRC). 2009. *Driving and the Built Environment: The Effects of Compact Development on Motorized Travel, Energy Use, and CO$_2$ Emissions*. Committee for the Study on the Relationship Among Development Patterns, Vehicle Miles Traveled, and Energy Consumption. Washington, DC: Transportation Research Board.

Nelson, A., J. Randolph, J. Schilling, J. McElfish, and J. Logan. 2009. *Environmental Regulation and Housing Cost*. Washington, DC: Island Press.

Parolek, D., C. Leinberger, and L. Pruitt. 2010. "Getting to Small Footprint Density, Responding to the Market Demand for Walkable Urban Living." New Partners for Smart Growth Conference, Seattle, WA.

Phillips, T., and P. Staeheli. 2010. "Evidence from Leading Green Affordable Communities: High Point Redevelopment." New Partners for Smart Growth Conference, Seattle, WA.

Portland Sustainability Institute (PSI). 2010. Portland EcoDistricts. www.pdxinstitute.org/index.php/ecodistricts.

Randolph, J., and G. M. Masters. 2008. *Energy for Sustainability: Technologies, Planning, Policy*. Washington, DC: Island Press.

Ranney, V., K. Kirley, and M. Sands. 2010. *Building Communities with Farms: Insights from Developers, Architects and Farmers on Integrating Agriculture and Community*. Prairie Crossing, Grayslake, IL: Liberty Prairie Foundation.

Retzlaff, R. 2008. "Green Building Assessment Systems: A Framework and Comparison for Planners." *Journal of the American Planning Association* 74(4):505–519.

Ritchie, A. 2009. "Sustainable Urbanism: Urban Design with Nature." *Journal of the American Planning Association*. 75(1):97–98.

Ritchie, A., and R. Thomas, eds. 2009. *Sustainable Urban Design*, 2nd ed. New York: Taylor & Francis.

Rocky Mountain Institute. 1998. *Green Development*. New York: Wiley.

Schilling, J. 2010. "Regeneration Planning and Policy for Shrinking Cities." New Partners for Smart Growth Conference, Seattle, WA.

Schilling, J., and J. Logan. 2008. "Greening the Rust Belt: A Green Infrastructure Model for Right Sizing America's Shrinking Cities." *Journal of the American Planning Association* 74(4):451–466.

Sentman, S. D., S. T. Del Percio, and P. Koerner. 2008. "A Climate for Change: Green Building Policies, Programs, and Incentives." *Journal of Green Building* 3(2):46–63.

Seskin, S. 2010. "Complete Streets 2010." New Partners for Smart Growth Conference, Seattle, WA.

Simmons, P., and R. Lang, 2001. *The Urban Turnaround: A Decade-by-Decade Report Card on Postwar Population Change in Older Industrial Cities*. Fannie Mae Foundation (FMF) Census Note 01. Washington, DC: FMF.

Slone, D. 2010. "Retrofitting Suburbia." New Partners for Smart Growth Conference, Seattle, WA.

Sohmer, R., and R. Lang. 2001. *Downtown Rebound*. Fannie Mae Foundation Census Note 03. Washington, DC: FMF.

Song, Y., and G. J. Knaap. 2004. "Measuring Urban Form: Is Portland Winning the War on Sprawl?" *Journal of the American Planning Association* 70(2):210–225.

Talen, E. 1999. "Sense of Community and Neighborhood Form: An Assessment of the Social Doctrine of New Urbanism." *Urban Studies* 36(8):1361–1379.

Talen, E. 2001. "Traditional Urbanism Meets Residential Affluence: An Analysis of the Variability of Suburban Preference." *Journal of the American Planning Association* 67 (2):199–216.

Talen, E., and A. Duany. 2002. "Transect Planning." *Journal of the American Planning Association* 68(3):245–266.

Urban Land Institute (ULI)/PricewaterhouseCoopers. 2006. "Best Bets: 2007." *Emerging Trends in Real Estate 2007*. Washington, DC: Author.

U.S. Department of Agriculture (USDA), NRCS. 2009. *National Resources Inventory*. Washington, DC: U.S. GPO. http://www.nrcs.usda.gov/technical/NRI/.

U.S. Environmental Protection Agency (EPA). 2001a. *Road Map to Understanding Innovative Technology Options for Brownfields Investigation and Cleanup*, 3rd ed. EPA 500-F-01-001. Washington, DC: U.S. EPA Office of Solid Waste and Emergency Response. Retrieved June 13, 2003, from http://clu-in.org/roadmap.

U.S. EPA. 2010a. "Brownfields." http://epa.gov/brownfields/.

U.S. EPA. 2010b. "Residential Construction Trends in America's Metropolitan Regions." 2010 edition. Development, Community, and Environment Division. Washington, DC.

U.S. EPA. 2010c. "Smart Growth Illustrated." http://www.epa.gov/smartgrowth/case .htm.

U.S. Government Accountability Office. 2004. *United States GAO Report to the Congressional Requesters: Brownfield Redevelopment* (Dec. 2004) (GAO-05-94).

U.S. Green Building Council (USGBC). 2010. http://www.usgbc.org/DisplayPage.aspx ?CMSPageID=1721.

Van der Ryn, S., and P. Calthorpe. 1986. *Sustainable Communities*. San Francisco: Sierra Club Books.

Wallace, McHarg, Roberts & Todd (WMRT). 1963. *The Plan for the Valleys*. Philadelphia: Author.

Wallace, Roberts & Todd (WRT). 2010. "Description of Plan for the Valleys." Retrieved from http://www.wrtdesign.com.

Yaro, R., R. Arendt, H. Dodson, and E. Brabec. 1988. *Dealing with Change in the Connecticut River Valley*. Center for Rural Massachusetts, Environmental Law Foundation, Lincoln Institute for Land Policy (LILP). Cambridge, MA: LILP.

Chapter 17

Arendt, R. 1994. *Rural by Design*. Chicago: American Planning Association Press.

Arendt, R. 1999. *Growing Greener, Putting Conservation into Local Plans and Ordinances*. Washington, DC: Island Press.

Arigoni, D. 2001. *Smart Growth and Affordable Housing*. Washington, DC: Smart-Growth Network.

Arlington, County of. 2011. "Columbia Pike Special Revitalization District: Form-Based Code." Retrieved from http://www.arlingtonva.us/departments/CPHD /forums/columbia/current/CPHDForumsColumbiaCurrentCurrentStatus.aspx.

Austin, City of. 2001. "Smart Growth Matrix." Retrieved from http://www.ci.austin.tx .us/smartgrowth/matrix.htm.

Austin, City of. 2010. "Austin Watershed Regulation Areas, Desired Development Zone and Drinking Water Protection Zone." Retrieved from http://www.ci.austin.tx.us/watershed/ordinances.htm.

Austin, City of. Undated. "Smart Growth Initiative." Retrieved from http://www.ci.austin.tx.us/smartgrowth/.

Benfield, F. K., J. Terris, and N. Vorsanger. 2001. *Solving Sprawl: Models of Smart Growth in Communities Across America.* Washington, DC: Natural Resources Defense Council.

Blacksburg, Town of. 2010a. "Comprehensive Plan." Retreived from http://www.blacksburg.gov/comp_plan/.

Blacksburg, Town of. 2010b. "Zoning Ordinance." Retrieved from http://www.blacksburg.gov/ordinances.php.

Boulder, City of. 2001. *Greenways Master Plan.* Boulder, CO: Author. Retrieved June 13, 2003, from http://www.ci.boulder.co.us/publicworks/depts/utilities/projects/greenways/index.htm.

Boulder Valley Comprehensive Plan. 1996. "Year 2000 Update." Retrieved June 13, 2003, from http://www.ci.boulder.co.us/planning/BVCP2000/bpbvcp2000.htm.

Boulder Valley Comprehensive Plan. 2010. BVCP Area I, II, III Map. Retrieved from http://www.bouldercolorado.gov/index.php?option=com_content&task=view&id=1482&Itemid=1611.

Center for Watershed Protection. 2004. Code and Ordinance Worksheet. Retrieved from http://www.cwp.org.

Coughlin, R. 1991. "Formulating and Evaluating Agricultural Zoning Programs." *Journal of the American Planning Association* 57(2):183–192.

Fairfax County, Virginia. 1991. *General Policy Plan.* Fairfax, VA: Author.

Fannie Mae Foundation. 2000. *Fair Growth.* Prepared for Association of Collegiate Schools of Planning Conference, November. Washington, DC: Author.

Fleissig, W., and V. Jacobsen. 2002. *Smart Growth Scorecard for Development Projects.* Congress for the New Urbanism. Washington, DC: U.S. EPA.

Greve, D., I. Miller, and S. Swenson. 2010. "Regional Growth and Conservation. Transfer of Development Rights." New Partners for Smart Growth Conference, Seattle, WA.

Hollis, L., and W. Fulton. 2002. *Open Space Protection: Conservation Meets Growth Management.* Washington, DC: Brookings Institution Center on Urban and Metropolitan Policy.

King County, Washington. 2010. "Comprehensive Plan. 2010." Retrieved from http://www.kingcounty.gov/property/permits/codes/growth/CompPlan.aspx.

King County, Washington. Undated. *Transfer of Development Rights Brochure.* http://www.kingcounty.gov/tdr.

Lucero, L., and J. Soule. 2002. "A Win for Lake Tahoe: The Supreme Court Validates Moritoriums in a Path-Breaking Decision." *Planning* 68(6):4–7.

Miami, City of. 2009. Miami21. "Types of Zoning." Miami: Miami Planning Department. Retrieved from http://www.miami21.org/TypesofZoningCodes.asp.

Montgomery County, Maryland. 2002. *Special Protection Area Program*, Annual Report 2001. Rockville, MD: Departments of Environmental Protection and Permitting Services. Retrieved June 13, 2003, from http://www.montgomerycountymd.gov/mc/services/dep/SPA/home.htm#Documents.

Montgomery County, Maryland. 2003. *Agricultural Preservation Initiatives.* Retrieved June 13, 2003, from http://www.montgomerycountymd.gov/siteHead.asp?page=/content/ded/AgServices/aginitiatives.html.

Montgomery County, Maryland. 2006. *TDR Program Overview.* Department of Economic Development Agricultural Services Division. Retrieved from http://www.montgomerycountymd.gov/content/ded/agservices/pdffiles/tdr_info.pdf.

Morris, D. 1982. *Self-Reliant Cities: Energy and the Transformation of Urban America.* San Francisco: Sierra Club Books.

Morris, M. 2009. *Smart Codes: Model Land Development Regulations.* PAS Report 556. Chicago: American Planning Association, Planning Advisory Service.

Natural Resources Defense Council (NRDC). 1977. *Land Use Controls in the United States.* New York: Dial Press/John Wade.

Nelson, A. C., and J. Duncan. 1995. *Growth Management: Principles and Practices.* Chicago: American Planning Association Press.

Nelson, K. 2010. "The Dollars and Sense of Sustainability Codes." New Partners for Smart Growth Conference, Seattle, WA.

New Hampshire Department of Environmental Services. 2008. "Innovative Land Use Planning Techniques." Retrieved from http://des.nh.gov/organization/divisions/water/wmb/repp/innovative_land_use.htm.

Northwest Environment Watch. 2002. "Sprawl and Smart Growth in Greater Seattle-Tacoma." Seattle: Author. Retrieved June 13, 2003, from http://www.northwestwatch.org/press/seattle_sprawl.pdf.

1000 Friends of Minnesota. 2003. "TDR Conceptual Overview." Retrieved June 23, 2003, from http://www.1000fom.org/Tool%20Box/TDR-concept.pdf.

Palo Alto, City of. 2009. *Palo-Alto Context-Based Design Code. Mixed-Use and Pedestrian and Transit-Oriented Overlay Zones.* Van Meter Williams Pollack LLP.

Parolek, D. 2010. "Form-Based Codes and Walkable Urbanism: How and Why Communities Are Making Decisions About Zoning Reform." New Partners for Smart Growth Conference, Seattle, WA.

Pelletier, M., R. Pruetz, and C. Duerksen. 2011. TDR-Less TDR Revisited. PAS Memo—May/June. Chicago: American Planning Association.

Pruetz, R. 2003. *Beyond Takings and Givings: Saving Natural Areas, Farmland and Historic Landmarks with Transfer of Development Rights and Density Transfer Charges.* Burbank, CA: Arje Press.

Randolph, J. 1981. "The Local Energy Future: A Compendium of Community Programs." *Solar Law Reporter* 3(2):253–282.

Richardson, J. 2002. *Dillon's Rule and Growth Management in 50 States.* Washington, DC: Brookings Institution.

Rocky Mountain Land Use Institute. 2009. "RMLUI Model Sustainability Code." http://www.law.du.edu/index.php/rmlui/sustainable-community-development-code-and-reform-initiative.

Seattle, City of. 2005. Comprehensive Plan Toward a Sustainable Seattle. Urban Village Element.

Seattle, City of. 2010. Comprehensive Plan: Toward a Sustainable Seattle. Update. Future Land Use Map.

SmartCode 9.2. 2010. SmartCode Central. http://www.smartcodecentral.org.

Somin, I., and J. Adler. "The Green Costs of Kelo: Economic Development Takings and Environmental Protection." *Washington University Law Review* 84:623–666.

U.S. Environmental Protection Agency (EPA). 2009. "Essential Smart Growth Fixes for Urban and Suburban Zoning Codes." Kevin Nelson, principal author. EPA 231 -k-09-00.3. Retrieved from http://www.epa.gov/smartgrowth/essential_fixes.htm.

Witten, J., and S. Horsley. 1995. *A Guide to Wellhead Protection*. Planning Advisory Service. U.S. EPA. PAS Report 457/458. Chicago: American Planning Association.

Chapter 18

American Planning Association (APA). 1999. *Planning Communities for the 21st Century*. Chicago: Author.

American Planning Association. 2002. *Planning for Smart Growth. State of the States*. Chicago: Author.

Barbour, E., and M. Teitz. 2006. Blueprint Planning in California: Forging Consensus on Metropolitan Growth and Development. Occasional Papers. Public Policy Institute of California, San Francisco.

California Attorney General's Office. 2009. "Climate Change, the California Environmental Quality Act, and General Plan Updates: Straightforward Answers to Some Frequently Asked Questions." Retrieved January 7, 2011, from http://ag.ca.gov /globalwarming/pdf/CEQA_GP_FAQs.pdf.

Calthorpe Associates. 2000. *St. Croix Valley Redevelopment Study*. Prepared for the Metropolitan Council (Minnesota). Berkeley, CA: Author.

Calthorpe, P., and W. Fulton. 2001. *The Regional City*. Washington, DC: Island Press.

ECONorthwest. 2000. *Willamette Valley Alternative. Futures Project*. Eugene, OR: Author.

Florida Department of Transportation. 2009. "Transportation Glossary of Terms." Office of Policy Planning. Retrieved from www.dot.state.fl.us/planning/glossary /glossary.pdf.

Frece, J. 1997. "Lessons from Next Door: 'Smart Growth' in Maryland." *Planning in Virginia 1997*. Midlothian, VA: American Planning Association (Virginia Chapter).

Frece, J. 2000. "Smart Growth in Maryland." Presentation at Blacksburg, Virginia, October.

Governors' Institute on Community Design. Undated. *Policies That Work: A Governors' Guide to Growth and Development*. Retrieved from http://www.govinstitute.org /policyguide.

Ingram, G., A. Carbonell, Y. Hong, and A. Flint. 2009. *Smart Growth Policies: An Evaluation of Programs and Outcomes*. Cambridge, MA: Lincoln Institute of Land Policy.

Leonard, H. J. 1982. *Managing Oregon's Growth: The Politics of Development Planning*. Washington, DC: Conservation Foundation.

Lewis, R., G. Knapp, and J. Sohn. 2009. "Managing Growth with Priority Funding Areas: A Good Idea Whose Time Has Yet to Come." *Journal of the American Planning Association* 75(4):457–478.

National Governors Association (NGA). 2001. "Growth and Quality of Life Tool Kit." Retrieved June 13, 2003, from http://www.nga.org/center/growth.

Natural Resources Defense Council (NRDC). 1977. *Land Use Controls in the United States*. New York: Dial Press/John Wade.

New Jersey Future. "Smart Growth Scorecard—Proposed Development." Retrieved from http://www.njfuture.org.

New Jersey Pinelands Commission. 2002. *The Third Progress Report on Implementation*. Retrieved June 13, 2003, from http://www.state.nj.us/pinelands/planrev.pdf.

New Jersey Pinelands Commission. Undated. "A Summary of the New Jersey Pinelands Comprehensive Management Plan." Retrieved June 13, 2003, from http://www.state.nj.us/pinelands/.

Northwest Environment Watch. 2002. "Sprawl and Smart Growth in Metropolitan Portland." Seattle: Author. Retrieved June 13, 2003, from http://www.northwest watch.org/press/portland_sprawl.html.

1000 Friends of Oregon. 2003. "Measure 7/Takings Information." Retrieved June 13, 2003, from http://www.friends.org/issues/m7.html.

Oregon Department of Land Conservation and Development. 1997. Oregon Statewide Planning Program. Salem, OR: Author. Retrieved June 28, 2003, from http://www.lcd.state.or.us/fastpdfs/brochure.pdf.

Phillips, C., and J. Randolph. 1998. "Has Ecosystem Management Really Changed Practices on the National Forests?" *Journal of Forestry* 96(5):40–45.

Portland Metro Council. 2010a. Transit-Oriented Development Program. *Annual Report July 2009–June 2010*.

Portland Metro Council. 2010b. Urban Reserve and Rural Reserve Map. Retrieved from http://www.oregonmetro.gov/index.cfm/go/by.web/id=24876.

Portland Metro Council and City of Portland. 2006. Metro 2040 Concept Map. Metro Data Resource Center.

Randolph, J. 1987. "Comparison of Approaches to Public Lands Planning: Forest Service, Park Service, Bureau of Land Management, Fish and Wildlife Service." *Trends* 24(2):36–45.

San Francisco Bay Conservation and Development Commission (BCDC). 1998. "San Francisco Bay Plan." Retrieved June 13, 2003, from http://www.bcdc.ca.gov/.

San Francisco Bay Conservation and Development Commission (BCDC). 2008. "San Francisco Bay Plan." Retrieved from http://www.bcdc.ca.gov/.

Schneider, K. 2007. *Smart Growth in the States: Survey of Recent Developments*. East Lansing: Michigan State University, Land Policy Institute.

State of Washington. 1998. *SEPA Handbook*. Olympia: Department of Ecology.

Tahoe Regional Planning Agency (TRPA). 1986. "Regional Plan for the Lake Tahoe Basin." Stateline, NV: Author. Retrieved June 2003 from http://www.trpa.org/Goals/preface.html.

Tahoe Regional Planning Agency (TRPA). 2002. *2001 Threshold Evaluation Report*. Stateline, NV: Author. Retrieved June 2003 from http://www.trpa.org/News/2001_Thresholds.html.

Tahoe Regional Planning Agency (TRPA). 2007. "Environmental Assessment for Threshold Updates for Regional Plan Update for the Lake Tahoe Region." South Lake Tahoe, CA: Author.

Tahoe Regional Planning Agency (TRPA). 2009. "Environmental Threshold Carrying Capacities (Thresholds) and Pathway Vision Statements." South Lake Tahoe, CA: Author.

Tahoe Regional Planning Agency (TRPA). 2011a. "Regional Plan Update. Restoring Lake Tahoe While Creating Sustainable Communities." July 20, 2011 Draft Documents. Retrieved from http://www.trpa.org/default.aspx?tabid=130.

Tahoe Regional Planning Agency (TRPA). 2011b. "Regional Plan Update Re-Scope." Attachment D: Proposed Threshold Amendments. South Lake Tahoe, CA: Author.

Tang, Z., E. Bright, S. Brody. 2009. "Evaluating California Local Land Use Plan's Environmental Impact Reports." *Environmental Impact Assessment Review* 29: 96–106.

Twin Cities Metropolitan Council (Minnesota). 2002. *Blueprint 2030.* St. Paul, MN: Author. Retrieved June 13, 2003, from http://www.metrocouncil.org/planning /blueprint2030/overview.htm.

Twin Cities Metropolitan Council. 2006. "Regional Development Framework." http:// www.metrocouncil.org.

Twin Cities Metropolitan Council. 2010a. MUSA Regional Map. Retrieved from http://general.metc.state.mn.us/gallery/Default.aspx.

Twin Cities Metropolitan Council. 2010b. *Natural Resources Data Atlas.* Retrieved from http://general.metc.state.mn.us/nrda/resources.asp.

Twin Cities Metropolitan Council. 2010c. "Regional Benchmarks: Measuring Our Progress." Retrieved from http://www.metrocouncil.org/planning/framework/bench marks.htm.

U.S. Council on Environmental Quality. 1974. *The Costs of Sprawl.* Washington, DC: U.S. Government Printing Office.

Chapter 19

Anacostia Watershed Restoration Partnership (AWRP). 2010. "Anacostia River Watershed Restoration Plan." Retrieved from http://www.anacostia.net/plan.html.

Bauer, M. 2001. "Collaborative Environmental Decisionmaking: A Power Sharing Process That Achieves Results Through Dialogue." Ph.D. dissertation, Environmental Design and Planning, Virginia Tech, Blacksburg, Virginia.

Bauer, M., and J. Randolph. 2000. "Characteristics of Collaborative Environmental Planning and Decision-Making Processes." *Environmental Practice* 2(2):156–65.

Chesapeake Bay Foundation (CBF). 2009. State of the Bay 2008. Annapolis, MD: Author.

Clements, J., C. Creager, A. Beach, J. Butcher, M. Marcus, and T. Schueler. 1996. "Framework for a Watershed Management Program." Alexandria, VA: Water Environment Research Foundation.

Clewell, A., J. Rieger, and J. Munro. 2000. *Guidelines for Developing and Managing Ecological Restoration Projects.* Retrieved June 23, 2003, from http://www.ser.org /reading.php?pg=guidelines4er.

Corbett, J., and T. Hayden. 1981. "Local Action for a Solar Future." *Solar Law Reporter* 2(5):957.

Doyle, M., and C. Drew, eds. 2008. *Large-Scale Ecosystem Restoration: Five Case Studies from the United States.* Washington, DC: Island Press.

Fitzsimmons, A. 1999. *Defending Illusions: Federal Protection of Ecosystems.* Lanham, MD: Rowman & Littlefield.

Frank, K. 2009. "The Role of Collaboration in Everglades Restoration." Ph.D. dissertation, City and Regional Planning. Georgia Institute of Technology, Atlanta, Georgia.

Goldstein, B. 1992. "The Struggle Over Ecosystem Management at Yellowstone." *BioScience* 42(3):183–187.

Gregory, R., D. Ohlson, and J. Arvai. 2006. "Deconstructing Adaptive Management: Criteria for Applications to Environmental Management. *Ecological Applications* 16(6):2411–2425.

Grumbine, R. 1994. "What Is Ecosystem Management?" *Conservation Biology* 8(1): 27–38.

Holst, D. 1999. "Statewide Watershed Protection and Local Implementation: A Comparison of Washington, Minnesota, and Oregon." Master's thesis, Master of Urban and Regional Planning, Virginia Tech, Blacksburg, Virginia.

Keuhl, D. 2001. "From Collaboration to Knowledge: Planning for Remedial Action in the Great Lakes." Ph.D. dissertation, Environmental Design and Planning, Virginia Tech, Blacksburg, Virginia.

Koontz, T., and J. Bodine. 2008. "Implementing Ecosystem Management in Public Agencies: Lessons from the U.S. Bureau of Land Management and the Forest Service." *Conservation Biology* 22(1):60–69.

Liu, J., T. Dietz, S. Carpenter, M. Alberti, C. Folke, E. Moran, A. Pell, P. Deadman, T. Kratz, J. Lubchenco, E. Ostrom, Z. Ouyang, W. Provencher, C. Redman, S. Schneider, and W. Taylor 2007. "Complexity of Coupled Human and Natural Systems." *Science* 317:1513.

National Research Council (NRC). 1992. *Restoration of Aquatic Ecosystems: Science, Technology, and Public Policy.* Washington, DC: National Academies Press.

National Research Council (NRC). 2004. *Adaptive Management for Water Resources Project Planning.* Washington, DC: National Academies Press.

National Research Council (NRC). 2008. *Progress Toward Restoring the Everglades: The Second Biennial Review, Committee on Independent Scientific Review of Everglades Restoration Progress.* Washington, DC: National Academies Press.

National Research Council (NRC). 2009. *Urban Stormwater Management in the United States,* Vol. xii. Washington, DC: National Academies Press.

Oregon Plan for Salmon and Watersheds. 2001. Retrieved from http://www.oregon-plan.org/.

Peterson, G., G. Cumming, and S. Carpenter. 2003. "Scenario Planning: A Tool for Conservation in an Uncertain World." *Conservation Biology* 17:358–366.

Phillips, C., and J. Randolph. 1998. "Has Ecosystem Management Really Changed Practices on the National Forests?" *Journal of Forestry* 96(5):40–45.

Phillips, C., and J. Randolph. 2000. "The Relationship of Ecosystem Management to NEPA and Its Goals." *Environmental Management* 26(1):1–12.

Randolph, J. 1987. "Comparison of Approaches to Public Lands Planning: Forest Service, Park Service, Bureau of Land Management, Fish and Wildlife Service." *Trends* 24(2):36–45.

Reitan, P. 2005. "Sustainability Science—and What's Needed Beyond Science." *Sustainability: Science, Practice, & Policy* 1(1):77–80.

Rowe, P., and T. Schueler. 2006. *The Smart Watershed Benchmarking Tool.* Ellicott City, MD: Center for Watershed Protection.

Schueler, T. 1997. "The Economics of Watershed Protection." *Watershed Protection Techniques* 2(4):469–481.

Schueler, T. 2000. "Basic Concepts of Watershed Planning." In *The Practice of Watershed Protection,* edited by T. Schueler and H. Holland, pp. 145–161. Ellicott City, MD: Center for Watershed Protection.

Schueler, T., and H. Holland, eds. 2000. *The Practice of Watershed Protection.* Ellicott City, MD: Center for Watershed Protection.

Schueler, T., A. Kitchell, D. Hirschman, M. Novotney, J. Zielinski, K. Brown, C. Swann, T. Wright, S. Sprinkle, R, Winer, and K. Cappiella. 2005, 2006. *Urban Subwatershed Restoration Manual.* Eleven volumes. Ellicott City, MD: Center for Watershed Protection.

Smith, T. 1995. *Habitat Conservation Planning Under the Endangered Species Act: Is It Ecosystem Management?* Master's thesis, Urban and Regional Planning, Virginia Tech, Blacksburg, Virginia.

Society for Ecological Restoration (SER). 2004. *The SER Primer on Ecological Restoration. Version 2.* Retrieved from http://www.ser.org/content/ecological_restoration_primer.asp.

Turner, B., P. Matsond, J. McCarthye, R. Corellf, L. Christensend, N. Eckleyg, G. Hovelsrud-Brodah, J. Kasperson, R. Kasperson A. Luersd, M. Martellof, S. Mathiesenj, R. Naylord, C. Polskya, A. Pulsipher, A. Schillerb, H. Selink, and N. Tyler. 2003. "Illustrating the Coupled Human-Environment System for Vulnerability Analysis: Three Case Studies." *Proceedings of the National Academy of Sciences* 100(14): 8080–8085.

U.S. Army Corps of Engineers. 2010. Comprehensive Everglades Restoration Plan. Report to Congress. Retrieved from http://www.evergladesplan.org/.

U.S. Department of Agriculture (USDA). U.S. Forest Service. 1992. *Ecosystem Management of the National Forests and Grasslands.* Memorandum 1330-1. Washington, DC: Author.

USDA. U.S. Forest Service. 2000. "National Forest System Land Resource Management Planning: Final Rule." *Federal Register* 65(218):67514–81.

U.S. Department of the Interior (DOI). 2009. *Adaptive Management: The U.S. Department of the Interior Technical Guide.* Retrieved from http://www.doi.gov/initiatives/AdaptiveManagement/.

U.S. Environmental Protection Agency (EPA). 1996. *The Watershed Protection Approach.* Office of Water. Washington, DC: Author.

U.S. EPA. 1997. *Top 10 Watershed Lessons Learned.* OWOW (4501F) EPA 840-F-97–001. Office of Water. Washington, DC: Author.

U.S. EPA. 2001. *Protecting and Restoring America's Watersheds: Status, Trends, and Initiatives in Watershed Management.* (4204) EPA-840-R-00–001. Office of Water. Washington, DC: Author.

U.S. EPA. 2008. *Handbook for Developing Watershed Plans to Restore and Protect Our Waters.* Office of Water. Washington, DC: Author.

U.S. EPA. Chesapeake Bay Program. 2010a. "Bay Barometer: A Health and Restoration Assessment of the Chesapeake Bay and Watershed in 2009." Annapolis, MD: Author. Retrieved from http://www.chesapeakebay.net/indicatorshome.aspx?menuitem=14871.

U.S. EPA. Chesapeake Bay Program. 2010b. "Final Chesapeake Bay Total Maximum Daily Load." Region 3 Water Protection Division, Region 3 Chesapeake Bay Program, Region 2. Division of Environmental Planning and Protection. Retrieved from http://www.epa.gov/chesapeakebaytmdl/.

U.S. EPA. 2010c. "Stormwater, TMDL, and Watershed Success Stories." http://www.epa.gov/owow_keep/tmdl/tmdlsatwork/index.html, http://www.epa.gov/owow/NPS/success/index.htm.

U.S. Global Change Research Program (USGCRP). 2009. *Global Climate Change Impacts in the United States.* Cambridge, England: Cambridge University Press. http://www.globalchange.gov/publications/reports/scientific-assessments/us-impacts.

Wicks, C., D. Jasinski, and B. Longstaff. 2007: *Breath of Life: Dissolved Oxygen in Chesapeake Bay.* Oxford, MD: EcoCheck. http://www.eco-check.org/pdfs/do_letter.pdf.

Yaffee, S., A. Phillips, I. Frentz, P. Hardy, S. Maleki, and B. Thorpe. 1996. *Ecosystem Management in the United States: An Assessment of Current Experience.* Washington, DC: Island Press.

Index

Note: page numbers followed by b, f, or t refer to boxes, figures, or tables, respectively.